LAURIE J MULLINS

MANAGEMENT AND ORGANISATIONAL BEHAVIOUR

Second edition

Pitman

To my wife, Pamela

PITMAN PUBLISHING
128 Long Acre, London WC2E 9AN
A Division of Longman Group UK Limited

© L J Mullins, 1985, 1989
First published in Great Britain 1985
Second edition 1989
Reprinted 1989

British Library Cataloguing in Publication Data
Mullins, Laurie J.
  Management and organisational behaviour – 2nd ed
  1. Man. Organisational behaviour
  I. Title
  158.7

ISBN 0 273 02985 1

Printed and bound in Great Britain

CONTENTS

PREFACE

I am grateful for encouragement in writing this book from colleagues in the Department of Business and Management Studies, Portsmouth Polytechnic, especially my head of department Gordon Oliver, Tom McEwan, and members of the behavioural studies team. Thanks are due to Brian Deverson and Phylippa Smithson for their helpful comments on the manuscript. I also wish to thank my publisher Simon Lake and his colleagues at Pitman Publishing for their help and guidance.

I wish to pay a special tribute for the constant interest, encouragement and support in completing this book from my wife and children, and my parents – of all of whom I am deeply appreciative.

Laurie Mullins

ABOUT THIS BOOK

This book presents a managerial approach to organisational behaviour. It is concerned with interactions among the structure and operation of organisations, the process of management and the behaviour of people at work. *The underlying theme of the book is the need for organisational effectiveness and the importance of the role of management as an integrating activity.*

The aims of this book are to:

- relate the study of organisational behaviour to that of management;
- provide an integrated view embracing both theory and practice;
- point out applications of behavioural science within work organisations and implications for management action;
- indicate ways in which organisational performance may be improved through the better use of human resources.

The book is written with a minimum of technical terminology and the format is clearly structured. Each chapter contains a short introduction, objectives, a synopsis of key points, review and discussion questions, notes and references, and assignment(s) and/or case(s).

It is hoped that the book will appeal to students at undergraduate, graduate or post experience level in business or management, or on related professional courses. It is also hoped that the book will appeal not only to those aspiring to a managerial position but to practising managers and supervisors who wish to expand their knowledge of the subject area.

The study of behavioural science, in one form or another, is now included in many courses on organisation and management. However, whilst a prior knowledge of behavioural science would prove useful to the reader, it is not assumed. Neither is such knowledge a necessary prerequisite for an understanding of the concepts and ideas discussed in this book.

No single book could hope to cover adequately all aspects of what is a wide and essentially multidisciplinary field of inquiry. It is not the intention to attempt to cover all aspects of individual or social behaviour. In order to attain a reasonable depth, this book concentrates on selected topics of particular relevance to problems of organisation and management in work situations, and which meet the needs of the intended audience. There are, of course, related areas of specialisms such as personnel and industrial relations, outlined in Chapter 8, which also bear upon management action and organisational effectiveness.

The concepts and ideas presented in this book provide a basis on which to formulate a critical appraisal of different perspectives on the structure, operation and management of organisations, and interactions among people who work in them. Hopefully this will encourage more awareness of, and sensitivity to, the organisational factors and management processes influencing the behaviour and performance of people at work.

The second edition

This second edition is completely revised and expanded with considerable new material, examples and references.

- There are four additional chapters on 'The nature of organisational behaviour', 'Staffing the organisation', 'Organisation development' and 'Management development and organisational effectiveness'.
- Other chapters have been reorganised and many include new sections or have been completely rewritten. There are also changes in the sequence of certain chapters.
- Each chapter now includes practical assignment(s) and/or case(s).
- There is a more structured layout and style to make the book more appealing to the reader.

PLAN OF THE BOOK

PART ONE
MANAGEMENT AND ORGANISATIONAL BEHAVIOUR

> **CHAPTER 1**
> The Nature of Organisational Behaviour

> **CHAPTER 2**
> Approaches to Organisation and Management

PART TWO
CONTEXT OF THE ORGANISATION

CHAPTER 3 The Organisational Setting	**CHAPTER 4** Organisational Goals and Objectives	**CHAPTER 5** Organisation Structure and Systems
		CHAPTER 6 Contingency Approach to Organisation Structure

PART THREE
STAFFING THE ORGANISATION

> **CHAPTER 7**
> Staffing the Organisation

PART FOUR
MANAGEMENT AS AN INTEGRATING ACTIVITY

CHAPTER 8 The Nature of Management	**CHAPTER 9** Managerial Behaviour and Effectiveness

PART FIVE
ORGANISATIONAL PROCESSES AND THE EXECUTION OF WORK

CHAPTER 10 Delegation	**CHAPTERS 11 & 12** Motivation and Job Satisfaction	**CHAPTERS 13 & 14** Groups and Group Behaviour	**CHAPTER 15** Leadership	**CHAPTER 16** Control

PART SIX
ORGANISATIONAL DEVELOPMENT AND EFFECTIVENESS

CHAPTER 17 Organisation Development	**CHAPTER 18** Management Development and Organisational Effectiveness

GUIDE TO YOUR STUDY OF THE BOOK

The book adopts an applied approach to help in the search for the most appropriate ways of improving organisational performance and effectiveness. The objective analysis of organisations is supported, where appropriate, by a more prescriptive stance. For example, in Chapter 5 the underlying need to establish a framework of order and system of command by which the work of the organisation is undertaken demands that attention be given to certain basic principles and consideration of structure.

Although the main focus of attention is the private enterprise business organisation, reference is made to other types of organisations for the purpose of comparisons and examples. General principles and prescriptions apply equally to all types of work organisations which achieve their goals and objectives through the process of management.

It is possible that the more practically minded reader may wish to concentrate greater attention on the latter parts of certain chapters. However, even a cursory examination of earlier sections of the chapter will help provide an understanding of underlying studies upon which discussion of practical applications is based.

You are invited to test your knowledge and understanding of the contents by attempting the review and discussion questions at the end of each chapter. These questions provide a basis for revision and review of progress. You are also invited to undertake the assignment(s) and/or case(s) at the end of each chapter. The questions, assignments and case studies provide an opportunity to relate ideas, principles and practices to specific work situations, to think and talk about major issues, and to discuss and compare views with colleagues.

The notes and references given at the end of each chapter are to encourage you to pursue further any issues of particular interest. A simple numbering system has deliberately been chosen in order to keep the main text uncluttered and easier to follow, to provide more detailed and specific referencing, and because this system appears to be favoured by most readers.

Although there is a logical flow to the sequencing of topic areas, each chapter is self-contained. The selection and ordering of chapters can be varied to suit the particular demands of your study courses or your interests.

You are encouraged to complement your reading of the book by drawing upon your own experience of work organisations. Search for and study examples of management and organisational behaviour. Look for good and bad examples of management activities and practices, and consider reasons for their apparent success or failure. Consider the manner in which concepts and ideas presented in this book can best be applied in particular work situations. Contemporary examples from your own observations should help further your interest in the subject area and illustrate practical applications to real-life situations.

ACKNOWLEDGEMENTS

We are all influenced by the work of other people. It is inevitable, therefore, that thoughts and ideas of other people tend to drift into the subconscious and are not always distinguished clearly from one's own. I have attempted to give references for sources of work by other writers but apologise to any concerned if acknowledgement of their work has inadvertently not been recorded.

Some of the ideas in this book have been influenced by work carried out in connection with management and professional courses organised by the Education Department of the National and Local Government Officers' Association. I am grateful to Regina Kibel, Education Officer, Michael Wilson and colleagues for asking me to be involved with this work.

Acknowledgements for Assignments and Case Studies

Chapter 1 'Inference–Observation' exercise is reprinted with permission from Haney, W. V. *Communications and Interpersonal Relations: Text and Cases*, Fifth edition, Irwin (1986) p. 393.

Chapter 3 'Our Organizational Society: Your Association with Organizations' is reprinted with permission from Kast, F. E. and Rosenzweig, J. E. *Experiential Exercises and Cases in Management*, McGraw-Hill (1976) pp. 13–15.

Chapter 4 'Square Deal PLC' is reprinted with permission from The Institute of Administrative Management, Diploma in Administrative Management Examination Paper, Summer 1983.

Chapter 5 The case study is adapted from that written originally by the late John Cluett and published in the journal *Administrative Management*, vol. 29, no. 3, November 1979. It is used with permission of the Institute of Administrative Management.

Chapter 7 'Sixth Time Lucky' is reprinted with permission from Chilver, J. *People, Communication and Organisation: A Case Study Approach*, Pergamon Press (1984) pp. 116–17. 'Wessex Computers' is reprinted with permission from the Institute of Administrative Management, Certificate in Administrative Management Examination Paper, Summer 1983.

Chapter 8 'What *is* Management?' is reprinted with permission from Doswell, R. and Nailon, P. *Further Case Studies in Hotel Management*, Century Hutchinson (1977) pp. 15–26.

Chapter 9 'Principle of Supportive Relationships Questionnaire' is reprinted with permission from Likert, R. *The Human Organization – Its Management and Value*, McGraw-Hill (1967) pp. 48–9. 'Managerial Style and Appraisal: Administrators in the NHS' is reprinted with permission from Clegg, C. W., Kemp, N. J. and Legge, K. *Case Studies in Organizational Behaviour*, Paul Chapman (1985) pp. 44–50.

Chapter 11 'Motivation Questionnaire' is reprinted from 'Motivation: A Feedback Exercise' in Jones, J. E. and Pfeiffer, J. W. (eds) *The Annual Handbook for Group Facilitators*, University Associates Inc., San Diego, CA (1973) pp. 43–5 and is used with permission. Assignment 3 is reprinted with permission from Hellriegal, D., Slocum, J. W. and Woodman, R. W. *Organizational Behavior*, Fourth edition, West Publishing Company (1986) p. 180.

Chapter 12 'The Wide Open Spaces' is reprinted with permission from Chilver, J. *People, Communication and Organisation: A Case Study Approach*, Pergamon Press (1984) pp. 118–19. Case Study 2 is reprinted with permission from the Institute of Chartered Secretaries and Administrators, Management: Principles and Policy Examination Paper, June 1985.

Chapter 13 The copyright of 'Hovertec PLC' case study rests with my colleague Tom McEwan, Portsmouth Polytechnic, and is reprinted with permission.

Chapter 14 'Wilderness Survival Work Sheet' is reprinted from 'Wilderness Survival: A Consensus-seeking Task' in Pfeiffer, J. W. and Jones, J. E. (eds) *The 1976 Annual Handbook for Group Facilitators*, University Associates Inc., San Diego, CA. (1976) pp. 19–25 and is used with permission.

Chapter 15 'Least Preferred Co-worker (LPC) Scale' is reprinted with permission of Professor F. E. Fiedler. 'Leadership Questionnaire' is reprinted from Pfeiffer J. W. and Jones, J. E. (eds) *A Handbook of Structured Experiences for Human Relations Training*, vol. 1, Revised edition, University Associates Inc., San Diego, CA. (1974). The questionnaire was adapted from the Sergiovanni, T. J., Metzcus, R. and Burden, L. version of the Leadership Behavior Description Questionnaire, *American Educational Research Journal*, vol. 6, no. 1, 1969, pp. 62–79 and is used with permission. 'Leader Effectiveness and Adaptability Description (LEAD)' is extracted with permission from Hersey, P. and Blanchard, K. H. *Rationale and Analysis of LEAD Instruments*, Center for Leadership Studies, Ohio University (1973).

Chapter 16 The case study is reprinted with permission from the Institute of Chartered Secretaries and Administrators, Management: Principles and Policy Examination Paper, June 1987.

Chapter 17 The case study is reprinted with permission from The Institute of Chartered Secretaries and Administrators, Management: Principles and Policy Examination Paper, December 1986.

Chapter 18 The practical assignment is adapted from material prepared by Dr John Bourn for a NALGO Education distance learning course and is used with permission of the Education Office.

Note I have unfortunately been unable to trace the copyright holder of 'The Enthusiastic Delegator', which appears as the case study in Chapter 10, and would appreciate any information which would enable me to do so.

PART ONE

MANAGEMENT AND ORGANISATIONAL BEHAVIOUR

1. THE NATURE OF ORGANISATIONAL BEHAVIOUR

The scope for the examination of behaviour in organisations is very wide. There is a multiplicity of interrelated factors which influence the behaviour and performance of people as members of a work organisation. It is important to understand the role of management as an integrating activity and as the cornerstone of organisational effectiveness. People and organisations need each other. The manager needs to understand the main influences on behaviour in work organisations and the nature of the people–organisation relationship.

Objectives

To: (i) Provide an introduction to management and organisational behaviour;
(ii) Explain the meaning and nature of organisational behaviour;
(iii) Detail main interrelated influences on behaviour in work organisations and explain the nature of behavioural science;
(iv) Examine the process of perception and identify problem areas in perceiving other people;
(v) Explain the importance of management as an integrating activity;
(vi) Assess the importance of the psychological contract;
(vii) Appreciate the complex nature of the behaviour of people in work organisations.

THE MEANING OF ORGANISATIONAL BEHAVIOUR

Organisations play a major and continuing role in the lives of us all, especially with the growth of large-scale business organisations and the divorce of ownership from management. We live in an organisational world. Organisations of one form or another are a necessary part of our society and serve many important needs. The decisions and actions of management in organisations have an increasing impact on individuals, other organisations and the community. It is important, therefore, to understand how organisations function and the pervasive influences which they exercise over the behaviour of people.[1]

The Behaviour of People

Organisational behaviour is concerned with the study of the behaviour of people within an organisational setting. It involves the understanding, prediction and control of human behaviour and the factors which influence the performance of people as members of an organisation.[2] There is a close relation between organisational behaviour and management theory and practice. Some writers seem to suggest that organisational behaviour and management are synonymous, but this is something of an over-simplification because there are many broader facets to management. Organisational behaviour does not encompass the whole of management; it is more accurately described in the narrower interpretation of providing a behavioural approach to management.

In most cases the term 'organisational behaviour' is, strictly, a misnomer: rarely do all members of an organisation, except perhaps very small organisations, behave collectively in such a way as to represent the behaviour of the organisation as a whole. In practice we are referring to the behaviour of individuals, or sections or groups of people, within the organisation. For example, when we talk about a 'caring organisation' we are really talking about the philosophy, attitudes and actions of top managers and/or departmental managers, or possibly an individual manager.

Nevertheless, the wording 'organisational behaviour' has become widely accepted and is found increasingly in textbooks and literature on the subject. The term 'organisational behaviour' is a convenient form of shorthand to refer to the multiplicity of interrelated influences on, and patterns of, behaviour of people within formal organisations.[3]

INFLUENCES ON BEHAVIOUR IN ORGANISATIONS

The formal organisation is a constantly changing network of interrelated activities and the behaviour of people cannot be studied in isolation. It is necessary to understand the interrelationships between human behaviour and other variables which together comprise the total organisation. The study of organisational behaviour therefore involves consideration of interaction among the formal structure, the tasks to be undertaken, the technology employed and methods of carrying out work, the behaviour of people, the process of management and the external environment.

These variables provide parameters within which can be identified a number of interrelated dimensions – the individual, the group, the organisation, and the environment – which collectively influence behaviour in work organisations.

The individual

Organisations are made up of their individual members. The individual is a central feature of organisational behaviour and a necessary part of any behavioural situation, whether acting in isolation or as part of a group, in response to expectations of the organisation, or as a result of influences of the external environment.

Where the needs of the individual and the demands of the organisation are incompatible, this can result in frustration and conflict. It is the task of management to provide a working environment which permits the satisfaction of individual needs as well as the attainment of organisational goals.

The group

Groups exist in all organisations and are essential to their working and performance. The organisation is comprised of groups of people and almost everyone in an organisation will be a member of one or more groups. Informal groups arise from the social needs of people within the organisation. People in groups influence each other in many ways, and groups may develop their own hierarchies and leaders.

Group pressures can have a major influence over the behaviour and performance of individual members. An understanding of group structure and behaviour complements a knowledge of individual behaviour and adds a further dimension to organisational behaviour.

The organisation

Individuals and groups interact within the structure of the formal organisation. Structure is created by management to establish relationships between individuals and groups, to provide order and systems and to direct the efforts of the organisation into goal-seeking activities. It is through the formal structure that people carry out their organisational activities in order to achieve aims and objectives.

Behaviour is affected by patterns of organisation structure, technology, styles of leadership and systems of management through which organisational processes are planned, directed and controlled. The focus of attention, therefore, is on the impact of organisation structure and design, and patterns of management, on the behaviour of people within the organisation.

The environment

The organisation functions as part of the broader external environment of which it is part. The environment affects the organisation through, for example, technological and scientific development, economic activity, social and cultural influences and governmental actions.

The effects of the operation of the organisation within its environment are reflected in terms of the management of opportunities and risks and the successful achievement of its aims and objectives. The increasing rate of change in environmental factors has highlighted the need to study the total organisation and the processes by which the organisation attempts to adapt to the external demands placed upon it.

Contrasting but related approaches

These different dimensions provide contrasting but related approaches to the understanding of human behaviour in organisations. They present a number of alternative pathways for the study of the subject and level of analysis. It is possible, for example, to adopt a *psychological* approach with the main emphasis on the individuals of which the organisation is comprised. Psychological aspects are important but, by themselves, provide too narrow an approach for the understanding of management and organisational behaviour. Our main concern is not with the complex detail of individual differences and attributes *per se*, but with the behaviour and management of people within an organisational setting.

3

It is also possible to adopt a *sociological* approach concerned with a broader emphasis on human behaviour in society. Sociological aspects can be important. A number of sociology writers seem set on the purpose of criticising traditional views of organisation and management. Many of the criticisms and limitations to which such writers refer are justified and help promote healthy academic debate. Unfortunately, however, much of the argument tends to be presented in the abstract and lacking in constructive ideas on how, in practical terms, action could be taken to improve organisational performance.

BEHAVIOURAL SCIENCE – AN INTERDISCIPLINARY APPROACH

The study of organisational behaviour cannot be undertaken entirely in terms of a single discipline. It is necessary to provide an interdisciplinary, behavioural science approach. (*See* Fig. 1.1.)

The wording 'behavioural science' has no strict scientific definition. It may be used as a collective term for the grouping of all the social sciences concerned with the study of people's behaviour. However, it is now more frequently used to refer to attempts to apply a selective, interdisciplinary approach to the study of human behaviour. *In particular, the term is often taken as applying more narrowly and specifically to problems of organisation and management in the work environment.*

Three main disciplines

There are areas of overlap among the various social sciences, their sub-divisions and related disciplines such as economics and political science. However, the study of behaviour can be viewed in terms of three main disciplines – psychology, sociology and anthropology. All three disciplines have made an important contribution to the field of organisational behaviour.

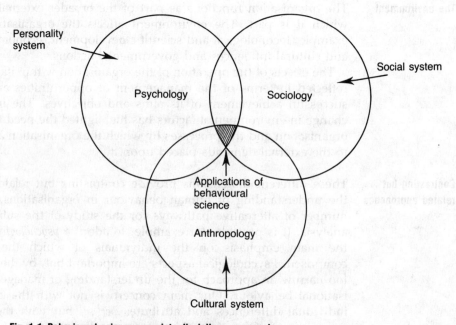

Fig. 1.1 Behavioural science – an interdisciplinary approach

- *Psychologists* are, broadly speaking, concerned with the study of human behaviour, with traits of the individual and membership of small social groups. The main focus of attention is on the individual as a whole person, or what can be termed the 'personality system'.
- *Sociologists* are more concerned with the study of social behaviour, relationships among social groups and societies, and the maintenance of order. The main focus of attention is on the social system.
- *Anthropologists* are more concerned with the science of mankind and the study of human behaviour as a whole. As far as organisational behaviour is concerned the main focus of attention is on the cultural system, the beliefs, customs, ideas and values within a group or society, and the comparison of behaviour among different cultures. People learn to depend on their culture to give them security and stability, and they can suffer adverse reactions to unfamiliar environments.

Personality system – Properties and traits of the individual, for example perception, attitudes, motives, feelings and processes.

Social systems – Analysis of social structures and positions in those structures, for example the relationship between the behaviour of leaders and followers.

Cultural system – Beliefs, customs, ideas and values within a society which affect the emphasis individuals place on certain activities, for example the importance to Muslim women of wearing trousers to work.

Contribution of behavioural science

The contribution of relevant aspects of psychology, sociology and anthropology aid our understanding of the behaviour of people in work organisations, and underpin the field of organisational behaviour.

Behavioural science attempts to structure organisations in order to secure the optimum working environment. It is concerned with reconciling the needs of the organisation for the contribution of maximum productivity, with the needs of individuals and the realisation of their potential. Emphasis is on the application of relevant aspects of psychological and sociological theory and practice, and cultural influences, to problems of organisation and management in the work situation.

You should not be confused by use of the word 'theory'. Most rational decisions are based on some form of theory. Theory contains a message on how managers might behave. This will influence attitudes towards management practice and lead to changes in actual behaviour. Theory helps in the building of generalised models applicable to all organisations. It further provides a conceptual framework and gives a perspective for the practical study of the subject. Thus theory and practice are inseparable. Together they lead to a better understanding of factors influencing patterns of behaviour in organisations and applications of the process of management.

THE PROCESS OF PERCEPTION

One characteristic feature of behaviour which has particular importance to the manager is the process of perception. We all see things in different ways. We all have our own, unique picture or image of how we see the 'real' world. Why is it, for example, that a memorandum from management to section heads to provide statistics of overtime worked within their section during the past six months and projection for the next six months, can provide such mixed reactions?

- One section head may see it as a reasonable and welcomed request to provide information which will help lead to improved future staffing levels.
- Yet, another section head may see it as an unreasonable demand, intended only to enable management to exercise closer supervision and control over the activities of the section.
- A third section head may have no objection to providing the information, but is suspicious that it may lead to possible intrusion into the running of the section.
- But a fourth section head may see it as a positive action by management to investigate ways of reducing costs and improving efficiency throughout the organisation.

Each of the section heads perceives the memorandum differently, and as perception becomes their reality of the situation each is likely to react accordingly.

Information from the environment The process of perception explains the manner in which information (stimuli) from the environment around us is selected and organised, to provide logic and meaning for the individual. Perception is the mental function of giving meaning and significance to stimuli such as shapes, colours, movement, taste, sounds, touch, smells, pain, pressures and feelings. Perception gives rise to individual behavioural responses to particular situations.

Despite the fact that a group of people may 'physically see' the same thing, each person has his or her own version of what is seen. It is the individual person's mental view of reality. Consider, for example, the shape

Fig. 1.2

in Fig. 1.2.[4] What do you see? Do you see a young, attractive, well-dressed woman? Or do you see an older, poor woman? Or can you now see both? Your response is likely to be based at least in part on your cultural experiences (*see* Fig. 1.3).

THE SELECTION AND ORGANISATION OF STIMULI

Through the process of *selection* attention is focused on certain specific stimuli, while others are screened or filtered out. After stimuli have passed through the selection process, they are *organised and arranged* in a way that is logical and meaningful to the individual.

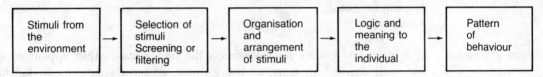

Fig. 1.3 The process of perception

Selection of stimuli The process of perceptual selection is based on both internal factors and external factors.

Internal factors are personality, learning, motives, preferences and expectations of what is to be perceived, and previous experiences. These factors give rise to an individual's *perceptual set*: that is the inclination or readiness to respond in certain ways to a given set of stimuli, but less inclination to respond to other stimuli.

People usually perceive stimuli that are likely to help satisfy their needs or prove pleasurable. For example, a manager deeply engrossed in preparing an urgent report may screen out ringing telephones, the sound of typewriters, people talking and furniture being moved in the next office; but respond readily to the smell of coffee brewing. The manager has been able to ignore the mildly disturbing stimuli but is likely to respond to more important ones, such as a fire alarm.

External factors refer to the nature and characteristics of the stimuli. There is usually a tendency to give more attention to stimuli which are, for example:

- large;
- moving;
- intense;
- loud;
- contrasted;
- bright;
- novel;
- repeated;
- stand out from the background.

Any number of these factors may be present at a given time or situation. It is, therefore, the *total pattern* of the stimuli and the *context* in which they occur that influence perception. For example, it is usually a novel or unfamiliar stimulus that is more noticeable, but a person is more likely to perceive the familiar face of a friend among a group of people all dressed in the same style uniform.

The sight of a fork-lift truck on the factory floor of a manufacturing organisation is likely to be perceived quite differently from one in the corridor of a polytechnic.

The word 'terminal' is likely to be perceived differently in the context of, for example, (i) a hospital, (ii) an airport or (iii) a computer firm.

Organisation of stimuli

The organisation and arrangement of stimuli is influenced by three important principles:

- figure and ground;
- grouping; and
- closure.

Figure and ground

In a *figure and ground* representation the figure may either appear as solid and well defined in front of the ground, or as a shapeless background. When there is no clear figure and ground pattern, individuals will tend to perceive the feature which most catches their attention.

Look at the example in Fig. 1.4.[5] What do you see? Do you see a white chalice (or small stand shape) in the centre of the frame? Or do you see the dark profiles of twins facing each other on the edges of the frame? Now look again to try and see the other.

Fig. 1.4

Grouping

The principle of *grouping* refers to the tendency to group stimuli into meaningful patterns according to continuity, proximity or similarity.

In Fig. 1.5(a) the workers are likely to be perceived as nine independent people; but in Fig. 1.5(b), because of the proximity principle, the workers may be perceived as three distinct sets of people.

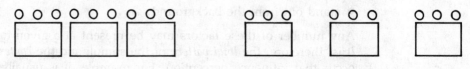

Fig. 1.5 (a)   Fig. 1.5 (b)

Taxi firms, for example, often use the idea of grouping to display their telephone number. In Fig. 1.6 which of the following numbers (a), (b) or (c) is most likely to be remembered easily?

265 265   265265   26 52 65
    (a)   (b)   (c)

Fig. 1.6

In Fig. 1.7 there is a tendency to see alternate lines of characters – crosses and noughts (or circles). This is because the horizontal similarity is usually greater than the vertical similarity. However, if the page is turned sideways the figure may be perceived as alternate noughts and crosses in each line. (It is also interesting to note that many people when asked to describe the figure refer to alternate lines of noughts and crosses – rather than crosses and noughts.)

X X X X X X X X X

O O O O O O O O O

X X X X X X X X X

O O O O O O O O O

Fig. 1.7

Closure

The principle of *closure* refers to the tendency to complete an object that is perceived as a whole, even though only parts of the object are in evidence. The object is completed in order to create the overall, mental picture and to provide a meaningful image. In the example in Fig. 1.8[6] most people are likely to perceive the blobs either as an unconnected letter B or the unconnected number 13, possibly depending on whether at the time they had been more concerned with written material or in dealing with numbers. However, for some people the pattern may remain as just a series of discrete blobs or be perceived as some other meaningful object.

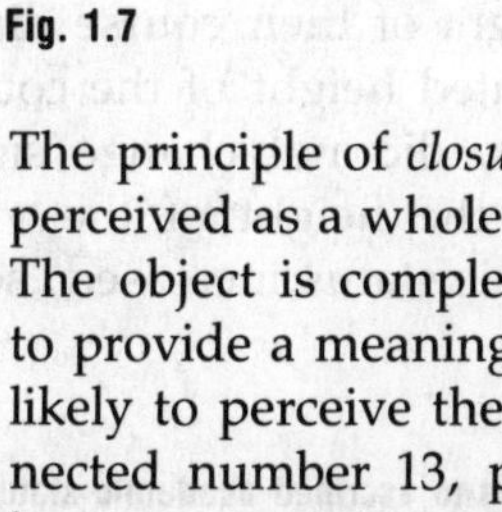

Fig. 1.8

OTHER FACTORS INFLUENCING PERCEPTION

Perception is also influenced by two other important factors:

- the situation, and
- perceptual judgement.

The knowledge of, familiarity with, or expectations about a *given situation*, or previous experiences, will influence perception.

Perceptual judgement applies particularly to perceptions about other people. A person may tend to organise perception of another person in terms of the 'whole' mental picture of that person. Perceptual judgement is influenced by reference to related characteristics associated with the person and the attempt to place that person in a complete environment.

In one example, an unknown visitor was introduced by the course director to 110 students, divided into five equal groups.[7] The visitor was described differently to each group as:

(i)   Mr England, a student from Cambridge;
(ii) Mr England, demonstrator in psychology from Cambridge;
(iii) Mr England, lecturer in psychology from Cambridge;
(iv) Dr England, senior lecturer from Cambridge;
(v)   Professor England from Cambridge.

After being introduced to each group, the visitor left. Each group of students were then asked to estimate his height to the nearest $\frac{1}{2}$ inch. They were also asked to estimate the height of their course director after he too had left the room. The mean estimated height of the course director, who had the same status for all groups, did not change significantly among groups. However, the estimate of the height of the visitor varied with perceived status: as ascribed academic status increased, so did the estimate of height. (*See* Table 1.1.)

Table 1.1 Estimated height according to ascribed academic status.

Group	Ascribed academic status	Average estimated height
(i)	Student	5' 9.9"
(ii)	Demonstrator	5' 10.14"
(iii)	Lecturer	5' 10.9"
(iv)	Senior lecturer	5' 11.6"
(v)	Professor	6' 0.3"

(Adapted from P. R. Wilson, 'Perceptual Distortion of Height as a Function of Ascribed Academic Status', *Journal of Social Psychology*, no. 74, 1968, pp. 97–102.)

Further examples Here are three further examples to help you judge your own perceptive skills.

In Fig. 1.9 try reading aloud the four words. It is possible that you find yourself in a perceptual set which means that you tend to pronounce 'machinery' as if it too was a Scottish surname.

In Fig. 1.10[8] which of the centre circles is the larger? The circle on the right may well appear larger because it is framed by smaller circles; and the circle on the left smaller because it is framed by larger circles. However, the two circles are the same size.

M – A – C – D – O – N – A – L – D

M – A – C – P – H – E – R – S – O – N

M – A – C – D – O – U – G – A – L – L

M – A – C – H – I – N – E – R – Y

Fig. 1.9

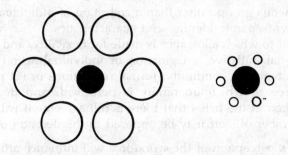

Fig. 1.10

Fig. 1.11

In Fig. 1.11[9] which of the three people is the tallest? Although the person on the right may appear the tallest, they are in fact all the same size.

PERCEIVING OTHER PEOPLE

The principles and examples of perceptual differences discussed above reflect the way we perceive other people and are the source of many organisational problems. In the work situation the process of perception and the selection of stimuli can influence a manager's relationship with subordinate staff. Some examples might be as follows.

- The way in which a manager may think of a number of staff: either working in close proximity; or with some common feature such as all clerical workers, all management trainees or all black workers; as a homogeneous group rather than a collection of individuals each with his or her own separate identity and characteristics.
- The extent to which allowance is made for flexibility, and tolerance given, for personal initiative, imagination or individual action by staff; rather than insistence on continuity, formal regulations or set procedures.
- The degree to which unanimity is perceived, and decisions made or action taken in the belief that there is full agreement with staff; when in fact a number of staff may be opposed to the decision or action.

A manager's perception of the workforce will influence attitudes in dealing with people and the style of managerial behaviour adopted. The way in which managers approach the performance of their jobs and the behaviour they display towards subordinate staff are likely to be conditioned by predispositions about people, human nature and work. An example of this is the style of management adopted on the basis of McGregor's Theory X and Y suppositions,[10] discussed in Chapter 9.

The perception of people's performance can be affected by the organisation of stimuli. In employment interviews, for example, interviewers are susceptible to contrast effects and the perception of a candidate is influenced by the rating given to immediately preceding candidates. Average candidates may be rated highly if they follow people with low qualifications, but rated lower when following people with higher qualifications.[11]

Perceptual distortions and errors

Differences in perception result in different people seeing different things and attaching different meanings to the same stimuli. Every person sees things in his or her own way and as perceptions become a person's reality this can lead to misunderstandings.

The accuracy of interpersonal perception and the judgements made about other people are influenced by:

- the nature of the relationship between the perceiver and the other person;
- the amount of information available to the perceiver and the order in which such information is received;
- the nature and extent of interaction between the two people.[12]

A manager might well know more about the 'type of person' A is – a member of staff who has become or was already a good friend, who is seen in a variety of social situations and with whom there is a close relationship – than about B – another member of staff, in the same section as A and undertaking similar duties, but with whom there is only a formal work relationship and a limited social acquaintanceship. These differences in relationship, information and interaction might well influence the manager's perception if asked, for example, to evaluate the work performance of A and of B.

Judgements of other people can also be influenced by perceptions of such stimuli as, for example:

- role or status;
- occupation;
- physical factors and appearance; and
- body language, for example inferences drawn from posture, the extent of eye contact, tone of voice or facial expression.

There are four main features which can create particular difficulties and give rise to perceptual errors, especially in dealings with other people – that is problems with people perception. These are:

- stereotyping;
- the halo effect;
- perceptual defence; and
- projection.

Stereotyping   This is the tendency to ascribe positive or negative characteristics to a person on the basis of a general categorisation and perceived similarities. The perception of that person may be based more on certain expected characteristics than on the recognition of that person as an individual. It is a form of typecasting.

Stereotyping is a means of simplifying the process of perception and making judgements of other people, instead of dealing with a range of complex and alternative stimuli. Examples of common stereotyping may be based on:

- Nationality – for example, all Germans are orderly and industrious;
- Occupation – for example, all accountants are boring;
- Age – for example, all young people are unreliable/no old person wants to consider new ideas;
- Physical – for example, all people with red hair have a fiery temperament;
- Sex – for example, all women are too emotional/all men are prejudiced;
- Education – for example, all graduates are clever;
- Social – for example, all unemployed people are lazy;
- Politics – for example, all labour voters are in favour of strong trade unions.

Halo effect   This is the process by which the perception of a person is formulated on the basis of one favourable or unfavourable trait or impression. The halo effect tends to shut out other relevant characteristics of that person. Some examples might be as follows:

- A candidate for employment who arrives punctually, is smart in appearance and friendly, may well influence the perception of the selectors –

who then place less emphasis on the candidate's technical ability, qualifications or experience for the job.

- A new member of staff who performs well in a first major assignment may be perceived as a likely person for promotion, even though that assignment is not typical of the usual duties the member of staff is expected to undertake.
- A single trait, such as good attendance and time keeping, may become the main emphasis for judgement of overall competence and performance, rather than other considerations such as the quantity, quality and accuracy of work.

A particular danger with the halo effect is that, where quick judgements are made on the basis of readily available stimuli, the perceiver may become 'perceptually blind' to subsequent stimuli at variance with the original perception, and (often subconsciously) notice only those characteristics which support the original judgement.

Perceptual defence This is the tendency to avoid or screen out certain stimuli that are perceptually disturbing or threatening. People may tend to select information which is supportive of their point of view and choose not to acknowledge contrary information. For example, a manager, who has decided recently to promote a member of staff against the advice of colleagues, may select only favourable information which supports that decision and ignore less favourable information which questions that decision.

Projection This is the tendency for people to project their own feelings, motives or characteristics to their perception of other people. Judgements of other people may be more favourable when they have characteristics largely in common with, and easily recognised by, the perceiver. Projection may also result in people exaggerating undesirable traits in others that they fail to recognise in themselves.

Perception is distorted by feelings and emotions. For example, a manager who is concerned about possible redundancy may perceive other managers to be even more concerned. People have a tendency to perceive others less favourably by projecting certain of their own feelings or characteristics to them. As another example, supervisors may complain that their manager did not work hard enough to secure additional resources for the department, when in fact the supervisors failed to provide the manager with all the relevant information and statistics.

Perception of 'self' and how people see and think of themselves, and the evaluation of themselves, are discussed in Chapter 14.

MANAGEMENT AS AN INTEGRATING ACTIVITY

Every work organisation is concerned with being effective, especially now in a difficult economic environment and in the face of fierce world competition. Organisational effectiveness should be the concern of everyone within the organisation. Upon the attainment of its aims and objectives will rest the success and ultimate survival of the organisation.

It is through the process of management that the efforts of members of

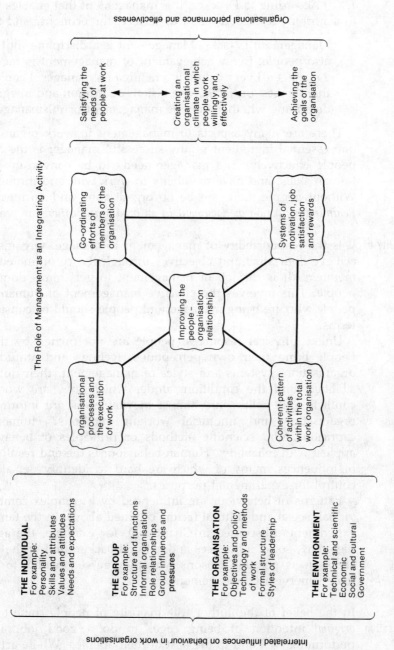

Organisational performance and effectiveness

Satisfying the needs of people at work ←→ Creating an organisational climate in which people work willingly and effectively ←→ Achieving the goals of the organisation

The Role of Management as an Integrating Activity

Go-ordinating efforts of members of the organisation

Systems of motivation, job satisfaction and rewards

Improving the people – organisation relationship

Organisational processes and the execution of work

Coherent pattern of activities within the total work organisation

THE INDIVIDUAL
For example:
Personality
Skills and attributes
Values and attitudes
Needs and expectations

THE GROUP
For example:
Structure and functions
Informal organisation
Role relationships
Group influences and pressures

THE ORGANISATION
For example:
Objectives and policy
Technology and methods of work
Formal structure
Styles of leadership

THE ENVIRONMENT
For example:
Technical and scientific
Economic
Social and cultural
Government

Interrelated influences on behaviour in work organisations

Fig. 1.12 Management as the cornerstone of organisational effectiveness

the organisation are co-ordinated, directed and guided towards the achievement of organisational goals. Management is therefore the cornerstone of organisational effectiveness, and is concerned with arrangements for the carrying out of organisational processes and the execution of work. (*See* Fig. 1.12.) According to Drucker, it is management that enables the organisation to contribute a needed result to society, the economy and the individual.

> Management is tasks. Management is a discipline. But management is also people. Every achievement of management is the achievement of a manager. Every failure is a failure of a manager. People manage rather than 'forces' or 'facts'. The vision, dedication and integrity of managers determine whether there is management or mismanagement.[13]

There are many aspects to management in work organisations, but the one essential ingredient of any successful manager is the ability to handle people effectively. The manager needs to be conversant with social and human skills, and have the ability to work with and through other people. Without people there can be no organisation and no meaningful activity. *Behind every action or document in an organisation there are people.*

The responsibility of management

It is the responsibility of management to manage. Organisations can only achieve their aims and objectives through the co-ordinated efforts of their members. It is the job of management to get things done through other people. This involves the effective management of human resources. It is people who are being managed and people should be considered in human terms.

Unlike physical resources, people are not owned by the organisation. People bring their own perceptions, feelings and attitudes towards the organisation, systems and styles of management, their duties and responsibilities, and the conditions under which they are working. Tensions, conflicts and politics are almost inevitable, as are informal structures of organisation and unofficial working methods. Human behaviour is capricious, and scientific methods or principles of behaviour cannot be applied with reliability. 'Human behaviour is the end result of a multiplicity of influences, many of which are hard to identify, let alone measure or control for experimental purposes.[14]

Patterns of behaviour are influenced by a complex combination of individual, social and cultural factors outlined above. In the famous Hawthorne experiments (discussed in Chapter 2), for example, the ages, 'sex power' hierarchy, social influences and cultural background of the women workers are seen as possible reasons why they agreed readily to participate with male supervisory management.

The people–organisation relationship

In the belief of the author, the majority of people come to work with the *original* intention of being eager to do a good job, and desirous of performing well and to the best of their abilities. Where actual performance fails to match the ideal this is largely a result of how staff perceive they are treated by management and the management function.

Many problems in the people–organisational relationship arise not so much from what management does, *but the manner in which it is done.* Often, it is *not so much the intent* but the *manner of implementation* that is the root cause of staff unrest and dissatisfaction. For example, staff may agree on the need to introduce new technology to retain the competitive efficiency of the organisation; but feel resentment about the lack of pre-planning, consultation, training programmes, participation in agreeing new working practices and similar considerations arising from the manner of its introduction.

Therefore, a heavy responsibility is placed on managers and the activity of management – on the processes, systems and styles of management. Accordingly, how managers exercise the responsibility for, and duties of, management is important. Attention must be given to the work environment, and appropriate systems of motivation, job satisfaction and rewards.

It is difficult to think of any aspect of the functioning of the organisation, or behaviour of people, which does not concern, or relate back to, management in some way. For example, even personality clashes between two individual members of staff could possibly be traced back to management procedures for recruitment and selection, induction and training, delegation or the level and style of supervision. And clearly the personality clashes are likely to affect the work performance of the members concerned and also affect the morale of other staff.

Providing the right balance

Management should, therefore, endeavour to create the right balance among the interrelated elements which make up the total organisation, and to weld these into coherent patterns of activity best suited to the external environment in which the organisation is operating. Consideration must be given to developing an organisational climate in which people work willingly and effectively.

People and organisations need each other. *Attention should be focused, therefore, on improving the people–organisation relationship.* Management is an integral part of this relationship. It should serve to reconcile the needs of people at work with the requirements of the organisation. Management is essentially an integrating activity which permeates every facet of the operations of the organisation.

THE PSYCHOLOGICAL CONTRACT

One particular aspect of the relationship between the individual and the organisation is the concept of the psychological contract. This is not a written document, but implies a series of mutual expectations and satisfaction of needs arising from the people–organisation relationship. It involves a process of giving and receiving by the individual and by the organisation. The psychological contract covers a range of expectations of rights and privileges, duties and obligations, which do not form part of a formal agreement but still have an important influence on people's behaviour.[15]

Individuals' expectations

The nature and extent of individual's expectations vary widely, as do the ability and willingness of the organisation to meet them. It is difficult to list the range of implicit expectations that individuals have, and they change over time, but they may include that the organisation will, for example:

- provide safe and hygienic working conditions;
- make every reasonable effort to provide job security;

- attempt to provide challenging and satisfying jobs and reduce alienating aspects of work;
- adopt equitable personnel policies and procedures;
- allow staff genuine participation in decisions which affect them;
- provide reasonable opportunities for personal development and career progression;
- treat members of staff with respect;
- demonstrate an understanding and considerate attitude towards personal problems of staff.

These expectations are notwithstanding any statutory requirements placed upon the organisation. Instead, they relate more to the idea of a social responsibility of management, which is discussed in Chapter 4.

The organisation's expectations

The organisation will also have implicit expectations of its members, for example:

- to accept the ideology of the organisation;
- to work diligently in pursuit of organisational objectives;
- not to abuse goodwill shown by management;
- to uphold the image of the organisation;
- to show loyalty;
- not to betray positions of trust.

The organisational side of the psychological contract places emphasis on expectations, requirements and constraints which often differ from, and may be in conflict with, an individual's expectations. For example, *French* suggests the following list of organisational expectations and requirements:

1. Achieving organisational goals that are different from the personal goals of individual members.
2. Having sufficient involvement, commitment, and initiative from organisational members.
3. Requiring individuals to take certain organisational roles.
4. Having people perform certain tasks effectively and efficiently.
5. Requiring participants to accept authority and to assume responsibilities.
6. Achieving the integration and coordination of activities.
7. Requiring adherence to policies, rules and procedures.
8. Attaining responsiveness to leadership and influence.
9. Developing sufficient loyalty to maintain the organisation as a social system.[16]

Process of balancing

It is unlikely that all expectations of the individual or of the organisation will be met fully. There is a continual process of balancing, and explicit and implicit bargaining. The nature of these expectations is not defined formally, and although the individual member and the organisation may not be aware consciously of them, they still affect relationships between them and have an influence on behaviour.[17]

The psychological contract is a useful concept in examining the socialisation of new members of staff to the organisation. According to *Kotter*, for example, early experiences have a major effect on an individual's subsequent career in an organisation, and influence job satisfaction, attitude and level of productivity. The extent of the matches between individual and organisational expectations also influences the willingness of people to stay with the organisation and of the organisation to continue to employ them.[18]

THE STUDY OF MANAGEMENT AND ORGANISATIONAL BEHAVIOUR

The use of separate topic areas is a recognised academic means of aiding study and explanation of the subject. In practice, however, the activities of an organisation and the job of management cannot be isolated, neatly, in discrete categories. The majority of actions are likely to involve a number of simultaneous functions that relate to the total processes of management.

Consider, for example, a manager briefing departmental staff on an unexpected, important and urgent task which has to be undertaken. Such a briefing is likely to involve consideration of goals and objectives, organisation structure, management system, process of delegation, systems of communication, leadership style, motivation and management control systems. The behaviour of the staff will be influenced by a combination of individual, group, organisational and environmental factors.

Topic studies in organisational behaviour should not be regarded, therefore, as entirely free-standing. Any study of organisation and management inevitably covers several aspects, and each study can be used to a greater or lesser extent to confirm generalisations made about particular topic areas. The use of the same studies to illustrate different aspects of management and organisational behaviour serves as useful revision and reinforcement, and helps to bring about a greater awareness and understanding of the subject.

No single, right answer

By now, you will probably be aware that a feature of the study of management and organisational behaviour is the invariable difficulty in identification of a single solution to a particular problem. The absence of one, right answer can make study of the subject complex and frustrating. But the area of study can also be interesting and challenging, stimulating creative thought and ideas, and it can be related to your own work experience.

A useful model for the study of management and organisational behaviour is to see the organisation as an open system, which is discussed in Chapter 3. The open system approach views the organisation within its broader, external environment and places emphasis on multiple channels of interaction. It provides a means of viewing the total organisation and of embracing different dimensions of analysis. The open system model provides a perspective for a managerial approach to organisational behaviour. It helps in the search for the most appropriate ways of influencing the behaviour of people within an organisational setting.

THE USE OF CASE STUDIES[19]

Case studies are becoming increasingly popular as a part of the study of management and organisational behaviour. There are a variety of types of case studies and they may be presented in a number of different ways. Case studies range from, for example, a brief account of events which may be actual, contrived or a combination of both; 'armchair' cases based on hypothetical but realistic situations, and developed to draw out and illustrate particular points of principle; to complex, multi-dimensional cases giving a fuller descriptive account of actual situations in real organisations. The term 'case study' may be extended to include critical incident analysis, role play and the in-tray (or in-basket) exercise, although these are more methods of training.[20]

A case study may require you to work on an individual basis or it may involve group work. It may also specify that you are to assume a particular role, for example as financial controller, manager or consultant.

Objectives of use of case studies

Whatever the nature or form of case studies, a major objective of their use is usually the application of theoretical knowledge to practical situations and/or the integration of knowledge drawn from a number of related disciplines or areas of study. Case studies are basically problem analysis and decision-making exercises. They provide a test of the ability to distinguish real issues from less significant matters. There is unlikely to be a single, right answer.

Case studies, therefore, provide the participants with an opportunity to demonstrate analytical ability, logical thinking, judgement and persuasiveness and skills of communication in the presentation of answers. If the case study is undertaken as a group exercise it provides, also, a means of assessing both the performance of the group as a whole and the ability of individuals to work effectively as members of the group.

Guidelines on tackling case studies

The level and depth of analysis, and the type of answer required, will depend upon the particular case study and the reasons for its use. However, despite variations in the nature and format of case studies it is possible to suggest general guidelines on how to tackle them.

(i) Read the whole of the case study. Try to get a 'feel' for what it is about and note what the question(s) asks you to do. Check on the time allowed.

(ii) Read the case study a second time. Look at the material carefully and try to identify with the situation. Check again on exactly what you are required to do and instructions on how to present your answer. For example, if a report is called for, your answer should be presented in proper report form. Check whether you are to assume a specific role and if your answer is to be directed at a specified audience, for example a senior manager, the board of directors or a committee.

(iii) If there are a number of different parts to the case study you should apportion available time and 'weight' your answers accordingly.

(iv) Approach your analysis of the case study with an open mind. Be conscious of any bias or prejudice you may have and avoid any predispositions which may influence your perception of the case material. Do not jump to hasty or unfounded conclusions. Do not formulate firm opinions or solutions until you have collated all the available evidence.

(v) Adopt a brainstorming approach and take the case apart by exploring all reasonably possible considerations. Remember there may be a number of separate problems with separate causes and a number of alternative courses of action.

(vi) You may need to search for hidden meanings and issues which are not at first readily apparent. Do not, however, make things unnecessarily complicated. Do not take the 'obvious' for granted and do not neglect simple responses which help to provide a satisfactory answer to the question as worded.

(vii) A particular feature of case study work is that you are likely to have only limited information. You should, therefore, make a point of studying all the details given in the case material, first, to make certain of the facts; and second, to identify what deductions or inferences can be drawn from these facts. You may feel it necessary to make certain assumptions. If so, these assumptions should follow *reasonably* from the case material and serve only to help clarify the situation. Even if not specifically requested to do so, it is recommended that you make clear any necessary assumptions as part of your answer.

(viii) The case study may set out deliberately to present a tangle of information, events or situations which need to be unravelled in order to clarify links and relationships, and to distinguish causes from effects, and symptoms from problems. Concentrate on what you see to be the more important matters as opposed to any irrelevant detail or possible red herrings which may confuse the real issues.

(ix) In your analysis of the case material you may find it helpful to emphasise key words or phrases, including emotive language and actions. You may also find it helpful to:
- list the people involved and draw a pen picture of them from the available information; and
- trace the sequence and timing of events which have led to the present situation.

The use of margin notes, underlining, numbering and/or lettering, colours or highlighting pens may all be useful but you should be careful not to make your analysis confused or too complicated.

(x) Where appropriate, relate your analysis of the case material to your theoretical studies, general points of principle and the work of leading writers. It is always valuable to be able to draw upon practical experience but make sure it is relevant to the particular circumstances. You may still be able to make use of knowledge gained from experience not related directly to the case study, but avoid the temptation to distort your perception of the situation as described to suit your own personal experience.

(xi) Bearing in mind the question, clearly identify existing or potential difficulties or problem areas and indicate where you see the need for most urgent action. Where you have identified a number of possible courses of action indicate your recommended priorities. Bear in mind also practical considerations such as timing, costs and existing personalities. Where appropriate give reasons in support of your recommendations.

(xii) Draw up a plan of key points as the basis of your answer.

(xiii) The use of visual displays such as diagrams, charts or tables may enhance the presentation of your answer. But make sure such visual displays are accurate, clear and relate directly to your analysis of the case material, and to the question as worded. Every visual display should be given a meaningful title, and serve to help the reading and interpretation of your answer. Do not be tempted to use visual displays for their own sake or to spend too much time on an over-elaborate display at the expense of more important matters.

(xiv) Allow time to read through and check your work.

Synopsis

Organisations play a major and continuing role in the lives of us all, especially with the growth of large-scale business organisations. The decisions and actions of management in organisations have an increasing impact on individuals, other organisations and the community. It is important, therefore, to understand how organisations function and the pervasive influences they exercise over the behaviour of people.

There are four main interrelated influences on the behaviour of people in work organisations: the individual, the group, the organisation and the environment. The study of organisational behaviour cannot be understood fully in terms of a single discipline. It is necessary to provide an interdisciplinary behavioural science approach drawing on selected aspects of psychology, sociology and anthropology. The main focus of attention of psychology is on the personality system; sociology on the social system; and, as far as organisational behaviour is concerned, anthropology on the cultural system.

One characteristic feature of behaviour of particular importance to the manager is the process of perception. People all see things differently and have their own unique picture or image of how they see things – the 'real' world. Perception gives rise to individual behavioural responses in particular situations through the selection and organisation of stimuli (information). With interpersonal perception there are four main features which give rise to perceptual distortions or errors: stereotyping, the halo effect, perceptual defence and projection. In the work situation perceptual differences reflect the way we perceive other people and are the source of many organisational problems.

It is through the process of management that efforts of members of the organisation are co-ordinated, directed and guided towards the achievement of organisational objectives. Management is therefore the cornerstone of organisational effectiveness, and is concerned with arrangements for the carrying out of organisational processes and the execution of work. How managers exercise the responsibility for, and duties of, management is important. Attention should be focused on improving the people–organisation relationship. Management is essentially an integrating activity which permeates every facet of the operations of the organisation.

One particular aspect of the relationship between the individual and the organisation is the concept of the psychological contract. This is not a formal, written document but implies a series of mutual expectations and satisfaction of needs arising from the people–organisation relationship. It involves a process of giving and receiving by the individual and by the organisation. There is a continual process of explicit and implicit bargaining.

The nature of expectations has an important influence on behaviour in work organisations.

The activities of an organisation and the job of management cannot be isolated, neatly, in discrete categories. The majority of actions are likely to involve a number of simultaneous functions that relate to the total process of management. A useful model for the study of management and organisational behaviour is to see the organisation as an open system within its broader external environment and with multiple channels of interaction. The use of case studies is becoming increasingly popular as part of the study of management and organisational behaviour. Whatever the nature or form of case studies, a major objective of their use is usually the application of theoretical knowledge to practical situations and/or the integration of knowledge drawn from a number of related disciplines or areas of study.

Review and discussion questions

1. Explain your understanding of (i) the nature of organisational behaviour; and (ii) the meaning of behavioural science.
2. Suggest main headings under which can be identified interrelated factors which influence behaviour in work organisations. For each of your headings give examples from your own organisation.
3. What do you understand by the process of perception? Why is the study of perception important to management and organisational behaviour?
4. What factors influence the judgements we make of other people? Explain main sources of distortions or errors in interpersonal perception. Support your answer with practical examples.
5. Discuss the role of management as an integrating activity. Give your own views on the responsibility of management and the manner in which you believe this responsibility should be exercised.
6. Explain the nature of the people–organisation relationship. Why is it important to distinguish between the 'intent' and the 'implementation' of management decisions and actions?
7. Explain what is meant by the 'psychological contract'. List (i) the personal expectations you have of your own organisation; and (ii) what you believe to be the expectations of the organisation. To what extent are these lists of expectations compatible?
8. Discuss what you believe are particular difficulties presented by the study of management and organisational behaviour. Where possible give practical examples based on your own experience.

Assignment 1 | INFERENCE–OBSERVATION

1. Read the following short story.
2. Then read the 15 statements about the story and check each to indicate whether you consider it true, false, or?
   'T' means that the statement is *definitely true* on the basis of the information presented in the stroy.
   'F' means that it is *definitely false*.
   '?' means that it may be either true or false and that you cannot be certain

which on the basis of the information presented in the story. If any part of a statement is doubtful, mark it '?'.

3. Answer each statement in turn. Do not go back to change any answer later and do not re-read any statements after you have answered them.

The Story

A businessman had just turned off the lights in the store when a man appeared and demanded money. The owner opened a cash register. The contents of the cash register were scooped up, and the man sped away. A member of the police force was notified promptly.

Statements about the story

1. A man appeared after the owner had turned off his store lights.	T	F	?
2. The robber was a *man*.	T	F	?
3. The man who appeared did not demand money.	T	F	?
4. The man who opened the cash register was the owner.	T	F	?
5. The store owner scooped up the contents of the cash register and ran away.	T	F	?
6. Someone opened a cash register.	T	F	?
7. After the man who demanded the money scooped up the contents of the cash register, he ran away.	T	F	?
8. While the cash register contained money, the story does *not* state *how much*.	T	F	?
9. The robber demanded money of the owner.	T	F	?
10. A businessman had just turned off the lights when a man appeared in the store.	T	F	?
11. It was broad daylight when the man appeared.	T	F	?
12. The man who appeared opened the cash register.	T	F	?
13. No one demanded money.	T	F	?
14. The story concerns a series of events in which only three persons are referred to: the owner of the store, a man who demanded money, and a member of the police force.	T	F	?
15. The following events occurred: someone demanded money, a cash register was opened, its contents were scooped up, and a man dashed out of the store.	T	F	?

4. After you have completed checking all 15 statements, work in small groups of three to five and discuss your individual answers.
   How much agreement is there among members of your group?
   On what basis did members of your group give different answers and how did their perception of the statements about the story differ?
   Do not change any of your first individual answers. However, if as a result of your group discussion you would now give a different answer to any of the statements, note this alongside your original answer.

| Case study |

John Adams was on duty as a member of the night service staff with ABC Hotel. After an overseas guest clicked her fingers and whistled for service Adams lost his temper. 'You're not the only guest in this hotel.' He then warned the guest that if she did not stop her obnoxious behaviour no one would provide her or anyone else with service. Next day the guest complained to a chambermaid. Adams was reprimanded by the personnel manager of the hotel and threatened with dismissal. In his defence Adams admitted that heated words were exchanged with the guest when she left the lounge late that night to go to her room. 'I did not swear at her but I did allow her to rile me. She started causing trouble as soon as she came into the lounge after the bar had closed. The day staff warned me about her when they went off duty. She was clicking her fingers and whistling for service all night. She threw the tray back at me when I took food to her room at 3 o'clock in the morning. I told her it was about time she stopped behaving like that. I just had enough of everything. I told her she would not get any more service if she treated people like that.'

(i) Analyse the main issue(s) of management and organisational behaviour identified in this situation.
(ii) Suggest how the issue(s) might best be resolved. Assuming you are the general manager of ABC Hotel, what action would you propose to take?

Assignment 2

From your own experience, preferably in a work situation, provide for class discussion a short description of a 'person problem'.

(i) Identify clearly the significant nature of the problem, which should be a definite inconvenience rather than just a minor irritation.
(ii) Where possible, choose a problem which is persistent rather than a one-off situation.
(iii) Describe the nature of the behaviour/actions involved.
(iv) Where appropriate explain what actions you have already taken to help overcome the problem and with what results.
and/or
What solutions would you now propose might be adopted?
(v) Limit your description to not more than 500 words.

Notes and references

1. A summary of some merits in understanding organisational behaviour theory and the role of management is given in Mullins, L. J. 'The Organisation and the Individual', *Administrator*, vol. 7, no. 4, April 1987, pp. 11–14.
2. See, for example: Luthans, F. *Organisational Behaviour*, Fourth edition, McGraw-Hill (1985).
3. For further details of recurring themes in organisational behaviour and premises about life in organisations see, for example: Porter, L. W., Lawler, E. E. and Hackman, J. R. *Behaviour in Organisations*, McGraw-Hill (1975).
4. Hill, W. E. *Puck*, 6 November 1915.
5. Berleson, B. and Steiner, G. A. *Human Behaviour*, Harcourt Brace and World (1967) p. 151
6. Morgan, C. T. and King, R. A. *Introduction to Psychology*, Third edition, McGraw-Hill (1966) p. 343.
7. Wilson, P. R. 'Perceptual Distortion of Height as a Function of Ascribed Academic Status', *Journal of Social Psychology*, no. 74, 1968, pp. 97–102.
8. Hellriegel, D., Slocum, J. W. and Woodman, R. W. *Organisational Behaviour*, Fourth edition, West Publishing (1986) p. 90.
9. Luthans, F. *Organisational Behaviour*, Fourth edition, McGraw-Hill (1985) p. 166.
10. McGregor, D. *The Human Side of Enterprise*, McGraw-Hill (1960), Penguin (1987).
11. Wexley, K. N., Yukl, G. A., Kovacs, S. Z. and Sanders, R. E. 'Importance of Contrast Effects in Employment Interviews', *Journal of Applied Psychology*, 56, 1972, pp. 45–8.

12. For a more detailed analysis of the accuracy of interpersonal perception and problems in judgement of others, see: Krech, D., Crutchfield, R. S. and Ballachey, E. L *Individual in Society*, McGraw-Hill (1962).
13. Drucker, P. F. *Management*, Pan Books (1979) p. 14.
14. Gellerman, S. W. *Behavioural Science in Management*, Penguin (1974) p. 10.
15. See, for example: Schein, E. H. *Organizational Psychology*, Third edition, Prentice-Hall (1980).
16. French, W. L., Kast, F. E. and Rosenzweig, J. E. *Understanding Human Behaviour in Organisations*, Harper and Row (1985) pp. 42–3.
17. See, for example: Argyris, C. *Understanding Organisational Behaviour*, Dorsey (1960).
18. Kotter, J. P. 'The Psychological Contract: Managing the Joining-up Process', *California Management Review*, vol. 15, no. 3, 1973, pp. 91–9.
19. Based on Mullins, L. J. 'Tackling Case Studies', *Student Administrator*, vol. 1, no. 5, June 1984.
20. There are a number of books which provide complementary case study material and practical exercises. See, for example: Chilver, J. *People, Communication and Organisation: A Case Study Approach*, Pergamon Press (1984); Clegg, C. W., Kemp, N. J. and Legge, K. *Case Studies in Organizational Behaviour*, Harper and Row (1985).

2. APPROACHES TO ORGANISATION AND MANAGEMENT

Management is a discursive subject and much has been written about it. The study of organisations and their management has, therefore, to proceed on a broad front. No single approach to organisation and management provides all the answers. It is the comparative study of the different approaches which will yield benefits to the manager. The study of organisations, their structure and management is important for the manager. Identification of major trends in management and organisational behaviour, and the work of leading writers provides a perspective on concepts and ideas discussed in more detail in other chapters.[1]

Objectives

To: (i) Explain the relationships between management theory and practice;
(ii) Identify major trends in the development of organisational behaviour and management thinking;
(iii) Contrast main features of different approaches to organisation and management;
(iv) Evaluate the relevance of these different approaches to the present-day management of organisations;
(v) Assess the value of the study of management theory and different approaches to organisation and management;
(vi) Recognise the relationship between the development of theory, behaviour in organisations and management practice;
(vii) Provide a basis for consideration of aspects of management and organisational behaviour discussed in following chapters.

MANAGEMENT THEORY

Writing on organisation and management, in some form or another, can be traced back thousands of years.[2] However, the systematic development of management thinking is viewed, generally, as dating from the end of the nineteenth century with the emergence of large industrial organisations, and the ensuing problems associated with their structure and management.

A central part of the study of organisation and management is the development of management thinking and what might be termed management theory. The application of theory brings about change in actual behaviour. Managers reading the work of leading writers on the subject might see in their ideas and conclusions a message of how they should behave. This will influence their attitudes towards management practice. As *McGregor* puts it:

Every managerial act rests on assumptions, generalizations, and hypotheses – that is to say, on theory. Our assumptions are frequently implicit, sometimes quite unconscious, often conflicting; nevertheless, they determine our predictions that if we do *a*, *b* will occur. Theory and practice are inseparable.[3]

Importance of management theory

The study of management theory is important, therefore, because:

- What leading writers say is an important part of the study of management;
- It is necessary to view the interrelationships between the development of theory, behaviour in organisations and management practice;
- An understanding of the development of management thinking helps in understanding principles underlying the process of management;
- Knowledge of the history helps in understanding the nature of management and organisational behaviour, and reasons for the attention given to main topic areas;
- Many of the earlier ideas are of continuing importance to the manager and later ideas on management tend to incorporate earlier ideas and conclusions.

DEVELOPMENTS IN MANAGEMENT AND ORGANISATIONAL BEHAVIOUR

It is helpful, therefore, to trace major developments in management and organisational behaviour, and what has led to the concentration of attention on such topics as structure, motivation, groups, leadership and organisation development.

Miner makes the point that the more that is known about organisations and their methods of operation, the better the chances of dealing effectively with them. Understanding may be more advanced than prediction, but both provide the opportunity to influence or to manage the future. Theory provides a sound basis for action.[4] However, if action is to be effective, the theory must be adequate and appropriate to the task and to improved organisational performance. It must be a 'good' theory.

In order to help identify main trends in the development of organisational behaviour and management theory it is usual to categorise the work of writers into various 'approaches', based on their views of organisations, their structure and management. This provides a framework in which to direct study and focus attention on the progression of ideas concerned with improving organisational performance. There are many ways of categorising these various approaches. For example, *Skipton* attempts a classification of eleven main schools of management theory.[5]

However, a commonly used analysis is the simpler three-fold heading of Classical, Human Relations and Systems. This form of analysis is found, although perhaps at different levels of refinement and detail, in much of the literature. *O'Shaughnessy*, for example, suggests that only these three broad approaches are still distinguished but acknowledges that 'Each of these could, however, have been broken down still further as this broad classification ignores many minor differences among writers that could give rise to sub-grouping and cross-grouping'.[6]

Some of these 'sub-groupings and cross-groupings' might be seen as mutually exclusive, others might be seen as sub-divisions of a broader approach or as an attempt to synthesise the ideas of earlier approaches. Whilst it is possible to argue with O'Shaughnessy that only three broad approaches are still distinguished, the categorisation of Classical, Human Relations and Systems provides a convenient broad framework as a basis for our discussions.

THE CLASSICAL APPROACH

The classical writers thought of the organisation in terms of its purpose and formal structure. They placed emphasis on the planning of work, the technical requirements of the organisation, principles of management, and the assumption of rational and logical behaviour. The analysis of organisation in this manner is associated with work carried out initially in the early part of this century, by such writers as *Taylor, Fayol, Urwick, Mooney* and *Reiley* and *Brech*.

A clear understanding of the purpose of an organisation is seen as essential to understanding how the organisation works and how its methods of working can be improved. Identification of general objectives would lead to the clarification of purposes and responsibilities at all levels of the organisation, and to the most effective structure. Attention is given to the division of work, the clear definition of duties and responsibilities, and maintaining specialisation and co-ordination. Emphasis is on a hierarchy of management and formal organisational relationships.

Sets of principles The classical writers (also variously known as the structural, formal or scientific management writers – although scientific management is really only a part of the classical approach) were concerned with improving the organisation structure as a means of increasing efficiency. They emphasised the importance of principles for the design of a logical structure of organisation. Their writings were in a normative style and they saw these principles as a set of 'rules' offering general solutions to common problems of organisation and management.

Most classical writers had their own set of principles but among the most publicised are those of *Fayol* and *Urwick*. Fayol recognised there was no limit to the principles of management but in his writing he advocated fourteen.[7] Urwick originally specified eight principles, but these were revised to ten in his later writing.[8] (*See* Chapters 5 and 8.)

Mooney and *Reiley* set out a number of common principles which relate to all types of organisations. They place particular attention on:

- *The principle of co-ordination* – the need for people to act together with unity of action, the exercise of authority and the need for discipline;
- *The scalar principle* – the hierarchy of organisation, the grading of duties and the process of delegation;
- *The functional principle* – specialisation and the distinction between different kinds of duties.[9]

Brech attempts to provide a practical approach to organisation structure based on tried general principles as opposed to the concentration on specific cases or complex generalisations of little value to the practising manager. He sets out the various functions in the organisation and the definition of formal organisational relationships.[10] Although clearly a strong supporter of the formal approach in some of his views such as, for example, on the principle of span of control, Brech is less definite than other classical writers and recognises a degree of flexibility according to the particular situation.

Brech does, however, place great emphasis on the need for written definition of responsibilities and the value of job descriptions as an aid to effective organisation and delegation. This work builds on from the ideas of earlier writers, such as Urwick, and provides, therefore, a comprehensive view of the classical approach to organisation and management.

Evaluation of the classical approach

The classical writers have been criticised generally for not taking sufficient account of personality factors, and of creating an organisation structure in which people can exercise only a limited control over their work environment. The idea of sets of principles to guide managerial action has also been subject to much criticism. For example, *Simon* writes: 'Organisational design is not unlike architectural design. It involves creating large, complex systems having multiple goals. It is illusory to suppose that good designs can be created by using the so-called "principles" of classical organisation theory.'[11] Research studies have also expressed doubt about the effectiveness of these principles when applied in practice.[12]

However, although the work of the classical writers is sometimes regarded as an out-of-date approach it does focus attention on important factors in the study of organisation and management. Technical and structural factors are important considerations in improving organisational performance. Yet, while attention to formal structure is important, it is also necessary to consider the people who work within the structure.

The classical approach attempts to provide some common principles applicable to all organisations. These principles are still of some relevance in that they provide general guidelines to the structuring and efficiency of organisations. They provide a useful starting point in attempting to analyse the effectiveness of the design of organisation structure. But, the application of these principles must take full account of:

- the particular situational variables of each individual organisation; and
- the psychological and social factors relating to members of the organisation.

Two major 'sub-groupings' of the classical approach are:

(i) Scientific Management, and
(ii) Bureaucracy.

SCIENTIFIC MANAGEMENT

Many of the classical writers were concerned with the improvement of management as a means of increasing productivity. At this time emphasis was on the problem of obtaining increased productivity from individual workers through the technical structuring of the work organisation and the provision of monetary incentives as the motivator for higher levels of output. A major contributor to this approach was *F. W. Taylor* (1856–1917) – the 'father' of scientific management.[13] Taylor believed that in the same way that there is a best machine for each job, so there is a best working method by which people should undertake their jobs. He considered that all work processes could be analysed into discrete tasks and that by scientific method it was possible to find the 'one best way' to perform each task. Each job was broken down into component parts, each part timed, and the parts rearranged into the most efficient method of working.

Principles to guide management

Taylor was a believer in the rational–economic needs concept of motivation. He believed that if management acted on his ideas, work would become more satisfying and profitable for all concerned. Workers would be motivated by obtaining the highest possible wages through working in the most efficient and productive way. Taylor was concerned with finding more efficient methods and procedures for co-ordination and control of work. He set out a number of principles to guide management. These principles are usually summarised as:

- The development of a true science for each person's work;
- The scientific selection, training and development of the workers;
- Co-operation with the workers to ensure work is carried out in the prescribed way;
- The division of work and responsibility between management and the workers.

In his famous studies at the Bethlehem Steel Corporation, Taylor, who was appointed as a management consultant, applied his ideas on scientific management to the handling of pig iron. A group of 75 men were loading an average of $12\frac{1}{2}$ tons per man per day. Taylor selected a Dutch labourer, called Schmidt, who he reported to be a 'high-priced' man with a reputation for placing a high value on money, and a man of limited mental ability. By following detailed instructions on when to pick up the pig iron and walk, and when to sit and rest, and with no back talk, Schmidt increased his output to $47\frac{1}{2}$ tons per day. He maintained this level of output throughout the three years of the study. In return Schmidt received a 60 per cent increase in wages compared with that paid to the other men.

One by one other men were selected and trained to handle pig iron at the rate of $47\frac{1}{2}$ tons per day and in return they received 60 per cent more wages. Taylor drew attention to the need for the scientific selection of the workers. When the other labourers in the group were trained in the same method only one in eight was physically capable of the effort of loading $47\frac{1}{2}$ tons per day, although there was a noticeable increase in their level of output.

Reactions against scientific management

There were strong criticisms of, and reaction against, scientific management methods from the workers who found the work boring and requiring little skill. Despite these criticisms Taylor attempted to expand the implementation of his ideas in the Bethlehem Steel Corporation. But fears of mass redundancies persuaded the management to request Taylor to moderate his activities. However, Taylor's belief in his methods was so strong that he would not accept management's interference and eventually his services were dispensed with.

Scientific management was applied for a time in other countries with similar criticisms and hostile reactions. The ideas of scientific management were also adopted in the American Watertown Arsenal despite the lingering doubts of the controller. He was not convinced about the benefits of paying bonuses based on methods which reduced time taken to complete a job; also the workers reacted unfavourably to time and motion studies, and he was fearful of a strike. The controller eventually gave way, however, and the approach of scientific management was adopted – to be followed almost immediately by a strike of moulding workers. The strike at Watertown Arsenal led to an investigation of Taylor's methods by a House of Representatives Committee which reported in 1912.

The conclusion of the committee was that scientific management did provide some useful techniques and offered valuable organisational suggestions, but gave production managers a dangerously high level of uncontrolled power. The studies at Watertown Arsenal were resumed but the unions still retained an underlying hostility towards scientific management. A subsequent attitude survey among the workers revealed a broad level of resentment and hostility, by both union and non-union members, to scientific management methods. Arising from this report Taylor's methods of time study were banned in defence establishments by the Senate.

Functional foremen *Taylor* also put forward the idea of functional foremanship under which workers would be responsible simultaneously to eight different, specialist first line supervisors. The eight supervisors were divided into two groups. *Planning*, concerned with (i) order of work, (ii) instruction cards, (iii) time and costing and (iv) discipline. *Performance*, concerned with (v) gang boss, (iv) speed boss, (vii) repair boss and (viii) inspector. The idea of functional foremen represented a practical application of the idea of specialisation and the belief that each person's work should, as far as possible, be confined to a single leading function. However, such an arrangement gives rise to problems of co-ordination, role conflict and unity of command. The idea of functional foremanship appears not to have become very popular and to have had little application in practice.[14]

Taylorism as management control There has also been considerable interest in 'Taylorism' as representing a system of management control over workers. *Taylor* placed emphasis on the content of a 'fair day's work' and on optimising the level of workers' productivity. A major obstacle to this objective was 'systematic soldiering' and what Taylor saw as the deliberate attempt by workers to promote their own best interests and to keep employers ignorant of how fast work, especially piece rate work, could be carried out.

According to *Braverman*, scientific management starts from the capitalist point of view and method of production, and the adaptation of labour to the needs of capital. Taylor's work was more concerned with the organisation of labour than with the development of technology. A distinctive feature of Taylor's thought was the concept of management control.[15] Braverman suggests that Taylor's conclusion was that workers should be controlled not only by the giving of orders and maintenance of discipline, but also by removing from them any decisions about the manner in which their work was to be carried out. By division of labour, and by dictating precise stages and methods for every aspect of work performance, management could gain control of the actual process of work. The rationalisation of production processes and division of labour tends to result in the deskilling of work and this may be a main strategy of the employer.[16]

Relevance of scientific management

While *Taylor*'s work is often criticised today it should be remembered that he was writing at a time of industrial reorganisation and the emergence of large, complex organisations with new forms of technology. Taylor's main concern was with the efficiency of both workers and management. He believed his methods of scientific management would lead to improved management–labour relations, and contribute to improved industrial efficiency and prosperity.

Taylor adopted an instrumental view of human behaviour together with the application of standard procedures of work. Workers were regarded as rational, economic beings motivated directly by monetary incentives linked to the level of work output. Workers were viewed as isolated individuals and more as units of production to be handled almost in the same way as machines. Hence, scientific management is often referred to as a machine theory model.

The work of Taylor continues to evoke much comment and extreme points of view. For example, *Rose* suggests that:

> It is difficult to discuss the 'contribution' of F. W. Taylor to the systematic study of industrial behaviour in an even-tempered way. The sheer silliness from a modern perspective of many of his ideas, and barbarities they led to when applied in industry, encourage ridicule and denunciation.[17]

The theme of inefficiency

Rose argues that Taylor's diagnosis of the industrial situation was based on the simple theme of inefficiency. Among his criticisms are that Taylor selected the best workers for his experiments and assumed that workers who were not good at one particular task would be best at some other task. There is, however, no certainty of this in practice. Taylor regarded workers from an engineering viewpoint and as machines, but the one best way of performing a task is not always the best method for every worker.

The reduction of physical movement to find the one best way is not always beneficial and some 'wasteful' movements are essential to the overall rhythm of work. Rose also argues that the concept of a fair day's pay for a fair day's work is not purely a technical matter. It is also a notion of social equity and not in keeping with a scientific approach.

On the other hand, however, *Drucker* claims that:

> Frederick Winslow Taylor may prove a more useful prophet for our times than we yet recognize. . . . Taylor's greatest impact may still be ahead . . . the underdeveloped and developing countries are now reaching the stage where they need Taylor and 'scientific management'. . . . But the need to study Taylor anew and apply him may be the greatest in the developed countries.[18]

According to Drucker, the central theme of Taylor's work was not inefficiency but the need to substitute industrial warfare by industrial harmony. Taylor sought to do this through: higher wages from increased output; the removal of physical strain from doing work the wrong way; development of the workers and the opportunity for them to undertake tasks they were capable of doing; and elimination of the boss by the duty of management to help the workers.

Drucker also suggests that Taylor's idea of functional foremen can be related to what is now known as matrix organisation (matrix organisation is discussed in the Chapter 5). Support for Drucker's views appears to come from Locke who asserts that much of the criticism of Taylor is based on a misunderstanding of the precepts and that many of his ideas are accepted by present-day managers.[19]

Impetus to modern management thinking

Whatever the opinions on scientific management, *Taylor* and his disciples, such as *Frank* and *Lilian Gilbreth*,[20] have left to modern management the legacy of such practices as work study, organisation and methods, payment by results, management by exception and production control.

The principles of Taylor's scientific approach to management appear still to have relevance today. We can still see examples of Taylorism alive and well, and management practices based on the philosophy of his ideas. Some workers appear content to adopt an instrumental view of work and are motivated almost solely by high financial rewards. Other workers, whatever the nature of their job, do not wish to accept responsibility at work. They seem to prefer, and respond better to, closely defined work tasks, and a more directed and controlled style of management.

Whatever else, Taylor did at least give a major impetus to the development of modern management thinking and the later development of organisational behaviour. It is difficult to argue against the general line of Taylor's principles but they are subject to misuse. What is important is the context and manner in which such principles are put into effect.

It seems that Taylor did not so much ignore (as is often suggested) but was more unaware of the complexity of human behaviour in organisations and the importance of the individual's own feelings and sentiments, group working, managerial behaviour and the work environment. However, we now have greater knowledge about social effects within the work organisation, and about the value of money, incentives, motivation, and job satisfaction and performance.

BUREAUCRACY

A form of structure to be found in many large-scale organisations is bureaucracy. Because of its importance in the development of organisation theory it is often regarded as a sub-division under the classical heading and studied as a separate approach to management and the organisation of work. The ideas and principles of the classical writers were derived mainly from practical experience. Writers on bureaucracy, however, tend to take a more theoretical view.

Weber, a German sociologist, showed particular concern for what he called 'bureaucratic structures', although his work in this area came almost as a side issue to his main study on power and authority.[21] He suggested that 'the decisive reason for the advance of bureaucratic organisation has always been its purely technical superiority over any other form of organisation'. Weber pointed out that the definition of tasks and responsibilities within the structure of management gave rise to a permanent administration and standardisation of work procedures notwithstanding changes in the actual holders of office.

The term 'bureaucracy' has common connotations with criticism of red tape and rigidity, though in the study of organisations and management it is important that the term is seen not necessarily in a deprecative sense but as applying to certain structural features of formal organisations. Weber analysed bureaucracies not empirically but as an 'ideal type' derived from the most characteristic bureaucratic features of all known organisations. He saw the development of bureaucracies as a means of introducing order and rationality into social life.

Main characteristics of bureaucracies

Weber did not actually define bureaucracy but did attempt to identify the main characteristics of this type of organisation. He emphasised the importance of administration based on expertise (rules of experts) and administration based on discipline (rules of officials).

- The tasks of the organisation are allocated as official duties among the various positions.
- There is an implied clear-cut division of labour and a high level of specialisation.
- A hierarchical authority applies to the organisation of offices and positions.
- Uniformity of decisions and actions is achieved through formally established systems of rules and regulations. Together with a structure of authority this enables the co-ordination of various activities within the organisation.
- An impersonal orientation is expected from officials in their dealings with clients and other officials. This is designed to result in rational judgements by officials in the performance of their duties.
- Employment by the organisation is based on technical qualifications and constitutes a lifelong career for the officials.[22]

The four main features of bureaucracy are summarised by *Stewart* as specialisation, hierarchy of authority, system of rules, and impersonality

- *Specialisation* applies more to the job than to the person undertaking the job. This makes for continuity because the job usually continues if the present job holder leaves.
- *Hierarchy of authority* makes for a sharp distinction between administrators and the administered, or between management and workers. Within the management ranks there are clearly defined levels of authority. This detailed and precise stratification is particularly marked in the armed forces and in the civil service.
- *System of rules* aims to provide for an efficient and impersonal operation. The system of rules is generally stable, although some rules may be changed or modified with time. Knowledge of the rules is a requisite of holding a job in a bureaucracy.

- *Impersonality* means that allocation of privileges and the exercise of authority should not be arbitrary, but in accordance with the laid-down system of rules. In more highly developed bureaucracies there tend to be carefully defined procedures for appealing against certain types of decisions. Stewart sees the characteristic of impersonality as the feature of bureaucracy which most distinguishes it from other types of organisations. A bureaucracy should not only be impersonal but seen to be impersonal.[23]

Criticisms of bureaucracy

Weber's concept of bureaucracy has a number of disadvantages and has been subject to severe criticism.

- The over-emphasis on rules and procedures, record keeping and paperwork may become more important in its own right than as a means to an end.
- Officials may develop a dependence upon bureaucratic status, symbols and rules.
- Initiative may be stifled and when a situation is not covered by a complete set of rules or procedures there is a lack of flexibility or adaptation to changing circumstances.
- Position and responsibilities in the organisation can lead to officious bureaucratic behaviour. There may also be a tendency to conceal administrative procedures from outsiders.
- Impersonal relations can lead to stereotyped behaviour and a lack of responsiveness to individual incidents or problems.

Weber's work has been criticised on the grounds that there is lack of attention to the informal organisation and the development of groups with goals of their own, and inadequate recognition of conflict in organisations. *Crozier*, in his study of two French bureaucratic systems, views bureaucracies not so much as static technical systems but as dynamic social systems.[24] Individuals have goals of their own and they devise ways of improving their position in the power struggle within organisations. Formal rules and the rigidity of the system will never fully remove this power struggle. There will always be areas of uncertainty which groups will want to claim and preserve for themselves. Crozier's view of bureaucracies as social systems with individuals having their own goals and expectations, and pursuing their own strategies, provides a link with the social action approach which is discussed later in this chapter.

One of the strongest critics of bureaucratic organisation, and the demands it makes on the worker, is *Argyris*.[25] He claims that bureaucracies restrict the psychological growth of the individual and cause feelings of failure, frustration and conflict. Argyris suggests that the organisational environment should provide: a significant degree of individual responsibility and self-control; commitment to the goals of the organisation; productiveness and work; and an opportunity for individuals to apply their full abilities.

When these ideas are related to the main features of bureaucracy discussed above such as specialisation, hierarchy of authority, system of rules and impersonality; it is perhaps easy to see the basis of Argyris's criticism.

Bureaucratic dysfunction

Another area of criticism comes from writers who question *Weber*'s concept of bureaucracy as an ideal type, and as highly functional with everything neatly in its place and contributing to the smooth running of the organisation. These writers are usually referred to under the heading of 'bureaucratic dysfunction' and include *Merton, Selznick* and *Gouldner*.

Merton refers to the development of 'bureaucratic personality' and fixation on rules and lack of adaptability as an unintended consequence of bureaucracy. There is also a tendency to 'goal displacement' where the means become ends in themselves and more important than the actual goals which the organisation is intended to achieve.[26]

Selznick also draws attention to the vulnerability of bureaucracies to goal displacement. Increased specialisation, and delegation and independence given to experts, can lead to the unintended consequences of the emergence of sub-groups with their own goals at variance with the goals of the organisation.[27]

Gouldner distinguishes three types of bureaucracy:

- *Mock* – where rules are formulated by an outside body but ignored by both managers and workers;
- *Representative* – where rules are formulated by management together with participation of the workers, and are considered to be reasonable;
- *Punishment centred* – where rules are formulated by one party but not accepted as legitimate by other parties.[28]

Gouldner also studied the unanticipated consequences of a bureaucratic system in a gypsum mine ('wildcat strike') and the effects of introducing tighter supervision and formal controls over the workers in order to increase efficiency. The workers responded by attempting to resist the changes, by reducing the amount of work they did and by submitting a wage claim. Although the wage claim was settled there were continuing problems at the plant which culminated in a wildcat strike.

Reasons for growth of bureaucracy

Much of the criticism of bureaucracy is valid, but much also appears to be unfair comment. In any case, whatever the validity of the criticism, it is difficult to envisage how modern large-scale organisations could function effectively without exhibiting at least some of the features of a bureaucratic structure.

The growth of bureaucracy has come about through the increasing size and complexity of organisations and the associated demand for effective administration. The work of the classical writers has given emphasis to the careful design and planning of organisation structure and the definition of individual duties and responsibilities. Greater specialisation and the application of expertise and technical knowledge has highlighted the need for laid-down procedures. In the case of public sector organisations in particular there is a demand for uniformity of treatment, regularity of procedures and accountability for their operations. This leads to adherence to specified rules and procedures which limit the degree of discretion exercised by management, and to the keeping of detailed records.

It is interesting to note that, despite the criticisms of bureaucracy, people in their dealings with public sector organisations often call for what amounts to increased bureaucracy, even though they may not use that term. One can frequently see letters to newspapers, for example, that call for a letter of law and a clearer set of rules in dealings with benefit claims from government departments instead of decisions made on the opinion of a particular manager in a particular office.

Structuralists

Sometimes the work of *Weber* is associated with what *Etzioni* calls the structuralist approach, which is 'a synthesis of the Classical (or formal) school and the Human Relations (or informal) one, drawing also on the work of Max Weber, and, to a degree, that of Karl Marx'.[29] Their line of thought was that the earlier approaches were incomplete and the 'structuralists' were concerned with relationships between the formal and informal aspects of the organisation and the study of conflict between needs of the individual and of the organisation, and between workers and management. They believed that all types of organisations have many things in common and studies should not be restricted to industrial organisations. Following Weber there was a broadening of these ideas which are now often associated as part of the human relations approach.

THE HUMAN RELATIONS APPROACH

The main emphasis of the classical writers was on structure and the formal organisation, but during the 1920s, the years of the great depression, greater attention began to be paid to the social factors at work and to the behaviour of employees within an organisation – that is, to human relations.

The Hawthorne experiments

The turning point in the development of the human relations movement ('behavioural' and 'informal' are alternative headings sometimes given to this approach) came with the famous Hawthorne experiments at the Western Electric Company in America (1924–32), and the subsequent publication of the research findings.[30,31]

The researchers included people from the National Research Council, the Harvard Business School and the Massachusetts Institute of Technology. Among the people who have written about the Hawthorne experiments was *Elton Mayo* (1880–1949) who is often quoted as a leader of the researchers. However there appears to be some doubt as to the extent to which Mayo was actually involved in conducting the experiments and his exact contribution to the human relations movement.[32]

There were four main phases to the Hawthorne experiments:

- the illumination experiments;
- the relay assembly test room;
- the interviewing programme;
- the bank wiring observation room.

The illumination experiments

The original investigation was conducted on the lines of the classical approach and was concerned, in typical scientific management style, with the effects of the intensity of lighting upon the workers' productivity. The workers were divided into two groups, an experimental group and a control group. The results of these tests were inconclusive as production in the experimental group varied with no apparent relationship to the level of lighting, but actually increased when conditions were made much worse. Production also increased in the control group although the lighting remained unchanged. The level of production was influenced, clearly, by factors other than changes in physical conditions of work. This prompted a series of other experiments investigating factors of worker productivity.

The relay assembly test room

In the relay assembly test room the work was boring and repetitive. It involved assembling telephone relays by putting together a number of small parts. Six women workers were transferred from their normal departments to a separate area. The researchers selected two assemblers who were friends with each other. They then chose three other assemblers and a layout operator. The experiment was divided into 13 periods during which the workers were subjected to a series of planned and controlled changes to their conditions of work, such as hours of work, rest pauses and provision of refreshments. The general environmental conditions of the test room were similar to those of the normal assembly line. During the experiment the observer adopted a friendly manner, consulting with the workers, listening to their complaints and keeping them informed of the experiment. Following all but one of the changes there was a continuous increase in the level of production. (*See* Table 2.1.) The researchers formed the conclusion that the extra attention given to the workers, and the apparent interest in them shown by management, was the main reason for the higher productivity.

The interviewing programme

Another significant phase of the experiments was the interviewing programme. The lighting experiment and the relay assembly test room drew attention to the form of supervision as a contributory factor to the workers' level of production. In an attempt to find out more about the workers' feelings towards their supervisors and their general conditions of work, a large interviewing programme was introduced. More than 20 000 interviews were conducted before the work was ended because of the depression.

Initially, the interviewers approached their task with a set of prepared questions, relating mainly to how the workers felt about their jobs. However, this method produced only limited information. The workers regarded a number of the questions as irrelevant; also they wanted to talk about other issues than just supervision and immediate working conditions. As a result, the style of interviewing was changed to become more non-directive and open-ended. There was no set list of questions and the workers were free to talk about any aspect of their work.

The interviewers set out to be friendly and sympathetic. They adopted an impartial, non-judgemental approach and concentrated on listening. They did not take sides or offer opinions, but if necessary would explain company policy and details of, for example, benefit schemes. The interviewers made verbatim notes of the interview, but it was made clear that everything said was in confidence. No identification would be given on the notes and no personal details revealed to management.

Arising from this approach, the interviewers found out far more about the

Table 2.1 Relay assembly test room experiment.

Period	Length in weeks	Conditions	Results
1	2	records kept on assembly line work	base rate established
2	5	operators enter test room, no other changes	production up slightly
3	8	payment rate changed to give higher reward for individual effort	production up
4	5	two five-minute rests, one morning and one afternoon	production up
5	4	rest breaks lengthened to ten minutes each	production up
6	4	six five-minute rest breaks	operators complain that too many breaks makes them lose the rhythm of the work; production up a little
7	11	15-minute morning break and ten-minute afternoon break; company provides refreshments	production up
8	7	work stops at 4:30 instead of 5:00; rest breaks as in period 7	production up
9	4	work stops at 4:00; rest breaks as in period 7	total daily production down slightly but hourly rate up
10	12	same as period 7	production up
11	9	Saturday work eliminated; rest breaks as in period 7	production up
12	12	same as period 3; no breaks	production drops slightly at first, then rises
13	31	same as period 7; but company supplies only coffee	production breaks all records

(From K. London, *The People Side of Systems*, McGraw-Hill (1976) p. 67.)

workers' true feelings and attitudes. They gained information not just about supervision and working conditions, but also about the company itself, management, work group relations and matters outside of work such as family life and views on society in general. Many workers appeared to welcome the opportunity to have someone to talk to about their feelings and problems, and to be able to 'let off steam' in a friendly atmosphere. The interviewing programme was significant in giving an impetus to present-day personnel management and the use of counselling interviews, and highlighting the need for management to listen to workers' feelings and problems.

The bank wiring observation room

Another experiment involved the observation of a group of 14 men working in the bank wiring room. It was noted that the men formed their own informal organisation with sub-groups or cliques, and with natural leaders emerging with the consent of the members. The group developed its own pattern of informal social relations and 'norms' of what constituted 'proper' behaviour. Despite a financial incentive scheme where the workers could receive more money for the more work produced, the group decided on a level of output well below the level they were capable of producing. Group pressures on individual workers were stronger than financial incentives offered by management. The group believed that if they increased their output management would raise the standard level of piece rates. The importance of group 'norms' and informal social relations is discussed in Chapter 13.

Evaluation of the human relations approach

There are a number of interpretations of the results of the Hawthorne experiments, including the possible implications of the 'sex power differential' between the two groups. In the relay assembly room where output increased the group was all female, whilst in the bank wiring room where output was restricted the group was all male. The workers in the relay assembly test room were all young unmarried women. All except one were living at home with traditional families of immigrant background. In the work environment of the factory the women had been subjected to frequent contact with male supervisors and therefore 'the sex power hierarchy in the home and in the factory were congruent'. It is suggested, therefore, that it was only to be expected that the women agreed readily to participate with management in the relay assembly test room experiment.[33]

Whatever the interpretation of the results of the Hawthorne experiments, they did generate new ideas concerning the importance of work groups and leadership, communications, output restrictions, motivation and job design. They placed emphasis on the importance of personnel management, and gave impetus to the work of the human relations writers.

Whereas supporters of the classical approach sought to increase production by rationalisation of the work organisation, the human relations movement has led to ideas on increasing production by humanising the work organisation.

The human relations approach recognised the importance of the informal organisation which will always be present within the formal structure. This informal organisation will influence the motivation of employees who will view the organisation for which they work through the values and attitudes of their colleagues. Their view of the organisation determines their approach to work and the extent of their motivation to work well or otherwise.

Human relations writers demonstrated that people go to work to satisfy a complexity of needs and not simply for monetary reward. They emphasised the importance of the wider social needs of individuals and gave recognition to the work organisation as a social organisation and the importance of the group, and group values and norms, in influencing individual behaviour at work. It has been commented that the classical school were concerned about 'organisations without people', and the human relations school about 'people without organisations'.

The human relations approach has been subjected to severe criticism. The Hawthorne experiments have been criticised, for example, on methodology and on failure of the investigators to take sufficient account of environmental factors – although much of this criticism is with the value of hindsight. The human relations writers have been criticised generally for the adoption of a management perspective, their 'unitary frame of reference' and their over-simplified theories.[34]

Other criticisms of the human relations approach are that it is insufficiently scientific, and that it takes too narrow a view. It ignores the role of the organisation itself in how society operates.[35]

41

However, the classical writers have been subjected to many similar criticisms and, whatever the validity of these criticisms, the Hawthorne experiments undoubtedly marked a significant step forward in providing a further insight into human behaviour at work and the development of management thinking. The Hawthorne experiments are regarded as one of the most important of all social science investigations and are recognised as probably the single most important foundation of the human relations approach to management and the development of organisational behaviour.

NEO-HUMAN RELATIONS

Certainly there were shortcomings in the human relations approach, and assumptions which evolved from such studies as the Hawthorne experiments were not necessarily supported by empirical evidence.

For example, the contention that a satisfied worker is a productive worker was not always found to be valid. However, the results of the Hawthorne experiments and the subsequent attention given to the social organisation and to theories of individual motivation gave rise to the work of those writers in the 1950s and 1960s who adopted a more psychological orientation. The major focus of concern was the personal adjustment of the individual within the work organisation, and the effects of group relationships and leadership styles. This group of writers is often (and more correctly) categorised separately under the heading of 'neo-human relations'. The works of these writers are examined in more detail in subsequent chapters but are summarised broadly here.

A major impetus for the neo-human relations approach was the work of *Maslow* who, in 1943, put forward a theoretical framework of individual personality development and motivation based on a hierarchy of human needs.[36] The hierarchy ranges through five levels from, at the lowest level, Physiological needs, through Safety needs, Love needs, Esteem needs, to the need for Self-actualisation at the highest level. Individuals only advance up the hierarchy as each lower-level need is satisfied. Although Maslow did not originally intend this need hierarchy to be applied necessarily to the work situation it has, nevertheless, had a big impact on modern management approaches to motivation and the design of work organisation to meet individual needs.

Some leading contributors

Among the best-known contributions to the neo-human relations approach are *Herzberg* and *McGregor*. Herzberg isolated two different sets of factors affecting motivation and satisfaction at work. One set of factors are those which, if absent, cause dissatisfaction. These are 'hygiene' or 'maintenance' factors which are concerned basically with job environment. However, to motivate workers to give of their best, proper attention must be given to a different set of factors, the 'motivators' or 'growth' factors. These are concerned with job content.[37]

McGregor argued that the style of management adopted is a function of the manager's attitudes towards human nature and behaviour at work. He put forward two suppositions called Theory X and Theory Y which are based on popular assumptions about work and people.[38]

Other major contributors to the neo-human relations approach include Likert whose work includes research into different systems of management;[39] and Argyris who considered the effects of the formal organisation on the individual and psychological growth in the process of self-actualisation.[40]

The neo-human relations approach has generated a prolific amount of writing and research not only from original propounders, but also from others seeking to establish the validity, or otherwise, of their ideas. This has led to continuing attention being given to such matters as organisation structuring, group dynamics, job satisfaction, communication and participation, leadership styles and motivation. It has also led to greater attention to the importance of interpersonal interactions, the causes of conflict and recognition of 'industrial relations' problems.

THE SYSTEMS APPROACH

More recently, attention has been focused on the analysis of organisations as 'systems' with a number of interrelated sub-systems.

The classical approach emphasised the technical requirements of the organisation and its needs – 'organisations without people'; the human relations approaches emphasised the psychological and social aspects, and the consideration of human needs – 'people without organisations'.

The systems approach attempts to reconcile these two earlier approaches and the work of the formal and the informal writers. Attention is focused on the total work organisation and the interrelationships of structure and behaviour, and the range of variables within the organisation. This approach can be contrasted with a view of the organisation as separate parts. The systems approach encourages managers to view the organisation both as a whole and as part of a larger environment. The idea is that any part of an organisation's activities affects all other parts.

Systems theory is not new and has been used in the natural and physical sciences for a number of years. One of the founders of this approach was the biologist *Ludwig von Bertalanffy* who used the term 'systems theory' in an article published in 1951, and who is generally credited with having developed the outline of General Systems Theory.[41] The Systems Approach to organisation has arisen, at least in part, therefore, from the work of biologists, and *Miller* and *Rice* have likened the commercial and industrial organisation to the biological organism.[42]

Using a general systems theory (GST) approach *Boulding* classified nine levels of systems of increasing complexity according to the state of development and knowledge about each level.[43] Organisations are complex social systems and are more open to change than lower-level simple dynamic or cybernetic systems. Boulding felt there were large gaps in both theoretical and empirical knowledge of the human level and the social organisations level of systems, although some progress has now been made with recent theories of organisational behaviour.

The business organisation as an open system

The business organisation is not a closed system, where there is no interaction between the system and the environment or where any such interaction is stabilised. It is an open system, there is continual interaction with the broader external environment of which it is part. The systems approach views the organisation within its environment and emphasises the importance of multiple channels of interaction. Criticisms of earlier approaches to organisation are based in part on the attempt to study the activities and problems of the organisation solely in terms of the internal environment.

The view of the organisation as an open system is examined in Chapter 3.

The organisation as a socio-technical system

The systems approach views the organisation as a whole and involves the study of the organisation in terms of the relationship between technical and social variables within the system. Changes in one part, technical or social, will affect other parts and thus the whole system. The concept of the organisation as a 'socio-technical' system directs attention to the transformation or conversion process itself, to the series of activities through which the organisation attempts to achieve its objectives. The socio-technical system is concerned with the interactions between the psychological and social factors and the needs and demands of the human part of the organisation, and its structural and technological requirements.

Longwall coal-mining study

The idea of socio-technical systems arose from the work of *Trist* and others, of the Tavistock Institute of Human Relations, in their study of the effects of changing technology in the coal-mining industry in the 1940s.[44] The increasing use of mechanisation and the introduction of coal-cutters and mechanical conveyors enabled coal to be extracted on a 'longwall' method.

Shift working was introduced with each shift specialising on one stage of the operation – preparation, cutting or loading. However, the new method meant a change in the previous system of working where a small self-selecting group of miners worked together, as an independent team, on one part of the coalface – the 'single place' or 'shortwall' method.

Technological change had brought about changes in the social groupings of the miners. It disrupted the integration of small groups and the psychological and sociological properties of the old method of working. There was a lack of co-operation between different shifts and within each shift, an increase in absenteeism, scapegoating and signs of greater social stress. The 'longwall' method was socially disruptive and did not prove as economically efficient as it could have been with the new technology.

The researchers saw the need for a socio-technical approach in which an appropriate social system could be developed in keeping with the new technical system. The result was the 'composite longwall' method with more responsibility to the team as a whole and shifts carrying out composite tasks, the reintroduction of multi-skilled roles and a reduction in specialisation. The composite method was psychologically and socially more rewarding and economically more efficient than the 'longwall' method.

Technology

The concept of socio-technical systems provides a link between the systems approach and a further sub-division, sometimes adopted, of a technology approach. Writers under the technology heading attempt to restrict generalisations about organisations and management, and emphasise the effects of varying technologies on organisation structure, work groups and individual performance and job satisfaction. This is in contrast with the socio-technical approach which did not regard technology, *per se*, as a determinant of behaviour.

Under the heading of the technology approach could be included the work of such writers as *Walker* and *Guest* (effects of the assembly-line production method on employee behaviour);[45] *Woodward* (relationships between application of principles of organisation and business success);[46] *Sayles* (relationship between technology and the nature of work groups);[47] and *Blauner* (problems of 'alienation' in relation to different work technologies).[48]

Decision making

Recognition of the need for decision making and the attainment of goals draws attention to a further sub-division of the systems approach, or a separate category, that of the decision-making (or decision theory) approach. Here the focus of attention is on managerial decision making and how organisations process and use information in making decisions.

The systems approach involves the isolation of those functions most directly concerned with the achievement of objectives and the identification of main decision areas or sub-systems. Viewing the organisation as a system emphasises the need for good information and channels of communication in order to assist effective decision making in the organisation.

O'Shaughnessy lists the following steps in the systems approach to organisation:

1 Specifying objectives.
2 Listing the sub-systems, or main decision areas.
3 Analysing the decision areas and establishing information needs.
4 Designing the communication channels for the information flow.
5 Grouping the decision areas to minimise the communications burden.[49]

Successful management lies in responding to internal and external change. This involves the clarification of objectives, the specification of problems, and the search for and implementation of solutions. The organisation is seen as an information-processing network with numerous decision points. An understanding of how decisions are made helps in understanding behaviour in the organisation. Decision-making writers seek to explain the mechanisms by which conflict is resolved and choices are made.

Some leading writers

Leading writers of the decision-making approach include *Barnard*, *Simon*, and *Cyert* and *March*. The scope of the decision-making approach, however, is wide, and it is possible to identify contributions from engineers, mathematicians and operational research specialists in addition to the work of economists, psychologists and writers on management and organisation.

Barnard stressed the need for co-operative action in organisations. He believed that people's ability to communicate, and their commitment and contribution to the achievement of a common purpose, were necessary for the existence of a co-operative system.[50] These ideas were developed further by Simon. He sees management as meaning decision making and his concern is with how decisions are made and how decision making can be improved.[51] Simon is critical of the implication of man as completely rational and proposes a model of 'administrative man' who, unlike 'economic man', 'satisfices' rather than maximises. Administrative decision making is the achievement of satisfactory rather than optimal results in solving problems.

Economic models of decision making, based on the assumption of rational behaviour in choosing from known alternatives in order to maximise objectives, can be contrasted with behavioural models based not so much on maximisation of objectives but on short-term expediency where a choice is made to avoid conflict and within limiting constraints. Managers are more concerned with avoiding uncertainties than with the prediction of uncertainties.[52]

MORE RECENT APPROACHES

The study of organisations, their structure and management, is a still developing field of inquiry and extends beyond the systems approach into more recent forms of analysis such as contingency theory and social action.

CONTINGENCY THEORY

Contingency theory, which is best viewed as an extension of the systems approach, highlights possible means of differentiating between alternative forms of organisation structures and systems of management. There is no one optimum state. For example, the structure of the organisation and its 'success' are dependent upon the nature of tasks with which it is designed to deal and the nature of environmental influences. The most appropriate structure and system of management is, therefore, dependent upon the contingencies of the situation for each particular organisation.

There is a close relationship between contingency theory and the technology approach discussed above. Contingency models of organisation such as those of *Woodward, Burns* and *Stalker,* and *Lawrence* and *Lorsch* are looked at briefly in Chapter 3 and are discussed in more detail in Chapter 6.

Another area of study which could be included under contingency theory is the programme of action research carried out by *Sadler* and *Barry* in the printing industry in this country from 1964 to 1967.[53] In their study of changing conditions in a printing group Sadler and Barry described the firms in terms of four interrelated dimensions: technology; the social system; formal organisation structure; and relations with the environment. Their research indicated wide differences between how, in theory, the organisation should have operated and what happened in practice.

Actual working arrangements relied heavily on the informal organisation, and on personalities and the teamwork of managers. The researchers proposed a programme of organisational change which included adapting the formal structure, hierarchical control and formal responsibilities and relationships to be more in keeping with the actual working arrangements and flow of communications. Change in the attitudes and behaviour of members of the organisation should be related to change in the design of the formal organisation structure.

SOCIAL ACTION

Social action represents a contribution from sociologists to the study of organisations. Social action writers attempt to view the organisation from the standpoint of individual members (actors) who will each have his or her own goals, and interpretation of the work situation in terms of the satisfaction sought and the meaning that work has for him or her. The goals of the individual, and the means selected and actions taken to achieve these goals, are affected by the individual's perception of the situation. Social action looks to the individual's own definition of the situation as a basis for explaining behaviour. Conflict of interests is seen as normal behaviour and part of organisational life. According to Silverman,[6] 'The action approach . . . does not, in itself, provide a theory of organisations. It is instead best understood as a method of analysing social relations within organisations.'[54]

Criticisms of earlier approaches

A main thrust of social action is the criticism of earlier approaches to organisation and management, and on what is claimed to be their failure to provide a satisfactory basis for the explanation or prediction of individual behaviour. For example, criticism is directed at approaches which focused on the goals and needs of the organisation, rather than on considerations of the effectiveness of an organisation in meeting the needs of its individual members.

The human relations approaches have been criticised because of their focus on generalised theories of good management, group psychology, and the suggestion of needs common to all individuals at work. The technology approach has been criticised for attributing feelings of alienation to the nature of technology and the status of work groups, rather than an analysis which focused on concern for the individual's expectations of, and reactions to, his or her work. The systems approach has been criticised for failure to examine the orientation of individual members to the organisation, the different expectations people have of their work or ways in which the environment influences expectations of work.

Unitary or pluralistic view

Important contributors to a social action approach include *Goldthorpe* (industrial attitudes and behaviour patterns of manual workers)[55] and *Fox*. In a research paper written for the Royal Commission on Trade Unions and Employers' Associations (the Donovan report), Fox suggests two major ways of perceiving an industrial organisation – a 'unitary' approach and a 'pluralistic' approach.[56]

With *the unitary approach* the organisation is viewed as a team with a common source of loyalty, one focus of effort and one accepted leader. From this approach, trade unions are seen as an unnecessary evil and restrictive practices are outmoded or caused by troublemakers. Conflict can be explained by, for example, poor communications, personality clashes or the work of agitators.

It was argued that a unitary view of industrial society will regard restrictive practices and resistance to change as the result of stupidity or outdated class rancour.

The pluralistic approach views the organisation as made up of competing sub-groups with their own loyalties, goals and leaders. These competing sub-groups are almost certain to come into conflict. From the pluralistic approach, conflict in organisations is seen as inevitable and induced, in part, by the very structure of the organisation. Restrictive practices may be seen as a rational response from a group which regards itself as being threatened. The role of the manager would be less commanding and enforcing, and more persuading and co-ordinating. Fox suggests that a pluralistic approach is a more realistic frame of reference. He argues the importance of viewing work situations through the different groups involved rather than attempting a wished for unitary approach. According to *Horn*, 'these views were widely acceptable, particularly to the trade unions, who saw this as legitimising their intervention into an increasing range of managerial prerogative areas'.[57]

Action theory

A theory of human behaviour from an 'action approach' is presented by *Bowey*.[58] She suggests that action theory, systems theory and contingency theory are not necessarily incompatible approaches to the understanding of behaviour in organisations. It would be possible to take the best parts of the different approaches and combine them into a theory that would model empirical behaviour, and also facilitate the analysis of large numbers of people in organisations. Bowey goes on to present such a theory as a particular form of an action theory approach. According to Bowey, action theory is not capable of dealing with the analysis of the behaviour of a large number of people in organisations. Her theory is based, therefore, on three essential principles of action theory, augmented by four additional concepts taken from systems theory.

The three essential principles of action theory are summarised as:

- sociology is concerned not just with behaviour, but with 'meaningful action';
- particular meanings persist through reaffirmation in actions;
- actions can also lead to changes in meanings.

Additional concepts

Bowey suggests that these three principles apply mainly to explanations of individual, or small-scale, behaviour. She gives four additional concepts, taken from systems theory, on which analysis of large-scale behaviour can be based. These concepts are redefined in accordance with an action approach.

- *Role* – this is needed for the analysis of behaviour in organisations. It explains the similar action of different people in similar situations within the organisation, and the expectations held by other people.
- *Relationships* – this is needed to explain the patterns of interaction among people and the behaviours displayed towards one another.
- *Structure* – the relationships among members of an organisation give rise to patterns of actions which can be identified as a 'transitory social structure'. The social factors, and non-social factors such as payment systems, methods of production and physical layout, together form the behavioural structure.

- *Process* – human behaviour can be analysed in terms of processes, defined as 'continuous interdependent sequences of actions'. The concept of process is necessary to account for the manner in which organisations exhibit changes in structure.

The three principles of action theory, together with the four additional concepts from systems theory, provide an action approach to the analysis of behaviour in organisations. Bowey goes on to illustrate her theory by case studies of five different types of organisations, all in the restaurant industry.

RELEVANCE OF APPROACHES TO ORGANISATION AND MANAGEMENT

The broad three-fold classification of classical, human relations and systems approaches provides a convenient framework in which to view developments of management and organisational behaviour. *See*, for example, the summary in Fig. 2.1.

However, we can now see that within the broad three-fold classification of classical, human relations and systems it is possible to identify a number of other approaches or at least sub-divisions of approaches. So far we have identified a possible nine-fold classification: classical (including scientific management); bureaucracy; human relations; neo-human relations; systems; technology; decision making; contingency; and social action – and if structuralists are included a ten-fold classification. This classification could be extended still further. For example, another more recent categorisation sometimes identified as a separate approach is Management Science – with emphasis on quantitative analysis, mathematic models, operational research and computer technology. (*See* Fig. 2.2.)

Different categorisations not a bad thing

It is possible then to distinguish a number of different approaches to the study of organisation and management, although there is no consensus on the categorisation of these different approaches or on the identification of the various contributors to one particular approach. The different possible categorisations are not necessarily a bad thing – they illustrate the discursive nature of management. The possible sub-divisions and cross-groupings help illustrate the many factors relevant to the study and practice of management and organisational behaviour. Discussion on the various categorisations of approaches and the identification of individual writers within a particular approach can provide a useful insight into the subject.

Positive advantages

Whatever form of categorisation is adopted the division of writers on organisation and management into various approaches offers a number of positive advantages.

- It is helpful to students in the arrangement and study of their material.
- It provides a setting in which to view the field of management, and to consider the contribution of individual writers.
- It traces the major lines of argument developed by writers seeking to advise practising managers on how they might improve performance.
- It provides a framework in which the principles enunciated can be set, and against which comparisons with management practice can be made.

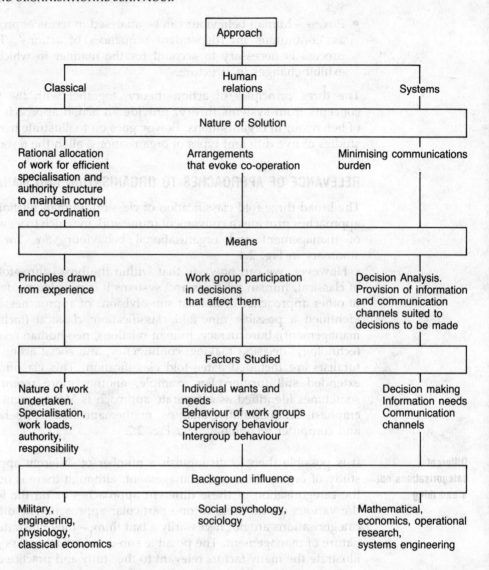

Fig. 2.1 Summary of classical, human relations and systems approaches
(From O'Shaughnessy, J. *Business organization*, Unwin Hyman Limited, London, 1966. Reproduced by permission of the publishers.)

- It helps in organisational analysis and in the identification of problem areas. For example, is the problem one of structure, of human relations, or of the socio-technical process?
- It enables the manager to take from the different approaches those ideas which suit best the particular requirements of the job. For example, in dealing with a problem of structure the ideas of the classical writers or of contingency theory might be adopted. When there is a problem relating to personnel management ideas from the human relations movement might be of most value. If the problem is one of environmental influence insights from the systems approach might prove most helpful. For problems of a more quantitative nature ideas from the decision-making approach or from management science might be applicable.

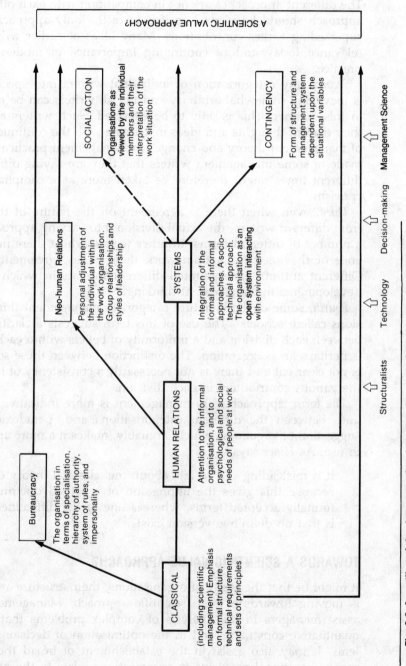

Fig. 2.2 An outline of developments of main approaches to organisation and management

A SCIENTIFIC VALUE APPROACH?

SOCIAL ACTION

Organisations as viewed by the individual members and their interpretation of the work situation

CONTINGENCY

Form of structure and management system dependent upon the situational variables

Neo-human Relations

Personal adjustment of the individual within the work organisation. Group relationships and styles of leadership

SYSTEMS

Integration of the formal and informal approaches. A socio-technical approach. The organisation as an **open system interacting** with environment

Bureaucracy

The organisation in terms of specialisation, hierarchy of authority, system of rules, and impersonality

HUMAN RELATIONS

Attention to the informal organisation, and to psychological and social needs of people at work

CLASSICAL

(including scientific management) Emphasis on formal structure, technical requirements and sets of principles

Management Science

Decision-making

Technology

Structuralists

51

Caveats to be noted There are, however, a number of important caveats which should be noted.

First, the various approaches represent a progression of ideas; each building on from the other and adding to it. Together they provide a pattern of complementary studies into the development of management thinking. The different approaches are not in competition with each other and no one approach should be viewed as if it were the only approach, replacing or superseding earlier contributions. Many ideas of earlier writers are still of relevance today and of continuing importance in modern management practice.

Second, any categorisation of individual writers into specific approaches is inevitably somewhat arbitrary and not all writers can be neatly arranged in this manner. This is only to be expected. Such writers are expounding their current thoughts and ideas in keeping with the continual development of management theory and changes in management practice. The comment made of some management writers that they are saying different things at different times might therefore be taken more as a compliment than as a criticism.

Third, even when there is agreement on the nature of the contribution from different writers, the actual division into varying approaches may take a number of different forms. In other words, whilst there might be acceptance of the need for a framework there is no agreement on its shape. Different authors have adopted different formats in which to set out the developments in management thinking.

Fourth, some of the literature categorises management thinkers into divisions called 'schools'. The use of this term suggests a clarity of distinction between each division and a uniformity of beliefs within each division. This is perhaps an exaggeration. The distinction between these so-called schools is not clear-cut and there is not necessarily a consistency of thinking among the various contributors in each division.

The term 'approaches' to management is more indicative of the obscure lines between the different categorisations and, paradoxically, it is the suggestion of vagueness which, arguably, makes it a more appropriate term to use. As *Hiner* says,

> It is misleading . . . to talk about 'the' classical theory of organisations because this gives the impression of a settled doctrine expressed in formally accepted terms, whereas one of the difficulties of the theory is that no definitive version exists.[59]

TOWARDS A SCIENTIFIC VALUE APPROACH?

It might be that the study of organisations, their structure and management is moving towards a more scientific approach. Management science can assist managers in the analysis of complex problems that are subject to quantitative constraints and in the optimisation of decisions to such problems. It may also assist in the establishment of broad theory. However, many operational problems in organisations relate to the nature of human behaviour and the people–organisation relationship, and do not lend themselves to the application of a scientific answer.

There are no definitive or final solutions to the problems of organisations.

The nature of work organisations and the environment in which they operate is becoming increasingly complex and subject to continual change. But at least we do understand more about the dynamics of management and organisational behaviour as a basis for the analysis of human behaviour in organisations.[60]

Research findings

The research findings of organisational behaviour are still inconclusive and contradictory but, according to *London*, there are a number of general features which can be identified.

- Modern organisations have failed to provide individuals with adequate outlets for creativity and self-actualisation, thus causing alienation and conflict.
- Conflict and tension, in themselves, are not necessarily undesirable. The nature of conflict needs to be understood so it can be utilised to help improve organisational performance.
- Organisation structures can be designed to allow individuals full scope for self-actualisation, and at the same time facilitate achievement of organisational goals and objectives.
- Different individuals have different levels of skills and ambitions. Managers must be able to manage if the organisation is to achieve its goals and objectives.
- Modern management has become too democratic. Without evoking excesses of Taylorism, there must be a return to more authoritarian attitudes of management.[61]

Balance between philosophy and science

Miner, however, suggests that although the degree of commitment to the scientific value system is increasing, as yet there is insufficient research to move the field entirely into science, completely divorced from philosophy. At present management theory is clearly in the 'schools' phase. As discussed earlier, it is possible to argue over the use of the term 'schools'. But whatever terminology is used, and whatever the state of our knowledge, the message from Miner is clear. '. . . schools of management thought are very much a reality, and the management student who approaches the field without at least a minimal understanding of them does so at some risk.'[62]

Whatever the balance between philosophy and science, a knowledge and understanding of management theory will help with the complexities of management in modern work organisations. No single approach to organisation and management provides all the answers. It is the comparative study of different approaches which will yield benefits to the manager.[63]

There are many aspects to management. There are no simple solutions, no one best way to manage. The study of organisations, their structure and management is important for the manager and an indispensable part of the job.

Synopsis

The study of organisation and management has to proceed on a broad front. A central part of this study is the development of management thinking and what might be termed management theory. In order to help identify main trends in the development of management thinking and organisational behaviour, it is usual to categorise the work of leading writers into various 'approaches' based on their views of organisations, their structure and management. This provides a framework in which to direct study and focus attention.

A commonly used analysis of approaches to organisation and management is the three-fold categorisation of classical, human relations and systems. The classical writers placed emphasis on purpose and structure, on the technical requirements of the organisation, on principles of management, and on the assumption of rational and logical behaviour. The human relations writers emphasised the importance of the informal organisation and the psychological and social needs of people at work. The systems approach attempts to integrate the work of the classical and human relations writers. Attention is focused on the organisation as a whole and the interactions between technical and social variables. The organisation is seen as an open system in continual interaction with the external environment.

The three-fold categorisation of classical, human relations and systems provides a useful starting point for the identification of main trends in the development of management thinking. It provides a framework in which to focus attention on different aspects of management theory and practice, and the development of organisational behaviour. Within this framework it is possible to identify a number of other approaches or sub-divisions of approaches, such as, for example, bureaucracy, neo-human relations, technology, decision making.

More recent forms of analysis include contingency theory and social action. Contingency theory highlights possible means of differentiating between alternative forms of structures and systems of management. Social action writers attempt to view the organisation from the position of individual members who will each have his or her own interpretation of the work situation in terms of the satisfaction sought and the meaning that work has for him or her.

The obscure lines between the different approaches, and the interrelationships among them, appear to support the use of the term 'approaches' to organisation and management as more appropriate than the term 'schools' which is used in some of the literature. Whatever form of categorisation is adopted, the division of writers on organisation and management into various approaches offers a number of advantages. For example, it helps in organisational analysis and the identification of problem areas. It enables the manager to take from the different approaches those ideas which suit best the particular requirements of the job. There are, however, a number of caveats which should also be noted.

It might be that the study of organisations is moving towards a more scientific value approach. But whatever the balance between philosophy and science, a knowledge of management theory will help with the complexities of management in modern work organisations. It is necessary to view the interrelationships among the development of theory, behaviour in organisations and management practice.

Review and discussion questions

1. Identify, and outline briefly, major trends in approaches to organisation and management since the beginning of this century.

2. Assess critically the relevance of scientific management to present-day management in organisations. Illustrate your answer with reference to your own organisation.

3. To what extent is there anything positive to be said for bureaucratic structures? Select a large-scale organisation of your choice and suggest ways in which it displays characteristics of a bureaucracy.

4. What are the main conclusions that can be drawn from the Hawthorne experiments? Discuss critically the relevance of these experiments for management and organisational behaviour today.

5. Summarise the main features of the neo-human relations approach to organisation and management. How does it differ from other approaches?

6. Evaluate the application of the systems approach to the analysis of work organisations. Suggest an example of a work situation in which the systems approach might be appropriate.

7. Contrast approaches to improving organisational performance based on attention to technical and structural requirements, with those based on concern for psychological and social factors.

8. Explain what is meant by a social action approach. Distinguish between 'unitary' and 'pluralistic' views of work situations.

9. Discuss the extent to which the study of the development of management theory has any practical value to the manager. What caveats should be noted?

10. Which *one* of the different approaches to organisation and management would you select as most relevant to the analysis of a particular work situation? Give a detailed assessment of the contributions and limitations of your selected approach.

| **Practical assignment** | In self-selecting groups of three or four, visit a work organisation of your choice, preferably that is well known to at least one member of your group. |

(i) Investigate those features of the structure, management and operations of the organisation which are characteristic of:
   (a) scientific management; and
   (b) bureaucracy.
   Comment critically on what you believe to be the practical effects of your set of characteristics, and give examples in support of your comments.

(ii) For the same, or a different, organisation: comment critically, with supporting examples, on the extent to which applications of the human relations approach to organisation and management have been applied in practice.

Notes and references

1. This chapter is based in parts on a development of the author's articles: Mullins, L. J. 'Approaches to Management', *Management Accounting*, vol. 57, no. 4, April 1979, pp. 15–18, and Mullins, L. J. 'Some Further Approaches to Management Theory', *Management Accounting*, vol. 58, no. 3, March 1980, pp. 30–3.
2. See, for example: George, C. S. *The History of Management Thought*, Second edition, Prentice-Hall (1972).

3. McGregor, D. *The Human Side of Enterprise*, McGraw-Hill (1960) p. 6.
4. Miner, J. B. *Theories of Organizational Behavior*, Holt, Rinehart and Winston (1980).
5. Skipton, M. D. 'Management and the Organisation', *Management Research News*, vol. 5, no. 3, 1983, pp. 9–15.
6. O'Shaughnessy, J. *Business Organization*, Allen and Unwin (1966) Preface. See also, for example: PA Management Consultants Ltd. *Company Organization*, Allen and Unwin (1970) and Rogers, E. M. and Agarwala-Rogers, R. *Communication in Organizations*, Free Press (1976).
7. Fayol, H. *General and Industrial Management*, Pitman (1949). See also: Gray I. *Henri Fayol's General and Industrial Management*, Pitman (1988).
8. Urwick, L. *Notes on the Theory of Organization*, American Management Association (1952).
9. Mooney, J. D. and Reiley, A. C. *The Principles of Organization*, Harper and Bros (1939); revised by Mooney, J. D., Harper and Row (1947).
10. Brech, E. F. L. *Organisation: The Framework of Management*, Second edition, Longman (1965).
11. Simon, H. A. *Administrative Behavior*, Third edition, Free Press (1976) p. xxii.
12. Woodward, J. *Industrial Organization: Theory and Practice*, Second edition, Oxford University Press (1980).
13. Taylor, F. W. *Scientific Management*, Harper and Row (1947). Comprises Shop Management (1903), Principles of Scientific Management (1911) and Taylor's testimony to the House of Representatives' Special Committee (1912).
14. Woodward, J. *Industrial Organization: Theory and Practice*, Second edition, Oxford University Press (1980).
15. Braverman, H. *Labor and Monopoly Capital*, Monthly Review Press (1974).
16. For a study of employers' labour relations policies, including comments on the work of Braverman, see: Gospel, H. F. and Littler, C. R. (eds), *Managerial Strategies and Industrial Relations*, Heinemann Educational Books (1983).
17. Rose, M. *Industrial Behaviour*, Penguin (1978) p. 31. See also: Rose, M. *Industrial Behaviour*, Second edition, Penguin (1988) Chapter 2.
18. Drucker, P. F. 'The Coming Rediscovery of Scientific Management', *The Conference Board Record*, vol. XIII, June 1976, p. 23–7. Reprinted in Drucker, P. F. *Towards the Next Economics and Other Essays*, Heinemann (1981).
19. Locke, E. A. 'The Ideas of Frederick W Taylor: An Evaluation', *Academy of Management Review*, vol. 7, no. 1, January 1982, pp. 14–24.
20. Gilbreth, F. B. and Gilbreth, L. M. *Applied Motion Study*, Sturgess and Walton (1917).
21. Weber, M. *The Theory of Social and Economic Organization*, Collier Macmillan (1964).
22. Blau, P. M. and Scott, W. R. *Formal Organizations*, Routledge and Kegan Paul (1966).
23. Stewart, R. *The Reality of Management*, Second edition, Pan Books (1986).
24. Crozier, M. *The Bureaucratic Phenomenon*, Tavistock Publications (1964).
25. Argyris, C. *Integrating the Individual and the Organization*, Wiley (1964).
26. Merton, R. K. *Social Theory and Social Structure*, Revised edition, Collier Macmillan (1968).
27. Selznick, P. *TVA and the Grass Roots*, Harper and Row (1966).
28. Gouldner, A W. *Patterns of Industrial Bureaucracy*, Free Press (1954), and *Wildcat Strike*, Harper and Row (1965).
29. Etzioni, A. *Modern Organizations*, Prentice-Hall (1964) p. 41.
30. There are many versions of the Hawthorne experiments. Among the most thorough accounts is that by: Roethlisberger, F. J. and Dickson, W. J. *Management and the Worker*, Harvard University Press (1939).
31. See also: Landsberger, H. A. *Hawthorne Revisted*, Cornell University Press, Ithaca (1958).
32. See, for example: Rose, M. *Industrial Behaviour*, Second edition, Penguin (1988).
33. Stead, B. A. *Women in Management*, Prentice-Hall (1978) p. 190.
34. Silverman, D. *The Theory of Organisations*, Heinemann (1970).
35. London, K. *The People Side of Systems*, McGraw-Hill (1976).
36. Maslow, A. H. 'A Theory of Human Motivation', *Psychological Review*, vol. 50, July 1943, pp. 370–96.
37. Herzberg, F. W., Mausner, B. and Snyderman, B. B. *The Motivation to Work*, Second edition, Chapman and Hall (1959).
38. McGregor, D. *The Human Side of Enterprise*, McGraw-Hill (1960).
39. Likert, R. *New Patterns of Management*, McGraw-Hill (1961). See also: Likert, R. *The Human Organization*, McGraw-Hill (1967), Likert, R. and Likert, J. G. *New Ways of Managing Conflict*, McGraw-Hill (1976).

40. Argyris, C. *Understanding Organizational Behavior*, Tavistock Publications (1960) and *Integrating the Individual and the Organization*, Wiley (1964).
41. Bertalanffy, L. von. 'Problems of General Systems Theory: A New Approach to the Unity of Science', *Human Biology*, vol. 23, no. 4, December 1951, pp. 302–12.
42. Miller, E. J. and Rice, A. K. *Systems of Organization*, Tavistock Publications (1967).
43. Boulding, K. 'General Systems Theory – The Skeleton of Science', *Management Science*, vol. 2, no. 3, April 1956, pp. 197–208.
44. Trist, E. L. *et al. Organizational Choice*, Tavistock Publications (1963).
45. Walker. C. R. and Guest, R. H. *The Man on the Assembly Line*, Harvard University Press (1952). See also: Walker, C. R., Guest, R. H. and Turner, A. N. *The Foreman on the Assembly Line*, Harvard University Press (1956).
46. Woodward, J. *Industrial Organization: Theory and Practice*, Second edition, Oxford University Press (1980).
47. Sayles, L. R. *Behavior of Industrial Work Groups*, Wiley (1958).
48. Blauner, R. *Alienation and Freedom*, University of Chicago Press (1964).
49. O'Shaughnessy, J. *Business Organization*, Allen and Unwin (1966) pp. 127–8.
50. Barnard, C. *The Functions of the Executive*, Oxford University Press (1938).
51. Simon, H. A. *The New Science of Management Decision*, Revised edition, Prentice-Hall (1977).
52. Cyert, R. M. and March, J. G. *A Behavioral Theory of the Firm*, Prentice-Hall (1963).
53. Sadler, P. J. and Barry, B. A. *Organizational Development*, Longman (1970).
54. Silverman, D. *The Theory of Organisations*, Heinemann (1970) p. 147.
55. Goldthorpe, J. H. *et al. The Affluent Worker*, Cambridge University Press (1968).
56. Fox, A. *Industrial Sociology and Industrial Relations*, HMSO (1966).
57. Horn, C. A. 'Management Style', *Administrator*, vol. 6, no. 4, April 1986, p. 14.
58. Bowey, A. M. *The Sociology of Organisations*, Hodder and Stoughton (1976).
59. Hiner, O. S. *Business Administration*, Longman (1969) p. 143.
60. See, for example: Klein S. M. and Ritti R. R. *Understanding Organizational Behavior*, Second edition, Kent Publishing (1984) Chapter 1.
61. London, K. *The People Side of Systems*, McGraw-Hill (1976).
62. Miner, J. B. *Management Theory*, Macmillan (1971) p. 145. See also: Miner, J. B. *Theories of Organizational Behavior*, Holt, Rinehart and Winston (1980) Chap. 1.
63. For a critical account on competing views about organisation theory and its applications, see: Perrow, C. *Complex Organizations*, Second edition, Scott, Foresman (1979). For a discussion of British and American ideas on conceiving and selling management theory, see: Foster, G. 'Management's Missing Ideas', *Management Today*, March 1980, pp. 72–5, 152–6.

CONTEXT OF THE ORGANISATION

3. THE ORGANISATIONAL SETTING

The application of organisational behaviour and the process of management take place not in a vacuum but within the context of an organisational setting. The organisation is a complex social system and is the sum of many interrelated variables. The operations of the organisation are influenced by the external environment of which it is part. The manager needs to understand the nature of organisations and the main features which affect the structure, management and functioning of the work organisation.

Objectives

To: (i) Explain the nature of organisations, and distinguish between the formal and the informal organisation;

(ii) Describe the basic components of an organisation;

(iii) Distinguish alternative types and classifications of organisations, and relate different organisations to these classifications;

(iv) Examine the organisation as an open system and the interrelated sub-systems within an organisation;

(v) Explain the significance of contingency models of organisation;

(vi) Appreciate the influence of technology in work organisations and the impact of information technology;

(vii) Recognise the importance of the organisational setting.

THE NATURE OF ORGANISATIONS

All organisations have some function to perform. Organisations exist in order to achieve objectives and to provide satisfaction for their members. Organisations enable objectives to be achieved that could not be achieved by the efforts of individuals on their own. Through co-operative action, members of an organisation can provide a synergistic effect. There are many different types of organisations which are set up to serve a number of different purposes and to meet a variety of needs.

Organisations come in all forms, shapes and sizes. Consider the diversification among such organisations as, for example:

Firm of accountants	Hotel
School	Leisure centre
Retail shop	Quarry works
Local authority	Government department
Airport	Pharmaceutical company
Motor car manufacturer	Bank
Hospital	Nationalised industry

The structure, management and functioning of these organisations will all vary because of differences in the nature and type of the organisation, their respective goals and objectives, and the behaviour of the people who work in them.

Let us now consider just two types of organisations towards the opposite ends of a possible continuum – say a maximum security prison and a university largely concerned with research – as a framework on which to focus attention.

We can appreciate readily that although both types of organisation will be concerned with the basic activities of organisation and management their goals and objectives, actual procedures and methods of operation, structure, systems and style of management, and orientation and behaviour of members will differ considerably.

Common factors in organisations

Despite the differences among various organisations there are, however, at least three common factors in any organisation:

- people,
- objectives,
- structure.

It is the interaction of *people* in order to achieve *objectives* which forms the basis of an organisation. Some form of *structure* is needed by which people's interactions and efforts are channelled and co-ordinated. To which we can add a fourth factor –

- management

Some process of *management* is required by which the activities of the organisation, and the efforts of its members, are directed and controlled towards the pursuit of objectives. (*See* Fig. 3.1.)

The actual effectiveness of the organisation will be dependent upon the quality of its people, its objectives and structure, and the resources available to it. There are two broad categories of resources:

- non-human – physical assets, materials and facilities; and
- human – members' abilities and influence, and their management.

The interrelationship of people, objectives and structure, together with the efficient use of available non-human and human resources, will determine the success or failure of the organisation and the extent of its effectiveness.

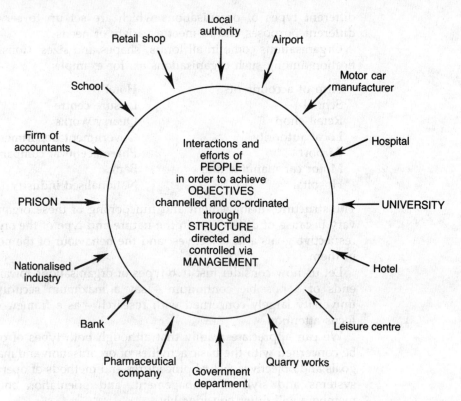

Fig. 3.1 Common factors in organisations

FORMAL AND INFORMAL ORGANISATIONS

The formal organisation

A *formal organisation* has been defined by *Schein* as 'the planned co-ordination of the activities of a number of people for the achievement of some common, explicit purpose or goal, through division of labor and function, and through a hierarchy of authority and responsibility'.[1] An organisation is a pattern of roles and a blueprint for their co-ordination. The object of co-ordination is activities, not people. The formal organisation can exist independently of the membership of particular individuals.

The formal organisation can be distinguished from the informal organisation. The difference between the formal and the informal organisation is a feature of the degree to which they are structured. The formal organisation is deliberately planned and created and is concerned with the co-ordination of activities. It is hierarchically structured with stated objectives, the specification of tasks, and defined relationships of authority and responsibility. An organisation chart, for example, gives a representation of the formal structure. Other examples of the formal organisation are rules and regulations, standing orders, job descriptions.

The informal organisation

Within this formal structure an informal organisation will always be present. The informal organisation arises from the interaction of people working in the organisation, their psychological and social needs, and the development of groups with their own relationships and norms of behaviour, irrespective of those defined within the formal structure. The informal organisation is flexible and loosely structured. Relationships may be left undefined. Membership is spontaneous and with varying degrees of involvement. Group relationships and norms of behaviour exist outside the official structure and the informal organisation may, therefore, be in conflict with the aims of the formal organisation. A summary of differences between the formal and the informal organisation is given in Table 3.1.

Table 3.1 Comparison of formal and informal organisation.

Characteristic	Formal organisation	Informal organisation
1. **Structure**		
A. Origin	Planned	Spontaneous
B. Rationale	Rational	Emotional
C. Characteristics	Stable	Dynamic
2. **Position terminology**	Job	Role
3. **Goals**	Profitability or service to society	Member satisfaction
4. **Influence**		
A. Base	Position	Personality
B. Type	Authority	Power
C. Flow	Top down	Bottom up
5. **Control mechanisms**	Threat of firing, demotion	Physical or social sanctions (norms)
6. **Communication**		
A. Channels	Formal channels	Grapevine
B. Networks	Well defined, follow formal lines	Poorly defined, cut across regular channels
C. Speed	Slow	Fast
D. Accuracy	High	Low
7. **Charting the organisation**	Organisation chart	Sociogram
8. **Miscellaneous**		
A. Individuals included	All individuals in work group	Only those 'acceptable'
B. Interpersonal relations	Prescribed by job description	Arise spontaneously
C. Leadership role	Assigned by organisation	Result of membership agreement
D. Basis for interaction	Functional duties or position	Personal characteristics, ethnic background, status
E. Basis for attachment	Loyalty	Cohesiveness

(Adapted from J. L. Gray and F. A. Starke, Organizational Behavior: Concepts and Applications, Fourth edition, Charles E. Merrill (1988) p. 432.)

Functions of the informal organisation

The informal organisation can serve a number of important functions.

- It provides satisfaction of members' social needs, and a sense of personal identity and belonging.
- It provides for additional channels of communication; for example, through the 'grapevine' information of importance to particular members is communicated quickly.
- It provides a means of motivation, for example, through status, social interaction, variety in routine or tedious jobs, and informal methods of work.
- It provides a feeling of stability and security, and through informal 'norms' of behaviour can exercise a form of control over members.

- It provides a means of highlighting deficiencies or weaknesses in the formal organisation, for example, areas of duties or responsibilities not covered in job descriptions or outdated systems and procedures. The informal organisation may also be used when formal methods would take too long, or not be appropriate, to deal with an unusual or unforeseen situation.[2]

The informal organisation, therefore, has an important influence on the morale, motivation, job satisfaction and performance of staff. It can provide members with greater opportunity to use their initiative and creativity in both personal and organisational development.

The importance and nature of groups, and reasons why people form into groups, both formal and informal, are discussed in Chapter 13.

At this stage we are concerned with consideration of the formal organisation. (In practice, however, it is not always possible to distinguish clearly between formal and informal organisations.) We are not concerned with what is sometimes referred to as the social organisation. Social organisations are groups or institutions, such as the family or friends, where human behaviour is socially organised and where members share common beliefs or interests. Social organisations arise from the interactions of individuals. There are no specially defined hierarchical structures and no explicit organisational goals.

The organisation as a coalition

The formal organisation can be seen as a coalition of individuals with a number of sub-coalitions.[3] Membership of the coalition will be dependent upon the type of organisation but could include, for example, managers, administrators, workers, elected representatives, appointed officials, volunteers, shareholders, suppliers, trade union officials, leaders of interest groups, customers, clients, patrons, donors, specialists, consultants, and representatives of external agencies.

It is difficult to define specific, permanent boundaries for an organisational coalition. However, by focusing on participants over a given period, or participants concerned with particular decision-making processes, it is possible to identify the main members of a coalition. Strategies adopted by particular sectional interests or sub-coalitions will sometimes be part of the formal organisation structure, for instance, in the pursuit of manifest managerial goals; and sometimes related to the informal structure, for example, heads of departments vying with each other for limited resources, or workers indulging in restrictive practices.

BASIC COMPONENTS OF AN ORGANISATION

Any organisation can be described, broadly, in terms of an operating component and an administrative component.[4]

The *operating component* comprises the people who actually undertake the work of producing the products, or providing the services.

The *administrative component* comprises managers and analysts, and is concerned with supervision and co-ordination.

Developing this description, we can identify five basic components of a work organisation: the operational core; operational support; organisational support; top management; and middle management. (*See* Fig. 3.2.)

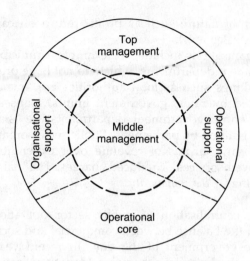

Fig. 3.2 Five basic components of an organisation

- *The operational core* is concerned with direct performance of the technical or productive operations and the carrying out of actual task activities of the organisation; for example, people putting together parts on an assembly line, teaching in a classroom, treating a patient, cooking meals in a hotel, serving in a bank, repairing a hole in the road.
- *Operational support* is concerned indirectly with the technical or productive process but closely related to the actual flow of operational work; for example, people working in quality control, work study, progress planning, storekeeping, works maintenance, technical services.
- *Organisational support* is concerned with provision of services for the whole organisation, including the operational core, but which are usually outside the actual flow of operational work; for example, people working in personnel, medical services, canteen, management accounting, office services.
- *Top management* is concerned with broad objectives and policy, strategic decisions, the work of the organisation as a whole and interactions with the external environment; for example, managing director, governors, management team, chief executive, board of directors, council members.
- *Middle management* is concerned with co-ordination and integration of activities; and providing links with operational support staff and organisational support staff, and between the operational core and top management.

PRIVATE AND PUBLIC SECTOR ORGANISATIONS

Organisations can, traditionally, be distinguished in terms of two generic groups:

- private enterprise organisations; and
- public sector organisations.

The distinction can be made on the basis of ownership and finance, and the profit motive. Private enterprise organisations are owned and financed by individuals, partners, or shareholders in a joint stock company. The main aim is of a *commercial* nature such as profit, return on capital employed, market standing or sales level.

Public sector organisations include, for example, municipal undertakings and central government departments, which do not have profit as their goal. Municipal undertakings such as local authorities are 'owned' by the ratepayers and financed by rates, government grants, loans and charges for certain services. Central government departments are 'state owned' and financed by funds granted by parliament. Public sector organisations do not distribute profits. Any surplus of revenue over expenditure may be reallocated by improved services or reduced charges. The main aim is a *service to* and the well-being of *the community*.

Privatisation

The extent of the centralisation of public sector operations, or of their 'privatisation', and the balance between commercial and social interests, are determined by the government of the day. In recent years, the present government has embarked upon a major 'denationalisation' programme involving the selling off of shares and subsidiaries, and increasing competition for public monopolies. There has been a vigorous policy of transfer of business undertakings to private hands (privatisation) involving such organisations as, for example, British Petroleum, National Freight Corporation, Jaguar, British Telecom, British Aerospace, British Gas, Rolls-Royce and British Airways.

There are other public sector organisations whose aims involve both a commercial interest and a service interest. Nationalised industries such as electricity, coal and the railways are, at present, run as public corporations with autonomy on day-to-day management, but with ultimate government control in the national interest. These public corporations are required to make efficient use of their resources by ensuring a given minimum rate of return on their investments and to charge prices based on the actual cost of supplying goods or services to certain groups of consumers. But provision may also be made for certain activities to be undertaken on social grounds as a service to the community even though these activities might be run at a financial loss.

It is, however, the present government's intention to further its privatisation programme, and there are plans to consider the transfer of, for example, water authorities and electricity industry to private hands.

A number of government functions have also been privatised; for example, motorway service areas and the Hydraulics Research Station. There has also been increasing moves to encourage contracting out of certain local authority services and putting them to competitive tender. Examples include cleansing services, vehicle maintenance, catering, parks services, refuse collection and social services transport. A greater degree of competition has also been introduced; for example, in the supply of communications apparatus; the provision to suspend the postal monopoly; and removal of restrictions on passenger road transport to allow increased competition among coach operators.

The increasing scale of privatisation and the blurring of commercial interests and social interests have led to an alternative classification of organisations:

- *profit*; and those clearly,
- *not-for-profit*.

Not-for-profit organisations include on one hand charities, private societies and most religious organisations, and on the other hand National Health Service hospitals, universities, prisons, and most government and local authority departments.

However, even in not-for-profit, public sector organisations there has been increased government pressure to ensure cost-effectiveness and efficiency and economy in their operations.

TYPES OF AUTHORITY AND ORGANISATIONS

In one of the earliest studies of formal organisations, *Weber* distinguished three types of authority: *traditional, charismatic* and *legal–rational*.[5] These types of authority are based on the form of control regarded as legitimate by subordinates, and their acceptance of the power of superiors. The three types of authority relate to different types of organisations.

- In *traditional organisations*, authority is legitimised by custom and a long-standing belief in the natural right to rule, or is possessed by traditional ('proper') procedure. Examples would be the authority of the pope, kings or queens or a paternalistic employer.
- In *charismatic organisations*, authority is legitimised by belief in the personal qualities of the leader; authority is based on the leader's strength of personality and inspiration. Winston Churchill might be quoted as an example. The practical need for some routine, for procedures and systems and for economic support means that if the movement is to continue it must become organised. On the impending demise of the charismatic leader the movement might collapse unless a 'legitimate' heir is found. This process tends to transform a charismatic organisation into either a traditional organisation or a bureaucratic organisation.
- In *bureaucratic organisations*, authority is based on the acceptance of the law of formal rules and procedures, and on impersonal principles. There is a legal–rational authority which stems from hierarchical position in the organisation and not from personality. Examples are the armed forces and the authority of government ministers or a college principal.

The concept of legal–rational authority is of most interest to us because most business organisations, particularly large-scale ones, tend to be of the bureaucratic type of structure, although there are variations in degree. Bureaucracy, as applying to certain structural features of organisation, is the most dominant type of formal organisation.

THE CLASSIFICATION OF ORGANISATIONS

In order to relate the study of management and organisational behaviour to one particular type of organisation as distinct from another, it is necessary to group similar types of organisations together. This enables generalisations to be made on the basis of certain characteristic features of organisations within a particular grouping. Organisations can be distinguished by, for example, their nature and type; goods or services provided; size; aims and objectives; and the people who are employed by or who work in them. Organisations can, therefore be classified in a number of ways and different writers have emphasised particular features of organisations.

Classification by major purpose

A common classification of organisations is by their major purpose. This leads to a distinction between, for example:

- business firms (economic organisations);
- armies, trade unions and police forces (protective organisations);
- clubs and societies (associative organisations);
- local authorities and hospitals (public service organisations); and
- churches (religious organisations).

Further distinctions could be made, for example, into political organisations, educational organisations, military organisations and voluntary organisations.

Such a distinction tends to lack refinement and not all organisations fit simply into one classification. Many universities combine research with teaching. Some hospitals are concerned as much with training and/or research as with treatment of patients. One could debate the main purpose of a prison; is it, for example, corrective, protective, penal or educational? The main purpose of a trade union is seen, presumably, as protection of the interests of its members through their wages and working conditions, but many trade unions also have strong social, educational and political interests.

Many organisations serve more than one goal; but although they are multi-purpose organisations it is usual to be able to identify one predominant goal (or purpose) by which the organisation can be classified, however crude this classification may be. It is, however, of interest to note the comment by *Etzioni* that: 'To the extent that such things can be measured, it appears that many multi-purpose organisations tend to serve each of their goals separately and all of them together more effectively and efficiently than single-purpose organisations of the same category.'[6]

Other alternative forms of classification have been constructed, among the best known of which are those by *Etzioni*, and by *Blau* and *Scott*.

Power and involvement

Etzioni, in a comparative analysis of complex organisations on power, involvement, and their correlates, considers the development of 'middle range' organisation theory – that is 'between high-level abstractions about the characteristics of organisations in general and detailed observations about single cases' and uses compliance as the basis for classification.[7] The Etzioni typology involves three dimensions: power; involvement; and the identification of kinds of power with kinds of involvement. Compliance is the relationship between the kinds of power applied by the organisation to control its members and the kinds of involvement developed by members of the organisation.

Power differs according to the means by which members of the organisation comply.

- *Coercive* power relies on the use of threats, or physical sanctions or force, for example, controlling the need for food or comfort;

- *Remunerative* power involves the manipulation of material resources and rewards, for example, through salaries and wages;
- *Normative* power relies on the allocation and manipulation of symbolic rewards, for example, esteem and prestige.

Involvement is the degree of commitment by members to the organisation.

- *Alienative* involvement occurs where members are involved against their wishes. There is a strong negative orientation towards the organisation.
- *Calculative* involvement occurs where attachment to the organisation is motivated by extrinsic rewards. There is either a negative orientation or a low positive orientation towards the organisation.
- *Moral* involvement is based on the individual's belief in, and value placed on, the goals of the organisation. There is a high positive orientation towards the organisation.

The identification of kinds of power with kinds of involvement

When considered together nine logical types of organisational relationships and compliance result from this typology. (See Fig. 3.3.)

Based on this analysis, *Etzioni* suggests that a particular kind of power usually goes with a particular kind of involvement.

- Coercive power with alienative involvement – relationship 1 (typified, for example, by prisons).
- Remunerative power with calculative involvement – relationship 5 (typified, for example, by business firms).
- Normative power with moral involvement – relationship 9 (typified, for example, by churches).

The matching of these kinds of power and involvement are congruent with each other, and represent the most common form of compliance in organisations. The other six types of organisational relationships are incongruent. Etzioni suggests that organisations with congruent compliance structures will be more effective than organisations with incongruent structures.

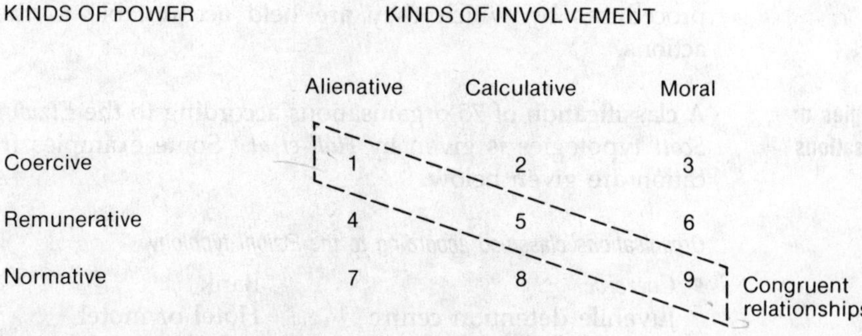

KINDS OF POWER   KINDS OF INVOLVEMENT

	Alienative	Calculative	Moral
Coercive	1	2	3
Remunerative	4	5	6
Normative	7	8	9

Congruent relationships

Fig. 3.3 Organisational relationships and compliance

(Adapted and reproduced with permission from: Etzioni, A., *A Comparative Analysis of Complex Organizations*, Revised edition. Copyright © The Free Press, a Division of Macmillan, Inc., 1975, p. 12.)

Prime beneficiary of the organisation

Blau and *Scott* propose a classification on the basis of the prime beneficiary.[8] Four groups of persons involved in a relationship with any organisation are categorised into:

- The members, or rank and file participants;
- The owner or managers of the organisation;
- The clients or, more generally, the 'public-in-contact' who are technically 'outside' the organisation yet have regular direct contact with it;
- The public at large, that is, the members of the society in which the organisation operates.

Organisations are then classified on the basis of who benefits, that is, which of the four categories is the prime beneficiary of its operations. Four types of organisation are identified on this basis:

- *Mutual-benefit associations*, where the prime beneficiary is the membership, such as political parties, trade unions and professional associations;
- *Business concerns*, where the owners are the prime beneficiaries, such as industrial and other firms privately owned and operated for profit;
- *Service organisations*, where the client group is the main beneficiary, such as hospitals, schools and welfare agencies;
- *Commonweal organisations*, where the prime beneficiary is the public-at-large, such as central government departments, the armed services and the police.

It is emphasised that the prime beneficiary is not necessarily the only beneficiary. Each of the various groups who make a contribution to an organisation do so only in return for certain benefits received.

Blau and Scott suggest that special problems are associated with each type of organisation.

In *mutual-benefit organisations* the main problem is that of providing for participation and control by the membership, and of maintaining internal democracy.

In *business concerns* the central problem is that of maximising operational efficiency in a competitive environment.

In *service organisations* the problem is reconciling conflict between professional service to clients and administrative procedures.

In *commonweal organisations* the important problem is ensuring democratic procedures by which they are held accountable to the public for their actions.

Typologies or organisations

A classification of 75 organisations according to the *Etzioni* and the *Blau* and *Scott* typologies is given by *Hall et al.*[9] Some examples from Hall's classification are given below.

Organisations classified according to the Etzioni typology

- *Coercive*
  Juvenile detention centre
  Law enforcement agency
  Prison
- *Utilitarian*
  (i.e. remunerative)

Bank
Hotel or motel
Insurance company
Trade union organisation
Manufacturing plant
Municipal airport

Post Office
Restaurant
Retail store
Trade association
- *Normative*
Church
Civil rights organisation
Local political party
Local authority recreation department
Farmers' federation

Fund-raising agency
Newspaper
Private country club
Private hospital
Private school
Private welfare agency
Psychiatric hospital
University

Organisations classified according to the Blau and Scott typology

- *Mutual-benefit*
Local political party
Farm co-operative
Trade union organisation
Local religious organisation
Private country club
Trade association

- *Business*
Bank
Hotel or motel
Manufacturing plant
Newspaper
Quarry
Restaurant
Retail store

- *Service*
Civil rights organisation
Insurance company
Juvenile detention centre
Private hospital
Private school
Private welfare agency
Psychiatric hospital
University

- *Commonweal*
Local authority recreation department
Fund-raising agency
Law enforcement agency
Municipal airport
Post Office
General hospital
Prison

Extracted and adapted from R. H. Hall, J. E. Haas and N. J. Johnson, 'An Examination of the Blau–Scott and Etzioni Typologies', *Administrative Science Quarterly*, vol. 12, 1967–8, pp. 120–1.

The Etzioni typology is based on the control structure as the dependent variable, and the organisation as the independent variable. The Blau and Scott typology, however, is based on the organisation as the dependent variable. Hall found that although the two typologies are not interchangeable, they are interrelated. For example, of the 75 organisations in the classification, 89 per cent of business organisations were also utilitarian, and 57 per cent of mutual-benefit organisations and 77 per cent of service organisations were also normative.

It is not easy to find a comprehensive classification into which all organisations can be simply and satisfactorily categorised; and a degree of generalisation, assumption and qualification is required. However, the classifications of Etzioni and Blau and Scott provide useful typologies of organisations. An alternative form of classification is provided by *Katz* and *Kahn*.

Primary activity of the organisation

The *Katz* and *Kahn* classification is based on 'genotypic (first-order) factors' and on 'second-order factors'.[10] In terms of the genotypic function, which is the primary activity of the organisation as a sub-system within the larger society, there are four broad types of organisations:

- *Productive or economic* – concerned with the creation of wealth, the manufacture of goods, and the provision of services for the public;
- *Maintenance* – for example, schools and churches, concerned with the socialisation of people to fulfil roles in other organisations and in society;
- *Adaptive* – for example, research establishments, concerned with the pursuit of knowledge and the development and testing of theory;
- *Managerial or political* – for example, government departments, trade unions and pressure groups. These are concerned with adjudication, co-ordination and control of physical and human resources and other sub-systems.

Organisations can then be described in terms of second-order factors. Among other things these factors relate to structure; the system of intrinsic or extrinsic rewards to attract and retain members and to achieve satisfactory performance from them; and the nature of the throughput – the transformation or processing of objects or the moulding of people as the end product of the organisation. A distinction can be made between:

- object-moulding organisations; and
- people-moulding organisations.

Object-moulding organisations are concerned with physical or material objects as the nature of work being carried out, for example, a manufacturing plant, a coal mine or an oil company.

People-moulding organisations are concerned with human beings as the basis of the nature of work being carried out, for example, a school or a leisure centre. In people-moulding organisations a further distinction can be made between: (i) people-processing organisations, for example, an employment agency or a social security benefit office; and (ii) people-changing organisations, for example, a mental hospital or an open prison.

THE ORGANISATION AS AN OPEN SYSTEM

We have seen that organisations differ in many important respects. But they also share common features. Organisations can be viewed as open systems (*see* Fig. 3.4) which take inputs from the environment (outputs from other systems) and through a series of activities transform or convert these inputs into outputs (inputs to other systems) to achieve some objective.[11]

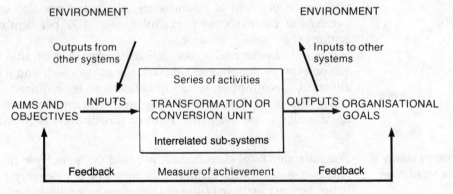

Fig. 3.4 The open systems model of organisations

In terms of this open systems model the business organisation, for example, takes in resources such as people, finance, raw materials and information from its environment; transforms or converts these; and returns them to the environment in various forms of outputs such as goods produced, services provided, completed processes or procedures in order to achieve certain goals such as profit, market standing, level of sales or consumer satisfaction.

There are, of course, differences in the activities and methods of operation of the various forms of business organisations. There will also be differences between business organisations of the same type, for example, in relation to their size and scale of activities. However, adopting the systems view of organisations, we can identify principles and prescriptions of organisation and management that apply to business organisations in general. Differences in the application and operation of these principles and prescriptions as between one business organisation and another is largely a matter only of degree and of emphasis.

Using this systems model the same form of analysis can be applied to all types of organisations. Viewing organisations as systems provides a common point of reference and enables us to take a general approach to the study of organisations, to analyse them and to derive general principles and prescriptions.[12]

Interaction with environment

The business organisation is an open system. It is in continual interaction with the external environment of which it is part. In order to be effective and maintain survival and growth, the organisation must respond to the opportunities and challenges, and the risks and limitations, presented by the external environment. Changes in the environment will affect inputs, and changes in inputs will affect the transformation or conversion process and hence the outputs. The open systems approach views the organisation within its total environment and emphasises the importance of multiple channels of interaction.

Fig. 3.5 Environmental influences on the organisation

The increasing rate of change in major environmental factors (technical, economic, social and governmental) has highlighted the need to study the total organisation and to adopt a systems approach. In addition to these major environmental factors, there is a multiplicity of constantly changing environmental influences which affect the operation of an organisation (*see* Fig. 3.5). In order to understand the operations of organisations, and to improve organisational performance, it is necessary to consider how they achieve an internal and external balance and how they are able to adapt to changes in their environment and the demands placed upon them.

The structure, management and functioning of an organisation is not only determined by internal considerations and choices, but is also strongly influenced by a range of external, environmental factors. Consider how the operations of a large comprehensive school, for example, might be affected by such external influences as: government proposals for reform of education; changing population trends; advances in information technology; changing views of the role of education in society; reports from Her Majesty's Inspectors; representations from employers' associations and trade unions; parent groups; equality campaigners.

Organisational performance and effectiveness will be dependent upon the successful management of the opportunities, challenges and risks presented by changes in the external environment.

Common features of organisations

All organisations need clear aims and objectives which will determine the nature of inputs, the series of activities to achieve outputs and the realisation of organisational goals. Feedback about the performance of the system, and the effects of its operation on the environment, are measured in terms of achieving the aims and objectives. Basic principles of organisation and management apply in any series of activities in any organisation.

Attention must be given to the design of a suitable structure. The common elements of management – clarification of objectives, planning, organising, directing and control – apply to a greater or lesser extent in all cases. Essential administrative functions must be carried out in all types of organisations. These common features make possible the application of general principles of management and organisational behaviour, and the meaningful study of organisation theory.

Whilst general principles and prescriptions apply to all organisations, differences in their aims and objectives, organisational goals, and environmental influences will result in differences in the input–conversion–output process and in the series of activities involved in this process. The nature of the inputs, the throughputs, and the form of the outputs will emphasise characteristic features of a particular organisation. These features highlight alternative forms of structure, management, methods of operation, and behaviour of people employed by or working in different types of organisations.

The study of organisations as systems serves, therefore, to indicate both the common features of organisations and the main distinguishing features between different types of organisations. It provides a useful framework for the comparative study of organisations. The systems view of organisations enables managers to view their own organisation in perspective, and to compare it in meaningful terms with other types of organisations.[13]

ORGANISATIONAL SUB-SYSTEMS

Whatever the type or classification of organisations, the transformation or conversion of inputs into outputs is a common feature of all organisations. Within the organisation (system) as a whole, each of the different transformation or conversion activities may themselves be viewed as separate sub-systems with their own input–conversion–output process interrelated to, and interacting with, the other sub-systems. The analysis of an organisation could perhaps be based upon the departmental structure as sub-systems. However, this could lead to an investigation concentrating on blinkered, sectional interests, rather than on the need to adopt a corporate approach based on the interrelationships and co-ordination of sub-systems in terms of the effectiveness of the organisation as an integrated whole.

The interrelationship and interdependence of the different parts of the system raise the question of the identification of these sub-systems. What are the boundaries that distinguish one sub-system from other sub-systems, and from the system as a whole? In practice the boundaries are drawn at the discretion of the observer and sub-systems are identified according to the area under study. These sub-systems may be identified, therefore, in a number of different ways, although there is a degree of similarity among the alternative models.

Socio-technical system

The work of *Trist* and others of the Tavistock Institute of Human Relations, in their study of changing technology in the British coal mines, gave rise to the idea of the socio-technical system.[14] The socio-technical system is concerned with the transformation or conversion process itself, and the relationships between technical efficiency, and social considerations and the effect on people. It was observed that new methods of work and changes in technology disrupted the social groupings of the miners, and brought about undesirable changes to the psychological and sociological properties of the old method of working. As a result, the new method of work was less efficient than it could have been despite the introduction of new technology.

The researchers saw the need for a socio-technical approach in which an appropriate social system could be developed in keeping with the new technical system. They suggested that there are three sub-systems common to any organisation:

- the *technological* sub-system;
- the sub-system of *formal role structure*;
- the sub-system of *individual members' feelings or sentiments*.

This form of analysis is taken a stage further by *Kast* and *Rosenzweig* who see the organisation as an open, socio-technical system with five major sub-systems.[15]

- *Goals and values* – the accomplishment of certain goals determined by the broader system and conformity with social requirements.
- *Technical* – the knowledge required for the performance of tasks, and the techniques and technology involved.
- *Psychosocial* – the interactions of individuals and groups, and behaviour of people in the organisation.

● *Structure* – the division and co-ordination of tasks, and formal relationships between the technical and psychosocial sub-systems.
● *Managerial* – covering the whole organisation and its relationship to the environment, setting goals, planning, structure and control.

Organisational functioning

Katz and *Kahn* also identify five sub-systems which describe organisational functioning.[16]

● *Production or technical* – concerned with the throughput, the work that gets done and the main productive process.
● *Supportive* – environmental transactions relating to input procurement or output disposal, or transactions supportive of the productive process.
● *Maintenance* – the equipment for getting the work done. Much of this 'equipment' relates to performance of people and to recruitment, socialisation and rewarding employees.
● *Adaptive* – concerned with sensing external changes and their effects on the organisation and its survival, for example, research and development.
● *Managerial* – organised activities for the direction, control and co-ordination of sub-systems and adjustment of the total system to its environment.

Interrelated sub-systems

An alternative model is suggested by *Hersey* and *Blanchard*, who identify four main interrelated sub-systems.[17]

● *Human/social* focuses on the needs and motivations of members of the organisation and styles of leadership.
● *Administrative/structural* focuses on authority and responsibility, and the structure within the organisation.
● *Informational/decision-making* focuses on key decisions and information needs necessary to keep the organisation operational.
● *Economic/technological* focuses on the work to be undertaken and its cost-effectiveness related to the goals of the organisation.

Another useful model is that of *Leavitt* who suggests the organisation consists of four main elements – task, structure, information and control, and people – which interact with each other and with the external environment.[18]

● *Task* – involves problem solving and improving organisational performance.
● *Structure* – refers to patterns of organisation authority and responsibility, communications.
● *Information and control* are techniques for controlling and processing information, such as accounting techniques.
● *People* – involves attitudes and interpersonal relations.

The analysis of work organisations

However these sub-systems are identified, it is the task of management to co-ordinate the sub-systems, and to ensure that the activities of the organisation as a whole are directed towards the accomplishment of its goals and objectives. We can suggest, therefore, five main interrelated sub-systems as a basis for the analysis of work organisations:

- *Task* – the goals and objectives of the organisation. The nature of inputs and outputs, and the work to be carried out in the transformation or conversion process.
- *Technology* – the manner in which the tasks of the organisation are carried out and the nature of work performance. The materials, systems and procedures, and equipment used in the transformation or conversion process.
- *Structure* – patterns of organisation, and formal relationships and channels of communication among members. The division of work and co-ordination of tasks by which the series of activities are carried out.
- *People* – the nature of the members undertaking the series of activities: such as their attitudes, skills and attributes; needs and expectations; interpersonal relations and patterns of behaviour. Group functioning and behaviour; informal organisation and styles of leadership.
- *Management* – co-ordination of task, technology, structure and people, and policies and procedures for the execution of work. Corporate strategy, direction of the activities of the organisation as a whole and its interactions with the external environment.

The attention given to organisational sub-systems can be related to developments in management thinking and organisational behaviour (discussed in Chapter 2). The classical approach emphasised the structural and the managerial sub-systems and the development of general principles of organisation. The human relations approach emphasised the psychological and sociological aspects and gave attention to the importance of people in the organisation and such factors as the social needs of individuals, motivation and group behaviour.

The systems approach focuses attention on the organisation as a whole, as a socio-technical system, and considers the interrelationships between the different sub-systems and the importance of environmental influences. The contingency approach concentrates on situational factors as determinants of alternative forms of organisation and management.

We have seen that adopting an open systems approach attempts to view the organisation as a purposeful, unified whole in continual interaction with its external environment. The organisation (system) is composed by a number of interrelated parts (sub-systems). Any one part of the organisation's activities affects other parts. Managers cannot afford to take a narrow, blinkered view. They need to adopt a broader view of the organisation's activities. Managers should recognise the interrelationships among various activities and the effects that their actions and decisions have on other activities.

Using the above framework of five main interrelated sub-systems – task, technology, structure, people, management – provides a useful basis for the analysis of organisational performance and effectiveness.

The manager must realise that in order to improve organisational effectiveness attention should be focused on the total work organisation and on the interrelationships among the range of variables which affect organisational performance. The organisation is best viewed as an open system and studied in terms of the interactions between technical and social considerations, and environmental influences. Changes in part of the system will affect other parts and thus the whole organisation. *The open systems approach provides a perspective in which to view different types of organisations and their methods of operation.*

CONTINGENCY MODELS OF ORGANISATION

The systems and contingency approaches highlight the complex nature of organisations. The analysis of organisational effectiveness requires an understanding of relationships within the organisation's structure, the inter-related sub-systems and the nature of its external environment.

Irrespective of the identification of sub-systems, the nature and scale of the series of activities involved in converting inputs to outputs will differ from one organisation to another in terms of the interrelationships between technology, structure, methods of operation, and the nature of environmental influences. 'Contingency' models of organisation such as, for example, those of *Woodward, Perrow, Burns* and *Stalker*, and *Lawrence* and *Lorsch*, highlight these interrelationships and provide a further possible means of differentiation between alternative forms of organisation and management.

These contingency models are examined in more detail in Chapter 6 but are introduced briefly here.

The contingency approach takes the view that there is no one best, universal form of organisation. There are a large number of variables, or situational factors, that influence organisational performance. Contingency models can be seen as an 'if–then' form of relationship. *If* certain situational factors exist, *then* certain organisational and managerial variables are most appropriate. Contingency models highlight differences between organisations. Managers can utilise these models to compare the structure and functioning of their own organisation.

Technological processes

Woodward, in her study of 100 manufacturing firms in south-east Essex found a relationship between technological processes and organisation structure.[19] Eleven different categories of production systems were identified in terms of their technological complexity, but these may be summarised under three broad headings: (i) unit and small batch production; (ii) large batch and mass production; and (iii) process production. Organisational patterns were found to be more related to similarity of objectives and production technique than to size, type of industry or the business success of the firm.

Perrow drew attention to two major dimensions of technology: (i) the extent to which the work task is predictable or variable, that is the number of exceptions encountered by the individual; and (ii) the extent to which technology and work tasks are broken down and highly specified, that is the extent to which procedures can be analysed.[20]

Combining the two dimensions provides a continuum of technology from routine, such as a mass production motor car factory; to non-routine, such as a mental hospital. *Perrow* suggests that by classifying organisations according to their technology and the predictability of work tasks, we should be able to predict the most effective form of structure.

Nature of the external environment

Burns and *Stalker* investigated 20 industrial firms in Scotland and analysed the relationship between their pattern of management and the nature of the external environment, and economic performance.[21] They identified two ideal types of organisation at opposite extremes of a continuum – the 'mechanistic' organisation and the 'organic' organisation. The mechanistic organisation is a rigid structure, and is appropriate to relatively stable conditions. The organic organisation is a more fluid structure and is appropriate to conditions of change and to uncertain environmental influences.

Differentiation and integration

Lawrence and *Lorsch* undertook a study of different organisations in the plastics, food and containers industries.[22] They analysed organisations in terms of 'differentiation' (differences in orientation among managers in different departments) and 'integration' (the degree of collaboration among departments) of the internal structure in relation to the external environment. Lawrence and Lorsch suggest that the extent of differentiation and integration in effective organisations will vary according to the demands of the particular environment. Organisations operating within a dynamic environment have to be both highly differentiated and highly integrated.

THE INFLUENCE OF TECHNOLOGY

The systems and contingency approaches have drawn attention to the importance of technology in the structure, management and functioning of work organisations.

The meaning of technology is interpreted broadly to include both:

- the physical aspects of machines, equipment, processes and work layout (machine technology) involved in the transformation or conversion process; and
- the actual methods, systems and procedures involved (knowledge technology) in carrying out the work of the organisation and transforming or converting inputs into outputs.

There is a close interrelationship between the machine side of technology and the specialist knowledge side of technology.[23]

The nature of technology can, therefore, be applied to the analysis of all organisations. For example, in a polytechnic the machine side of technology would include: blackboards or whiteboards; overhead projectors; computers; televisions and video recorders, closed circuit television; scientific and engineering equipment; library facilities. The knowledge side of technology would include: lectures, seminars and tutorials; case studies; role playing; practical laboratory work; visiting speakers; project and assignment work; examinations.

The work processes of a polytechnic, and other educational establishments, give rise to the specialist study of educational technology.[24] A polytechnic will receive inputs of students and, through the process of educational technology, 'transform' them and return them as outputs into the broader society.

Technology and the behaviour of people

The nature of technology can influence the behaviour of people in work organisations in many ways including, for example, the following.

- It influences the specific design of each member's pattern of work including the nature and variety of activities performed, and the extent of autonomy and freedom of action.
- It affects the nature of social interactions, for example the size and nature of work groups, the extent of physical mobility and of contacts with other people. A person working continuously on a single, isolated machine in a mass production factory will have very limited social interactions compared with, say, a team of receptionists in a large conference hotel.
- It can affect role position and the nature of rewards. People with higher levels of specialist technical knowledge and expertise such as engineers or systems analysts tend to receive higher status and pay than machine operators on an assembly line.
- It can impose time dimensions on workers and may require set times for attending to operations and a set pace of work; for example, the mechanical pacing of work on a mass production assembly line.
- It can result in distinguishing features of appearance; for example, the requirement to wear a standard uniform or protective clothing, compared with a personal choice of smart clothes.[25]

Technology is a major influence on the general climate of the organisation and the behaviour of people at work. For example, according to *Buchanan* and *Huczynski*:

> The organization of work around a given technology can be used to control labour costs, to control decision making, to control the relative status of different groups in an organization and to control promotion and career prospects. Managers may be able to manipulate employees in these ways by appealing to the technological determinist argument: 'We have to do this because the technology demands it.' Technological determinism may thus be used to justify unpopular management decisions.[26]

The nature of technology is also a potential source of tension and stress and affects motivation and job satisfaction: this is discussed in Chapter 12.

The systems approach should serve to remind managers that activities managed on the basis of technical efficiency alone are unlikely to lead to optimum improvements in organisational performance. It is important to maintain the balance of the socio-technical system. Changes to the work organisation as a result of new developments in technology must take account of human and social factors as well as technical and economic factors.

Information technology

The importance of the effective management of technical change has been highlighted by recent and continuing developments in information technology. Advances in technical knowledge, the search for improved economic efficiency and government support for information technology have all prompted a growing movement towards more automated procedures of work.

The impact of information technology will demand new patterns of work organisation, especially in relation to administrative procedures. It will affect the nature of individual jobs, and the formation and structure of work groups. There will be a movement away from large-scale, centralised organisation to smaller working units. Processes of communication will increasingly be linked to computer systems with the rapid transmission of information and immediate access to other national or international offices. Improvements in telecommunications mean, for example, that support staff need no longer be located within the main 'production' unit. Modern methods of communication may reduce the need for head office clerical jobs.

Individuals may work more on their own, from their personal work stations or even from their own homes, or work more with machines than with other people. One person may be capable of carrying out a wider range of activities. There will be changes in the nature of supervision and in the traditional hierarchical structure of jobs and responsibilities. Computer-based information and decision support systems provide an additional dimension of structural design. They will affect choices such as division of work, individual tasks and responsibilities. The introduction of information technology will undoubtedly transform, significantly, the nature of work and employment conditions for staff.

Advances in technical knowledge tend to develop at a faster rate than, and in isolation from, consideration of related human and social consequences. For example, fatigue and low morale are two major obstacles to the efficiency of staff. Research is now being conducted into possible health hazards such as eye strain, backache, general fatigue and irritability for operators of visual display units. This concern has prompted union proposals for recommended working practices for VDU operators. The Trades Union Congress has called for regular health checks and eye sight tests for operators, and a 20-minute break every 2 hours.

Managing technical change

Failure to match technical change to the concomitant human and social considerations means that staff may become resentful, suspicious and defensive. People's cognitive limitations, and their uncertainties and fears, may result in a reluctance to accept change. There may be strong opposition from staff and unions to the introduction of new technology. Fears are often expressed over such matters as employment levels and job security, the de-skilling of work, loss of job satisfaction, wage rate differentials, changes to social structures and working conditions, loss of individual control over work, and greater in-built management control.

The psychological and social implications of technical change, such as information technology and increased automation, must not be underestimated. New ideas and innovations should not be seen by members of staff as threats. The manager has to balance the need for adaptability in meeting opportunities presented by new technology with an atmosphere of stability and concern for the interests of staff. The manner in which technical change is introduced into the organisation will influence people's attitudes to work, the behaviour of individuals and groups, and their level of performance.[27]

Continued technical change is inevitable and likely to develop at an even greater rate. Managers must be responsive to such change. Information technology and automation create a demanding challenge. Managers need to develop working practices based on an accurate understanding of human behaviour and the integration of people's needs with organisational needs.

It is important to avoid destructive conflict, alienating staff including managerial colleagues, or evoking the anger and opposition of unions. At the same time, it is important to avoid incurring increased costs or a lower level of organisational performance caused by delays in the successful implementation of new technology. What needs to be considered is the impact of technical change on the design of the work organisation, and the attitudes and behaviour of staff. It will be necessary for managers and supervisors to develop more agile skills in organisation. This calls for the effective management of human resources and a style of managerial behaviour which helps to minimise the problems of technical change. (The management of conflict and organisational change is discussed further in Chapter 17.)

ORGANISATIONAL GOALS

Whatever the form and structure of the transformation or conversion process, the activities of an organisation are directed towards some end, some organisational goal. A goal is a future expectation, it is something the organisation is striving to accomplish. The goals of an organisation will determine the nature of its outputs and the series of activities through which those outputs are achieved. Organisational goals and objectives are discussed in the following chapter.

| **Synopsis** | The application of organisational behaviour and the process of management take place not in a vacuum but within the context of an organisational setting. Organisations come in all forms, shapes and sizes. However, despite the differences among various organisations there are at least three common factors in any organisation: people, objectives and structure. To which can be added a fourth factor – management. The qualities of these factors determine organisational effectiveness.

The formal organisation can be distinguished from the informal organisation and from the social organisation. The formal organisation is deliberately planned and created, and is concerned with the co-ordination of activities. Five basic components of a formal organisation are: operational core, operational support, organisational support, top management and middle management. The informal organisation arises from the interaction of people. It serves a number of important functions and has an influence on the morale, motivation, job satisfaction and performance of staff.

There are many different types of organisations which are set up to serve a variety of needs. Organisations can, traditionally, be distinguished in terms of two generic groups: private enterprise and public sector. The increasing rate of privatisation has led, however, to a blurring of commercial interests and service to the community. In order to relate the study of management and organisational behaviour to one particular type of organisation as distinct from another, it is necessary to group similar types of organisations together. A number of alternative forms of classification have been constructed. These classifications help provide useful typologies of organisations.

The structure, management and functioning of organisations will differ according to their nature and type, aims and objectives, and the behaviour of people who work in them. Organisations differ in many important respects but they also share common features. Business organisations can be viewed as open systems in continual interaction with the external environment of which they are part. Within the organisation as a whole there are a number of sub-systems interrelating to and interacting with each other. Contingency models of organisation draw attention to interrelationships among technology, structure, methods of operation and environmental influences. They highlight differences among organisations resulting from particular situational variables.

The systems and contingency approaches have drawn attention to the importance of technology in work organisations. The nature of technology can influence the behaviour of people at work in many ways. The impact of technical change has been highlighted by recent developments in information technology and automation. It is important to maintain the balance of the socio-technical system. This calls for effective management of human resources and a style of managerial behaviour which helps to minimise problems of technical change.

Review and discussion questions

1. Why do organisations exist? What are the common factors in any organisation?
2. Distinguish between the formal and the informal organisation, and explain their main characteristics. What functions are served by the informal organisation?
3. Explain the basic components of a work organisation. Support your answer with examples from your own organisation.
4. Contrast various organisations, including your own, in terms of classifications based on: (i) power and involvement, (ii) prime beneficiary and (iii) primary activity.
5. Discuss the extent to which differences among various organisations limit the value of the study of management and organisational behaviour.
6. Explain the organisation as an open system. What is meant by organisational sub-systems and how might they be identified? Illustrate each of these sub-systems by reference to your own organisation.
7. Assess the practical value to both the student and the manager of adopting a systems view of organisational analysis. What do you understand by contingency models of organisation?
8. Discuss the importance of technology in the structure, management and functioning of work organisations. Give practical examples of how the nature of technology can influence the behaviour of people at work.

| Assignment 1 | OUR ORGANIZATIONAL SOCIETY: YOUR ASSOCIATION WITH ORGANIZATIONS

Learning objectives

1. To identify some of the important organizations in your life.
2. To determine relevant, specific characteristics of organizations.

3. To describe some of the important functions of management in organizations.

Advance preparation

Read the Overview and Procedure Sections. Complete the form 'Profile of Organizations'.

Overview

Undoubtedly, you have had recent experiences with numerous organizations. Ten to fifteen minutes of reflective thinking should result in a fairly large list of organizations. Don't be misled by thinking that only large organizations, such as your college or General Motors, are relevant for consideration. How about the clinic with the doctor(s), nurse(s) and secretary/bookkeeper? Or the corner garage or service station? The local tavern, McDonald's and the neighborhood theater are all organizations. You should not have any difficulty in listing a number of organizations with which you have had recent contact.

The second part of the exercise, however, gets tougher. You are asked to describe several of the key characteristics of the organizations that you have listed. One of the major issues in studying and describing organizations is deciding *what* characteristics or factors are important. Some of the more common characteristics considered in the analysis of organizations are:

1. Size (small to very large)
2. Degree of formality (informal to highly structured)
3. Degree of complexity (simple to complex)
4. Nature of goals (what the organization is trying to accomplish)
5. Major activities (what tasks are performed)
6. Types of people involved (age, skills, educational background, etc.)
7. Location of activities (number of units and their geographic location)

You should be able to develop a list of characteristics that you think are relevant for each of your organizations.

Now, to the third, final, and most difficult task. Think about what is involved in the *management* of these organizations. For example, what kinds of functions do their managers perform? How does one learn the skills necessary to be an effective manager? Would you want to be a manager in any of these organizations?

In effect, in this exercise you are asked to think specifically about organizations you have been associated with recently, develop your own conceptual model for looking at their characteristics, and think more specifically about the managerial functions in each of these organizations. You probably already know a great deal more about organizations and their management than you think. This exercise should be useful in getting your thoughts together.

Procedure

Step 1

Prior to class, list up to 10 organizations (e.g., work, living group, club) in which you have been involved or with which you have had recent contact.

Step 2

Enter five organizations from your list on the form 'Profile of Organizations'.

a. List the organization.

b. Briefly outline the characteristics that you consider most significant.

c. Describe the managerial functions in each of these organizations.

Step 3

During the class period, meet in groups of five or six to discuss your list of organizations, the characteristics you consider important, and your descriptions of their management. Look for significant similarities and differences across organizations.

Step 4

Basing your selections on this group discussion, develop a list entitled 'What We Would Like to Know about Organizations and Their Management'. Be prepared to write this list on the board and to share your list with other groups in the class.

PROFILE OF ORGANIZATIONS		
Organization	*Key characteristics*	*Managerial functions*
1. _____		
2. _____		
3. _____		
4. _____		
5. _____		

Assignment 2

With the aid of a diagram, depict your own organisation, or some other organisation well known to you, in terms of an open system.

(i) Indicate, clearly:
- main aims and objectives;
- inputs;
- the nature of the transformation or conversion process;
- outputs;
- measurements of effectiveness in achieving organisational goals.

(ii) Give specific examples of ways in which the structure, management and functioning of the organisation are affected by external environmental influences.

How effective is the organisation in adapting to changes in its external environment?

(iii) Analyse the transformation or conversion process in terms of main interrelated sub-systems. (Use a model or framework of your own choice.)

How effective are the interactions and interrelationships among the sub-systems? Provide practical examples to support your views.

(iv) Comment critically on the *effectiveness of management* in co-ordinating the sub-systems and directing the activities of the organisation as a unified whole towards the accomplishment of its goal and objectives. Give specific examples in support of your comments.

Notes and references

1. Schein, E. H. *Organizational Psychology*, Third edition, Prentice-Hall (1980) p. 15.
2. For a detailed account of the nature and function of the informal organisation, see: Gray, J. L. and Starke, F. A. *Organizational Behavior: Concepts and Applications*, Fourth edition, Charles E. Merrill (1988).
3. Cyert, R. M. and March, J. G. *A Bahavioral Theory of the Firm*, Prentice-Hall (1963).
4. Mintzberg, H. *The Structuring of Organizations*, Prentice-Hall (1979).
5. Weber, M. *The Theory of Social and Economic Organization*, Collier Macmillan (1964).
6. Etzioni, A. *Modern Organizations*, Prentice-Hall (1964) p. 14.
7. Etzioni, A. *A Comparative Analysis of Complex Organizations*, Revised edition, Free Press (1975).
8. Blau, P. M. and Scott, W. R. *Formal Organizations*, Routledge and Kegan Paul (1966).
9. Hall, R. H., Haas, J. E. and Johnson, N. J. 'An Examination of the Blau–Scott and Etzioni Typologies', *Administrative Science Quarterly*, vol. 12, 1967–8, pp. 118–39.
10. Katz, D. and Kahn, R. L. *The Social Psychology of Organizations*, Second edition, Wiley (1978).
11. A summary of the systems view of organisations, and its value in distinguishing between private and public organisations, is given in: Mullins, L. J. 'The Organisation – A Systems View', *Professional Administration*, vol. 11, no. 2, February 1981, pp. 20–2.
12. See, for example: Mullins, L. J. 'Is the Hotel and Catering Industry Unique?' *Hospitality*, no. 21, September 1981, pp. 30–3.
13. For an interesting collection of readings on the systems view of organisations see: Lockett, M. and Spear, R. (eds) *Organizations as Systems*, Open University Press (1980).
14. Trist, E. L. *et al. Organizational Choice*, Tavistock Publications (1963).
15. Kast, F. E. and Rosenzweig, J. E. *Organization and Management*, Fourth edition, McGraw-Hill (1985).
16. Katz, D. and Kahn, R. L. *The Social Psychology of Organizations*, Second edition, Wiley (1978).
17. Hersey, P. and Blanchard, K. *Management of Organizational Behavior*, Fifth edition, Prentice-Hall (1988).
18. Leavitt, H. J. *Managerial Psychology*, Fourth edition, University of Chicago Press (1978).
19. Woodward, J. *Industrial Organization – Theory and Practice*, Second edition, Oxford University Press (1980).
20. Perrow, C. *Organizational Analysis: A Sociological View*, Tavistock (1967).
21. Burns, T. and Stalker, G. M. *The Management of Innovation*, Tavistock Publications (1966).
22. Lawrence, P. R. and Lorsch, J. W. *Organization and Environment*, Irwin (1969).
23. For a fuller discussion on the meaning of technology, see: Kast, F. E. and Rosenzweig, J. E. *Organization and Management*, Fourth edition, McGraw-Hill (1985).
24. See, for example: Davies, I. K. *The Management of Learning*, McGraw-Hill (1971).
25. Developed from French, W. L., Kast, F. E. and Rosenzweig, J. E. *Understanding Human Behavior in Organizations*, Harper and Row (1985) pp. 321–2.
26. Buchanan, D. A. and Huczyanski, A. A. *Organizational Behaviour: An Introductory Text*, Prentice-Hall (1985) p. 243.
27. See: Mullins, L. J. 'Information Technology – The Human Factor', *Administrator*, vol. 5, no. 5, September 1985, pp. 6–9.

4. ORGANISATIONAL GOALS AND OBJECTIVES

The activities of a work organisation are directed towards an end, towards certain goals. Organisations pursue a variety of goals which are not mutually exclusive and which may conflict with each other. Goals are translated into objectives and policy in order to provide corporate guidelines for the operations and management of the organisation. Organisational goals, objectives and policy are therefore important features in the study of work organisations and their management.

Objectives

To: (i) Explain the nature of, and functions served by, organisational goals;

(ii) Detail different classifications of organisational goals;

(iii) Examine the need for objectives and policy, and assess the importance of the profit objective to business organisations;

(iv) Assess the need for corporate strategy and identify criteria for evaluating an appropriate mix of business;

(v) Explain the nature of opportunities and risks in relation to business strategy;

(vi) Examine the social responsibilities of management;

(vii) Recognise the importance of organisational goals, objectives and policy for the effective management of a work organisation.

THE NATURE OF ORGANISATIONAL GOALS

All organisations have some function to perform, some contribution to make to the environment of which they are part. The function of the business organisation may be seen, for example, as the creation and/or supply of goods and services. This involves bringing together the factors of production in appropriate units of organisation, and their successful mix and direction, in order to create value added. Others might see the function of business organisations as, for example, providing a source of employment and of income.

In addition to performing some function, all organisations also have some incentive for their existence, and for their operations. The goals of an organisation are the reason for its existence. The activities of the organisation are directed to the attainment of its goals.

A goal is a future expectation, some desired future state. It is something the organisation is striving to accomplish. The meaning of a goal is, however, subject to a number of interpretations. It can be used in a very broad sense to refer to the overall purpose of an organisation, for example to produce television sets. A goal may also be used to refer to more specific desired accomplishments, for example to produce and sell a given number of a range of television sets within a given period of time.

The concept of organisational goals is more specific than that of the function of an organisation. The goals of an organisation will determine the nature of its inputs and outputs, the series of activities through which the outputs are achieved, and interactions with its external environment. The extent to which an organisation is successful in attaining its goals is a basis for the evaluation of organisational performance and effectiveness.

Goal model approach

The goal model approach concentrates on the study of organisational goals and the measurement of success against the realisation of goals. *Etzioni* suggests a potential disadvantage of this approach.[1] Goals are ideals and more attractive than actual achievement. Organisations are characterised by low effectiveness. They rarely achieve their goals with any degree of finality and can, therefore, almost always be reported as a failure. The goal model approach results in attention being focused on the organisation's lack of success in attaining goals at the expense of more meaningful forms of analysis. Instead of comparing organisations in terms of their stated goals, performance may be assessed relatively against different organisations.

The concept of organisational goals is ambiguous. Goals may be expressed very simply: in the case of business organisations, for example, to make a profit, or to increase productivity. Such broadly based goals might be taken for granted and they tell us little about the emphasis placed on the various activities of the organisation in meeting its goals. In any case, profit might more correctly be interpreted as a reward to the shareholders or providers of capital, and a means of ensuring the continued existence of the organisation and maintaining its growth and development.

Goals have been defined by *Simon* as value premises which serve as inputs to decisions.[2] Goals at different levels within the organisation contribute to alternatives for decision making. Simon compares goal setting with the mathematical approach of linear programming and he sees goals more as sets of constraints which the organisation must satisfy. For example: profit for shareholders, or a minimum rate of return on investments; satisfying demands of consumers; complying with government legislation on safety standards; providing job satisfaction for staff; pacifying environmental groups such as Friends of the Earth. Goals limit the scope of actions and decision making at lower levels of the organisation. Constraints may themselves be regarded as goals in that they represent objectives which management is trying to meet.

THE FUNCTIONS OF GOALS

Despite the problems associated with the goal model approach, the concept of organisational goals serves a number of important functions.[3]

- Goals provide a standard of performance. They focus attention on the activities of the organisation and the direction of the efforts of its members.

- Goals provide a basis for planning and management control related to the activities of the organisation.
- Goals provide guidelines for decision making and justification for actions taken. They reduce uncertainty in decision making and give a defence against possible criticism.
- Goals influence the structure of the organisation and help determine the nature of technology employed. The manner in which the organisation is structured will affect what it will attempt to achieve.
- Goals help to develop commitment of individuals and groups to the activities of the organisation. They focus attention on purposeful behaviour and provide a basis for motivation and reward systems.
- Goals give an indication of what the organisation is really like, its true nature and character, both for members and for people outside of the organisation.
- Goals serve as a basis for the evaluation of change and organisation development.
- Goals are the basis for objectives and policies of the organisation.

Goals are therefore an important feature of work organisations. To be effective goals should be emphasised, stated clearly and communicated to all members of the organisation. The goal-setting process is of importance to all types of organisations and facilitates the attainment of objectives. In the public sector for example, organisations such as hospitals, local authorities and universities have complex, diverse and competing goals. The clarification of goals and objectives is the basis for corporate planning, and a planning, programming, budgeting systems (PPBS) approach to decision making.

INTEGRATION OF GOALS

Strictly, organisations have no goals, only people do. Organisational goals are established by people, either individually, or, more usually, by a number of individuals co-operating together. For example, a group of senior managers may collectively agree on a particular desired course of action which may then come to be referred to as an organisational goal; but this is still the goal of those managers who initially determined it. Success of the organisation is measured by the progress of people towards goals set by people. This gives rise to the questions:

- How far are the goals of management compatible with the goals of the organisation?
- To what extent do individual members obtain satisfaction of their own goals through the attainment of organisational goals?

Informal goals Members of the organisation have different, and often conflicting, goals. As a result, the goals which the organisation actually pursue (informal goals) may be distinguished from the officially stated goals (formal goals) which are set out in broad terms as the reasons for the purpose of the organisation. Informal goals may be inferred from the actual decisions made and actions taken within the organisation. All members of the organisation will have:

(i) their own perception of the goals of the organisation, for example to produce high-quality television sets which satisfy requirements of the customers; and

(ii) their personal goals, for example to earn high wages, to gain social satisfaction, to achieve status; which they expect to fulfil by participating in the activities of the organisation. (*See* Fig. 4.1.)

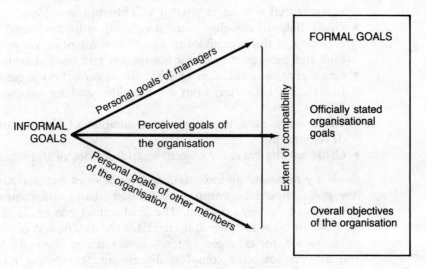

Fig. 4.1 Compatibility of goals within an organisation

If organisational goals and personal goals are pulling in different directions conflict will arise and performance is likely to suffer. An organisation will be more effective when personal goals are compatible with organisational goals. Organisational performance will depend ultimately on the extent to which individuals are provided with the opportunity to satisfy their own goals by contributing to the goals of the organisation.[4]

Management has a responsibility to clarify organisational goals and to attempt to integrate personal goals (including their own) with the overall objectives of the organisation. Only when organisational goals are shared by all members of the organisation will complete integration be achieved. In practice, this is unlikely. As *McGregor* points out:

> Perfect integration of organizational requirements and individual goals and needs is, of course, not a realistic objective. In adopting this principle, we seek that degree of integration in which the individual can achieve his goals *best* by directing his efforts towards the success of the organization.[5]

Management should endeavour, therefore, to structure the organisation so that people may realise their own (personal) goals by helping the organisation to satisfy its goals. One attempt at integrating organisational goals with the needs of the individual members of the organisation is provided by the approach of Management by Objectives. This is discussed in Chapter 9.

CLASSIFICATION OF ORGANISATIONAL GOALS

We have seen that goals are an important feature in the management of organisations. The goals of an organisation may be classified in a number of different ways.

The concept of compliance

Etzioni provides a classification which distinguishes three types of organisational goals in terms of their relationship with the concept of compliance discussed in Chapter 3.[6]

- *Order goals* are negative and attempt to place some kind of restraint upon members of the organisation and to prevent certain forms of behaviour.
- *Economic goals* are concerned with the production of goods and/or services for people outside of the organisation.
- *Cultural goals* are concerned with symbolic objects and with creating or maintaining value systems of society. Social goals, which serve the various needs of members of the organisation, are classified as a sub-type under cultural goals.

Most organisations would be expected to display one of three central combinations of organisational goals and compliance structure. Although there are other possibilities the three most usual combinations are:

- Organisations with order goals and a coercive compliance structure, for example closed prisons.
- Organisations with economic goals and a utilitarian compliance structure, for example business firms.
- Organisations with culture goals and a normative compliance structure, for example professional bodies.

Organisations may, of course, serve more than one goal which do not fall, necessarily, into the same category. Usually, however, there is one main goal which maintains a relationship with compliance structure in keeping with one of the three central combinations.

Goals as the outcome of bargaining

According to *Cyert* and *March*, goals result from the outcome of bargaining among members of a coalition. They identify five organisational goals related specifically to a business firm.[7]

- *Production goal* – related to minimising variations in the range of production operations over a given period of time, and to the overall level of production.
- *Inventory goal* – aspirations related to levels of completed goods. The inventory goal acts as a buffer between production and sales.
- *Sales goal* – aspirations related to the level of sales, either in monetary terms, number of units, or both. The sales goal provides some general criteria of sales effectiveness.
- *Market share goal* – concerned with a measure of sales effectiveness or with comparative success. The market share goal can be used as an alternative to the sales goal, or both can be used.
- *Profit goal* – linked to accounting procedures for determining profit and loss. The profit goal may be an aspiration relating to amount of monetary profit, or profit share, or return on investment.

The five goals are not listed in any necessary order of importance, but all the goals must be satisfied. Cyert and March suggest that most of the time no order of importance is necessary, although there may be an implicit order of priority in different organisations.

A systems view of organisational goals

Another form of classification is provided by *Perrow*, who distinguishes five categories of goals.[8]

- *Societal goals* which refer to society in general and large classes of organisations that strive to satisfy the needs of society.
- *Output goals* which refer to the organisation and the consumers towards which products and/or services are directed.
- *System goals* refer to desired conditions of the organisation and to its functioning, as opposed to the goods or services it provides.
- *Product goals* refer to the organisational characteristics of the actual goods or services produced.
- *Derived goals* refer to the influence of the organisation in a broader sense and the impact of its power on the environment. Derived goals arise from the pursuit of the other goals. The power generated by the organisation is used to influence its own members and the environment, independently of product goals or system goals.

Using Perrow's categorisation as a basis and adapting this to the systems view of organisations we can distinguish four main types of organisational goals:

- *Consumer goals*. These relate to the nature of outputs in terms of the market to be served and consumer satisfaction. That is, the range and nature of goods and/or services produced or supplied in order to meet the needs of customers or clients. For example: consumer products, educational services, health care.
- *Product goals*. These relate to the nature and characteristics of the outputs themselves, that is the goods and/or services provided. This is the main area in which organisations deliberately attempt to distinguish themselves from other organisations, for example in the range, design, quality and availability of their outputs.
- *Operational goals*. These relate to the series of activities involved in providing outputs, and to the operation and functioning of the organisation. For example: the management of opportunities and risks, the choice of structure, the nature of technology, and management processes.
- *Secondary goals*. These relate to goals that are not the main aim of the organisation. They arise from the manner in which the organisation uses its power and influence in pursuit of its outputs, and in undertaking the series of activities to achieve these outputs. Political aims; aid to the community; the development of staff; and social responsibilities would come under this heading.

A general model of organisational goals

A more general model of organisational goals is provided by *Gross* who gives a list appropriate to all types of organisations.[9]

- *Satisfaction of interests*. Organisations exist to satisfy multiple interests of various people, both members of the organisation and outsiders. These interests are hard to identify and overlapping. This category of purpose might be referred to as welfare, utility, benefit or payoff.

* *Output of services or goods.* The output of products, goods or services (tangible or intangible) which the organisation makes available to clients.
* *Efficiency or profitability.* The efficient use of available, scarce inputs relative to outputs. Inputs and outputs, and the relationship between them, may be calculated in a number of ways. 'Profitability' is applicable when both outputs and inputs can be expressed in monetary terms.
* *Investment in organisational viability.* The diversion of inputs from the production of output to investment in physical, human and organisational assets in order to maintain survival and growth.
* *Mobilisation of resources.* The organisation must mobilise resources for inputs in order to produce goods or services and to invest in viability.
* *Observance of codes.* Usually expressed in terms of acceptable margins of deviation. Codes include both formal and informal rules developed by the organisation and patterns of behaviour imposed by law, moral considerations and standards of professional ethics.
* *Rationality.* Actions which are regarded as satisfactory in terms of desirability, feasibility and consistency. Rationality applies to both technical and administrative (managerial) considerations.

Organisational goals are not necessarily the same for any one group of people, for example top management. Rather they are representative of the organisation as a collection of individuals and groups, and define the characteristics and activities of the whole organisation as a system. All organisations have multiple goals. It is difficult to develop criteria of performance against such broadly based goals and they need to be translated into more specific goals capable of measurement in particular organisations.

Alteration of goals Survival of the organisation will depend upon its ability to adapt to change and to the demands of its external environment. In practice, however, organisations usually appear to alter their goals only on a gradual basis. Commitment to the objectives and policies of the organisation, people's cognitive limitations and their uncertainties and fears, may mean a reluctance to accept change. Organisations may also find it difficult to make short-term, rapid changes in resource allocation. The very complexity of environmental influences may itself hinder rapid change. (See also the discussion on organisational change in Chapter 17.)

It is important, however, that the organisation does not restrict innovation but is ready to respond positively to changing circumstances and, increasingly, to anticipate future change. Management has to balance the need for adaptability in meeting the challenges and opportunities presented by change with, at the same time, preserving an atmosphere of stability and continuity in the interests of members of the organisation.

OBJECTIVES AND POLICY

Goals are translated into objectives and policy.

* *Objectives* set out more specifically the goals of the organisation, the aims to be achieved and the desired end-results.

- *Policy* is developed within the framework of objectives. It provides the basis for decision making and the course of action to follow in order to achieve objectives.

Objectives are, therefore, the 'what': policies the 'how', 'where' and 'when', the means that follow the objectives.

The relationship between the organisation, its objectives and management is illustrated by *Fayol* who stated that one of the managerial duties of an organisation is to: 'See that the human and material organization is consistent with the objective, resources and requirements of the concern'.[10] The establishment of objectives and policy is therefore an integral part of the process of management, and a necessary function in every organisation. A distinction between objectives and policy is given by *O'Shaughnessy*.[11]

> Objectives emphasize aims and are stated as expectations, but policies emphasize rules and are stated in the form of directives. For example:
>
> *Marketing* Objective: complete market coverage
> Policy: the Company *will* sell to every retail outlet that is creditworthy, as decided by the Company Accountant.
> *Production* Objective: low unit costs from long production runs
> Policy: the Company *will not* produce one-off jobs without the specific authority of the Board.
> *Finance* Objective: to maintain adequate liquidity
> Policy: accountant will draw up a cash budget and inform the Board if working capital is likely to fall below a specified limit.
> *Personnel* Objective: good labour relations
> Policy: set up and maintain schemes for: Joint Consultation, Job Evaluation, Wage Incentives.

The objectives of an organisation are related to the input–conversion–output cycle. In order to achieve its objectives and satisfy its goals the organisation takes inputs from the environment, through a

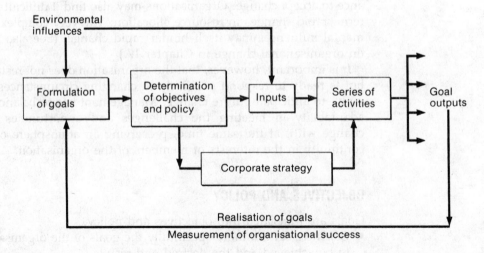

Fig. 4.2 A systems view of organisational goals and objectives

series of activities transforms or converts these inputs into outputs and returns them to the environment as inputs to other systems. The organisation operates within a dynamic setting and success in achieving its goals will be influenced by a multiplicity of interactions with the environment. (*See* Fig. 4.2.)

Whatever the type of organisation, there is need for lines of direction through the establishment of objectives and determination of policy. Objectives and policy form a basis for the process of management.

Objectives

The choice of objectives is an essential part of the decision-making process involving future courses of action. Objectives may be set out either in general terms or in more specific terms. General objectives are determined by top management. Specific objectives are formulated within the scope of general objectives and usually have more defined areas of application and time limits.

Objectives may be just implicit but the formal, explicit definition of objectives will help highlight the activities which the organisation needs to undertake and the comparative importance of its various functions. An explicit statement of objectives may assist communications and reduce misunderstandings, and provide more meaningful criteria for evaluating organisational performance. However, objectives should not be stated in such a way that they detract from the recognition of possible new opportunities, potential danger areas, the initiative of staff or the need for innovation or change.

Policy

A policy is a guideline for organisational action and the implementation of goals and objectives. Policy is translated into rules, plans and procedures; it relates to all activities of the organisation, and to all levels of the organisation. Policy provides guiding principles for areas of decision making and delegation. *For example*, specific decisions relating to personnel policy could include:

- to give priority to promotion from within the organisation;
- to enforce retirement at government pensionable age;
- whenever possible to employ only graduate or professionally qualified accountants;
- to permit line managers, in consultation with the personnel manager, to appoint staff up to a given salary/wage level.

Some policy decisions are directly influenced by external factors, for example government legislation on racial and sexual discrimination.[12]

Fundamental elements of policy

Brech suggests two fundamental elements which make up the policy of an organisation: ethical foundation; and organisational or operational foundation.[13]

- *Ethical foundation* embodies the basic principles which govern the external and internal relations of the organisation. *External relations* concern standards of fair trading and relations with, for example, the general public, customers and suppliers. *Internal relations* are concerned with fair standards of employment and relations with members of the organisation, including authorised trade union representatives.

- *Organisational or operational foundation* is concerned with the structure and conduct of the activities of the organisation. This also has external and internal aspects relating to the operation of the organisation. *External aspects* relate to, for example, operations such as channels of distribution and methods of trading. *Internal aspects* include methods of production, use of equipment and management practices relating to organisational performance, productivity and profitability.

Certain aspects of an organisation's policy may be so dominant that it becomes the 'hallmark' of that organisation and places constraints on other policy areas. For example, the highest-quality hallmark of Rolls-Royce cars would presumably prevent entry into the cheaper, mass production market. Another example is the high-quality standard of Marks and Spencer's merchandise, no changing rooms but a 'no questions asked' refund policy. Also Marks and Spencer's explicit policy of buying primarily from British sources.[14] A further example is The Body Shop whose overriding byword is honesty. Their policy is: 'We WILL be the most honest cosmetic company.'[15]

Objectives and policy together provide corporate guidelines for the operations and management of the organisation. The activities of the organisation derive their significance from the contribution they make to achieving objectives in the manner directed. The formulation of objectives and policy, and the allocation of resources, provide the basis for strategic planning which is the first stage in the planning and control processes of business organisations.[16]

THE PROFIT OBJECTIVE

In order to be successful the primary objectives of the business organisation may be seen as:

- to continue in existence, that is to *survive*:
- to maintain *growth and development*; and
- to make a *profit*.

All three objectives are inextricably linked and it is a matter of debate whether the organisation survives and develops in order to provide a profit, or makes a profit by which it can survive and develop.

If we accept survival as the ultimate objective of the business organisation, then this involves the need for a steady and continuous profit. Organisations must be prepared to accept the possibility of a reduction in short-term profitability in order to provide for future investments. The profit goal is achieved through the process of management and the combined efforts of members of the organisation. (*See* Fig. 4.3.)

Not a sufficient criterion for effective management

Although the objective of profit maximisation is undoubtedly of great importance, it is not, by itself, a sufficient criterion for the effective management of a business organisation. In practice, there are many other considerations and motivations which affect the desire for the greatest profit or maximum economic efficiency and the accompanying assumptions which underlie the economic theory of the firm.

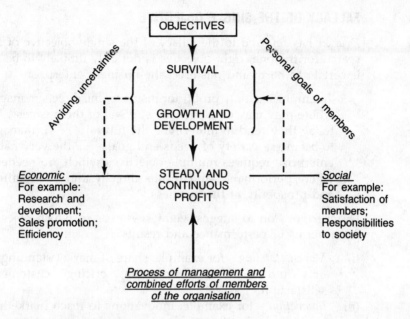

Fig. 4.3 Objectives of a business organisation

The meaning of 'profit maximisation' is not, by itself, very clear. Consideration has to be given to the range and quality of an organisation's products or services, to the costs of its operations and to environmental influences. Reducing attention to longer-term 'investments' such as quality and after-sales service, research and development, sales promotion, management development, satisfaction of staff and their employment conditions may increase profitability in the short term; but is likely to jeopardise future growth and development, and possibly even the ultimate survival of the organisation.

A business organisation has to provide some commodity or service by which it contributes to the economic and/or social needs of the community. It also has broader social responsibilities to society. (Social responsibilities are discussed later in this chapter.) Profit can be seen as the incentive for an organisation to carry out its activities effectively. Profit does at least provide some broad measure of effectiveness and highlights the difficulty in evaluating the effectiveness of not-for-profit organisations such as National Health Service hospitals or universities.

Managers are more concerned with avoiding uncertainties than with prediction of uncertainties. Economic models of decision making, based on the assumption of rational behaviour in choosing from known alternatives in order to maximise objectives, can be contrasted with behavioural models based not so much on maximising of objectives, but on short-term expediency where a choice is made to avoid conflict and within limiting constraints.[17]

Also, as discussed earlier, members of the organisation will have their own personal goals and their own perception of the goals of the organisation.

FALLACY OF THE SINGLE OBJECTIVE

Drucker has referred to the fallacy of the single objective of a business. The search for the one, right objective is not only unlikely to be productive, but is certain to harm and misdirect the business enterprise.

> To emphasize only profit, for instance, misdirects managers to the point where they may endanger the survival of the business. To obtain profit today they tend to undermine the future. . . . To manage a business is to balance a variety of needs and goals . . . the very nature of business enterprise requires multiple objectives which are needed in every area where performance and results directly and vitally affect the survival and prosperity of the business.[18]

Drucker goes on to suggest eight key areas in which objectives should be set in terms of performance and results.

(i) *Market standing* – for example: share of market standing; range of products and markets; distribution; pricing; customer loyalty and satisfaction.

(ii) *Innovation* – for example: innovations to reach marketing goals; developments arising from technological advancements; new processes and improvements in all major areas of organisational activity.

(iii) *Productivity* – for example: optimum use of resources; use of techniques such as operational research to help decide alternative courses of action; the ratio of 'contributed value' to total revenue.

(iv) *Physical and financial resources* – for example: physical facilities such as plant, machines, offices and replacement of facilities; supply of capital and budgeting; planning for the money needed; provision of supplies.

(v) *Profitability* – for example: profitability forecasts and anticipated time scales; capital investment policy; yardsticks for measurement of profitability.

(vi) *Manager performance and development* – for example: the direction of managers and setting up their jobs; the structure of management; the development of future managers.

(vii) *Worker performance and attitude* – for example: union relations; the organisation of work; employee relations.

(viii) *Public responsibility* – for example: demands made upon the organisation, such as by law or public opinion; responsibilities to society and the public interest.

Allocation of resources and decision making

The organisation therefore must give attention to all those areas which are of direct and vital importance to its survival and prosperity. *Etzioni* makes the point that:

> The systems model, however, leads one to conclude that just as there may be too little allocation of resources to meet the goals of the organization, so there may also be an over-allocation of these resources. The systems model explicitly recognizes that the organization solves certain problems other than those directly involved in the achievement of the goal, and that excessive concern with the latter may result in insufficient attention to other necessary organizational activities, and to a lack of

coordination between the inflated goal activities and the de-emphasized non-goal activities.[19]

Individuals in the organisation are not necessarily guided at all times by the primary goal(s) of the organisation. *Simon* illustrates this in respect of the profit goal.

Profit may not enter directly into the decision-making of most members of a business organisation. Again, this does not mean that it is improper or meaningless to regard profit as a principal goal of the business. It simply means that the decision-making mechanism is a loosely coupled system in which the profit constraint is only one among a number of constraints and enters into most sub-systems only in indirect ways.[20]

We have seen, then, that although the profit objective is clearly of importance, by itself it is not a sufficient criterion for the effective management of a business organisation. There are many other considerations and motivations which affect the desire for the greatest profit or maximum economic efficiency.

THE NEED FOR STRATEGY

Objectives and policy are formalised within the framework of a corporate strategy. *Tilles* has suggested that without an explicit statement of strategy it becomes more difficult for expanding organisations to reconcile co-ordinated action with entrepreneurial effort.[21] An explicit strategy for the business organisation is necessary for the following reasons. First, there is the need for people to co-operate together in order to achieve the benefits of mutual reinforcement. Second, there are the effects of changing environmental conditions.

The absence of an explicit concept of strategy may result in members of the organisation working at cross-purposes. The intentions of top management may not be communicated clearly to those at lower levels in the hierarchy who are expected to implement these intentions. Obsolete patterns of behaviour become very difficult to modify. Change comes about from either subjective or intuitive assessment, and becomes increasingly unreliable as the rate of change increases. Developing a statement of strategy demands a creative effort. If strategic planning is to be successful it requires different methods of behaviour and often fundamental change in the nature of interactions among managers.

Appropriate mix of business

Tilles goes on to suggest that once objectives have been established, the appropriate mix of business engaged in can be evaluated against the following criteria.

Criteria related to individual performance

- *Probable contribution* – the estimated contribution of existing businesses to corporate performance given no major changes in competitive practice.
- *Minimum standards* – disengagement from unsatisfactory situations. Where standards of performance cannot be achieved with the existing mix of businesses, performance may frequently be improved by disinvestment of some businesses. As well as identifying attractive new opportunities,

a well-managed company will have an active procedure for disengaging from unsatisfactory situations.

- *Trade-offs* – the requirement for trade-off decisions in establishing standards for unit performance, for example growth versus profitability, or short-term profitability versus long-term profitability.

Criteria related to the total mix

- *Risk level* – the degree of risk represented by the portfolio. Groups of businesses may be associated together within a single company because the risk inherent in the total is less than would be present if the businesses were separate.

- *Synergism* – the nature and extent of mutual reinforcement which individual businesses provide for the whole. This may be either operational reinforcement, where two businesses operated jointly improve the company's strategic advantage; or financial reinforcement because of the different patterns in funding or timing, or because of the appeal of the whole to the financial community.

- *Extrapolation* – the range of additional opportunities for which an appropriate mix of businesses provides a platform. Where the company may go from its present position and what is required to do so. This may be expressed as the 'n + 1' situation. What should be the next business added to the existing portfolio?

- *Funds requirements* – the constraint of balancing the funds requirements and resources available in order to meet successfully the corporate strategy. If strategy is to be assessed rationally it must be translated into funds flow projections.

Corporate approach in local government

Some form of corporate strategy or planning is necessary for all organisations, particularly large organisations and including those in the public sector. In local government, for example, the Bains report urged local authorities to adopt a corporate approach to their affairs in order to ensure that their resources are deployed most effectively. The report makes the following comments:

> Local government is not, in our view, limited to the narrow provision of a series of services to the local community, though we do not intend in any way to suggest that these services are not important. It has within its purview the overall economic, cultural and physical well-being of that community, and for this reason its decisions impinge with increasing frequency upon the individual lives of its citizens. . . . This corporate approach should be displayed not only within the authority itself but also in its relations with other spheres of local government and with public bodies. . . . We believe that the need for a corporate approach is beyond dispute if local government is to be efficient and effective.[22]

To give effect to this corporate approach, the Bains report proposed the establishment of a central Policy and Resources Committee responsible for the formulation of the structure plan for a local authority county or district. The Policy and Resources Committee would aid the council in setting its objectives and priorities, be instrumental in co-ordinating and controlling their implementation, and in monitoring and reviewing the performance of the authority in the achievement of its defined objectives.

In the public sector, the establishment of objectives and policy requires clarification of the respective roles of both elected members and permanent officials. This dual nature of management requires harmonious relationships between the two parties and emphasises the need for a corporate approach.[23]

THE CONCEPT OF SYNERGY

An important aspect of corporate strategy and the growth and development of organisations is the concept of synergy which was developed in management applications by *Ansoff*.[24] Synergy results when the whole is greater than the sum of its component parts. It can be expressed, simply as 2 + 2 = 5.

Synergy is usually experienced in situations of expansion or where one organisation merges with another, such as an organisation responsible for the development and production of a product merging with an organisation which markets the product. An example could be a television manufacturer merging with a television rental organisation. The new organisation could benefit from the combined strengths and opportunities, skills and expertise, and from the streamlining and economy of its operations. Another example could be the merger of a computer firm expert in the design and marketing of hardware, with a firm expert in software manufacture and systems design.

It is possible, however, to experience negative synergy or the 2 + 2 = 3 situation. Such a situation might arise when a merger occurs between organisations operating in different fields, with different markets or with different methods, or where the new organisation becomes unwieldy or loses its cost-effectiveness. The original merger which resulted in the formation of British Leyland could, perhaps, be quoted as an example of negative synergy.

SWOT ANALYSIS

Ansoff has also referred to the analysis of strengths and weaknesses of organisations following the formulation of objectives;[25] and to threats and opportunities in the process of strategic change.[26] This can be developed into what is known as SWOT analysis, which focuses on the Strengths, Weaknesses, Opportunities and Threats facing organisations.

- *Strengths* are those positive aspects of the organisation which it can build upon, for example through the pursuit of diversification. By searching out opportunities which match its strengths the organisation can optimise the effects of synergy.
- *Weaknesses* are those deficiencies in the present skills and resources of the organisation which need to be corrected and action taken to minimise their effect on the organisation.
- *Opportunities* usually arise from the nature of environmental change. The organisation needs to be sensitive to the problems of business strategy and responsive to change in, for example, products, markets or technology.

- *Threats* are the converse of opportunities and refer to external developments which are likely to endanger the operations of the organisation, for example the introduction of a radically new product by competitors. Organisations need to be responsive to changes that have already occurred, and to plan for anticipated significant changes in the environment and be prepared to meet them.

THE MANAGEMENT OF OPPORTUNITIES AND RISKS

Every business needs to have a strategy and this strategy must be related to changing environmental conditions. In order to survive and maintain growth and expansion top management must protect the business from potentially harmful influences, and be ready to take maximum advantage of the challenges and opportunities presented. Whilst top management must always accept the need for innovation there is still the decision as to which opportunities it wishes to develop in relation to its resources, and those it chooses not to pursue. An effective business strategy depends upon the successful management of opportunities and risks.

Drucker suggests that strategy should be based on the priority of maximising opportunities, and that risks should be viewed not as grounds of action but as limitations on action.[27] He classifies three kinds of opportunities and four kinds of risks.

Opportunities

- *Additive* – arise from chances to exploit more fully existing resources, for example by establishing additional markets for existing product lines. Additive opportunities do not change the basic character of the business. Risks involved should be small and additive opportunities should not be permitted to take resources away from higher priority opportunities.
- *Complementary* – consist of the addition of new products or activities which complement existing business and provide a synergistic effect. Complementary opportunities change the structure of the business and require at least one new area of expertise. There is a higher level of risk and such opportunities should be evaluated in terms of the likely wealth-producing capacity to the business as a whole. *Drucker* gives the example of establishing a paper company in the plastics field through purchasing packaging machines which use both paper and plastics.
- *Break-through* – changes the fundamental characteristics of the business. Break-through opportunities demand first-class resources, particularly human resources, great effort and high expenditure on research and development. Risks are always high and such opportunities need to be evaluated in terms of a correspondingly high return. Examples of break-through opportunities would appear to arise from developments in the field of information technology.

Risks

- *The risk one must accept* – this is inherent in the very nature of the business and must be accepted to ensure survival. *Drucker* quotes the example of the development and marketing of new systemic drugs when not enough is known about the behaviour of the human body to test for all possible effects. A recent example could be the American company Eli Lilly Industries who have offered compensation payments, without admission of liability, to alleged victims of the banned arthritis drug Opren.

- *The risk one can afford to take* – this is the risk of lost effort and money in pursuit of an opportunity where even the worst failure would not cripple the business. An example might be an unsuccessful drilling exploration for oil or gas. If the costs involved are greater than the business can lose and still survive it cannot afford the opportunity.
- *The risk one cannot afford to take* – this is, in part, the opposite of the risk one can afford to take. The major risk under this heading is being unable to exploit success through lack of capital, knowledge, technical skill or market information. For example, a new venture into the field of information technology is unlikely to be successful without sufficient technical expertise, full knowledge of the potential market and the likely direction of future technological developments.
- *The risk one cannot afford not to take* – this is associated with the breakthrough opportunity where the business cannot afford to be left out of possible major new developments; for example, as in the potential development of atomic energy as a practical source of electric power. Such a risk must be justified by very high rewards should the effort prove successful. For example, manufacturers of watches could hardly have ignored the development of quartz crystals and the fashion for digital display. Another example could be the need for expenditure by oil companies on the search for alternative sources of energy.

Drucker points out that while it is not possible to ensure that the right opportunities are chosen, it is certain that the right opportunities will not be selected unless:

(i) the focus is on maximising opportunities rather than on minimising risks;

(ii) major opportunities are scrutinised collectively and in respect of their characteristics rather than singly and in isolation;

(iii) opportunities and risks are understood in terms of the appropriateness of their fit to a particular business; and

(iv) a balance is struck between immediate and easy opportunities for improvement, and more difficult, long-range opportunities for innovation and changing the character of the business.

If the business is to be successful then its organisation structure must be related to its objectives and to its strategy. The structure must be designed so as to be appropriate to environmental influences, the continued development of the business, and the management of opportunities and risks. The nature of organisation structure is discussed in Chapter 5.

SOCIAL RESPONSIBILITIES OF MANAGEMENT

Organisations play a major and increasingly important role in the lives of us all, especially with the growth of large-scale business and the divorce of ownership from management.

The decisions and actions of management in organisations have an increasing impact on individuals, other organisations and the community.

The power and influence which many business organisations now exercise should be tempered, therefore, by an attitude of responsibility by management.

In striving to satisfy its goals and achieve its objectives the organisation cannot operate in isolation from the environment of which it is part. The organisation requires the use of factors of production and other facilities of society. The economic efficiency of organisations is affected by governmental, social, technical and cultural variables. In return, society is in need of the goods and services created and supplied by organisations, including the creation and distribution of wealth. Organisations make a contribution to the quality of life and to the well-being of the community.

Organisational survival is dependent upon a series of exchanges between the organisation and its environment. These exchanges and the continual interaction with the environment give rise to a number of broader responsibilities to society in general. These broader responsibilitiies, which are both internal and external to the organisation, are usually referred to as social responsibilities. These social responsibilities arise from the interdependence of organisations, society and the environment.

The importance of social responsibilities

The importance of the exercise of social responsibility by business and by managers is emphasised by *Drucker*. This responsibility

> can no longer be based on the assumption that the self-interest of the owner of property will lead to the public good, or that self-interest and public good can be kept apart and considered to have nothing to do with each other. On the contrary, it requires of the manager that he assume responsibility for the public good, that he subordinate his actions to an ethical standard of conduct, and that he restrain his self-interest and his authority wherever their exercise would infringe upon the common weal and upon the freedom of the individual.[28]

The recognition of the importance of social responsibilities can be gauged in part by the extent of government action and legislation on such matters as, for example, employment protection, employee participation, companies acts, consumer law, product liability and safeguarding the environment. This has formalised certain areas of social responsibilities into a legal requirement. It is doubtful, however, if legislation alone is sufficient to make management, or other members of an organisation, behave in what might be regarded as a 'proper' manner.

There has been a growing attention to the subject of social responsibilities and an increasing amount of literature on the subject. For example, a recent report by a British Institute of Management working party seeks to provide practical guidance relevant to both social and managerial needs.[29] Managers in BIM branches identified two prominent issues of social policy with which they were most concerned: (i) assisting small businesses and enterprise agencies; and (ii) the establishing of links with public bodies and the educational world. As a general rule the key to the process of business social policy is seen widely as a partnership with national and local government and with not-for-profit organisations. The report gives guidance on what organisations and individual managers can do in relation to: assisting small enterprise and employment; links between industry and education; environmental enhancement; participating in political, civil and judicial activities; managing secondments; financial assistance and charitable donations.

In keeping with many recognised professional bodies, BIM has also published a *Code of Conduct* which is binding on all corporate members of the institute, together with supporting *Guides to Good Management Practice*.[30] The guides supplement the code and set out the standards of conduct which members of the institute are expected to adhere to in pursuit of the objective of good management.

A number of business organisations also emphasise the importance of social responsibilities. For example, a Unilever educational publication sets out a commentary on social responsibility in terms of the manager's role, the company and society and the accountability of management. The report makes the point that 'social responsibility involves more than spending a little time and money on society's affairs. It is an attitude of mind which

ought to be adopted by managers as a normal part of their professional outlook'.[31]

It should, however, be recognised that the distinction is blurred between (i) the exercise of a genuine social responsibility; and (ii) actions taken in pursuit of good business practice and the search for organisational efficiency. One approach is that attention to social responsibilities arises out of a moral or ethical motivation and the dictates of conscience; that is out of genuine philanthropic objectives. An alternative approach is not motivation is through no more than enlightened self-interest and the belief that, in the long term, attention to social responsibilities is simply good business sense. In practice, it is a matter of degree and balance, or combining sound economic management with an appropriate concern for broader responsibilities to society. (*See* Fig. 4.4.)

A LESSON IN CARING FROM ANITA THE BODY SHOP BOSS

Love is ... giving away your profits to those who need the money most

A WOMAN tycoon stunned the captains of industry yesterday with a challenge to bring a little love into their business lives.

Body Shop founder Anita Roddick, 44, had just collected an award for Most Enterprising Company of the year from the CBI.

She responded with a spirited attack on Britain's biggest companies, describing them as 'mindless, faceless, soulless bureaucracies'.

One couple walked out muttering 'Disgraceful, extraordinary' after she

added: 'Big business has taught us nothing. We see tired executives in a tired system. They are dying of boredom and inertia. We believe they are doomed.'

Mrs Roddick is managing director and her husband Gordon chairman of Body Shop, which they founded 11 years ago with a £4,000 overdraft and now has a £17,500,000 international turnover. The company, which sells natural cosmetics in plain plastic bottles, has put some of its profits into third world aid, environmental causes and the inner cities.

But other companies think only of

money, Mrs Roddick told the Confederation of British Industry at a Savoy Hotel lunch.

'Why is altruism in business seen as suspect?' she demanded. 'Private greed never automatically translates into public benefit. The word love is never mentioned in big business. The responsibility on profit is to help society.'

The woman who once stripped naked in Japan to show women the beneficial effect of her own products said her firm encouraged its workers to have a sense of fun and enthusiasm.

Anita Roddick:Challenge

Fig. 4.4 An example of the social responsibilities of management
(From *Daily Mail*, 27 November 1987. Reproduced by permission of Mail Newspapers plc.)

Main areas of social responsibility   Whatever the approach, social responsibilities may be considered under the following main headings.

Employees   People and organisations need each other. Social responsibilities to employees extend beyond terms and conditions of the formal contract of employment and give recognition to the worker as a human being. People today have wider expectations of the quality of working life, including: justice in treatment; democratic functioning of the organisation and opportunities for consultation and participation; training in new skills and technologies; effective personnel and industrial relations policies and practices; and provision of social and leisure facilities.

Organisations should also, for example, give due consideration to the design of work organisation and job satisfaction, make every reasonable effort to give security of employment, and provide employment opportunities for minority groups. Many organisations now choose to report details of their financial results and performance direct to all employees. Under the Employment Protection Acts a general duty is placed on an employer to disclose to authorised representatives of independent trade unions, on request, information for the purposes of collective bargaining and which it would be good industrial relations practice to disclose. There is also a greater thrust for increased participation by employees. This has come about through social pressures for change and encouragement by legislation. The Employment Act 1982 requires that annual reports of all companies with more than 250 employees contain a statement concerning the introduction, maintenance or development of arrangements to involve employees.

Shareholders or other providers of capital

Joint stock companies are in need of the collective investments of shareholders in order to finance their operations. Shareholders are drawn from a wide range of the population. Between 22 and 25 per cent of the shareholding on the Stock Exchange is held, currently, by private individuals.[32] Many people also subscribe indirectly as shareholders through pension funds and insurance companies who act as trustees for the individual contributors. Shareholders expect a fair financial return as payment for risk bearing and the use of their capital. In addition, social responsibilities of management extend to include the safeguarding of investments, and the opportunity for shareholders to exercise their responsibility as owners of the company, to participate in policy decisions and to question top management on the affairs of the company. Management has a responsibility to declare personal interests, and to provide shareholders with full information presented in a readily understood form.

In the case of public sector organisations, finance may be provided by government grants/subsidies – which are funded 'compulsorily' by the public through taxation and rates – as well as loans, and charges for services provided. There is, therefore, a similar range of social responsibilities to the public as subscribers of capital.

Consumers

To many people, responsibilities to consumers may be seen as no more than a natural outcome of good business. There are, however, broader social responsibilities including: providing good value for money; the safety and durability of products/services; standard of after-sales service; prompt and courteous attention to queries and complaints; long-term satisfaction, for example serviceability, adequate supply of products/services, and spare and replacement parts; fair standards of advertising and trading; full and unambiguous information to potential consumers.

Increasing concern for social responsibilities to consumers can be seen by the activities of such bodies as the Consumers' Association, and the number of television and radio programmes devoted to this subject. In the case of public corporations there are User's National Councils which are independent bodies that look after the interests of customers. In the case of local government there is a system of Commissioners for Local Administration (popularly referred to as 'Ombudsmen') designed to provide an independent investigation of citizens' complaints alleged to have been caused through maladministration.

Local government electors also have a right of access to the district auditor or 'approved' auditor, to make objections and to question the auditor about any of a local authority's accounts. If requested the district auditor is required to give a written statement of reasons in view of the right of an unsatisfied complainant to appeal to the courts.

Community

It is in the area of concern for the community at large that social responsibilities can be seen most clearly. Organisations have a responsibility not to misuse the scarce factors of production upon which the wealth of the country depends. Organisations have a responsibility to society, to respect environmental considerations and take care of amenities. Examples under this heading include: the effects and potential dangers of pollution, noise, disposal of waste; the siting and appearance of new buildings; transportation policies, such as the routeing of heavy vehicles through narrow village roads; and avoidance of excessive packaging and more use of bio-degradable materials.

A specific example is the protest against aerosol sprays containing chloro-fluoro-carbons. These have been blamed for damaging the ozone layer protecting the earth from harmful ultraviolet rays from the sun.

Other possible areas of responsibility

Another important area of social responsibility could be to the *government*. Organisations should, or course, respect and obey the law even where they regard it as not in their best interests. But what is debatable is the extent to which organisations should co-operate voluntarily with actions requested by the government. Some examples are: restraint from trading with certain overseas countries, and the acceptance of controls over imports or exports; actions designed to combat inflation, for example limits on the level of wage settlements; assisting in the control of potential social problems, for example advertising and sale of tobacco and the display of health warnings.

The potential range of social responsibilities is numerous. Other groups to whom organisations might be regarded as having a social responsibility, or obligation, are *suppliers, business associates* and even *competitors*. Examples of social responsibilities to these groups might include: fair standards of trading; honouring terms and conditions of purchase or sale, and settlement dates, for example payment of accounts; assistance to smaller organisations; engagement only in fair competition; respect for copyright and patents.

Some organisations extend the range of social responsibilities even further by, for example: giving recognition to the needs of developing countries; limiting the extent of political involvement or campaigning; donations to, or sponsorship of, the arts, educational or research institutions, sporting organisations or charities.

Social reports The difficulties in reporting on an organisation's social responsibilities are well known. For example how can one calculate the well-being created by, and the satisfaction with, its products or services, or the personal fulfilment of its members? The recognition of corporate social responsibilities does, however, imply a case for reporting on how such responsibilities have been discharged.

An increasing number of business organisations do attempt to produce some form of 'social' report. For example, IBM UK publish a Stakeholder Report summarising information under the following main headings:

- *Employees* – population, earnings, graduates recruited, student employment, opinion survey comments, equal opportunity.
- *Customers* – customer satisfaction, price/performance, customer training, customer visits to IBM centres.
- *Suppliers* – amount of business, percentage of expenditure with British suppliers, investment in land and buildings, major construction projects.
- *The community* – secondments to community projects, support for enterprise agencies, schools and further education, contributions to charities, youth training, sponsorships, community projects.

The purpose and usefulness of the present level of social reporting is, however, open to question. For example, *Deverson* suggests:

> The best approach would appear to be to recognize the integrated nature of corporate activity, and seek to develop a more sophisticated, wider-ranging annual report of use to a variety of stakeholders. Progress in this direction would be a major advance towards a better understanding of the role and contribution of industry.[33]

Business organisations might also consider the idea of a 'social responsibility audit' with a checklist of specific areas in which management can review its actions in relation to the internal and external environment. There is, however, an argument against this approach. A social responsibility audit might widen unnecessarily the number of objectives, managers might be confused by ill-defined standards of performance, and there could be a tendency for social responsibilities to detract from the aim of maximising the growth of profits. The suggestion is that social responsibilities should be built into the profit motive.[34]

Profit and effective performance Whether or not organisations have a social responsibility audit, management has as its priority the need to ensure the survival and effective performance of the organisation. As *Drucker* puts it:

> The first responsibility to society is to operate at a profit, and only slightly less important is the necessity for growth. The business is the wealth-creating and wealth-producing organ of our society. Management must maintain its wealth-producing resources intact by making adequate profits to offset the risk of economic activity. And it must besides increase the wealth-creating and wealth-producing capacity of these resources and with them the wealth of society.[35]

The attention given to social responsibilities must involve weighing the costs of meeting these responsibilities against the benefits derived. Provided the cost/benefit analysis is not detrimental to economic and/or competitive performance, management must then determine the extent to which, and the manner in which, the organisation will attempt to satisfy its social responsibilities. The recognition of social responsibilities should form an integral part of strategy and the establishment of objectives and policies of the organisation.

Synopsis

All organisations have some function to perform, and some incentive for their existence and for their operations. The activities of the organisation are directed to the service of its goals. The goals of an organisation will determine the nature of its outputs and the series of activities through which the outputs are achieved. The goal model approach concentrates on the study of organisational goals and the measurement of success against the realisation of these goals. There are potential disadvantages and limitations with this approach, but the concept of organisational goals serves a number of important functions.

Strictly, organisations have no goals, only people do. Members of an organisation have different and often conflicting goals. Management has a responsibility to clarify organisational goals and to attempt to integrate personal goals with the overall objectives of the organisation. Adopting a systems view of organisations, we can distinguish four main types of goals: consumer, product, operational and secondary. Organisational goals can, however, be classified in a number of different ways.

Goals are translated into objectives and policy. Objectives set out more specifically the goals of the organisation, the aims to be achieved, the desired end-results. The choice of objectives is an essential part of the decision-making process involving future courses of action. Policy is developed within the framework of objectives. It provides the basis for decision making and the course of action to follow in order to achieve objectives. Policy is made up of two fundamental elements: ethical foundation which embodies the basic principles governing the organisation's external and internal relations; and organisational or operational foundation concerned with the structure and conduct of the activities of the organisation.

Objectives and policy, together, provide corporate guidelines for the operation and management of the organisation. Although the objective of profit maximisation is undoubtedly important, it is not by itself a sufficient criterion for the effective management of a business organisation. In practice there are many other considerations and motivations which affect the desire for the greatest profit or maximum economic efficiency. Attention must be given to all those areas which are of direct and vital importance to the survival and prosperity of the organisation.

Objectives and policy are formalised within the framework of a corporate strategy. An explicit strategy is necessary in order that people may co-operate and because of the effects of changing environmental conditions. Once objectives have been set, the appropriate mix of business engaged in can be evaluated. An effective business strategy depends upon the successful management of opportunities and risks. Some form of corporate strategy or planning is necessary for all organisations, particularly large organisations, and including those in the public sector.

In striving to satisfy its goals and achieve its objectives, the organisation cannot operate in isolation from the environment of which it is part. Organisation survival is dependent upon a series of exchanges between the organisation and its environment. These exchanges and the continual interaction with the environment give rise to a number of broader responsibilities to society in general – the social responsibilities of management. The potential range of social responsibilities is numerous but may be considered under the main headings of: employees; shareholders or other providers of capital; consumers; and the community. Another important area of social responsibility could be to the government. An increasing number of business organisations produce some form of social report on how social responsibilities have been discharged. However, the purpose and usefulness of the present level of social reporting is open to question.

Review and discussion questions

1. What are goals and what functions are served by organisational goals? Suggest a classification of organisational goals and relate this to your own organisation.

2. Illustrate the systems view of organisational goals and objectives. Give examples of how the goals of an organisation may change over time. Why is it that in practice organisational goals usually tend to be altered only on a gradual basis?

3. Distinguish between objectives and policy. Identify examples of objectives and policy in your own organisation, and comment on how effectively you believe they have been implemented.

4. Discuss the extent to which profit maximisation is a sufficient criterion for the effective management of a business organisation. What other indicators might be applied in terms of organisational performance and results?

5. Explain the need for a corporate strategy and attempt to examine the corporate plan for your own or some other organisation. Suggest criteria for the evaluation of an appropriate mix of activities.

6. Assess the practical relevance of (i) the concept of synergy, and (ii) a SWOT analysis.

7. How might the opportunities and risks facing an organisation be classified? Give examples of specific opportunities and risks facing your own organisation.

8. What do you understand by the concept of social responsibility? What factors should be borne in mind by the management of an organisation in seeking to meet social responsibilities? Give examples of how your own organisation attempts to satisfy (and/or has failed to satisfy) its social responsibilities or obligations.

| Case study | SQUARE DEAL PLC |

Square Deal PLC is a newly formed subsidiary company of Square Deal International Inc. The intention is to use it to unify the efforts and improve the profitability of the hitherto separate UK subsidiaries of Arnold PLC,

Carlton PLC and Foodrich PLC. At present it has a managing director, an administrative/financial controller and a typist all sharing a large temporary office in central London.

Arnold PLC has 69 food stores, all within a radius of 30 miles from London. Most of them contain either a small restaurant or snack bar and occupy high street or suburban shopping centre locations. It owns one small bakery whose total production supplies ten stores with bread and cakes. Perishables for both re-sale and restaurant use are bought locally but all other products are bought centrally and distributed from one large warehouse. These products are charged to the stores at selling price on computer-printed internal invoices. Store managers are judged solely on revenue. Accounts for each store are produced on the batch computer system at head office which is an old building on the edge of a dockland redevelopment site in East London. The company owns the freehold, as it does of about half of its food stores.

Carlton PLC has joint managing directors, one in charge of 21 restaurants and one in charge of property development. To date it has built four shopping centres and has plans for three more, all as part of schemes to regenerate old city centres in the north of England, around 150 miles from London. It leases out the shops with the exception of one per centre which it operates as a restaurant. Both MDs rigidly pursue a 15 per cent annual return on investment as their measure of achievement.

Foodrich PLC was, until last year, a family firm which canned fruit and vegetables from its one factory situated about 100 miles from London, in the west of England. It was bought by Square Deal International Inc with the idea that it would supply 'own label' products to Arnold PLC and large catering packs to both Arnold's and Carlton's restaurants. To do this, Foodrich was obliged to deny supplies to some of its regular customers and re-equip part of its plant to handle the large catering packs. The MD, son of the founder, has worked there for nearly 40 years and runs the company, making all decisions, both long-term and operational, using his experience and intuition. He is furious to learn that Arnold has not put all its 'own label' business in his direction and Carlton is still buying most catering packs from Foodrich's competitors while its new plant is grossly underused. Both Arnold's head buyer and the head chef at Carlton's claim they get the same quality cheaper from other companies. These recent changes at Foodrich have overwhelmed the MD and one result is that the financial year end accounts up until April will not be ready until some time in August. The accounts are the only defined measure of performance and are usually drawn up by the MD.

The MD of Square Deal PLC has just spent a week touring parts of these three subsidiaries and has returned to the office with a variety of ideas and concerns about ways to unify efforts and improve profitability. To help crystallise some of these ideas he asks the administrator/controller to prepare written statements on various points. Assume you are this administrator/controller.

(1) Discuss the benefits and drawbacks of judging performance on a single criterion such as:
   a revenue, in the case of the store managers.

b return on investment, in the case of Carlton's MDs.

(2) Explain to what extent Arnold's head buyer and Carlton's head chef are justified in buying catering packs from other companies.

(3) Describe how further computerisation might help in this quest for unification and profit improvement.

After you have finished this task, the MD tells you he is toying with the idea of regrouping the company under the name of Square Deal PLC and dividing it into the following divisions, each operating as a profit centre:

Square Deal PLC

Restaurants division	Property division	Food retail division	Canning division	Bakery division

He is concerned about the effects of such a change on the morale of the managers and other employees so he asks you for a further statement.

(4) Discuss ideas that should maintain or improve morale if this regrouping were to take place.

(5) Highlight any other advantages or difficulties that you foresee in the regrouping idea.

Notes and references

1. Etzioni, A. *Modern Organizations*, Prentice-Hall (1964).
2. Simon, H. A. 'On the Concept of Organizational Goal', *Administrative Science Quarterly*, vol. 10, June 1964, pp. 1–22.
3. See, for example: Porter, L. W., Lawler, E. E. and Hackman, J. R. *Behavior in Organizations*, McGraw-Hill (1975), and Kast, F. E. and Rosenzweig, J. E. *Organization and Management*, Fourth edition, McGraw-Hill (1985).
4. A view expressed by a number of writers including, for example: Argyris, C. *Integrating the Individual and the Organization*, Wiley (1964).
5. McGregor, D. *The Human Side of Enterprise*, Penguin (1987) p. 55.
6. Etzioni, A. *A Comparative Analysis of Complex Organizations*, Revised edition, Free Press (1975).
7. Cyert, R. and March, J. G. *A Behavioral Theory of the Firm*, Prentice-Hall (1963).
8. Perrow, C. *Organizational Analysis*, Tavistock Publications (1970).
9. Gross, B. M. *Organizations and their Managing*, Free Press (1968).
10. Fayol, H. *General and Industrial Management*, Pitman (1949) p. 53.
11. O'Shaughnessy, J. *Business Organization*, Allen and Unwin (1966) pp. 24–5.
12. For further information on policy decisions, see: Massie, J. L. *The Essentials of Management*, Fourth edition, Prentice-Hall (1987).
13. Brech, E. F. L. (ed.) *The Principles and Practice of Management*, Third edition, Longman (1975).
14. Tse, K. K. *Marks & Spencer*, Pergamon Press (1985).
15. Cowley, D. 'The Woman from the Body Shop', *Reader's Digest*, vol. 131, no. 785, September 1987, p. 41.
16. For a summary of the nature of strategic planning, see: Drucker, P. F. *Management*, Pan Books (1979).
17. Cyert, R. and March, J. G. *A Behavioral Theory of the Firm*, Prentice-Hall (1963).
18. Drucker, P. F. *The Practice of Management*, Pan Books (1968) pp. 82–3.
19. Etzioni, A. *Modern Organizations*, Prentice-Hall (1964) p. 17.
20. Simon, H. A. 'On the Concept of Organizational Goal', *Administrative Science Quarterly*, vol. 10, June 1964, p. 21.
21. Tilles, S. 'Making Strategy Explicit', in Ansoff, H. I. (ed.) *Business Strategy*, Penguin (1969).
22. Department of the Environment, *The New Local Authorities: Management and Structure* (the Bains report), HMSO (1972) pp. 6–7.

23. For an account of corporate planning in central government and in local government, see: Bourn, J. *Management in Central and Local Government*, Pitman (1979).
24. Ansoff, H. I. (ed.) *Business Strategy*, Penguin (1969).
25. Ansoff, H. I. *Corporate Strategy*, Revised edition, Penguin (1987).
26. Ansoff, H. I. (ed.) *Business Strategy*, Penguin (1969).
27. Drucker, P. F. *Managing for Results*, Pan Books (1964). See also: Drucker, P. F. *Managing in Turbulent Times*, Heinemann (1980).
28. Drucker, P. F. *The Practice of Management*, Pan Books (1968) pp. 454–5.
29. BIM Working Party 'Business Social Policy – What Is It?' British Institute of Management (March 1987).
30. BIM *Code of Conduct* and supporting *Guides to Good Management Practice*, Revised edition, July 1984. British Institute of Management.
31. Kuin, P. 'Social Responsibility: There's More to Management', a Unilever Educational Publication, reprinted from *Unilever Magazine*, 1978, p. 3.
32. Estimate provided by Valentine S. Head, Wider Share Ownership, Public Affairs Department, Stock Exchange, January 1988.
33. Deverson, B. 'Corporate Social Responsibility in Industry Year 1986' *Business Graduate Journal*, October 1986, pp. 42–5.
34. Elliott, K. 'Management by Subjectives', *Management Today*, September 1975, pp. 19, 22, 26.
35. Drucker, P. F. *The Practice of Management*, Pan Books (1968) p. 459.

5. ORGANISATION STRUCTURE AND SYSTEMS

In order to achieve its goals and objectives the work of an organisation has to be divided among its members. Some structure is necessary to make possible the effective performance of key activities and to support the efforts of staff. Structure provides the framework of an organisation and for its pattern of management. It is by means of structure that the purpose and work of the organisation is carried out. The manager needs to understand the importance and effects of organisation structure and systems.

Objectives

To: (i)   Explain the meaning and nature of organisation structure;
    (ii) Identify levels of organisation and dimensions of organisation structure;
    (iii) Explain the importance of good structure and consequences of a deficient structure;
    (iv) Evaluate main factors to be considered in the design of organisation structure;
    (v) Detail different methods for division of work and grouping together of activities;
    (vi) Assess the nature of the relationship between the structure of an organisation and the people who work within it;
    (vii) Recognise the importance of structure in influencing organisational performance.

THE MEANING AND NATURE OF ORGANISATION STRUCTURE

Structure is the pattern of relationships among positions in the organisation and among members of the organisation. The purpose of structure is the division of work among members of the organisation, and the co-ordination of their activities so they are directed towards achieving the goals and objectives of the organisation. The structure defines tasks and responsibilities, work roles and relationships, and channels of communication. Structure makes possible the application of the process of management and creates a framework of order and command through which the activities of the organisation can be planned, organised, directed and controlled.

In the very small organisation there will be few, if any, problems of structure. The distribution of tasks, the definition of authority and responsibility, and the relationship between members of the organisation can be established on a personal and informal basis. But with increasing size there is greater need for a carefully designed and purposeful form of organisation. There is need for a formal structure. There is also need for a continual review of structure to ensure that it is the most appropriate form for the particular organisation, and in keeping with its growth and development. As we shall see later, size is an important situational variable in the structure of an organisation

Objectives of structure

The objectives of structure may be summarised as to provide for:

- the economic and efficient performance of the organisation and the level of resource utilisation;
- monitoring the activities of the organisation;
- accountability for areas of work undertaken by groups and individual members of the organisation;
- co-ordination of different parts of the organisation and different areas of work;
- flexibility in order to respond to future demands and developments, and to adapt to changing environmental influences; and
- the social satisfaction of members working in the organisation.[1]

These objectives provide the criteria for structural effectiveness. Structure is not an end in itself but a means of improving organisational performance.

Drucker suggests that the organisation structure should satisfy three requirements.[2]

It must be organised for business performance

The more direct and simple the structure the more efficient it is because there is less change needed in the individual activities directed to business performance and results. Structure should not rest on past achievements but be geared to future demands and growth of the organisation.

The structure should contain the least possible number of management levels

The chain of command should be as short as possible. Every additional level makes for difficulties in direction and mutual understanding, distorts objectives, sets up additional stresses, creates inertia and slack, and increases the difficulties of the development of future managers moving up through the chain. The number of levels will tend to grow by themselves without the application of proper principles of organisation.

Organisation structure must make possible the training and testing of future top management

In addition to their training, future managers should be tested before they reach the top. They should be given autonomy in positions of actual managerial responsibility while still young enough to benefit from the new experience. They should also have the opportunity of at least observing the operation of the business as a whole, and not be narrowed by too long an experience in the position of a functional specialist.

In order to satisfy these three requirements Drucker suggests that the organisation structure must be based preferably on the principle of federal decentralisation', with activities integrated into autonomous product businesses with their own product and market, and with responsibility for their profit and loss. If federal decentralisation is not possible then the organisation structure should be based on the principle of 'functional decentralisation' with integrated units having the maximum responsibility for major and distinct stages of the business process.

LEVELS OF ORGANISATION

Organisations are layered. The determination of policy and decision making, the execution of work, and the exercise of authority and responsibility are carried out by different people at varying levels of seniority throughout the organisation structure. It is possible to look at organisations in terms of interrelated levels in the hierarchy of control. *Parsons*, for example, identifies three systems in the hierarchical structure of organisations: the technical level, the managerial level and the community level.[3]

The technical level is concerned with specific operations and discrete tasks, with the actual job or tasks to be done, and with performance of the technical function. For example: the physical production of goods in a manufacturing firm; administrative processes giving direct service to the public in government departments; the actual process of teaching in an educational establishment.

The technical level interrelates with *the managerial level*, or organisational level, which is concerned with the co-ordination and integration of work at the technical level. Decisions at the managerial level relate to the resources necessary for performance of the technical function, and to the beneficiaries of the products or services provided. Decisions will be concerned with: (i) mediating between the organisation and its external environment, such as the users of the organisation's products or services, and the procurement of resources; and (ii) the 'administration' of the internal affairs of the organisation including the control of the operations of the technical function.

In turn, the managerial level interrelates with *the community level* or institutional level, concerned with broad objectives and the work of the organisation as a whole. Decisions at the community level will be concerned with the selection of operations, and the development of the organisation in relation to external agencies and the wider social environment. Examples of the community level within organisations are: the board of directors of joint stock companies; governing bodies of educational establishments which include external representatives; trustees of non-profit organisations. Such bodies provide a mediating link between the managerial organisation and co-ordination of work of the technical organisation, and the wider community interests. Control at the institutional level of the organisation may be exercised, for example, by legislation, codes of standards or good practice, trade or professional associations, political or governmental action, public interest.

Interrelationship of levels

In practice there is not a clear division between determination of policy and decision making, co-ordination of activities and the actual execution of work. Most decisions are taken with reference to the execution of wider decisions, and most execution of work involves decision. Decisions taken at the institutional level determine objectives for the managerial level, and decisions at the managerial level set objectives for the technical level. If the organisation as a whole is to perform effectively there must be clear objec-

OBJECTIVES – STRUCTURE – COMMUNICATIONS

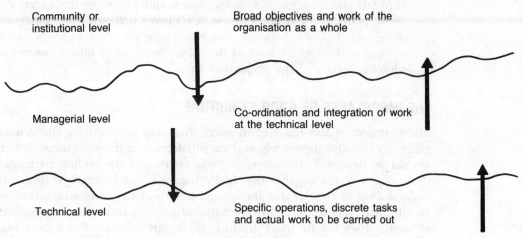

Community or
institutional level

Broad objectives and work of the
organisation as a whole

Managerial level

Co-ordination and integration of work
at the technical level

Technical level

Specific operations, discrete tasks
and actual work to be carried out

Fig. 5.1 Interrelated levels of organisation

tives; a soundly designed structure; and good communications, both upwards and downwards, among the different levels of the organisation. (*See* Fig. 5.1.)

The managerial level, for example, would be unable to plan and supervise the execution of work of the technical function without the knowledge, expertise, practical know-how and enthusiasm of people who are closest to the actual tasks to be undertaken. People operating at the technical level should, therefore, make known to higher levels the practical difficulties and operational problems concerning their work. It is the duty of the managerial level to take appropriate action on this information, and to consult with people at the community or institutional level.

Not all activities concerned with the management of an organisation can be considered, necessarily, in terms of these three levels of work. There will be certain activities which are analysed more meaningfully in terms of a greater, or possibly a fewer, number of levels. However, the three broad levels provide a basis for an analysis of the interrelated activities of the organisation.

An example of the interrelationship between the different levels of an organisation can be seen from the comments in the Bains report on management in local government.[4] The report recognises that elected members remain responsible for ultimate direction and control of the authority, key decisions on objectives and plans to attain them, and reviewing progress and performance of services. However, the report also refers to the dual nature of management and to the changing relationship between permanent officers and elected members at the different stages of the management process.

The report concludes:

> We doubt whether it is possible to divide the total management process into two separate halves, one for members and the other for officers. . . . That process itself can be seen as a scale, with the setting

of objectives and allocation of major resources at one end, moving through the designing of programmes and plans, to the execution of those plans at the other end. As one moves through that management scale, the balance between the two elements changes from member control with officer advice at the 'objective' end to officer control with member advice at the 'execution' end.[5]

THE IMPORTANCE OF GOOD STRUCTURE

The structure of an organisation affects not only productivity and economic efficiency but also the morale and job satisfaction of the workforce. Structure should be designed, therefore, so as to encourage the willing participation of members of the organisation and effective organisational performance.

According to *Drucker* it is the correct design of structure which is of most significance in determining organisational performance. 'Good organization structure does not by itself produce good performance. But a poor organization structure makes good performance impossible, no matter how good the individual managers may be. To improve organization structure . . . will therefore always improve performance.'[6]

The importance of good structure is also emphasised by *Child*.

> The allocation of responsibilities, the grouping of functions, decision-making, co-ordination, control and reward – all these are fundamental requirements for the continued operation of an organization. The quality of an organization's structure will affect how well these requirements are met.[7]

The functions of the formal structure and the activities and defined relationships within it, exist independently of the members of the organisation who carry out the work. However, personalities are an important part of the working of the organisation. In practice, the actual operation of the organisation and success in meeting its objectives will depend upon the behaviour of people who work within the structure and who give shape and personality to the framework. As *Meyer* puts it, 'organizational structure is but a simplification of complex patterns of human behavior'.[8]

The human element The overall effectiveness of the organisation will be affected both by sound structural design and by the individuals filling the various positions within the structure. Management will need to acknowledge the existence of the informal organisation (discussed in Chapter 3) which arises from the interactions of people working in the organisation. The organisation is a social system and people who work within it will establish their own norms of behaviour, and social groupings and relationships, irrespective of those defined in the formal structure.

The human relations writers are critical of the emphasis on the formal organisation. They favour a structure in which there is increased participation from people at all levels of the organisation, greater freedom for the individual, and more meaningful work organisation and relationships. One of the strongest critics of the formal organisation is *Argyris*.[9] He claims that the formal, bureaucratic organisation restricts individual growth and self-fulfilment and, in the psychologically healthy person, causes a feeling of failure, frustration and conflict. Argyris argues that the organisation should provide a more 'authentic' relationship for its members.

The view of the human relations writers represents more of an attitude towards organisation than specific proposals, but it reminds us of the importance of the human element in the design of structure. Managers need to consider how structural design and methods of work organisation influence the behaviour and performance of members of the organisation. For example, as we discussed in Chapter 3, changes in structure and working methods in the coal industry disrupted the miners' social relationships. As a result there was a lack of co-operation, an increase in absenteeism scapegoating and signs of greater social stress. The new method of work did not prove as efficient economically as it could have been.[10]

Relationship between people and organisation

The operation of the organisation and actual working arrangements will be influenced by the style of management, the personalities of members and the informal organisation. These factors may lead to differences betwen the formal structure of the organisation and what happens in practice. *Stewart* found the relationship between people and organisation to be reciprocal.

> People modify the working of the formal organization, but their behaviour is also influenced by it. The method of work organization can determine how people relate to one another, which may affect both their productivity and morale. Managers, therefore, need to be conscious of the ways in which methods of work organization may influence people's attitudes and action.[11]

Structure must be designed, therefore, so as to maintain the effectiveness of the socio-technical system and of the organisation as a whole. Attention must be given to the interactions between both the structural and techno-

```
┌──────────────────────────────────┐
│ People–organisation relationship │
└──────────────────────────────────┘
```

- CLARIFICATION OF OBJECTIVES
- DIMENSIONS OF STRUCTURE
- DIVISION OF WORK AND CO-ORDINATION OF ACTIVITIES
- CENTRALISATION AND DECENTRALISATION
- TASK AND ELEMENT FUNCTIONS
- 'PRINCIPLES' OF ORGANISATION
- SPAN OF CONTROL AND SCALAR CHAIN
- FORMAL ORGANISATIONAL RELATIONSHIPS
- PARTICULAR FORMS OF STRUCTURE
  For example:
  line and staff organisation
  matrix organisation

```
┌──────────────────────────────────┐
│ Maintain effectiveness of the    │
│ socio-technical system and the   │
│ organisation as a whole          │
└──────────────────────────────────┘
```

Fig. 5.2 Considerations in design of organisation structure

logical requirements of the organisation; and social factors and the needs and demands of the human part of the organisation. There is, however, in the final analysis, an underlying need to establish a framework of order and system of command by which the work to be undertaken is accomplished successfully. This demands that attention be given to certain basic considerations in the design of organisation structure, or in reviewing the effectiveness of an existing structure. (*See* Fig. 5.2.)

THE DESIGN OF ORGANISATION STRUCTURE

Structure provides the framework for the activities of the organisation and must harmonise with its goals and objectives. The first step, therefore, is to examine the objectives of the organisation. Only when objectives have been clearly defined can alternative forms of structure be analysed and compared. A clear definition of objectives is necessary in order to provide a basis for the division of work and grouping of duties into sub-units. The objectives for these sub-units must be related to the objectives of the organisation as a whole in order that an appropriate pattern of structure can be established.

Clarification of objectives

Clearly stated and agreed objectives will provide a framework for the design of structure, and a suitable pattern of organisation to achieve those objectives. The nature of the organisation and its strategy will indicate the most appropriate organisational levels for different functions and activities, and the formal relationships between them. Clearly defined objectives will help facilitate systems of communication between different parts of the organisation and the extent of decentralisation and delegation. The formal structure should help make possible the attainment of objectives. It should assist in the performance of the essential functions of the organisation and the major activities which it needs to undertake.

DIMENSIONS OF STRUCTURE

The variables which determine the dimensions of organisation structure can be identified in a number of ways but are usually taken to include the grouping of activities, the responsibilities of individuals, levels of hierarchical authority (the scalar chain), span of control and formal organisational relationships.[12] The dimensions of structure can, however, be identified in a number of ways.

Primary dimensions of structure

From an examination of literature on organisations *Pugh* defined six primary dimensions of organisation structure.[13]

- *Specialisation* – concerned with the division of labour and the allocation of tasks among different positions.
- *Standardisation* – the standardisation of procedures (rules or definitions that have regularity of occurrence and purport to cover all circumstances). This is a basic aspect of organisational structure.
- *Formalisation* – denotes the extent to which rules, procedures, instructions and communications are set out in written documents.
- *Centralisation* – concerned with the locus of authority to make decisions

affecting the organisation, determined by the last person whose assent is necessary before legitimate action can be taken.

- *Configuration* – is the 'shape' of the structure, for example long or short chain of command. This would be illustrated by a hypothetical organisation chart showing literally every role in the organisation.
- *Traditionalism* – the extent to which an organisation is standardised by customs or by rules.

Pugh constructed 64 scales to measure various aspects of the first five of these primary dimensions. Data were collected from 52 varying organisations from both the private and public sector in the Birmingham area, in order to test the internal consistency of the scales. From these scales, 16 were selected as most representative of the variables and as most distinctive; for example, functional specialisation, overall role specialisation, standardisation procedures controlling selection, overall centralisation, autonomy of the organisational unit, chief executive's span, line chain of command, percentage of total employees concerned with direct output.

A principal components analysis of the 16 scales indicated four empirically established, underlying dimensions of organisation structure.

- *Structuring of activities* – degree to which employee behaviour is defined by specialisation, standardisation and formalisation.
- *Concentration of authority* – degree to which decision making is concentrated at the top of the organisation or outside the organisation in part of a larger company.
- *Line control of work flow* – degree of control exercised by line personnel over direct output rather than impersonal procedures.
- *Relative size of support component* – relative number of non-productive personnel performing auxiliary activities to main work flow.

Components of organisation structure

In a replication study of *Pugh*'s work, *Child* used a similar measuring procedure on a sample of 82 business organisations, all whole units without subsidiaries, and located throughout the country.[14] Child found agreement with three of Pugh's factors: the structuring of activities; line control of work flow; and size of the support component. He did not discover a separate 'centralisation' factor but found that structuring of activities and centralisation were correlated negatively, resulting in the disappearance of the concentration of authority factor.

Child also suggests six major dimensions as components of an organisation structure:

- allocation of individual tasks and responsibilities, job specialisation and definition;
- formal reporting relationships, levels of authority and spans of control;
- grouping together of sections, departments, divisions and larger units;
- systems for communication of information, integration of effort and participation;
- delegation of authority and procedures for monitoring and evaluating the use of discretion;
- motivation of employees through systems for appraisal of performance and reward.[15]

Essential design parameters

Another approach to the identification of dimensions of structure is suggested by *Mintzberg* who gives a set of nine essential design parameters which form the basic components of organisation structure.

- How many tasks should a given position in the organization contain and how specialised should each task be?
- To what extent should the work content of each position be standardized?
- What skills and knowledge should be required for each position?
- On what basis should positions be grouped into units and units into larger units?
- How large should each unit be; how many individuals should report to a given manager?
- To what extent should the output of each position or unit be standardized?
- What mechanisms should be established to facilitate mutual adjustment among positions and units?
- How much decision-making power should be delegated to the managers of line units down the chain of authority?
- How much decision-making power should pass from the line managers to the staff specialists and operators?[16]

These nine design parameters can be grouped under four broad headings: design of position; design of superstructure; design of lateral linkages; and design of decision-making system.

Information technology

An additional dimension of structural design is *information technology*. The importance of information technology was discussed in Chapter 3. *Robey*, for example, suggests that although not strictly a separate area of design, computer-based information and decision-support systems affect other choices in design such as strategic decisions on markets, customer and products, division of work and individual tasks, organisational relationships and control systems. Because of the impact of automated systems 'managers must develop an appreciation for the interface between computing and organization'.[17]

A minister of state for industry and information technology has referred to the immense potential of information technology, and how the speed in development is changing the nature and organisation of work.

> This move towards an information-based economy is having a profound effect upon the nature and organization of work. There will be fewer people in factories making things and more people in smaller units: processing, storing, creating and handling information. Administrators and managers in these smaller units will have to develop new and more agile skills in organization. The winners will be those who are mobile and flexible, and the losers will be the over-centralized bureaucratic hierarchies.[18]

The impact of information technology will have significant effects on the structure, management and functioning of most organisations. (The importance of information technology and managing technical change was discussed in Chapter 3.) The introduction of new technology will demand new patterns of work organisation. It will affect individual jobs, the formation and structure of groups, the nature of supervision and managerial roles. Technology results in changes to lines of command and authority, and influences the need for restructuring the organisation and attention to job design.[19]

The Work Research Unit points out that new technology has typically resulted in a 'flatter' organisational pyramid with fewer levels of management required. In the case of new office technology it allows the potential for staff at clerical/operator level to carry out a wider range of functions and to check their own work. The result is an erosion in the traditional supervisory function. The role of the supervisor is likely to change and there are likely to be fewer supervisors.[20]

THE DIVISION OF WORK

Within the formal structure of an organisation work has to be divided among its members and different jobs related to each other. The division of work and the grouping together of people should, wherever possible, be organised by reference to some common characteristic which forms a logical link between the activities involved. It is necessary to maintain a balance between an emphasis on subject matter or function at higher levels of the organisation, and specialisation and concern for staff at the operational level.

Work can be divided, and activities linked together, in a variety of different ways.

(i) *By a major purpose or function* which is the most commonly used basis for grouping activities according to specialisation, the use of the same set of resources, or the shared expertise of members of staff. It is a matter for decision in each organisation as to which activities are important enough to be organised into separate functions, departments or sections. Work may be departmentalised and based, for example, on differentiation between task and element functions. In manufacturing firms the usual task functions are those concerned with research and development, production, marketing and finance. (*See* Fig. 5.3.) Element functions provide for the application of shared expertise and resources serving a number of different operational areas, products or services. For example, personnel, management accounting, maintenance and public relations provide supportive advisory functions common to the organisation as a whole.

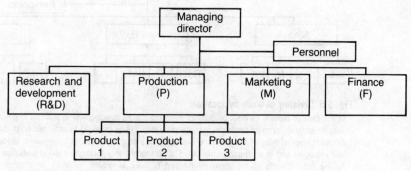

Fig. 5.3 Division of work by major purpose or function

(ii)   *By product or service* when the contributions of different specialists are integrated into separate, semi-autonomous units with collective responsibility for a major part of the business process or for a complete cycle of work. This form of grouping is more common in the larger diversified organisations and may be used as a means of sub-dividing departments into sections. For example, the bringing together of all activities concerned with a particular production line, product or service. (*See* Fig. 5.4.) Another example is a hospital where medical and support staff are grouped together in different units dealing with particular treatments such as accidents and emergency, medical or surgery. With grouping by product or service there is a danger that the divisions may attempt to become too autonomous, presenting management with a problem of co-ordination and control.

(iii)   *By location* when different services are provided by area or geographical boundaries according to particular needs or demands, the convenience of consumers, or for ease of administration. (*See* Fig. 5.5.) For example, the provision of local authority services for people living in a particular locality; the siting of hospitals or post offices; the provision of technical or agricultural further education in industrial or rural areas; sales territories for business firms; or the grouping of a number of retail shops under an area manager. Another example is provided by organisations with multi-site working and the grouping of a range of similar activities or functions located together on one site.

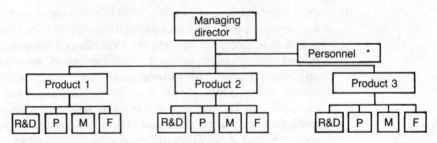

Fig. 5.4 Division of work by product or service

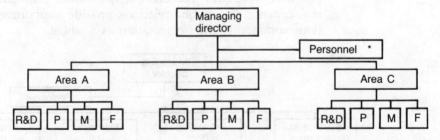

Fig. 5.5 Division of work by location

* In the case of division of work by product or service, or by geographical location, it is possible that certain aspects of support services, such as personnel management, may also be assigned to individual units of the organisation. However, the main responsibility of the personnel manager, as a separate entity, is to provide a specialist advisory service to all unit managers and to ensure implementation of personnel policy throughout the organisation as a whole. Responsibility for the main aspects of the personnel function is likely to remain, therefore, in a direct line of authority from top management.

A problem with grouping by location is the definition of the geographical boundaries and the most appropriate size for a given area. The improvement in communications, particularly telecommunications, tends, however, to reduce the importance of location. For example, administrative staff may no longer need to be located within the main production unit.

(iv) *By nature of the work to be performed* where there is some special common feature of the work such as the need for speedy decisions, accuracy, confidentiality/security, or where local conditions require first-hand knowledge not immediately available elsewhere. Another example may be the grouping together of equipment or machinery which is noisy or which produces dust, fumes or unpleasant odours.

(v) *By common time scales* such as shift working and the extent to which different tasks should be undertaken by different shifts. In a further education college there may be separate departments or groupings to deal with the different needs of full-time day students and part-time evening students. Another example of activities grouped according to time is in a hotel. Activities in the kitchen tend to be short term, especially when guests in the restaurant are waiting to be served, and a range of different tasks have to be co-ordinated very quickly. Other activities, for example market research and forecasting future room occupancy, are longer-term decisions, and subject to different organisational requirements.

(vi) *By common processes* which are used in a range of different activities. This method of grouping is similar to the division by nature of the work, but includes, for example, the decision whether to establish a centralised typing pool for all departments of the organisation, or to allow each department to have its own service. With manufacturing industries a range of products may pass through a common production facility or configuration of machines which may be grouped together in a single unit, for example a batch production engineering firm having departments based on like skills or methods of operation. Services using expensive equipment such as mainframe computers may need to be grouped together in this way for reasons of efficiency and economy.

(vii) *By the staff employed* when the allocation of duties and responsibilities is according to experience, or where a particular technical skill or special qualification is required. For example, the division of work between surgeons, doctors and nurses; or between barristers, solicitors and legal executives. Another example is the sharing of routine work processes among members of a supervised group. In smaller organisations the allocation of work may be on an *ad hoc*, personal basis according to the knowledge and skills contributed by individuals. Work may also be planned deliberately to give a variety of tasks and responsibilities to provide improved job satisfaction or to assist in the training of staff.

(viii) *By type of customer/people to be served* and the establishment of separate groups dealing with different consumer requirements. For example, the division between trade or retail customers, or between home or export sales. In hospitals there are different groupings dealing with, for example, patients in the gynaecology, geriatric and children's wards. In large clothes shops there may be separate departments for men's, women's and children's clothing. Government departments are often grouped by this method and work is divided according to for whom the services are provided; for example, the unemployed, low-pay families, students, young people or senior citizens. A further example is the provision of canteen services which may be grouped by customer demand according to price; range or standard of meals available, speed of service; or type of customer; this gives rise to separate facilities such as the directors' dining room, or for staff and students in educational establishments.

Combination of groupings

These different ways of dividing work can be combined in various forms and most organisations will contain examples of alternative combinations for grouping activities. Some activities might be grouped according to one method and other activities according to a different method. Decisions on the methods of grouping will include considerations of:

- the need for co-ordination;
- the identification of clearly defined divisions of work;
- economy;
- the process of managing the activities;
- avoiding conflict; and
- the design of work organisation which takes account of the nature of staff employed, their interests and job satisfaction.

Management must decide upon the most significant factors which will determine the methods for division of work and linking of activities appropriate to the changing circumstances within the particular organisation.

Co-ordinating mechanisms

The division of work among members of the organisation and the co-ordination of their activities is at the essence of structure. *Mintzberg* identifies five basic elements of structure which serve as co-ordinating mechanisms for the work of the organisation:

- mutual adjustment;
- direct supervision;
- standardisation of work processes;
- standardisation of work output; and
- standardisation of worker skills.

These co-ordinating mechanisms are 'the glue that holds organisations together'.[21]

Mutual adjustment involves the ability of specialists to adapt to each other in discovering the activities which need to be undertaken. Under mutual adjustment, control of the work rests with the members of the organisation themselves and is achieved through the process of informal communication. This form of co-ordinating mechanism is used in small and very simple organisations, but it may also be necessary in highly complex organisations where work is undertaken in difficult circumstances.

Direct supervision arises in the larger organisations and involves clearly defined division of labour and the formal co-ordination of work. Members of the organisation are distinguished by the work they do. With direct supervision co-ordination is achieved by an individual having responsibility for the work of others and by the giving of instructions and the monitoring of their performance.

Apart from mutual adjustment or direct supervision, work can be co-ordinated by standardisation. Work processes, the outputs of work, and the knowledge and skills of the workers can all be designed to meet pre-determined standards.

Standardisation of work processes involves the specification or programming of the contents of the work. Co-ordination is achieved through the design of the work organisation. An example is assembly-line production where the workers require little direct supervision or informal communication with their colleagues.

Standardisation of work output involves predetermining the interrelationships between completed work tasks rather than the methods or operations of work. End-results are specified, for example the dimensions of the finished product or the standard of performance provided.

Standardisation of worker skills involves the specification of the kind of training required to perform the work. When neither the nature of the work itself nor the finished outputs can be standardised, co-ordination and control are achieved through standardisation of the knowledge and skills of the worker. In most cases this is achieved by requiring a specified form of training before the worker joins the organisation, for example doctors joining a hospital.

Mintzberg suggests that these five co-ordinating factors appear to fall into a rough order according to the complexity of the work of the organisation. As work becomes more complicated the preferred means of co-ordination moves through:

mutual adjustment → *direct supervision* → *standardisation;*
first of work processes, next of work output and then of worker skills;
→ back finally to *mutual adjustment.*

CENTRALISATION AND DECENTRALISATION

One particular problem which arises from division of work and grouping of activities is the extent of centralisation or decentralisation. Most organisations necessarily involve a degree of decentralisation arising from such features as an increase in size, the geographical separation of different parts of the organisation, or the need to extend activities or services to remote areas. Our main concern is with decentralisation in terms of specific delegation to sub-units or groups within the organisation such that they enjoy a measure of autonomy or independence.

The advantages often claimed for centralisation include:

- the easier implementation of a common policy for the organisation as a whole;
- prevents sub-units becoming too independent;
- makes for easier co-ordination;
- improved economies of scale and a reduction in overhead costs;
- greater use of specialisation, including better facilities and equipment;

- improved decision making which might otherwise be slower and a result of compromise because of diffused authority.

Arguments against centralisation

However, such advantages frequently are not realised fully, and do not lead to an actual improvement in service. There are a number of contrary arguments against centralisation, including the criticism that it creates a more mechanistic structure and may result in lengthening the scalar chain. There are also positive arguments in favour of decentralisation:

- it enables decisions to be made closer to the operational level of work;
- support services, such as administration, are more likely to be effective if provided as close as possible to the activities they are intended to serve;
- it provides opportunities for training in management;
- usually, it has an encouraging effect on the motivation and morale of staff.

The advisability of decentralisation must be considered in terms of: the nature of the product or service provided; policy making; the day-to-day management of the organisation; and the need for standardisation of procedures, or conditions or terms of employment of staff.

Decentralisation generally tends to be easier to implement in private sector organisations than in the public sector organisations where there is a greater demand for the accountability of their operations, regularity of procedures and uniformity of treatment.

TASK AND ELEMENT FUNCTIONS

In order to produce some good, or provide some service, there are four essential functions that the organisation must perform.

(i) The need to develop the good or service.

(ii) The creation of something of value. In the case of the business organisation this might be the production or manufacture of a product; in the case of the public sector organisation the provision of a service.

(iii) The products or services must be marketed. They must be distributed or made available to those who are to use them.

(iv) Finance is needed in order to make available the resources used in the development, creation and distribution of the products or services provided.

These essential functions of developing the good or service, manufacturing the good or providing the service, marketing them, and financing the organisation, are what *Woodward* refers to as the 'task' functions. These are the basic activities of the organisation which are related to the actual completion of the productive process and directed towards specific and definable end results. To ensure the efficient achievement of overall objectives of the organisation the results of the task functions must be co-ordinated.[22]

Other activities of the organisation are not directed towards specific and definable ends but are supportive of the task functions and an intrinsic part of the management process. These are referred to as 'element' functions and include, for example, personnel, planning, management services, quality control and maintenance. In other organisations, noticeably in service indus-tries, personnel can be seen as closely associated with a task function. But in the majority of organisations the personnel function does not normally have any direct accountability for the performance of a specific end-task.

Implications for organisation

The two kinds of functions, task and element, differ in a number of ways and these differences have important implications for organisation. Failure to distinguish between the two types of functions can lead to confusion in the planning of structure and in the relationships between members of the organisation.

For example, in her study of the management organisation of firms in this country, *Woodward* comments on the bad relationships between accountants and other managers referred to during the study. One reason for this hostility was the bringing together of two quite separate financial functions essential to the efficient operation of a business.

> People concerned with works accounting tended to assume responsi-bility for end results that was not properly theirs; they saw their role as a controlling and sanctioning one rather than as a servicing and supportive one. Line managers resented this attitude and retaliated by becoming aggressive and obstructive.[23]

According to Woodward, activities concerned with raising funds for the business, keeping accounts and determination of financial policy are task functions. But management accounting, concerned with prediction and control of production administration, is an element function, and is primarily a servicing and supportive one. Relationships between the accountants and other managers seemed better when the two functions were organisationally separate. This was noticeable especially in division-alised organisation when each product division had its own accounting staff providing line managers with the necessary information to control their own departments. In these cases the task function of finance was completely divorced from the element function of management accounting in which the servicing and supportive role is of most importance.

PRINCIPLES OF ORGANISATION

The classical writers placed emphasis on the definition of structure in terms of division of work, chain of command, span of control and reporting relationships. Attention was focused on the requirements of the formal organisation and the search for a common set of principles applicable to all circumstances. Probably the leading authority in the country was *Lyndall Urwick*, who originally specified eight principles of organisation, but revised these to ten in his later writing.[24]

(i) *The principle of the objective*
'Every organisation and every part of the organisation must be an expression of the purpose of the undertaking concerned, or it is mean-ingless and therefore redundant.'

(ii) *The principle of specialisation*
'The activities of every member of any organised group should be

confined, as far as possible, to the performance of a single function.'

(iii) *The principle of co-ordination*

'The purpose of organising *per se*, as distinguished from the purpose of the undertaking, is to facilitate co-ordination: unity of effort.'

(iv) *The principle of authority*

'In every organised group the supreme authority must rest somewhere. There should be a clear line of authority to every individual in the group.'

(v) *The principle of responsibility*

'The responsibility of the superior for the acts of the subordinate is absolute.'

(vi) *The principle of definition*

'The content of each position, both the duties involved, the authority and responsibility contemplated and the relationships with other positions should be clearly defined in writing and published to all concerned.'

(vii) *The principle of correspondence*

'In every position, the responsibility and the authority should correspond.'

(viii) *The principle of span of control*

'No person should supervise more than five, or at the most, six direct subordinates whose work interlocks.'

(ix) *The principle of balance*

'It is essential that the various units of an organisation should be kept in balance.'

(x) *The principle of continuity*

'Re-organisation is a continuous process: in every undertaking specific provision should be made for it.'

Relevance of principles

As we mentioned in Chapter 2, the idea of common sets of principles on organisation and management has been subject to much criticism. Many of the principles are bland statements expressed in non-operation terms and give little basis for specific managerial action, and they tend to view people as 'a given rather than a variable in the system'.[25] However, the principles do provide general guidance on the structuring of organisations and much of the more recent writing on the subject appears to be based on the original statements. The basic concept can be of value to the practical manager if modified to suit the demands of the particular situation, including the nature of staffing in the organisation. The proper application of these principles is likely to help improve organisational performance. Two of the more specific principles of general interest in the structuring of organisations are (i) the span of control and (ii) the scalar chain.

SPAN OF CONTROL AND SCALAR CHAIN

The span of control arises in line authority and refers to the number of subordinates who report *directly* to a given manager or supervisor. It does not refer to the total of subordinate operating staff, that is those staff who report first to the subordinate. Hence the term 'span of responsibility' or 'span of supervision' is sometimes considered to be more appropriate.

The classical writers tended to suggest a definite figure for the span of control. *Brech* suggested that it should be limited to a reasonable number of interrelated executive or supervisory subordinates, but for only the most exceptional person would this number exceed single figures.[26] *V. A. Graicunas* developed a mathematical formula for the span of control.[27] The limitation of the number of subordinates who can be effectively supervised is based on the total of direct and cross relationships.

$$R = n\left(\frac{2^n}{2} + n - 1\right)$$

where n is the number of subordinates, and R is the number of interrelationships.

For example, with 5 subordinates the total number of interrelationships requiring the attention of the manager is 100, with 6 subordinates the number of interrelationships is 222. *Urwick* supports the idea of Graicunas and, as we have seen from his list of principles, states that the span of control should not exceed five, or at the most six direct subordinates whose work interlocks. At lower levels of the organisation, however, where there is less interlocking, or where responsibility is concerned more with the performance of specific tasks, the span of control may be larger.

Practical studies of span of control, however, show that it varies widely in different organisations and that the average span is larger than suggested by Graicunas and Urwick. In *Woodward*'s study of 100 manufacturing firms in south-east Essex she found that the size of span of control varied directly with technology and type of production system.[28]

In the case of the chief executive, the span of control in unit production firms was a median of 4, with a range of 2–9.

In large batch and mass production firms the median was 7, with a range of 4–13.

In process production firms the median was 10, with a range of 5–19.

There was also a wide variation in the span of control of first line supervisors (usually the foreman).

In unit production firms the average was 23, with a range of less than 10–41 to 50.

In large batch and mass production firms the average was 49, with a range of 11 to 20–81 to 90.

In process production firms the average was 13, with a range of less than 10–31 to 40.

Factors influencing span of control

In addition to the type of production system there are a number of other factors that will influence the limit of span of control. These include:

- the nature of the organisation, the complexity of the work and the similarity of functions, and the range of responsibilities;
- the ability and personal qualities of the manager including the capacity to cope with interruptions;
- the amount of time the manager has available from other activities to spend with subordinates;

- the ability and training of subordinate staff, and the extent of direction and guidance needed;
- the effectiveness of co-ordination and the nature of communication and control systems;
- the physical location or geographical spread of subordinates;
- the length of the scalar chain, that is the number of different levels in the hierarchical structure of the organisation.

If the span of control is too wide it becomes difficult to supervise subordinates effectively and places more stress on the manager. With larger groupings informal leaders and sub-groups or cliques are more likely to develop and these may operate contrary to the policy of management. There may be lack of time to carry out all activities properly. Planning and development, training, inspection and control may suffer in particular, leading to poor job performance. A wide span of control may limit opportunities for promotion. Too wide a span of control may also result in a slowness to adapt to change or to the introduction of new methods or procedures.

If the span of control is too narrow this may present a problem of co-ordination and consistency in decision making, and hinder effective communications across the organisation structure. Morale and initiative of subordinates may suffer as a result of too close a level of supervision. Narrow spans of control increase administrative costs and can prevent the best use being made of the limited resource of managerial talent. They can lead to additional levels of authority in the organisation creating an unnecessarily long scalar chain.

The scalar chain   This refers to the number of different levels in the structure of the organisation, the chain of hierarchical command. The scalar chain establishes the vertical graduation of authority and responsibility, and the framework for superior–subordinate relationships (*see* Fig. 5.6). Every person must know his or her position within the structure of the organisation. The very act of organising introduces the concept of the scalar chain. Most organisation charts demonstrate that this principle is used widely as a basis for organisational design. A clear line of authority and responsibility is necessary for the effective operation of the organisation.

It seems to be generally accepted, however, that for reasons of morale and to help decision making and communications there should be as few levels as possible in the scalar chain. There is the danger of adding to the structure in such a way that it results in increased hierarchical authority and control, leads to the risk of empire building and the creation of unnecessary work in justification of the new position. But if efforts are made to reduce the number of levels this may bring about an increase in the span of control with the resulting difficulties already discussed. The design of structure necessitates, therefore, maintaining an appropriate balance between span of control and scalar chain.

The combination of span of control and scalar chain determines the overall pyramid shape of the organisation and whether the hierarchical structure is 'flat' or 'tall'. (*See* Fig. 5.7.) The pyramid represents the structure of authority. Broader spans of control and few levels of authority result in a flat hierarchical structure as tends to be found, for example, in universities and

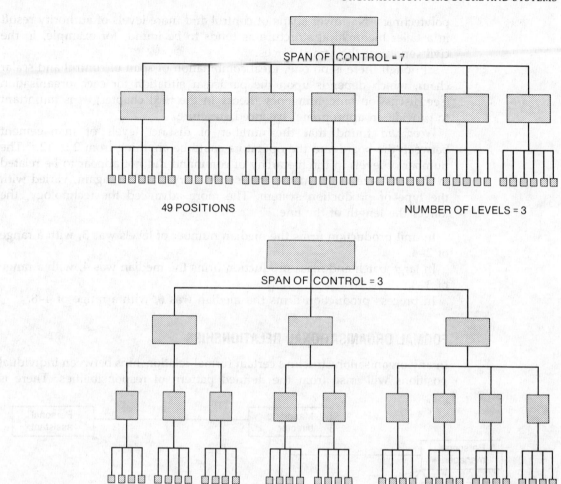

SPAN OF CONTROL = 7

49 POSITIONS

NUMBER OF LEVELS = 3

SPAN OF CONTROL = 3

49 POSITIONS

NUMBER OF LEVELS = 4

Fig. 5.6 How span of control and scalar chain affects organisation structure

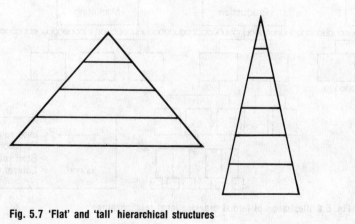

Fig. 5.7 'Flat' and 'tall' hierarchical structures

polytechnics. Narrower spans of control and more levels of authority result in a taller hierarchical structure as tends to be found, for example, in the civil service or the armed forces.

Although there is no one, ideal combination of span of control and scalar chain, which depends upon the particular situation for each organisation (see discussion on contingency theory in the next chapter), it is important to provide an appropriate, balanced structure.

Woodward found that the number of distinct levels of management between the board and the operators could be anything from 2 to 12.[29] The number of levels in the hierarchy of command did not appear to be related to the total size of the managerial/supervisory staff but, again, varied with the type of production system. The more advanced the technology, the longer the length of the line.

In unit production firms the median number of levels was 3, with a range of 2–4.

In large batch and mass production firms the median was 4, with a range of 3–8.

In process production firms the median was 6, with a range of 4–8.

FORMAL ORGANISATIONAL RELATIONSHIPS

In any organisation structure certain formal relationships between individual positions will arise from the defined pattern of responsibilities. There is

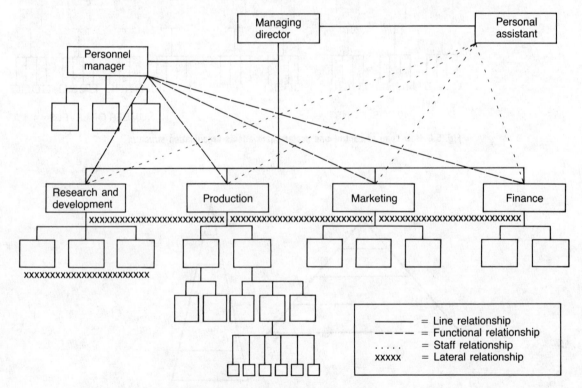

Fig. 5.8 Illustration of formal organisational relationships

often confusion over the meaning of different terms and their implications for organisational structure, but these *individual* authority relationships may be identified as line, functional, staff or lateral [30] (*See* Fig. 5.8.) The design of organisation structure in terms of the principle of line, functional, staff or lateral, determines the pattern of role relationships and interactions with other roles (see Chapter 13).

Line relationships
In *line relationships*, authority flows vertically down through the structure, for example from the managing director to managers, section leaders, supervisors and other staff. There is a direct relationship between superior and subordinate, with each subordinate responsible to only one person. Line relationships are associated with functional or departmental division of work and organisational control. Line managers have authority and responsibility for all matters and activities within their own department.

Functional relationships
Functional relationships apply to the relationship between people in specialist or advisory positions, and line managers and their subordinates. The specialist offers a common service throughout all departments of the organisation, but has no direct authority over those who make use of the service. There is only an indirect relationship. For example, the personnel manager has no authority over staff in other departments – this is the responsibility of the line manager. But as the position and role of the personnel manager would have been sanctioned by top management other staff might be expected to accept the advice which is given. The personnel manager, however, could be assigned some direct, executive authority for certain specified responsibilities such as, for example, health and safety matters throughout the whole organisation. Note, however, that specialists in a functional relationship with other managers still have a line relationship with both their own superior and their own departmental subordinate staff.

Staff relationships
Staff relationships arise from the appointment of personal assistants to senior members of staff. Persons in a staff position have no direct authority in their own right but act as an extension of their superior and exercise only 'representative' authority. Normally there is no direct relationship between the personal assistant and other staff except where delegated authority and responsibility has been given for some specific activity. In practice, personal assistants often do have some influence over other staff, especially those in the same department or grouping. This may be partially because of the close relationship between the personal assistant and the superior, and partially dependent upon the knowledge and experience of the assistant, and the strength of the assistant's own personality.

Lateral relationships
Lateral relationships exist between individuals in different departments or sections, especially individuals on the same level. These lateral relationships are based on contact and consultation and are necessary to maintain co-ordination and effective organisational performance. Lateral relationships may be specified formally but in practice they depend upon the co-operation of staff and in effect are a type of informal relationship.

LINE AND STAFF ORGANISATION

An area of management which causes particular difficulty is the concept of line and staff. As organisations develop in size and work becomes more complex, the range of activities and functions undertaken increases. People with specialist knowledge have to be integrated into the managerial structure. Line and staff organisation is concerned with different functions which are to be undertaken. It provides a means of making full use of specialists while maintaining the concept of line authority. It creates a type of informal matrix structure (*see* Fig. 5.9).

Again, confusion can arise from conflicting definitions of terminology. In the line and staff form of organisation, the individual authority relationship defined previously as 'functional' now becomes part of the actual structure under the heading of staff relationships.

One viewpoint is that line organisation relates to those functions

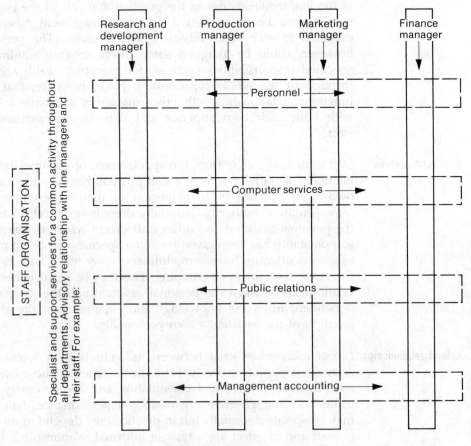

Fig. 5.9 Representation of line and staff organisation

concerned with specific responsibility for achieving the objectives of the organisation and to those people in the direct chain of command. Staff organisation relates to the provision of specialist and support functions for the line organisation and creates an advisory relationship. This is in keeping with the idea of task and element functions discussed earlier.

Difficulties with line and staff relations

The concept of line and staff relations presents a number of difficulties. With the increasing complexity of organisations and the rise of specialist services it becomes harder to distinguish clearly between what is directly essential to the operation of the organisation, and what might be regarded only as an auxiliary function. The distinction between a line manager and a staff manager is not absolute. There may be a fine division between offering professional advice and the giving of instructions.

Friction inevitably seems to occur between line and staff managers. Neither side may fully understand nor appreciate the purpose and role of the other. Staff managers are often criticised for unnecessary interference in the work of the line manager and for being out of touch with practical realities. Line managers may feel that the staff managers have an easier and less demanding job because they have no direct responsibility for producing a product or providing a service for the customer, and are free from day-to-day operational problems.

Staff managers may feel that their own difficulties and work problems are not appreciated fully by the line manager. Staff managers often complain about resistance to their attempts to provide assistance and co-ordination, and the unnecessary demands for departmental independence by line managers. A major source of difficulty is to persuade line managers to accept, and act upon, the advice and recommendations which are offered.

The line and staff relationship can also give rise to problems of 'role congruence'; see Chapter 13.

PROJECT TEAMS AND MATRIX ORGANISATION

The division of work and methods of grouping described earlier tend to be relatively permanent forms of structure. With the growth in newer, complex and technologically advanced systems it has become necessary for organisations to adapt traditional structures in order to provide greater integration of a wide range of functional activities. In recent years greater attention has been given, therefore, to more flexible forms of structure and the creation of groupings based on project teams and matrix organisation. Members of staff from different departments or sections are assigned to the team for the duration of a particular project.

A project team may be set up as a separate unit on a temporary basis for the attainment of a particular task. When this task is completed the project team is disbanded or members of the unit are reassigned to a new task. Project teams may be used for people working together on a common task or to co-ordinate work on a specific project such as the design and development, production and testing of a new product; or the design and implementation of a new system or procedure. For example, project teams have been used in many military systems, aeronautics and space programmes. A project team is more likely to be effective when it has a clear objective, a well-defined task, a definite end-result to be achieved, and the composition of the team is chosen with care.

The matrix organisation

The matrix organisation is a combination of:

(i) functional departments which provide a stable base for specialised activities and a permanent location for members of staff; and

(ii) units that integrate various activities of different functional departments on a project team, product, programme, geographical or systems basis.

The matrix organisation therefore establishes a grid, or matrix, with a two-way flow of authority and responsibility (*see* Fig. 5.10). This can result in problems of co-ordination. 'By using matrix structure, the organisation avoids choosing one basis of grouping over another; instead, it chooses both . . . as a result, matrix structure sacrifices the principle of unity of command.'[31] There may be a limited number of staff reporting directly to the project manager but assistance is required from other departmental managers who assign staff to provide help with particular projects.

Within the functional departments authority and responsibility flow vertically down the line, but the authority and responsibility of the project manager flow horizontally across the organisation structure. Matrix organisation offers the advantage of flexibility; greater security and control of project information; and opportunities for staff development. There is, however, the problem of defining the extent of the project manager's auth-

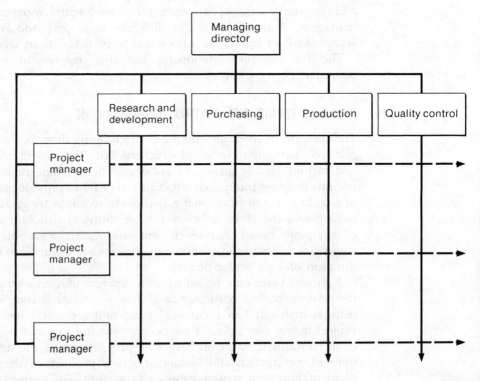

Fig. 5.10 Outline of matrix organisation structure
Solid lines = *line authority* exercised over departmental staff through direct chain of command. Broken lines = *project authority* exercised over selected staff assigned from departments as appropriate.

ority over the staff from other departments, and of gaining the support of other functional managers and their co-operation with the project. Matrix organisation can result in a more complex structure. Functional groups may tend to neglect their normal duties and responsibilities. There may be a feeling of ambiguity. As a result staff may be reluctant to accept constant change and prefer the organisational stability from membership of their own functional grouping.

A matrix design might be adopted where there is:

(i) *more than one critical orientation to the operations of the organisation*, for example an insurance company that has to respond simultaneously to both functional differentiation such as life, fire, marine, motor; and to different geographical areas;

(ii) *a need to process simultaneously large amounts of information*, for example a local authority social services department seeking help for an individual will need to know where to go for help from outside agencies such as police, priest, community relations officer; and at the same time whom to contact from internal resources within the organisation such as the appropriate social worker, health visitor or housing officer;

(iii) *the need for sharing of resources* which could only be justified on a total organisational basis such as the occasional or part-time use by individual departments of specialist staff or services.

Developing an effective matrix organisation, however, takes time, and a willingness to learn new roles and behaviour which means that matrix structures are often difficult for management to implement effectively.[32]

ORGANISATION CHARTS

The structure of an organisation is depicted usually in the form of an organisation chart. This will show, at a given moment in time, how work is divided, the levels of authority and formal organisational relationships. The organisation chart provides a pictorial representation of the structural framework of an organisation. Some charts are very sketchy and give only a minimum amount of information. Other charts give varying amounts of additional detail such as an indication of the broad nature of duties and responsibilities of the various units. Some charts give the names of postholders and even photographs; and some give the salary gradings for individual positions.

Charts are usually displayed in a traditional, vertical form such as those already depicted in Fig. 5.6 above. They can, however, be displayed either horizontally with the information reading from left to right, or concentrically with top management at the centre. The main advantage of both the horizontal and the concentric organisation charts is that they tend to reduce the indication of superior or subordinate status. They also offer the practical advantage of more space on the outer margin. In addition, the concentric chart may help to depict the organisation more as a unified whole.

Organisation charts are useful in explaining the outline structure of an organisation. They may be used as a basis for the analysis and review of structure, for training and management succession, and for formulating changes. The chart may indicate apparent weaknesses in structure such as too wide a span of control, too long a scalar chain or poor lines of communication.

Limitations of organisation charts

There are, however, a number of limitations with traditional organisation charts. They depict only a static view of the organisation, and show how it looks and what the structure should be. They do not describe how the organisation actually works or the behaviour of people represented on the chart. *Gray* and *Starke* give a humorous but perhaps realistic illustration of how an organisation actually works.[33] (*See* Fig. 5.11.) Charts do not show the comparative authority and responsibility of positions on the same level, or lateral contacts and informal relations. Neither do charts show the extent of personal delegation from superior to subordinates, or the precise relationships between line and staff positions. Organisation charts can become out of date quickly and are often slow to be amended to reflect changes in the actual structure.

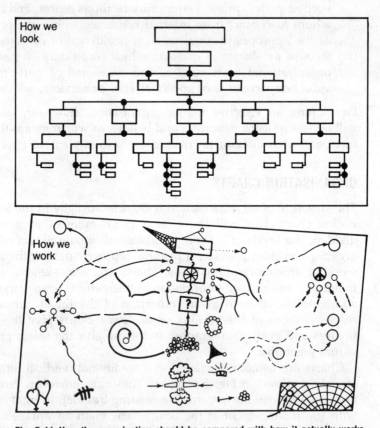

Fig. 5.11 How the organisation should be compared with how it actually works
(From Gray, J. L. and Starke, F. A., *Organizational Behavior: Concepts and Applications*, 4th edition, Merrill Publishing Co., Columbus, Ohio (1988) p. 431. Reproduced by permission of the publishers.)

Comprehensible form of organisation chart

Despite these limitations, the organisation chart is a valuable and convenient way of illustrating the framework of structure – provided the chart is drawn up in a comprehensible form. There is always the question of what the chart does not show and what the observer interprets from it.[34] Some charts add a rider, for example: 'position of boxes does not necessarily indicate importance of status or level of authority', or 'the chart indicates lines of communication and not necessarily lines of authority'. Such comments may only serve to add to the doubts, and it is quite possible that the chart really does indicate what the rider attempts to disclaim.

There are a number of conventions in drawing up organisation charts. It is not our purpose to go into specific details, but it is important to remember that the chart should always give:

- the date when it was drawn up;
- the name of the organisation, branch or department (as appropriate) to which it refers;
- whether it is an existing or proposed structure;
- the extent of coverage, for example if it refers to the management structure only, or if it excludes servicing departments;
- a reference to identify the person who drew up the chart.

EFFECTS OF A DEFICIENT ORGANISATION STRUCTURE

It is not easy to describe, in a positive manner, what constitutes a 'good' or an effective organisation structure although, clearly, attention should be given to the design principles discussed above. However, the negative effects of a poorly designed structure can be identified more easily. In his discussion on the principles of organisation and co-ordination, *Urwick* suggests that: 'Lack of design is Illogical, Cruel, Wasteful and Inefficient'.[35]

- *It is illogical* because in good social practice, as in good engineering practice, design should come first. No member of the organisation should be appointed to a senior position without identification of the responsibilities and relationships attached to that position and its role within the social pattern of the organisation.
- *It is cruel* because it is the individual members of the organisation who suffer most from lack of design. If members are appointed to the organisation without a clear definition of their duties or the qualifications required to perform those duties, it is these members who are likely to be blamed for poor results which do not match the vague ideas of what was expected of them.
- *It is wasteful* because if jobs are not put together along the lines of functional specialisation then new members of the organisation cannot be trained effectively to take over these jobs. If jobs have to be fitted *to members* of the organisation, rather than members of the organisation *to jobs*, then every new member has to be trained in such a way so as to aim to replace the special, personal experience of the previous job incumbent. Where both the requirements of the job and the member of the organisation are unknown quantities this is likely to lead to indecision and much time wasted in ineffective discussion.
- *It is inefficient* because if the organisation is not founded on principles, managers are forced to fall back on personalities. Unless there are clearly established principles, which are understood by everyone in the organisation, managers will start 'playing politics' in matters of promotion and similar issues.

Urwick lays emphasis on the technical planning of the organisation and determining and laying out structure before giving any thought to the individual members of the organisation. Although Urwick acknowledges that the personal touch is important, and part of the obvious duty of the manager, it is not a substitute for the need for definite planning of the structure. 'In short, a very large proportion of the friction and confusion in current society, with its manifest consequences in human suffering, may be traced back directly to faulty organisation in the structural sense.'[36]

Consequences of badly designed structure

Urwick's emphasis on the logical design of organisation structure rather than the development around the personalities of its members is typical of the classical approach to organisation and management. Despite this rather narrow view, more recent writers have drawn similar conclusions as to the consequences of badly designed structure.

For example, *Child*, points out that:

> There are a number of problems which so often mark the struggling organization and which even at the best of times are dangers that have to be looked for. These are low motivation and morale, late and inappropriate decisions, conflict and lack of co-ordination, rising costs and a generally poor response to new opportunities and external change. Structural deficiencies can play a part in exacerbating all these problems.[37]

Child then goes on to explain the consequences of structural deficiencies.

- *Low motivation and morale* may result from apparently inconsistent and arbitrary decisions; insufficient delegation of decision making; lack of clarity in job definition and assessment of performance; competing pressures from different parts of the organisation; and managers and supervisors overloaded through inadequate support systems.
- *Late and inappropriate decisions* may result from: lack of relevant, timely information to the right people; poor co-ordination of decision makers in different units; overloading of decision makers due to insufficient delegation; and inadequate procedures for evaluation of past decisions.
- *Conflict and lack of co-ordination* may result from: conflicting goals and people working at cross-purposes because of lack of clarity on objectives and priorities; failure to bring people together into teams or through lack of liaison; and breakdown between planning and actual operational work.
- *Poor response to new opportunities and external change* may result from: failure to establish specialist jobs concerned with forecasting environmental change; failure to give adequate attention to innovation and planning of change as main management activities; inadequate co-ordination between identification of market changes and research into possible technological solutions.
- *Rising costs* may result from: a long hierarchy of authority with a high proportion of senior positions; an excess of administrative work at the expense of productive work; and the presence of some, or all, of the other organisational problems.

It is clear, then, that it is essential to give full attention to the structure of an organisation. Consideration should be given to both the formal and technological requirements, and to social factors, and the needs and demands of the human part of the organisation. Structure should be designed as to maintain the balance of the socio-technical system, and to encourage the willing participation of members and effective organisational performance.

| Synopsis |

Structure provides the framework of an organisation and makes possible the application of the process of management. Some structure is necessary to make possible the effective performance of key activities and to support the efforts of staff. Organisations are layered and within the hierarchical structure there are three broad, interrelated levels: technical, managerial and community. The dimensions of structure can be identified in a number of ways but are usually taken to include the grouping of activities, responsibilities of individuals, levels of hierarchical authority, span of control and formal organisational relationships. An additional, important dimension of structure is the impact of information technology.

The structure of an organisation affects not only productivity and economic efficiency but also the morale and job satisfaction of its members. The overall effectiveness of the organisation will be influenced both by sound structural design, and by the behaviour of people who work within the structure. Attention must be given to maintaining the socio-technical system and to integrating the structural and technological requirements of the organisation, and the needs and demands of the human part of the organisation. A badly designed structure is likely to give rise to inefficiency, low motivation and morale, late and inappropriate decisions, conflict, rising costs and lack of development.

There is an underlying need to establish a framework of order and system of command through which the activities of the organisation can be planned, organised, directed and controlled. This demands attention to certain basic considerations in the design of organisation structure, such as: clarification of objectives; dimensions of structure; division of work and co-ordination of activities; centralisation; task and element functions; principles of organisation; span of control and scalar chain; and formal organisational relationships.

The essence of structure is the division of work among members of the organisation and the co-ordination of their activities. Work can be divided and activities linked in a number of ways. Most organisations will contain examples of alternative combinations for grouping activities and relating different jobs to each other. A particular form of structure which can cause difficulty is the line and staff organisation. With the growth in newer, complex and technologically advanced systems, and the need to provide integration of a wide range of functional activities, greater attention has been given to more flexible forms of structure, such as matrix organisation.

The structure of an organisation is depicted usually in the form of an organisation chart which provides, at a given moment in time, a pictorial representation of the structural framework of an organisation. Charts may be used as a basis for the analysis and review of structure, and may indicate apparent weaknesses. There are, however, limitations with traditional organisation charts. There are also a number of conventions in drawing up the charts.

Review and discussion questions

1 What are the objectives of organising? Distinguish different levels in the hierarchical structure of an organisation.
2 Summarise the major dimensions of organisation structure and give examples from your own organisation.
3 What is the importance of good structure? How does structure relate to the overall effectiveness of an organisation?
4 How might the work of a large organisation be divided among its members? Give examples where each method might be most appropriate. Examine the means for division of work in your own organisation and comment upon their effectiveness.
5 Explain the main factors to be considered in the design of organisation structure. Is there one best way to design an organisation and of what value are the 'principles' of organisation?
6 Distinguish between 'span of control' and 'scalar chain'. Discuss the practical implications of span of control and scalar chain for the structure and effective operation of an organisation.
7 To what extent would you agree with the contention that a logical structure for organisation is better for efficiency and morale than a structure allowed to develop around personalities? What are the likely consequences of a poorly designed structure?
8 Prepare diagrams to help explain (i) line and staff organisation, and (ii) a matrix form of organisation structure. What are the reasons for adopting each of these forms of structure and what problem areas might arise?

| **Practical assignment** | Examine arrangements for the division of work and linking together of activities in your own or some other organisation of your choice. |

(i)   Investigate and make notes on the variety of ways in which work is divided and combinations for grouping of activities within the organisation.
(ii) Comment critically on the apparent effectiveness of:
    (a) different methods adopted for the division of work among members of the organisation; and
    (b) mechanisms designed to achieve co-ordination of the work of the organisation as a whole.
(iii) Give reasons, and where possible practical examples, in support of your comments.
    Explain any changes you would recommend in order to help improve organisational performance.

| **Case study** | *Part One* |

The personal assistant to the commercial director of a large manufacturing group is at present looking into the costing systems of the metal furniture division employing some 500 people, 30 of whom are in the general offices at the works.

The division manufactures metal furniture in the Home Counties for industrial and business use, selling catalogue lines from stock mainly to retailers.

The works takes in raw material and parts at the receiving bay, then machines batches of components, assembles, finishes and dispatches orders to customers in the firm's transport or by carrier from the warehouse at the other end of the works.

The office manager is responsible for all the clerical and commercial functions except the sales and general ledgers which are kept at Head Office. The sales manager is at the London showrooms, but all customers' orders are handled by office staff at the works.

One afternoon, the secretary to the commercial director's personal assistant comes into the office and says that her friend Cynthia is in tears. Mr Smith, the personal assistant, protests that it is not his concern but is persuaded to listen. In due course he discovers that Cynthia is the computer operator in the general office and that she is upset because she is worried about her work.

Mr L. O. Kate, the senior cost clerk, complains that the period overhead rates have not been calculated; Mr T. Clarke says his jobs should have been done first; Mr I. Payem insists that the bonus figures and tax computations for the wages which are due for payment the very next day must be ready by lunchtime. The buyers want the batches of incoming invoices checked; the sales statistics clerk is looking for percentages and cumulative figures.

Cynthia does not really get on with most of the other girls in the offices, who are typists and resent the fact that she is paid more. Mr Jones, the office manager, does not seem to notice that she exists and his secretary, who has been around longer than anyone else, orders Cynthia and everyone else about.

Mr Smith, trying to be tactful, has a quiet word with Mr Jones. Mr Jones says that Mr Smith is quite right to come to him about the matter. He is also always ready to make his 30 years' experience available to 'you smart young people'. He adds that he is sure there is nothing for Mr Smith to worry about – all his staff report directly to him and he would not have it any other way. He will, however, have a word with Tom, his chief clerk, and ask him to keep an eye on her. Tom is rather busy with a small buying problem, and with balancing the wages, and one or two other things at the moment – but he will tell him about the girl.

Still a trifle concerned, Mr Smith has a word with the local personnel assistant, who reminds him that the division's personnel department deals only with shop-floor people. On his next visit to Head Office, he has a look in the office staff files, but can find no sign that job descriptions or charts of an organisation were ever compiled for the office staff at the division.

(1) Comment on the nature of the relationships among people in the office.
(2) Suggest a preferred organisation structure which may help to resolve some of the problems involved.

Part Two

Mr Smith, the personal assistant to the commercial director, has now been appointed office manager of the division after the early retirement of Mr Jones. The appointment as office manager took place some time after the events outlined in part one of the case study and the office staff had just moved into a large open-plan office instead of being spread in several rooms around the building.

It is assumed that the preferred organisation you designed after the incidents described in part one of the case study is slowly being introduced as it becomes possible to persuade the staff to change their attitudes and methods of working.

One day early in February, the commercial director's secretary rings up to ask about the monthly return of packing and carriage for December. The office manager explains that he is not aware of any delay but will inquire and ring back. He sends for the chief clerk (who is rather vague about the return) and who asks permission to work overtime in the buying section that evening. The office manager agrees, with some reservations, and takes his inquiries further.

He finds from a few moments' conversation in the office that the clerk who deals with incoming invoices is clear and to the point. He has the whole month's charges for packing materials neatly summarised, the internal debit note from the garage cost centre, and the haulage contractors' accounts okayed by the dispatch supervisor. So total costs are ready; and that leaves the income side, the amounts 'recovered' from each of the customers' orders for the month.

The office manager finds that this is dealt with by Mrs B., who takes each copy invoice for the month and evaluates notional percentages incorporated in the price to cover packing and carriage which varies according to the sales area zone. These details are then summarised in a very large book which, it turns out, no one else in the office understands at all.

Mrs B. has not finished the December figures yet because she is busy with some special data the sales manager in London has asked her to provide. She also mentions that the packing and carriage return for January is due at Head Office at the end of next week – and if she had been asked, she would have said.

Mr Smith, the office manager, considers that the procedure she has just outlined is a long-winded way of getting a general indication that recovery matches expense during the year. Still a bit put out by the chief clerk's lack of interest, he rashly tells her that the procedure is poor.

Mrs B. stiffens and says she has always tried very hard at her job and done what she was told to do, and it was always satisfactory in the past. If Mr Smith cared he could ask Mr Jones – but things aren't the same any more, she adds.

Mr Smith mumbles reassurances and asks if she could possibly clear up the December figures by Friday. Mrs B. agrees reluctantly – but what shall she do about finishing off the sales manager's request? Then, almost as an afterthought, she reminds him that it has already been agreed that she shall take next week off as special leave.

Later that afternoon the chief clerk puts his head round the door and drops his small bomb – Mrs B. has given a month's notice.

Mr Smith rings Head Office to ask the chief accountant if he can tell him anything more about the packing and carriage return. The chief accountant promises to send Mr Smith a photocopy of an old file note he has unearthed.

But relief is short-lived for the chief accountant goes on to darken the day still more by asking if Mr Smith has heard the managing director's latest? An official announcement will be made shortly: 'In view of anticipated trading difficulties, overtime working will now be strictly limited, no new staff may be recruited, and replacements will be restricted to works direct labour only. Capital expenditure will be halted and all managers are required to exercise the strictest economy.'

(1) What do you see as the main issues or problem areas?
(2) Suggest what actions you recommend be taken to help resolve the present situation and overcome future difficulties.

Notes and references

1. Adapted from Knight, K. (ed.) *Matrix Management: a Cross-functional Approach to Organization*, Gower (1977) pp. 114–15.
2. Drucker, P. F. *The Practice of Management*, Pan Books (1968).
3. Parsons, T. 'Some Ingredients of a General Theory of Formal Organization', in Litterer, J. A. *Organizations: Structure and Behaviour*, Third edition, Wiley (1980).
4. Department of the Environment, *The New Local Authorities: Management and Structure* (The Bains report), HMSO (1972).
5. Ibid., pp. 10–11.
6. Drucker, P. F. *The Practice of Management*, Pan Books (1968) p. 273.
7. Child, J. *Organization: A Guide to Problems and Practice*, Second edition, Harper and Row (1984) p. 4.
8. Meyer, M. W. *Theory of Organizational Structure*, Bobbs-Merrill (1977) p. 44.
9. Argyris, C. *Integrating the Individual and the Organization*, Wiley (1964).
10. Trist, E. L. *et al. Organizational Choice*, Tavistock Publications (1963).
11. Stewart, R. *The Reality of Management*, Second edition, Pan Books (1986) p. 127.
12. For a summary of empirical literature on the determination of structural dimensions see: Blackburn, R. S. 'Dimensions of Structure: A Review and Reappraisal', *Academy of Management Review*, vol. 7, no. 1, January 1982, pp. 59–66.
13. Pugh, D. S., Hickson, D. J., Hinings, C. R. and Turner, C. 'Dimensions of Organization Structure', *Administrative Science Quarterly*, vol. 13, June 1968, pp. 65–105.
14. Child, J. 'Organizational Structural and Strategies of Control; A Replication of the Aston Study', *Administrative Science Quarterly*, vol. 17, 1972, pp. 163–76.
15. Child, J. *Organization: A Guide to Problems and Practice*, Second edition, Harper and Row (1984).
16. Mintzberg, H. *The Structuring of Organizations*, Prentice-Hall (1979) p. 66.
17. Robey, D. *Designing Organizations*, Irwin (1982) p. 33.
18. Baker, K. 'What I. T. is all about'. *The British Journal of Administrative Management*, vol. 32, no. 9/10, December 1982/January 1983, pp. 293–4.
19. See, for example, Atkinson, P. 'The Impact of Information Technology and Office Automation on Administrative Management', *British Journal of Administrative Management*, vol. 35, no. 3, June 1985, pp. 100–5.
20. Thompson, L. 'New Office Technology', Work Research Unit Occasional Paper no. 34, Department of Employment, April 1985.
21. Mintzberg, H. *The Structuring of Organizations*, Prentice-Hall (1979) p. 3.
22. Woodward, J. *Industrial Organization: Theory and Practice*, Second edition, Oxford University Press (1980).
23. Ibid., p. 113.
24. Urwick, L. *Notes on the Theory of Organization*, American Management Association (1952).
25. March, J. G. and Simon, H. A. *Organizations*, Wiley (1958) p. 29.

26. Brech, E. F. L. *Organisation: The Framework of Management*, Second edition, Longman (1965).

27. Graicunas, V. A. 'Relationship in Organization', in *Papers on the Science of Administration*, University of Columbia (1937).

28. Woodward, J. *Industrial Organization: Theory and Practice*, Second edition, Oxford University Press (1980).

29. Ibid.

30. See, for example: Brech, E. F. L. *Organisation: The Framework of Management*, Second edition. Longman (1965).

31. Mintzberg, H. *The Structuring of Organizations*. Prentice-Hall (1979) p. 169.

32. Adapted from Kolondy, H. F. 'Managing in a Matrix'. *Business Horizons*, March/April 1981 pp. 17–24.

33. Gray, J. L. and Starke, F. A. *Organizational Behavior: Concepts and Applications*, Fourth edition, Charles E. Merrill (1988).

34. For a light-hearted account of the function of organisation charts, see: Tolputt, B. 'Up the Organization Chart'. *BIM Bulletin*, vol. 5, no. 2, 1972, and 'Further Up the Organization Charts', *BIM Bulletin*, vol. 6, no. 2, 1973.

35. Urwick, L. *The Elements of Administration*, Second edition, Pitman (1947) p. 38.

36. Ibid. p. 39.

37. Child, J. *Organization: A Guide to Problems and Practice*, Second edition, Harper and Row (1984) pp. 5, 6.

6. CONTINGENCY APPROACH TO ORGANISATION STRUCTURE

There are many variables which influence the design of the most appropriate organisation structure. The contingency approach rejects earlier views based on one best form of structure. Instead, it attempts to analyse structure in terms of relationships among its components, and the environment of the organisation. The 'fit' between structure, systems and style of management, and the behaviour of people, will depend upon (be *contingent* upon) situational variables for each particular organisation.

Objectives

To: (i) Explain the meaning and nature of the contingency approach;
(ii) Contrast the contingency approach with earlier approaches to organisation and management;
(iii) Examine main contingency models and assess their implication for management;
(iv) Analyse structure in terms of relationships among its components and the environment of the organisation;
(v) Evaluate the relevance and practical value of the contingency approach;
(vi) Recognise the importance of situational variables for organisational design;
(vii) Appreciate the importance of human nature and what may happen in practice in organisations.

THE MEANING AND NATURE OF THE CONTINGENCY APPROACH

Both the classical and human relations approaches to organisation and management believed in one best form of structure and tended to concentrate on limited aspects of organisation. Both approaches also tended to study the organisation in isolation from its environment.

The *classical approach* focused attention on the formal structure, technical requirements of the organisation and general sets of principles. There was an assumption of rational and logical behaviour. The identification of general objectives and the clarification of purposes and responsibilities at all levels of the organisation would lead to the most effective structure. Bureaucracy, as a sub-group of the classical approach, views the structure of the organisation in terms of specialisation, hierarchy of authority, system of rules and impersonality.

The *human relations approach* focused attention on the informal organisation, and on the psychological and social needs of people at work. The neo-human relations writers concentrated on the personal adjustment of individuals within the structure of the organisation. Members were assumed to be committed to achieving the goals of the organisation. Attention was given to design of a structure which removed alienating aspects of work and restrictions on effective performance.

The *open systems view* of organisation and management recognised the importance of the environment. The contingency approach can be seen as an extension of the systems approach and goes a stage further in relating the environment to specific structures of organisation.

The contingency approach

The contingency approach takes the view that there is no one best, universal structure and that there are a large number of variables, or situational factors, which influence organisational design and performance. *Hunt* explains the concept of contingency as follows:

> The concept of contingency also implies that there is no one, absolute 'best' design; rather, there is a multitude of possibilities and the best or preferred choice will be contingent on the situation being analysed. Universal models designed to suit all situations are therefore rejected. And this is consistent with the fact that most organizations are networks of a variety of bits of design rather than conforming, as one entity, to a particular model. So we might find units of bureaucracy, units of matrix structures, units with project teams, units with extremely loose, almost *ad hoc* structures – and all of these within, say, the same oil company. In this sense, the contingency theorists merely reflected the findings of hundreds of researchers. There are common elements in the hierarchies of different organizations but there are also very many differences peculiar to the local situation.[1]

The most appropriate structure is dependent, therefore, upon the contingencies of the situation for each individual organisation. These situational factors account for variations in the structure of different organisations.

Situational factors

The contingency approach can be seen as a form of 'if–then' matrix relationship.[2] *If* certain situational factors exist, *then* certain variables in organisation structure and systems of management are most appropriate. A simplified illustration of contingency relationships is given in Fig. 6.1.

Situational factors may be identified in a number of ways. The more obvious bases for comparison include the type of organisation and its purpose (which was discussed in Chapter 3); the characteristics of the members of the organisation such as their abilities, skills and experience and their needs and motivations. Other important variables are size, technology and environment. A number of studies have been carried out into the extent to which these contingency factors influence organisational design and effectiveness.

Contingency models

Among the best-known contingency 'models' are those shown in Fig. 6.2.

SIZE OF ORGANISATION

The size of an organisation has obvious implications for the design of its structure. In the very small organisation there is little need for a formal structure. But with increasing size, and the associated problems of the

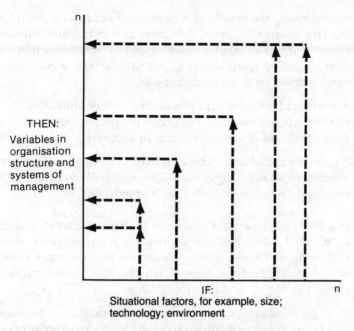

Fig. 6.1 The 'if – then' contingency relationship

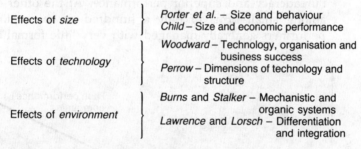

Fig. 6.2 Examples of contingency models

execution of work and management of staff, organisations may be divided into departments, or semi-autonomous sub-units; or in large business organisations distinct fields or industries. In larger organisations there are likely to be more formalised relationships and greater use of rules and standardised procedures. Studies such as those undertaken by the University of Aston[3] suggest that size has important implications for organisational design. Size explains best many of the characteristics of organisation structure, for example the importance of standardisation as a mechanism for co-ordination in larger organisations.

Size, however, is not a simple variable. It can be defined and measured in different ways, although the most common indication of size is the number of persons employed by the organisation. There is the problem of distinguishing the effects of size from other organisational variables. And there is conflicting evidence on the relationship of size to the structure and operation of the organisation.

Relationship between size and behaviour

Summarising the results of a number of studies on the relationship between the size of organisational sub-units and individual attitude and behaviour, *Porter et al.* found that in the larger size sub-units there appeared to be a clear, negative relationship to job satisfaction, absenteeism and staff turnover. Subject to three qualifications:

- that accident rates and productivity were equivocal;
- most studies involved rank and file employees; and
- the problem of distinguishing among types of sub-units.

Porter concluded that: 'The weight of evidence would seem to make a strong indictment against large-sized subunits, both from the individual's point of view and from the organization's standpoint'.[4]

Size and economic performance

In a study of the effects of size on the rate of growth and economic performance, *Child* acknowledges the tendency for increased size to be associated with increased bureaucracy. He argues that the more bureaucratised, larger organisations perform better than the less bureaucratised, larger organisations (*see* Fig. 6.3). Child found that:

> Much as critics may decry bureaucracy . . . the more profitable and faster growing companies, in the larger size category of 2,000 employees and above, were those that had developed this type of organization. The larger the company, the greater the association between more bureaucracy and superior performance. At the other end of the scale, among small firms of only a hundred or so employees, the better performers generally managed with very little formal organization.[5]

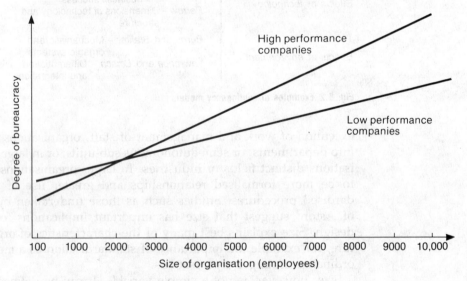

Fig. 6.3 Size of organisation, bureaucracy and performance
(From Child, J., *Organization: A Guide to Problems and Practice*, 2nd edition, Harper & Row (1984) p. 222.)

TECHNOLOGY

Two important studies under this heading are by *Woodward* and *Perrow*.

THE WOODWARD STUDY

A major study of the effects of technology on organisation structure was carried out by *Joan Woodward*.[6] Her work presents the results of empirical study of 100 manufacturing firms in south-east Essex and the relationships between the application of principles of organisation and business success. The main thesis was 'that industrial organizations which design their formal organizational structures to fit the type of production technology they employ are likely to be commercially successful'.[7]

Information was obtained from each of the firms under the four headings of:

(i)   History, background and objectives.
(ii) Manufacturing processes and methods.
(iii) Forms and routines used in the organisation and operation of the firm.
(iv) Information relating to an assessment of commercial success.

The researchers then studied differences in the structure, management, organisation and operation of the firms, and their efficiency and business success. The assessment of business success was made through an examination of profits made and capital investment in expansion programmes; together with other considerations such as rate of development in personnel and plant, fluctuation of shares on the Stock Exchange, level of salaries to senior management, reputation of the firm and staff turnover. Firms were classified into three broad groups: 'average', 'above average' and 'below average'.

Types of production systems
The firms were divided into different types of production systems, from least to most technological complexity, with three main groupings of:

- *Unit and small batch production*

  (i)   production of units to customer's requirements;
  (ii) production of prototypes;
  (iii) fabrication of large equipment in stages;
  (iv) production of small batches to customer's orders.

- *Large batch and mass production*

  (v)   production of large batches;
  (vi) production of large batches on assembly lines;
  (vii) mass production.

- *Process production*

  (viii) intermittent production of chemicals in multi-purpose plant;
  (ix)   continuous flow production of liquids, gases and crystalline substances.

The research showed that the firms varied considerably in their organisation structure and that many of the variations appeared to be linked closely with differences in manufacturing techniques.

Types of organisation structure
The researchers examined the organisation structure of the firms under three main types:

35 firms had essentially a *line* type of organisation.

 2 firms were organised *functionally* (as suggested by F. W. Taylor).

59 firms had varying degrees of *line staff* organisation.

(4 firms were unclassified.)

There was a trend for the line staff type of organisation to be developed highly in the middle ranges of the scale. The two firms with a functional type of organisation and fifteen of the firms with a predominantly line organisation were in the process production grouping. The other firms with line organisations were in the unit production grouping.

Eight firms which had a simple organisation structure based on line specialisation of basic task functions only were all in the 'average' or 'above average' success classification. Three of these firms employed less than 500 people, four employed between 500 and 1000 people, and one employed more than 1000 people. All firms were in either the unit production or process production groupings. No successful firms with large batch or mass production had this simple form of organisation structure.

Patterns of organisation and technology

Organisational patterns were found to be related more to similarity of objectives and production techniques than to size, type of industry, or the business success of the firm. Among the organisational characteristics showing a direct relationship to technology were span of control and scalar chain (which we have discussed in Chapter 5), percentage of total turnover allocated to wages and salaries, ratio of managers to total personnel, and ratio of clerical and administrative staff to manual workers. Details of levels of management and span of control are summarised in Table 6.1.

Table 6.1 Summary of levels of management and span of control.

Number of levels of management authority			
No. of firms	Type of production	Range of levels	Median
24	Unit and small batch	2 to 4	3
31	Large batch and mass production	3 to 8 or more	4
25	Process production	4 to 8 or more	6
Average span of control of first line supervisor			
No. of firms	Type of production	Range of span	Median
24	Unit and small batch	Less than 10 to 51–60	23
31	Large batch and mass production	11–20 to 81–90	49
25	Process production	Less than 10 to 31–40	13

(Adapted from Joan Woodward, *Industrial Organization: Theory and Practice*, Second edition, Oxford University Press (1980) pp. 52 and 69.)

Woodward acknowledges that technology is not the only variable which affects organisation but is one that could be isolated more easily for study. She does, however, draw attention to the importance of technology, organisation and business success.

The figures relating to the span of control of the chief executive, the number of levels in the line of command, labour costs, and the various labour ratios showed a similar trend. The fact that organizational characteristics, technology and success were linked together in this way suggested that not only was the system of production an important variable in the determination of organizational structure, but also that one particular form of organization was most appropriate to each system of production. In unit production, for example, not only did short and relatively broad based pyramids predominate, but they also appeared to ensure success. Process production, on the other hand, would seem to require the taller and more narrowly based pyramid.[8]

Principles of organisation and business success

There appeared to be no direct link between principles of organisation and business success. As far as organisation was concerned, the 20 outstandingly successful firms had little in common.

The classical approach appeared to fail in providing a direct and simple basis for relating organisational structure and business success. There was, however, a stronger relationship between organisation structure and success within each of the three main groupings of production systems. Twenty firms were placed in the 'above average' classification of business success – five unit production, five mass production, six process production – and the remainder with combined systems. Seventeen firms were classified as 'below average' – five unit production, six mass production, four process production, and two with combined systems.

It was found that within each production grouping the successful firms had common organisational characteristics which tended to be clustered round the medians for the grouping as a whole. Figures for those firms classified as 'below average' tended to be at the extremes of the range. It was also found that in terms of the *Burns* and *Stalker* analysis (discussed below), successful firms in the large batch production range tended to have a mechanistic management system, while successful firms outside of this range tended to have organic management systems.

Relationship between development, production and marketing

Another important finding of *Woodward*'s study was the nature of the actual cycle of manufacturing and the relationship between three key 'task' functions of development, production and marketing. The most critical of these functions varied according to the type of production system. (*See* Fig. 6.4.)

Unit and small batch. Production was based on firm orders only with marketing the first activity. Greater stress was laid on technical expertise, and the quality and efficiency of the product. Research and development were the second, and most critical, activities. Because of the need for flexibility, close integration of functions and frequent personal contacts, an organic structure was required.

Large batch and mass. Production schedules were not dependent directly on firm orders. The first phase of manufacturing was product development, followed by production which was the most important function, and then third, marketing. The three functions were more independent and did not rely so much on close operational relationships among people responsible for development, production and sales.

Process. The importance of securing a market meant that marketing was the central and critical activity. Products were either impossible or difficult to store, or capacity for storage was very limited. The flow of production

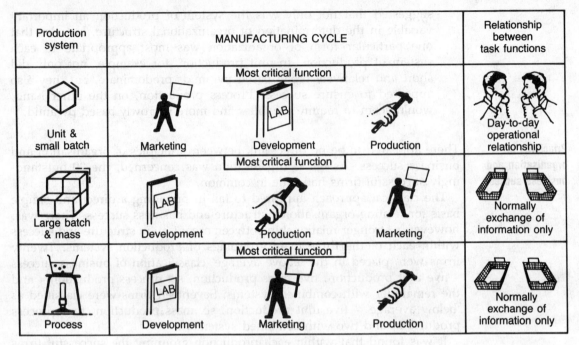

Fig. 6.4 Characteristics of production systems
(From Woodward, Joan, *Industrial Organization: Theory and Practice*, 2nd edition, Oxford University Press (1980) p. 128.)

was directly determined, therefore, by the market situation. Emphasis of technical knowledge was more on how products could be used than on how they could be made.

A subsequent study by *Zwerman* supported, very largely, the findings of Woodward. Zwerman's study involved a slightly different sample of organisations and was carried out in Minneapolis, America.[9] In other respects, however, the study attempted to replicate Woodward's work. Zwerman reached a similar conclusion, that the type of production technology was related closely to variations in organisation structure.

MAJOR DIMENSIONS OF TECHNOLOGY: THE WORK OF PERROW

The work by *Woodward* was extended by *Perrow* who drew attention to two major dimensions of technology:

* the extent to which the work task is predictable or variable; and
* the extent to which technology can be analysed.[10]

Variability refers to the number of exceptional or unpredictable cases and the extent to which problems are familiar. For example, a mass production factory is likely to have only a few exceptions but the manufacture of a designer range of clothing would have many exceptional and unpredictable cases.

The analysis of technology refers to the extent to which the task functions are broken down and highly specified, and the extent to which problems can be solved in recognised ways or by the use of routine procedures.

Combining the two dimensions provides a continuum of technology from

	FEW EXCEPTIONS	MANY EXCEPTIONS
PROBLEMS CANNOT BE ANALYSED	*Craft technology* Making a whole product probably in the same way each time, e.g. fine glassware	*Non-routine technology* E.g. psychiatric care in a mental hospital; manufacture of nuclear fuel systems
PROBLEMS CAN BE ANALYSED	*Routine technology* Manufacture of standard products; highly mechanised mass production	*Engineering technology* E.g. made-to-order machines such as electrical components; research consultancy

Fig. 6.5 Matrix of technology variables

(Adapted from Perrow, C., *Organizational Analysis: A Sociological View*, Tavistock Publications (1970) p. 78, and Mitchell, T. R., *People in Organizations*, 2nd edition, McGraw-Hill (1982) p. 32.)

Routine → Non-routine. With non-routine technology there are a large number of exceptional cases involving difficult and varied problem solving.

The two dimensions of variability and the analysis of problems can also be represented as a matrix. (*See* Fig. 6.5.)

Technology and structure

The classification of each type of technology relates to a particular organisation structure. *Perrow* suggests that by classifying organisations according to their technology and predictability of work tasks, we should be able to predict the most effective form of structure.

Variables such as the discretion and power of sub-groups, the basis of co-ordination and the interdependence of groups result from the use of different technologies. In the *routine type of organisation* there is minimum discretion at both the technical and supervisory levels, but the power of the middle management level is high; co-ordination is based on planning; and there is likely to be low interdependence between the two groups. This arrangement approaches a bureaucratic structure. In the *non-routine type of organisation* there is a high level of discretion and power at both the technical and supervisory levels; co-ordination is through feedback; and there is high group interdependence. This model resembles an organic structure.

ENVIRONMENT

Two important studies, those by *Burns* and *Stalker* and by *Lawrence* and *Lorsch*, focused not just on technology but on the effects of uncertainty and a changing external environment on the organisation, and its management and structure.

BURNS AND STALKER STUDY

The study by *Burns* and *Stalker* was an analysis of 20 industrial firms in the United Kingdom and the effects of the external environment on their pattern of management and economic performance.[11] The firms were drawn from a number of different industries: a rayon manufacturer; a large engineering company; Scottish firms attempting to enter the electronics field; and English firms operating in varying sectors of the electronics industry.

Mechanistic and organic systems

From an examination of the settings in which the firms operated, *Burns* and *Stalker* distinguished five different kinds of environments ranging from 'stable' to 'least predictable'. They also identified two divergent systems of management practice and structure – the *'mechanistic' system* and the *'organic' system*. These represented the polar extremes of the form which such systems could take when adapted to technical and commercial change. Burns and Stalker suggested that both types of system represented a 'rational' form of organisation which could be created and maintained explicitly and deliberately to make full use of the human resources in the most efficient manner according to the circumstances of the organisation.

The mechanistic system is a more rigid structure and more appropriate to stable conditions. The characteristics of a mechanistic management system are similar to those of bureaucracy. It is characterised by:

- the specialisation of tasks;
- closely defined duties, responsibilities and technical methods;
- a clear hierarchical structure;
- knowledge centred at the top of the hierarchy;
- the tendency for vertical interaction between superior and subordinate;
- the use of instructions and decisions by superiors on methods of operation and working behaviour; and
- insistence on loyalty to the organisation and obedience to superiors.

MECHANISTIC		ORGANIC
High, many and sharp differentiations	SPECIALISATION	Low, no hard boundaries, relatively few different jobs
High, methods spelled out	STANDARDISATION	Low, individuals decide own methods
Means	ORIENTATION OF MEMBERS	Goals
By superior	CONFLICT RESOLUTION	Interaction
Hierarchical based on implied contractual relation	PATTERN OF AUTHORITY CONTROL AND COMMUNICATION	Wide net based upon common commitment
At top of organisation	LOCUS OF SUPERIOR COMPETENCE	Wherever there is skill and competence
Vertical	INTERACTION	Lateral
Directions, orders	COMMUNICATION CONTENT	Advice, information
To organisation	LOYALTY	To project and group
From organisational position	PRESTIGE	From personal contribution

Fig. 6.6 Characteristics of mechanistic and organic organisations
(From Litterer, J. A., *The Analysis of Organizations*, 2nd edition, John Wiley (1973) p. 339.)

The organic system is a more fluid structure appropriate to changing conditions. It appears to be required when new problems and unforeseen circumstances arise constantly and require actions outside defined roles in the hierarchical structure. The organic system is characterised by:

- the contribution of special knowledge and experience to the tasks of the organisation;
- the adjustment and continual redefinition of tasks;
- a network structure of control, authority and communication;
- technical or commercial knowledge located throughout the organisation, not just at the top;
- superior knowledge not coinciding necessarily with positional authority;
- a lateral direction of communication, and communication based more on information and advice than instructions and decisions;
- commitment to the common task of the organisation; and
- the importance and prestige attached to individual contribution.

A summary of the characteristics of mechanistic and organic organisations is provided by Litterer.[12] (*See* Fig. 6.6.)

Location of authority Although the organic system is not hierarchical in the same sense as the mechanistic system, *Burns* and *Stalker* emphasise that it is still stratified, with positions differentiated according to seniority and greater expertise. The location of authority, however, is by consensus and the lead is taken by the 'best authority', that is the person who is seen to be most informed and capable. Commitment to the goals of the organisation is greater in the organic system, and it becomes more difficult to distinguish the formal and informal organisation. The development of shared beliefs in the values and goals of the organisation in the organic system runs counter to the co-operation and monitoring of performance achieved through the chain of hierarchical command in the mechanistic system.

Burns and Stalker point out that there are intermediate stages between the two extreme systems which represent not a dichotomy but a polarity. The relationship between the mechanistic and organic systems is not rigid. An organisation moving between a relatively stable and a relatively changing environment may also move between the two systems.

'Mixed' forms of organisation structure Many organisations will be hybrid – that is a mix of both mechanistic and organic structures. And often this is an uneasy mix which can lead to tension and conflict! For example, where a group of people engaged on a set of broad functional activities prefer, and perform best, in an organic structure; whilst another group tend to prefer a mechanistic structure and to work within established rules, systems and procedures.

The different perceptions of appropriate organisational styles and working methods present a particular challenge to management. There is need for a senior member of staff, in an appropriate position in the hierarchy and who has the respect of both groups, to act in a bridging role and to help establish harmony between them.[13] A typical example of a hybrid organisation could be a university or large polytechnic with differences in perception between the academic staff and the non-teaching staff. The non-teaching staff have an important function in helping to keep the organisation operational and working effectively, and may fail to understand why academics appear to find it difficult, or resent, working within prescribed administrative systems and procedures. The academic staff may well feel that they can only work effectively within an organic structure, and to tend to see non-teaching staff as bureaucratic and resistant to novel or different ideas.

Polytechnics may also tend to be more mechanistic at top management level with an apparent proliferation of committees and sub-committees, and because of their dealings with, for example, government bodies and local authority administrators.

The distinction between mechanistic and organic structures is often most pronounced between 'production' and 'service' functions of an organisation. An example of a hybrid organisation from the private sector could be a large hotel. Here the work tasks and operations of the kitchen (the production element) suggest that a more mechanistic structure might be appropriate. Other departments, more concerned with a service element, such as front office reception, may work better with a more organic structure.

LAWRENCE AND LORSCH STUDY

Lawrence and *Lorsch* undertook a study of six firms in the plastics industry followed by a further study of two firms in the container industry and two firms in the consumer food industry.[14] They attempted to extend the work of *Burns* and *Stalker* and examined not only the overall structure, but also the way in which specific departments were organised to meet different aspects of the firm's external environment.

Lawrence and Lorsch sought to answer the following questions:

(i) What are the differences in the environmental demands facing various organisations, and how do these demands relate to the internal functioning of effective organisations?

(ii) Do organisations operating in a stable environment make greater use of the formal hierarchy to achieve integration, and if so, why? Is it because less integration is required, or because decisions can be made more effectively at higher levels of the organisation or by fewer people?

(iii) Is the same degree of differentiation in orientation and departmental structure found in organisations in different industrial environments?

(iv) If greater integration is required among functional departments in different industries, does this influence problems of integrating different parts of the organisation and the methods of achieving integration?

Differentiation and integration

The word 'functional' was used to indicate major aspects or departments of the organisation such as research, production and marketing. The first stage of the study was an investigation of six firms in the plastics industry which were operating in relatively comparable, dynamic environments. The internal structures of the firms were analysed in terms of *'differentiation' and 'integration'*.

Differentiation describes 'the difference in cognitive and emotional orientation among managers in different functional departments' with respect to:

- the goal orientation of managers, for example the extent to which attention was focused on particular goals of the department;
- the time orientation of managers and relation to aspects of the environment with which they are concerned, for example longer-term horizons, or short-term horizons and problems requiring immediate solutions;
- the interpersonal relations of managers to other members, for example a managerial style based on concern for the task, or on concern for people relationships; and
- the formality of structure, for example the extent of mechanistic or organic design.

Integration describes 'the quality of the state of collaboration that exists among departments that are required to achieve unity of effort by the demands of the environment'. It is the degree of co-ordination and co-operation between different departments with interdependent tasks.

Lawrence and *Lorsch*'s view of integration was not the minimising of differences between departments and the provision of a common outlook. It was the recognition that different departments could have their own distinctive form of structure according to the nature of their tasks, and the use of mediating devices to co-ordinate the different outlooks of departments.

Different structures for individual departments

Given the possibility that different demands of the environment are characterised by different levels of uncertainty, then it follows that individual departments may develop different structures. The study of the firms in the plastics industry supported this hypothesis and *Lawrence* and *Lorsch* found a clear differentiation between the major departments of research, production and sales, for example:

- *Research* was more concerned with the long-run view and was confronted with pressures for new ideas and product innovation. The department operated in a dynamic, scientific environment and had the least bureaucratic structure.
- *Production* was more concerned with the here and now, short-term problems such as quality control and meeting delivery dates. The department operated in a fairly stable, technical environment and had the most bureaucratic structure.
- *Sales* was in the middle between research and production. The department was concerned with chasing production and had a moderately stable market environment.

The two most successful firms were those with the highest degree of integration and were also among the most highly differentiated.

Organisation structure and different environments

This view of differentiation and integration was confirmed in the subsequent study of firms in the container and consumer food industries. In this part of the study a comparison was made of both high and low performance firms operating in different environments. The aim was to discover what forms of organisation structure were required for different environments.

It was concluded that the extent of differentiation and integration in effective organisations will vary according to the demands of the particular environment.

- The more diverse and dynamic the environment, the more the effective organisation will be differentiated and highly integrated.
- In more stable environments, less differentiation will be required but a high degree of integration is still required. Differences in the environment will require different methods of achieving integration.

Integrating mechanisms

The mechanisms used to achieve integration depend on the amount of integration required and the difficulty in achieving it.

- In mechanistic structures, integration may be attempted through the use of policies, rules and procedures.
- In organic structures, integration may be attempted through teamwork and mutual co-operation.
- As the requirements for the amount of integration increase, additional means may be adopted, such as formal lateral relations, committees and project teams.
- When there is a high degree of differentiation, the use of assigned 'integrators' or possibly a separate unit with a number of integrators were suggested. Because they are not dominated by any particular perspective these integrators can help resolve problems of co-ordination and work programming between different departments.

Lawrence and *Lorsch* do not see the classical and human relations approaches as being out of date but as part of a continuum of patterns of organisation and management related to the environment in which they operate. The work of Lawrence and Lorsch is an extension of this continuum and their case for 'a contingency theory of organisations' has provided a further insight into the relationship between organisation structure and the demands of the environment.

EVALUATION OF CONTINGENCY APPROACH

The contingency approach draws attention to the situational factors which account for variations in the structure of organisations. It is more concerned with differences among organisations than with similarities. It rejects a number of assumptions of the classical and human relations approaches, and the idea of one best form of structure. For its part, however, the contingency approach tends to assume that organisational performance is dependent upon the degree to which the structure of the organisation matches the prevailing contingencies.

In order to operationalise the 'if–then' contingency approach, *Luthans* suggests a three-dimensional matrix model comprising: situational variables; management variables; and different levels of performance effectiveness.[15] If sufficient information is available to diagnose the situational variables and the management variables, the matrix could predict the resultant level of performance. However, Luthans suggests that it is still debatable whether this can be done in a meaningful way.

Criticisms/ limitations

As with other approaches to organisation and management, contingency theory has been subject to a number of criticisms or doubts about its practical value to management. Among the writers who have assessed the contribution and relevance of the contingency approach are *Child*,[16] *Dawson*[17] and *Mintzberg*.[18]

The criticisms, difficulties and limitations of the contingency approach usually revolve around seven main issues.

(i) *Causal relationship*

The nature of the causal relationship between organisation and performance. Most contingency models imply a causal relationship between structure, as an intervening variable, and performance as a dependent variable. It is probable, however, that certain factors such as the personal characteristics of management and staff, and changes in product markets and market conditions, influence performance independently of structure. These factors cannot be coped with just by changes in structure. In addition to the possible effects organisation has on performance, it is also possible that organisational performance is an influence on structural design. Managers may be stimulated to make changes to structure as a result of feed-back of information on performance.

Poor performance may result in less organisational slack and opportunities to make use of expensive integrating devices. *Child* suggests that it is possible the poor performance firms identified by *Lawrence* and *Lorsch* as not having solved the problem of integration were unable to do so because of lack of resources, existing conditions of poor performance, and the tendency to centralise decision making and increase control.

(ii) *Organisational performance*

Implicit in contingency theory is the notion that the fit among components of the organisation and situation variables is related to maximising organisational performance. However, organisational performance is multi-faceted and the measurement of performance applied in many of the contingency studies has not been precise. It is impossible to derive a single criterion for the appropriateness of the fit among various features of organisation and improved performance. (Recall, for example, the discussion on the fallacy of the single objective and the eight key areas of performance and results, in Chapter 4.)

(iii) *Independent variables*

The supposed status of the independent 'contingent' variables as the 'given' and beyond the control of members of the organisation is open to question. Large organisations may be in a position to exercise control over certain aspects of their environment. For example, an organisation may be in a monopoly position or have its own protected niche in the environment. Organisations may also be able to influence their environment through, for example, advertising or political pressure groups. Some organisations, therefore, may be less dependent upon their environment and in a more secure position compared with other organisations. Any mismatch in contingency factors is likely to have less severe consequences for survival and level of performance.

(iv) *Multiple contingencies*

Different patterns of contingency factors have distinctive implications for organisational design. Organisations face multiple contingencies and there is potential for multi-way relationships among the range of organisational variables. Different contingencies may result in the need for different patterns of structure (as with a hybrid form of organisation discussed above); for example, a department operating within a dynamic environment and demanding a more organic structure, within an organisation where other departments function within a more bureaucratic structure.

(v) *Planned change*

Contingency models of organisation fail to give sufficient emphasis to unanticipated consequences of planned change; for example, the effects of the introduction of new technology on the internal working of the organisation or on the social interactions among groups of people engaged in certain activities.

(vi) *Power factors*

Organisation structure is not necessarily determined only by impersonal contingency conditions, but also by what are referred to as 'power' factors. The pressure of external control – such as government control of public sector organisations; the political context; the power needs of various members and managerial preferences; the culture of the organisation and the power of social norms – also enters into the design of structure.

(vii) *Timing of organisational change*

Most organisations operate under conditions of constant change, and this raises the question of the frequency and timing of organisational change. Developing organisations cannot, without difficulty, change their formal structure at too frequent an interval. There must be a significant change in contingency factors before an organisation will respond. Changes in structure tend to lag behind situational change. There is, therefore, a degree of luck whether at any moment in time there is a good fit between structure and prevailing contingency factors.

Contribution of contingency theory

Despite the criticisms and limitations of contingency theory it has provided a further insight into our understanding of relationships among factors influencing the structure, management and operations of work organisations. An appropriate form of organisation will help prevent problems caused by unsuitable structures. The contingency approach has relevance in terms of, for example, division of work and co-ordination of activities; hierarchy and definition of responsibilities; methods of work; motivation and commitment of staff; and style and systems of management.

The contingency approach also draws attention to the importance of different structures for different activities of the organisation. The design of an organisation is an exercise in matching structures, systems and style of management, and the people employed, to the various activities of the organisation. If there is a mismatch, then problems can arise. *Parris* gives an example from the television programme 'M * A * S * H' (Mobile Army Surgical Hospital):

Activities that are concerned with keeping things going but work in unstable conditions is an area where mismatching can occur as they contain elements of work that could be made systematic and simplified but as a consequence of their need to react quickly to changes to systematisation could make them less flexible. *However* since they are often dealing with complex problems a degree of systematisation is necessary. An example of this would be the 4077th MASH where to meet the demands of treating emergencies in battle they need to react quickly. But to treat complex injuries with complex technology and maintain records etc, for the future treatment and other associated administration, a certain level of routine is necessary. Similarly when the unit is overloaded and necessary medical supplies are not available, considerable 'negotiation' and 'dealing' with other units etc is undertaken. The organisation that has evolved is a sort of Task Culture where everyone works as a team to process the work with easy working relationships etc, but it does have role elements in the efficiency with which paperwork is processed. It has power culture elements for Radar [the Company Clerk] to negotiate and bargain with other units and the unit commander has to use personal intervention to keep the unit going and protect it from the rest of the organisation in which it exists.

The problems of imposing an inappropriate organisational design exists in the shape of Majors Burns, Hoolahan and the occasional CIA agent. These represent the dominant role organisation in which the unit exists. Their attempts to impose military rules and procedures and impose the formal rank in the unit are seen as highly inappropriate, often farcical.[19]

Over-emphasis of differences

Robey suggests that modern contingency theory can contribute to a more successful organisation. It provides an increasing amount of empirical research, it defines variables ignored in earlier work, and it directs the attention of the manager to the contingencies to be considered in the design of organisation structure. However, the contingency approach runs the risk of concluding that 'it all depends on everything', and the greatest danger is the over-emphasis on differences between organisations and the exclusion of similarities.

If the contingency approach is to be useful in guiding organisation design it should not treat every situation as being unique. 'Rather it must strike a balance between universal prescriptions and the statement that all situations are different (which is really no theory at all). Thus, modern theory uses a limited number of contingencies to help explain structural differences between organizations.'[20]

ORGANISATIONAL PRACTICES

To conclude our discussion on the contingency approach to organisation it is convenient, here, to consider two sets of observations on the nature of human behaviour and what may actually happen, in practice, in organisations. Although these observations on organisational practice are presented in a satirical manner, they nevertheless make a serious point about the structure, management and functioning of organisations.

PARKINSON'S LAW

A major feature of Parkinson's Law is that of the 'Rising Pyramid', that is: *'Work expands so as to fill the time available for its completion.'*[21] General recognition of this is illustrated in the proverb, 'It is the busiest person who has time to spare.' There is little, if any, relationship between the quantity of work to be done and the size of the staff doing it. Underlying this general tendency are two almost axiomatic statements: (i) an official wants to multiply subordinates, not rivals; and (ii) officials make work for each other.

Parkinson goes on to give the following example. If a civil servant A believes he is overworked there are three possible remedies: (i) resignation; (ii) ask to half the work by having it shared with a colleague, B; or (iii) seek the assistance of two subordinates, C and D. The first two options are unlikely. Resignation would involve loss of pension rights, and sharing work with a colleague on the same level would only bring in a rival for promotion. So A would prefer the appointment of two junior members of staff, C and D. This would increase A's status. There must be at least two subordinates so, that by dividing work between C and D, A will be the only person to understand the work of them both. Also, each subordinate is kept in order by fear of the other's promotion.

When, in turn, C complains of overwork, A, with the agreement of C, will advise the appointment of two assistants, E and F. But as D's position is much the same and to avoid internal friction, two assistants, G and H, will also be recommended to help D. There are now seven people, A, C, D, E, F, G, H, doing what one person did before, and the promotion of A is almost certain.

People making work for each other With the seven people now employed, the second stage comes into operation. The seven people make so much work for each other they are all fully occupied and A is actually working harder than ever. For example, an incoming document comes before each of them in turn. E decides it is F's concern, who places a draft reply for C, who makes drastic amendments before consulting with D, who asks G to action it. But then G goes on leave and hands the file to H, who drafts a minute signed by D and returned to C, who revises the first draft and puts the new version before A.

What does A do? A could find many excuses for signing C's draft unread. But being a conscientious person, and although beset with problems created by subordinates both for A and for themselves, A reads through the draft carefully, deletes the fussy paragraphs added by C and H, and restores it to the format presented in the first instance by F.

To illustrate his point about the size of an organisation and the relative size of the administrative staff component, Parkinson gives the case of admiralty statistics relating to the Royal Navy between 1914 and 1928. During these years the capital ships in commission decreased by 68 per cent, and officers and other ranks in the Royal Navy by 31 per cent. But over the same period, the number of dockyard workers increased by 9 per cent, dockyard officials and clerks by 40 per cent and admiralty officials by 78 per cent.

Other features of organisational practice

Among other features of organisational practice that Parkinson discusses are: principles of personnel selection; the nature of committees; personality screen; high finance – and the 'Law of Triviality' which means in a committee that the time spent on any agenda item will be in inverse proportion to the sum involved; layout of the organisation's administration block; and 'injelitis' – the disease of induced inferiority.

Relevance of observations

Despite the light vein of Parkinson's writing, the relevance of his observations can be gauged from comments in the Introduction by H.R.H. The Duke of Edinburgh. 'The most important point about this book for serious students of management and administration is that it illustrates the gulf that exists between the rational/intellectual approach to human organization and the frequent irrational facts of human nature' and

> The law should be compulsory reading at all business schools and for all management consultants. Management structures solve nothing if they do not take the facts of human nature into proper consideration, and one of the most important facts is that no one really likes having to make decisions. Consequently structures may generate a lot of activity but little or no useful work.[22]

THE PETER PRINCIPLE

This is concerned with the study of occupational incompetence and the study of hierarchies. The analysis of a hundred of cases of occupational incompetence led to formulation of the 'Peter Principle', this is: '*In a hierarchy every employee tends to rise to his level of incompetence.*'[23]

Employees competent in their position are promoted and competence in each new position qualifies for promotion to the next higher position until a position of incompetence is reached. The principle is based on perceived incompetence at all levels of every hierarchy – political, legal, educational and industrial – and ways in which employees move upwards through a hierarchy, and what happens to them after promotion.

Among the many examples quoted by Peter are those from the teaching occupation.

A is a competent and conforming college student who becomes a teacher following the textbook, curriculum guide and timetable schedule, and who works well except when there is no rule or precedent available. A never breaks a rule or disobeys an order but will not gain promotion because, although competent as a student, A has reached a level of incompetence as a classroom teacher.

B, a competent student and inspiring teacher, although not good with paperwork, is promoted to head of the science department because of success as a teacher. The head of science is responsible for ordering all science supplies and keeping extensive records and B's incompetence becomes evident.

C, a competent student, teacher and head of department is promoted to assistant principal, and being intellectually competent is further promoted to principal. C is now required to work directly with higher officials. But by working so hard at running the school, C misses important meetings with superiors and has no energy to become involved with community organisations. C thus becomes regarded as an incompetent principal.

Means of promotion Peter suggests two main means by which a person can affect promotion rate: 'Pull' and 'Push'.

Pull is an employee's relationship – by blood, marriage or acquaintance – with a person above the employee in the hierarchy.

Push is sometimes manifested by an abnormal interest in study, vocational training and self-improvement. In small hierarchies, push may have a marginal effect in accelerating promotion; in larger hierarchies the effect is minimal. Pull is, therefore, likely to be more effective than Push. 'Never stand when you can sit; never walk when you can ride; never Push when you can Pull.'[24]

Synopsis

Earlier approaches to organisation and management believed in one best form of structure and tended to concentrate on limited aspects of organisation. The classical and human relations approaches also tended to study the organisation in isolation from its environment. The contingency approach, however, takes the view that there is no one best structure, and there are a large number of variables, or situational factors, which influence organisational design and performance.

The most appropriate structure is dependent upon the contingencies of the situation for each individual organisation. It is more concerned with differences among organisations than with similarities. The contingency approach can be seen as a form of 'if–then' matrix relationship. *If* certain situational factors exist, *then* certain variables in organisation structure and systems of management are most appropriate.

Situational factors may be identified in a number of ways and a number of studies have been carried out into the extent to which these contingency factors influence organisational design and effectiveness. These include the work of Porter and of Child (size of organisations); Woodward and Perrow (technology); and Burns and Stalker, and Lawrence and Lorsch (environment).

As with other approaches to organisation and management, the contingency approach has been subject to a number of criticisms or doubts about its practical value to management. However, despite the criticisms and limitations of contingency theory it has provided a further insight into our understanding of relationships among factors influencing the structure, management and operations of organisations. An appropriate form of organisation will help prevent problems caused by unsuitable structures. The contingency approach also draws attention to the importance of different structures for different activities of the organisation.

It is also necessary to consider the nature of human behaviour and what may actually happen, in practice, in organisations. One example of organisational practice is Parkinson's Law: 'Work expands so as to fill the time available for its completion.' Another example is the Peter Principle: 'In a hierarchy every employee tends to rise to his level of incompetence.'

Review and discussion questions

1. Explain what is meant by the contingency approach to organisation. How does the contingency approach differ from other approaches to organisation and management?
2. Discuss ways in which different types of production systems have implications for the design of organisation structure. Give examples relating to the 'production' system of your own organisation compared with that of some other organisation.
3. Contrast 'mechanistic' and 'organic' systems of management practice and structure. What is the significance of this distinction? Suggest ways in which your own organisation tends towards one type of system or the other.
4. What do you understand by a 'hybrid' form of organisation structure? What particular problems might arise with this form of structure? Where possible support your answer with a practical example.
5. Explain what is meant by 'differentiation' and 'integration' of the internal structure of an organisation. What are the implications of differentiation and integration, and what mechanisms might be adopted to achieve integration?
6. Summarise the main criticisms, difficulties and limitations which could be claimed of contingency theory.
7. Assess the positive value and contribution of contingency theory to the structure, management and operation of work organisations. Give your own examples of situational factors which are likely to account for variations in the structure and management of different organisations.
8. Explain your understanding of (i) Parkinson's Law and (ii) the Peter Principle as observations on the nature of human behaviour. What are the implications of these observations for organisational practice?

Practical assignment

In self-selecting groups of three or four, visit a work organisation of your choice.

(i) Investigate and make notes about:
   (a) the nature and main purpose of the organisation;
   (b) its size;
   (c) the nature of technology/'production' systems;
   (d) characteristics of the staff employed;
   (e) main environmental influences; and
   (f) any other relevant factors.
(ii) Obtain, or prepare, a chart depicting the structural design of the organisation.
(iii) Using your knowledge of the *contingency* approach, comment on the apparent effectiveness of the structure of the organisation and/or particular departments of the organisation. Identify what you believe to be good and bad examples of structure.
(iv) Explain, with supporting reasons, what changes to structure you would recommend in order to help improve organisational performance.
(v) Where appropriate, prepare a revised organisation chart.

Notes and references

1. Hunt, J. W. *Managing People at Work*, Second edition, McGraw-Hill (1986) p. 172.
2. See, for example: Luthans, F. *Organizational Behavior*, Fourth edition, McGraw-Hill (1985).
3. Pugh, D. S. *et al.* 'A Conceptual Scheme for Organizational Analysis', *Administrative Science Quarterly*, vol. 8, December 1963, pp. 289–315.
4. Porter, L. W., Lawler, E. E. and Hackman, J. R. *Behavior in Organizations*, McGraw-Hill (1975) p. 250.
5. Child, J. *Organization: A Guide to Problems and Practice*, Second edition, Harper and Row (1984) p. 221.
6. Woodward, J. *Industrial Organization: Theory and Practice*, Second edition, Oxford University Press (1980).
7. Dawson, S. and Wedderburn, D. Introduction to Woodward, J. *Industrial Organization: Theory and Practice*, Second edition, Oxford University Press (1980) p. xiii.
8. Ibid. pp. 69, 71.
9. Zwerman, W. L. *New Perspectives on Organization Theory*, Greenwood (1970).
10. Perrow, C. *Organisational Analysis*, Tavistock Publications (1970).
11. Burns, T. and Stalker, G. M. *The Management of Innovation*, Tavistock Publications (1966).
12. Litterer, J. A. *The Analysis of Organizations*, Second edition, Wiley (1973).
13. Wilkins, R. 'The Management Challenge of Hybrid Organisations', *Administrator*, vol. 7, no. 8, September 1987, p. 3.
14. Lawrence, P. R. and Lorsch, J. W. *Organization and Environment*, Irwin (1969).
15. Luthans, F. *Organizational Behavior*, Fourth edition, McGraw-Hill (1985).
16. Child, J. *Organization: A Guide to Problems and Practice*, Second edition, Harper and Row (1984).
17. Dawson, S. 'Organisational Analysis and the Study of Policy Formulation and Implementation', *Public Administration Bulletin*, 31, December 1979 pp. 52–68.
18. Mintzberg, H. *The Structuring of Organizations*, Prentice-Hall (1979).
19. Parris, J. 'Designing your Organisation', *Management Services*, vol. 23, no. 10, October 1979, p. 14.
20. Robey, D. *Designing Organizations*, Irwin (1982) p. 59.
21. Parkinson, C. N. *Parkinson's Law*, Penguin (1986) p. 14.
22. H.R.H. The Duke of Edinburgh Introduction to Parkinson, C. N. *Parkinson's Law*, Penguin (1986) pp. 9, 10.
23. Peter, L. J. and Hull, R. *The Peter Principle*, Pan Books (1970) p. 22.
24. Ibid. p. 56.

PART THREE

STAFFING THE ORGANISATION

7. STAFFING THE ORGANISATION

> Whatever the structure of the organisation, it has to be staffed with people of the right quality. The effectiveness of any organisation inevitably depends very largely upon the staff it employs. All managers are concerned with the success of the personnel function in their own department and for the management of their own staff. Managers much recognise the importance of a planned and systematic approach to staffing the structure, and to the recruitment and selection of staff.
>
> ### Objectives
>
> To: (i)   Explain the importance of, and main stages in, manpower planning;
>   (ii) Examine the process of job analysis;
>   (iii) Detail the main stages in a planned and systematic approach to recruitment and selection;
>   (iv) Assess different methods of staff selection;
>   (v) Examine interviewing style and skills of interviewing;
>   (vi) Suggest how the effectiveness of the recruitment and selection process might be evaluated;
>   (vii) Recognise the importance to all managers of effective staff selection.

THE CONCERN OF ALL MANAGERS

Most managers are likely to be faced with the frequent need to recruit and select staff. Larger organisations may, perhaps, have a designated personnel manager and specialist personnel staff with responsibility for the administration of recruitment and selection procedures. But this does not detract from the concern of all managers for the success of the personnel function in their own department and for the management of their own staff. It is only right and sensible, therefore, that managers and supervisors have at least some say in the appointment of their own staff or those staff whose work they have to supervise.

Unit managers/supervisors would be expected to consult with the personnel department and to seek specialist knowledge and advice. The recruitment and selection of staff can rightly be regarded as a specialist activity, but all managers and supervisors should be well acquainted with the basic procedures and skills involved. In smaller organisations it is likely that unit managers will have a greater responsibility for staffing the organisation.

The message for all managers is to recognise the importance of recruitment and selection; to assess the effectiveness of present procedures; and to improve methods, skills and techniques of selection. The manner in which staff are appointed is a major factor in determining the quality of product produced and/or service offered, and the behaviour and performance of the workforce, and in meeting satisfactorily the objectives of the organisation.

Top management have overall control of personnel policies and final responsibility for their success. The style and effectiveness of recruitment and selection are influenced by the underlying philosophy of top management and the attitude which is brought to bear upon the development and maintenance of a good working climate in the particular organisation.

Organisational context

Procedures for recruitment and selection must themselves be put into an organisational context. The prerequisites of an effective recruitment and selection policy include:

- *the clarification of corporate objectives*;
- *design of an effective structure* – the allocation of work and network of jobs – in order to achieve these objectives;
- *a system of manpower planning* – providing the link between objectives and organisation structure, and a framework within which personnel policies, including a systematic approach to recruitment and selection, are planned and operated.

MANPOWER PLANNING

In recent years increasingly more attention has been given to the importance of planning manpower resources as well as other economic resources such as capital, materials, machinery and equipment. At both the national and the organisational level it is essential that human resources are utilised as effectively as possible.

National manpower planning

The basic aim of manpower planning at the national level is to review the economic performance of manpower in different industries in line with anticipated future economic growth. Government action is geared towards overcoming problems of overstaffing/understaffing and the movement (redeployment) of workers accordingly. There is a wide range of activities undertaken by the Department of Employment and the Manpower Services Commission related to employment, training and enterprise programmes.[1]

Effective manpower planning at the national level, however, presents a number of difficulties.[2] But our concern here is with manpower planning at the organisational level, although clearly there are links with national manpower planning.

Organisational manpower planning

Manpower planning has been defined as: 'A strategy for the acquisition, utilisation, improvement and retention of an enterprise's human resources.'[3]

Whatever the nature of the organisation, manpower planning should not be regarded in isolation but as an integral part of the broader process of corporate planning. Manpower planning is linked to the development of the organisation as a whole, and should be related to corporate objectives and to an organisation structure capable of achieving those objectives.

The organisation will need to clarify the extent and scope of the manpower plan; the target date, that is the length of the forecasting period; the types of occupations and skills for which forecasts are to be made; and the amount of information and detail required.

Main stages in manpower planning

Whatever the scope and nature of the manpower plan, it is possible to identify four main stages. (*See* Fig. 7.1.)

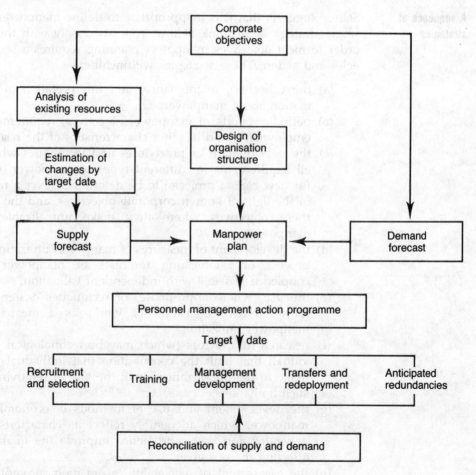

Fig. 7.1 Main stages in manpower planning

- *An analysis of existing staffing resources.* This requires an effective system of personnel records and a manpower inventory.
- *An estimation of likely changes in resources by the target date.* This includes consideration of changes and losses to the organisation; incremental improvements in staff performance and current programmes of staff development; and external environmental factors such as the likely availability of labour.
- *A forecast of staffing requirements necessary to achieve corporate objectives by the target date.*
- *A series of measures to ensure that the required staffing resources are available as and when required.* This reconciliation of supply and demand is the basis of the manpower plan.

The manpower planning process should also take account of broader environmental factors, such as: changes in population trends; patterns of employment, for example part-time workers; level of competition from other organisations for labour; changes in the educational system; government initiatives on employment, training or enterprise programmes, and employment legislation; developments in information technology and automation.

A sequence of strategies

Stainer suggests that it is inappropriate to define manpower planning as a single strategy or to think of it as concerned only with the long term. In order to meet objectives manpower planning requires a sequence of strategies and action. These strategies will include:

(a) the collection, maintenance, and interpretation of relevant information about manpower;

(b) periodic reports of manpower objectives, requirements and actual employment, and of other characteristics of the resource;

(c) the development of procedures and techniques which will enable all requirements for different types of manpower (including those for new capital projects) to be determined over a range of periods in the light of known corporate objectives; and the modification of these objectives where they make unrealizable demands for manpower;

(d) the development of measures of manpower utilization as part of the process of establishing forecasts of manpower requirements, coupled if possible with independent validation;

(e) the use, where appropriate, of techniques designed to result in more effective allocation of work, as a means of improving manpower utilization;

(f) research into factors (which may be technological, social, or individual) that limit the contribution that individuals or groups can make to the organization, with the aim of removing or modifying such limitations;

(g) the development and use of methods of economic evaluation of manpower which adequately reflect its characteristics as income-generator and cost, and hence improve the quality of decisions affecting the resource;

(h) the assessment of availability, acquisition, promotion, and retention, in the light of the forecast requirements of the organization, of individuals whom it has been established are likely to perform well;

(i) the analysis of the dynamic processes of recruitment, promotion, and loss to which an organization is subject, and the control both of these processes and of the organizational structure; so that as far as possible the maximum performance of individuals and groups is encouraged without excessive cost.[4]

Concepts of manpower planning

The concepts of manpower planning are basically straightforward and so are most of the methods involved. However, a number of more sophisticated statistical and quantitative techniques have been developed.[5] Computer programs are also available for more complex models of manpower planning. These techniques can be helpful but should be applied only as appropriate to the amount of detail and accuracy required. The real importance is in recognition of the need for effective manpower planning to suit the requirements of the particular organisation.

The value of manpower planning

Manpower planning involves considerable uncertainty and mistakes are bound to occur. However, the use of manpower planning can assist organisations to foresee changes and identify trends in staffing resources, and to adopt personnel policies which help to avoid major problems. A manpower plan provides the trigger for a personnel management action programme aimed at reconciling differences between supply and demand. It provides a framework in which action can be taken to help overcome staffing difficulties facing the organisation.

Effective manpower planning can help anticipate potential future difficulties while there is still a choice of action. Forward planning should enable the organisation to develop effective personnel strategies related to such activities as: recruitment and selection; training and re-training; management development and career progression; transfers and redeployment; early retirements; wage/salary levels; anticipated redundancies; and accommodation requirements.

Coupled with good communications, and meaningful consultation and participation with staff involved, including where appropriate union and/or staff association representatives, effective manpower planning should help alleviate potentially harmful effects to individual members of staff or to the performance of the organisation.

RECRUITMENT AND SELECTION OF STAFF

There are three important and fundamental considerations which should underlie the recruitment and selection of staff.

First, recruitment and selection should not be considered in isolation, that is simply finding someone to do a particular job, but in the context of the overall manpower plan and personnel management action programme. For example, it will be necessary to investigate the potential of the persons appointed for training, development and future promotion; and their flexibility and adaptability to possible new methods, procedures or working conditions.

Second, the need to consider not just technical competence but also, and equally important, how new members of staff will fit into the cultural and social structure of the organisation. There is nothing to be gained by appointing someone who although competent and technically efficient is unlikely to work in harmonious relations with other staff, customers or suppliers; or who is likely to upset the cohesiveness of work groups.

Indeed, if such is the case, there is plenty that the organisation can lose in terms of its overall performance and effectiveness. Sociability may be of particular significance in certain jobs or in certain types of organisations, but it is an important consideration in any work organisation. This is another reason for close involvement of the immediate head of department, and where appropriate the section leader/supervisor, in the recruitment and selection procedure.

Third, the necessity to comply fully with all legal requirements relating to employment, and to ensure justice and fair treatment to all applicants/candidates.

Staff turnover

One of the many adverse consequences of poor recruitment and selection is the possibility of a high level of staff turnover. A particular, although perhaps extreme, example is in the hotel and catering industry. A report from the Hotel and Catering Industry Training Board confirmed a high level of staff turnover in the industry. Gross annual turnover rates were identified as 55 per cent for craftspeople, 65 per cent for operatives and 94 per cent for supervisors.

Although much of the turnover is movement within the industry, this does not alter the frequency with which staff have to be replaced or the need for retraining in particular working practices. The report makes clear that

> the costs of high staff turnover cannot be ignored – not just the direct costs of recruiting and inducing replacement staff, but also the intangible costs of possible customer dissatisfaction caused by staff shortages, and the disruptive cost of managerial time spent on filling vacant posts.[6]

A very important additional intangible cost is the effect of high staff turnover on the morale, motivation and job satisfaction of staff, and on the level of organisational performance. Other industries may not face the same high levels of staff turnover but *all organisations* face potentially high costs, both direct and intangible, arising from ineffective recruitment and selection procedures.

So what can be done to select the best available staff in the first place and to retain them for a reasonable length of time? The need is for a planned and systematic approach.

A planned and systematic approach

When selecting staff, managers should ask themselves two basic questions.

(i) If you do not know what you are looking for, how will you recognise a suitable person when you see one?

(ii) If you do not know what you want your staff to do, how can you judge their ability to do a good job, effectively train or develop them, or assess their performance?

There are at least five basic stages in a planned and systematic approach to recruitment and selection.[7]

- The need to know about the job to be filled.
- The need to know about the type of person and qualities required to perform the job effectively.
- The need to know the likely means of best attracting a range of suitable applicants.
- The need to know how best to assess the applicants' likely suitability for the job.
- The need for induction and follow-up.

JOB ANALYSIS

Central to a planned and systematic approach is job analysis. This is the process by which you derive, first, a job description, leading to, second, a job specification.[8]

Job descriptions

A job description tells you about the total requirements of the job: exactly what it is; its purpose; what it entails; the duties, activities and responsibilities attached to it; and its position within the formal structure of the organisation. The scope of the job description, and the amount of detail it gives, may vary among different jobs and different organisations. An example of a possible list of contents, illustrated with reference to the hotel and catering industry, is given in Fig. 7.2.

Results-orientated job descriptions

There are many ways in which a job description can be prepared. For example, instead of jobs being described traditionally in terms of the duties, tasks or activities to be undertaken, job descriptions can be written in terms of results. This should help to make people feel important and to let them know why they do what they do, why their work is important to the organisation and what it is intended to accomplish.[9] (*See* Fig. 7.3.)

Job specifications

The job specification is an extension of the job description. It not only tells you about the job but also provides a blueprint of the 'ideal' person to do that job. The job specification details the personal attributes and qualities associated with successful performance of the job; for example, experience, technical skills, physical characteristics, health and appearance, motivation, intellectual ability, formal qualifications, personality and temperament, and any special requirements, such as the need for mobility. In drawing up the job specification regard must be given to the provisions of the Sex Discrimination Act 1975 and the Race Relations Act 1976.[10] Consideration should also be given to whether the job could satisfactorily be performed by a disabled person.[11] See, for example, the following extract from *Employment News*.[12]

Companies awarded for encouraging disabled people

A company whose bosses learnt sign language in order to speak to their deaf employees is among the 100 winners of the 1987 Fit for Work awards.

Job title (whether a new or replacement appointment)

Department/section and location

Wage/salary range

Duties and responsibilities – including *ad hoc* or occasional requirements.
It may be appropriate here to give precise and detailed information or it may only be necessary to set out the general scope and level of the job. Details may be quantified wherever possible. For example, an *average* of, or perhaps a *minimum* or *maximum* of: meals produced each day; rooms to be cleaned; covers per service; bills prepared each week for departing guests.

Duties and responsibilities can also be broken down into *approximate* percentage of time likely (or expected) to be devoted to each main activity over the *average* of, say, a week or a month. For example: % organisation of daily servicing and cleaning of guests' rooms; % training of kitchen staff; or % opening and distribution of incoming mail.

Specific limitations on authority
For example, not to authorise cash purchases above £X per item without prior approval of General Manager; not to accept payment by cheque for bills exceeding £X without authorisation of Head Receptionist.

Responsible to – that is, the job title of immediate superior.
(This superior would normally expect to be involved in the selection, induction and training programme for the new member of staff.)

Responsible for – that is, the number and job titles of direct subordinates.

Specific functional contacts – main lateral communications and working relationships with staff in other departments/sections.

Signature of head of department/section

Date job description prepared

Fig. 7.2 List of contents for job description

At a reception for the winners in London last month, employment secretary Norman Fowler emphasised the message – that disabled workers are good and reliable employees who are keen to develop their abilities and potential.

To qualify for an award employers have to put into practice seven policy guidelines based on a Code of Good Practice.

Designed to encourage and recognise a positive approach to employing disabled people, the award scheme has the support of the Government, the CBI, the TUC and the National Advisory Council on the Employment of Disabled People.

Other winners of the award include:

- A high-tech company in Ayrshire – **Digital Equipment Scotland** – employs 70 disabled men and women in a workforce of 1,000. The company spent £15,000 on new car parking facilities, ramps and toilets at its Ayr plant to help their disabled employees.
- **Lloyds of Stafford**, a Ford dealer, employs eight disabled people; makes every effort to retain them, and encourages applications from

Results-oriented vs. Duty-oriented style	
Patient Receptionist in a Dental Clinic	
Duty-oriented	Results-oriented
1. Greets patients and visitors and refers them to the appropriate area.	1. Helps patients and visitors by greeting them and referring them to the appropriate area.
2. Notifies provider (dentist or hygienist) of patient's arrival, reviews adherence to schedule, and reminds provider of excessive delays.	2. Ensures that patient appointments are on schedule by notifying provider of patient's arrival, reviewing adherence to schedule, and reminding provider of excessive delays.
3. Anticipates patient's anxieties, answers questions, and maintains an orderly reception area.	3. Comforts patients by anticipating anxieties, answering questions, and maintaining an orderly reception area.
4. Schedules appointments in person or by telephone.	4. Optimizes patients' satisfaction, providers' time, and treatment-room utilization by scheduling appointments in person or by telephone.
5. Enters and retrieves patient scheduling data on a computer terminal while maintaining confidentiality	5. Completes and updates scheduling files by entering and retrieving data on a computer terminal while maintaining confidentiality.
6. While stationed at the main desk: Receives and redirects all incoming calls. Operates the central paging and music system. Monitors the hazard warning systems and notifies the appropriate person of deviations. Opens and closes specified rooms and appliances while maintaining security precautions.	6. Provides centralized referral and control when stationed at the main desk by: Receiving and redirecting all incoming calls. Operating the central paging and music system. Monitoring the hazard warning systems and notifying the appropriate person of deviations. Opening and closing specified rooms and appliances while maintaining security precautions.
7. Responds to emergencies.	7. Assists patients in distress by responding to emergencies.
8. Performs other related duties which may be necessary from time to time.	8. Helps out when necessary by performing other related duties which may be necessary from time to time.

Fig. 7.3 Comparison of results-oriented and duty-oriented style of job description
(Reprinted by permission of the publisher, from 'Writing Job Descriptions That Get Results, by Roger J. Plachy, from *Personnel*, vol. 64, no. 10, October 1987, p. 58. © 1987 American Management Association, New York. All rights reserved.)

disabled people via the local job-centres. They also operate a Sheltered Placement Scheme for one of their workers.

• Company policy at **Harris and Company** in Worcester is to retain employees who become disabled through accidents.

For example, machinist Peter Dyer lost an arm in an accident 25 years ago. After a period of rehabilitation, he still works in the wood-cutting shop.

All these cases demonstrate some major aspects of the Fit for Work guidelines, including: an effective policy on the employment of disabled people; full and fair consideration for all disabled people who apply for jobs; and retention in suitable employment for employees who become disabled.

You are, of course, unlikely to find the perfect or absolutely ideal candidate. The job specification should therefore be written in a practical way and not unduly restrict the possible need for flexibility. The process of job analysis should provide you with a realistic set of objectives for the requirements of the job and the person to do it. It may be helpful to consider persons you have known to perform the job successfully and to analyse their attributes and qualities.

A widely used classification for the basis of a job specification is the Rodger Seven Point Plan (discussed below). The headings in this plan, which may be related to both the job and the individual, are: Physical make-up; Attainments; General intelligence; Special aptitudes; Interests; Disposition; Circumstances.

Difficulties and distastes

The job specification is even more meaningful if it includes the 'difficulties' and 'distastes' of the job.[13] Difficulties and distastes may often go together but this is not necessarily the case. Difficulties are those aspects of the job which are regarded as particularly demanding or hard to perform competently. Examples, again from the hotel and catering industry, might be the bar manager dealing with drunken or unruly guests; a waiter/waitress serving a large number of unexpected customers arriving together; a washer-up scrubbing heavy copper pans; a receptionist dealing with complaints or awkward guests; section heads operating within budget limits. For the 'right' members of staff, however, *certain* difficulties might be seen as an attractive feature of the job. Some people may enjoy what they see as the challenge or responsibility that the difficulties of the job present.

Distastes are those aspects of the job or working conditions which are regarded as tedious or unpleasant. Examples might be a waiter/waitress polishing silver before each service; a commis chef preparing the same vegetables for a standard menu; the kitchen porter emptying swill bins; a chambermaid cleaning baths or changing soiled bed linen; a waiter/waitress unblocking the restaurant toilet. For some people, however, the 'easier' aspects of the job might be disliked and seen as distastes; for example, because of the lack of variety, challenge or responsibility in the job, or because they prefer to be kept active.

Although these examples relate to the hotel and catering industry, the nature of difficulties and distastes for jobs in other organisations can readily be appreciated. And effective managers should be well aware of the difficulties and distastes of particular jobs in their own department of their organisation.

Concealing difficulties and distastes

There is little to be gained from concealing the difficulties and distastes of the job. If staff are appointed without full knowledge of the difficulties and distastes, or are not trained to deal with them, then once they find out what the job really involves they are likely to join the numbers who leave within a short period of time. This only adds to the 'induction crisis' and means starting the recruitment and selection process all over again! Even if staff do stay there is likely to be loss of goodwill, and an adverse effect on their attitude, job satisfaction and performance.

A study of insurance agents by *Weitz* showed that more realistic expectations about the job did not deter the number of applicants, but did reduce the six-month staff turnover rate.[14] One company introduced a revised recruitment booklet which gave attention to the less glamorous aspects of the job; for example, being turned down in a second interview after spending several hours preparing an insurance programme for a family, or being subjected to uncomplimentary and unwarranted comments about sales people.

Fifty agencies used the revised style booklet and another 50 agencies continued to use the original booklet which emphasised only the positive aspects of the job. As many applicants were recruited for the job with the revised booklet as with the original booklet. But the number of agents recruited with the revised booklet and still employed after six months (71 per cent) was greater than the number recruited with the original booklet and still employed after six months (57 per cent).

Staff are more likely to stay with your organisation for a reasonable time and provide a satisfactory standard of work if:

- the job and working conditions have been explained fully prior to their acceptance of the appointment;
- they understand exactly what will be expected of them including the difficulties and distastes of the job;
- their personal attributes and qualities match closely those required for successful performance of the job and/or potential future jobs; and
- there is an effective induction and training programme.

If candidates are not prepared, or are unable, to accept the difficulties and distastes then clearly they should not be offered the job. It is preferable, however, that unsuitable potential applicants do not apply in the first place or that unsuitable candidates decide to withdraw their application before the selection decision. The other side of the recruitment and selection process is the applicant's assessment of you and your organisation. *The more information given to applicants the more self-selection there will be.* From the job specification can be distilled the job advertisement and further particulars available to inquirers.

The importance of job analysis

From the job specification can also be drawn up the interview plan, including areas to be covered in assessing the candidate's willingness and ability to cope with the difficulties and distastes. Each of the headings in your interview plan can be related to the requirements of the job, and to the essential or desirable attributes and qualities looked for in the candidates.

The job specification is, therefore, the basis of the recruitment and selection process. It provides guidelines for the objective assessment of applicants and aids the all-important selection decision. Upon appointment, successful candidates can be given a copy of, at least, the job description part of the job specification. New members of staff might be asked to sign and return a duplicate copy as an indication of their acceptance of its contents and requirements.

The process of job analysis is not only an essential preliminary to effective staff selection; it is basic to the solution of most staffing problems. Job analysis provides the basis for performance review and appraisal, training, reward systems, staff development and career progression, and the design of working methods and practices. The study of difficulties and distastes helps provide a more thorough understanding of the jobs staff have to do and the working conditions under which they have to do them. Without such an understanding you are less able to assess the true performance of staff, including recognition of the shirkers and fiddlers.

A carefully prepared job specification is a focus for describing the requirements of the job, the working conditions, and the personal attributes and qualities necessary for successful performance. Any significant changes in the requirements of the job or the person to do it can be used as the basis for review of wage/salary rates, promotion prospects or training needs. Once agreed with the member of staff these changes can be formalised by incorporating them in a revised job specification.

ATTRACTING SUITABLE APPLICANTS

It is clearly important to know where suitable applicants are likely to be found, how best to make contact with them and to secure their application. This involves a thorough knowledge of sources of labour and methods of recruitment. The most appropriate means of attracting suitable applicants will depend upon the nature of the organisation, the position to be filled, and possibly the urgency of the need to make the appointment.

Among potential sources to be considered are: employment service agencies; universities, colleges and schools; private employment agencies;[15] professional appointments registers; personal introductions; and, of course, advertising. Vacancies may be advertised in the national and/or local press, professional or trade journals, and possibly on local commercial radio and television. Exhibitions and career conventions can also be considered under this heading. With advertising, not only is the choice of media important, but so also is the design, layout and content of the advertisement.

Application form The question of letters of application and/or specially designed, standard application forms, and preliminary, informal interviews must also be considered. Again, procedures will vary from organisation to organisation, and possibly with the nature of the vacancy. A common procedure is to invite inquirers to complete a standard application form (often, and preferably, typewritten) accompanied by a short, handwritten letter of application. Where appropriate a curriculum vitae (c.v.) may also be requested. Note Marks and Spencer's use of a computer program to screen application forms (see appendix to this chapter.)

METHODS OF SELECTION

Methods of selection involve the short-listing of applicants, collecting information (provided by other people) about the applicants, and the design and preparation of the selection process. The drawing up of the short-list can be undertaken by comparing applications against the information provided by job analysis, and consideration of the number of potentially suitable people applying for the position. After short-listing, selected applicants are referred to as 'candidates'.

Information provided about the applicants/candidates includes references and testimonials; university, college or school reports; service discharge documents; and possibly a medical report. Another possible source of information is from graphology – the analysis of the handwriting on the letter of application. Information provided by the candidates will come from the application form/letter of application, curriculum vitae and examples of past work, and during the course of the selection process.

There are a variety of methods which can be used in staff selection. These include: peer rating; in-tray exercises; selection tests and personality questionnaires; group exercises; and individual (one to one) or panel or board interviews. The choice, combination and application of methods should be appropriate to the nature of the organisation; the position, tasks and responsibilities of the vacant job; and the number and nature of candidates. *As an example, details of Marks and Spencer's revised management selection procedure are set out in the appendix to this chapter.*

Planning the selection process[16]

Whatever selection process is adopted, it requires careful planning and preparation. Selectors must plan their work commitments to give adequate time and undivided attention to the candidates, free from interruptions or distractions. Time should be allowed to read through carefully all the papers and documents. A check should be made on the physical environment – accommodation, seating, facilities; arrangements for reception of candidates; and, where appropriate, arrangements for tea/coffee and lunch.

The manner in which the selection process is conducted is doubly important. It should, of course, be efficient in its own right to ensure that every effort is made to reach the 'best' decisions. Equally important, however, is that for most candidates the selection process is the first point of contact with the organisation. *The other side of the selection process is the candidate's assessment of you and your organisation.* Candidates will tend to judge the organisation by the manner in which the selection process is conducted, looking upon this as an indication of how it manages itself and its staff, and whether they would wish to work for the organisation.

Peer rating

This involves the candidates nominating other candidates, usually on the basis of a sociability rating. Typical questions might be: 'Which of the other candidates would you choose to go on holiday with?' or 'If you had a personal problem (or a sensitive work problem) which of the other candidates would you choose to talk to?' Peer rating is clearly only appropriate if candidates are together long enough to become sufficiently well acquainted with each other; for example, if they are involved in a week-end selection programme. (Peer rating is also discussed in Chapter 14.)

In-tray (or in-basket) exercises

In-tray exercises are designed to simulate a state of affairs that participants can recognise as relevant to an actual working situation. Typically, the exercise presents a number of problems, and a range of material in the form of, for example, letters, memoranda, instructions and messages. Prepared plans of action may be disrupted by the receipt of further diverse communications. In-tray exercises require careful and detailed planning, and sufficient time needs to be allowed for their completion. They are perhaps normally more useful as a training device than in staff selection.

SELECTION TESTS AND QUESTIONNAIRES

Much has been written about the value of selection tests and questionnaires and they are subject to a number of criticisms. It should be noted that the word 'test' is often taken to refer to measures of intelligence, achievement and developed abilities, and aptitude for particular tasks. Measures of interests, social attitudes, emotional stability or traits of personality are usually referred to as questionnaires or profiles, or similar. Answers are regarded as common or uncommon, typical or untypical, rather than right or wrong, good or bad. The word 'test' is therefore usually avoided in such measures, such as for example in the Cattell 16 PF Questionnaire.

According to a joint British Institute of Management and Institute of Personnel Management survey of management selection, based on data from 335 organisations, tests were relatively little used at management level in British industries. And tests were not held to be a particularly useful method of selection. Where general intelligence and aptitude tests are used these appear to be applied most to computer staff. Personality 'tests' are more often used for sales and marketing posts.[17]

It does appear, however, that a number of large organisations do use tests as part of their selection procedures at management trainee level. For example, the Post Office uses a number of different aptitude tests related to the areas of work of candidates for appointment, including management entrants. All candidates called for testing are issued with a test description handout giving one or two examples of the different tests together with answers.

Objective tests which help to discover whether candidates are likely to possess the necessary skills for a job and to meet the demands made by the job can form a useful part of the selection process. Such tests help in the comparison of one candidate against another.[18]

Personality questionnaires

The general feeling about the value of personality 'tests' seems to have been well summarised by *Barrett*:

> A dismal history has been recorded by personality tests. There have been a few scattered successes with some modern techniques, but on the whole the typical personality questionnaire, test, or inventory has not proved to be useful. In many of them, the 'right' answers (which exist despite the naive disclaimer that there are no right answers) are so obvious that everyone comes out a model of healthy adjustment. But even if all applicants were to answer each question with complete candor, the value of their answers for predicting success would still be in doubt because the complexities of human personality are as yet poorly understood.[19]

The potential usefulness of typical behaviour tests in personnel selection and placement is also questioned by *Dunnette*: 'Though widely used as aids in making selection decisions, the evidence regarding their accuracy for predicting job behaviour is far from impressive.'[20]

There is no test of completely general application and it is necessary to undertake a detailed study of the position for which a candidate is going to be tested. 'A test is only useful when one knows exactly what one is testing, and the minimum scores which will be needed in order to carry out the job. This is a particularly complicated problem where personality variables are concerned.'[21]

Great skill is required in the administering of a 'personality questionnaire' and in the interpretation of results. This would probably entail the services of a consultant psychologist, which would add to the cost of the selection process. A suitable physical environment is also important. The possible reaction of candidates must be considered. Some might find any form of 'test' something of an ordeal or regard it as an unpleasantness.

Another important consideration in the possible use of selection tests is whether they contravene the provisions of the Race Relations Act 1976 by having a discriminatory effect on a racial group which an employer cannot show to be justified. A degree of cultural bias in an assessment procedure means that standard assessment techniques may be a potential source of unfair discrimination in employment decision making.[22]

Even when selection tests *are* used, they should be part of a comprehensive selection process and applied in appropriate circumstances to supplement the interview, never as a substitute for it.

GROUP EXERCISES

A group exercise is where a number of candidates are brought together and seen simultaneously by the selector(s). A number of group selection procedures are available, including discussions and debates, business games and problem-solving exercises. The group exercise is most effective when it simulates or resembles a practical 'real-life' situation which is reasonably representative of the task or type of situation that the person appointed might be concerned with in the organisation. The exercise might be guided or 'led' by a member of the selectors or by a nominated candidate, or it may be leaderless allowing the group to establish their own patterns of interaction.

Leaderless group discussions

A major possible criticism of 'techniques' such as leaderless group discussions (LGDs) is that they only highlight candidates who are proficient at that kind of activity rather than candidates who might be suitable for the job position. However, according to *Anastasi*: 'Validity studies suggest that LGD techniques are among the most effective applications of situational tests.'[23] The advantage of the group exercise is that it establishes a social situation. It enables candidates to demonstrate personal qualities and how well they are likely to get on with their peers. It provides a different slant on the candidates – as people in a working group.

The behaviour of candidates can be observed directly. A number of 'scoring' measures have been designed for LGDs (these are discussed in Chapter 14) and it is recommended that a set plan and observation sheet be used by the observer. This would assist in observing and rating each candidate's performance and allow a more meaningful interpretation of results. Note should also be made of body language, eye contact and other non-verbal clues. It is useful to have a short, informal discussion with the group at the end of the exercise. The observer could then explain any points arising from the exercise and candidates given a chance to make any comments.

Sociability is an important consideration in the appointment of staff. An appropriate group exercise can be a valuable part of the selection process. It could be used, for example, in the appointment of a member of staff who has direct contact with 'customers' or who is the focal point for complaints and criticisms; or for staff who face frequent problem-solving situations or difficult tasks to accomplish. Group exercises are also commonly used in the selection of management trainees.

THE SELECTION INTERVIEW

Despite its criticisms the interview is usually the central and indispensable element of the selection process, and the most widely used method of selection.[24] In order to make a fair assessment of candidates you must know what information is needed and how best to collect this from the interview. *A clear interview plan is necessary.* A popular example is the Rodger Seven Point Plan.[25] (*See* Fig. 7.4.) Another well-known classification is the Munro Fraser Five Point Plan covering:[26]

---

1. *Physical make-up*
   Are there any defects of health or physique that may be of occupational importance? How agreeable are appearance, bearing and speech?
2. *Attainments*
   What type of education? How well achieved educationally? What occupational training and experience had already? How well done occupationally?
3. *General intelligence*
   How much general intelligence can be displayed? How much general intelligence ordinarily displayed?
4. *Special aptitudes*
   Any marked mechanical aptitude, manual dexterity, facility in the use of words or figures, talent for drawing or music?
5. *Interests*
   To what extent are interests intellectual, practical–constructional, physically active, social, artistic?
6. *Disposition*
   How acceptable to other people? Influence on other people? Steady and dependable? Self-reliant?
7. *Circumstances*
   What are the domestic circumstances? What do the other members of the family do for a living? Are there any special openings available?

Fig. 7.4 The seven point plan
(Adapted from Rodger, Alec, *The Seven Point Plan*, 3rd edition, National Foundation for Educational Research (1970).)

(i) *Impact on others* – such as an individual's appearance, speech and manner.

(ii) *Qualifications and experience* – the knowledge and skills required by different types of work.

(iii) *Innate abilities* – the speed and accuracy with which an individual's mind works.

(iv) *Motivation* – the kind of work that appeals to an individual and how much effort the individual is prepared to apply to it.

(v) *Emotional adjustment* – the amount of stress involved in living and working with other people.

Interview plan

Many organisations have their interview plan/checklist. The important thing is that some suitable plan is used, and that the plan is appropriate to the desired characteristics of the candidates. Specific interview checklists may be drawn up for particular appointments. An example of a checklist and rating scale for trainee social workers in a local authority is given in Fig. 7.5. *However, interviewers should avoid the impression of just 'going through a list'.* Candidates should be encouraged to do most of the talking and asked questions that will encourage them to describe experiences and develop ideas. Information under each heading of the interview plan can then be assembled as it is encountered and not in any set order. At the end of the interview all points in the plan should have been covered adequately.

Panel interview

If a panel, or board, interview is used the plan can serve as a basis of the division of questioning among selectors. It enables a clear allocation to be made of which areas are to be covered by which interviewer and the part which each is to play in the selection interview.

An advantage of the panel interview is that candidates may be seen simultaneously by a number of people who have an interest in the appointment. This would enable all aspects of the candidate's application to be explored and suitability for the appointment considered from both the technical competence and the broader organisational viewpoints. Typically, for example, the panel might include a member of top management, the head of department, the immediate supervisor and a member of the personnel department.

A disadvantage of the panel interview is that it tends to be a formal affair and sometimes rather intimidating to some candidates. Each additional member on the panel can add to the difficulties of putting candidates at ease and encouraging them to talk freely.

Interview on the move

The traditional face-to-face interview can usefully be augmented by taking candidates round the organisation and conducting a two-way interview on the move. This will enable candidates to gain a fuller appreciation of the job, equipment and methods, and actual working conditions; to meet some of the staff and see them at work; and to ask further questions. The interview on the move will also aid the selectors' assessment of candidates by allowing them to observe what are likely to be more natural responses to actual situations.

X	1	2	3	4	5	Y
1. Good bearing and address						Unprepossessing
2. Health appears to be good						Doubtful if strong enough for social work
3. Quick in intellectual grasp						Slow in intellectual grasp
4. Expresses self well						Difficulty in expressing thoughts
5. Shows resource and initiative						Might have difficulty in coping with the unexpected
6. Personality seems warm						Seems cold
7. Appears tolerant						Inclined to be rigid
8. Response seems sensitive						Seems insensitive
9. Inspires confidence						Does not inspire confidence
10. Permissive						Inclined to be authoritative
11. Likely to get on well with colleagues						Might not be able to co-operate well
*12. Seems balanced and mature in relation to age						Seems immature
*13. Has strong sense of responsibility						Sense of responsibility doubtful

Please tick appropriate box

Fig. 7.5 Ratings of selection panel for trainee social workers
(1. X applies: 2. Tendency to X: 3. Average: 4. Tendency to Y: 5. Y applies)

*12 *Maturity of age*: This quality necessarily overlaps with others and might be regarded as a summing up, and an answer to the question – 'Is there promise of good all round personal development?'
   Important considerations appear to be acceptance of one's own abilities and limitations; tolerance of opposition; variety of interests; resilience, humour and integrity.

*13 *Sense of responsibility*: Used in relation both to professional work and training. Important qualities seem to be a steady sense of value, forethought, consistency, persistence. Might be regarded as the answer to the question: 'Is this candidate likely to accept and fulfil reasonable conditions of training and employment and give good measure?'

INTERVIEWING STYLE

Candidates tend to copy the mannerisms and postures of the interviewer(s). A seating arrangement which is comfortable and allows some indication of informality helps the candidates to be more at ease and reduces the element of confrontation.

Skilled interviewers will know how to change their interview style and form of questions according to the different behaviour of candidates and the extent of their social skills. The type of question asked influences the candidate's reply. By using the right form of question you are better able to control the interview and the candidate's behaviour.

Types of questions Interviewers should avoid the temptation to suggest possible answers to their own questions. They should also avoid 'leading' questions, that is questions which indicate the sort of response you expect to get and lead the candidate towards the 'right' answer. In most cases, a successful interview will contain a balance of open questions, direct or closed questions, and reflective remarks or questions.

Examples of leading questions

- Timekeeping is important in this job. Are you a good timekeeper?
- I guess you regret that now, do you?
- This is a very busy office and often we are short-staffed. Do you mind working under pressure?

Examples of open questions

- What made you decide to . . .?
- Tell me about . . .
- How did you happen to . . .?

Examples of direct or closed questions

- What grades did you receive in each of your subjects?
- Exactly how many staff report directly to you?
- How many months did you work with . . .?

Examples of reflective remarks/questions

These are helpful in correcting any misunderstandings and to show the candidates that they are being listened to attentively.

- You appear to prefer working in a busy office.
- So you are interested in all outdoor sports?
- It seems that you do not respond well to personal criticism.

The purpose of the questions Interviewers should probe the candidate and ask meaningful, searching and practical questions. Candidates should not be able to avoid particular questions or to give only a cursory reply. Interviewers should listen with care and note the way a candidate responds to a question. *Often this can tell you as much about the candidate as the actual answer to the question.* Candidates' reactions should be noted, and interviewers need to be responsive to both verbal and non-verbal cues.

All interviewers tend to have their own favourite questions, and sometimes very deep or philosophical questions are asked of candidates. For example: 'Tell me [pause] what do you do when you feel really lonely?' Usually such questions are avoided or the candidate tends to talk around the question, or to give only a superficial reply. The value of such questions seems doubtful, and in any case depends upon whether any meaningful interpretation can be placed on the answers given. If any question is worth asking in the first place, the interviewer should persevere and attempt to continue to tease out the information from the candidate.

The interview involves an interaction of personalities and the perception of other people. Bear in mind the possibility of perceptual distortions and errors (such as the 'halo' effect and stereotyping) which were discussed in Chapter 1.

Towards the end of the interview, the interviewer might be expected to do more talking in explaining conditions of employment and in answering questions the candidate has been invited to ask. It is important to remember the other side of the selection process – the acceptance of you and your organisation by the candidate.

THE SELECTION DECISION

The selection decision is all important and the culmination of the entire selection process. It should be as objective as possible and every effort made to reach the 'right' decision. This decision making is greatly assisted by job analysis, a clear interview plan containing meaningful comments, and a grading scheme.

The need for good reporting

If the selection decision is to be effective, *good reporting* as well as good interviewing is important. The use of a grading scheme, for example, might introduce some degree of objectivity. It would encourage selectors to rationalise their comments and bring some level of uniformity to their assessment of candidates.

The description attaching to each grade should be carefully laid out, and the grading system and how to use it well known to all selectors. An example of a grading scheme is given below.

> **A** *Outstanding candidate*. No weaknesses on technical competence or personal grounds. Could be appointed with confidence.
> **B** *Above average candidate*. Many strengths and no serious weaknesses. Could be appointed with reasonable confidence.
> **C** *Average candidate*. Strengths outweigh weaknesses. Could be appointed subject to any special comments noted on interview plan.
> **D** *Below average candidate*. Number of weaknesses. Appointment doubtful. Normally a rejection (but acceptance might be possible subject to circumstances).
> **E** *Definite rejection* (even if the only candidate). Weaknesses outweigh strengths to extent that appointment cannot be supported.

All five grades should be used and selectors should avoid the temptation to cluster candidates around the C grading. No pluses or minuses should be used.

It should always be borne in mind that there is the N *(number of candidates) + 1 option. That is that no appointment is made.* However much the pressure there is to appoint a member of staff, it is clearly very short-sighted to appoint someone who is not really considered suitable or who is 'the best of a poor bunch'. Despite the costs, effort and time involved in going through another round of the selection process, it is in the long-term interests of the organisation to persist until a suitable candidate is found.

Induction

Induction involves the introduction of a new member of staff to the environment of the organisation, and to its policies and practices. Effective induction is a continuous process covering the first few months at work but it can be viewed as an extension of the recruitment and selection procedure starting with the selection process.

The first impressions of an organisation and its managers are seldom forgotten. New members of staff face an unfamiliar environment and have to make a number of personal adjustments. A warm welcome, initial introductions, and a properly planned and designed induction programme will do much to reassure members, and aid their motivation and attitudes to the work performance.

COSTS OF THE SELECTION PROCESS

Cost is obviously a major consideration in any selection process. However, the costs should not be considered in isolation. They should be weighed against the costs of selection failure, either by the appointment of an unsuitable member of staff or by the rejection of a candidate who would have made a 'successful' member of staff. The financial costs of the selection process are immediately apparent and usually clearly identified, for example selectors' time and administrative expense. The contributions from an efficient and effective selection process and the benefits derived by the organisation are not readily apparent and less easy to identify.

Control is a vital part of a manager's job. Control over the performance of staff is not easy nor is it achieved without cost. The more efficient the selection process, the easier the process of control and the lower the effort and expenditure. Teamwork and co-operation are necessary ingredients of a good staff and are more likely to be achieved the higher the stability of the labour force. Better staff morale leading to improved work performance and increased goodwill will improve the quality of products produced and/or service offered and assist in meeting satisfactorily the objectives of the organisation.

In the long term the costs of improving the selection process must be more than justified in improving the effectiveness of the organisation. Mistakes in selection are expensive, not only in the possible effects on staff morale and performance, but especially now that there is increased job security as a result of government legislation. To keep mistakes to a minimum the need is for a planned and systematic approach to recruitment and selection.

EFFECTIVENESS OF THE RECRUITMENT AND SELECTION PROCESS

We have said that the contribution from an effective selection process and the benefits derived by the organisation are not always readily apparent nor easy to identify. Over a period of time, however, some quantified measures might help to give a possible indication of its success. For example:

- Staff turnover – especially in the short term or at the end of any probationary period of employment;
- Labour costs;

- Absenteeism/timekeeping;
- Errors in work;
- Breakages, scrap or waste;
- Accidents at work;
- Complaints, for example from clients or customers;
- Promotions/staff development;
- Discipline/grievance procedures;
- Dismissals.

Information might also be obtained from: feedback from candidates; staff attitude surveys; performance appraisal schemes; exit interviews. Other possible indicators might be: the number and quantity of applicants for positions in the organisation; the exercise of 'social' responsibilities, for example the employment of YTS staff, registered disabled people or ethnic minorities; full compliance with all legal provisions relating to employment.

However, it must be appreciated that it is always difficult to isolate a single variable. It is, of course, quite possible that a number of other factors, apart from recruitment and selection, contribute to, or are the main reasons for, favourable or unfavourable figures or indicators.

Basic principles

Drucker makes the point that there is no magic to good staffing (and promotion) decisions and no such thing as an infallible judge of people. 'If I put a person into a job and he or she does not perform, I have made a mistake. I have no business blaming that person, no business invoking the "Peter Principle", no business complaining. I have made a mistake.'[27]

Drucker goes on to suggest five basic principles for matching jobs and people.

- *Think through the job requirements.* Job descriptions may last a long time and remain unchanged for many years. It is important to look at the nature of the job and what is at the heart of the job.
- *Look at the number of potentially qualified people.* Formal qualifications are a minimum for consideration because their absence disqualifies the candidate automatically. In order to make an effective decision the manager should look at three to five qualified candidates.
- *Think hard about how to look at these candidates.* The central question is the strengths each possesses and are these the right strengths for the job.
- *Discuss each of the candidates with several people.* All of us have first impressions, prejudices, likes and dislikes. We need to listen to what other people think.
- *Make sure the appointee understands the job.* After the appointee has been in a new job for three to four months, he or she should be focusing on the demands of that job rather than on the requirements of preceding jobs.

A crucial determinant of the success of recruitment and selection is how well the new member of staff adapts to the requirements of the organisation and makes an effective contribution to the development of the organisation.[28] Despite difficulties in evaluation, this should be an ultimate measure of the effectiveness of the recruitment and selection process.

Synopsis

Whatever the structure of the organisation it has to be staffed with people of the right quality. Most managers are likely to be faced with the frequent need to recruit and select staff. Managers and supervisors should have at least some say in the appointment of their own staff or those staff whose work they supervise. Procedures for recruitment and selection must themselves be put into an organisational context. Manpower planning provides the link between corporate objectives and organisation structure, and is the basis of a personnel management action programme.

There are three important considerations which should underlie the recruitment and selection of staff: (i) the context of the overall manpower plan; (ii) how new members of staff will fit into the cultural and social structure of the organisation; and (iii) full compliance with all legal requirements. In order to select the best available staff, and to retain them for a reasonable length of time, the need is for a planned and systematic approach to recruitment and selection. Central to such an approach is the process of job analysis from which is derived, first, a job description, leading to, second, a job specification. The job specification is more meaningful if it includes the 'difficulties' and 'distastes' of the job.

It is important to have a thorough knowledge of sources of labour and methods of recruitment. There are a variety of methods which can be used in staff selection. The choice, combination and application of methods should be appropriate to the nature of the organisation, the vacant job and the number and nature of candidates. Whatever selection process is adopted, it requires careful planning and preparation. The other side of the selection process is the candidate's assessment of you and your organisation.

Group exercises and selection tests and questionnaires may be used to supplement the interview. Despite criticisms, the interview is usually the central and indispensable element of the selection process. A clear interview plan/checklist is necessary. If a panel or board interview is used the plan can serve as a basis for division of questioning among selectors. Skilled interviewers will know how to change their interview style and form of questions according to the different behaviour of candidates, and the extent of their social skills.

In most cases, a successful interview will contain a balance of open questions, direct or closed questions, and reflective remarks or comments. Interviewers should probe the candidate and ask meaningful, searching and practical questions. Interviewers should listen with care and note the way a candidate responds to a question. If the selection decision is to be effective, good reporting as well as good interviewing is important. The use of a grading scheme, for example, might introduce some degree of objectivity.

Cost is obviously a major consideration in any selection process. However, costs should be weighed against the costs of selection failure; the contributions from an efficient and effective selection process, and benefits derived by the organisation, should be taken into account. These benefits are not always readily apparent or easy to identify, but over a period of time some quantified measures might help to give a possible indication of the success of the selection process. However, there is no magic to good staffing decisions and no such thing as an infallible judge of people.

| Appendix | MARKS AND SPENCER plc – SELECTION PROCEDURE CANDIDATES FOR MANAGEMENT POSITIONS |

Research and design

Our Target Job for management recruitment is 4/5 years into the Company. Our Target Jobs are Deputy Commercial Manager, Personnel Manager, Administration Manager, Operations Manager. We expect all candidates re-cruited into management to have reached these levels within this period of time. We are not recruiting candidates who will reach a ceiling at supervis-ory level or assistant manager level.

To establish the selection criteria for the four management careers within stores we embarked upon a criteria setting exercise:

- First we interviewed 25 Managers (i.e. one level above the Target Job). From them we elicited a range of criteria related to successful performance on-the-job.
- From this information we designed a questionnaire listing 64 criteria with definitions.
- These questionnaires were sent to every Store Manager to complete on each of the four management categories.
- The information from all the questionnaires (nearly 500) was analysed by computer.
- The top 20 criteria were discussed with a working party who considered the needs of the business going forward and a list of 14 criteria was established.
- Following this we introduced a new approach to interviewing called Criteria Based Interviewing. Briefly this is a technical skill whereby inter-viewers are taught to ask questions relevant to the criteria. The inter-viewer will observe and then record the candidates' behaviour, the behaviour is then classified in relation to the criteria, and then finally evaluated. After all the criteria have been evaluated the yes/no decision is taken.
- Next stage was to re-design Selection Centres. We carried out a Job Content survey to identify the job tasks and situations relevant to each of the specific Target Jobs. From this we found there to be similarities in the way in which the different categories of management spend their time. In general the tasks and situations can be broken down into three main areas:

1–1 situations
Group situations
Analytical/Scheduling Work

- From this information we were able to design a Selection Centre that could be used to select all categories of management staff with our stores.
- We also knew from the survey the period of time in the centre to allocate to the various situations and the type of tasks that a candidate needed to handle within these situations.
- The last stage of the development work was to train a group of Assessors and a group of Chairmen to run the Selection Centres. All Assessors had

first been CBI trained, and all Chairmen had been CBI trained and Assessor trained prior to their Chairman training.
– Volume – in 1988 we will run 58 Selection Centres
We have trained 250 Interviewers
                     85 Assessors
                     25 Chairmen

The selection process

We have three sources of recruitment for management positions with stores.

– 'A' level entrants
– Graduates
– Job Changers

'A' level entrants

First Stage   – An Initial Interview in a store (by a CBI trained inter-viewer); the interviewer can be a Store Manager, a Personnel Manager or an Administration Manager. Before the interview the applicant will have a store tour.
Second Stage – A Selection Board. Here the candidate is interviewed by two CBI trained managers.

Graduates

Graduates usually apply to us through the milkround.

First Stage   – An Initial Interview in a hotel near to the university or sometimes on campus.
Second Stage – A Selection Centre. Each centre has 8 candidates, 4 Assessors and a Chairman, the centre runs from 12:00 noon in day 1 to 12:00 noon in day 2. Candidates work through 4 exercises plus an interview. The exercises are designed to give multiple observations of behaviour against our range of Selection Criteria. All exercises are relevant to on-the-job situations, and performance is measured against what would be required on-the-job. Successful candidates from centres are required to have a short store attachment before the offer is confirmed.

Job Changers (applicants with previous work experience)

First Stage   – An Initial Interview in a store followed by a store tour.
Second Stage – A Selection Board. Those interviewers who interview Job Changers are, in addition to being CBI trained, experienced in interviewing slightly older applicants and obviously they look for their evidence in relation to the criteria mainly from the applicants' previous work experience.

Application form

The initial stage of the selection procedure is the application form. This form is screened in Head Office. On the form the questions are designed to give the applicant the ability to show some evidence against some of the criteria. In addition to academic qualifications plus bio-data we ask for information relating to work experience plus leadership and responsibilities.

For the past 6 months we have been working on the design of a computer program to screen application forms. This system is now live. It has been designed using the knowledge of the experts who previously screened the forms. This is a fairer method as it enables uniformity of standards. It is essentially a screen to reject. Our main aim, at this stage, is to screen out those candidates who should not be selected for initial interview. The program has not been designed to highlight, from application form, those candidates who should be recruited into the business.

I am grateful to Mrs Sandra Fell, Recruitment Department, Marks and Spencer plc, for providing the above information.

Review and discussion questions

1. Why is the recruitment and selection of staff the concern of all managers in an organisation? What are the prerequisites of an effective recruitment and selection policy?
2. Explain the importance of, and main stages involved in, organisational manpower planning. What do you understand by a personnel management action programme?
3. Explain (i) the fundamental considerations which should underlie the recruitment and selection of staff; and (ii) the basic stages in a planned and systematic approach to recruitment and selection.
4. Central to a systematic approach to staff selection is the process of 'knowing the job and the person to do it'. Explain how you would ensure this process is carried out effectively in a large organisation.
5. Assess the main methods of staff selection, *apart* from the interview, and give examples of when each method might be most appropriate.
6. Draw up (i) a suggested selection interview plan; and (ii) a suggested grading scheme for reporting the interview. Make clear the nature of the appointment to which your interview plan and grading scheme refer.
7. Discuss the main points to bear in mind in adopting an appropriate interviewing style. Give your own examples of the different types of questions that might be asked.
8. Suggest how the management of an organisation might attempt to evaluate the effectiveness of its recruitment and selection process. Give practical examples relating to your own organisation.

| Case study 1 | SIXTH TIME LUCKY |

Pink Passion Products Ltd.

Scene: The pleasantly appointed office of Don Rennie, the Personnel Manager.

Players: The said Don Rennie – his secretary,. Shani Lewis – and a very ruffled and agitated Production Manager, Tony Grey.

Time: The present.

Don is discussing a job description with Shani when Tony bursts in, un-announced. He is waving a piece of paper in his hand.

Tony: He's done it. You wouldn't believe it was possible. Here it is, Crab-tree's letter of resignation. A record this time. He stayed six weeks.
(Don takes the letter and reads it to himself)

Don: I remember interviewing him when he came for the job. He seemed really keen. According to this letter, he's got a more interesting job – he didn't mention money. Poor old Tony. You're certainly unlucky with your quality-control men. This is the fifth one you've lost in a twelvemonth isn't it?

Tony: It's too bad, Don. I don't think we're getting the right sort of fellows applying for the job. Can't you make the advertisement more attractive next time so that we can have a better choice, at least?

Don: I think the trouble is we've made the job sound *too* attractive. It's a routine job – just checking the tubs. But we've got to have a qualified man in the job.

Tony: Do everything you can, Don, that's all I ask. This situation is getting ridiculous.

Don: You can't say I haven't tried. I did some calculations last time we advertised this job. We've spent £1200 on advertisements alone in the last two years.
(As Tony goes through the door, Shani brings out the Job Description)

Shani: Assistant Quality Control Manager – analyse ingredients in samples before they are used on the production line. M'm. Quite an important job. Some chemicals cause skin cancer don't they?

What advice would you offer Don Rennie and Tony Grey in this situation?

| Case study 2 | WESSEX COMPUTERS

Wessex Computers has been running for five years now, and it is still virtually a 'one-man business' though there are 20 employees. While the firm sells books, magazines and small 'micro' games, its business is predominantly in microcomputers. Staff thus spend their time in selling computers and persuading clients that package programs are applicable to their business or in providing software packages to suit individual require-ments. The employees are nearly all in the 20–25 age group, and very keen and interested in their jobs, obviously involved in learning a trade which has every prospect going for it in the years ahead. Every opportunity is taken to display their wares at computer shows and exhibitions and to help in running courses on micros in an effort to make people aware of the 'user-friendly' nature of the equipment.

The site of the main part of the business is in what was once a main shop-ping street but has now become bypassed, and is in fact a cul-de-sac. The premises consist of a small shop front with 600 sq ft of shopping area in which are displayed microcomputers, books, computer games, calculators and standard software. Behind is a workroom, and above more workrooms and office space, in all 3000 sq ft. Over the shop itself lived a tenant, who has just left the property so that another 1000 sq ft has become available. The proprietor hopes to use this to solve the storage problems and to create one large room which can be used for setting up a permanent training section. His idea is to charge customers a moderate fee so that their employees can be taught how to run their computers. The staff currently consists of the proprietor, a secretary/bookkeeper, three receptionists/assistants and seven programmers/customer support staff. As this is a small organisation and somewhat overworked the specific tasks are flexible and depend on individual preferences.

The other part of the premises is about five miles away in Embridge; three years ago Wessex Computers won a local 'Enterprise' competition run by the Corporation, for which the prize was this site rented at a reduced cost. It is used as working quarters for five programmers, two customer support staff involved in repairing and servicing the microcomputers and two administrative staff. Control of these staff and effective charging-out of their work to customers has not proved very satisfactory.

As far as Wessex Computers is concerned, some success has been achieved by lending out the microcomputers free of charge for about ten days or by renting them out at a minimal charge for a month or two so that customers have a chance to get acquainted with them. Ninety per cent of such clients end by buying the machine and to some extent the rental could be offset against the capital cost. The owner is considering going into the leasing business as potential buyers are worried about machines becoming quickly outdated; a financing company deals with the funding of this side of the business. Maintenance work has to be done at times, although most frequently problems are caused by either mishandling of floppy disks by the customers, or failure to read the instruction handbooks carefully. Staff has to spend about one or two hours with each customer teaching them to use the machines even though comprehensive instruction manuals are available.

Some six months ago, with everyone working particularly hard, the record keeping was neglected, and the overdraft increased rapidly. The bank became nervous and was only reassured when an independent accountant was called in to complete the year's accounts, and to produce a report and cash flow forecast for a few months ahead.

Among the accountant's remarks was the comment that the owner was working far too hard, for too many hours, trying to be sales manager, general manager and office manager. Obviously this pressure of work could not be maintained and some aspect of his work had to be shed. Since the least interesting part of the business for him was the 'paper work', and the most interesting was selling microcomputers, meeting people and solving problems with them, he decided to appoint an office manager to take control of office procedures, in the most convenient way.

Make clear any reasonable assumptions you feel are necessary.

(1) Produce a job specification for the appointment of the office manager.
(2) Prepare a press advertisement covering the vacancy and list other sources which could be used.
(3) Describe the methods of employment selection which could be used.

Notes and references

1. For a summary, see: *Action for Jobs*, Department of Employment, April 1986.
2. Bartholomew D. J. (ed.) *Manpower Planning*, Penguin (1976) Part Four.
3. Department of Employment *Company Manpower Planning*, HMSO (1974).
4. Stainer, G. *Manpower Planning*, Heinemann (1971) pp. 3–4.
5. See, for example: Civil Service Department *Some Statistical Techniques in Manpower Planning*, HMSO (1970).
6. HCITB Research Report *Manpower Flows in the Hotel and Catering Industry*, Hotel and Catering Industry Training Board, September 1984.
7. Mullins, L. J. 'Systematic Staff Selection', *HCIMA Journal*, no. 65, May 1977.
8. Developed from Mullins, L. J. 'Job Analysis – Know the Job and the Person to Do It', *International Journal of Hospitality Management*, vol. 4, no. 4, 1985, pp. 181–3.
9. Plachy, R. J. 'Writing Job Descriptions that get Results', *Personnel*, vol. 64, no. 10, October 1987, pp. 56–63.
10. For practical guidance, see: Commission for Racial Equality *Race Relations: Code of Practice*, July 1983.
11. For a summary of legal provisions and voluntary guidelines, see: Manpower Services Commission, *Code of Good Practice on Employment of Disabled People*, October 1984.
12. *Employment News*, Department of Employment newspaper, no. 61, January 1988.
13. Rodger, A. and Cavanagh, P. 'Personnel Selection and Vocational Guidance', in Welford, A. T. *et al.* (eds) *Society: Problems and Methods of Study*, Revised edition, Routledge and Kegan Paul (1967).
14. Weitz, J. 'Job Expectancy and Survival', *Journal of Applied Psychology*, no. 40, 1956, pp. 245–7.
15. See, for example: Page, B. 'Do You Use Your Recruitment Agency Correctly?' *British Journal of Administrative Management*, vol. 35, no. 2, May 1985, pp. 54–5.
16. Some of the ideas expressed are based on the author's study of the selection process for long-term volunteers with the United Nations Association International Service.
17. *Selecting Managers: How British Industry Recruits*. BIM Management Survey Report no. 49 / IPM Information Report no. 34. British Institute of Management / Institute of Personnel Management (1980).
18. See, for example: Toplis, J., Dulewicz, V. and Fletcher, C. *Psychological Testing: A Practical Guide for Employers*, Institute of Personnel Management (1987).
19. Barrett, R. S. 'Guide to Using Psychological Tests', in Fleishman, E. A. (ed.) *Studies in Personnel and Industrial Psychology*, Revised edition, Dorsey Press (1967) p. 58.
20. Dunnette, M. D. *Personnel Selection and Placement*, Tavistock (1966) p. 63.
21. Kingston, N. *Selecting Managers*, BIM Management Survey Report no. 4, British Institute of Management (1971) p. 22.
22. For example, see: Mottram, R. and Pearn, M. 'Can Selection Tests be Colour Blind?' *Personnel Management*, vol. 10, no. 6, June 1978, pp. 40–1.
23. Anastasi, A. *Fields of Applied Psychology*, McGraw-Hill (1964) p. 71.
24. See, for example: *Selecting Managers: How British Industry Recruits*. BIM Management Survey Report no. 49 / IPM Information Report no. 34. British Institute of Management / Institute of Personnel Management (1980).
25. Rodger, A. *The Seven Point Plan*, Third edition (1970). Originally devised for the National Institute of Industrial Psychology; now available from the National Foundation for Educational Research.
26. Fraser, J. M. *Employment Interviewing*, Fifth edition, Macdonald and Evans (1978).
27. Drucker, P. F. 'Getting Things Done: How to Make Good People Decisions', *Harvard Business Review*, vol. 4, July–August 1985, p. 22.
28. Tyson, S. and Fell, A. *Evaluating the Personnel Function*, Hutchinson (1986).

PART FOUR

MANAGEMENT AS AN INTEGRATING ACTIVITY

8. THE NATURE OF MANAGEMENT

Organisations can only achieve their goals and objectives by the co-ordinated efforts of their members and it is the task of management to get work done through other people. It is by the process of management and execution of work that the activities of the organisation are carried out. Management is an integral part of the people–organisation relationship. It is essentially an integrating activity which permeates every facet of the operations of an organisation. Management is fundamental to the effective operation of work organisations.

Objectives

To: (i) Explain the meaning of management;

(ii) Examine main activities, or functions, of management;

(iii) Analyse the essential nature of managerial work;

(iv) Contrast management in private enterprise and public sector organisations;

(v) Examine the nature of the personnel function as an essential part of the process of management;

(vi) Explain the work of a manager and outline empirical studies on the nature of managers' jobs;

(vii) Appreciate the importance of management to the effective performance of work organisations.

THE MEANING OF MANAGEMENT

Management is a generic term and subject to many interpretations. A number of different ideas are attributed to the meaning of management and to the work of a manager. In certain respects everyone could be regarded as a manager to some extent. Everyone has some choice whether or not to do something, and some control, however slight, over the planning and organisation of their work. But we are concerned with management as being responsible for the attainment of objectives, taking place within a structured organisation and with prescribed roles. This involves people looking beyond themselves and exercising formal authority over the activities and performance of other people.

For our purposes we can, therefore, regard management as being

- within a structured organisational setting;
- directed towards aims and objectives;
- through the efforts of other people;
- using systems and procedures.

Manager as a job title

Even within a work organisation you cannot identify, necessarily, a manager by what a person is called or by his or her job title. In some organisations there is a liberal use of the title 'manager' in an apparent attempt to enhance the status and morale of staff. As a result there are a number of people whose job title includes the term manager but who, in reality, are not performing the full activities of a manager.

On the other hand, there are many people whose job title does not include the term manager (for example group accountant, head chef, chief inspector, captain, head of a comprehensive school, production controller, district nursing officer, company secretary), but who, in terms of the activities they undertake and the authority and responsibility they exercise, may be very much a manager.

Drucker sees management as denoting a function as well as the people who discharge it, a social position and authority, and also a discipline and field of study. 'Management is tasks. Management is a discipline. But management is also people. Every achievement of management is the achievement of a manager. Every failure is a failure of a manager.'[1]

Other writers, however, take the view that management is not a separate discipline. The problem is identifying a single discipline which encompasses the work of a manager, or agreeing the disciplines that a manager needs in order to carry out effectively this work.

Management and administration

There is often confusion over different interpretations of the two terms 'management' and 'administration'. One of the main reasons for this confusion would seem to result from the translation of *Fayol*'s book *Administration industrielle et générale* from the French into English. In the original (1929) English edition there was a direct translation of administration, but in the wider republication of the book in 1949 the term 'management' replaced 'administration' in the title. In the introduction to the revised edition *Urwick* indicates regret at this change.[2] He refers to Fayol's use of the word administration as indicating a specific function which enters all tasks involving supervision of the work of others. It is not concerned with the status of those who exercise this function.

Urwick also expresses concern at the possible division between management being seen to apply only to business organisations, and (public) administration as applying to the same functions in public service organisations.

Dictionary definitions tend to see the two words as synonymous.

Management is sometimes referred to as 'administration of business concerns' and administration as 'management of public affairs'. There is clearly an overlap between the two terms and they tend to be used, therefore, in accordance with the convenience of individual writers. This confirms the feeling that although most people perceive a difference between the two terms this difference is not easy to describe.

Administration is still used sometimes to refer to the highest level of management (top management) and to the functions of establishing the overall aims and formulating policy for the organisation as a whole. The use of the term administration has been associated more popularly, however, with public sector organisations. But even in the public sector the term management is now used increasingly. This can be seen, for example, in local government with the publication of the Bains report of the study group appointed to 'examine management principles and structures in local government at both elected member and officer levels'. The report includes a chapter on 'Local government management – its nature and purpose' and makes frequent reference to corporate management, the management process, and the management team.[3]

There appears, therefore, to be growing acceptance of the term management as the general descriptive label and administration as relating to the more specific function of the operation of procedures used by management. Administration can be seen as taking place in accordance with some sort of rules or procedures, whereas management implies a greater degree of discretion.

For our purposes administration is interpreted as part of the management process, and concerned with the design and implementation of systems and procedures to help meet stated objectives.

Managers born or made? Management an art or a science? There is frequent debate about whether managers are born or made; or whether management is an art or a science. Briefly, the important point is that neither of these is a mutually exclusive alternative. The answer to either question is surely a combination of both. Even if there are certain innate qualities which make for a potentially good manager these natural talents must be encouraged and developed through proper guidance, education and training, and planned experience.

Clearly, management must always be something of an art, especially in so far as it involves personal judgement and dealing with people. However, it still requires knowledge of the fundamentals of management, and competence in the application of specific skills and techniques – as illustrated, for example, with developments in information technology.

THE PROCESS OF MANAGEMENT

The nature of management is variable. Management relates to all activities of the organisation and is undertaken at all levels of the organisation. Management is not a separate, discrete function. It cannot be departmentalised or centralised. An organisation cannot have a department of management in the same way as a department for other functions such as, for example, production, marketing, accounting or personnel. Management is seen best, therefore, as a process common to all other functions carried out within the organisation. Management is essentially an integrating activity.

The overall responsibility of management can be seen as the attainment of the given objectives of the organisation. Objectives are the desired end-results the organisation is striving to achieve. Within the framework of objectives, policy provides the guidelines for the operations and activities of the organisation.

Policy determines the manner in which the affairs of the organisation are to be conducted. The establishment of objectives and the formulation of policy rest with the board of directors (or their equivalent) and it is part of their responsibility for determining the direction of the organisation as a whole and for its survival, development and profitability. Clarification of objectives and policy is a prerequisite if the process of management is to be effective. But what does the process of management actually involve, and what activities does it encompass?

Management is a complex and discursive subject. Despite the widespread use of the term and the large amount written about the subject, it is not easy to find agreement on a simple yet comprehensive definition of management or of a manager. And 'management' is not homogeneous. It takes place in different ways and at different levels of the organisation. One approach, especially favoured by classical writers, is to analyse the nature of management and to search for common activities (or functions, or elements) applicable to managers in all organisations.

Common activities of management

One of the first, and most widely quoted, analysis is that given by *Henri Fayol*, who analysed the activities of industrial undertakings into six groups: technical (production, manufacture and adaption); commercial (buying, selling, exchange and market information); financial (obtaining capital and making optimum use of available funds); security (safeguarding property and persons); accounting (information on the economic position, stock-taking, balance sheet, costs, statistics); and managerial. (The term 'management' is a translation of the French term 'administration'.)[4]

The managerial activity is divided into five elements of management, which are defined as; 'to forecast and plan, to organise, to command, to co-ordinate and to control'. Fayol describes these elements as:

- *Planning* – (translated from the French *prevoyance* = to foresee, and taken to include forecasting) examining the future, deciding what needs to be achieved and developing a plan of action.
- *Organising* – providing the material and human resources and building the structure to carry out the activities of the organisation.
- *Command* – maintaining activity among personnel, getting the optimum return from all employees in the interests of the whole organisation.
- *Co-ordination* – unifying and harmonising all activities and effort of the organisation to facilitate its working and success.
- *Control* – verifying that everything occurs in accordance with plans, instructions, established principles and expressed command.

Principles of management

Fayol also suggests that a set of well-established principles would help concentrate general discussion on management theory. But he emphasises that these principles must be flexible and adaptable to changing circumstances. Fayol recognised that there was no limit to the principles of management but in his writing advocated fourteen.

(i) *Division of work* – the object is to produce more and better work from the same effort, and the advantages of specialisation. However, there are limits to division of work which experience and a sense of proportion tell us should not be exceeded.

(ii) *Authority and responsibility* – responsibility is the corollary of authority. Wherever authority is exercised, responsibility arises. The application of sanctions is essential to good management, and is needed to encourage useful actions and to discourage their opposite. The best safeguard against abuse of authority is the personal integrity of the manager.

(iii) *Discipline* – is essential for the efficient operation of the organisation. Discipline is in essence the outward mark of respect for agreements between the organisation and its members. The manager must decide on the most appropriate form of sanction in cases of offences against discipline.

(iv) *Unity of command* – in any action an employee should receive orders from one superior only; if not, authority is undermined and discipline, order and stability threatened. Dual command is a perpetual source of conflicts.

(v) *Unity of direction* – in order to provide for unity of action, co-ordination and focusing of effort, there should be one head and one plan for any group of activities with the same objective.

(vi) *Subordination of individual interest to general interest* – the interest of the organisation should dominate individual or group interests.

(vii) *Remuneration of personnel* – remuneration should as far as possible satisfy both employee and employer. Methods of payment can influence organisational performance and the method should be fair, encourage keenness by rewarding well-directed effort, but not lead to over-payment.

(viii) *Centralisation* – is always present to some extent in any organisation. The degree of centralisation is a question of proportion and will vary in particular organisations.

(ix) *Scalar chain* – the chain of superiors from the ultimate authority to the lowest ranks. Respect for line authority must be reconciled with activities which require urgent action, and with the need to provide for some measure of initiative at all levels of authority.

(x) *Order* – includes material order and social order. The object of material order is avoidance of loss. There should be an appointed place for each thing, and each thing in its appointed place. Social order involves an appointed place for each employee, and each employee in his or her appointed place. Social order requires good organisation and good selection.

(xi) *Equity* – the desire for equity and for equality of treatment are aspirations to be taken into account in dealing with employees throughout all levels of the scalar chain.

(xii) *Stability of tenure of personnel* – generally, prosperous organisations have a stable managerial personnel. But changes of personnel are inevitable and stability of tenure is a question of proportion.

(xiii) *Initiative* represents a source of strength for the organisation and should be encouraged and developed. Tact and integrity are required to promote initiative and to retain respect for authority and discipline.

(xiv) *Esprit de corps* – should be fostered as harmony and unity among members of the organisation is great strength in the organisation. The principle of unity of command should be observed. It is necessary to avoid the dangers of divide and rule of one's own team; and the abuse of written communication. Wherever possible verbal contacts should be used.

A number of these principles relate directly to, or are influenced by, the organisation structure in which the process of management takes place. Fayol's set of principles can be compared therefore with those given by Urwick and discussed in Chapter 5.

Management as a social process

Another well-known analysis is given by *Brech* who defines management as:

A social process entailing responsibility for the effective and economical planning and regulation of the operations of an enterprise, in fulfilment of given purposes or tasks, such responsibility involving:

(a) judgment and decision in determining plans and in using data to control performance and progress against plans;

(b) the guidance, integration, motivation and supervision of the personnel composing the enterprise and carrying out its operations.[5]

Brech identifies four main elements of management:

- *Planning* – determining the broad lines for carrying out operations, preparing methods by which they are carried out and setting standards of performance.

- *Control* – checking actual performance against standards to ensure satisfactory progress and performance, and recording as a guide to possible future operations.

- *Co-ordination* – balancing and maintaining the team by ensuring a suitable division of work and seeing that tasks are performed in harmony.

- *Motivation* – or inspiring morale. Getting members of the team to work effectively, to give loyalty to the group and to the task, to carry out properly their tasks, and to play an effective part in the activities of the organisation. With this general inspiration is a process of supervision or leadership to ensure the teams are carrying out their activities properly.

Other analyses

Many other writers have provided an analysis of the elements of management. At first sight these analyses may appear to differ in certain aspects, but on closer study they show a basic similarity. Debate on the inclusion or exclusion of a particular element of management tends to revolve round the use and interpretation of different terms, and the emphasis which is placed upon them.

For example, what *Fayol* calls *command* – maintaining activity among personnel and getting optimum return from employees – might be taken to mean what *Brech* refers to as *motivation* – getting members of the team to work effectively and to carry out properly the activities allocated to them. Brech does not use the term *organising* but this appears to be covered under the headings of *planning* and *co-ordination*.

Authority over subordinate staff

Based on his experience as chief executive of the Glacier Metal Company, *Wilfred* (now Lord) *Brown* defines the concept of a 'manager' in terms of someone who has more work than he or she can perform personally, who arranges for some of this work to be carried out by others, and who is accountable to a higher authority for the manner in which all of this work is carried out. Brown gives a boundary definition of a managerial role as:

> a role from which some work has to be delegated to subordinate roles. The occupant of the managerial role is accountable for his subordinates' work and must at least have authority to veto the appointment of persons to the subordinate roles, to insist that they be removed from these roles if they are unsatisfactory, and to determine which portions of his own work shall be carried out by each subordinate.[6]

This is a very demanding definition. Strict adherence to these requirements, and in particular the authority to veto the appointment of subordinates and to insist that they be removed if unsatisfactory, would rule out the majority of people who actually carry the title of manager in modern organisations. The definition does, however, remind us of the changing nature of the extent of the manager's individual authority over subordinate staff.

THE TASKS AND CONTRIBUTION OF A MANAGER

Another approach to describing management is given by *Drucker* who identifies three tasks, equally important, but essentially different, that have to be performed:

- fulfilling the specific purpose and mission of the institution, whether business enterprise, hospital, or university;
- making work productive and the worker achieving;
- managing social impacts and social responsibilities.[7]

Drucker then goes on to identify five basic operations in the work of the manager:

- *Sets objectives* – determines objectives and the goals for each area of objectives, and describes what needs to be done to achieve these objectives.
- *Organises* – analyses the activities, decisions and relations required, classifies and divides work, creates organisation structure, and selects staff.
- *Motivates and communicates* – creates a team out of people responsible for various jobs.
- *Measures* – establishes targets and measurements of performance which focus on both the individual and the organisation as a whole.
- *Develops people* – directs, encourages and trains. How well subordinates develop themselves depends on the way a manager manages.

These categories require a combination of analytical ability, synthesising ability, integrity, human perception and insight, and social skill.

Drucker argues that the traditional definition of management based on the responsibility for the work of other people is unsatisfactory and too narrow, and emphasises a secondary rather than a primary characteristic. There are people, often in responsible positions, who are clearly 'management' but who do not have responsibility for the work of other people.

A person's function and contribution may be unaffected by the number of subordinate staff. A 'manager' is someone who performs the tasks of management whether or not he or she has power over others.

> Who is a manager can be defined only by that person's function and by the contribution he or she is expected to make. And the function that distinguishes the manager above all others is the function no one but the manager can perform. The one contribution a manager is uniquely expected to make is to give others vision and ability to perform. It is vision and moral responsibility that, in the last analysis, define the manager.[8]

Other definitions

There are numerous other definitions of management. Many of these definitions reflect the influence of a particular approach to management thinking. *Simon*, for example, sees management as synonymous with decision making.[9] Other examples include such definitions as 'management is delegation', or 'the task of management is to create teams out of individuals'.

There are other definitions such as 'the responsibility of management is to achieve results', or 'management is the ordering and co-ordination of functions to achieve a given purpose', which tell us little about the actual process of management. These definitions may all be correct as far as they go, but on their own are too narrow or too vague to provide an adequate description of management.

ESSENTIAL NATURE OF MANAGERIAL WORK

The essential nature of managerial work is not easy to describe, therefore, as aspects which are common in many applications escape us in others.

However, if we look at how people at work actually spend their time we should be able to distinguish between those whose main occupation is the carrying out of discrete tasks and the actual doing of work themselves; and those who spend proportionally more of their time in determining the nature of work to be undertaken by other people, the planning and organising of their work, issuing them with instructions and giving advice, and checking on their performance.

'Managing' and 'doing'

By distinguishing 'managing' from 'doing' in this way we can see management as clarifying objectives and the planning of work, organising the distribution of activities and tasks to other people, direction of subordinate staff and controlling the performance of other people's work. This provides us with a convenient description and summary of managerial work as: clarification of objectives, planning, organising, directing and controlling. (*See* Fig. 8.1.) The degree of emphasis given to these different activities may vary

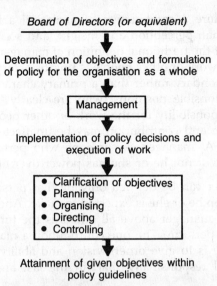

Board of Directors (or equivalent)

Determination of objectives and formulation
of policy for the organisation as a whole

Management

Implementation of policy decisions and
execution of work

- Clarification of objectives
- Planning
- Organising
- Directing
- Controlling

Attainment of given objectives within
policy guidelines

Fig. 8.1 Summary of essential nature of managerial work

widely, however, from one manager to another. Some managers are likely to spend more time on certain activities than other managers. The application of these activities reflects a wide range of management practice and managerial style.

There are, of course, many other ways of conceptualising the nature of managerial work, and relying on the 'classical' activities (or functions) of management might, to some, appear outdated. However, in an evaluation of the usefulness of the classical functions perspective for describing managerial work, *Carroll* and *Gillen* conclude:

> There seems to be some confusion about what managers do. . . . The classical functions still represent the most useful way of conceptualizing the manager's job, especially for management education, and perhaps this is why it is still the most favored description of managerial work in current management textbooks. The classical functions provide clear and discrete methods of classifying the thousands of different activities that managers carry out and the techniques they use in terms of the functions they perform for the achievement of organisational goals.[10]

The setting of objectives and formulation of policy takes place at different levels in the organisation, but as part of the same process. The board of directors, or similar body, establish objectives and formulate policy (direction) for the organisation as a whole.

Management is responsible for the implementation of policy decisions and the execution of work designed to meet these objectives. However, as mentioned in the discussion on levels of organisation in Chapter 5, it is not easy to distinguish between policy and its execution. In the same way that the board of directors are concerned with planning, organisation and control as part of their responsibility for the operations of the organisation as a whole, so the execution of policy will involve the manager in decision making and the clarification of objectives for subordinate staff.

Direction and motivation

Having already identified direction (of the organisation as a whole) as a responsibility of the board of directors it is tempting to use the term 'motivating' instead of 'directing' in our definition of the activities of management. This would avoid possible confusion over terminology. But is motivating an adequate description? It is certainly part of the manager's job to motivate staff but it involves more than this. Subordinate staff also need development and guidance. They need to be motivated to *perform well in the right areas*. The manager has a responsibility to see that subordinate staff are effective as well as efficient. Their efforts must be *directed* towards the achievement of given objectives in accordance with stated policy.

As we have seen, 'co-ordination' is often included as one of the activities of management. But the harmonising of effort to meet objectives (co-ordination) is not so much a separate activity; it is of a more general nature and involves all the activities of management. Co-ordination, like communication and decision making, is inherent in the process of management. It permeates all the activities of management and is descriptive more of how the work of the manager is carried out.

A popular view of management

Despite the view expressed by *Drucker*, one of the most popular ways of defining management is that it involves getting work done second-hand, that is *through the efforts of other people*. Managers are judged not just on their own performance but on the results achieved by subordinate staff. There are, then, many ways of looking at the meaning of management. The basic criteria must be a compromise between the ideas of some of the more lucid writers on the subject.

Stewart attempts to integrate the various definitions of management and summarises the manager's job, broadly defined as:

> deciding what should be done and then getting other people to do it. A longer definition would be concerned with how these two tasks are to be accomplished. The first task comprises setting objectives, planning (including decision-making), and setting up formal organization. The second consists of motivation, communication, control (including measurement), and the development of people.[11]

The definition of management as 'getting work done through the efforts of other people' may not perhaps meet all criteria, or satisfy everyone's perception of the nature of managerial work. It does, however, have the advantage of simplicity and focuses on what in reality is at the heart of effective management.

The importance of management

However the essential nature of managerial work is said to be, the importance and responsibility of management are widely, and rightly, recognised. Among the many writers emphasising this is *Drucker*:

> The responsibility of management in our society is decisive not only for the enterprise itself but for management's public standing, its success and status, for the very future of our economic and social system and the survival of the enterprise as an autonomous institution.[12]

MANAGEMENT IN PRIVATE ENTERPRISE AND PUBLIC SECTOR ORGANISATIONS

There are differences between management in the private and public sectors. These differences arise from particular features of public sector organisations, such as:

- the aims are concerned with providing a service for, and for the well-being of, the community rather than with just a commercial nature;
- the scale, variety and complexity of their operations;
- the tendency for them to be subject more to press reports on their activities;
- the political environment in which they operate, and in the case of local government, for example, the relationship between elected members and permanent officers;
- the generally high level of trade union involvement;
- the difficulties in measuring standards of performance of services provided compared with profitability;
- the demand for uniformity of treatment and public accountability for their operations; and
- the tendency for more rigid personnel policies, for example specific limitations on levels of authority and responsibility, fixed salary gradings based on general pay scales, long-term career structures and set promotion procedures.

A number of these features combine to result in increased bureaucracy within public sector organisations.

General problems of management

Both private enterprise and public sector organisations, however, face the same general problems of management. Both are concerned with the efficiency and effectiveness of their operations; with the clarification of aims and objectives; with the design of a suitable structure; and with carrying out essential administrative functions. Basic principles of management apply in any series of activities in any organisation. The common activities of management apply to a greater or lesser extent in both private enterprise and public sector organisations.

Based on an analysis of management development in central and local government, *Bourn* suggests management as a set of interrelated activities:

(i) forecasting, setting objectives and planning;

(ii) the definition of problems that need to be solved to achieve these objectives;

(iii) the search for various solutions that might be offered to these problems;

(iv) the determination of the best or most acceptable solutions;

(v) the securing of agreement that such solutions should be implemented;

(vi) the preparation and issue of instructions for carrying out the agreed solutions;

(vii) the execution of the solutions;

(viii) the devising of an auditing process for checking whether such solutions are properly carried out and, if they are, that they do in fact solve the problems for which they were devised;

(ix)   the design, introduction and maintenance of the organizational structures which are most appropriate for these activities;

(x)   the selection, training, development and management of the appropriate staff.[13]

Clearly, this set of activities is of equal relevance to management in business organisations, and can be seen as an extension of the generalised definition of clarification of objectives, planning, organising, directing and controlling suggested above. Although greater emphasis might be placed on certain activities this analysis helps demonstrate the degree of commonality between the basic process of management in both private and public sector organisations.

THE PERSONNEL FUNCTION

However the activities of management are identified, an essential part of the process of management is that proper attention be given to the personnel function. The effectiveness of any work organisation is dependent upon the efficient use of resources, in particular human resources. The human element plays a major part in the overall success of the organisation. Proper attention to the personnel function will help improve the efficiency of the labour force and the level of organisational performance.

In her study of industrial organisations, *Woodward* identified the personnel function not as one of the main 'task' functions which are related to the actual completion of the productive process or directed towards specific and definable end results, but as an 'element' function and an intrinsic part of the management process.[14] In the majority of organisations the personnel function does not normally have any direct accountability for the performance of a specific end-task. In certain organisations, however, such as employment agencies, personnel will be a task function. In other organisations, noticeably in the service industries, personnel can be seen as closely associated with a task function. For example, in the hotel and catering industry many members of the workforce are in direct contact with the customer and are seen as being involved in achieving the objectives of the organisation. People are part of the finished product for which the customer is paying. Customer satisfaction is likely to be affected as much by the courtesy, helpfulness and efficiency of the staff as by the standard of accommodation and food and beverage.[15]

Personnel policies   Whatever the nature of the work organisation, a manager achieves results through the performance of other people. Understanding the needs and wants of staff, and the nature of their grievances, goes a long way in motivating them to perform well. The efficiency of staff, their commitment to the aims of the organisation, and the skills and attitudes which they bring to bear on their work performance are fostered by good human relationships. Success in the field of human relationships stems from good personnel policy and practice, and an effective personnel function.

Personnel policy and the effective management of people are influenced by the philosophy of top management and the attitudes they bring to bear on relationships with staff, and the problems which affect them. Personnel policies should emanate from the top of the organisation. They should be defined clearly and communicated through managers and supervisors to staff at all levels.

Personnel policies should be based on underlying principles, such as the recognition of people's needs, stability of employment and opportunity for advancement, equitable levels of remuneration, good conditions of service, justice in treatment, democratic functioning of the organisation, and observance of all laws relating to employment.

In overall terms, personnel policies can be seen to embrace:

- designing an effective organisation structure;
- manning the structure with suitable people;
- defining work roles and relationships; and
- securing optimum working arrangements.

The objective is to develop and maintain a level of morale and human relationships which evokes willing and full co-operation of all persons in the organisation in order to attain optimum operational effectiveness. This is the total concept of the personnel function. A system of manpower planning will provide the link between objectives and organisation structure and clarification of personnel policies. Manpower planning provides a framework within which personnel activities are planned and put into operation.

Range of personnel activities   The range and scope of personnel activities are wide but they may be considered within the framework of the following main headings.

- Manpower planning and employment.
- Salary and wage administration including related reward systems.
- Organisational design.
- Education, training and development.
- Employee services, welfare, health and safety.
- Industrial relations.

Inherent in these activities is the need to give proper regard and attention to employment legislation and other legal requirements.

Smaller organisations may not justify a specialist personnel manager or a separate personnel department. But it is still necessary to have an effective personnel *function*, whether it be the responsibility of, for example, the owner, the manager or the secretary. Even in the smallest organisations, or in organisations where a specialist personnel department has not been established, there will be the need to recruit staff, to train them, to motivate them and to reward them, and to comply with the law relating to employment. Personnel work must still be carried out even if an organisation is too small to justify a separate personnel department, or chooses not to establish one.

In the larger concerns, where more time is taken up with problems of organisation and personnel management, there is greater need for a specialist member of staff to whom is delegated full-time responsibilities for advising top management on personnel matters and for the implementation of clearly defined policies which permit consistent personnel practices. For example, high staffing costs together with increased employment legislation suggest that greater attention must be given to the process of recruitment and selection. This is a central part of the personnel function.

Other examples include: pressures for a greater social responsibility towards employees through schemes of worker participation, including European Commission proposals on employee involvement; government involvement in employment legislation and incomes policies; the development of behavioural science; the role of industrial tribunals and the Advisory, Conciliation and Arbitration Service (ACAS); and the important role of trade unions and their officials. All suggest that industrial relations is an area of increasing specialisation.

The personnel manager

Even where personnel work is established as a separate, specialist function, it is not easy to define closely the activities of the personnel department. The range of responsibilities varies from one organisation to another, as do the title and status of the head of the personnel department (for ease of reference we shall use the term personnel manager) and position in the management structure. In very large organisations, personnel activities might be divided between two or more specialists, so that it would be possible to have, for example, a personnel officer, a training officer and an industrial relations adviser. Whatever the range of responsibilities, the personnel manager operates by consent, by delegated authority. How much consent is dependent upon the attitudes of top management, the role which they see the personnel specialist(s) performing and formal organisational relationships with 'line' managers.

Line managers

Line managers are departmental or unit managers with responsibility for the 'production' process – for the operational functions directly related to the purpose and aims of the organisation. They form a hierarchical level in the line of command throughout the organisation structure. Line managers report directly to higher management for the activities within their own department and for its operational efficiency. There is unity of command, a clear line of authority and a direct boss – subordinate relationship between line managers and their staff. Line managers are responsible for the management of their own staff and for the success of the personnel function in their own department.

However, although line managers are specialists in their own area of work, they are not necessarily specialists on personnel matters. Just as line managers need help and guidance on planning, organisation and control, and turn to specialists on legal and accounting matters and the use of the computer, so they will need help and guidance, and specialist advice on personnel matters. *Thomason* suggests that the personnel manager is probably the only specialist in the organisation whose role can be distinguished by the virtually exclusive concern with the management of human assets. All other managers will also have some direct concern with the management of physical assets.[16]

Relationship with other managers

The personnel manager, as a separate entity, operates in terms of a 'functional' relationship, that is as a specialist adviser on personnel matters and on the implementation of personnel policies throughout all departments of the organisation. It is the job of the personnel manager to provide specialist knowledge and services for line managers, and to support them in the performance of their jobs.

It is not the job of the personnel manager to manage people, other than direct subordinates. The personnel manager has no direct control over other staff except where a specific responsibility is delegated directly by top management, for example if nominated as safety officer under the Health and Safety at Work Act 1974. The personnel manager has executive authority for such delegated responsibility and for the management of the personnel department and its staff.

In all other respects the personnel manager's relationship with other managers, supervisors and staff of the organisation is indirect; that is, an advisory or 'functional' relationship. It is the line managers who have control and authority over staff in their departments, and who have the immediate responsibility for personnel management, although there will, of course, be times when they need the help and advice of the personnel specialist. There has to be co-operation and consultation between line managers and the personnel manager.

Line managers have responsibility for the management of their own staff. They have the technical expertise and a detailed knowledge of their own areas of work and working conditions of staff. The personnel manager is responsible for the interpretation and implementation of the organisation's personnel policies. The personnel manager sees the overall effect throughout all departments of the organisation, and is responsible for keeping a balance between departments and for a sense of fair play. The personnel manager has professional expertise and a specialist knowledge of personnel work.

Two levels of operation

The personnel function can be seen, therefore, as operating at two levels: the organisational level, and the departmental or unit level. (*See* Figure 8.2.)

At *the organisational level* the detailed involvement of several departments, available time and need for specialisation suggest that the personnel manager has a prominent role to play, and is the main executor of personnel policy acting in consultation with, and taking advice from, line managers.

At *the departmental or unit level* line managers may assume the prominent role for day-to-day personnel matters with the personnel manager as adviser, and if necessary as arbitrator.

On this basis the personnel manager would be concerned mainly with the broader aspects of personnel policies which affect staff generally or the organisation as a whole, such as: manpower planning; job analysis; systems of recruitment and selection; induction; problems of labour turnover; consultations with trade union representatives; compliance with the law relating to employment; maintaining records and statistics; and liaison with outside bodies such as ACAS, training boards, professional associations and wages councils.

Every line manager a personnel manager

Line managers would be more concerned, at least in the first instance, with operational aspects of personnel activities within their own departments, such as: the organisation of work and allocation of duties; minor disciplinary

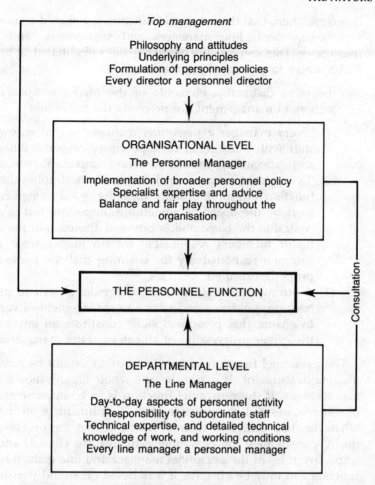

Top management

Philosophy and attitudes
Underlying principles
Formulation of personnel policies
Every director a personnel director

ORGANISATIONAL LEVEL

The Personnel Manager

Implementation of broader personnel policy
Specialist expertise and advice
Balance and fair play throughout the
organisation

THE PERSONNEL FUNCTION

Consultation

DEPARTMENTAL LEVEL

The Line Manager

Day-to-day aspects of personnel activity
Responsibility for subordinate staff
Technical expertise, and detailed technical
knowledge of work, and working conditions
Every line manager a personnel manager

Fig. 8.2 The personnel function as a shared responsibility

matters; standards of work performance; safety; communication of information; on the job training; and grievances from staff. Line managers have both the right and the duty to be concerned with the effective operation of their own department, including the management and well-being of their staff.

In this respect it could be said that *all line managers are their own personnel manager*. Line managers are on hand to observe directly the performance of their staff. They will actually see, and be directly affected by, for example, lateness of staff, unsatisfactory work, insufficient training, low morale, staff unrest, or poor planning of work duties and responsibilities. As an element function, the management of personnel is an integral part of any managerial activity. It is part of the generality of management. All managers are required to work with other people and to get things done through the efforts of other people. All managers are concerned with the personnel function to some extent. The personnel function is an essential part of every manager's responsibilities.

Personnel function: a shared responsibility

It is clear, then, that the personnel function is a shared responsibility among top management, line managers and supervisors, and the personnel manager.[17] This can be illustrated by the enlightened approach of Marks and Spencer to personnel management.

the most distinctive elements of the Marks & Spencer approach to personnel management are precisely the following:

(1) 'Every manager a personnel manager' – that is, every member of staff with managerial or supervisory responsibilities is trained in, and expected to perform, a certain important personnel function.

(2) 'Every director a personnel director' – this implies that the personnel function – or more broadly speaking, good human relations – is not seen by the board as something 'important but peripheral' but as central to the basic philosophy and approach of the entire business. Board members responsible for no matter what area share the common responsibility for ensuring that the personnel function is properly executed.

(3) A strong, well-trained team of personnel staff to provide support, training, guidance and advice to management of various levels and to ensure that personnel skills constitute an important element in the career progression of all categories of managerial staff.[18]

The personnel function of an organisation cannot be housed within one discrete department. It permeates the whole organisation and all phases of management. If the personnel function is to be implemented successfully, it also requires the co-operation and commitment of all members of staff, whatever their duties or their positions within the organisation. However the responsibilities for personnel activities are shared, and whatever the respective roles of the personnel manager and line managers, the personnel function can only be effective if it is based on sound personnel policies.

INDUSTRIAL RELATIONS

Sound personnel policies help to foster good industrial relations. Broadly defined, industrial relations is concerned with the relationships between the policies and practices of the organisation and its staff, and the behaviour of work groups.

The nature and contents of an industrial relations policy will be influenced by such factors as:
- the type and size of organisation;
- its structure and methods of operation;
- arrangements for collective bargaining;
- the structure and strength of trade unions;
- preference of the parties for freedom of action from outside influences; and
- the philosophy of top management and their attitudes towards the management of industrial relations.

Industrial relations is often associated, in particular, with the activities of trade unions and their officials. Trade unions may be seen as existing, primarily, to promote the best interests of their members, and to improve their quality of working life and general standard of living. Through the process of collective bargaining trade unions endeavour to improve their members' terms of employment and conditions of work.

Industrial relations is not limited, however, to management–trade union relationships and employment legislation. It covers relationships among employers, management and other staff, and other organisations and their members concerned with the total employment process. For this reason the term 'labour relations' or 'employee relations' may be adopted as an alternative to 'industrial relations'.[19]

The shop steward

The shop steward, as an elected union representative of the employees, acts as spokesperson on behalf of the work group, initiates negotiations with management and may also be involved in grievance and disciplinary procedures. The shop steward will be responsible for communications with both full-time union officers and members about union matters and developments in working practices.

Shop stewards require knowledge of the trade union movement and its services, an awareness of the law relating to employment, the role of ACAS and industrial tribunals, as well as an understanding of the policies and practices of the organisation, its structure, the role of managers, supervisors and personnel specialists, group situations, and how best to handle the problems affecting individual union members. Shop stewards are therefore an important part of the effective operation of the organisation. They undertake a range of activities broadly similar to those of managers and they require similar skills.

Involvement of line managers

It is sometimes suggested that in many organisations the responsibility for industrial relations still lies with line managers who are often sceptical or even hostile towards personnel ideas and techniques, and who frequently reject the concept of an industrial relations policy because it hampers their work and limits their flexibility. For example, *Clegg* argues that:

> If line managers are left to handle industrial relations issues for themselves, the pressures of production are likely to lead to ad hoc and contradictory decisions. . . . If a personnel policy is introduced to promote consistent decisions on industrial relations issues, its effectiveness may depend on granting authority to the personnel department to override the natural priorities of line managers.[20]

According to Cuming, however, the increase in industrial relations legislation has resulted in a trend for personnel matters, particularly wage negotiations, to be transferred from line management to personnel departments. At the same time there has been a deterioration in management–worker relations in many places and a failure to introduce changes in work methods necessary for effective competition and organisational effectiveness.

> Personnel departments as such are clearly not to blame for these developments; much more guilty are those line managers at the highest level who have opted out of their most important function, that of managing people. They are especially blameworthy for allowing communication channels to become the province of personnel departments and trade

215

union organizations, so that complaints are now frequently heard from first-line managers that they hear news of changes likely to affect them from their departmental shop stewards.[21]

As with other aspects of the personnel function it is important that line managers are involved, at least to some extent, with industrial relations. But there must be good communications and close consultation with the personnel department. There should be team-work and a concerted organisational approach to the management of industrial relations. This is made easier when top management, who retain ultimate responsibility for the personnel function, take an active part in fostering goodwill and co-operation between departments and with official union representatives, and agree clear terms of reference for both the personnel manager and line managers within the framework of sound personnel policies.

Attention to the personnel function

Proper attention to the establishment of good personnel policies and to the operation of the personnel function, including industrial relations, will help to improve the efficiency of the workforce and the level of organisational performance. Full use should be made of personnel specialists, the involvement of line managers, and modern methods of personnel management.

This, of course, will cost money. Cost is obviously a major consideration but should not be viewed in isolation. Not every activity of the organisation can be identified clearly as making a direct contribution to profitability. A balance must be kept between the more easily identified financial costs of the personnel function and the less readily apparent, but very important, long-term benefits which also make a positive contribution to organisational effectiveness and the achievement of objectives.

The attitudes, behaviour and performance of staff will be influenced by good personnel policies and an effective personnel function. This is something that every manager in the organisation would do well to remember.

THE ATTRIBUTES OF A MANAGER

In order to carry out the process of management and the execution of work, the manager requires a combination of technical competence, social and human skills, and conceptual ability (Fig. 8.3). Social and human skills reflect the ability to get along with other people, and are important attributes at all levels of management. The degree of technical competence or conceptual ability required will vary according to the level of the organisation at which the manager is working.

As the manager advances up the organisational hierarchy, greater emphasis is likely to be placed on conceptual ability, and proportionately less on technical competence. This can be illustrated by reference to the levels of organisation discussed in Chapter 5.

Technical competence relates to the application of specific knowledge, methods and skills to discrete tasks. Technical competence is likely to be required more at the supervisory level and for the training of subordinate staff, and with day-to-day operations concerned in the actual production of goods or services.

Social and human skills refer to interpersonal relationships in working with

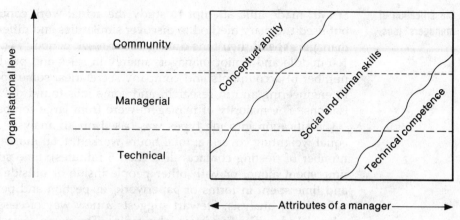

Fig. 8.3 The combination of attributes of a manager

and through other people, and the exercise of judgement. It involves effective team-work and the direction and leadership of staff to achieve co-ordinated effort. Under this heading can be included sensitivity to particular situations, and flexibility in adopting the most appropriate style of management.

Conceptual ability is required in order to view the complexities of the operations of the organisation as a whole, including environmental influences. It also involves decision-making skills. The manager's personal contribution should be related to the overall objectives of the organisation and to its strategic planning.

THE WORK OF A MANAGER

Despite similarities in the general activities of management, the jobs of individual managers will differ widely. The work of the manager is varied and fragmented. In practice it will be influenced by such factors as:

- the nature of the organisation, its objectives and size;
- the type of structure;
- technology and methods of performing work;
- environmental conditions;
- the nature of people employed; and
- the level in the organisation at which the manager is working.

These differences exist not just between organisations in the private and public sectors, but are often more a matter of degree. For example, many large business organisations may have more in common in their management and operations with public sector organisations than with small private firms.

More recent studies have been based on wider observation and research, and have concentrated on the diversity of management and differences in the jobs of managers. Among the best-known empirical studies on the nature of managers' jobs, and how managers actually spend their time, are those by *Stewart*, *Mintzberg* and *Kotter*.

Classification of managers' jobs

Stewart made little attempt to study the actual work content of managers, but used the diary method to discover similarities and differences in the way managers spend their time during a four-week period.[22] The sample covered 160 middle and senior managers mainly in sales and production, a smaller number of accountants and company secretaries, some specialist managers in engineering and in research, and some jobs found only in larger organisations. The majority of managers were from large companies.

Classification into job types was based on an analysis of 25 variables of equal weighting covering: total hours worked; total number of entries; total number of fleeting contacts (less than 5 minutes); time spent in travelling; time spent alone, or with other people inside or outside the organisation; and time spent in forms of paperwork, inspection and personnel matters.

From her analysis, Stewart suggests a new way of classifying managers' jobs and identifies five basic job profiles. The name of each group indicates very broadly one of its main characteristics. There are: (i) the emissaries; (ii) the writers; (iii) the discussers; (iv) the trouble shooters; and (v) the committee people.

The emissaries – These managers are in close touch with the world outside the organisation and spend much of their time dealing with people other than employees. They work long hours but their day is less fragmented than that of other groups. There were 45 managers who fell into this group. Main examples were sales managers, and general managers who act as public figures and whose work takes them away from the organisation.

The writers – In comparison with other groups these managers spend more of their time by themselves in reading, writing, dictating and figure work. Working hours were shorter than those for other groups. They spent the least amount of time in group contacts and were less subject to pressure than other groups. There were 33 managers in this group. Main examples were specialist engineering advisers, also some sales managers who spent time on office administration, and a few accountants and company secretaries.

The discussers – These managers tend to be the 'average' managers for the whole sample with less distinguishing characteristics than the other groups. They spent most of their time with their colleagues and with other people. There were 35 in this group which contained a wider variety of managers than other groups, and covered a diverse range of activities.

The trouble shooters – These managers spend more of their time in coping with crises and they had the most fragmented pattern of work. More of their time was involved with subordinates than with peers. A relatively large amount of time was spent on inspection. Main external contacts were with suppliers. There were 33 managers in this group. Main examples were factory managers or works managers, also a few engineering managers, and a few general managers concerned with works management in small organisations.

The committee people – This group differs noticeably from other groups because of the wide range of internal contacts, and the large amount of time managers spend in group discussion. Internal contacts were both horizontal and vertical with few outside contacts. For most managers a lot of time was spent in committees. They also spent more time on personnel work.

Managers in this group worked in large organisations. There were 14 in the group, mostly production or works managers.

Main types of jobs
In a later study, *Stewart* looked at the work patterns of several hundred managers, and the demands and choices of different types of managers' jobs.[23] In a sample of 250 jobs, 12 definable types were identified on the basis of the pattern of contacts required (*see* Fig. 8.4). The job types were grouped into four main types: (i) Hub; (ii) Peer dependent; (iii) People management; and (iv) Solo.

Hub – where management of people takes a lot of time; there is contact with peers, other seniors and juniors, the job depends upon co-operation of people in other departments; and contact time is usually over 50 per cent. Hub jobs are immersed most in the network of organisational relationships and require an ability to establish relationships with a wide variety of people. Examples are works manager, group accountant, marketing manager, quality controller.

Peer dependent – where contacts with people at the same level is high; it is important to obtain co-operation from people over whom the manager has no authority; contact time with peers is usually over 50 per cent; and conflicting demands are a usual part of the job. Unless managers with peer dependent jobs can get co-operation from people within the organisation over whom they have no authority, they may find they have no job to do. Examples are personnel manager, management accountant, market research manager, product manager.

People management – where peer contact is low, and there is little dependence on other people over whom the manager has no authority except for external contacts. People management jobs have responsibility for a separate

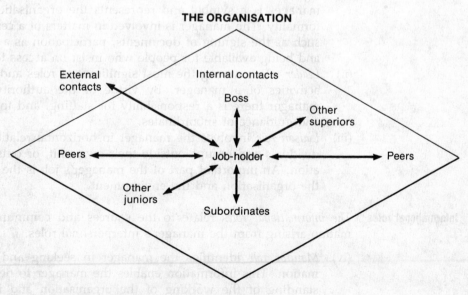

Fig. 8.4 The possible category of contacts of a manager
(Reproduced with permission from; Stewart, Rosemary, *Contrasts in Management*. Copyright © McGraw-Hill Book Co. (UK) Limited (1976) p. 7.)

unit or fairly self-contained section. For two of the job types in this group the primary social skill required is that of people management, and there is high contact time with subordinates. Examples are store manager, office manager, works manager. With the third job type many of the people management aspects are delegated in order to concentrate on a wide range of external contacts. Examples are bank manager, branch manager. The fourth job type is more specialist and concerned with bargaining with a limited range of external contacts. Examples are head buyer, sales manager.

Solo – where contact time is under 50 per cent; demands on relationships are low; sustained attention is required; there are few subordinates; there is a low level of uncertainty, and a high proportion of time is spent in meeting deadlines. Examples are company accountant, research manager and head office inspector.

MANAGERIAL ROLES

Based on the study of the work of five chief executives of medium to large organisations, *Mintzberg* classifies the activities which constitute the essential functions of a top manager's job.[24] He recognises that people who 'manage' have formal authority over the unit they command, and this leads to a special position of status in the organisation. As a result of this formal authority and status, managerial activities can be seen as a set of ten roles which may be divided into three groups: (i) interpersonal roles; (ii) informational roles; and (iii) decisional roles (*see* Fig. 8.5).

Interpersonal roles *The interpersonal roles* are relations with other people arising from the manager's status and authority.

(i) *Figurehead role* is the most basic and simple of managerial roles. The manager is a symbol and represents the organisation in matters of formality. The manager is involved in matters of a ceremonial nature, such as the signing of documents, participation as a social necessity, and being available for people who insist on access to the 'top'.

(ii) *Leader role* is among the most significant of roles and it permeates all activities of a manager. By virtue of the authority vested in the manager there is a responsibility for staffing, and for the motivation and guidance of subordinates.

(iii) *Liaison role* involves the manager in horizontal relationships with individuals and groups outside their own unit, or outside the organisation. An important part of the manager's job is the linking between the organisation and the environment.

Informational roles *The informational roles* relate to the sources and communication of information arising from the manager's interpersonal roles.

(iv) *Monitor role* identifies the manager in seeking and receiving information. This information enables the manager to develop an understanding of the working of the organisation and its environment. Information may be received from internal or external sources, and may be formal or informal.

(v) *Disseminator role* involves the manager in transmitting external infor-

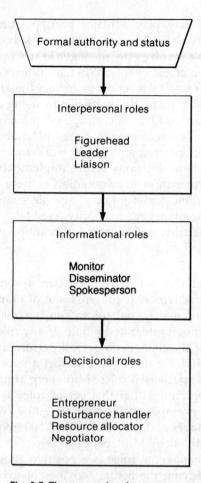

Fig. 8.5 The manager's roles
(From Mintzberg, Henry, *The Nature of Managerial Work*, p. 59. Copyright © 1973 by Henry Mintzberg. Reprinted by permission of Harper & Row, Publishers, Inc.)

mation through the liaison role into the organisation, and internal information through leader role between the subordinates. The information may be largely factual or may contain value judgements. The manager is the nerve centre of information. If the manager feels unable, or chooses not, to pass on information this can present difficulties for delegation.

(vi) *Spokesperson role* involves the manager as formal authority in transmitting information to people outside the unit, such as the board of directors or other superiors, and the general public such as suppliers, customers, government departments and the press.

Decisional roles *The decisional roles* involve the making of strategic organisational decisions on the basis of the manager's status and authority, and access to information.

(vii) *Entrepreneurial role* is the manager's function to initiate and plan controlled change (that is, voluntary), through exploiting opportunities or solving problems, and taking action to improve the existing situation. The manager may play a major part, personally, in seeking improvement, or may delegate responsibility to subordinates.

(viii) *Disturbance handler role* involves the manager in reacting to involuntary situations and unpredictable events. When an unexpected disturbance occurs the manager must take action to correct the situation.

(ix) *Resource allocator role* involves the manager in using formal authority to decide where effort will be expended, and making choices on the allocation of resources such as money, time, materials and manpower. The manager decides the programming of work and maintains control by authorising important decisions before implementation.

(x) *Negotiator role* is participation in negotiation activity with other individuals or organisations, for example a new agreement with a trade union. Because of the manager's authority, credibility, access to information, and responsibility for resource allocation, negotiation is an important part of the job.

Arbitrary division of activities

Mintzberg emphasises that this set of ten roles in a somewhat arbitrary division of the manager's activities. It presents one of many possible ways of categorising the view of managerial roles. The ten roles are not easily isolated in practice but form an integrated whole. If any role is removed this affects the effectiveness of the manager's overall performance.

The ten roles suggest that the manager is in fact a specialist required to perform a particular set of specialised roles. Mintzberg argues that empirical evidence supports the contention that this set of roles is common to the work of all managers. An example of this is provided by *Wolf* who analysed the work of the audit manager and assigned critical task requirements to the ten managerial roles identified by Mintzberg.[25]

Mintzberg's model of managerial roles is a positive attempt to provide a realistic approach to classifying the actual activities of management. There are, however, criticisms that the roles lack specificity and that a number of items under each role are related not to a single factor but to several factors. For example, *McCall* and *Segrist* found that activities involved in figurehead, disseminator, disturbance handler and negotiator were not separate roles but overlapped too much with activities under the six other roles.[26]

Why organisations need managers

As a result of describing the nature of managerial work in terms of a set of ten roles, *Mintzberg* suggests six basic purposes of the manager, or reasons why organisations need managers:

- to ensure the organisation serves its basic purpose and the efficient production of goods or services;
- to design and maintain the stability of the operations of the organisation;
- to take charge of strategy making and adapt the organisation in a controlled way to changes in its environment;
- to ensure the organisation serves the ends of those people who control it;
- to serve as the key informational link between the organisation and the environment; and
- as formal authority to operate the organisation's status system.

PATTERNS OF MANAGERIAL WORK AND BEHAVIOUR

Based on earlier studies of managerial jobs, *Stewart* has developed a model for understanding managerial work and behaviour.[27] The model directs attention to the generalisations that can be made about managerial work, and differences which exist among managerial jobs. It acknowledges the wide variety, found from previous studies, among different managers in similar jobs in terms of how they view their jobs and the work they do.

Demands, constraints and choices

The three main categories of the model are demands, constraints and choices. These identify the flexibility in a managerial job.

- *Demands* are what anyone in the job *has* to do. They are not what the manager ought to do, but only what must be done. For example, meeting minimum criteria of performance, work which requires personal involvement, complying with bureaucratic procedures which cannot be avoided, meetings that must be attended.
- *Constraints* are internal or external factors which limit what the manager can do. For example, resource limitations, legal or trade union constraints, the nature of technology, physical location, organisational constraints, attitudes of other people.
- *Choices* are the activities that the manager is free to do, but does not have to do. They are opportunities for one job-holder to undertake different work from another, or to do the work in a different way. For example, what work is done within a defined area, to change the area of work, the sharing of work, participation in organisational or public activities.

The flexibility of managerial jobs

Stewart suggests that the model provides a framework for thinking about the nature of managerial jobs, and about the manner in which managers undertake them. To understand what managerial jobs are really like it is necessary to understand the nature of their flexibility. Account should be taken of variations in behaviour and differences in jobs before attempting to generalise about managerial work. Study of managers in similar jobs indicates that their focus of attention differs. Opportunities for individual managers to do what they believe to be most important exist to a greater or lesser extent in all managerial jobs. Stewart also concludes that the model has implications for organisational design, job design, management effectiveness, selection, education and training, and career decisions.

Behaviour pattern of general managers

From a detailed study of 15 successful general managers involved in a broad range of industries, *Kotter* found that the managers spent most of their time interacting with other people. Many of these other people were in addition to their boss or direct subordinates. Meetings provided exchanges of information over a wide range of topics in a short period of time. Many of the contacts were 'network building' and concerned more with the requirements of other managers than the managers' own needs.[28]

On the basis of interviews, observations, questionnaires and relevant documents, Kotter found the following features of a typical pattern in daily behaviour for a general manager (GM).

(i)   They spent most of their time with others.
(ii) The people they spent time with included many in addition to their superior and direct subordinates.
(iii) The breadth of topics covered in discussions was very wide.
(iv) In these conversations, GMs typically asked a lot of questions.
(v)   During these conversations GMs rarely seemed to make 'big' decisions.
(vi) Discussions usually contained a considerable amount of joking, kidding, and non-work-related issues.
(vii) In not a small number of these encounters, the substantive issue discussed was relatively unimportant to the business or organisation.
(viii) In such encounters, the GMs rarely gave 'orders' in a traditional sense.
(ix) Nevertheless, GMs frequently attempted to influence others.
(x)   In allocation of time with other people, GMs often reacted to the initiatives of others.
(xi) Most of their time with others was spent in short, disjointed conversations.
(xii) They worked long hours. (The average GM studied worked just under 60 hours per week. Although some work was done at home, and whilst commuting or travelling, they spent most of their time at work.)

How restaurant managers spend their time

Using a similar methodology to *Kotter*, a study of nine restaurant managers was undertaken by *Ferguson* and *Berger*. From observation and documentation of the activities of the managers, their time was categorised as being used in one of five ways:

Desk sessions	17%
Telephone calls	13%
Scheduled meetings	29%
Unscheduled meetings	35%
Tours	6%

Ferguson and *Berger* see the two categories of desk sessions and scheduled meetings as suggesting a reasonable level of structure and organisation; and conducive to organising, planning and deciding. However, from their study, the activities of the restaurant managers seemed far from the textbook description of planner, organiser, co-ordinator and controller. 'Planning seems to have been eclipsed by reacting; organizing might be better described as simply carrying on; coordination appears more like juggling; and controlling seems reduced to full time watching.'[29]

THE NATURE OF MANAGEMENT

We have seen, then, that 'management' is a generic term subject to many interpretations. A number of different ideas are attributed to the meaning of management. Despite similarities in the general activities of management the jobs of individual managers will differ widely. A number of studies have been conducted into the work of the manager.

A summary of main points considered in this chapter is given in Fig. 8.6. This provides a framework for looking at the nature of management.

'MANAGEMENT' – A GENERIC TERM AND SUBJECT TO MANY INTERPRETATIONS

- Structured organisation
- Aims and objectives
- Through people
- Systems and procedures

The essential nature of managerial work

- 'Management' distinguished from 'administration'
- Common activities or elements of management (for example *Fayol, Brech, Drucker*)
- Management a social process (*Brech*)
- Managers as having subordinates' roles, able to veto appointments of and remove subordinates (*Lord Brown*)
- Managers defined by their function and contribution (*Drucker*)
- 'Managing' distinguished from 'doing'
- *Generalised description and summary of management as: clarify objectives; planning; organisation; direction, control*
- Popular view of management as getting work done through the efforts of other people

Applications to particular types of organisations/situations

- Differences in management between, for example: private and public sector organisations; large and small scale; production or service
- Analysis of managerial activities in central and local government (*Bourn*)
- General principles of management relevant to all types of organisations but varying applications and emphasis on certain activities, and varying systems and styles of management
- Work activities of particular managers, for example, restaurant managers (*Ferguson* and *Berger*)
- Systems approach, and contingency models, to help analyse common features and differences in structure, management and operations of organisations

Empirical studies on the work of the manager (for example Stewart; Mintzberg; Kotter)

MANAGEMENT AS A COMMON PROCESS. ESSENTIALLY AN INTEGRATING ACTIVITY

Fig. 8.6 A framework for looking at the nature of management

Synopsis

'Management' is a generic term and subject to many interpretations. Our concern is with management as taking place within a structured organisation and with prescribed roles. It involves the exercise of formal authority over the work of other people. For our purposes we can regard management as being: within a structured organisational setting; directed towards aims and objectives; through the efforts of other people; and using systems and procedures.

The nature of management is variable and is seen best as a process which permeates all other aspects of the organisation. Management can be distinguished from administration. Management is both an art and a science; and it is a combination of both innate qualities, and education and training.

It is not easy to find agreement on the definition of management, or of a manager. And management is not homogeneous. It takes place in different ways in different levels of the organisation. One approach is to analyse the nature of management and to identify common activities. By distinguishing 'managing' from 'doing' we can summarise the nature of managerial work as clarification of objectives, planning, organising, directing and controlling. The degree of emphasis given to these different activities may vary widely, however, from one manager to another. A popular definition of management is getting work done through the efforts of other people. Although there are differences in management in the private and public sectors, both face the same general problems of management and apply the same basic principles.

An essential part of the process of management is the personnel function. This is a shared responsibility among top management, line managers and supervisors, and the personnel manager. The personnel function can be seen as operating at two levels; the organisational level, and the departmental or unit level. As an element function the management of personnel is part of the generality of management and a responsibility of every manager.

The shop steward, as an elected union representative of the employees, also has an important part to play in the effective operation of the organisation. Proper attention to the establishment of good personnel policies and to the personnel function, including industrial relations, will help to improve the efficiency of the labour force and the level of organisational performance.

In order to carry out the process of management and execution of work, the manager requires a combination of technical competence, social and human skills, and conceptual ability. The jobs of individual managers differ widely. Recent empirical studies have concentrated on the diversity of management and differences in the nature of managerial work. These studies have drawn attention to such features as: the classification of managers' jobs; main types of jobs; managerial roles; the manager's contacts; demands, constraints and choices in a managerial job; behaviour patterns and how managers actually spend their time. Studies have also illustrated the flexibility of a managerial job.

Review and discussion questions

1. Explain what you understand by the term 'management'. Distinguish management from administration.

2. How would you summarise the essential nature of managerial work? In what ways does the job of a manager differ from any other job in a work organisation?

3. From your own experience, identify with examples main activities of management. What do you see as the main attribute(s) required of a manager in undertaking each of these activities?

4. To what extent is it possible to establish rules or principles of good management? In what ways might you expect to find differences between management in private sector and public sector organisations?

5. 'Every director should be a personnel director; every line manager a personnel manager.' In the light of this statement discuss what you see

as the role and functions of the personnel manager in a large business organisation.

6. Explain arrangements for the sharing of responsibilities of the personnel function in your own, or some other, organisation. Where appropriate, identify the role of the shop steward. Give your views on the effectiveness of these arrangements.

7. Explain managerial activities as a set of interrelated roles. Give examples of each of these roles from your own organisation.

8. Why do organisations need managers? Suggest how the flexibility in managerial jobs might be identified, and compare and contrast any two different managerial jobs.

| Case study | WHAT *IS* MANAGEMENT?

A thing may look specious in theory, and yet be ruinous in practice; a thing may look evil in theory, and yet be in practice excellent.

EDMUND BURKE

Adam Smith sat at his desk and reflected that it was now exactly twelve months since he had been appointed general assistant to Charles Gaynor, Managing Director of Gaynor Hotels. During this time he had been used as adviser, counsellor, internal consultant and therapist. He had investigated problems, developed concepts, established principles and generally contributed to the decision taking process which took place in the mind of his employer, Gaynor.

His attention had been attracted by an article he had been reading, which said:

In order to maintain its internal dynamic which is essential to progress, a company needs the existence of a rebel group which is primarily concerned with challenging company policy; a group which regards as its main function the generation of sceptical attitudes towards the company's methods of operation, organization and policies. Such a group should adopt as a working principle the slogan, 'if it works it's obsolescent'. In other words the mere fact that a system is working satisfactorily should in itself be sufficient reason for its re-examination.*

Adam ruminated on this and considered that with Carson, his assistant, they really had created a two-man management services activity since they had concentrated on looking at, and solving, old problems in new ways. A pocket of rational thought in a wilderness of emotionalism – if only that were really true, thought Adam!

He felt depressed, although he realised that some progress had been made, it seemed infinitesimal when one looked at the company as a whole. Where is the real answer to the achievement of progress, thought Adam, if only one could put one's finger on it. Particular aspects, methods, solutions and so on were looked at which all seemed part of the answer,

* Ward, T. R., Management Services – The Way Ahead, *National O & M Conference*, 1964; published as an Anbar Monograph, Anbar Publications, 1965.

but where was the whole answer? Charles Gaynor, although a man inculcated at an early age with the attitudes and ways of traditional hotelkeeping, was most receptive to new ideas; indeed, he could generate them himself and boasted of his preparedness to accept necessary change. But nothing much seemed to have changed in these twelve months; Gaynor Hotels was still making a profit, its managers were still 'managing' but problems continued to abound and there seemed just as many unanswered questions.

Adam leaned forward on his desk with his head in his hands, he wondered if the company was really progressing, if things were any better, and whether he was just deceiving himself. Perhaps the problem was that the company was just 'managing', that it was just getting by, just keeping its head above water. Is it really geared to grow and develop and prosper, is it really looking ahead and ready to exploit the changing circumstances of a changing world? That's the central question, thought Adam, and I wish I could answer it confidently.

Management! It is all in the management, a handful of men cannot carry a company – it is in the strength and depth of *all* the people who form the firm. His thoughts were interrupted by the door opening and Gaynor appearing with a benevolent smile, and a friendly 'Good afternoon, Adam.'

Gaynor: I thought I would let you know it looks as though I will have to fire a manager, or to put it euphemistically, to ask him to resign.

Adam: Who is it, sir?

Gaynor: Hedges, at the Zephyr. Nasty business and the sort of scandal I deplore. I had a letter from a Mr. Coloniki; his wife is secretary to Hedges who, he asserted, has been sleeping with her. I thought there couldn't be anything in it and I referred it to our Mr. Hedges never expecting anything other than a denial. Well the damn fool confirmed it as being true, he *has* been sleeping with his secretary. Doesn't leave me much alternative, does it? I can't compromise my principles and I will not have my hotel executives entering into this sort of relationship with their staff. My goodness! What sort of an example is it? Oh, the stupid man, and he was doing quite a good job for us.

Adam: Well, sir, there's an old Hungarian proverb which says that when a man's fancy is titillated his brain goes to water.

Gaynor: How very true! But a little control, a little sense of responsibility, a little maturity, that's all I ask. It isn't even as if he was serious about her; as he told me, it was just his 'little indiscretion' and he hoped that I wouldn't find out. By the way, you didn't already know about it, did you?

Adam: No, certainly not, sir. I haven't heard the slightest suggestion.

Gaynor: Well, back to the old problem of finding a new manager; as if good managers grew on trees! They are such rare animals, they take such a great deal of finding, such a great deal of raising.

Adam: How about his assistant, Gripple, do you think that he might be ready to take over?

Gaynor: He might. . . . I don't know, even if we knew what job we were really picking him for; I mean, what *is* management, what is it *really*? What are we looking for?

Adam: Well, quite honestly, sir, I do not think that he's ready. I think he could develop into a manager, but he needs more time.

Gaynor: All right, we will have to find somebody. I'll tell you what we can do: you take over as manager of the Zephyr for the next month or so. During that time I will find a new manager. This *has* caught us unawares, I can't think of anybody suitable in the company at present.

Adam: But I've never actually managed an hotel!

Gaynor: Well, it will be an excellent experience for you. Anyway, I have no doubt about *your* management abilities. But you still didn't answer my question just now. What actually *is* management – do you know what it is?

Adam: Strange you should ask me that this afternoon, I think that I was just to ask myself the same question just as you walked in.

Gaynor: Fine, but can you answer it?

Adam: Well, it's obviously to do with concern for profits and its equally to do with concern for people and creating a climate where they can grow and develop.

Gaynor: That's rather vague.

Adam: Well, let me go on, sir. If it's to do with concern for profits then it is also to do with knowledge of modern management methods and techniques and how to use them. If it's to do with concern for people, then it's also to do with knowledge of human behaviour and its applications.

Gaynor: You're struggling, Adam, I remember we talked about the purpose of business and it must lead on from there. We agreed that this was the satisfaction of the needs, wants and desires of those who control the business and generally, but not always, this involved a certain level of profitability. Now purpose must define or set the aims and objectives. Subsequently the policy indicates the means as to how to accomplish these. Policy acts then as the firm guide in all decision making at an operational level. Management, therefore, is the implementation of policy to achieve company aims and objectives. Yes, I rather like that – I must remember to use it again.

Adam: I know you won't mind Mr. Gaynor, but I can't agree with you.

Gaynor: Go on then, I am not very busy at the moment.

Adam: I don't disagree with what you say, but really I am concerned with the assumptions which are being made. Indeed, the business purpose sets aims or objectives but this implies that the business purpose has been established, is commonly perceived and is accepted. You next assume that policy is rationally formulated and promulgated, that managers are aware of it, and take their decisions within its limitations.

Gaynor: Perhaps that describes the ideal situation, but I would still maintain that what I said – what was it – management is the implementation of policy to achieve company aims and objectives, is a good description.

Adam: May I ask what policy Mr. Hedges offended?

Gaynor: Ah well, now there are several. First it is unethical; second, if it became known it would damage our image and create havoc in staff relationships, and there are more besides.

Adam: But Mr. Hedges took a decision, presumably with a knowledge of the policies you mention, whose effects could militate against our aims and objectives as well as damage his career.

Gaynor: And a damn fool he was, too!

Adam: Were it a less serious affair, and something which was only a minor departure from Company policy, I can't help wondering how he or we would know that a departure had occurred. For example, if a manager gave

11% commission to travel agents during the winter to obtain some preference from them, would this be stopped if you became aware of it?

Gaynor: I hope that he would have discussed this with me first, but I can appreciate the point. After all we must be flexible enough to deal with special situations.

Adam: Doesn't this, then, highlight the problem of what we mean by policy? Earlier you said that policy acts as a firm guide, but payment of commission is pretty well fixed at 10% although you would be prepared to consider exceptions. I hope I am not splitting hairs if I suggest that our policy is to pay commissions, a procedure has been established which fixes this at 10%.

Gaynor: I think, in this case, you are tending to split hairs but I see what you are getting at; a confusion exists between policy and procedures. I must admit that I have confused these at times, yes I see the point – policy should act as a guide. But formulating policy in this way must make it so general that it cannot provide much of a guide, a paradox in fact. Another thought that occurs to me is that if the policy is to be an effective guide it should be written out and available for the manager to consult. I must say that this would be an unenviable task!

Adam: Reading text-books about management I have found the exhortation to have a written policy a common theme. I have never actually seen one so far for an hotel and one can appreciate why this is so. At the same time I would think it comparatively easy to spell out some policies; in the financial areas, for example, this would seem a fairly straightforward exercise.

Gaynor: Yes, and I think it could be done in the operating area too. I must admit, though, that I am not sure that I would like to have an exhaustive written policy document. I feel it would be a restriction on me.

Adam: I believe this is a fairly common feeling among senior executives; Glacier Metal Company introduced a written policy and their experience was that flexibility *increased* since when a change had to be made, everybody could be informed and a written amendment incorporated. This makes sense to me, but I have always had a sneaking feeling that they wrote a procedure manual rather than a policy handbook.

Gaynor: So you are back to your distinction between policy and procedures! Am I to take it, then, that you are advocating that we should try to produce a policy document for the Company?

Adam: No, sir, I may tend to overstate the case, but I would think that the existence of such a document represents a failure of management. At a unit level, and indeed at company level, it is essential to have *procedure* manuals since these provide a means of establishing and maintaining standards as well as a basis for training. I would also say that it is essential for a company to spend a lot of time clarifying its objectives and aims at the top level. The real problem is that many so-called policy documents are little more than a public relations handout. If a company is clear about what it wants to be, surely it should make every effort for everybody to understand and accept these aims and behave in a supportive way towards them.

Gaynor: I would have thought that having a written policy would help to do this, since people could see just what the aims are and act accordingly.

Adam: I am sure that this is partly true, but what I am trying to say is that if, starting at the top, members of an organization demonstrate by their behaviour what the policy is, this will be reflected downwards. If the senior executives behave as though they believed the customer was important, then other employees will adopt similar behaviour.

Gaynor. In other words, people will learn by example; I am rather intrigued that you should have such a charming old-fashioned idea!

Adam: By example, yes. But it is a little more than this. Put into the jargon, I would say that it is minimizing corporate discrepancy. That is, reducing the difference between what a company as a collection of people say, and what in fact they do.

Gaynor: Very well, I agree with what you say but I must say there are some grave dangers of misinterpretation. If the conclusion without the supporting argument is adopted it can become an excuse for avoiding the necessary analytical thinking at the top level. We seem to have strayed a long way from my attempt to define management; taking into account all you have said we still have a good description.

Adam: I agree, but the whole problem of vocabulary in management continues to be a stumbling-block. I always remember a lecturer at college who said at his first lecture to us that he had to devise a vocabulary to talk to us which we would automatically adopt, but never to attempt to use it outside. Since there is no generally accepted or defined vocabulary he had to fashion his own to communicate with us. We all forgot, of course, and it took some time to stop using our private language when we went into industry.

Gaynor: You still forget sometimes!

Adam: Sorry! If we do understand that policy and company aims and objectives are in some way related to individual interpretation, depending on the perceptions of the people involved, then I think it is a good *des*cription. But shouldn't a definition of this sort be a *pres*cription? By saying what it is, it gives some indication of how to do it?

Gaynor: Description, prescription, you're chopping words again. I will accept, although I think you are trying to find a philosopher's stone if a definition can tell a manager how to do his job!

Adam: To come back to the definition, sir, suppose the policy is wrong or the aims and objectives are wrong. Is it true to say that an individual is managing if he keeps things going to achieve these and doesn't have the wit or the insight to besiege his superiors for a change of direction?

Gaynor: Ah! Now you are introducing value judgements about 'good' management and 'bad' management!

Adam: No Mr Gaynor. You will accuse me of sophistry again, but I would say that a person who is a manager is managing effectively. If he is ineffective, then he is not a manager.

Gaynor: Save me from quibblers! But do go on.

Adam: When I was in America I was given an assignment to collect together as many definitions of management as I could find. It really was a fascinating exercise but eventually I found myself in such a muddle that I could hardly think straight. The things that people have to say about this process, which hundreds of thousands of people go about for five days a week, year in and year out is amazing. The one that I remember, and considered the most banal of a very sad bunch, was 'Management is getting things done through people.'

Gaynor: Oh! I always considered that a truism.

Adam: Well, yes. But it doesn't advance our understanding. Bus conductors, waitresses and supervisors get things done through people – but they are not managers.

Gaynor: Very interesting; so you don't think supervisors are managers?

Adam: No. Managers are tacticians; that is they are the people who are once-removed from the actual operators who serve the food or make the beds. Managers are concerned with the deployment of resources. A manager *says* what has to be done, a supervisor frequently *shows* people what has to be done. The supervisor is a technician, the manager is a tactician. In this sense he is *always* 'getting things done through other people' and the other people are his supervisors.

Gaynor: Well then why does this 'getting things done through other people grate on you so much?

Adam: Chiefly because of its lack of prescription. Would you say that a person is an effective manager who spends all his time with his supervisors, guiding, instructing, directing and giving decisions?

Gaynor: No, certainly not. I would expect him to set the guide lines – policy, if you like – and by his selection and development of the supervisors, reach a stage where they got on with the work and left him time to think.

Adam: Exactly. I think it has been sufficiently demonstrated from studies of managers' and supervisors' behaviour that these are very different roles. We must be careful, however, about actual titles that go with a job.

Gaynor: Yes indeed. It was always a source of amusement to me, when I had the title of General Manager, to sit next to people, with the same designation, at conferences who ran an hotel with twenty bedrooms. I would be the first to insist that we belonged to the same industry, but our needs and problems were vastly different! Do we have any common ground, I wonder? The other thing that concerns me is the entrepreneurial aspect. The owner of a twenty bedroom hotel is an entrepreneur, whereas Kimble at the Diana is a manager employed by the Company. Yet he is responsible for about twenty times the turnover of this entrepreneur!

Adam: I have often pondered about this. In many ways it is a very personal thing. Occasionally I meet people who ask me why I work for Gaynor Hotels when I could be my own boss running a small hotel in the Cotswolds and probably able to take each afternoon off for golf. But it really depends on what you mean by being one's own boss. I am sure there is great satisfaction in being personally involved with the customer in the small business, but the real boss is then the bank manager and there is a very real dependence on suppliers. I think that one can over-emphasize the differences between the entrepreneur and the manager. Probably the owner of a small hotel spends about five per cent of his time on entrepreneurial decisions and the rest of the time he is a manager. So Kimble and the proprietor have a 95% of common activity if they are running similar establishments.

Gaynor: I suppose I am the professional entrepreneur of this Company, but I have never been able to find any courses which deal with this topic! But we are still groping about. You have the advantage of your research on definitions of management, what are your conclusions? After all, people like me that just manage, what time do we have for all this introspection?

Adam: Now I am in difficulties! On the one hand I am asked to offer my conclusions against your experience, and on the other hand I am asked to sit in judgement on the multitude of writers on management!

Gaynor: I thought this is what you did anyway, but please! You know that I want to know about your ideas and that I shall use my experience to challenge you where I think you are wrong. I know that you will produce research findings, that I have never heard of, like rabbits from a hat. But I am still interested in your ideas.

Adam: Sorry, Mr. Gaynor, but I just realised the enormity of what you asked me to do. It is one thing to make comments about a definition that somebody proposes; it is quite another thing to be asked, from limited experience, to fly in the face of the savants!

Gaynor: I quite understand, but go ahead.

Adam: Well, the early writers about management became heavily involved in trying to define management but I think because they were engineers or technologists, they wanted it cut and dried. They saw the world in mechanical terms and placed all the emphasis on what should be done to create orderliness and an organization which works like a smoothly oiled machine.

Gaynor: Then the social scientists came along and started to demonstrate that most of the problems were centred round people who did not behave like machines. In fact they were unpredictable.

Adam: Yes, but I think that the success of techniques in advertising show that there are quite a lot of predictable elements in people's behaviour. But the effect of the behavioural scientists' findings tended to tip the balance with a lot of managers from concern for production to concern for people. In fact I sometimes think this still persists today to a large extent; from the way some people talk, one would think that the Hawthorne experiments were the only studies which have been conducted in this field.

Gaynor: You mean that a manager should be involved in maintaining a balance between his concern for people and for production?

Adam: Yes. This means that management is a process which involves achieving business goals while at the same time providing a means of satisfaction for the individual needs or goals of employees. Now I think that the real danger to maintaining this balance might be described as the return on invested time. A comparatively short time spent in replanning a layout of a kitchen, or the desirability of installing a room state indicator, can quickly produce economies. We can see that more meals can be produced or customers allocated rooms speedily. But to increase people's effectiveness, requires a much greater investment in time to establish what goals they are seeking to achieve.

Gaynor: I think most managers would agree with you and that they appreciate the need for developing people, but there is always the pressure of other things to be done and the consequent shortage of time. And what about decision taking, I would think that this is a basic and fundamental part of managing?

Adam: The problem of time is something I would like to come back to. I must admit that I feel slightly nervous when decision taking is regarded as some prerogative of managers. After all, everybody is involved in taking decisions every day. A housewife faces a major problem in a supermarket when she has to decide between paying 28p for a family-sized pack of detergent or 32p for a special large size accompanied by a free plastic flower!

Gaynor: I see what you mean, but surely we cannot divorce this business of making decisions from a process of management? I keep reading that use of computers is likely to remove a lot of decision taking from middle management in the future. But I don't think this will come for a long time and I certainly think that in running hotels there will continue to be a lot of decisions which would defy any computer. We will still need the reception manager who can fit an unexpected regular customer into the hotel which the computer says is full.

Adam: Yes indeed, we cannot ignore that decisions have to be taken in business organizations and it needs some careful thinking to distinguish between normal human decision taking and the special characteristics of those in business.

Gaynor: That should not be too difficult. I am sometimes very conscious of spending time collecting information in order to make a decision. In a similar way, you or the chief accountant sometimes spend time preparing briefs about the possible alternatives available and the likely results. A lot of this involves figures and projections and so on. With no disrespect to you, most of this could be done better on a computer, but I will still have to make the decision about which line to follow. I would also think that the unit managers will have to continue making similar decisions; perhaps these are less important in that a wrong one will be unlikely to damage the company, whereas mine might! In these decisions, at both levels, we have to use experience and our personal judgement.

Adam: If most of the operating decisions at unit level are to be made by computers in the future, the manager's role becomes one of a human relations mechanic.

Gaynor: I don't see it that way. I hope that they will use information from the computer in reaching operating decisions; I suppose I am agreeing with your balance between people and production. My concern, however, is that this is the only method I can see for developing executives. As you know, we are a fairly decentralised company and I want my managers to feel that they are more than what you call 'human relations mechanics'. This really goes back to what I was thinking earlier when I used the word 'policy'. One would like to feel, as a company, that decisions are made in accordance with the policy and this is the paradox you saw. I am reluctant to start writing everything down, but I do want decisions made which support what we are trying to be as a company. Perhaps it would be a better way of describing this to say that I would like to create an ethos or spirit that ensures this.

Adam: I would say that creating this environment of ethos is a very important part of the management process. It can probably be compared to the training we have as children; having confidence in social situations because we have a good idea of what is the 'right thing to do' like not putting our elbows on the table.

Gaynor: I thought only great-aunts worried about that nowadays! But I think you have something. Tell me, where does problem solving come into all this? I certainly seem to spend a significant part of my time dealing with problems and I am sure it is the same with all managers.

Adam: Just before you came in I was thinking about this; after a year I am still involved in solving problems and I find this rather disappointing.

Gaynor: This is what I mean. Surely you can't expect problems to stop requiring solving, I would think that this is almost the core of what management is about.

Adam: This makes me feel uncomfortable. Identifying problems and solving them certainly is a significant part of managing. But I can't help feeling that this is catching hold of the wrong end of the stick. Surely if we concentrated on identifying the *causes* of problems and removing those we could be much more effective?

Gaynor: I am not sure I understand you.

Adam: Perhaps I can illustrate it with the problem we had at the Apollo. Rather, I should say, problems; no potential managers were being produced, there was a high labour turnover and so on. We could have attempted to solve these by introducing different methods of selection, higher pay and various other means. These might have had some effect but in the long run we hadn't identified and remedied the cause. That was Whitstone, whose autocratic behaviour as a manager was the cause of the problems.

Gaynor: Yes, I see what you mean. It is like worrying about the problem of high labour costs at Head Office when the cause is people wanting to have things in writing as a protection.

Adam: Exactly. But having said that, I am not sure just how this fits in with the management process. Undoubtedly managers are involved in solving problems and now it sounds as though I am saying they shouldn't be.

Gaynor: From what you say, and it is certainly a new slant for me, I would see this as part of the ethos. It involves analysing the cause of problems rather than saying 'we have a problem'. This reminds me of one of the British Institute of Management's luncheons when Peter Drucker spoke. It was very impressive to me when he said something like 'We are concerned with effective management rather than efficient management, because a manager can be very efficient at doing something that does not need to be done'. I remember that I was disturbed for several days afterwards!

Adam: This really typifies how one can see a whole new dimension to the task of managing by taking a step sideways and looking at the words we use. I sometimes think that words and clichés are like old slippers, they are comfortable until you notice the holes in them.

Gaynor: Comfortable, but not presentable! What about communication? I recall that we have said something about this before. It must come in somewhere.

Adam: I think on that occasion you quoted Thoreau and said, 'How can I hear what you say, when what you are keeps drumming in my ears.'

Gaynor: Ah yes! A favourite quote of mine.

Adam: Well, the way I see it is that if your ethos exists, then communication will occur. Most people in talking about communication generally emphasize the skills of writing, speaking and reading. Sometimes they also include the skill of listening. These are, of course, important, but I would think that the emotional and social context are important. Which is just what Thoreau was saying.

Gaynor: So you don't consider communication is a part of managing.

Adam: Oh, I think it is, but if we mix Drucker with Thoreau and add a dash of your observation on the ethos of the enterprise, we can see that communication is a function of the internal environment. If trust exists and people appreciate the objectives, then communication will occur. If not, then no communication.

Gaynor: In some ways I would describe it as 'good' and 'poor' communication, but I am a little worried that you might take me to task on these words! Look, I have a lunch appointment and must go in a few minutes. This has been a very interesting discussion, what shall I do, sum up what we have been saying or leave it to you to prepare a memo?

Adam: I would rather you summarized, Mr. Gaynor. After all, I don't want to land myself with solving a problem of overloaded Head Office typists!

Gaynor: Your motives are suspect, but let me see. The Management Process seems to be concerned with creating an environment in which a balance between concern for production and concern for people is maintained as well as providing a guide to decision taking. It is directed towards an analysis of the causes from which problems arise and seeks to provide for achievement of organizational objectives whilst satisfying individual needs. Is that adequate?

Adam: It really is a concise statement of what we have been talking about.

Gaynor: Does it satisfy your demands for prescription?

Adam: I think it does because it stresses the things that a manager must do. Creating the environment, for example. But I wonder how long this takes to achieve.

Gaynor: You have a chance to find out, Adam. Tell me about it when you come back from the Zephyr! Goodbye for now, and enjoy yourself.

Notes and references

1. Drucker, P. F. *Management*, Pan Books (1979) p. 14.
2. Fayol, H. *General and Industrial Management*, Pitman (1949). See also: Gray, I. *Henri Fayol's General and Industrial Management*, Pitman (1988).
3. Department of the Environment *The New Local Authorities: Management and Structure* (the Bains report), HMSO (1972).
4. Fayol, H. *General and Industrial Management*, Pitman (1949).
5. Brech, E. F. L. *Principles and Practice of Management*, Third edition, Longman (1975) p. 19.
6. Brown, W. *Organization*, Penguin (1974) p. 45.
7. Drucker, P. F. *People and Performance*, Heinemann (1977) p. 28.
8. Ibid. p. 59.
9. Simon, H. A. *The New Science of Management Decision*, Revised edition, Prentice-Hall (1977).
10. Carroll, S. J. and Gillen, D. J. 'Are the Classical Management Functions Useful in Describing Managerial Work?' *Academy of Management Review*, vol. 12, no. 1, 1987, p. 48.
11. Stewart, R. *The Reality of Management*, Second edition, Pan Books (1986) p. 12.
12. Drucker, P. F. *The Practice of Management*, Pan Books (1968) p. 455.
13. Bourn, J. *Management in Central and Local Government*, Pitman (1979) pp. 17–18.
14. Woodward, J. *Industrial Organization: Theory and Practice*, Second edition, Oxford University Press (1980).
15. Mullins, L. J. 'The Personnel Function', *HCIMA Journal*, no. 94, October 1979, pp. 22–5.
16. Thomason, G. F. *A Textbook of Personnel Management*, Fourth edition, Institute of Personnel Management (1981).
17. Mullins, L. J. 'The Personnel Function – A Shared Responsibility', *Administrator*, vol. 5, no. 5, May 1985, pp. 14–16.
18. Tse, K. K. *Marks & Spencer*, Pergamon Press (1985) p. 129.
19. See, for example: Hotel and Catering Industry Training Board *Employee Relations*, Fifth edition (March 1984). Previous editions of this booklet were titled *Industrial Relations, A Guide for Managers*.

20. Clegg, H. A. *The Changing System of Industrial Relations in Great Britain*, Basil Blackwell (1980) p. 129.
21. Cuming, M. W. *The Theory and Practice of Personnel Management*, Sixth edition, Heinemann (1989) p. 20.
22. Stewart, R. *Managers and Their Jobs*, Macmillan (1967).
23. Stewart, R. *Contrasts in Management*, McGraw-Hill (1976).
24. Mintzberg, H. *The Nature of Managerial Work*, Harper and Row (1973).
25. Wolf, F. M. 'The Nature of Managerial Work: An Investigation of the Work of the Audit Manager', *Accounting Review*, vol. LVI, no. 4, October 1981, pp. 861–81.
26. McCall, M. W. and Segrist, C. A. *In Pursuit of the Manager's Job: Building on Mintzberg*, Centre for Creative Learning: Greenboro NC (1980).
27. Stewart, R. *Choices for the Manager*, McGraw-Hill (1982).
28. Kotter, J. P. 'What Effective General Managers Really Do', *Harvard Business Review*, vol. 60, no. 6, November–December 1982, pp. 156–67.
29. Ferguson, D. H. and Berger, F. 'Restaurant Managers: What Do They *Really* Do?' *Cornell H.R.A. Quarterly*, May 1984, p. 30.

9. MANAGERIAL BEHAVIOUR AND EFFECTIVENESS

It is the responsibility of management to manage and to achieve results through the efforts of other people. This involves the effective management of human resources. Consideration must be given to the management of people. The way in which managers exercise the responsibility for, and duties of, management is important. Managers are only likely to be effective if they adopt an appropriate style of behaviour.

Objectives

To: (i) Contrast different attitudes and assumptions of managers about human nature and behaviour at work;

(ii) Examine managerial styles in terms of concern for production and concern for people;

(iii) Assess different systems of management and relate these systems to organisational characteristics;

(iv) Appreciate the importance of adopting a caring and positive approach to the management of people;

(v) Evaluate Management by Objectives as a means of improving organisational performance;

(vi) Explain managerial effectiveness and suggest criteria for evaluating the effectiveness of managers;

(vii) Recognise the importance of adopting an appropriate style of managerial behaviour.

MANAGERIAL BEHAVIOUR

The behaviour of managers and their style of management will influence the effort expended and level of performance achieved by subordinate staff.

To repeat the point made in Chapter 1 – in the belief of the author, the majority of people come to work with the *original* intention of being eager to do a good job, and desirous of performing well and to the best of their abilities. Where actual performance fails to match the ideal this is largely a result of how staff perceive they are treated by management. There is, therefore, a heavy responsibility on managers and on the styles and systems of management adopted.

The way in which managers approach the performance of their jobs and the behaviour they display towards subordinate staff is likely to be conditioned by predispositions about people, and human nature and work.

MANAGERS' ATTITUDES TOWARDS PEOPLE

Drawing on *Maslow*'s hierarchy of needs model (which is discussed in Chapter 11), *McGregor* put forward two suppositions about human nature and behaviour at work. He argues that the style of management adopted is a function of the manager's attitudes towards people and assumptions about human nature and behaviour. The two suppositions are called Theory X and Theory Y, and are based on polar assumptions about people and work.[1]

Theory X approach to human nature

Theory X represents the assumptions on which traditional organisations are based, and was widely accepted and practised before the development of the human relations approach. Its assumptions are that:

- the average person is lazy and has an inherent dislike of work;
- most people must be coerced, controlled, directed and threatened with punishment if the organisation is to achieve its objectives; and
- the average person avoids responsibility, prefers to be directed, lacks ambition and values security most of all.

The central principle of Theory X is direction and control through a centralised system of organisation and the exercise of authority. Motivation occurs only at the physiological and security levels of *Maslow*'s hierarchy.

McGregor questions whether the Theory X approach to human nature is correct, and the relevance today of management practices which are based upon it. His argument is based on the belief that changing social structures, educational and occupational opportunities have changed people's expectations of others.

A style of management which rests on Theory X assumptions, and the use of rewards and sanctions exercised by the nature of the manager's position and authority, is no longer appropriate in the modern organisational setting. McGregor implies that most people have the potential to be self-motivating and can best achieve their personal goals through self-direction of their own efforts towards meeting the goals of the organisation. Managers should develop practices based more on an accurate understanding of the nature of human behaviour and motivation.

Theory Y approach to human nature

At the other extreme to Theory X is Theory Y which represents the assumptions consistent with current research knowledge. *The central principle of Theory Y is the integration of individual and organisational goals.* Its assumptions are:

- that work is as natural as play or rest;
- people will exercise self-direction and self-control in the service of objectives to which they are committed;
- commitment to objectives is a function of rewards associated with their achievement;
- given the right conditions, the average worker can learn to accept and to seek responsibility;

- the capacity for creativity in solving organisational problems is distributed widely in the population; and
- the intellectual potential of the average person is only partially utilised.

McGregor implies that a Theory Y approach is the best way to elicit co-operation from members of an organisation. It is the task of management to create the conditions in which individuals may satisfy their motivational needs, and in which they achieve their own goals through meeting the goals of the organisation.

Under Theory Y, motivation is assumed to occur at the affiliation, esteem and self-actualisation levels of *Maslow*'s hierarchy as well as the physiological and security levels. McGregor develops an analysis of the implications of accepting Theory Y in regard to performance appraisal, administration of salaries and promotions, participation, staff–line relationships, leadership, management development and the managerial team.

Demands of the situation

Although Theory X and Theory Y are based on polar extremes and are an over-simplification, they do represent identifiable philosophies which influence managerial behaviour and strategies. The two views tend to represent extremes of the natural inclination of managers towards a particular style of behaviour. In practice, however, the actual style of management behaviour adopted will be influenced by the demands of the situation.[2]

Where the job offers a high degree of intrinsic satisfaction or involves a variety of tasks, an element of problem solving and the exercise of initiative, or where output is difficult to measure in quantitative terms, an informal, participative approach would seem to be more effective. It is more likely to lead to a higher level of staff morale. In many cases this would apply to work of a scientific, technical or professional nature. Where commitment to the goals of the organisation is almost a prerequisite of membership, such as in certain volunteer or charity organisations, for example, then a Theory Y approach would clearly seem to be most appropriate.

However, even if a manager has a basic belief in Theory Y assumptions there may be occasions when it is necessary, or more appropriate, to adopt a Theory X approach. When the nature of the job itself offers little intrinsic reward or limited opportunities to satisfy higher level needs, a more dictatorial style of management might work best. Some jobs are designed narrowly, with highly predictable tasks, and output measured precisely. This is the case, for example, with many complex production processes in manufacturing firms. With these types of jobs a Theory X approach may be needed if an adequate level of performance is to be maintained.

A Theory X approach is also indicated in emergency situations, or where shortage of time or other overriding factors demand the use of authority in directing actions to the tasks in hand. For example, in the hustle, heat and noise of a busy hotel kitchen preparing fresh meals for a large banquet, with many tasks to be co-ordinated over very short time scales, it seems to be recognised that a Theory X style of management is most appropriate. In such circumstances this style of management appears to be accepted by the kitchen staff.

If subordinates match the Theory Y assumptions of the manager, then this style of management may well be effective. However, there are many staff who, whatever the nature of their job, do not wish to accept responsibility at work. They seem to prefer, and respond better to, a more directed and controlled style of management. There are times, therefore, when the manager may be justified in adopting Theory X assumptions about staff.

JAPANESE 'THEORY Z' ENVIRONMENT

A comparison of management style and practice in different cultural settings is provided by *Ouchi*. In contrast to the traditional, more bureaucratic American organisational environment, Ouchi recommends a Japanese style 'Theory Z' environment.

> The problem of productivity in the United States will not be solved with monetary policy nor through more investment in research and development. It will only be remedied when we learn how to manage people in such a way that they can work together more effectively. Theory Z offers several such ways.[3]

The characteristics of a Theory Z organisation are described by Ouchi as:

- long-term employment, often for a lifetime;
- relatively slow process of evaluation and promotion;
- development of company-specific skills, and moderately specialised career path;
- implicit, informal control mechanisms supported by explicit, formal measures;
- participative decision making by consensus;
- collective decision making but individual ultimate responsibility;
- broad concern for the welfare of subordinates and co-workers as a natural part of a working relationship, and informal relationships among people.

In Britain, the operations of the successful Marks and Spencer organisation have been likened to a manner that approaches the typical Japanese company, and with close similarities to the characteristics of a Theory Z organisation.[4]

BEHAVIOURAL IMPLICATIONS OF MANAGEMENT ACCOUNTING

As part of a study of behavioural implications of management accounting and working theories held by accountants, *Caplan* provided a questionnaire on information about the use of standard costs and variance analysis.[5] The questionnaire was given to 20 accountants and a total of 20 production and general managers in different organisations. A series of questions were asked under three broad headings of:

(i) Organisation goals;
(ii) Management accounting goals; and
(iii) The standard cost system.

Although based on a small sample, responses to the questionnaire suggest a widely held belief in Theory X assumptions.

What is the principal (i.e., single most important) goal or objective of your company?

	Accountants	Production and general managers
Achieve maximum profits	75%	25%
Achieve satisfactory profits	5%	40%
Produce high quality product at a competitive cost and reasonable profit	15%	30%
Leader in the industry	–	5%
Stay in business	5%	–

Is it necessary to control costs in your company?

	Accountants	Production and general managers
Yes, because employees will either be deliberately wasteful or lazy, or will, at best, make no real effort to reduce costs	55%	50%
Yes, because management might try to reduce costs on their own but would not have information to do so	45%	45%
No, because employees would do better without such control	–	5%

Would the company be better off if it discontinued use of standard costing and/or variance analysis?

	Accountants	Production and general managers
No	100%	90%
Yes	–	10%

In accomplishing the major goal of the company would it be better for management to become more or less lenient in analysing variances and enforcing standards?

	Accountants	Production and general managers
More lenient	–	30%
Less lenient	85%	60%
About right as is	–	10%
Don't know	15%	–

What is the definition of the term management authority?

	Accountants	Production and general managers
Traditional definition; authority goes with the position and/or delegated from above	80%	65%
Some awareness of modern organisation theory; view of authority as that which others accept	20%	15%
Don't know	–	20%

What is the attitude of line production foremen and workers to the use of standard costs as a control technique?

	Accountants	Production and general managers
Foremen		
In favour	90%	65%
Not in favour	10%	35%
Workers		
In favour	60%	50%
Not in favour	30%	35%
Unaware of system or indifferent	10%	15%

(Extracted and adapted with permission from: E. H. Caplan, *Management Accounting and Behavioral Science*, © 1971, Addison-Wesley, Reading, Massachusetts. Pp. 71–81.)

THE MANAGERIAL GRID

One means of describing and evaluating different styles of management is the *Blake* and *Mouton* Managerial Grid® (*see* Fig. 9.1), first published in 1964, and restated in 1978 and 1985.[6] The managerial grid provides a basis for comparison of managerial styles in terms of two principal dimensions:

(i) concern for production; and
(ii) concern for people.

Concern for production, that is the amount of emphasis which the manager places on achieving production, getting results or profits, is represented along the horizontal axis of the Grid.

Concern for people, that is subordinates and colleagues as individuals, is represented along the vertical axis of the Grid.

Each axis is on a scale of 1–9 indicating varying degrees of concern that the manager has for either production or for people. The manner in which these two concerns are linked together depends upon the use of the hierarchy, the 'boss aspect', and assumptions that the manager makes about how to achieve production with and through people, and the use of power.

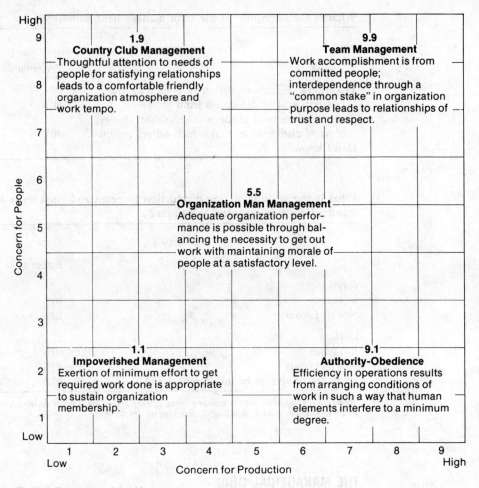

Fig. 9.1 The managerial grid
(Reproduced with permission from Blake, Robert R. and Mouton, Jane Srygley, *The Managerial Grid III*. Copyright © Gulf Publishing Company, Houston (1985) p. 12.)

Five basic combinations

Blake and *Mouton* define 'concern for' not as how much concern, but as indicating the character and strength of assumptions which underlie the manager's own basic attitudes and style of management. The significant point is 'how' the manager expresses concern about production or about people. The four quadrants of the Grid provide five basic combinations of degree of concern for production coupled with degree of concern for people:

- *the impoverished manager* (1,1 rating), low concern for production and low concern for people;
- *the authority–obedience (or task) manager* (9,1 rating), high concern for production and low concern for people;
- *the country club manager* (1,9 rating), low concern for production and high concern for people;
- *the organisation man (or middle-of-the-road) manager* (5,5 rating), moderate concern for production and moderate concern for people; and
- *the team manager* (9,9 rating), high concern for production and high concern for people.

Managers with a 1,1 rating tend to be remote from their subordinates and believe in the minimum movement from their present position. They do as little as they can with production or with people. Too much attention to production will cause difficulties with staff and too much attention to the needs of staff will cause problems with production.

Managers with a 9,1 rating are autocratic. They tend to rely on a centralised system and the use of authority. Staff are regarded as a means of production and motivation is based on competition between people in order to get work done. If staff challenge an instruction or standard procedure they are likely to be viewed as unco-operative.

The 1,9 rating managers believe that a contented staff will undertake what is required of them and achieve a reasonable level of output. Production is secondary to the avoidance of conflict and maintenance of harmony among the staff. Managers will seek to find compromises between staff and solutions acceptable to everyone. Although innovation may be encouraged, they tend to reject good ideas if likely to cause difficulties among the staff.

The 5,5 rating is the middle-of-the-road management with the approach of 'live and let live' and a tendency to avoid the real issues. This style of management is the 'dampened pendulum' with managers swinging between concern for production and concern for people. Under pressure, this style of management tends to become task management (9,1). But where this strains relations and causes resentment from staff, pressure is eased and managers adopt a compromise approach. If there is a swing too much the other way (towards 1,9) managers are likely to take a tighter and more hardened approach.

Managers with a 9,9 rating believe in the integrating of the task needs and concern for people. They believe in creating a situation whereby people can satisfy their own needs by commitment to the objectives of the organisation. Managers will discuss problems with the staff, seek their ideas and give them freedom of action. Difficulties in working relationships will be handled by confronting staff directly and attempting to work out solutions with them.

Blake and Mouton then go on to provide a comprehensive analysis of each of the major Grid styles in terms of: motivations; managing conflict; behavioural elements; management practice; consequences; recognising behaviour of the Grid style; suggestions for change.

Framework for patterns of behaviour

These five styles of management represent the extremes of the managerial Grid. With a nine point scale on each axis there is a total of 81 different 'mixtures' of concern for production and concern for people. Most people would come up with a score somewhere in an intermediary position on the managerial Grid.

Although the managerial Grid is a simplified concept it does provide a framework in which managers can identify, study and review their patterns of behaviour. Instead of viewing management styles as a dichotomy of 'either/or', *Blake* and *Mouton* claim the managerial Grid illustrates that the manager can gain the benefits of maximising, simultaneously, methods which are both production-oriented and people-oriented. Blake and Mouton maintain that the 9,9 position, although an ideal, is worth working for.

Based on their experience of using the original Grid, Blake and Mouton give three reasons why it is important to consider which style of management is used to achieve production through people.

- The 9,9 style of management correlates positively with bottom line productivity.
- 9,9 oriented managers enjoy maximum career success.
- There is now greater knowledge about the correlation between extreme grid styles of management, and mental and physical health.

Blake and Mouton provide a self-assessment questionnaire in two parts. First, there are five different descriptions of managerial behaviour which are to be ranked 5 to 1 as most to least typical. Second, there is a series of five statements relating to the different descriptions, under each of six headings: (1) decisions, (2) convictions, (3) conflict, (4) temper, (5) humour and (6) effort. From each heading is selected the one statement which describes best the person's behaviour. Results obtained from the questionnaire give an indication of the person's likely dominant style of management. Responses to the questionnaire can be compared with those of typical managers who are generally successful.

Dominant style of management

From their research, *Blake* and *Mouton* found that managers tend to have one dominant style of management which they use more often than any other. They found also that many managers have a 'back-up' style which they adopt if their dominant style does not work in a particular situation. Blake and Mouton suggest that the dominant style of management is influenced in any particular situation by any of four conditions.

- *Organisation* – the nature of the organisation in which the manager is employed, and the extent to which there are rigid rules and regulations.
- *Values* – the personal values, beliefs or ideals which the manager holds concerning how to treat people or to manage results.
- *Personal history* – the deep-rooted personal history of the manager may be an important factor, and lead to a preference for a particular approach because that style may have been experienced frequently in the past.
- *Chance* – the manager may not have been confronted with, or had personal experience of, alternative sets of assumptions about how to manage. 'Chance' has not provided the manager with an opportunity to learn.

Organisation development programme

Blake and *Mouton* have designed an organisation development programme based on group dynamics which is aimed at bringing about a style of management with a 9,9 concern for production and concern for people. The programme consists of six phases divided into two parts. Part one involves management development through: (i) laboratory-seminar training and introduction to the concepts of the Grid; and (ii) team building. Part two involves helping managers work towards organisation development through: (iii) intergroup development; (iv) designing organisational strategy; (v) implementing development; and (vi) consolidation, and stabilising progress made during the earlier phases. (*See also* Chapter 17.)

MANAGEMENT SYSTEMS

Work by *McGregor*, and by *Blake* and *Mouton*, suggests that an organisation is more likely to harness effectively its staffing resources if there is a participative style of management. This view is supported by the work of *Likert*. On the basis of a questionnaire to managers in over 200 organisations and research into the performance characteristics of different types of organisations, Likert identifies a four-fold model of management systems.[7] These systems are designated by number:

System 1 (Exploitive authoritative);
System 2 (Benevolent authoritative);
System 3 (Consultative);
and System 4 (Participative group).

System 1 – Exploitive authoritative – decisions are imposed on subordinates, motivation is based on threats, there is very little team-work or communication, responsibility is centred at the top of the organisational hierarchy.

System 2 – Benevolent authoritative – there is a condescending form of leadership, motivation is based on a system of rewards, there is only limited team-work or communication, there is responsibility at managerial levels but not at lower levels of the organisational hierarchy.

System 3 – Consultative – leadership involves some trust in subordinates, motivation is based on rewards but also some involvement, there is a fair degree of team-work, and communication takes place vertically and horizontally, responsibility for achieving the goals of the organisation is spread more widely throughout the hierarchy.

System 4 – Participative group – leadership involves trust and confidence in subordinates, motivation is based on rewards for achievement of agreed goals, there is participation and a high degree of team-work and communication, responsibility for achieving the goals of the organisation is widespread throughout all levels of the hierarchy.

Profile of organisational characteristics

Likert has also established a 'profile of organisational characteristics' describing the nature of the four different management systems. The profile compares the four systems in terms of a table of organisational variables under the headings of:

(i)   leadership processes;
(ii) motivational forces;
(iii) communication process;
(iv) interaction–influence process;
(v)   decision-making process;
(vi) goal setting or ordering; and
(vii) control processes.

Using this table, Likert undertook a survey of several hundred managers comprising different groups from a wide range of experience, and in both line and staff positions. His studies confirmed that least productive departments or units tended to employ management practices within Systems 1 and 2, and the most productive departments or units employed management practices within Systems 3 and 4.

Organisational variables	System 1 Exploitive Authoritative	System 2 Benevolent Authoritative	System 3 Consultative	System 4 Participative Group	Item no.
Leadership					
How much confidence and trust is shown in subordinates?	Virtually none	Some	Substantial amount	A great deal	1
How free do they feel to talk to superiors about job?	Not very free	Somewhat free	Quite free	Very free	2
How often are subordinates' ideas sought and used constructively?	Seldom	Sometimes	Often	Very frequently	3
Motivation					
Is predominant use made of 1 fear, 2 threats, 3 punishment, 4 rewards, 5 involvement?	1, 2, 3 occasionally 4	4, some 3	4, some 3 and 5	5, 4 based on group set goals	4
Where is responsibility felt for achieving organisation's goals?	Mostly at top	Top and middle	Fairly general	At all levels	5
How much co-operative teamwork exists?	Very little	Relatively little	Moderate amount	Great deal	6
Communication					
What is the usual direction of information flow?	Downward	Mostly downward	Down and up	Down, up and sideways	7
How is downward communication accepted?	With suspicion	Possibly with suspicion	With caution	With a receptive mind	8
How accurate is upward communication?	Usually inaccurate	Often inaccurate	Often accurate	Almost always accurate	9
How well do superiors know problems faced by subordinates?	Not very well	Rather well	Quite well	Very well	10
Decisions					
At what level are decisions made?	Mostly at top	Policy at top, some delegation	Broad policy at top, more delegation	Throughout but well integrated	11
Are subordinates involved in decisions related to their work?	Almost never	Occasionally consulted	Generally consulted	Fully involved	12
What does decision-making process contribute to motivation?	Not very much	Relatively little	Some contribution	Substantial contribution	13
Goals					
How are organisational goals established?	Orders issued	Orders, some comments invited	After discussion by orders	By group action (except in crisis)	14
How much covert resistance to goals is present?	Strong resistance	Moderate resistance	Some resistance at times	Little or none	15
Control					
How concentrated are review and control functions?	Very highly at top	Quite highly at top	Moderate delegation to lower levels	Widely shared	16
Is there an informal organisation resisting the formal one?	Yes	Usually	Sometimes	No ... same goals as formal	17
What are cost, productivity and other control data used for?	Policing, punishment	Reward, punishment	Reward some self-guidance	Self-guidance problem solving	18

Fig. 9.2 Short form profile of organisational characteristics

(Adapted and reproduced with permission from: Likert, R. and Likert, J. G., *New Ways of Managing Conflict*, McGraw-Hill (1976) p. 75.)

A shorter and simpler form of the profile of organisational characteristics is provided by Likert and Likert (Fig. 9.2).[8]

Systems 1 and 2 management

Systems 1 and 2 can be related to *McGregor's* Theory X. System 4 provides the basic assumptions and approaches of Theory Y, and is based on involvement, supportive relationships and participation. Organisational decisions are improved as they are based on more accurate information and there is greater motivation to implement the decisions. *Likert* found, for example, that: 'In Systems 1 and 2 organizations . . . high performance goals by superiors, coupled with high-pressure supervision using tight budgets and controls, yield high productivity initially because of compliance based on fear.'[9]

However, because of unfavourable attitudes, poor communication, lack of co-operative motivation and restriction of output, the long-term result is high absence and labour turnover, and low productivity and earnings. Likert suggests that the nearer the behavioural characteristics of an organisation approach System 4 the more likely this will lead to long-term improvement in labour turnover and high productivity, low scrap, low costs and high earnings.

System 4 management

Likert sets out three fundamental concepts of System 4 management. These are the use of:

- the principle of supportive relationships among members of the organisation and in particular between superior and subordinate;
- group decision making and group methods of organisation and supervision; and
- high performance aspirations for all members of the organisation.

Supportive relationships are intended to enhance self-esteem and ego building, contribute to subordinates' sense of personal worth and importance, and maintain their sense of significance and dignity. The superior's behaviour is regarded as supportive when this entails:

- mutual confidence and trust;
- help to maintain a good income;
- understanding of work problems and help in doing the job;
- genuine interest in personal problems;
- help with training to assist promotion;
- sharing of information;
- seeking opinions about work problems;
- being friendly and approachable; and
- giving credit and recognition where due.

Group decision making and supervision use an overlapping form of structure. Individuals known as 'linking-pins' are members not only of their own group but also of the next superior group and, where appropriate, of peer groups. This enables each work group to be linked to the rest of the organisation. (The linking-pin process is discussed further in Chapter 13.)

In System 4 management interaction and decision making rely heavily on group processes, and discussions focus on the decisions to be made. Likert emphasises that group methods of decision making should not be confused with the use of committees. With the group method of decision making the superior is held responsible for the quality and implementation of decisions. The superior is responsible for developing subordinates into an effective group.

In considering high performance aspirations, Likert refers to studies which suggest that employees generally want stable employment and job security, opportunities for promotion, and satisfactory compensation. They want, also, to feel proud of their organisation, and its performance and accomplishments. In System 4 management, superiors should therefore have high performance aspirations, but so also should every member of the organisation. To be effective, these high performance goals should not be imposed but set by a participative mechanism involving group decision making and a multiple overlapping group structure. The mechanism should enable employees to be involved in setting high performance goals which help to satisfy their own needs.

Employee-centred or job-centred supervision

Likert provides a contrast between employee-centred and job-centred styles of supervision, and orientation towards employees.

> The point of view of an assistant manager of a low-production department illustrates job-centered supervision: 'This interest-in-people approach is all right, but it's a luxury. I've got to keep pressure on for production, and when I get production up, then I can afford to take time to show an interest in my employees and their problems.'

This contrasts with the view of a manager of a high-producing division.

> One way in which we accomplish a high level of production is by letting people do the job the way they want to so long as they accomplish the objectives. I believe in letting them take time out from the monotony. Make them feel that they are something special, not just the run of the mill. As a matter of fact, I tell them if you feel that job is getting you down get away from it for a few minutes. . . . If you keep employees from feeling hounded, they are apt to put out the necessary effort to get the work done in the required time.
>
> I never make any decisions myself. Oh, I guess I've made about two since I've been here. If people know their jobs I believe in letting them make decisions. I believe in delegating decision-making. Of course, if there's anything that affects the whole division, then the two assistant managers, the three section heads and sometimes the assistant section heads come in here and we discuss it. I don't believe in saying that this is the way it's going to be. After all, once supervision and management are in agreement there won't be any trouble selling the staff the idea.
>
> My job is dealing with human beings rather than with the work. It doesn't matter if I have anything to do with the work or not. The chances are that people will do a better job if you are really taking an interest in them. Knowing the names is important and helps a lot, but it's not enough. You really have to know each individual well, know what his problems are. Most of the time I discuss matters with employees at their desks rather than in the office. Sometimes I sit on a waste paper basket or lean on the files. It's all very informal. People don't seem to like to come into the office to talk.[10]

Causal, intervening and end-result variables

Likert refers to three broad classes of variables relating to the firm's human organisation and its operations: (i) causal, (ii) intervening and (iii) end-result.

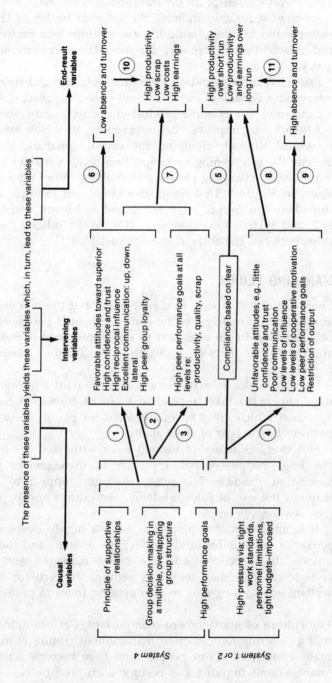

Fig. 9.3 Simplified diagram of relationships among variables for System 1 or 2 and System 4 operation
(Reproduced with permission from Likert, R., *The Human Organization*, McGraw-Hill (1967) p. 137.)

Causal variables are independent variables which can be amended by the organisation and its management, for example management policies, the structure of an organisation, leadership strategies. Causal variables determine development of an organisation and the results it achieves.

Intervening variables indicate the internal health of the organisation, for example the loyalties, attitudes, motivations and performance of members and their collective capacity for interaction, communication and decision making.

End-result variables indicate the final outcome and reflect the influences of intervening variables. The end-result variables reflect the achievement of the organisation, for example productivity, costs, scrap, earnings.

Attempts to improve the intervening variables are likely to be more successful through changing the causal variables, rather than changing directly the intervening variables. End-result variables are most likely to be improved by changing the causal variables, rather than the intervening variables. In Figure 9.3 Likert gives a simplified example of the interrelationships between causal, intervening and end-result variables in the System 1 or 2, and System 4 management. The arrows indicate the pattern of relationships between the three classes of variables.

MANAGING PEOPLE

There are many aspects to management but the one essential ingredient of any successful manager is the ability to handle people effectively. The work of *Likert* has drawn attention to the importance of System 4 management and a people-centred approach to managing people within a work organisation.

Popular books on management and the nature of organisational effectiveness appear to take a positive view of human nature and support an approach which gives encouragement for people to work willingly and to perform to the best of their ability.[11]

However, as many of us will have witnessed for ourselves, an understanding, people-centred approach to management seems often to be lacking in practice. Too many managers appear to attempt to manage through the use of rules, systems, procedures and paperwork, rather than *with and through people*.

It is important that managers have a highly developed sense of *people-perception*, and understand the feelings of staff, and their needs and expectations. It is people who are being managed and people should be considered in human terms. A genuine concern for people and for their welfare goes a long way in encouraging them to perform well.

The culture of management

The culture of management is important. For example, *Freemantle* suggests that a festering deficiency in management culture is that managers are not really concerned about people until they become a problem. As a result: 'management thinking has become corrupted by two major obessions: (1) An obsession with developing sophisticated systems for managing people more successfully (paper panaceas); (2) An obsession with trade union power (union paranoia)'.[12]

According to Freemantle, the perception of 'people as costs' leads to relatively little weight being given to people management and leadership skills when appointing managers. Many companies tend to appoint technical specialists to managerial positions, neglecting the vital task of managing people. Chief executives and personnel managers have allowed middle managers to opt out of the key task of leading their people in favour of filling in even more forms (the paper panacea). However, Freemantle does point out exceptions such as Mars, IBM, and Marks and Spencer, who in pursuit of excellence devote a high priority to people management and considerable time, energy and effort to the vital process of managing people.

In order to eliminate the corruption of management thinking, it is important to remove the paper panaceas and divert attention from paranoia about trade unions. Freemantle believes that managers must get back to the basics and concentrate their minds on five essential principles (which are very much in line with the views of the author).

- The successful management of people based on honesty, trust, openness, mutual respect, co-operation and support.
- Developing a perception of employees as an essential asset to be invested in, rather than a variable cost to be minimised.
- Ensuring managers have a clearly established set of principles (such as the above) which they can apply on a minute-by-minute basis in their daily management task.
- Fundamentals of leadership (as opposed to leadership systems) relating to vision, charisma and ability to gain team commitment and co-operation.
- The establishment of basic but essential practices, such as: clarity about their accountabilities; knowing how to care for people; knowing how to command respect; knowing the difference between a leader and a manager; knowing how to set high standards and achieve them; knowing how to manage people successfully and to achieve individual managerial excellence.

A caring and positive approach

There are, of course, organisations that do adopt a caring and positive approach to the management of people. One example of an interesting and enlightened people approach is put forward by Mary Kay Ash of Mary Kay Cosmetics in America.[13] Founded in 1963, the company had grown in 20 years to a multi-million corporation with a sales force of 200,000 people. The UK branch opened in 1984.

Ash writes about the intentional development of a management concept that allows fairness to flourish in business, the belief that people will shine if given a chance, and methods that are applicable to any organisation. Her concept of the management of people is based on the Golden Rule 'Do unto others as you would have them do unto you', with emphasis on being a 'people company'. (Again, this is a philosophy very much in line with the views of the author.)

> People come first at Mary Kay Cosmetics – our beauty consultants, sales directors and employees, our customers, and our suppliers. We pride ourselves as a 'company known for the people it keeps.' Our belief in caring for people, however, does not conflict with our need as a corporation to generate a profit.[14]

The philosophy of 'Golden Rule Management' is applied in such ways as, for example:

- *Treat people fairly but according to merit.* In order to balance responsibilities to the company, the employee, and all other employees, every manager must be able to say 'no'. But employees should be encouraged to turn a 'no' into the motivation to accomplish more.
- However busy you are, *make the other person feel important*, and let people know you appreciate them.
- *Motivate people through giving praise.* A good manager must understand the value of praising people to success.
- *Encourage feedback* and don't undervalue the ability to listen.
- *Sandwich every bit of criticism between two layers of heavy praise.*
- *An open-door philosophy.*
- *Help other people get what they want* – and you will get what you want. Good managers' success is reflected in the success of their people.
- *Never hide behind policy or pomposity.*

The human cost of poor management

The style of managerial behaviour has an obvious and direct effect both on the well-being of staff and on their level of work performance. Managers decide the manner in which work duties and responsibilities are to be undertaken. Different styles of management may be appropriate in managing different people in different circumstances. And a more autocratic management may not *necessarily* be a bad thing.

However, the environment of the work organisation and the nature of the manager–subordinate relationship can cause tension and stress. Increasing attention is being given to the number of health problems that are classified as stress-related and affected by working conditions. It is important to remember both the effects on organisational performance *and* the potentially high human cost of inappropriate management.[15]

MANAGEMENT BY OBJECTIVES

One particular approach to the activities involved in planning, organisation, direction and control, and to the execution of work, is Management by Objectives (MBO). MBO is a phrase used to describe a style or system of management which attempts to relate organisational goals to individual performance and development through the involvement of all levels of management. The basis of a system of MBO is:

- the setting of objectives and targets;
- participation by individual managers in agreeing unit objectives and criteria of performance; and
- review and appraisal of results.

The phrase Management by Objectives appears to have been introduced by *Drucker* in 1954.[16] The approach was taken up by *McGregor* who advocated its use as a preferred means of goal setting, appraisal of managerial performance and self-assessment. It was developed and popularised by writers such as *Odiorne* and *Humble*. As a result of work by these and other writers,[17] the system of MBO has been adopted in a wide range of organisational settings, in the public as well as the private sector.[18] Odiorne describes Management by Objectives as:

> a process whereby the superior and subordinate managers of an organization jointly identify its common goals, define each individual's major areas of responsibility in terms of the results expected of him, and use these measures as guides for operating the unit and assessing the contribution of each of its members.[19] (Figure 9.4)

A system of MBO means that instead of subordinates being told exactly how to do their work, they are given definite tasks and results to be achieved. Within agreed limits and the policies of the organisation, the subordinates are given freedom of action to decide how best to achieve these results. Measurement of performance is in terms of the subordinates' degree of accomplishment rather than the ability to follow instructions on how to undertake their work. *A system of Management by Objectives can be contrasted, therefore, with a style of management based on direction and control, and the adherence to rules.*

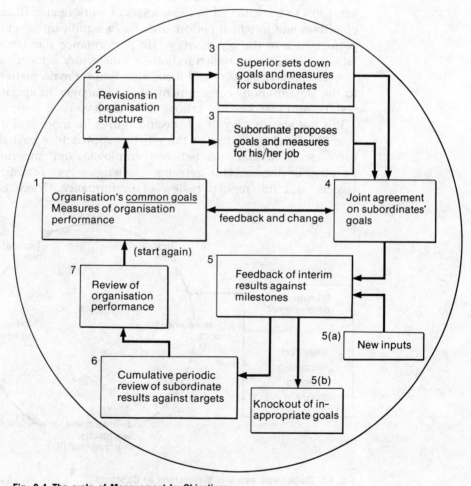

Fig. 9.4 The cycle of Management by Objectives
(From Odiorne, G. S., *Management by Objectives*, Pitman Publishing (1965) p. 78.)

Main stages of MBO The main stages of MBO are set out by *Humble* (*see* Fig. 9.5) as a continuous process of:

- the critical review and restatement of strategic and tactical plans for the organisation;
- the contribution of individual managers in clarifying their key results areas and standards of performance;
- agreement on a job improvement plan through which the manager can make a contribution to improved organisational performance;
- provision of a flexible organisation structure and system of management control information which makes for self-control and quicker decisions;
- the use of performance review to appraise progress in achieving results, and potential review to identify potential for advancement;
- development of management training plans and the acceptance of responsibility for self-development; and
- effective selection, salary and succession plans in order to strengthen the motivation of the manager.[20]

A key results analysis will identify: (i) the main purpose of the job, and the key tasks to be achieved in those areas of work related directly to achieving objectives and in which performance has a significant effect on the economic performance of the organisation; (ii) performance standards, either quantitative or qualitative, which indicate a satisfactory achievement of results.

A job improvement plan will focus attention on main matters of importance to the organisation, commitment of the manager to specific improvement results, and standards of actions to be achieved.

It is not always easy to set specific figures for more senior jobs, but whatever the level or nature of the job the approach is basically the same. It involves: (i) discussions between employee and superior on the basic purpose of the job; (ii) agreeing challenging yet realistic and attainable targets; and (iii) regular review of performance. There is, however, the

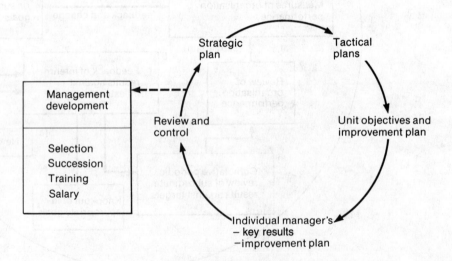

Fig. 9.5 The dynamic nature of Management by Objectives
(Reproduced with permission from Humble, J. W., *Management by Objectives*, Management Publications Limited for The British Institute of Management (1972) p. 32.)

danger that objectives which are more difficult to specify and measure in precise terms are neglected because of the emphasis on objectives which are more easily monitored. A system of MBO may also be more difficult to apply in a dynamic environment, or where objectives are subject to continual and rapid change.

Applications of MBO   A number of writers refer to MBO as a 'technique'. For example, *Argenti* describes MBO as a technique by which job descriptions are studied carefully to give precise details of results expected. Key words are translated into figures. For example: 'operate the doggling machine efficiently' is translated to 'maintain oil pressure at 60, revolutions per minute at 27, and rate of output at 425 per hour over a period of 6.8 hours a day'.[21] This might, perhaps, be appropriate at the operator level and in the example given by Argenti, but MBO is broader than this. It can take a number of different forms in different organisations and is more correctly described as *a style or system of management.*

MBO draws attention to the objectives for individual members of the organisation and how these objectives relate to the objectives for the organisation as a whole. MBO can be integrated into a system of corporate planning and top level management decisions on long-term objectives for the organisation as a whole. In public sector organisations, such as local government, MBO can be integrated into a planning, programming, budgeting system and decisions on the allocation of resources.

MBO is usually regarded as applying to subordinate managers and to the clarification of objectives for the units under their control. However, there is no reason why the principles of MBO cannot be applied to staff throughout all levels of an organisation. The introduction of MBO for managers may result in them adopting a more participative style of management with their subordinate staff.

Potential advantages of MBO   MBO is potentially an attractive system. It provides an opportunity for staff to accept greater responsibility and to make a higher level of personal contribution. There is much to recommend it to both the organisation and individual managers. Advantages generally claimed for MBO include:

- concentrates attention on main areas where it is important for the organisation to be effective;
- identifies problem areas in progress towards achievement of objectives;
- improves management control information and performance standards;
- leads to a sound organisation structure, clarifies responsibilities, and aids delegation and co-ordination;
- identifies where changes are needed and seeks continual improvement in results;
- aids management succession planning;
- identifies training needs, and provides an environment which encourages personal growth and self-discipline;
- improves appraisal systems, and provides a more equitable procedure for determining rewards and promotion plans;
- improves communications and interpersonal relationships; and
- encourages motivation to improve individual performance.

Based on a review of specific organisational MBO programmes, *Carroll* and *Tosi* conclude that 'the adoption of this approach can improve managerial performance, managerial attitudes, and organizational planning'.

However, they point out that their research also indicates that 'MBO programs require considerable time and effort expenditures for successful adoption, and unless they are given adequate support and attention and are well integrated into the organization, they will fail or not live up to expectations'.[22]

Requirements of a successful MBO programme

If an MBO programme is to be successful it requires:

- the commitment and active support of top management;
- specialist advice on implementation of the system and a thorough understanding by all the staff concerned;
- careful attention to the setting of key tasks, target figures and performance standards;
- objectives which are profitable to the organisation, clearly defined, realistically attainable, and capable of measurement;
- genuine participation by staff in agreeing objectives and targets;
- the right spirit and interest from staff concerned and effective team-work;
- avoidance of excessive paperwork and forms which lead to a mechanistic approach; and
- maintaining the impetus of the system.

Criticisms and limitations of MBO

MBO has been likened to a modern form of scientific management. It is also subject to the same possible criticisms of too great an emphasis on individual job definitions together with a management authority structure, and the assumption of no conflict between individual and organisational goals. MBO should not be applied simply as a pressure device by which management apply increasingly demanding targets which staff are expected to achieve.[23]

The system of MBO is usually associated with a sophisticated performance appraisal scheme and rating scales. But this approach may cause people to lose sight of the underlying principles and to regard the system as a substitute for the successful management of people.[24]

The practical effectiveness of MBO appears to be a matter of debate and many of the criticisms or limitations are related to the formulation of appraisal schemes. *Kane* and *Freeman* explain a number of common problems which are inherent flaws in any MBO-based appraisal scheme.

(i)   *The rate-setting phenomenon.* When rewards are based on performance appraisals employees can be expected to adopt an economic rationality orientation towards their objectives, and to attempt to set and maintain objectives at the lowest level possible to maximise the probability of attaining them.

(ii) *Lack of comparability in performance standards.* It is impossible to set standards for attaining each rating level which are comparable in difficulty. To the extent that members of staff participate in setting their own objectives their difficulty is determined more by relative bargaining skills than by concern for equity.

(iii) *Basing performance appraisal on MBO results in the forcing of objectives to fit the boundaries of individual jobs* rather than work groups or organisational subdivisions.

(iv) *Excessive emphasis on short-term accomplishment.* When appraisal results are used for personnel decisions (such as pay, merit awards, promotion or retention) such decisions are usually made within an annual period. The organisation must, therefore, set objectives related to short-term perspectives.

(v) *Substitution of supervisory discretion for measurement.* A performance appraisal scheme must satisfy the requirements of a measurement system. If cases occur that are not covered by any of the assignment rules, the measurement process falls under the control of the subjective whims of the measurers.

(vi) *Lost flexibility.* Most organisations go through periods of change and uncertainty when it is necessary for the nature or emphasis of activities to shift. Staff are bound to perceive that it is risky to respond to contingencies at their own discretion and sacrifice progress towards their objectives.

(vii) *Distortion of accountability.* The philosophy of MBO has been that objectives should refer to the expected output levels of a manager's work unit rather than to the expected effectiveness of the manager's performance. A highly effective manager can receive low appraisal ratings when the work unit fails to achieve its objectives for reasons outside the control of the manager. An ineffective manager can still receive high ratings when the work unit achieves its objective despite the incompetence of the manager.

(viii) *Uselessness as a predictor for promotion decisions.* Performance in a lower-level job can predict performance in a higher-level job only if the two jobs share common functions. Performance measurements on specific functions cannot be isolated when an MBO-based appraisal scheme is used.

(ix) *The bottleneck syndrome.* Objectives must be set for every work unit at the onset of the organisation's annual period of operation, and all 'come due' at the same time. This creates a tremendous administrative bottleneck for managers and supervisors.[25]

MANAGERIAL EFFECTIVENESS

The overall responsibility of management can be seen as the attainment of the given objectives of the organisation. Upon the attainment of its aims and objectives will rest the success and ultimate survival of the organisation. There is therefore a clear and important need for effective management. And this need is just as strong in public sector organisations as in private enterprise organisations. Indeed, it could be argued that in local government, for example, the accountability of public servants to elected members for their actions means that professional standards of management of the highest order are even more essential.[26] But whether in private or public sector organisations, managerial effectiveness is a difficult concept both to define and to measure.

Efficiency and effectiveness

Writers such as *Reddin* and *Drucker*[27] distinguish managerial efficiency from managerial effectiveness.

Efficiency is concerned with 'doing things right', and relates to inputs and what the manager does.

Effectiveness is concerned with 'doing the right things', and relates to outputs of the job and what the manager actually achieves.

Drucker also relates managerial effectiveness to essential practices such as: the management of time; an outward contribution in terms of results rather than work; building on existing strengths of people and in the situation; concentration on major areas of performance and establishing priorities; and judgement in decision making.[28]

To be efficient the manager must attend therefore to the input requirements of the job – to clarification of objectives, planning, organisation, direction and control. *But in order to be effective*, the manager must give attention to outputs of the job – to performance in terms of such factors as obtaining best possible results in the important areas of the organisation, optimising use of resources, increasing profitability, and attainment of the aims and objectives of the organisation.

Effectiveness must be related to the achievement of some purpose, objective or task – to the performance of the process of management and the execution of work. Criteria for assessing the effectiveness of a manager should be considered in terms of measuring the results that the manager is intended to achieve. *But what is also important is the manner in which the manager achieves results and the effects on other people.* This may well influence effectiveness in the longer term. Managerial effectiveness results from a combination of personal attributes and dimensions of the manager's job in meeting the demands of the situation, and satisfying the requirements of the organisation.

Measures of effectiveness

Management involves getting work done through the co-ordinated efforts of other people. Managers are judged, not just on their own performance, but also on the results achieved by subordinate staff. The manager's effectiveness may be assessed in part, therefore, by such factors as

- the strength of motivation and morale of staff;
- the success of their training and development; and
- the creation of an organisational environment in which staff work willingly and effectively.

The difficulty is determining objective measurement of such factors. Some possible indication might be given by, for example:

- the level of staff turnover;
- the incidence of sickness;
- absenteeism;
- poor time keeping; and
- accidents at work.

However, such figures are likely to be influenced also by broader organisational or environmental considerations, for example poor job security due to the economic climate, which are outside the direct control of the individual manager. In any case, there is the general question of the extent to which such figures bear a direct relationship to the actual performance of subordinate staff. *Other criteria which may give some indication of managerial effectiveness include the efficiency of systems and procedures, and the standard of service afforded to other departments.* Again, however, there is the question of how to determine objective measurement of such criteria.

For some management jobs it might be possible to identify more quantitative factors which *may* give an indication of managerial effectiveness, including:

- meeting important deadlines;
- accuracy of work carried out by the department, perhaps measured by the number of recorded errors;
- level of complaints received from other departments, customers or clients, suppliers, the public;
- adherence to quality standards, and the amount of scrap or waste material;
- keeping within agreed cost or budgetary control limits; and
- productivity.

Manager's checklist *Stewart* suggests that it is often salutary for managers to compare what they think they do against what happens in practice. Answers to the following questions will help managers decide what, if anything, they should check.[29]

1. Am I giving adequate attention to current activities, to reviewing the past and to planning for the future? In particular, am I giving enough thought to the future?
2. Am I dividing my time correctly between different aspects of my job? Is there, perhaps, one part of my job on which I spend too much of my time?
3. Have I allowed for the effects of changes which have taken place in the content of my job on my objectives and on the organization of my work?
4. Am I certain that I am not doing any work that I ought to have delegated?
5. Who are the people that I ought to be seeing? Am I spending too much or too little time with any of them?
6. Do I organize my working day and week, as far as possible, according to priorities, or do I tend to deal with each problem as it turns up, without stopping to think whether there is something more important that I should be working on?
7. Am I able to complete a task, or am I constantly interrupted? If the latter, are all these interruptions an essential part of my work?
8. What have I done recently to further my own development? How long is it since I read a book or article in my field?

There are three questions that managers should ask of any of their activities.

Should it be done at all?
If so, when should it be done?
Should it be delegated?

(The nature of delegation is discussed in the following chapter.)

3-D MODEL OF MANAGERIAL BEHAVIOUR

However effectiveness is measured, managers are only likely to be effective if they adopt the most appropriate style of behaviour.

A development of the *Blake* and *Mouton* Managerial Grid, discussed earlier, is the three-dimensional (3-D) model of managerial behaviour suggested by *Reddin*.[30] By adding a third dimension of managerial effectiveness to task orientation and relationship orientation, the 3-D model identifies eight possible styles of managerial behaviour.

Task orientation (TO) is the extent to which the manager directs both personal and subordinates' efforts through planning, organisation and control.

Relationship orientation (RO) is dependent upon the manager's personal job relationships. This is characterised by consideration for subordinates' feelings, mutual trust and encouragement.

The combination of TO and RO determines the manager's basic style of behaviour. The four possible basic styles (*see* Fig. 9.6) are similar to those identified by Blake and Mouton in the Managerial Grid.

Each of these four basic styles of management can be effective or ineffective depending on the situation in which they are applied. *Effectiveness* is defined by Reddin as 'the extent to which a manager achieves the output requirements of his position. . . . Managerial effectiveness has to be defined in terms of output rather than input, by what a manager achieves rather than by what he does'.[31]

Reddin distinguishes managerial effectiveness from (i) apparent effectiveness, and from (ii) personal effectiveness.

Apparent effectiveness is the extent to which the behaviour of the manager – for example punctuality, giving prompt answers, tidiness, making quick decisions and good public relations – gives the appearance of effectiveness. Such qualities may or may not be relevant to effectiveness.

Personal effectiveness is the extent to which the manager achieves personal objectives – for example power and prestige – rather than the objectives of the organisation.

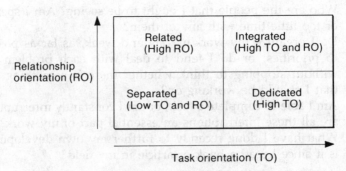

Fig. 9.6 The four basic styles of management behaviour

Eight styles of managerial behaviour

Applying the third dimension of managerial effectiveness provides eight styles of managerial behaviour – four effective styles, which achieve output requirements, and four ineffective styles (*see* Fig. 9.7). For each of the basic styles – separated, dedicated, related or integrated – there is a more effective

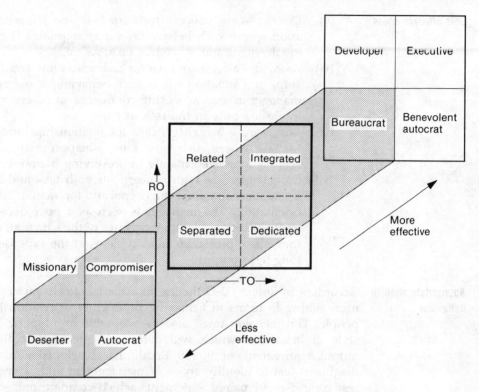

Fig. 9.7 The 3-D model of managerial effectiveness
(Reproduced with permission from Reddin, W. J., *Managerial Effectiveness*, McGraw-Hill (1970) p. 206.)

or less effective version. Effectiveness results from the appropriateness of a particular style of management to the demands of the situation in which it is applied. When one of the basic styles (for example 'separated') is adopted in an appropriate situation, a more effective style ('bureaucrat') results. When the basic style is adopted in an inappropriate situation, the result is a less effective style ('deserter').

The eight styles of management may be described briefly as follows.

More effective styles

(i) *Bureaucrat* – a low concern for both task and relationships. The manager adopting this style is seen as being interested mainly in rules and procedures to control the situation, and as conscientious.

(ii) *Benevolent autocrat* – a high concern for task and a low concern for relationships. Managers adopting this style know what they want and how to achieve it without causing resentment.

(iii) *Developer* – a high concern for relationships and a low concern for task. The manager adopting this style is seen as having implicit trust in people and concerned mainly with developing them as individuals.

(iv) *Executive* – a high concern for both task and relationships. The manager adopting this style is seen as a good motivator, sets high standards, treats people as individuals, and favours team management.

Less effective styles

(v) *Deserter* – low concern for both task and relationships in a situation where such behaviour is inappropriate. The manager lacks involvement and is passive or negative.

(vi) *Autocrat* – a high concern for task and a low concern for relationships in a situation where such behaviour is not appropriate. The manager is seen as lacking confidence in others, unpleasant, and interested only in the task in hand.

(vii) *Missionary* – a high concern for relationships and a low concern for task where such behaviour is inappropriate. The manager is seen as interested mainly in preserving harmony.

(viii) *Compromiser* – a high concern for both task and relationships in a situation requiring high concern for neither, or for only one orientation. The manager is seen as a poor decision-maker, too easily influenced by the pressures of the situation, and as avoiding immediate pressures and problems at the expense of maximising long-term output.

Appropriate style of behaviour

According to *Reddin*'s 3-D theory, managerial effectiveness cannot be measured simply in terms of achieving production or relationships with other people. The manager must also be adaptable in adopting the appropriate style of behaviour which will determine effectiveness in achieving the output requirements of the job. Reddin has developed a 'management-style-diagnosis' test to identify styles of management and of organisations. The test comprises 64 paired statements which compare one style of management with another. From each pair of statements is selected the one statement which describes best the manager's behaviour in his or her present job. Analysis of the answers can help the manager to evaluate his or her own perceived style of management.

GENERAL CRITERIA OF MANAGERIAL EFFECTIVENESS

From a review of the work of a number of writers, *Langford* identifies four broad groups of criteria of managerial effectiveness, and a single overall criterion of effectiveness.[32]

- *The manager's work* – decision making, problem solving, innovation, management of time and handling information.
- *The manager himself/herself* – motivation, role perception, coping with stress/ambiguity, seniority, and average salary grade for age.
- *The manager's relationships with other people* – subordinates, superiors, peers and clients; handling conflict and leadership/power.
- *The manager as part of the organisation* – maintenance of the organisation, and technical and financial control.
- *Criterion of general effectiveness* – allocation of resources, achieving purpose, goal attainment, planning, organising, co-ordinating, controlling.

Langford found that the most frequently mentioned criterion was overall effectiveness, followed by relationships with subordinates. Next in order of importance were the criteria of decision making, problem solving, self-development of the manager and maintenance of the organisation. Coping with ambiguity and the handling of conflict were seen as relatively unimportant criteria, although Langford suggests this might be related to the circumstances at the time when the various works were written.

Synopsis

It is the responsibility of managers to manage and to achieve results through the efforts of other people. This involves the effective management of human resources. The way in which managers exercise their authority and carry out their responsibilities is important. The style of management adopted, and the behaviour displayed towards subordinate staff, is likely to be conditioned by predispositions about people, human nature and work. One particular, cultural based, approach to management style and practice is the Japanese 'Theory Z' environment.

One means of describing different styles of management is the Blake and Mouton Managerial Grid, and the combination of concern for production and concern for people. The four quadrants of the Grid provide five basic combinations. Managers tend to have one dominant style of management, and many managers also have a 'back-up' style. A four-fold model of management systems is exploitive authoritative, benevolent authoritative, consultative, and participative group. These systems can be related to a profile of organisational characteristics.

There are many aspects to management but one essential ingredient of any successful manager is the ability to handle people effectively. It is important that managers have a highly developed sense of 'people-perception' and understand the feelings of staff, and their needs and expectations. It is people who are being managed, and people should be considered in human terms.

Work by leading writers suggests that a participative style of management is more likely to harness effectively the human resources of an organisation. One particular style or system of management is Management by Objectives (MBO). Participation is inherent if MBO is to work well, and there is an assumption that most people will work willingly if given freedom of action to decide how best to achieve agreed objectives. MBO is potentially an attractive and rewarding style of management. However, there are a number of limitations and possible shortcomings, particularly in respect of associated performance appraisal schemes.

There is a clear and important need for managerial effectiveness. The concept of managerial effectiveness, however, is difficult both to define and to measure. Effectiveness can be distinguished from efficiency.

The combination of task orientation and relationship orientation results in four basic styles of behaviour. Each of these styles can be effective or ineffective depending on the situation in which it is applied. Broad groupings of criteria of managerial effectiveness are: the manager's work, the manager himself/herself, relationships with other people; the manager as part of the organisation; together with an overall criterion of general effectiveness.

Review and discussion questions

1. Distinguish between different sets of attitudes and assumptions about people at work that might be held by managers. Give examples, pref-

erably from your own experience, of how these different attitudes and assumptions might influence actual managerial behaviour.

2. Discuss the extent to which you believe the characteristics of a Theory Z environment could successfully be applied to work organisations in this country.

3. Using the Blake and Mouton Managerial Grid, identify your likely dominant style of behaviour in dealing with subordinate staff. In what situations might you need to adopt a back-up style of behaviour and what style is that likely to be?

4. From your own experience, explain fully a situation which you believe demonstrates an effective way of dealing with subordinate staff. To what extent can you relate this situation to the application of theories or principles of management?

5. Discuss what you see as the most important considerations in adopting a people-centred approach to management. What do you understand by the culture of management?

6. Critically assess the value of Management by Objectives (MBO) as a means of improving organisational performance. In what ways might MBO be applied (or has MBO been applied) to your own organisation? What difficulties/problems might arise (or have arisen) from the introduction of MBO?

7. How would you attempt to distinguish between an effective and an ineffective manager? Give specific examples of the criteria you would apply to assess the effectiveness of a particular managerial job of your choice.

8. Explain Reddin's 3-D model of managerial behaviour. Give a practical example of situations which demonstrate (i) a more effective style, and (ii) a less effective style.

| Assignment | PRINCIPLE OF SUPPORTIVE RELATIONSHIPS QUESTIONNAIRE |

To test whether a superior's (and the organisation's) behaviour is supportive, consider the following questions.

1. How much confidence and trust do you feel your superior has in you? How much do you have in him?

2. To what extent does your boss convey to you a feeling of confidence that you can do your job successfully? Does he expect the 'impossible' and fully believe you can and will do it?

3. To what extent is he interested in helping you to achieve and maintain a good income?

4. To what extent does your superior try to understand your problems and do something about them?

5. How much is your superior really interested in helping you with your personal and family problems?

6. How much help do you get from your superior in doing your work?
   a. How much is he interested in training you and helping you learn better ways of doing your work?
   b. How much does he help you solve your problems constructively – not tell you the answer but help you think through your problems?

    c. To what extent does he see that you get the supplies, budget, equipment, etc., you need to do your job well?

  7. To what extent is he interested in helping you get the training which will assist you in being promoted?

  8. To what extent does your superior try to keep you informed about matters related to your job?

  9. How fully does your superior share information with you about the company, its financial condition, earnings, etc., or does he keep such information to himself?

10. Does your superior ask your opinion when a problem comes up which involves your work? Does he value your ideas and seek them and endeavour to use them?

11. Is he friendly and easily approached?

12. To what extent is your superior generous in the credit and recognition given to others for the accomplishments and contributions rather than seeking to claim all the credit himself?

Practical assignment

In self-selecting groups of three or four visit a work organisation of your choice, preferably that is well known to at least one member of your group.

(i) Using Likert's short form of *profile of organisational characteristics*, investigate the organisational variables and circle what you believe to be the most accurate answer for each of the 18 questions.

(ii) Make clear any necessary assumptions, and where possible give brief supporting reasons for your choice of answers.

(iii) Summarise the extent to which your answers suggest a clear inclination towards one particular model of management system.

(iv) Explain the conclusions you draw from your investigation and the pattern of your answers.

Case study

MANAGERIAL STYLE AND APPRAISAL: ADMINISTRATORS IN THE NHS*

Rosemary Stewart and Pauline Wingate

Organizational setting

This is a study of a district administrator (DA) in the National Health Service (NHS). The NHS is divided into geographical districts each responsible for a population of about 250 000, though some districts are somewhat smaller and others larger. Above the districts are regional authorities and regional officers. Each district is controlled by a District Health Authority (DHA) whose members are appointed, not elected as in local government. The officers are appointed by, and report to, the DHA. The chairman of a DHA receives a small, part-time salary.

    The DA's job at the time of the case study had three main aspects: management of the administrative staff; secretary to the DHA and member

* The research for this and two other case studies was financed by the King Edward's Hospital Fund for London.

of the district management team (DMT). Since the study a new post has been created – that of district general manager. At the time of the study the district management team had no permanently designated head but members took it in turn to act as chairman.

The district in this case study is a mixture of urban and rural, but is mainly urban. It serves a population of 300 000. The district has a full-time staff equivalent to over 4000 and a budget of over £4 million (1983 figures).

Background to the case

The district administrator (DA) is in his early forties. He had been DA in the same district since 1975 and had worked there for two years before that.

The case study was carried out shortly after the 1982 reorganization which abolished the middle tier in the geographical structure of the NHS, that of the area. It gave each district its own District Health Authority. This meant that the DA and other senior officers were for the first time reporting directly to a DHA, and that the DA was working directly to the chairman. The impact of these changes on the DA's job was considerable in terms of extra work and new responsibilities.

The Problem

This case is not about a particular problem but about how this senior manager saw his role and priorities and how his colleagues judged his effectiveness.

The DA's priorities

The DA is ambitious for his district, working to build for it a progressive and dynamic reputation. He makes every effort to find people with new ideas and is always ready to offer the district as a proving ground for new schemes. He feels he needs to be seen to be making changes. He must ensure that the organization remains dynamic. This means he must seize on new ideas and opportunities – even in the middle of reorganization – and he must make them work.

He places great emphasis on publicity for the district. He contributes to the district's reputation and opportunities for development through his membership of a whole range of national and regional committees.

He is now resigning from some of his external committees because he feels the DHA must have prior claim on his time. He is the executive arm of the DMT and the DHA. This is his biggest, most serious responsibility.

The DA sees himself as an overall manager of the district rather than just the administrator and thinks his title not well suited to the role he plays. He is interested in and feels the need to keep in touch with everything that goes on in the district. He makes no distinction between hospitals and community and doesn't confine his interest simply to the work and to his own staff. He does a fair amount of visiting because it gives him a better understanding of the problems and atmosphere. He sees it as part of the overall management monitoring process.

The DA's Views of His Role in Administration

The administration must see him as the boss 'otherwise I can't exist in any meaningful sense'. This 'depends on being seen to be a winner, a man of sound judgement, someone capable of protecting their interests and of doing something about the problems'. He gets involved in issues 'if it's necessary in order for us to win'.

He delegates established administrative work to his subordinates. He expects high standards of volume and thoroughness and trusts them to get on with it. In the last year though, he has had to delegate more and be involved in operational detail less than he would like, which he finds very worrying. He still makes time for visits.

The DA attaches importance to understanding the work of different staff. For example, he spent a couple of days with health visitors to see them in action and a day in the laundry, and another two in a medical records department.

Guidelines and problems are discussed at administrative meetings: for his immediate subordinates a debriefing session immediately after the formal DMT meeting followed by an informal general debate; a more formal meeting once a quarter for a wide group of senior officers.

For day to day matters on which he is trying to keep tabs, he has an envelope on his desk for each of his senior staff and colleagues and at least once a month calls them in to discuss progress. He feels that this system is not going to be good enough in the future. Something much more specific will be needed and must be developed once they are into the new organization.

The DA has individual discussions every six months with his subordinates specifically about their career development and how effective they are in their work. This is a pilot experiment which originated with the Regional Staff Development Committee for Administrative and Clerical Staff. It is an example of the kind of innovation that the DA welcomes.

He thinks that being 'opportunistic', seizing opportunities, is one of his most significant contributions to the effectiveness of the administration.

How the DA's Subordinates See Him

The DA is seen as a man of power and influence, virtually the chief executive, because of his responsibility for the overall coordination of the organization. He uses the power that comes from (1) his position as secretary to the DMT and DHA, giving him influence over what is discussed by them and when; (2) his very wide range of contacts throughout the health service, giving him access to information and to people with money and influence; (3) the length of time he has been in the district.

He spends a lot of time on his public relations role: on his relationships with other bodies in the district, with businessmen who might donate money or services, with the media, with colleagues in other districts, and on a whole range of national and regional administrative committees. He is also the politician, 'striking the bargains with consultant staff in the corridors of the hospitals . . . negotiating between clinical specialities . . . the person with the most power to shift resources'.

His main skill was described as follows: 'negotiating, finding a way through, manipulating pressure groups, avoiding head-on collision, keeping the whole thing going in order to achieve aims . . . he uses this skill widely, between people, between districts, with trade unions, in the local population. . . . It's an ability to wheel and deal. It means being very pragmatic.'

This approach was seen to have disadvantages. The DA can be too pragmatic. Pragmatism and compromise are not inspiring: 'It would be better if he sometimes looked for the best decision as this can be needed to get commitment from people.' The district lacked leadership and a sense of direction before the arrival of the DHA and the chairman's vision of patient care in the future.

The DA was seen as very effective at representing the views of administration and protecting their interest: 'If you persuade him to do something you know he will have the clout to carry it through . . . nothing worse than a boss who hasn't.' 'He is a fighter who believes in success and he does win.'

He can delegate completely: 'He respects his senior officers. He doesn't have to watch over them. There is terrific mutual respect. That is not to say he is not interested. It is proper delegation.' 'In tackling a problem he goes directly to individuals, but he would get more commitment if he brought people together to work in teams. . . . He can also get involved in too much detail and become too personally involved.' He can bypass the formal structure in order to work with a person he needs on a project, or issue a press release which can leave their immediate boss asking, 'Shouldn't I have known . . .?'

Contact between the DA and his subordinates is usually very business-like and infrequent. The DA's style is fairly formal at administrative meetings. He 'dominates the group more than is good for other members of it'. 'Senior officers' meetings tend to be a monologue.' He is out of the office a great deal: 'I can go six or seven weeks without seeing him.' 'It is not that there is any barrier.' 'He is potentially interested in everything and can show a surprising attention to detail . . . is extremely patient. But his style and the atmosphere of his office is such that I would not wish to trouble him with mundane issues. . . . I am aware of the level at which he is operating and of what it is appropriate to tell him.'

At times people can feel the need for greater guidance on objectives and for a greater interest in their work: 'Initially, I felt quite lost . . . there is a sense of isolation.' However, 'You do grow in confidence (if you don't become despondent). You learn to manage without the encouragement. It's great if you're a self-starter . . . it gives you freedom of action.'

He is very popular and his own energy and enthusiasm can rub off on others. He can be very good at involving his staff positively in what is happening, making them feel that they are in a very go-ahead district and must live up to it. He will always take up challenges at meetings. However, 'He's bad in that he doesn't always take into account the resources available to fulfil the commitments he made on behalf of his staff. People don't like to let him down but they can wear themselves out and he is not always aware of the strain on them, or of what work was put aside or neglected for the job he wants done.'

Other People's Views on the DA as Head of Administration

There was some criticism of the efficiency of his own department, which he has not been able to improve even though he has been in the district a long time: 'There are many practical areas of administration, a lot of the underlying systems and procedures, which are very poor . . . a DA with a different approach would have given priority to ensuring that the mechanics of the administration were operating smoothly.'

He tends, it was suggested, to credit his subordinates with qualities that they do not possess: 'He can produce reports very quickly and well, dictate 30–40 letters in a day and do meetings going into the evening. Other people cannot do this . . . . He delegates very substantially . . . too readily . . . and he does not keep an overview.'

There is regret that the organization is not geared up to cope with the DA's enthusiasm to accept challenges, to seize opportunities, the flashes of inspiration which he thinks can be immediately implemented. He is less aware of the stress and strain in the organization than he might be – 'He really is too innovative.'

The Chairman's View of the DA's Role

The DA's part in seeing that the decisions of the DHA are carried out is crucial: 'He should be an effective enabler and make things happen.' He must keep the chairman fully informed and should know where to find any information. He is the link between all the disciplines and must control any complex interdepartmental planning and be the voice of the DMT to the chairman. He is very influential in projecting the image of the authority.

The chairman has an office next to the DA and shares his secretary. There is quite a bit of contact, including dropping in on each other, although the chairman feels that they do not have enough time together. The chairman gets very frustrated by delays: 'Everything takes too long, but it is not his fault. He is very understaffed.'

The DA's View of His Role

The DA takes his responsibilities to the DHA very seriously, feeling that he has had to adjust his work style to fulfil the role required of him. This has meant that he has not been able to spend as much time with his subordinates as he would have wished since reorganization. The DA feels that he must be seen to be supporting the chairman, that he must persuade the DMT of the importance of coming to DHA meetings, that he must write good briefing papers and take action on behalf of the DHA.

He now feels the need to have some oversight of other departments so as to ensure that action is taken and to keep an eye on any possible trouble spots. This has to be done tactfully. He is aware that the DHA and the chairman see him as 'first man' – some even as chief executive. He thinks that this is mistaken but accepts that it is 'absolutely the DA's responsibility to see that the DHA's decisions are carried out'. He must also make sure that the members of the DHA are fully aware of the consequences of any decisions that they make, particularly if they are against DMT advice. He accepts that the members of the DHA see him as the voice of the DMT.

Above all, the DA wishes to use the abilities of the members of the DHA and to encourage them to go on producing new ideas. He sees broadening their knowledge as part of his role.

The DA and the DMT

Organization of the DMT and the Role of the DA. The DMT recently went on a week's workshop at the suggestion of the DA. They agreed that their most pressing problem was that meetings were taking far too long; the DA mentioned one which took 15 hours over two weeks. They concluded that the agenda was overloaded, badly structured and that there was a need for greater discipline in discussion. The team leaves the composition of the agenda to the DA and most of the items come through the administration. The DA has been aware of these criticisms but preferred to 'err on the side of over-communication'. He now agrees that there are other ways of sharing ideas and communicating them and cuts out half the items, particularly matters arising, which was used for a continuous updating process.

The DA plays the role of initiator of items, because most of the organization's mail comes to him, and adds items of which the team has asked to be reminded. He tends to talk to introduce each item because of time pressures and lack of administrative support. The team decided at the workshop that the DA should write a background note for each item.

There is criticism that the DMT is too slow in making decisions. The DA might be able to help them to be more decisive. However, he believes in consensus because 'you get a greater input, a wider range of debate, more ideas come out and greater commitment to the decision'. He often acts as judge of what decision the team has come to as a result of the discussion.

How Other Members See the DMT and the DA's Role. The team workshop, 'an example of very effective DA action', was considered very worthwhile because the objectives which would lead to improving the team's effectiveness had been identified and accepted. They appreciate the DA's reorganization of the agenda, particularly putting the difficult problems first. But meetings still go on too long, as the new chairman understands very well.

The DA probably talks more than anyone else 'because of his personality, definite views and involvement'. Most of the items are processed through his department: 'Those who are not officers defer to him because they don't know what is going on. They think that he is a good DA and trust him.' The DA's skill in taking the views of the team and making sense of them was valued. There is a suggestion that the DA could do more to help the team to be more decisive, but, said one of the medical members, 'I don't see why he should. They ought to do it as a team. And the DMT work happily together.'

Other members would find it helpful to have more time to prepare their own input to the meeting: 'The agenda comes out on Friday for Tuesday's formal meeting. This is not long enough to get feedback and information. . . . I need to make inquiries from my own department.' Sometimes papers were on the table for meetings, which is hopeless: 'We had all complained and the DA was more aware of the problem than anyone.'

The DMT appreciate the DA's excellent follow-up: 'We depend very heavily on the minutes. They are the bring forward system, the check-up.' 'The follow-up process takes up half the agenda . . . but it is better to be secure.' The team also appreciate the way the DA 'will gently prod the chairman or will himself suggest who will take on responsibility for action when this is not immediately clear'. 'He doesn't annoy people.'

General Comments on the Role and Personality of the DA

The DA's colleagues were united in their praise of his personal qualities and abilities: 'charming', 'gracious', 'calm', 'personable', 'a great sense of humour', 'sociable', 'enthusiastic', 'optimistic', 'involved', 'committed', 'energetic', 'a hell of a nice guy'. They appreciated his skill in handling people: 'keeping them happy', 'making them feel he thinks their problems are important', 'calming them down', 'not upsetting them', 'drawing them out because he is a good listener', 'keeping them up to the mark'. They praised his skill and energy in and commitment to public relations, to building up a good image for the district which, they expect, will attract a better calibre of people to the district and build up the staff's and public's confidence in the district. It also helps a lot in keeping industrial relations smooth and trouble free.

The DA is not seen as a particularly strong or effective head of administration. He is excellent as a coordinator of day to day matters and never loses sight of an issue. He is not good as a coordinator of planning, ensuring that the process is properly set up and timetabled, bringing in all the other disciplines. The DA was criticized for being careless of communication, 'holding his cards too close to his chest', creating mistrust by saying 'that's all you need to know, trust me' or 'taking risks on getting things through by the back door without people noticing'. He is seen as not tough enough. He 'bows to the strongest wind' and 'tries too hard to be all things to all men'.

The DA's colleagues praised his intellectual ability ('a good brain', 'a clear, incisive thinker', 'a skilled debater', 'knowledgeable', 'a superb grasp of what is going on in the district'), his industry ('his work load is enormous'), and his personal efficiency ('very well organized . . . can use his time well . . . never wastes five minutes').

Case study tasks

1 What are this DA's objectives? Consider both the explicit and implicit ones.
2 What are his main focuses of attention? Are these right for the current situation?
3 Would you like to work for him? Why? Why not?
4 What is the output of the DA's job? How would you judge his effectiveness in terms of output?
5 What are his weaknesses? In what ways is he ineffective?
6 What should he look for in others to compensate for his weaknesses?
7 What else do you think that he could do to improve his effectiveness?

Reading

Stewart, R. (1982) *Choices For The Manager: A Guide to Managerial Work and Behaviour*, McGraw-Hill (see Chapters 1, 2, 8, 11, 12, of which Chapters 1 and 11 are the minimum).

Notes and references

1. McGregor, D. *The Human Side of Enterprise*, Penguin (1987).
2. See, for example: Mullins, L. J. 'Management and Managerial Behaviour', *International Journal of Hospitality Management*, vol. 4, no. 1, 1985, pp. 39–41.
3. Ouchi, W. G. *Theory Z: How American Business can Meet the Japanese Challenge*, Addison-Wesley (1981) p. 4.
4. Tse, K. K. *Marks & Spencer*, Pergamon Press (1985).
5. Caplan, E. H. *Management Accounting and Behavioral Science*, Addison-Wesley (1971).
6. Blake, R. B. and Mouton, J. S. *The Managerial Grid*, Gulf Publishing Company (1964); *The New Managerial Grid*, Gulf Publishing Company (1978); *The Managerial Grid III*, Gulf Publishing Company (1985).
7. Likert, R. *New Patterns of Management*, McGraw-Hill (1961).
8. Likert, R. and Likert, J. G. *New Ways of Managing Conflict*, McGraw-Hill (1976).
9. Likert, R. *The Human Organisation*, McGraw-Hill (1967) p. 138.
10. Likert, R. *New Patterns of Management*, McGraw-Hill (1961) pp. 7–8.
11. See, for example: Blanchard, K. and Johnson, S. *The One Minute Manager*, Willow Books (1983).
12. Freemantle, D. 'The People Factor', *Management Today*, December 1985, p. 68.
13. Ash, M. K. *On People Management*, Macdonald & Co. (1985).
14. Ibid. p. xix.
15. See, for example: Rockledge, S. 'The Human Cost of Bad Management', *Administrator*, vol. 7, no. 1, January 1987, p. 13.
16. Drucker, P. F. *The Practice of Management*, Pan Books (1968).
17. For example, see also: Reddin, W. J. *Effective MBO*, Management Publications Limited for the British Institute of Management (1971).
18. See, for example: Glendenning, J. W. and Bullock, R. E. H. *Management by Objectives in Local Government*, C. Knight (1973).
19. Odiorne, G. S. *Management by Objectives*, Pitman (1965) pp. 55–6. See also: Odiorne, G. S. *MBO II: A System of Managerial Leadership for the 80's*, Second edition, Pitman (1979).
20. Humble, J. W. *Management by Objectives*, Management Publications Limited for the British Institute of Management (1972).
21. Argenti, J. *Management Techniques*, Allen and Unwin (1969) p. 148.
22. Carroll, S. J. and Tosi, H. L. *Management by Objectives: Applications and Research*, Macmillan (1973) p. 16.
23. For a discussion on the way managers react to MBO, see: Jamieson, B. D. 'Behavioral Problems with Management by Objectives', in Huseman, B. D. and Carroll, A. B. *Readings in Organizational Behavior*, Allyn and Bacon (1979).
24. Freemantle, D. 'The People Factor', *Management Today*, December 1985, pp. 68–71.
25. Kane, J. S. and Freeman, K. A. 'MBO and Performance Appraisal: A Mixture That's Not a Solution', *Personnel*, vol. 63, no. 12, December 1986, pp. 26–36.
26. Charsley, W. F. 'Effective Management – So You Think You've got it Right?' *British Journal of Administrative Management*, vol. 1, November 1986, pp. 11–12.
27. Drucker, P. F. *People and Performance*, Heinemann (1977).
28. Drucker, P. F. *The Effective Executive*, Pan Books (1970).
29. Stewart, R. *Managers and Their Jobs*, Macmillan (1967) pp. 146–7.
30. Reddin, W. J. *Managerial Effectiveness*, McGraw-Hill (1970).
31. Ibid. p. 3.
32. Langford, V. 'Managerial Effectiveness: A Review of the Literature', in Brodie, M. and Bennett, R. (eds) *Perspectives of Managerial Effectiveness*, Thames Valley Regional Management Centre (1979).

PART FIVE

ORGANISATIONAL PROCESSES AND THE EXECUTION OF WORK

10. THE NATURE OF DELEGATION

A particular feature of work organisations is the need for delegation. The various activities of the organisation have to be distributed among its members. Management involves getting work done through the efforts of other people. This entails the process of delegation and the creation of a special manager–subordinate relationship. Delegation is a necessary function of management. The manager needs to understand the process of delegation and how best to implement it in order to improve organisational effectiveness.[1]

Objectives

To: (i)   Explain dimensions of, and approaches to, delegation;
    (ii) Examine the process of delegation;
    (iii) Identify the benefits of delegation to the manager and to subordinate staff;
    (iv) Explain the need for management control;
    (v) Detail a planned and systematic approach to delegation, and recognise delegation as an art;
    (vi) Assess why managers may fail to delegate and other factors influencing opportunities for delegation;
    (vii) Appreciate the importance of successful delegation to the effective performance of the organisation.

DIMENSIONS OF DELEGATION

In order to manage it is necessary to manage the work of other people. This involves the process of delegation. In the case of the very small organisation where one person does everything alone, the question of delegation does not arise. But as soon as additional members of staff are employed it is necessary to plan, organise, direct and control their activities. It is a fundamental principle of management that for organisational effectiveness there must be delegation.

Delegation can be seen as taking place either at the organisational level or at the individual level.

The organisational level

The structure of the organisation (as depicted in organisation charts, for example) is itself a result of delegation. If there is no delegation, then there is no structure. As organisations grow in size, so the extent of delegation increases. Delegation is therefore a function of size. It relates to the location of decision making within the organisation. Delegation involves the passing on of authority and responsibility to various levels throughout the organisation.

At the organisational level, delegation involves consideration of centralisation/decentralisation, and divisionalisation or departmentalisation. Decentralisation may be federal or functional.[2] *Federal decentralisation* is the establishment of autonomous units operating in their own market with self-control and with the main responsibility of contributing profit to the parent body. *Functional decentralisation* is based on individual processes or products.

Divisions or departments may be established on the basis of 'task' or 'element' functions of the organisation. Task functions are directed towards specific and definable end-results and are basic activities of the organisation, for example research and development, production, marketing and finance. Element functions are ancillary to the basic activities and provide specialist support services, for example personnel, management accounting, quality control and maintenance.[3] The extent of decentralisation and divisionalisation provides the basic structural pattern of the formal organisation.

The nature of organisation structure has already been discussed in earlier chapters. In this chapter we are concerned with delegation at the individual, or personal, level and with the nature of the manager–subordinate relationship.

The individual level

Within the structure of the organisation the various activities that have to be undertaken must be distributed among individual members of the workforce.

At the individual (or personal) level, delegation is the process of entrusting authority and responsibility to others.

Delegation is not just the arbitrary shedding of work. It is not just the issuing and following of orders. Delegation is the systematic allocation of duties and responsibilities. It is the authorisation to undertake activities that would otherwise be carried out by someone in a more senior position.

APPROACHES TO DELEGATION

The concept of delegation may appear to be straightforward. But anyone with experience of a work situation is likely to be aware of the importance of delegation and the consequences of badly managed delegation. Successful delegation is a social skill. Where managers lack this skill, or do not have a sufficient awareness of people-perception, there are two extreme forms of behaviour which can result.

At one extreme is the almost total lack of meaningful delegation. Subordinate staff are only permitted to operate within closely defined and often routine areas of work, with detailed supervision. Staff are treated as if they are incapable of thinking for themselves and given little or no opportunity to exercise initiative or responsibility.

At the other extreme there can be an excessive zeal for so-called 'delegation' when a manager leaves subordinates to their own resources, often with only minimal guidance or training, and expects them to take the consequences for their own actions or decisions. And somehow, such managers often contrive not to be around when difficult situations arise. Such a form of behaviour is not delegation, it is an abdication of the manager's responsibility.

Either of these two extreme forms of behaviour can be frustrating and potentially stressful for subordinate staff, and unlikely to lead to improved organisational effectiveness. The nature of delegation can have a significant effect on the morale, motivation and work performance of staff. In all but the smallest organisation the only way to get work done effectively is through delegation.

A manager's approach to delegation is, therefore, of considerable importance and should not be underestimated. But what does the process of delegation actually involve? And how can it be carried out successfully?

THE PROCESS OF DELEGATION

It is possible to have delegation upwards, for example when a manager temporarily takes over the work of a subordinate who is absent through illness or holiday. It is also possible to delegate laterally to another manager on the same level. However, delegation is usually interpreted as a movement down the organisation. *Delegation creates a special manager–subordinate relationship.*

> Delegation means the conferring of a specified authority by a higher authority. In its essence it involves a dual responsibility. The one to whom authority is delegated becomes responsible to the superior for doing the job, but the superior remains responsible for getting the job done. This principle of delegation is the centre of all processes in formal organization.[4]

Authority and responsibility

Delegation is founded on the concepts of authority and responsibility.

Authority is the right to take action or make decisions that the manager would otherwise have done. It involves more than just carrying out specified duties according to detailed instructions. Authority legitimises the exercise of power within the structure and rules of the organisation. It enables the subordinate to issue valid instructions for others to follow.

Responsibility involves an obligation by the subordinate to perform certain duties or make certain decisions and having to accept possible reprimand from the manager for unsatisfactory performance.

Authority and responsibility are at the basis of the manager–subordinate relationship and recognised as 'rules' or principles of management. Responsibility is a corollary of authority. Wherever authority is exercised, responsibility arises. Sanctions are needed to encourage useful actions and to discourage others.[5]

Some writers argue that responsibility cannot be delegated,[6] but this is too simple a view. Authority without responsibility gives rise to a possible abuse of delegation. For example, if a manager gives a subordinate authority to incur expenditure on certain items up to the value of £100 without prior reference, the subordinate should be held responsible to the manager for incurring such expenditure. The subordinate is obligated to exercise due care and attention to actions taken and decisions made.

In his revised list of management principles, *Urwick* makes the point that responsibility and authority should correspond in every position.[7] This principle has been challenged by *Haire* as a mythology of organisation theory.[8] However, Haire's argument is based on a particular interpretation of the meaning of the two terms 'authority' and 'responsibility'. Most textbooks appear to support writers of the classical approach to management who argued in support of the principle that authority should be commensurate with responsibility.

Delegation, therefore, embraces both authority and responsibility. It is not practical to delegate one without the other.

- There should be sufficient responsibility to match the authority which is delegated.
- Responsibility should be sufficient to give the subordinate freedom of action within agreed terms of reference and to avoid excessive supervision.
- Part of the manager's job is the development of subordinates. Subordinates need the feeling of responsibility to help in the performance of their tasks, and in dealing with other staff.
- Delegated duties are sometimes delegated further down the structure.

Ultimate responsibility

The meaning of the term 'responsibility' is, however, subject to possible confusion: although delegation embraces both authority *and* responsibility, effective delegation is not abdication of responsibility.

Ultimate responsibility cannot be delegated. Managers have to accept 'responsibility' for the control of their staff, for the performance of all duties allocated to their department/section within the structure of the organisation, and for the standard of results achieved.

The manager is in turn responsible to higher management. This is the nature of the 'dual responsibility' of delegation. The manager is answerable to a superior and cannot shift responsibility back to subordinates. The responsibility of the superior for the acts of subordinates is absolute.[9]

If a manager delegates some task to a subordinate member of staff who does a bad job, then the manager must accept ultimate responsibility for the subordinate's actions. It is the manager who is answerable to a superior. It is not for the manager to say: 'Don't blame me boss, you don't expect me to do everything myself. You knew I would have to ask a member of my staff to do the work, I can't help it if "x" did a bad job.' The manager should accept the blame as the person who was obligated to the boss for the performance of the task, and accountable to see that the task was completed satisfactorily. *Managers should protect and support subordinate staff and accept, personally, any reprimand for unsatisfactory performance.* It is up to managers to sort out things in their own department/section, to counsel members of staff concerned and to review their system of delegation.

Accountability

In order to help clarify the position of 'dual responsibility' in delegation, it might be better expressed as 'The subordinate is *responsible* to the manager for doing the job, while the manager is responsible for seeing that the job gets done. The manager is *accountable* to a superior for the actions of subordinates.' Accountability is interpreted as meaning ultimate responsibility. Although in practice there is little difference between 'responsibility' and 'accountability', the use of these two terms helps to explain the nature of delegation of responsibility. (*See* Fig. 10.1.)

Responsibility must be supported by authority, and by the power to influence the areas of performance for which the subordinate is to be held responsible. Authority can be delegated readily, but many problems of delegation stem from failure to provide the necessary information and resources in order to achieve expected results, or from failure to delegate sufficient authority to enable subordinates to fulfil their responsibilities.

For example, if a section head is held responsible to a departmental manager for the performance of junior staff but does not have the power (authority) to influence their selection and appointment, their motivation, the allocation of their duties, their training and development, or their sanctions and rewards; then the section leader can hardly be held responsible for unsatisfactory performance of the junior staff.

To hold subordinates responsible for certain areas of performance without also conferring on them the necessary authority to take action and make decisions within the limits of that responsibility is an abuse of delegation.

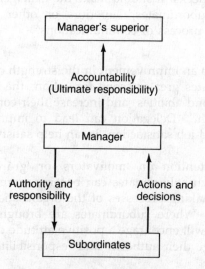

Fig. 10.1 The process of delegation

BENEFITS OF DELEGATION

Delegation is not an easy task. It involves behavioural as well as organisational and economic considerations, and it is subject to a number of possible abuses. Delegation is, however, as essential function of management. It is necessary for organisational effectiveness and, properly handled, offers many potential advantages to both the manager and subordinates.

Best use of time

Time is one of the most valuable, but limited, resources and it is important that the manager utilises time to the maximum advantage.[10] By delegating those activities which can be done just as well by subordinate staff the manager is using to advantage the human resources of the organisation. Managers are also giving themselves more time in which to manage.

Successful delegation will help to overcome Gresham's Law of Planning which states that programmed activity tends to drive out non-programmed activity. Programmed activity involves decisions which are repetitive and routine; non-programmed activity involves decisions which are novel and unstructured.[11]

Successful delegation frees managers from day-to-day routine duties and enables them to concentrate more of their time on non-programmed activities. This simple, but important, point was made many years ago by Sir Ian Hamilton in a study of the organisation of military units.

> the higher up the ladder you climb the less you have to do; provided (1) you have some courage; (2) you have some trust; (3) you have your office so organised that you don't have to deal with more than three of four responsible heads. If big men are overwhelmed with detail it is always their own fault.[12]

Delegation leaves the manager free to make profitable use of time, to concentrate on the more important tasks and to spend more time in managing and less in doing. This should lead to a more even flow of work and a reduction of bottlenecks. It should make the manager more accessible for consultation with subordinates, superiors or other managers. This should also improve the process of communications.

Strength of the workforce

Delegation should lead to an improvement in the strength of the workforce. It should give subordinates greater scope for action, the opportunities to develop their aptitudes and abilities, and increase their commitment to the goals of the organisation.[13] Delegation can lead to improved morale by increasing motivation and job satisfaction. It can help satisfy the employee's higher level needs.

Delegation focuses attention on 'motivators' or 'growth' factors and creates a climate in which subordinates can become more involved in the planning and decision-making processes of the organisation. Delegation is a form of participation. Where subordinates are brought to accept and welcome delegation this will encourage a positive attitude to their work and a willingness to discharge their authority and responsibilities.

A means of training

Delegation provides a means of training and of testing the subordinate's suitability for promotion. It can be used as a means of assessing the likely performance of a subordinate at a higher level of authority and responsibility. Delegation thereby helps to avoid the 'Peter Principle' – that is: 'In a hierarchy every employee tends to rise to his level of incompetence'.[14]

If managers have trained, competent subordinates capable of taking their place this will not only aid organisational progress but should also enhance their own prospects for further advancement. *Managers should therefore be encouraged to delegate in order to make themselves dispensable.*

Specialist knowledge and skills

As organisations become more complex there is an increasing need for staff with specialist knowledge and skills. This need is reinforced, for example, by the rate of change in environmental influences (technical, economic, social and governmental) which give rise to areas of specialist interest and knowledge. Delegation enables specific aspects of management to be brought within the province of a number of specialist staff for greater efficiency.

Geographical location

Another reason for delegation is the geographical separation of departments or sections of the organisation. For example, where a branch office is located some distance away from the head office the branch manager will need an adequate level of delegation in order to maintain the day-to-day operational efficiency of the office.

Sound economics

Successful delegation benefits both the manager and the subordinate and enables them both to play their respective roles in improving organisational effectiveness. It is a principle of delegation that decisions should be made at the lowest level in the organisation compatible with efficiency. If decisions are made at a higher level than necessary they are being made at greater cost than necessary. Delegation is therefore a matter of sound economics as well as good organisation.

THE NEED FOR CONTROL

The concept of ultimate responsibility gives rise to the need for effective management control over the actions and decisions of subordinate staff. Whatever the extent of their delegated authority and responsibility, subordinates remain accountable to the manager who should, and hopefully would, wish to be kept informed of their actions and decisions. Subordinates must account to the manager for the discharge of the responsibilities which they have been given. The manager will therefore need to keep open the lines of delegation and to have an upward flow of communication. The manager will need to be kept informed of the relevance and quality of decisions made by subordinates.

The concept of accountability is therefore an important principle of management. The manager remains accountable to a superior not just for the work carried out personally but for the total operation of the department/section. This is essential in order to maintain effective co-ordination and control, and to maintain the chain of command.

Authority, responsibility and accountability must be kept in parity throughout the organisation. The manager must remain in control. The manager must be on the lookout for subordinates who are more concerned with personal empire building than with meeting stated organisational objectives. The manager must prevent a strong personality exceeding the limits of formal delegation.

Control is, therefore, an integral part of the system of delegation. But control should not be so close as to inhibit the effective operation or benefits of delegation. *It is a question of balance.* (*See* Fig. 10.2.) In order to achieve this balance it is necessary to set up an effective scheme of delegation in which subordinates know exactly what is expected of them, what has to be achieved, the boundaries within which they have freedom of action, and

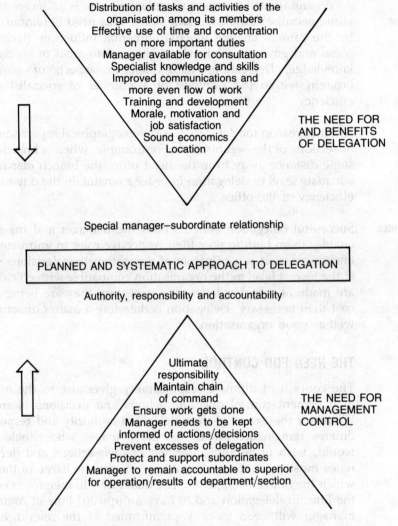

Distribution of tasks and activities of the
organisation among its members
Effective use of time and concentration
on more important duties
Manager available for consultation
Specialist knowledge and skills
Improved communications and
more even flow of work
Training and development
Morale, motivation and
job satisfaction
Sound economics
Location

THE NEED FOR
AND BENEFITS
OF DELEGATION

Special manager–subordinate relationship

PLANNED AND SYSTEMATIC APPROACH TO DELEGATION

Authority, responsibility and accountability

Ultimate
responsibility
Maintain chain
of command
Ensure work gets done
Manager needs to be kept
informed of actions/decisions
Prevent excesses of delegation
Protect and support subordinates
Manager to remain accountable to superior
for operation/results of department/section

THE NEED FOR
MANAGEMENT
CONTROL

Fig. 10.2 The balance between delegation and control

how far they can exercise independent decision making. Delegation must
be properly planned and approached in a systematic manner.

A SYSTEMATIC APPROACH TO DELEGATION

Setting up a successful system of delegation involves the manager examining three basic questions.

- What opportunities are there for subordinate staff to learn and develop
  by undertaking delegated tasks and responsibilities?
- How should the increased responsibilities be implemented and to whom
  should they be given?
- What forms of control system would be most appropriate?

It is then possible to identify six main stages in a planned and systematic
approach to delegation:

- Clarification of objectives and design of structure;
- Agreement on terms of reference;
- Acceptance of authority and responsibility;
- Briefing, guidance and training;
- Time limits, check points and performance standards; and
- Freedom of action within agreed terms of reference.

Clarification of objectives

The first stage in a planned and systematic approach to delegation is the *clarification of objectives and the design of suitable patterns of organisation* to achieve these objectives. There must be a clear chain of command with effective communications and co-ordination between the various levels of authority (scalar chain) within the organisation structure. Policies and procedures must be established and defined in order to provide a framework for the exercise of authority and the acceptance of responsibility. Managers must be clear about the opportunities and limitations of their own job.

Agreement on terms of reference

The manager can then *agree the subordinate's role prescription and terms of reference*. Those areas of work in which the subordinate is responsible for achieving results should be identified clearly. Emphasis should generally be placed on end-results rather than a set of detailed instructions. When, however, the manner in which delegated activities are to be carried out is of particular importance, this should be discussed fully with the subordinate who should understand the reasons for, and nature of, any limitations or restrictions imposed. The division of activities and responsibilities between the manager and subordinate should be established and agreed.

Acceptance of authority and responsibility

It is important to *make sure that subordinates accept the extent of, and restrictions on, the authority and responsibility delegated to them*. This involves the acceptance theory of authority. *Davis* explains this as follows:

> Although authority gives persons power to act officially within the scope of their delegation, this power becomes somewhat meaningless unless those affected accept it and respond to it. In most cases when delegation is made, a subordinate is left free to make responsive choices within a certain range of behavior. But even when an employee is told to perform one certain act, the employee still has the choice of doing it or not doing it and taking the consequences. It is, therefore, the subordinate who always controls the response to authority. Managers cannot afford to overlook this human fact when they use authority.[15]

Briefing, guidance and training

Subordinates should be properly briefed, given guidance and any necessary training. They should be told where, and to whom, they can go for further advice or help. The manager should make clear to other staff the nature and extent of delegation, and obtain their co-operation. Where the delegation is likely to involve contact or consultation with people in other departments or sections or requests for information, the manager should also communicate with other managers and seek their consent and support.

This simple process of smoothing the pattern of communications should ordinarily require little effort by the manager. Not only is it a courtesy but it can do much to enlist the co-operation of other staff and help avoid any possible misunderstandings. For example, a member of the personnel department X has been delegated by the personnel manager to draw up a comprehensive staffing report which requires certain information from the finance office. The personnel manager should consult with the finance manager and obtain agreement for X to have access to this information and to speak directly with Y in the finance office, who hopefully will then be informed of the situation by the finance manager.

Not only should this pattern of communication enable Y to understand why X is seeking information, it should also help to make for an easier working relationship between them. The finance manager will also now understand what is going on if X and Y are seen going through finance office files.

Time limits, check points and performance standards

It is necessary to agree time limits for delegation (such as a target date for completion of a task) and check points at which to review progress within the terms of reference agreed. For example, to discuss progress with the manager at the end of each week. Or to discuss the first draft of a report before it progresses further, and by an agreed date.

Delegation is not an irrevocable act and can always be withdrawn.

It is also important to agree on performance standards (wherever practically possible in quantitative terms) and how performance in each area is to be evaluated.

Freedom of action

The subordinate should then be left alone to get on with the job. One of the most frustrating aspects of delegation is the manager who passes on authority but stays close behind the subordinates' shoulders keeping a constant watch over their actions. This is contrary to the nature of delegation. The true nature of successful delegation means that the subordinate is given freedom of action *within the boundaries established and agreed in the previous stages.*

A planned and systematic approach means that effective delegation can be achieved without loss of control. Modern methods of management can also assist the effectiveness of delegation. Procedures such as management by exception and staff appraisal are useful means of helping to maintain control without inhibiting the growth of delegation. Delegation can be increased under a system of Management by Objectives. Management by Objectives (in which, through participation, specification of jobs and key tasks is related to the organisation's objectives; key results areas are identified; and standards of performance agreed) allows staff to accept greater responsibility and to make a greater personal contribution.[16]

However, recall the possible problems with MBO-based appraisal schemes, discussed in Chapter 9. There is also the danger that, if MBO is not implemented in a spirit of genuine trust, then the system will tend to be perceived simply as a control mechanism and may well result in reduced levels of performance.[17]

THE ART OF DELEGATION

The art of delegation is to agree clear terms of reference with subordinates, to give them the necessary authority and responsibility and then to monitor their performance without undue interference or the continual checking of their work. Wherever possible, delegation should be related to some form of 'reward' system, such as improved job satisfaction, or enhanced opportunities for promotion or personal development.

Reliance on other people
Delegation entails reliance on other people. It is important that the manager chooses the right subordinates to whom to delegate authority and responsibility. The manager must know what to delegate, when and to whom. Matters of policy and disciplinary power, for example, usually rest with the manager and cannot legitimately be delegated. Delegation is a matter of judgement and of trust and involves the question of discretion.

Jacques suggests that individuals differ in their capacity for discretion.[18] The 'time-span of discretion' refers to the maximum length of time that an individual can operate without a review of the quality of his or her performance. Certain tasks may involve a very short time-span, while the work of some senior managers may be measured in a time-span of years.

Confidence and trust
Delegation is also a matter of confidence and trust – both in subordinates and in the manager's own performance and system of delegation. In allowing freedom of action to subordinates within agreed terms of reference and the limits of authority, managers must accept that subordinates may undertake delegated activities in different manner from themselves. This can be one of the most difficult aspects of successful delegation. It involves the manager adopting an approach along the following lines of thought and action.

'There are a number of alternative, but equally acceptable, ways in which this task could be undertaken. After discussions with C to whom the task has been delegated, C has chosen that particular way. It would not have been the way I would have done it. However if C undertakes the task satisfactorily within our agreed terms of reference and performance criteria, then this is fine and credit should be given to C. If, however, things go wrong, then in effect C's way has become my way. I must be supportive of C, accept ultimate responsibility and any possible criticism from my superior.'

This is at the basis of the true nature of delegation. But learning to put trust in other people is one of the most difficult lessons for many managers, and some never learn it.[19]

Delegation is also a matter of courage. Mistakes will inevitably occur and the subordinate will need to be supported by the manager, and protected against unwarranted criticism. The acceptance of ultimate responsibility highlights the educational aspect of the manager's job. The manager should view mistakes as part of the subordinate's training and an opportunity for further development.

REASONS FOR LACK OF DELEGATION

With so many good reasons for delegation, why is it that managers often fail to delegate or do not delegate successfully? There are many factors which affect the amount of delegation, and its effectiveness. Delegation is influenced by the manager's perception of subordinate staff. It is also influenced by the subordinate's perception of the manager's reasons for delegation. *Failure to delegate often results from the manager's fear.*

- The manager may fear that the subordinate is not capable of doing a good job.
- Conversely, the manager may fear that the subordinate will do too good a job and show the manager in a bad light.

The manager should, of course, remember that the task of management is to get work done through the efforts of other people. If the subordinate does a particularly good job this should reflect favourably on the manager.

Dependence upon other people

As *Stewart* points out, managers who think about what can be done only in terms of what they can do, cannot be effective. Managing is not a solo activity.

> Managers must learn to accept their dependence upon people. A key part of being a good manager is managing that dependence. Managers who say that they cannot delegate because they have poor subordinates may genuinely be unfortunate in the calibre of the subordinates that they have inherited or been given. More often this view is a criticism of themselves: a criticism either of their unwillingness to delegate when they could and should do so, or a criticism of their selection, training and development of their subordinates.[20]

Lack of training

Managers may not have been 'trained' themselves in the skills and art of delegation. They may lack an awareness of the need for, and importance of, effective delegation, or what it entails. Another reason for a reluctance to delegate may, in part, be due to the fact that throughout childhood and in college life delegation is usually discouraged. There are few opportunities to learn how to delegate. Hence when people first become managers they tend to display poor delegation skills.[21]

Obstacles to delegation

Newman has identified some of the main obstacles to effective delegation in terms of the attitudes of the manager, and reasons why the subordinate shrinks from accepting new responsibilities. Reasons for reluctance to delegate are:

(i) the 'I can do it better myself' fallacy;
(ii) lack of ability to direct;
(iii) lack of confidence in subordinates;
(iv) absence of selective controls which give warning of impending difficulties; and
(v) a temperamental aversion to taking a chance.

Subordinates avoid responsibility because

(i) They find it easier to ask the boss to make decisions;
(ii) the fear of criticism for mistakes;
(iii) they believe they lack the necessary information and resources to do a good job;
(iv) the subordinates may already have more work than they can do;
(v) lack of self-confidence; and
(vi) positive incentives may be inadequate.[22]

Assumptions about human nature and behaviour

A reluctance to delegate might arise from the manager's belief in, and set of assumptions about, human nature and behaviour.[23] The Theory X manager believes that people have an inherent dislike of work, wish to avoid responsibility, and must be coerced, controlled direct and threatened with punishment in order to achieve results. Such a manager is likely, therefore, to be interested in only limited schemes of delegation, within clearly defined limits and with an easy system of reward and punishment.

On the other hand, the Theory Y manager believes that people find work a natural and rewarding activity, they learn to accept and to seek responsibility, and they will respond positively to opportunities for personal growth and to sympathetic leadership. Such a manager is more likely to be interested in wider schemes of delegation based on consultation with subordinates, and with responsibility willingly accepted out of personal commitment.

OTHER FACTORS INFLUENCING DELEGATION

Apart from the manager's own possible reluctance to delegate, there are a number of other organisational factors which may influence the opportunities for effective delegation.

Management system

The type of management system will influence the likely extent and nature of delegation. For example, *Likert* identified four types of management systems: System 1 (exploitive authoritative); System 2 (benevolent authoritative); System 3 (consultative) and System 4 (participative group).

System 4 is based on involvement, group decision making, supportive relationships and participation.[24] Real delegation is therefore likely to be greater under System 4 management.

Design of organisation structure

Opportunities for personal delegation will also be affected by the actual design of the organisation structure. For example, the degree of centralisation and the nature of divisionalisation, the extent to which role prescriptions are defined formally, the span of control of individual managers and the scalar chain (the number of levels of authority within the structure).

In practice, however, people rarely act in the manner which is officially expected. Within the formal organisation structure there will always be an informal structure which arises from the social interaction of people working in the organisation and the development of groups with their own relationships and norms of behaviour, irrespective of those defined within the formal structure. Delegation will therefore also be affected by the informal organisation.

Nature of organisation structure

Another factor affecting the amount of delegation is the nature of the organisation structure, for example in terms of whether the organisation is 'mechanistic' or 'organic'.[25] *The mechanistic system*, is a more rigid structure and is characterised by specialisation, a clear hierarchical structure, closely defined duties and responsibilities, and formal downward flow of information.

The *organic system* is a more fluid structure and is characterised by a network structure of control, authority and communication, the continual adjustment and redefinition of jobs, and communication based on information and advice rather than instructions. New problems constantly arise and require actions which cannot be allocated among defined roles in the hierarchical structure. The nature of the organic system suggests both a greater opportunity for delegation, and a greater willingness to delegate.

The characteristics of a mechanistic system are similar to those of a bureaucratic structure. Large-scale organisations are almost certain to exhibit many of the characteristics of bureaucracy and this is most noticeable within the public sector. In the case of public sector organisations there is a particular demand for uniformity of treatment, regularity of procedures and accountability for their operations. It might be seen therefore that opportunities for personal delegation will be greater in small organisations, especially within the private sector.

Flexibility of job descriptions/gradings

Where detailed job descriptions are adopted and applied rigidly as part of the philosophy of the organisation, then this can inhibit personal delegation. Staff may be reluctant to accept additional responsibilities which appear to fall outside the scope of their job description. Grading standards may also be an important factor and it may be expected that work is seen to be done at the 'proper' level. An example is the Civil Service where, to some extent, the decision as to who does what is bound by the grading of duties.[26]

Individual characteristics

Notwithstanding any other consideration the extent and nature of delegation will ultimately be affected by the nature of individual characteristics. The ages, ability, training, attitude, motivation and character of the subordinates concerned will, in practice, be major determinants of delegation.

An example is where a strong and forceful personality overcomes the lack of formal delegation. Or where an inadequate manager is supported by a more competent subordinate who effectively acts as the manager. Failure to delegate successfully to a more knowledgeable subordinate may mean that the subordinate emerges as an informal leader and this could have possible adverse consequences for the manager, and for the organisation.

DELEGATION AND WORK STRESS

Not only does poor delegation fail to take advantage of the potential benefits to both the individual and the organisation, but it can also be a potential source of work stress. For example, research into managers in various types of organisations in Western Australia showed that delegation of responsibility to middle managers required great skill, which was too seldom present. Replies from 532 managers in 36 organisations indicated a clear correlation between lack of autonomy and stress at work.[27]

Stress was often caused by the hierarchical structure of the organisation not permitting sufficient autonomy. As a result, projects were frequently delayed and also managers' authority within their own departments was undermined.

| **Synopsis** | It is a fundamental principle of management that for organisational effectiveness there must be delegation. The structure of the organisation is itself

a result of delegation. If there is no delegation, then there is no structure. At the organisational level, delegation involves consideration of centralisation/decentralisation and divisionalisation or departmentalisation.

At the individual, or personal, level delegation is the process of entrusting authority and responsibility to others. It is the authorisation to undertake activities that would otherwise be carried out by someone in a more senior position. It is possible to have delegation upwards, and also laterally. However, delegation is usually interpreted as a movement down the organisation. Delegation creates a special manager–subordinate relationship. A manager's approach to delegation is important and should not be underestimated.

Authority is the right to take actions of make decisions that the manager would otherwise have done. Responsibility involves an obligation by the subordinate to perform certain activities and having to accept possible reprimand from the manager for unsatisfactory performance. Delegation embraces both authority and responsibility. Ultimate responsibility, however, cannot be delegated. Managers remain accountable to a superior for the actions of subordinates and the performance of all duties allocated to their department/section.

Delegation is not an easy task. It involves behavioural as well as organisational and economic considerations, and it is subject to a number of possible abuses. But if delegation is properly planned and implemented it offers a number of potential benefits both to the manager and to subordinate staff.

Control is an integral part of the system of delegation. But control should not be so close as to inhibit the effective operation of delegation. It is a question of balance. Delegation must be properly planned and approached in a systematic manner. Subordinates must know exactly what is expected of them, what has to be achieved, and the boundaries within which they have freedom of action.

The art of delegation is to agree clear terms of reference with subordinates, give them the necessary authority and responsibility, and then monitor their performance without undue interference or the continual checking of their work. A planned and systematic approach means that the full benefits of delegation can be achieved without loss of control. Delegation entails the reliance on other people. It is also a matter of confidence and trust, and of courage.

Managers often fail to delegate or to delegate successfully. There are many factors which affect the extent and effectiveness of delegation. Some of the main obstacles to delegation are the attitudes of managers, and subordinates who shrink from accepting new responsibilities. Delegation is also affected by the style of leadership and system of management, the organisation structure, the informal organisation, and the personalities of the people concerned. Individual characteristics are a major determinant of delegation. Whatever the problem areas, however, delegation is an essential feature of organisational effectiveness and a necessary function of management.

Review and discussion questions

1. What do you understand by delegation in work organisations? How would you explain the relationship between a manager and subordinate

staff that is created by the process of delegation?

2. Discuss the extent to which you accept the contention that lack of delegation results in management at too low a level. Support your answer with examples from your own or some other organisation.

3. Analyse the nature of delegation in terms of the following two statements:

   (i) 'If you want a job done properly, do it yourself'; and
   (ii) 'The higher up the ladder you are, the less you should have to do yourself'.

4. What are the reasons for delegation in work organisations? What benefits would you expect to result, for both the manager and subordinate staff, from successful delegation?

5. Explain what you believe are the qualities required of an effective delegator. What is meant by the art of delegation?

6. Explain why you think it is that delegation, whilst often advocated, is not always practised fully.

7. As a departmental manager, explain fully how you would attempt to realise the full advantages of delegation without loss of control over subordinate staff.

8. Give practical examples of the factors which are likely to influence the extent of delegation in a particular work organisation/work situation of your choice.

| **Practical assignment** | Examine a process of delegation in your or some other organisation. |

(i) Note the extent to which the three basic questions concerning the setting up of a successful system of delegation appear to have been considered.

(ii) Examine the extent to which the six main stages in a planned and systematic approach to delegation appear to have been followed. In particular, explain:

   (a) the nature of the briefing, guidance and training given to the subordinate(s); and
   (b) the form of time limits, check points and performance standards for delegation.

(iii) Attempt to inquire of (a) the manager undertaking the delegation and (b) the member(s) of staff concerned what benefits they have each gained from the delegation and any difficulties experienced.

(iv) Explain ways in which you believe the process of delegation appears to be successful, or not. Where appropriate, suggest ways in which you think the process of delegation could be made more effective.

| **Case study** | THE ENTHUSIASTIC DELEGATOR |

When Charles Turner was told, on his fortieth birthday, that he was to be promoted manager of the Electrical Insulation Materials Sales Department of the big Climax Fibre and Textile Company Limited, his gratification was strongly tempered by doubts about his own personal adequacy for the job.

Climax had only started to market its 'Highohm' range of electrical insulation materials two years previously. Though the Highohm products were not easy to sell – their small but definite technical advantages over competing products were more or less cancelled out by higher prices – their entry to the market had been spectacularly successful. Existing production capacity was already almost fully sold, and a big new plant, which would more than double capacity, was under construction and expected to start up in six to nine months' time. Turner was left in no doubt by his sales director that, as manager, he would be expected, through his small sales force, to ensure that sales of Highohm products continued to increase and that most of the extra capacity of the new plant was sold within no more than a year of production commencing. In addition, he was expected personally to service the 'house accounts' – five very large customers who between them were responsible for over 25 per cent of all Highohm purchases. The biggest of them, Bucks Electrical Cables, was reputed to be extremely awkward to deal with, and one of Turner's immediate worries in his new appointment was that he would lose this account and 10 per cent of his sales in one dreadful moment of catastrophe.

This was not his only worry. He wondered how Jim Ferris, who managed the Northern and Scottish Area would react to his appointment. Turner did not know Ferris very well, though his predecessor as sales manager, Frank Spofforth, had often spoken of him in glowing terms. He was a self-confident man in his late twenties, reputedly very dynamic, highly intelligent, and a brilliant salesman of industrial products. He had achieved remarkable success in running the Northern and Scottish Area: 44 per cent of all Highohm sales were made there, as against only 28 per cent from the South and Midlands Area, which Turner had managed prior to his promotion. (Remaining sales came from the 'house accounts' and from exports.) Turner, in fact, wondered why he, and not Ferris, had been promoted.

A further worry for Turner was the new plant. He had always felt that it was much too big and he was extremely dubious that more than a small part of the extra capacity it provided could be rapidly taken up in increased sales.

Most of all, however, Turner doubted his own abilities. He knew that he was thorough, methodical, painstaking and cautious, but these were hardly the qualities essential for managing a sales operation. His caution tended to make him slow and hesitant. He rarely produced new ideas and he disliked making decisions unless he had all the facts and had gone over them several times. He thought he was by nature fitted to keep an existing successful operation going, but he gravely doubted his ability as a leader of a dynamic pioneering effort.

Turner had hoped that he would have a long period of changeover working alongside his predecessor, Spofforth. In fact, Spofforth was urgently wanted in the new post to which he had been promoted, and Turner, within a few days of being told of his new appointment, found himself in sole command. The organisation which he inherited was as follows:

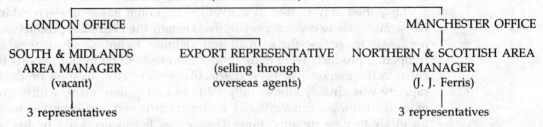

SALES MANAGER
(C. T. B. Turner)

LONDON OFFICE   MANCHESTER OFFICE

SOUTH & MIDLANDS   EXPORT REPRESENTATIVE   NORTHERN & SCOTTISH AREA
AREA MANAGER   (selling through   MANAGER
(vacant)   overseas agents)   (J. J. Ferris)

3 representatives   3 representatives

One of his immediate problems was to fill the South and Midlands Area manager vacancy. There were others, however; the plant had developed an intermittent defect which slowed production and meant that many deliveries were late. Several customers, notably Bucks Electrical Cables, were protesting vigorously. Furthermore, the sales director wanted two major reports. Each, Turner thought, would take at least a week of his time and severely tax his ability to produce new ideas and constructive proposals as well as his ability to write lucidly and elegantly. Yet he could not delay their production, or make anything less than a first-rate job of them, for fear of beginning his new appointment by disappointing the sales director.

Turner decided that he would ask Ferris to come to London for a few days. Apart from enabling him to obtain Ferris's views on the problems he faced, it would give him the opportunity to try to smooth out any resentment at his promotion.

Much to Turner's gratification, Ferris was extremely helpful. He made short work of Turner's reports. He was an abundant producer of ideas, and soon sketched out what seemed to Turner an eminently satisfactory set of proposals for both reports. He then offered to draft the reports for Turner, and dictated both during one afternoon. Turner, who normally made several laborious pencil drafts before attempting to finalise a report, was astonished at Ferris's facility. The drafts seemed to him quite perfect, and he signed them and sent them to the sales director.

Ferris next offered to go to 'pacify' Bucks Electrical Cables. Turner demurred saying it was his duty to deal personally with this problem, but Ferris insisted that Turner was too busy with managerial problems to spare the time. Turner was secretly relieved at not having to deal with these awkward customers. Ferris later telephoned to say that he had just taken three Bucks Electrical directors to lunch and they had all parted the best of friends.

Finally Ferris put forward an idea about the area manager vacancy. He, Ferris, would take over the South and Midlands Area and his senior representative in the north, Palmer, could be promoted Northern and Scottish Area manager. Turner was strongly attracted by the prospect of having Ferris's services 'on tap' in London, and readily agreed to this proposal.

Ferris tackled his new job as South and Midland's Area manager with characteristic vigour and sales were soon moving upwards – indeed, the production people had to make Herculean efforts to squeeze out the additional product needed to cope with the increased orders. He found time, however, to give substantial personal help to Turner, and Turner came increasingly to rely on him. Whenever he had a problem to solve, a decision to make, or a report to write, he consulted Ferris. Normally it was Ferris who supplied the solution, suggested the decision to be adopted, or wrote the report.

Turner often felt guilty about the extent to which he relied on Ferris and sometimes apologised to him for 'leaning' so much on him. Ferris, however, had a soothing answer. This, he explained, was the normal process of delegation. It would be quite wrong for Turner to be continually involved in detail problems; his function was to formulate the problems and leave his subordinates to solve them. Gradually, Turner came to accept the idea that his relationship with Ferris was no more than sound management; he even began to boast to his manager friends about the 'delegation' that he practised and the trouble-free life he led.

The new plant and the reorganisation

Thus, as the start-up of the new plant became imminent, Turner had a plan ready – Ferris's plan. Several new representatives had been recruited and Britain was to be divided into four sales areas – South, Midlands, North and Scotland. Ferris would continue to look after the South and Palmer the North; a nominee of Ferris, Murdoch, would manage Scotland; the Midlands Area was to be managed by Blackham, who was an older, senior representative recently transferred to Electrical Insulation Sales from another department. A new two-man technical service section was to be formed at the London office to service customers throughout Britain; and an additional export representative was to be engaged to participate in a drive for more overseas sales.

Ferris took on a wide range of new responsibilities through the reorganisation. Apart from managing the southern area and continuing to give personal assistance to Turner, he had persuaded Turner that he should in future service the 'house accounts'. He would also 'keep an eye on exports', and would accompany the export representatives on flying visits overseas when agents needed gingering up. It had been Ferris's idea that a technical service section should be formed and it was natural that he should direct its work. To free him from too much detailed work in managing the southern area, he was given an extra senior representative. The new organisation was therefore in practice as follows:

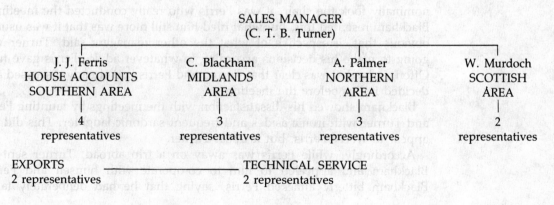

	SALES MANAGER		
	(C. T. B. Turner)		
J. J. Ferris	C. Blackham	A. Palmer	W. Murdoch
HOUSE ACCOUNTS	MIDLANDS	NORTHERN	SCOTTISH
SOUTHERN AREA	AREA	AREA	AREA
4	3	3	2
representatives	representatives	representatives	representatives

EXPORTS   TECHNICAL SERVICE
2 representatives   2 representatives

This organisation was not shown on the published charts, since both Turner and Ferris agreed that it would look better if exports and technical service were shown as formally responsible to Turner.

The first few months for the new organisation was difficult. The new plant came into production, but sales hardly rose at all. Ferris visited all the areas to coach representatives and accompany them on calls to major potential customers. He sent the technical service representatives out to scour the country, making contact with the development staffs of possible users of Highohm materials. He made numerous trips to European and Commonwealth countries to exhort the overseas agents to greater endeavour.

At length, sales began to increase – at first slowly, but then in a steep curve that took the new plant up to 80 per cent of capacity. Exports were responsible for the biggest part of the increase, but all the UK areas showed good growth, with the Midlands slightly ahead of the others.

Turner, who had only been saved from utter despondency during the months of difficulty by Ferris's unvarying confidence and optimism, now began to regain his serenity. He was congratulated by the board on the achievement of his department in selling the output of the new plant, and was given a substantial increase in salary. He became rather more self-confident, though he would still take no decision of importance without reference to Ferris.

Strains in the organisation

The area managers soon discerned something of the extent to which Turner depended on Ferris. Palmer and Murdoch, who were both protégés of Ferris, regarded it as natural. Blackham, the Midlands Area manager, however, began to make it clear that he strongly disapproved of what he called the 'imbalance of power' in the department. He pressed for more responsibility to be delegated to him. In particular, he asked to take over the two 'house accounts' in the Midlands Area. He also asked that all the area managers should be consulted before important decisions were taken.

On Ferris's advice, Turner told Blackham that he had enough to do already in developing sales in the Midlands without taking over the 'house accounts'. In any case, these important customers were best served by someone they knew and trusted. Turner and Ferris agreed, however, that more consultation with the area manager was desirable and monthly 'area manager meetings' were instituted.

These did little to decrease Blackham's dissatisfaction. Though Turner nominally took the chair, it was Ferris who really conducted the meetings. Blackham resented this, but what riled him still more was that it was usually obvious that, irrespective of what the other managers said, Turner was going to make his decisions according to whatever advice Ferris gave him. Often, indeed, it was clear that Turner and Ferris had already discussed and decided issues before the meeting.

Blackham showed his dissatisfaction with the meetings by taunting Ferris and Turner with ironic asides and frequent sardonic laughter. This did not appear to worry Ferris, but it upset Turner.

Accordingly, while Ferris was away on a trip abroad, Turner sent for Blackham and appealed to him to co-operate with himself and Ferris. Blackham bitterly attacked Ferris, saying that he had deliberately taken advantage of Turner's good nature to build up his own personal 'empire' within the department. Turner protested that this was not the case; it was just that he believed in delegation and since Ferris was exceptionally able, experienced, vigorous and willing to accept responsibility, it was natural that considerable responsibility should be delegated to him.

Blackham laughed sardonically. Turner did not delegate responsibility, he said, he abdicated it. Ferris did not just accept responsibility, he made a series of take-over bids for it.

Turner defended the system. At least it worked, he said. The department had great successes to its credit.

Blackham insisted that he was just as able and willing to accept responsibility as Ferris. It was unfair of Turner to delegate only to Ferris. The other area managers should be given the chance to show what they could do.

The meeting ended inconclusively, but Turner, who prided himself on being fair-minded, was half-persuaded that Blackham and the other area managers should be given more responsibility. As soon as Ferris returned, he consulted him on what changes in organisation might be made.

Ferris strongly opposed giving any further responsibility to the area managers, especially to Blackham, whose recent behaviour, he said, must make his judgement and temperament strongly suspect. What was wrong in the department was that the particular responsibilities he himself carried were not accompanied by appropriate formal authority. Ferris therefore proposed that he should be appointed deputy manager of the department. He was not seeking extra salary and would be quite content with only a status promotion, but he felt the time had come for it to be made clear that he was senior to Blackham and the other area managers.

This idea appealed to Turner. He felt it was only just that Ferris should be given some form of promotion. He also believed that promotion for Ferris might silence some of Blackham's criticisms.

He therefore went to ask the sales director for permission to create the new position of deputy manager, and for Ferris to be promoted to it. The sales director demurred. He said he felt that Turner's department was too small to warrant the appointment of a full-time deputy manager, and, in any case, Ferris was rather young to be promoted to such a post over the heads of older men such as Blackham. Turner pressed his case by outlining the range of duties undertaken by Ferris. The sales director questioned him closely upon this, and Turner was forced to reveal a great deal about the organisation of the department, and of his relationship with Ferris. He also mentioned his troubles with Blackham.

The sales director was obviously not at all pleased with what he had discovered. He said, 'I have always assumed that since your department has produced good results, its organisation, staffing and personal relationships have been satisfactory. Now I must consider whether or not I should intervene and impose changes.'

Questions

(i) When an inadequate manager is supported by a more able subordinate, is it likely that the subordinate will become the effective manager of the unit? Is it desirable? If not, what steps (apart from replacement of the manager) could be taken to prevent it?

(ii) Where are the boundaries between proper delegation of authority and abdication of responsibility? Was Turner, in fact, guilty of the latter?

(iii) Where does willingness to accept responsibility end and personal 'empire building' begin? Was Ferris an 'empire builder'? If so, with what motives?

(iv) How far can a theoretically undesirable system be justified on the ground that 'it works'?

(v) Should the sales director intervene in Turner's organisational and personal relations problems? If so, what should he do?

Notes and references

1. Parts of this chapter are based on the author's article: Mullins, L. J. 'Delegation and Management', *British Journal of Administrative Management*, vol. 31, no. 7, October 1981, pp. 218–24.
2. Drucker, P. F. *The Practice of Management*, Pan Books (1968).
3. Woodward, J. *Industrial Organization: Theory and Practice*, Second edition, Oxford University Press (1980).
4. Mooney, J. D. *The Principles of Organization*, Revised edition, Harper and Row (1947) p. 17.
5. Fayol, H. *General and Industrial Management*, Pitman (1949). See also: Gray, I. *Henri Fayol's General and Industrial Management*, Pitman (1988).
6. See, for example: Koontz, H. and O'Donnell, C. *Principles of Management*, Sixth edition, McGraw-Hill (1976).
7. Urwick, L. F. *Notes on the Theory of Organization*, American Management Association (1952).
8. Haire, M. (ed.) *Organization Theory in Industrial Practice*, Wiley (1962).
9. Urwick, L. F. *Notes on the Theory of Organization*, American Management Association (1952).
10. See, for example: Drucker, P. F. *The Practice of Management*, Pan Books (1968).
11. Simon, H. A. *The New Science of Management Decision*, Revised edition, Prentice-Hall (1977).
12. Hamilton, Sir Ian *The Soul and Body of an Army*, Arnold (1921) p. 236.
13. See, for example: Vinton, D. 'Delegation for Employee Development', *Training and Development Journal*, vol. 41, no. 1, January 1987, pp. 65–7.
14. Peter, L. J. and Hull, R. *The Peter Principle*, Pan Books (1970) p. 22.
15. Davis, K. *Human Behavior at Work*, Fifth edition, McGraw-Hill (1977) pp. 199–200.
16. Humble, J. W. *Management by Objectives*, Management Publications Limited for the British Institute of Management (1972).
17. Handy, C. B. *Understanding Organizations*, Third edition, Penguin (1985).
18. Jacques, E. A. *A General Theory of Bureaucracy*, Third edition, Heinemann (1981).
19. Stewart R. *The Reality of Management*, Second edition, Pan Books (1986).
20. Ibid. p. 190.
21. Hunt, J. W. *Managing People at Work*, second edition, McGraw-Hill (1986).
22. Newman, W. H. 'Overcoming Obstacles to Effective Delegation', *Management Review*, January 1956, pp. 36–41.
23. McGregor, D. *The Human Side of Enterprise*, Penguin (1987).
24. Likert, R. *New Patterns of Management*, McGraw-Hill (1961).
25. Likert, R. and Likert, J. G. *New Ways of Managing Conflict*, McGraw-Hill (1976).
26. Burns, T. and Stalker, G. M. *The Management of Innovation*, Tavistock Publications (1966).
27. Civil Service Department *Guide for New Managers*, HMSO (1975).
28. Hall, K. and Savery, L. K. 'Stress Management', *Management Decision*, vol. 25, no. 6, 1987 pp. 29–35.

11. THE NATURE OF WORK MOTIVATION

The activities of an organisation can only be achieved through the combined efforts of its members. The relationship between the organisation and its members is governed by what motivates them to work and the satisfaction they derive from it. The manager needs to understand how to elicit the co-operation of staff and direct their performance to achieving the goals and objectives of the organisation. The manager must know how best to motivate staff so that they work willingly and effectively.

Objectives

To: (i) Explain the meaning and underlying concept of motivation;
(ii) Identify main types of needs and expectations of people at work;
(iii) Explain possible reactions to frustration at work;
(iv) Outline different approaches to work motivation;
(v) Explain the nature of different theories of motivation;
(vi) Examine main theories of motivation and evaluate their relevance to particular work situations;
(vii) Appreciate the complex nature of work motivation.

THE MEANING OF MOTIVATION

The study of motivation is concerned, basically, with why people behave in a certain way. In general terms, motivation can be described as the direction and persistence of action. It is concerned with why people choose a particular course of action in preference to others, and why they continue with a chosen action, often over a long period, and in the face of difficulties and problems.[1]

From a review of motivation theory, *Mitchell* identifies four common characteristics which underlie the definition of motivation.[2]

- *Motivation is typified as an individual phenomenon.* Every person is unique and all the major theories of motivation allow for this uniqueness to be demonstrated in one way or another.
- *Motivation is described, usually, as intentional.* Motivation is assumed to be under the worker's control, and behaviours that are influenced by motivation, such as effort expended, are seen as choices of action.
- *Motivation is multifaceted.* The two factors of greatest importance are: (i) what gets people activated (arousal); and (ii) the force of an individual to engage in desired behaviour (direction or choice of behaviour).
- *The purpose of motivational theories is to predict behaviour.* Motivation is not the behaviour itself, and it is not performance. Motivation concerns

action, and the internal and external forces which influence a person's choice of action.

On the basis of these characteristics. Mitchell defines motivation as 'the degree to which an individual wants and chooses to engage in certain specified behaviours'.

Underlying concept of motivation

The underlying concept of motivation is some driving force within individuals by which they attempt to achieve some goal in order to satisfy some need or expectation. This concept gives rise to the basic motivational model, which is illustrated in Fig. 11.1.

People's behaviour is determined by what motivates them. Their performance is a product of both ability level and motivation.[3]

$$\text{Performance} = \text{function (ability} \times \text{motivation)}$$

Therefore, if the manager is to improve the work of the organisation, attention must be given to the level of motivation of its members. The manager must also encourage staff to direct their efforts (their driving force) towards the successful attainment of the goals and objectives of the organisation.

But what is this driving force? What are people's needs and expectations, and how do they influence behaviour and performance at work? Motivation is a complex subject and is influenced by many variables. Individuals have a variety of changing, and often conflicting, needs and expectations which they attempt to satisfy in a number of different ways.

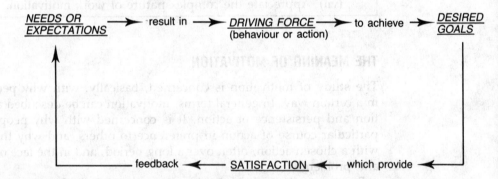

Fig. 11.1 A simplified illustration of the basic motivational model

Needs and expectations at work

These various needs and expectations can be categorised in a number of ways, for example the simple divisions into physiological and social motives; or into intrinsic or extrinsic motivation. As a starting point, the following is a useful, broad, three-fold classification for the motivation to work.[4]

- *Economic rewards* – such as pay, fringe benefits, material goods and security. This is an *instrumental* orientation to work and concerned with 'other things'.
- *Intrinsic satisfaction* – which is derived from the nature of the work itself, interest in the job, and personal growth and development. This is a *personal* orientation to work and concerned with 'oneself'.

- *Social relationships* – such as friendships, group working, and the desire for affiliation, status and dependency. This is a *relational* orientation to work and concerned with 'other people'

A person's motivation, job satisfaction and work performance will be determined by the comparative strength of these sets of needs and expectations, and the extent to which they are fulfilled. For example, some people may make a deliberate choice to forgo intrinsic satisfaction and social relationships (particularly in the short term or in the earlier years of their working life) in return for high economic rewards. Other people are happy to accept comparatively lower economic rewards in favour of a job which has high intrinsic satisfaction and/or social relationships.

The psychological contract

In addition to the above categories, the motivation to work is also influenced by the concept of the 'psychological contract', which was discussed in Chapter 1. The psychological contract involves a series of expectations between the individual member and the organisation. These expectations are not defined formally, and although the individual member and the organisation may not be aware consciously of them, they still affect the relationship between them.[5]

FRUSTRATION

If a person's motivational driving force is blocked before reaching a desired goal, there are two possible sets of outcomes: constructive behaviour or frustration. (*See* Fig. 11.2.)

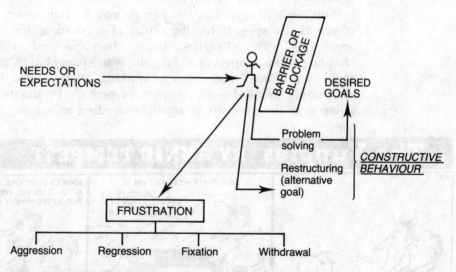

Fig. 11.2 A basic model of frustration

Constructive behaviour

This is a positive reaction to the blockage of a desired goal and can take two main forms: problem solving or restructuring.

- *Problem solving* is the removal of the barrier; for example repairing a damaged machine, or by-passing an unco-operative superior.

- *Restructuring*, or compromise, is the substitution of an alternative goal: although such a goal may be of a lower order, for example taking an additional part-time job because of failure to be promoted to a higher grading.

Note: Even if a person engages in constructive behaviour in response to a barrier or blockage it could be said that the person was 'frustrated', if only mildly or in the short term, in an attempt to satisfy a desired goal. However, the term frustration is usually interpreted as applying to *negative responses* to a barrier or blockage which prevents satisfaction of a desired goal.

Frustration (negative responses)

This is a negative response to the blockage of a desired goal and results in a defensive form of behaviour. There are many possible reactions to frustration caused by the failure to achieve a desired goal. These can be summarised under four broad headings: aggression; regression; fixation; withdrawal.[6] However, these categories are not mutually exclusive. Most forms of frustration-induced behaviour at work are a combination of aggression, regression and fixation.

Aggression is a physical or verbal attack on some person or object; for example, striking a supervisor, rage or abusive language, destruction of equipment or documents, malicious gossip about a superior. This form of behaviour may be directed against the person or object which is perceived as the source of frustration, that is the actual barrier or blocking agent.

However, where such direct attack cannot be made, because, for example, the source of frustration is not clear or not specific, or where the source is feared, such as a powerful superior, then aggression may be displaced towards some other person or object.

With *displaced aggression* the person may find an easier, safer person or object as a scapegoat for the outlet of frustration; for example, picking arguments with colleagues, being short-tempered with subordinates, shouting at the cleaners or kicking the waste-paper bin. A more constructive form of displaced aggression is working off frustrated feelings through demanding physical work or sport, or perhaps by shouting/cursing when alone or in the company of an understanding colleague.

Fig. 11.3 An example of displaced aggression!

(Cartoon by Annie Tempest reproduced with permission from the *Daily Mail*, 26 February 1988. Copyright © Mail Newspapers plc)

Regression is reverting to childish or a more primitive form of behaviour; for example, sulking, crying, tantrums, or kicking a broken machine or piece of equipment.

Fixation is persisting in a form of behaviour which has no adaptive value and continuing to repeat actions which have no positive results; for example, the inability to accept change or new ideas, repeatedly trying a machine which clearly will not work, insisting on applying for promotion even though not qualified for the job.

Withdrawal is apathy, giving up or resignation; for example, arriving at work late and leaving early, sickness and absenteeism, refusal to accept responsibility, avoiding decision making, passing work over to colleagues, or leaving the job altogether.

Factors influencing frustration

Among the factors which determine an individual's reaction to frustration are:

- the level of need;
- the degree of attachment to the desired goal;
- strength of motivation;
- perceived nature of the barrier or blocking agent; and
- the personality characteristics of the individual.

It is important that managers attempt to reduce potential frustration through, for example:

- effective recruitment, selection and training;
- job design and work organisation;
- equitable personnel policies;
- recognition and rewards;
- effective communications;
- participative styles of management.

APPROACHES TO MOTIVATION AT WORK

The development of different approaches to organisation and management has highlighted the changing concept of motivation at work.[7]

Economic needs motivation

Earlier writers, such as *F. W. Taylor*, believed in economic needs motivation. Workers would be motivated by obtaining the highest possible wages through working in the most efficient and productive way. Performance was limited by physiological fatigue. For Taylor, motivation was a comparatively simple issue – what the workers wanted from their employers more than anything else was high wages.[8] This approach is *the rational–economic concept of motivation*.

Social concept of motivation

The human relations writers, however, demonstrated that people go to work to satisfy a range of different needs, and not simply for monetary reward. They emphasised the importance of the social needs of individuals, and gave recognition to the work organisation as a social organisation. This was illustrated, for example, in the Hawthorne experiments. The human relations approach to organisation and management led to *the social concept of motivation*.

301

The systems approach also supports the social concept of motivation. The socio-technical system is concerned with the interactions between both the psychological and social factors, and the needs and demands of people; and the structural and technical requirements of the organisation. The longwall coal-mining study, for example, demonstrated the importance of redesigning work in a manner which provides opportunities for team-work and social interaction.

Self-actualisation

The findings of the Hawthorne experiments, and the subsequent attention to the social organisation and theories of individual motivation, gave rise to the work of the neo-human relations writers. These writers adopted a more psychological orientation to motivation. Greater attention was focused on the content and meaning of the task, and attempts to make work more intrinsically satisfying. The major focus of concern was the personal adjustment of the individual within the work situation. This approach is *the self-actualisation concept of motivation*.

Complex-person concept of motivation

The contingency approach to organisation and management takes the view that there are a large number of variables, or situational factors, which influence organisational performance. Contingency theory is concerned more with differences between organisations than with similarities. Managers must be adaptable, and vary their behaviour according to the particular situation, and the different needs and motivations of staff. The varying situational factors together with the complicated nature of human behaviour lead to *the complex-person concept of motivation*.

THEORIES OF MOTIVATION

There are many competing theories which attempt to explain the nature of motivation. These theories are all, at least, partially true, and all help to explain the behaviour of certain people at certain times. However, the search for a generalised theory of motivation at work appears a vain quest. A major determinant of behaviour is the particular situation in which individual workers find themselves. Motivation varies over time and according to circumstances. It is often most acute for people at a mid-career position, and especially for those who find opportunities for further advancement or promotion are blocked.

Differences in patterns of motivation are illustrated by, for example, *Hunt* who has developed average 'goal profiles' showing the relative importance of different categories of needs for people in different occupations, and changes in profiles at different stages for an average manager.[9] The complex nature of motivation is supported by the work of *Vroom*. Citing more than 500 research investigations he concludes that there is no all-embracing theory of motivation to work.[10]

Value of different theories

It is because of the complexity of motivation, and the fact that there is no single answer to what motivates people to work well, that these different theories are important to the manager. They show there are many motives which influence people's behaviour and performance. The different theories provide a framework within which to direct attention to the problem of how best to motivate staff to work willingly and effectively.

It is important to emphasise, however, that these various theories are not conclusive. They all have their critics, particularly the content theories of motivation, or have been subject to alternative findings which purport to contradict the original ideas. Many of these theories were not intended, originally, to have the significance that some writers have subsequently placed upon them. It is always easy to quote an example which appears to contradict any generalised observation on what motivates people to work. However, these different theories provide a basis for study and discussion, and for review of the most effective motivational style.

The manager, therefore, must judge the relevance of these different theories, how best to draw upon them, and how they might effectively be applied in particular work situations. The manager should be aware of at least the main theories of motivation.

Content theories and process theories

The usual approach to the study of motivation is through an understanding of internal cognitive processes. That is, what people feel and how they think. This understanding should help the manager to predict likely behaviour of staff in given situations. These different cognitive theories of motivation are usually divided into two contrasting approaches: content theories and process theories.

Content theories attempt to explain those specific things which actually motivate the individual at work. These theories are concerned with identifying people's needs and their relative strengths, and the goals they pursue in order to satisfy these needs. Content theories place emphasis on *what motivates*.

Process theories attempt to identify the relationship among the dynamic variables which make up motivation. These theories are concerned more with *how* behaviour is initiated, directed and sustained. Process theories place emphasis on the actual *process of motivation*.

CONTENT THEORIES OF MOTIVATION

Major theories under this heading include:

- *Maslow*'s hierarchy of needs model;
- *Alderfer*'s modified need hierarchy model;
- *Herzberg*'s two-factor theory; and
- *McClelland*'s achievement motivation theory.

MASLOW'S HIERARCHY OF NEEDS THEORY

A useful starting point is the work of *Maslow*, and his theory of individual development and motivation, published originally in 1943.[11] Maslow's basic proposition is that people are wanting beings, they always want more, and what they want depends on what they already have. He suggests that human needs are arranged in a series of levels, a hierarchy of importance.

The hierarchy ranges through five levels, from at the lowest level physiological needs, through safety needs, love needs, esteem needs, to the need for self-actualisation at the highest level. The hierarchy may be shown as

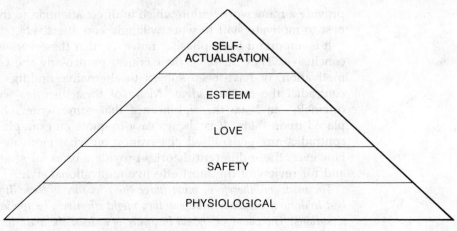

Fig. 11.4 Maslow's hierarchy of needs model

a series of steps, but is usually displayed in the form of a pyramid (Fig. 11.4). This is an appropriate form of illustration as it implies a thinning out of needs as people progress up the hierarchy.

- *Physiological needs*. These include homeostasis (the body's automatic efforts to retain normal functioning) such as satisfaction of hunger and thirst, the need for oxygen and to maintain temperature regulation. Also sleep, sensory pleasures, activity, maternal behaviour, and arguably sexual desire.
- *Safety needs*. These include safety and security, freedom from pain or threat of physical attack, protection from danger or deprivation, the need for predictability and orderliness.
- *Love needs* (often referred to as social needs). These include affection, sense of belonging, social activities, friendships, and both the giving and receiving of love.
- *Esteem needs* (sometimes referred to as ego needs). These include both self-respect and the esteem of others. Self-respect involves the desire for confidence, strength, independence and freedom, and achievement. Esteem of others involves reputation or prestige, status, recognition, attention and appreciation.
- *Self-actualisation needs*. This is the development and realisation of one's full potential. Maslow sees this as: 'What humans can be, they must be', or 'becoming everything that one is capable of becoming'. Self-actualisation needs are not necessarily a creative urge, and may take many forms which vary widely from one individual to another.

Once a lower need has been satisfied it no longer acts as a strong motivator. The needs of the next higher level in the hierarchy demand satisfaction and become the motivating influence. Only unsatisfied needs motivate a person. Thus Maslow asserts that *a satisfied need is no longer a motivator*.

Not a fixed order   Although *Maslow* suggests that most people have these basic needs in about the order indicated, he also makes it clear that the hierarchy is not necessarily a fixed order. There will be a number of exceptions to the order indicated. For some people there will be a reversal of the hierarchy, for example:

- Self-esteem may seem to be more important than love to some people. This is the most common reversal of the hierarchy. It is often based on the belief that the person most loved is strong, confident or inspires respect. People seeking love try to put on a show of aggressive, confident behaviour. They are not really seeking self-esteem as an end in itself but for the sake of love needs.
- For some innately creative people the drive for creativity and self-actualisation may arise despite lack of satisfaction of more basic needs.
- Higher level needs may be lost in some people who will continue to be satisfied at lower levels only. For example, the person who has experienced chronic unemployment.
- Some people who have been deprived of love in early childhood may experience the permanent loss of love needs.
- A need which has continued to be satisfied over a long period of time may be undervalued. For example, people who have never suffered from chronic hunger may tend to underestimate its effects, and regard food as rather an unimportant thing. Where people are dominated by a higher level need this may assume greater importance than more basic needs.
- People with high ideals or values may become martyrs and give up everything else for the sake of their beliefs.

Maslow claims that the hierarchy is relatively universal between different cultures, but he recognises that there are differences in an individual's motivational content in a particular culture.

Degrees of satisfaction

Maslow points out that a false impression may be given that a need must be satisfied fully before a subsequent need arises. He suggests a more realistic description is in terms of decreasing percentages of satisfaction along levels of the hierarchy. For example, arbitrary figures for the average person who may be, perhaps: satisfied 85 per cent in physiological needs; 70 per cent in safety needs; 50 per cent in love needs; 40 per cent in esteem needs; and 10 per cent in self-actualisation needs. There is a gradual emergence of a higher level need as lower level needs become more satisfied. The relative importance of these needs changes during the psychological development of the individual.

Maslow subsequently modified his views by noting that satisfaction of self-actualisation needs by growth motivated individuals can actually enhance these needs rather than reduce them. Also, he accepted that some higher level needs may still emerge after long deprivation of lower level needs, rather than only after their satisfaction.

Evaluation of Maslow's theory

Based on *Maslow's* theory, once lower levels needs have been satisfied (say at the physiological and safety levels) giving more of the same does not provide motivation. Individuals advance up the hierarchy as each lower level need becomes satisfied. Therefore, to provide motivation for a change in behaviour, the manager must direct attention to the next higher level of needs (in this case, love or social needs) that seek satisfaction.

However, there are a number of problems in relating Maslow's theory to the work situation. These include the following:

- People do not necessarily satisfy their needs, especially higher level needs, just through the work situation. They satisfy them through other areas of their life as well. Therefore the manager would need to have a complete understanding of people's private and social life, not just their behaviour at work.
- There is doubt about the time which elapses between the satisfaction of a lower level need and the emergence of a higher level need.
- Individual differences mean that people place different values on the same need. For example, some people prefer what they might see as the comparative safety of working in a bureaucratic organisation to a more highly paid and higher status position, but with less job security, in a different organisation.
- Some rewards or outcomes at work satisfy more than one need. Higher salary or promotion, for example, can be applied to all levels of the hierarchy.
- Even for people within the same level of the hierarchy, the motivating factors will not be the same. There are many different ways in which people may seek satisfaction of, for example, their esteem needs.
- Maslow viewed satisfaction as the main motivational outcome of behaviour. But job satisfaction does not necessarily lead to improved work performance.

An examination of Maslow's need hierarchy theory in an organisational setting was undertaken by *Hall* and *Nougaim*.[12] This was a longitudinal study, over a five-year period, of 49 young managers in the American Telephone and Telegraph Company. The top four levels of Maslow's hierarchy were used, with physiological needs excluded. An attempt was made to test the developmental change aspect of Maslow's theory. Researchers conducted lengthy interviews, each year, with the managers. Part of the study involved an analysis, for each year, of a comparison between the satisfaction score for one need with the strength score for the next higher level need. The comparison was undertaken by independent coders.

Although a positive relationship was found between need strength and need satisfaction, there was only a low statistical significance. Hall and Nougaim suggest the results indicate needs changed more because of developing career concern than the strength of need satisfaction. This study appears to provide only very limited support for the developmental theory of Maslow.

A somewhat similar study on 187 managers in two organisations was undertaken by *Lawler* and *Suttle*.[13] They used different samples and somewhat different methods of analysis from Hall and Nougaim. But, again, although some positive relationship to Maslow's theory was found, there were few findings of statistical significance.

Maslow's theory is difficult to test empirically and has been subject to various interpretations by different writers. Reviews of the need hierarchy model suggest little clear or consistent support for the theory and raise doubts about the validity of the classification of basic human needs.[14]

However, it is important to stress that Maslow himself recognised the limitations of his theory and did not imply that it should command wide-spread, empirical support. He suggested only that the theory should be considered as a framework for future research and points out: 'It is easier to perceive and to criticise the aspects in motivation theory than to remedy them.'

Although Maslow did not originally intend that the need hierarchy should necessarily be applied to the work situation, it still remains popular as a theory of motivation at work. Despite criticisms and doubts about its limitations, the theory has had a significant impact on management approaches to motivation and the design of organisations to meet individual needs. It is a convenient framework for viewing the different needs and expectations that people have, where they are in the hierarchy, and the different motivators that might be applied to people at different levels.

The work of Maslow has drawn attention to a number of different motivators and stimulated study and research. The need hierarchy model provides a useful base for the evaluation of motivation at work.

ALDERFER'S MODIFIED NEED HIERARCHY MODEL

A modified need hierarchy model has been presented by *Alderfer*.[15] This model condenses *Maslow's* five levels of need into only three levels based on the core needs of existence, relatedness and growth (ERG theory).

- *Existence needs* are concerned with sustaining human existence and survival, and cover physiological and safety needs of a material nature.
- *Relatedness needs* are concerned with relationships to the social environment, and cover love or belonging, affiliation, and meaningful interpersonal relationships of a safety or esteem nature.
- *Growth needs* are concerned with the development of potential, and cover self-esteem and self-actualisation.

A continuum of needs

Like *Maslow*, *Alderfer* suggests that individuals progress through the hierarchy from existence needs, to relatedness needs, to growth needs, as the lower level needs become satisfied. (*See* Table 11.1.) However, Alderfer suggests these needs are more a continuum than hierarchical levels. More than one need may be activated at the same time. Individuals may also progress down the hierarchy. There is a frustration–regression process. For example, if an individual is continually frustrated in attempting to satisfy growth needs, relatedness needs may reassume most importance. The lower level needs become the main focus of the individual's efforts.

Table 11.1 Relationships among Maslow's, Alderfer's and Herzberg's theories of motivation.

Maslow's hierarchy of needs	Alderfer's ERG theory	Herzberg's two-factor theory
PHYSIOLOGICAL	EXISTENCE	HYGIENE FACTORS
SAFETY		
LOVE	RELATEDNESS	
ESTEEM	GROWTH	MOTIVATORS
SELF-ACTUALISATION		

Alderfer proposed a number of basic propositions relating to the three need relationships. Some of these propositions followed Maslow's theory, some were the reverse of the theory. A number of studies were undertaken to test these propositions across different samples of people in different types of organisations.

Results from the studies were mixed. For example, the proposition that the less existence needs are satisfied the more they will be desired, received constant support from all six samples. However, the proposition that satisfaction of existence needs activates desire for relatedness needs was not supported in any of the six samples.

Unlike Maslow's theory, the results of Alderfer's work suggest that lower level needs do not have to be satisfied before a higher level need emerges as a motivating influence. The results, however, do support the idea that lower level needs decrease in strength as they become satisfied.

ERG theory states that an individual is motivated to satisfy one or more basic sets of needs. Therefore if a person's needs at a particular level are blocked then attention should be focused on the satisfaction of needs at the other levels. For example, if a subordinate's growth needs are blocked because the job does not allow sufficient opportunity for personal development, then the manager should attempt to provide greater opportunities for the subordinate to satisfy existence and relatedness needs.

HERZBERG'S MOTIVATION–HYGIENE THEORY

Herzberg's original study consisted of interviews with 203 accountants and engineers, chosen because of their growing importance in the business world, from different industries in the Pittsburgh area of America.[16] He used the critical incident method. Subjects were asked to relate times when they felt exceptionally good or exceptionally bad about their present job or any previous job. They were asked to give reasons and a description of sequence of events giving rise to that feeling. Responses to the interviews were generally consistent, and revealed that there were two different sets of factors affecting motivation and work – the two-factor theory of motivation and job satisfaction.

Hygiene and motivating factors

One set of factors are those which, if absent, cause dissatisfaction. These factors are related to job context, they are concerned with job environment and extrinsic to the job itself. *These factors are the 'hygiene' factors* (analogous to the medical term meaning preventive and environmental) or 'maintenance' factors. They serve to prevent dissatisfaction.

Table 11.2 Herzberg's two-factor theory.

Hygiene factors (dissatisfiers)	Motivators (satisfiers)
Company policy and administration	Achievement
Supervision	Recognition
Salary	Nature of the work
Interpersonal relations – Supervisor	Responsibility
Working conditions	Growth and advancement

The other set of factors are those which, if present, serve to motivate the individual to superior effort and performance. These factors are related to job content of the work itself. *They are the 'motivators' or growth factors*. The strength of these factors will affect feelings of satisfaction or no satisfaction, but not dissatisfaction (*see* Table 11.2).

The hygiene factors can be related roughly to Maslow's lower level needs and the motivators to Maslow's higher level needs. (*See* Table 11.1.)

Proper attention to the hygiene factors will tend to prevent dissatisfaction, but does not by itself create a positive attitude or motivation to work. It brings motivation up to a zero state. *The opposite of dissatisfaction is not satisfaction but, simply, no dissatisfaction*. To motivate workers to give of their best the manager must give proper attention to the motivators or growth factors.

Comparison of satisfiers and dissatisfiers

Herzberg emphasises that hygiene factors are not a 'second class citizen system'. They are as important as the motivators, but for different reasons. Hygiene factors are necessary to avoid unpleasantness at work and to deny unfair treatment. 'Management should never deny people proper treatment at work.' The motivators relate to what people are allowed to do at work. They are the variables which actually motivate people.

A comparison of satisfiers and dissatisfiers is shown in Fig. 11.5. The length of each box represents the frequency with which the factor occurred in the events described. The width of each box indicates the length of time over which the good or bad attitude to the job lasted, in terms of short duration or long duration. Short duration of attitude change lasted no longer than two weeks. Long duration of attitude change may have lasted for years.

Evaluation of Herzberg's work

The motivation–hygiene theory has extended *Maslow*'s hierarchy of needs theory and is more directly applicable to the work situation. *Herzberg*'s theory suggests that if management is to provide positive motivation then attention must be given not only to hygiene factors, but also to the motivating factors. The work of Herzberg indicates that it is more likely good performance leads to job satisfaction rather than the reverse.

Since the original study the theory has been replicated many times with different types of workers, including scientists, engineers, technicians, professional workers, nurses, food handlers, assemblers, maintenance staff. The samples have covered a number of different nationalities. Results of these studies have been largely consistent with the original findings.[17]

Herzberg's theory is, however, a source of frequent debate. There have been many other studies to test the theory. The conclusions have been mixed. Some studies provide support for the theory.[18] However, it has also been attacked by a number of writers. For example, *Vroom* claims that the two-factor theory was only one of many conclusions that could be drawn from the research.[19]

From a review of the research *House* and *Wigdor* draw attention to the influence of individual differences.[20] A given factor may be the cause of job satisfaction for one person but job dissatisfaction for another person, or vice versa. Within the sample of people, a given factor can be the source of both satisfaction and dissatisfaction. House and Wigdor conclude that the two-factor theory is an over-simplification of the sources of satisfaction and job satisfaction.

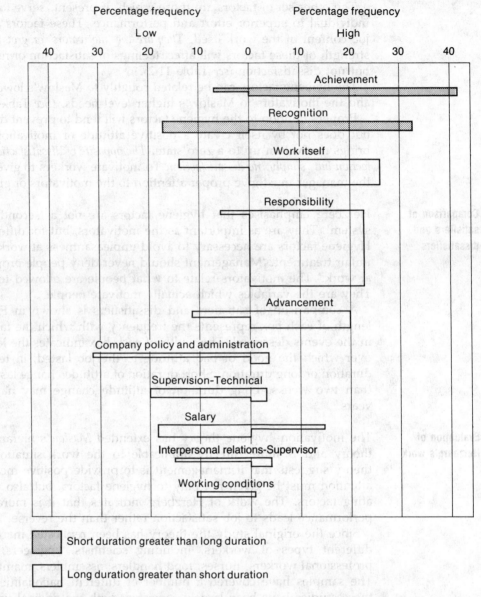

Fig. 11.5 Comparison of satisfiers and dissatisfiers.
(Reproduced with permission from Herzberg, F., *Work and the Nature of Man*, Granada Publishing Ltd. (1974) p. 73.)

Different interpretations

King suggests that there are at least five different theoretical interpretations of *Herzberg*'s model which have been tested in different studies.[21] Each interpretation places a different slant on the model. This suggests doubts about the clarity of statement of the theory.

(i) Do all motivators combined contribute more to satisfaction than to dissatisfaction, and all hygiene factors combined contribute more to dissatisfaction than to satisfaction?

(ii) Do all motivators combined contribute more to satisfaction than do all the hygiene factors combined, and all the hygiene factors combined contribute more to dissatisfaction than all motivators combined?

(iii) Does each motivator contribute more to satisfaction than to dissatisfaction, and each hygiene factor contribute more to dissatisfaction than to satisfaction?

(iv) Does each principal motivator contribute more to satisfaction than does any hygiene factor, and does each principal hygiene factor contribute more to dissatisfaction than does any motivator?

(v) Is it only motivators which determine satisfaction and only hygiene factors which determine dissatisfaction?

King concludes that theories (i) and (ii) are subject to the defensive bias of the respondents, and have not been tested adequately. Theories (iii), (iv) and (v) appear to be supported by other studies but are invalid because they reflect bias in the research.

Common general criticisms

There are two common general criticisms of *Herzberg*'s theory. One criticism is that the theory has only limited application to 'manual' workers. The other criticism is that the theory is 'methodologically bound'.

It is often claimed that the theory applies least to people with largely unskilled jobs or whose work is uninteresting, repetitive and monotonous, and limited in scope. Yet these are the people that often present management with the biggest problem of motivation. Some workers do not seem greatly interested in the job content of their work, or with the motivators or growth factors.

For example, in *Goldthorpe*'s study of manual workers on assembly-line and other factory work, he found a group of workers who adopted an 'instrumental orientation' to their job.[22] The workers' primary concern was with economic interests – pay and security – rather than with the nature of the work or the satisfaction of social needs. Their earnings were well in excess of the average manual wage at the time, the 'affluent' workers. Work was seen as a means to an end, a means of earning money through which to satisfy outside demands and interests.

However, later work by *Blackburn* and *Mann* suggests that not all manual workers share an instrumental orientation to work. From a sample of 1000 workers in relatively low-skilled jobs, they found a variety of work orientations. These included primary concerns for outdoor work or indoor work, autonomy, intrinsic aspects, worthwhileness of the job, work colleagues, working conditions, hours of work, promotion, as well as economic rewards.[23]

A second, general criticism concerns methodology. It is claimed that the critical incident method, and the description of events giving rise to good or bad feelings, influences the results. People are more likely to attribute satisfying incidents at work, that is the motivators, as a favourable reflection on their own performance. The dissatisfying incidents, that is the hygiene factors, are more likely to be attributed to external influences, and the efforts of other people. Descriptions from the respondents had to be interpreted by the interviewers. This gives rise to the difficulty of distinguishing clearly between the different dimensions, and to the risk of possible interviewer bias. When studies have been conducted without the use of the critical incident method, results generally are different from those predicted by the two-factor theory.[24]

Importance of job design

Whatever the validity of the two-factor theory much of the criticism is with the value of hindsight, and *Herzberg* did at least attempt an empirical approach to the study of motivation at work. Also his work has drawn attention to the importance of job design in order to bring about job enrichment. Herzberg has emphasised the importance of the 'quality of work life'. He advocates the restructuring of jobs to give greater emphasis to the motivating factors at work, to make jobs more interesting and to satisfy higher level needs. Job design and job enrichment are discussed in the following chapter.

McCLELLAND'S ACHIEVEMENT MOTIVATION THEORY

McClelland's work originated from investigations into the relationship between hunger needs and the extent to which imagery of food dominated thought processes. From subsequent research McClelland and colleagues identified three main arousal-based, and socially developed, motives:

- Affiliation (n-Aff);
- Power (n-Pow); and
- Achievement (n-Ach).[25]

These three motives correspond, roughly, to *Maslow's* love, esteem and self-actualisation needs.

The relative intensity of affiliation, power and achievement motives varies between individuals. It also tends to vary between different occupations. Managers appear to be higher in achievement motivation than in affiliation motivation. McClelland saw the achievement need (n-Ach) as the most critical for a country's economic growth and success. The need to achieve is linked to entrepreneurial spirit and the development of available resources.

Use of projective tests

Research studies by *McClelland* use a series of projective 'tests'. For example, individuals are shown a number of pictures in which some activity is depicted. Respondents are asked to look, briefly (10–15 seconds) at the pictures, and then to describe what they think is happening, what the people in the picture are thinking and what events have led to the situation depicted. The descriptions are used as a basis for analysing the strength of the individual's motives.

Despite the apparent subjective nature of the judgements, McClelland has, over years of empirical research, identified three common characteristics of people with high achievement needs: the preference for personal responsibility; the setting of moderate goals; and the desire for concrete feedback.[26]

- They like situations in which they can assume *personal responsibility* for solving problems. They like to attain success through their own efforts rather than by team-work or chance factors outside their control. Personal satisfaction is derived from the accomplishment of the task, and recognition need not come from other people.
- They tend to set *moderate achievement goals* with an intermediate level of difficulty, and to take calculated risks. If the task is too difficult or too

risky, it would reduce the chances of success and of gaining need satis-faction. If the course of action is too easy or too safe, there is little chal-lenge in accomplishing the task and little satisfaction from success.

- They want clear and unambiguous *feedback* on how well they are performing. A knowledge of results within a reasonable time is necessary for self-evaluation. Feedback enables them to determine success or failure in the accomplishment of their goals, and to derive satisfaction from their activities.

Extent of achievement motivation

The extent of achievement motivation varies between individuals. Some people think about achievement a lot more than others. Some people rate very highly in achievement motivation. They are challenged by opportuni-ties and work hard to achieve a goal. Other people rate very low in achieve-ment motivation. They do not care much and have little urge to achieve.

For people with a high achievement motivation, money may serve as a means of giving feedback on performance. They seem unlikely to remain long with an organisation that does not pay them well for good perform-ance. Money may seem to be important to high achievers, but they value it more as symbolising successful task performance and goal achievement. For people with low achievement motivation money may serve more as a direct incentive for performance.

McClelland's research has attempted to understand the characteristics of high achievers. He suggests that n-Ach is not hereditary but results from environmental influences, and he has investigated the possibility of training people to develop a greater motivation to achieve. McClelland suggests four steps in attempting to develop achievement drive.

- Striving to attain feedback on performance. Reinforcement of success serves to strengthen the desire to attain higher performance.
- Developing models of achievement by seeking to emulate people who have performed well.
- Attempting to modify their self-image and to see themselves as needing challenges and success.
- Controlling day-dreaming and thinking about themselves in more posi-tive terms.

McClelland was concerned with economic growth in underdeveloped coun-tries. He has designed training programmes intended to increase the achievement motivation and entrepreneurial activity of managers.

McClelland has also suggested that the effective manager should possess a high need for power.[27] However, the effective manager also scores high on inhibition. Power is directed more towards the organisation and concern for group goals, and is exercised on behalf of other people. This is 'social-ised' power. It is distinguished from 'personalised' power which is characterised by satisfaction from exercising dominance over other people, and personal aggrandisement.

PROCESS THEORIES OF MOTIVATION

Process theories attempt to identify the relationships among the dynamic variables which make up motivation. They provide a further contribution

313

to our understanding of the complex nature of work motivation. Many of the process theories cannot be linked to a single writer, but major approaches and leading writers under this heading include:

- Expectancy-based models – *Vroom*, and *Porter* and *Lawler*
- Equity theory – *Adams*
- Goal theory – *Locke*
- Attribution theory – *Heider*, and *Kelley*

Expectancy theories of motivation

The basis of expectancy theory is that people are influenced by the expected results of their actions. Motivation is a function of the relationship between effort expended and the perceived likely outcomes, and the expectation that reward will be related to performance. Performance depends upon the perceived expectation regarding effort expended and the desired outcome. For example, the desire for promotion will result in high performance only if the person believes there is a strong expectation that this will lead to promotion.

If, however, the person believes promotion to be based solely on age and length of service there is no motivation to achieve high performance. A person's behaviour reflects a conscious choice between the comparative evaluation of alternative behaviours. *The choice of behaviour is based on the expectancy of the most favourable consequences.*

Expectancy theory cannot be linked to a single individual writer. There are a number of different versions and some of the models are rather complex. More recent approaches to expectancy theory have been associated with the work of *Vroom*, and *Porter* and *Lawler*.

VROOM'S EXPECTANCY THEORY

Vroom was the first person to propose an expectancy theory aimed specifically at work motivation.[28] His model is based on three key variables: *valence, instrumentality and expectancy* (VIE theory or expectancy/valence theory). The theory is founded on the idea that people prefer certain outcomes from their behaviour over others. They anticipate feelings of satisfaction should the preferred outcome be achieved.

Valence

The feeling about specific outcomes is termed *valence*. *This is the attractiveness of, or preference for, a particular outcome to the individual.* Positive valence is where the person prefers achieving the outcome to not achieving it. Negative valence is where there is a preference for avoiding the outcome. Where the person is indifferent to achieving or not achieving the outcome, there is zero valence. *Vroom* distinguishes valence from value. A person may desire an object but then gain little satisfaction from obtaining it. Alternatively, a person may strive to avoid an object but finds, subsequently, that it provides satisfaction. *Valence is the anticipated satisfaction from an outcome.* This may differ substantially from value, which is the actual satisfaction provided by an outcome.

The valence of certain outcomes may be derived in their own right, but more usually they are derived from the other outcomes to which they are expected to lead. An obvious example is money. Some people may see money as having an intrinsic worth and derive satisfaction from the actual accumulation of wealth. Most people, however, see money in terms of the many satisfying outcomes to which it can lead. Vroom suggests that means acquire valence as a consequence of their expected relationships to ends.

Instrumentality

The valence of outcomes derive, therefore, from their *instrumentality*. This leads to a distinction between first level outcomes and second level outcomes.

The first level outcomes are performance-related. They refer to the quantity of output or to the comparative level of performance. Some people may seek to perform well 'for its own sake' and without thought to expected

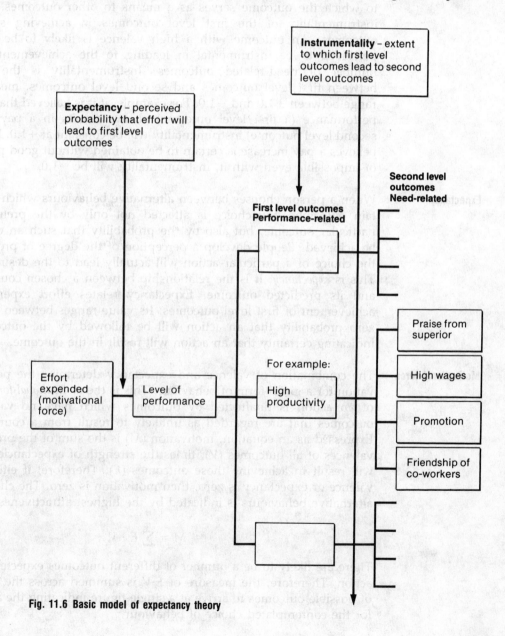

Instrumentality – extent to which first level outcomes lead to second level outcomes

Expectancy – perceived probability that effort will lead to first level outcomes

First level outcomes Performance-related

Second level outcomes Need-related

Praise from superior

High wages

Promotion

Friendship of co-workers

For example:

Effort expended (motivational force)

Level of performance

High productivity

Fig. 11.6 Basic model of expectancy theory

consequences of their actions. Usually, however, performance outcomes acquire valence because of the expectation that they will lead to other outcomes as an anticipated source of satisfaction – second level outcomes.

The second level outcomes are need-related. They are derived through achievement of first level outcomes, that is through achieving high performance. Many need-related outcomes are dependent upon actual performance rather than effort expended. People generally receive rewards for what they have achieved, rather than for effort alone or through trying hard.

On the basis of *Vroom's* expectancy theory it is possible to depict a general model of behaviour. (*See* Fig. 11.6.)

The strength of the valence of an outcome is dependent upon the extent to which the outcome serves as a means to other outcomes. This is the instrumentality of the first level outcomes in achieving second level outcomes. An outcome with a high valence is likely to be one that is perceived to be instrumental in leading to the achievement of a large number of need-related outcomes. Instrumentality is the association between first level outcomes and second level outcomes, measured on a range between $+1.0$ and -1.0. For example, if it is believed that good work performance (a first level outcome) always results in a pay increase (a second level outcome) instrumentality will be constant at $+1.0$. If the person believes a pay increase is certain to be obtained without good performance, or impossible even with it, instrumentality will be -1.0.

Expectancy

When a person chooses between alternative behaviours which have uncertain outcomes, the choice is affected not only by the preference for a particular outcome, but also by the probability that such an outcome will be achieved. People develop a perception of the degree of probability that the choice of a particular action will actually lead to the desired outcome. This is *expectancy*. It is the relationship between a chosen course of action and its predicted outcome. Expectancy relates effort expended to the achievement of first level outcomes. Its value ranges between 0, indicating zero probability that an action will be followed by the outcome, and 1, indicating certainty that an action will result in the outcome.

Motivational force

The combination of valence and expectancy determine the person's motivation for a given form of behaviour. This is the *motivational force*. The force of an action is unaffected by outcomes which have no valence, or by outcomes that are regarded as unlikely to result from a course of action. Expressed as an equation, motivation (M) is the sum of the products of the valences of all outcomes (V), times the strength of expectancies that action will result in achieving these outcomes (E). Therefore, if either, or both, valence or expectancy is zero, then motivation is zero. The choice between alternative behaviours is indicated by the highest attractiveness score.

$$M = \sum^{n} E \cdot V$$

There are likely to be a number of different outcomes expected for a given action. Therefore, the measure of $E \cdot V$ is summed across the total number of possible outcomes to arrive at a single figure indicating the attractiveness for the contemplated choice of behaviour.

Among the studies to test *Vroom*'s model was an investigation undertaken by *Galbraith* and *Cummings*.[29] They studied 32 workers in a firm manufacturing heavy equipment. Productivity figures were compared with measures of job-related (second level) outcomes such as pay, fringe benefits, promotion, style of supervision, and popularity with co-workers. The overall results suggested little significant support for the model as a whole. They did, however, indicate a marked interaction between valence and instrumentality in the case of support and consideration from supervisors, and high performance. Where workers wanted support from their supervisors, and believed this would be achieved by good performance, the workers had a high level of productivity.

THE PORTER AND LAWLER EXPECTANCY MODEL

Vroom's expectancy/valence theory has been developed by *Porter* and *Lawler*.[30] Their model goes beyond motivational force and considers performance as a whole. They point out that effort expended (motivational force) does not lead directly to performance. It is mediated by individual abilities and traits, and by the person's role perceptions. They also introduce rewards as an intervening variable. Porter and Lawler see motivation, satisfaction and performance as separate variables, and attempt to explain the complex relationships among them.

These relationships are expressed diagrammatically (Fig. 11.7) rather than mathematically. In contrast to the human relations approach which tended to assume that job satisfaction leads to improved performance, Porter and Lawler suggest that satisfaction is an effect rather than a cause of performance. It is peformance that leads to job satisfaction.

Value of reward (Box 1) is similar to valence in Vroom's model. People desire various outcomes (rewards) which they hope to achieve from work. The value placed on a reward depends on the strength of its desirability.

Perceived effort–reward probability (Box 2) is similar to expectancy. It refers to a person's expectation that certain outcomes (rewards) are dependent upon a given amount of effort.

Effort (Box 3) is how hard the person tries, the amount of energy a person exerts on a given activity. It is broadly similar to force in Vroom's model. Effort is associated more with motivation than performance. It does not relate to how successful a person is in carrying out an activity. The amount of energy exerted is dependent upon the interaction of the input variables of value of reward, and perception of the effort–reward relationship.

Abilities and traits (Box 4). Porter and Lawler suggest that effort does not lead directly to performance, but is influenced by individual characteristics. Factors such as intelligence, skills, knowledge, training and personality affect the ability to perform a given activity.

Role perceptions (Box 5) refer to the way in which individuals view their work and the role they should adopt. This influences the type of effort exerted. Role perceptions will influence the direction and level of action which is believed to be necessary for effective performance.

Performance (Box 6) depends not only on the amount of effort exerted but also on the intervening influences of the person's abilities and traits, and their role perceptions. If the person lacks the right ability or personality, or

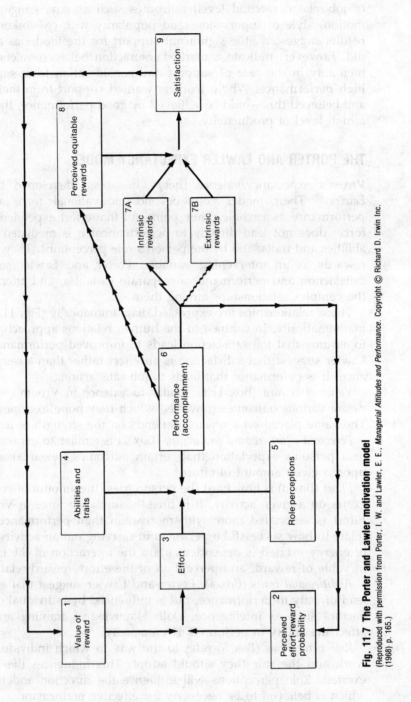

Fig. 11.7 The Porter and Lawler motivation model

(Reproduced with permission from Porter, I. W. and Lawler, E. E., *Managerial Attitudes and Performance*. Copyright © Richard D. Irwin Inc. (1968) p. 165.)

has an inaccurate role perception of what is required, then the exertion of a large amount of energy may still result in a low level of performance, or task accomplishment.

Rewards (Boxes 7) are desirable outcomes. Intrinsic rewards derive from the individuals themselves and include a sense of achievement, a feeling of responsibility and recognition (for example Herzberg's motivators). Extrinsic rewards derive from the organisation and the actions of others, and include salary, working conditions and supervision (for example Herzberg's hygiene factors). The proportion of intrinsic and extrinsic rewards will vary among individuals and in different work situations, but there must be a minimum of both. Porter and Lawler see both intrinsic and extrinsic rewards to be important and desirable outcomes. They suggest, however, that intrinsic rewards are more likely to produce job satisfaction related to performance than are extrinsic rewards.

Perceived equitable rewards (Box 8). This is the level of rewards people feel they should fairly receive for a given standard of performance. Most people have an implicit perception about the level of rewards they should receive commensurate with the requirements and demands of the job, and the contribution expected of them.

Satisfaction (Box 9). This is not the same as motivation. It is an attitude, an individual's internal state. Satisfaction is one of the variables in the Porter and Lawler model. Satisfaction is determined by both actual rewards received, and perceived level of rewards from the organisation for a given standard of performance. If perceived equitable rewards are greater than actual rewards received, the person experiences dissatisfaction. The experience of satisfaction derives from actual rewards which meet or exceed the perceived equitable rewards.

Performance and rewards

The *Porter* and *Lawler* model recognises that job satisfaction is more dependent upon performance than performance is upon job satisfaction. Satisfaction only affects performance through a feedback loop to value of reward. When satisfaction follows receipt of a reward it tends to influence the value of that reward. Also to the extent that performance results in reward, this tends to increase the effort–reward relationship.

Originally, Porter and Lawler included rewards as a single variable. After empirical testing the model was redrawn to divide rewards into two variables – intrinsic rewards and extrinsic rewards. The relationship between performance and intrinsic rewards is shown as a jagged line. This is because the extent of the relationship depends upon the nature of the job. If the design of the job permits variety and challenge, so that people feel able to reward themselves for good performance, there is a direct relationship. Where job design does not involve variety and challenge, there is no direct relationship between good performance and intrinsic rewards. The wavy line between performance and extrinsic rewards indicates that such rewards do not often provide a direct link to performance.

A second revision to the original model involved the drawing of a link between performance and perceived equitable rewards. Porter and Lawler suggest that self-rating of performance links directly with the perceived equitable reward variable. Higher levels of self-rated performance are associated with higher levels of expected equitable rewards. The heavily arrowed line indicates a relationship from the self-rated part of performance to perceived equitable rewards.

Investigations of the model

Porter and *Lawler* conducted an investigation of their own model. This study involved 563 questionnaires from managers in seven different industrial and government organisations. The main focus of the study was on pay as an outcome. The questionnaires obtained measures from the managers for a number of variables such as value of reward, effort–reward probability, role perceptions, perceived equitable rewards, and satisfaction. Information on the managers' effort and performance was obtained from their superiors. The results indicated that where pay is concerned, value of reward and perceived effort–reward probability do combine to influence effort.

Those managers who believed pay to be closely related to performance outcome received a higher effort and performance rating from their superiors. Those managers who perceived little relationship between pay and performance had lower ratings for effort and performance. The study by Porter and Lawler also demonstrated the interaction of effort and role perceptions to produce a high level of performance. Their study suggested, also, that the relationship between performance and satisfaction with their pay held good only for those managers whose performance was related directly to their actual pay.

A study by *Graen*, into the factors contributing to job satisfaction and performance, provided results which were generally supportive of expectancy theory.[31] A total of 169 women were engaged in part-time, temporary clerical tasks in a stimulated work organisation. One group of workers received verbal recognition directly related to their prior performance. A second group received a pay increase in the hope that they would do much better. The third group received no special treatment. Questionnaires were used to obtain measures of the different variables of the theory, and details of job satisfaction and performance. In general, intrinsic rewards were found to contribute substantially more to job satisfaction and performance than did the extrinsic rewards.

LAWLER'S REVISED EXPECTANCY MODEL

Following the original Porter and Lawler model, further work was undertaken by *Lawler* (*see* Fig. 11.8).[32] He suggests that in deciding on the attractiveness of alternative behaviours, there are two types of expectancies to be considered: effort–performance expectancies ($E \rightarrow P$); and performance–outcome expectancies ($P \rightarrow O$).

The first expectancy ($E \rightarrow P$) is the person's perception of the probability that a given amount of effort will result in achieving an intended level of performance. It is measured on a scale between 0 and 1. The closer the perceived relationship between effort and performance, the higher the $E \rightarrow P$ expectancy score.

The second expectancy ($P \rightarrow O$) is the person's perception of the probability that a given level of performance will actually lead to particular need-related outcomes. This is measured also on a scale between 0 and 1. The closer the perceived relationship between performance and outcome, the higher the $P \rightarrow O$ expectancy score.

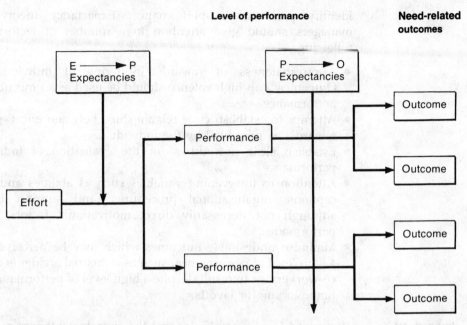

Fig. 11.8 An illustration of the Lawler expectancy model

Motivational force to perform

The multiplicative combination of the two types of expectancies, $E \rightarrow P$ and the sum of the products $P \rightarrow O$, determines expectancy. The motivational force to perform (effort expended) is determined by multiplying $E \rightarrow P$ and $P \rightarrow O$ by the strength of outcome valence (V).

$$E(\text{Effort}) = (E \rightarrow P) \times \Sigma[(P \rightarrow O) \times V]$$

The distinction between the two types of expectancies arises because they are determined by different conditions. $E \rightarrow P$ expectancy is determined in part by the person's ability and self-confidence, past experience, and the difficulty of the task. $P \rightarrow O$ expectancy is determined by the attractiveness of the outcomes and the belief about who controls the outcomes, the person him/herself or other people.

IMPLICATIONS FOR MANAGERS OF EXPECTANCY THEORIES

There are a number of different versions of expectancy theory. The main elements tend to be very similar, however, and this suggests the development of a generally accepted approach. Numerous research studies aimed at testing expectancy models appear to suggest general support for the theory, but they also highlight difficulties with some of the concepts involved and with methodology. Expectancy models are not always easy to understand, or to apply. There are many variables which affect behaviour at work. A problem can arise in attempting to include a large number of variables or in identifying those variables which are most appropriate in particular situations.

Expectancy theory does, however, draw attention to the complexities of work motivation. It provides further information in helping to explain the nature of behaviour and motivation in the work situation, and helps to identify problems in performance. Expectancy theory indicates that managers should give attention to a number of factors, including the following.

- Appropriateness of rewards in terms of individual performance. Outcomes with high valence should be used as an incentive for improved performance.
- Attempt to establish clear relationships between effort–performance and rewards, as perceived by the individual.
- Establish clear procedures for the evaluation of individual levels of performance.
- Attention to intervening variables such as abilities and traits, role perceptions, organisational procedures, and support facilities, which, although not necessarily direct motivational factors, may still affect performance.
- Minimise undesirable outcomes which may be perceived to result from a high level of performance, such as industrial accidents or sanctions from co-workers; or to result despite a high level of performance, such as short-time working or layoffs.

Just a model Porter and Lawler emphasise that the expectancy theory model applies only to behaviours which are under the voluntary control of the individual. The two general types of choices over which individuals have voluntary control of work performance in organisations are:

(i) the amount of effort and energy expended; and
(ii) the manner in which they go about performing their work.

Porter and *Lawler* also emphasise that the expectancy model is just a model.

> People rarely actually sit down and list their expected outcomes for a contemplated behaviour, estimate expectancies and valences, multiply, and add up the total unless, of course, they are asked to do so by a researcher. Yet people *do* consider the likely outcomes of their actions, do weigh and evaluate the attractiveness of various alternatives, and do use these estimates in coming to a decision about what they will do. The expectancy model provides an analytic tool for mirroring that process and for predicting its outcome, but it does not purport to reflect the actual decision-making steps taken by an individual.[33]

EQUITY THEORY OF MOTIVATION

One of the major variables of satisfaction in the Porter and Lawler expectancy model is perceived equitable rewards. This leads to consideration of another process theory of motivation – equity theory. Applied to the work situation, equity theory is usually associated with the work of *Adams*.[34]

Equity theory focuses on people's feelings of how fairly they have been treated in comparison with the treatment received by others. It is based on exchange theory. People evaluate their social relationships in the same way as buying or selling an item. People expect certain outcomes in exchange for certain contributions, or inputs.

Social relationships involve an exchange process. For example, a person may expect promotion as an outcome of a high level of contribution (input) in helping to achieve an important organisational objective. People also compare their own position with that of others. They determine the perceived equity of their own position. Feelings about the equity of the exchange is affected by the treatment they receive when compared with what happens to other people.

Most exchanges involve a multiple of inputs and outcomes. According to equity theory, people place a weighting on these various inputs and outcomes according to how they perceive their importance. When the ratio of a person's total outcomes to total inputs equals the perceived ratio of other people's total outcomes to total inputs there is *equity*.

When there is an unequal comparison of ratios the person experiences a sense of *inequity*. The feeling of inequity might arise when an individual's ratio of outcomes to inputs is either less than, or greater than, that of other people. For example, Adams suggests that workers prefer equitable pay to overpayment. Workers on piece-rate incentive payment schemes who feel they are overpaid will reduce their level of productivity in order to restore equity.

Behaviour as consequences of inequity

A feeling of inequity causes tension, which is an unpleasant experience. The presence of inequity therefore motivates the person to remove or to reduce the level of tension and the perceived inequity. The magnitude of perceived inequity determines the level of tension. The level of tension created determines the strength of motivation. *Adams* identifies six broad types of possible behaviour as consequences of inequity (*see* Fig. 11.9).

- *Changes to inputs* – a person may increase or decrease the level of his or her inputs, for example through the amount or quality of work, absenteeism, or working additional hours without pay.
- *Changes to outcomes* – a person may attempt to change outcomes such as pay, working conditions, status and recognition, without changes to inputs.
- *Cognitive distortion of inputs and outcomes* – in contrast to actual changes, people may distort, cognitively, their inputs or outcomes to achieve the same results. Adams suggests that although it is difficult for people to distort facts about themselves, it is possible, within limits, to distort the utility of those facts. For example, the belief about how hard they are really working, the relevance of a particular qualification, or what they can or cannot obtain with a given level of pay.
- *Leaving the field* – a person may try to find a new situation with a more favourable balance. For example, by absenteeism, request for a transfer, resigning from a job or from the organisation altogether.
- *Acting on others* – a person may attempt to bring about changes in others, for example to lower their inputs or accept greater outcomes. Or the person may cognitively distort the inputs and outcomes of others. Alternatively, a person may try to force others to leave the field.
- *Changing the object of comparison* – this involves changing the reference group with whom comparison is made. For example, where another person with a previously similar outcome–input ratio receives greater

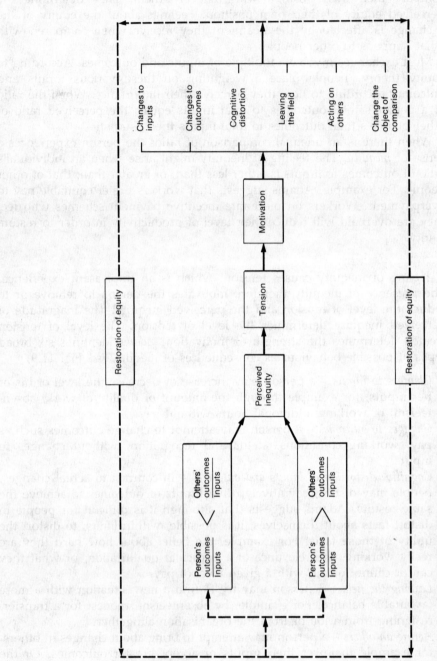

Fig. 11.9 An illustration of Adams's equity theory of motivation

outcomes without any apparent increase in contribution, that other person may be perceived as now belonging to a different level in the organisation structure. The comparison need not necessarily be made with people who have the same inputs and outcomes. The important thing is a similar ratio of outcomes to inputs.

GOAL THEORY

Another theory sometimes considered under the heading of motivation to work is goal theory, or the theory of goal setting (*see* Fig. 11.10). This theory is based mainly on the work of *Locke*.[35]

The basic premise of goal theory is that people's goals or intentions play an important part in determining behaviour. Locke accepts the importance of perceived value, as indicated in expectancy theories of motivation, and suggests that these values give rise to the experience of emotions and desires. People strive to achieve goals in order to satisfy their emotions and desires. Goals guide people's responses and actions. Goals direct work behaviour and performance, and lead to certain consequences or feedback.

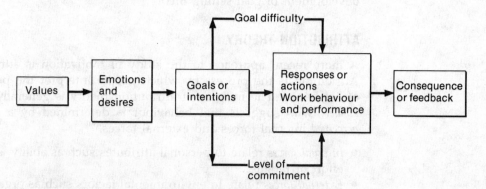

Fig. 11.10 An illustration of Locke's theory of goal setting

Goal setting and performance

The combination of goal difficulty and the extent of the person's commitment to achieving the goal regulates the level of effort expended. People with specific quantitative goals, such as a defined level of performance, or a given deadline for completion of a task, will perform better than people with no set goal or only a vague goal such as 'do the best you can'. People who have difficult goals will perform better than people with easier goals.

A number of research studies have attempted to examine the relationship between goal setting and performance. Although, almost inevitably, there are some contrary findings, the majority of evidence suggests strong support for the theory, and its effects on motivation.[36] *Locke* subsequently pointed out that 'goal-setting is more appropriately viewed as a motivational technique rather than as a formal theory of motivation'.[37] But, however it is viewed, the theory of goal setting provides a useful approach to work motivation and performance.

Practical implications for the manager

Goal theory has a number of practical implications for the manager.

- Specific performance goals should systematically be identified and set in order to direct behaviour and maintain motivation.
- Goals should be set at a challenging but realistic level. Difficult goals lead to higher performance. However, if goals are set at too high a level, or are regarded as impossible to achieve, performance will suffer, especially over a longer period.
- Complete, accurate and timely feedback and knowledge of results is usually associated with high performance. Feedback provides a means of checking progress on goal attainment and forms the basis for any revision to goals.
- Goals can be determined either by a superior or by individuals themselves. Goals set by other people are more likely to be accepted when there is participation. Employee participation in the setting of goals may lead to higher performance.[38]

Much of the theory of goal setting can be related to the system of Management by Objectives (discussed in Chapter 9). MBO is often viewed as an application of goal setting, although MBO was devised originally before the development of goal setting theory.

ATTRIBUTION THEORY

A more recent approach to the study of motivation is attribution theory. Attribution is the process by which people interpret the perceived causes of behaviour. The initiator of attribution theory is generally recognised as *Heider*, who suggests that behaviour is determined by a combination of *perceived* internal forces and external forces.[39]

- *Internal forces* relate to personal attributes such as ability, skill, amount of effort or fatigue.
- *External forces* relate to environmental factors such as organisational rules and policies, the manner of superiors, or the weather.

Behaviour at work may be explained by the *locus of control*, that is whether the individual perceives outcomes as controlled by themselves, or by external factors. Judgements made about other people will also be influenced strongly by whether the cause is seen as internal or external.

Basic criteria in making attributions

In making attributions and determining whether an internal or external attribution is chosen, *Kelley* suggests three basic criteria: distinctiveness, consensus and consistency.[40]

- *Distinctiveness.* How distinctive or different was the behaviour or action?
- *Consensus.* Is the behaviour or action in keeping with that displayed by most other people in the same situation?
- *Consistency.* Is the behaviour or action associated with an enduring personality or motivational characteristic, or a one-off situation caused by external factors.

An example of these criteria related to a student who fails a mid-sessional examination in a particular subject is given in Table 11.3.[41]

Table 11.3 Example of criteria in making attributions.

	Distinctiveness	Consensus	Consistency
Internal attribution	Student fails all mid-sessional examinations	Student is the only one to fail	Student also fails final examination
External attribution	Student gains high marks on other mid-sessional examinations	All students in the class get low marks	Student obtains a good mark in final examination

(Adapted from Terence R. Mitchell, *People in Organizations*, Second edition, McGraw-Hill (1982) p. 104.)

Classification of attributions

An additional consideration in the evaluation of task performance within an organisational setting is whether the cause of behaviour was due to 'stable' or 'unstable' factors.

- *Stable factors* are ability, or the ease or difficulty of the task.
- *Unstable factors* are the exertion of effort, or luck.[42]

The combination of internal and external attributions, and stable and unstable characteristics, results in four possible interpretations of a person's task performance (Table 11.4).

Table 11.4 Classification of possible attributions for performance.

	Internal attributions	External attributions
Stable factors	ABILITY	TASK DIFFICULTY
Unstable factors	EFFORT	LUCK

Implications of attribution theory

Employees with an internal control orientation are more likely to believe that they can influence their level of performance through their own abilities, skills or efforts. Employees with an external control orientation are more likely to believe that their level of performance is determined by external factors beyond their influence.

Studies appear to support the idea that staff with an internal control orientation are generally more satisfied with their jobs, are more likely to be in managerial positions, and satisfied with a participatory style of management, than staff with an external control orientation.[43] As a generalisation it might be implied that internally controlled managers are more effective than those who are externally controlled. However, this does not appear to be always the case.[44]

People with a high achievement motivation may perceive that successful performance is caused by their own internal forces, and their ability and effort, rather than by the nature of the task or by luck. If members of staff fail to perform well on their tasks they may believe that external factors are the cause, and as a result may reduce the level of future effort. On the other hand, if staff perform well but the manager perceives this as due to an easy task or to luck, the appropriate recognition and reward may not be given. If the staff perceive that good performance was due to ability and/or effort the lack or recognition and reward may well have a demotivating effect.

Synopsis

The study of motivation is concerned with why people behave in a certain way, with why they choose a particular course of action in preference to others. The underlying concept of motivation is some driving force within individuals by which they attempt to achieve some goal in order to satisfy some need or expectation. Individuals have a variety of changing, and often competing, needs and expectations which they attempt to satisfy in a number of different ways.

One useful three-fold classification of individual needs and expectations at work is economic, intrinsic and social. If a person's motivational driving force is blocked before reaching a desired goal, there are two possible sets of outcomes – constructive behaviour or frustration. Main reactions to frustration are aggression, regression, fixation and withdrawal.

The development of different approaches to organisation and management has highlighted the changing concept of motivation at work. These different approaches have led through the rational–economic concept of motivation, the social concept of motivation, the self-actualisation concept of motivation, to the complex-person concept of motivation.

There are many competing theories which attempt to explain motivation at work. These theories are not conclusive and all have their critics or have been subject to alternative findings, particularly the content theories. However, it is because of the complexity of motivation that these different theories are important to the manager. They show that there are many motives which influence people's behaviour at work. They provide a framework within which to direct attention to the problem of how best to motivate staff to work willingly and effectively.

The different theories of motivation may be divided into two contrasting groups: content theories and process theories. Content theories place emphasis on what motivates and are concerned with identifying people's needs and their relative strengths, and the goals they pursue in order to satisfy these needs. Main content theories include: Maslow's hierarchy of needs model; Alderfer's modified need hierarchy model; Herzberg's two-factor theory; and McClelland's achievement motivation.

Process theories place emphasis on the actual process of motivation. These theories are concerned with the relationships among the dynamic variables which make up motivation, and with how behaviour is initiated, directed and sustained. Many of the process theories cannot be linked to a single writer, but major approaches under this heading include: expectancy-based models; equity theory; goal theory; and attribution theory.

It is always easy to quote an example which appears to contradict any generalised observation on what motivates people to work. However, these different theories provide a basis for study and discussion, and for review of the most effective motivational style. The manager must judge the relevance of these different theories and how best to apply them to particular work situations.

Review and discussion questions

1. Explain what you understand by motivation and the underlying concept of motivation. Summarise the main needs and expectations to be taken into account in considering the motivation of people at work.
2. What do you understand by the term frustration? Explain the main forms

of frustrated-induced behaviour and give a practical example, preferably from your own experience, of each form of behaviour.

3. Why is the study of the different theories of motivation important to the manager? Distinguish between content and process theories of motivation.

4. Discuss, critically, the practical value of Maslow's hierarchy of needs model to improving the motivation of people at work. Which of these needs do you consider are most often satisfied in industrial work situations?

5. Critically assess the contribution of Herzberg's two-factor theory to an understanding of work motivation. Give examples of the extent to which the theory could meaningfully be applied to the motivation of staff in your own organisation.

6. Explain your understanding of expectancy-based theories of motivation. Use a simple diagram to help explain an expectancy theory of your choice. What implications do expectancy theories of motivation have for the manager?

7. Give practical examples of situations in which each of the following theories of motivation might be appropriate: (i) achievement motivation; (ii) equity theory; (iii) goal theory.

8. Explain what is meant by attribution theory. What are the basic criteria in making attributions? What do you believe to be the practical implications of attribution theory?

| Assignment 1 |

1. List, as far as possible in rank order, the specific needs and expectations which are most important to you as an individual. (Do *not* include *basic* physiological needs such as to satisfy thirst or hunger, or a reasonable place to live.)

2. Explain, briefly, to what extent these needs and expectations are met currently from your present work situation; and/or to what extent you anticipate they will be met from your future career ambitions.

3. Think of any work experience which you have had – even a short-term, vacation or part-time job. Briefly describe
   (a) those aspects of the job and/or experiences which motivated you to work well; and
   (b) those which had a demotivating influence on your behaviour/actions.

4. Be prepared to share your feelings and comments as part of a class discussion.

| Assignment 2 |

MOTIVATION QUESTIONNAIRE

The following questions have seven possible responses:

1. Please mark one of the seven responses by circling the number that corresponds to the response that fits your opinion. For example, if you 'strongly agree,' circle the number '+3'.

2. Complete every item. You have about ten minutes to do so.

	Strongly agree	Agree	Slightly agree	Don't know	Slightly disagree	Disagree	Strongly disagree
	+3	+2	+1	0	−1	−2	−3
1. Special wage increases should be given to employees who do their jobs very well.	+3	+2	+1	0	−1	−2	−3
2. Better job descriptions would be helpful so that employees will know exactly what is expected of them.	+3	+2	+1	0	−1	−2	−3
3. Employees need to be reminded that their jobs are dependent on the company's ability to compete effectively.	+3	+2	+1	0	−1	−2	−3
4. Supervisors should give a good deal of attention to the physical working conditions of their employees.	+3	+2	+1	0	−1	−2	−3
5. Supervisors ought to work hard to develop a friendly working atmosphere among their people.	+3	+2	+1	0	−1	−2	−3
6. Individual recognition for above-standard performance means a lot to employees.	+3	+2	+1	0	−1	−2	−3
7. Indifferent supervision can often bruise feelings.	+3	+2	+1	0	−1	−2	−3
8. Employees want to feel that their real skills and capacities are put to use on their jobs.	+3	+2	+1	0	−1	−2	−3
9. The company retirement benefits and share programmes are important factors in keeping employees on their jobs.	+3	+2	+1	0	−1	−2	−3
10. Almost every job can be made more stimulating and challenging.	+3	+2	+1	0	−1	−2	−3
11. Many employees want to give their best in everything they do.	+3	+2	+1	0	−1	−2	−3

	Strongly agree	Agree	Slightly agree	Don't know	Slightly disagree	Disagree	Strongly disagree
	+3	+2	+1	0	−1	−2	−3
12. Management could show more interest in the employees by sponsoring social events after hours.	+3	+2	+1	0	−1	−2	−3
13. Pride in one's work is actually an important reward.	+3	+2	+1	0	−1	−2	−3
14. Employees want to be able to think of themselves as 'the best' at their own jobs.	+3	+2	+1	0	−1	−2	−3
15. The quality of the relationships in the informal work group is quite important.	+3	+2	+1	0	−1	−2	−3
16. Individual incentive bonuses would improve the performance of employees.	+3	+2	+1	0	−1	−2	−3
17. Visibility with upper management is important to employees.	+3	+2	+1	0	−1	−2	−3
18. Employees generally like to schedule their own work and to make job-related decisions with a minimum of supervision.	+3	+2	+1	0	−1	−2	−3
19. Job security is important to employees.	+3	+2	+1	0	−1	−2	−3
20. Having good equipment to work with is important to employees.	+3	+2	+1	0	−1	−2	−3

After you have circled one number for each of the twenty questions, compare your responses with those of your colleagues.

Assignment 3

1. Study the picture below for 10–15 seconds.
2. What is going on in this picture?
   What is the person thinking?
   What has led up to this situation?
3. Write your own short story about the picture.

After you have written your story, compare your response with those of your colleagues.

Fig. 11.11 Sample picture used in a projective test

Notes and references

1. Krech, D., Crutchfield, R. S. and Ballachey, E. L. *Individual in Society*, McGraw-Hill (1962).
2. Mitchell, T. R. 'Motivation: New Directions for Theory, Research, and Practice', *Academy of Management Review*, vol. 7, no. 1, January 1982, pp. 80–8.
3. See, for example: Vroom, V. H. and Deci, E. L. (eds) *Management and Motivation*, Penguin (1970).
4. See, for example: Bennett, R. *Managing Personnel and Performance*, Business Books (1981).
5. See, for example: Argyris, C. *Understanding Organizational Behavior*, Dorsey (1960).
6. For example, see: Brown, J. A. C. *The Social Psychology of Industry*, Penguin (1954 and 1986).
7. For a development of this approach, see: Schein, E. H. *Organizational Psychology*, Third edition, Prentice-Hall (1980).
8. Taylor, F. W. *Scientific Management*, Harper and Row (1947).
9. Hunt, J. W. *Managing People at Work*, Second edition, McGraw-Hill (1986).

10. Vroom, V. H. *Work and Motivation*, Wiley (1964). (Also published by Krieger (1982).)

11. Maslow, A. H. 'A Theory of Human Motivation', *Psychological Review*, 50, July 1943, pp. 370 96 and Maslow, A H. *Motivation and Personality*, Third edition, Harper and Row (1987).

12. Hall, D. T. and Nougaim, K. E. 'An Examination of Maslow's Need Hierarchy in an Organizational Setting', *Organizational Behavior and Human Performance*, vol. 3, February 1968, pp. 12–35.

13. Lawler, E. E. and Suttle, J. L. 'A Casual Correlational Test of the Need Hierarchy Concept', *Organizational Behaviour and Human Performance*, vol. 7, 1972, pp. 265–87.

14. Wahba, M. A. and Bridwell, L. G. 'Maslow Reconsidered: A Review of Research on the Need Hierarchy Theory', *Organizational Behavior and Human Performance*, vol. 15, 1976, pp. 212–40.

15. Alderfer, C. P. *Existence, Relatedness and Growth*, Collier Macmillan (1972).

16. Herzberg, F., Mausner, B. and Synderman, B. B. *The Motivation to Work*, Second edition, Chapman and Hall (1959).

17. Herzberg, F. *Work and the Nature of Man*, Granada Publishing Ltd (1974).

18. For examples, see: (i) Bockman, V. M. 'The Herzberg Controversy', *Personnel Psychology*, vol. 24, Summer 1971, pp. 155–89. This work analyses existing evidence from a wide variety of studies. (ii) Filley, A. C., House, R. J. and Kerr, S. *Managerial Process and Organizational Behavior*, Second edition, Scott Foresman (1976). A number of different sets of interviews found a high level of validity for the theoretical prediction.

19. Vroom, V. H. *Work and Motivation*, Wiley (1964). (Also published by Krieger (1982).)

20. House, R. J. and Wigdor, L. A. 'Herzberg's Dual-Factor Theory of Job Satisfaction and Motivation. A Review of the Evidence and a Criticism'. *Personnel Psychology*, vol. 20, Winter 1967, pp. 369–90.

21. King, N. 'A Clarification and Evaluation of the Two-Factor Theory of Job Satisfaction', *Psychological Bulletin*, vol. 74, July 1970, pp. 18–31.

22. Goldthorpe, J. *et al*. *The Affluent Worker*, Cambridge University Press (1968).

23. Blackburn, R. M. and Mann, M. *The Working Class in the Labour Market*, Macmillan (1979).

24. See, for example: Hulin, C. L and Smith, P. A. 'An Empirical Investigation of Two Implications of the Two-Factor Theory of Job Satisfaction', *Journal of Applied Psychology*, vol. 51, October 1967, pp. 396–402.

25. McClelland, D. C. *The Achieving Society*, Van Nostrand Reinhold (1961). (Also published by Irvington (1976).)

26. McClelland, D. C. 'Business Drive and National Achievement'. *Harvard Business Review*, vol. 40, July–August 1962, pp. 99–112.

27. McClelland, D. C. and Burnham, D. H. 'Power is the Great Motivator', *Harvard Business Review*, vol. 54, March–April 1976, pp. 100–10.

28. Vroom, V. H. *Work and Motivation*, Wiley (1964). (Also published by Krieger (1982).)

29. Galbraith, J. and Cummings, L. L. 'An Empirical Investigation of the Motivational Determinants of Task Performance', *Organizational Behavior and Human Performance*, vol. 2, 1967, pp. 237–57.

30. Porter, L. W. and Lawler, E. E. *Managerial Attitudes and Performance*, Irwin (1968).

31. Graen, G. 'Instrumentality Theory of Work Motivation', *Journal of Applied Psychology Monograph*, vol. 53, no. 2, 1969, part 2.

32. Lawler, E.E. *Motivation in Work Organizations*, Brooks/Cole (1973).

33. Porter, L. W., Lawler, E. E. and Hackman, J. R. *Behavior in Organizations*, McGraw-Hill (1975), pp. 57–8.

34. Adams, J. S. 'Injustice in Social Exchange', in Berkowitz, L. (ed.) *Advances in Experimental Social Psychology*, Academic Press (1965). Abridged in Steers, R. M. and Porter. L. W. *Motivation and Work Behavior*, Second edition, McGraw-Hill (1979), pp. 107–24.

35. Locke, E. A. 'Towards a Theory of Task Motivation and Incentives', *Organizational Behavior and Human Performance*, vol. 3, 1968, pp. 157–89.

36. For examples, see: (i) Latham, G. P. and Yukl, G. A. 'A Review of the Research on the Applications of Goal Setting in Organizations', *Academy of Management Journal*, vol. 18, 1975, pp. 824–45. (ii) Latham, G. P. and Locke, E. A. 'Goal Setting: A Motivational Technique that Works', *Organizational Dynamics*, Autumn 1979, pp. 28–80.

37. Locke, E. A. 'Personal Attitudes and Motivation', *Annual Review of Psychology*, vol. 26, 1975, pp. 457–80.

38. For a summary or research supporting these conclusions, see: Miner, J. B. *Theories of Organizational Behavior*, Holt, Rinehart and Winston (1980).
39. Heider, F. *The Psychology of Interpersonal Relations*, John Wiley and Sons (1958).
40. Kelly, H. H. 'The Process of Causal Attribution', *American Psychologist*, February 1973, pp. 107–28.
41. Mitchell, T. R. *People in Organizations*, Second edition, McGraw-Hill (1982).
42. Bartunek, J. M. 'Why Did You Do That? Attribution Theory in Organizations', *Business Horizons*, September–October 1981, pp. 66–71.
43. Mitchell, T. R., Smyser, C. M. and Weed, S. E. 'Locus of Control: Supervision and Work Satisfaction', *Academy of Management Journal*, September 1975, pp. 623–31.
44. Durand, D. E. and Nord, W. R. 'Perceived Leader Behavior as a Function of Personality Characteristics of Supervisors and Subordinates', *Academy of Management Journal*, September 1976, pp. 427–38.

12. JOB SATISFACTION AND WORK PERFORMANCE

To make the best use of people as a valuable resource of the organisation, attention must be given to the relationship between staff and the nature and content of their jobs. The nature of the work organisation and the design of jobs can have a significant effect on the job satisfaction of staff. Attention needs to be given to the quality of working life. The manager needs to understand how best to make work more satisfying for staff and to overcome obstacles to effective performance.

Objectives

To: (i)   Explain the meaning and nature of job satisfaction;
    (ii) Examine dimensions of job satisfaction;
    (iii) Assess the importance of job design to job satisfaction and organisational performance;
    (iv) Detail main approaches to improving job design and work organisation;
    (v) Explain the concept of the quality of working life and the work of the Work Research Unit;
    (vi) Assess the potential value of quality circles;
    (vii) Evaluate the relationships among motivation, job satisfaction and work performance.

THE MEANING AND NATURE OF JOB SATISFACTION

Motivation to work well is usually related to job satisfaction, but the nature of this relationship is not clear. One view is that the motivation required for a person to achieve a high level of performance is satisfaction with the job. However, although the level of job satisfaction may well affect the strength of motivation, this is not always the case.

Satisfaction is not the same as motivation. *Job satisfaction is more of an attitude, an internal state. It could, for example, be associated with a personal feeling of achievement, either quantitative or qualitative.* Motivation is a process which may lead to job satisfaction.

Content theories of motivation and job satisfaction

The content theories of motivation are related more to satisfaction. In particular, *Herzberg*'s two-factor theory is essentially a theory of job satisfaction. His belief is that job enrichment should give people the opportunity to use their talents and abilities, and to exercise more self-control over the job. Inherent in the job should be a learning and growth experience.[1] Herzberg distinguishes job enrichment from job enlargement. Job enlargement involves making a job structurally bigger. It expands the job horizontally. Job enrichment, however, involves vertical job loading. It provides greater opportunities for psychological growth. Building on from the two-factor

335

theory, Herzberg has identified a number of factors as part of an approach to job design and job enrichment.[2]

In an attempt to test Herzberg's two-factor theory, *Myers* reports on an extensive, six-year study of motivation research undertaken by the management of Texas Instruments in America.[3] Conclusions drawn from the study include the following:

- What motivates employees to work effectively is a challenging job which allows a feeling of achievement, responsibility, growth, advancement, enjoyment of work itself and earned recognition.
- What dissatisfies workers is mostly factors which are peripheral to the job – work rules, lighting, coffee breaks, titles, seniority, rights, wages, fringe benefits and the like.
- Workers become dissatisfied when opportunities for meaningful achievement are eliminated and they become sensitised to their environment and begin to find fault.

Motivation seekers and maintenance seekers

Using *Herzberg*'s model, *Myers* identified two distinctive groups of people: motivation seekers and maintenance seekers.

The *motivation seekers* are motivated primarily by the nature of the task and have a high tolerance of poor environmental factors. They achieve a high level of satisfaction from a sense of accomplishment. Motivation seekers are more often inner-directed and self-sufficient people.

The *maintenance seekers* are motivated primarily by the nature of their environment and tend to avoid motivation opportunities. They show little interest in the nature and quality of work, and realise little satisfaction from a sense of accomplishment. They are preoccupied, and dissatisfied, with maintenance factors such as pay, security, supervision and working conditions. Maintenance seekers are usually outer-directed and may be highly reactive or ultra-conservative.

Although individual orientation as a motivation seeker or maintenance seeker tended to be fairly permanent, this orientation can be influenced by the characteristics of various roles and the nature of the work environment. Effective job performance depends on the fulfilment of both motivation needs and maintenance needs.

Myers found that satisfaction of the motivation needs arose typically from such factors as delegation, access to information, freedom of action, atmosphere of approval, involvement, goal setting, problem solving, performance appraisal, merit increases, discretionary awards, profit-sharing, utilised aptitudes, work itself, inventions, publications, company growth, promotions, education and training, memberships.

As a result of this study, Texas Instruments proceeded to implement job enrichment. Supervisors were trained to evaluate subordinates' jobs in terms of their potential for facilitating maintenance and motivation needs. A formalised attitude measurement programme was introduced to appraise total organisational effectiveness in both the maintenance-need and motivation-need areas.

JOB SATISFACTION AND WORK PERFORMANCE

The content theories of motivation also assume a direct relationship between job satisfaction and improved performance. The expectancy theories of motivation, however, recognise the complexity of work motivation and consider in more detail the relationship between motivation, satisfaction and performance.

Job satisfaction does not necessarily lead to improved work performance. For example, from the results of twenty studies, *Vroom* found no simple relationship, and only a low median correlation (0.14), between job satisfaction and job performance.[4]

Argyle suggests a probable relationship between satisfaction and productivity for highly skilled workers, or for those workers involved deeply with their work. However, individual differences cloud the position. The 'average' workers do work hard when satisfied. But some workers may work hard in order to forget their lack of contentment, and other workers are more content when their work requires little effort.[5] (*See* Fig. 12.1.)

Argyle also examined the relationship between job satisfaction and absenteeism, and labour turnover. Both are affected by factors other than job satisfaction, but it is concluded that there is a lower level of voluntary absenteeism, and of labour turnover, when there is a high level of job satisfaction.

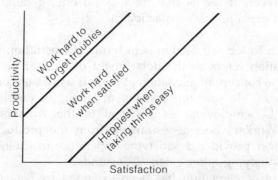

Fig. 12.1 The relation between productivity and satisfaction
(Reproduced with permission from Argyle, M., *The Social Psychology of Work*, Penguin Books Ltd. (1974) p. 239.)

Generally recognised points of view

The relationship between job satisfaction and performance is an issue of continuing debate and controversy. *Luthans* suggests that three generally recognised points of view have emerged:

(i)   that satisfaction leads to performance, a view associated with the early human relations approach;

(ii) that the relationship between satisfaction and performance is moderated by a number of variables, a view which is still reflected in research studies; and

(iii) a more recent view that performance leads to satisfaction.[6]

DIMENSIONS OF JOB SATISFACTION

Job satisfaction is itself a complex concept and difficult to measure objectively. The level of job satisfaction is affected by a wide range of variables relating to individual, social, cultural, organisational and environmental factors.

- *Individual factors* include: personality, education, intelligence and abilities, age, marital status, orientation to work.
- *Social factors* include: relationships with co-workers, group working and norms, opportunities for interaction, informal organisation.
- *Cultural factors* include: attitudes, beliefs and values.
- *Organisational factors* include: nature and size, formal structure, personnel policies and procedures, industrial relations, nature of the work, technology and work organisation, supervision and styles of leadership, management systems, working conditions.
- *Environmental factors* include: economic, social, technical and governmental influences.

These different factors all affect job satisfaction of certain individuals in a given set of circumstances but not necessarily in others. The various studies of job satisfaction all have some validity.

There is some doubt whether job satisfaction consists of a single dimension or a number of separate dimensions. Some workers may be satisfied with certain aspects of their work and dissatisfied with other aspects. There does, however, appear to be a positive correlation between satisfaction in different areas of work. This suggests a single overall factor of job satisfaction. However, it seems that there is no one, general, comprehensive theory which explains job satisfaction.[7]

Alienation at work

One approach to job satisfaction is in terms of frustration and alienation at work. Alienation refers to the detachment of the person from his or her work role. The concept of alienation at work is associated originally with the views of *Marx*.[8] He saw the division of labour in pursuit of profit, and exploitation by employers, as a denial of the workers' need for self-expression. Workers became estranged from the product of their work. Work no longer provided a satisfying experience in itself, but represented a means to satisfying other external demands.

The concept of alienation has been extended by *Blauner*.[9] He describes alienation in terms of four dimensions: powerlessness, meaninglessness, isolation and self-estrangement.

- *Powerlessness* – this denotes the workers' lack of control over management policy, immediate work processes, or conditions of employment.
- *Meaninglessness* – stems from standardisation and division of labour. It denotes the inability to see the purpose of work done, or to identify with the total production process or finished product.
- *Isolation* – is not belonging to an integrated work group or to the social work organisation, and not being guided by group norms of behaviour.
- *Self-estrangement* – the failure to see work as an end in itself or as a central life issue. Workers experience a depersonalised detachment, and work is seen solely as a means to an end.

Blauner examined these dimensions in a comparative analysis of four different technologies: craft, machine minding, assembly line and automated process. He suggested that all modern bureaucratic organisations have inherent alienating tendencies and found most manual workers were alienated to some degree. The extent of alienation experienced is likely to be a function of the nature of technology. Assembly-line technology was found to be most alienating. Machine minding and automated process were in the middle. Craft technology was the least alienating.

There is, of course, no reason to suggest that the experience of alienation at work is limited, necessarily, to manual workers. Marx emphasised that the social organisation of production in pursuit of profit led to alienation for all persons involved irrespective of their position in the organisation. *Weber* linked the growth of bureaucratic organisations, generally, with an increase in alienation at work.[10]

The nature of technology

The nature of technology and work organisation is a major influence on job satisfaction.

In a study in a new American car assembly plant, *Walker* and *Guest* examined the effects of mass production, assembly-line work on employee behaviour.[11] They describe the characteristics of assembly-line work as: repetitious and machine paced; involving a minimum of skill; using predetermined techniques with no choice of tools or methods; and closely defined divisions of the production process. The workers were able to perform their jobs with only 'surface mental attention'.

The nature of the job, the technological layout and the high level of noise restricted the amount of social interaction and contacts that workers could have with each other. The opportunities for interpersonal relationships were important, and when these opportunities were missing the workers felt deprived. The workers' main contact with authority was through the supervisors and this was an important factor in job satisfaction. There was little contact with the managers and as a result relationships with management were of little importance.

Workers in jobs involving a high degree of the characteristics of mass production disliked those aspects of their jobs. They also had a higher rate of absenteeism than workers in jobs with fewer of the characteristics of mass production.

Mass production work and stress

From an analysis of the results of two surveys of employee attitudes conducted by the University of Michigan and the Swedish Institute for Social Research, *Karasek* examined the relationship between mass production work and stress.[12] It was suggested that stress was related to two main job characteristics: (i) workload; and (ii) discretion in how to do the work. The most stressful jobs were those that combined high workload with low discretion.

Both the American and Swedish surveys supported this argument. High-stress jobs in America included: assembly-line workers; garment stitchers; goods and material handling; nurses' aids and orderlies; and telephone operators. Karasek suggests that the use of mental ability, exercising judgement and making decisions is not usually stressful. Stress can be reduced, therefore, if workers are given greater discretion in how their work is performed. As discretion can be increased without changing workloads, mental health could be improved without affecting productivity.

Meaningful work

From an extension of earlier studies at Texas Instruments, *Myers* examined the nature of meaningful work. An example of how the meaningfulness of a job can be determined is through a series of questions: (i) in terms of the supervisor's insight into the scope of meaningful work; and (ii) an analysis of work by the job incumbents themselves.[13] (*See* Fig. 12.2.)

From discussions on the emerging role of the supervisor it was concluded that an effective supervisor is one who 'provides a climate in which people have a sense of working for themselves'. In terms of day-to-day relationships the primary role of the supervisor was 'staying out of the way to let people manage their work'.[14]

Sample Items From Supervisor Worksheet for Analysing Meaningfulness of Work

Planning. Can the individual or group –
- Name customers and state delivery dates for products or services?
- State the product quality and quantity commitments?
- Organise their work layout and influence personnel assignments?
- Set goals and standards based on customer needs and fix priorities?
- State the sources of their materials and problems in obtaining them?
- List direct and overhead costs, selling price and other profit and loss information?

Doing. Does the job –
- Utilise people's talents and require their attention?
- Enable people to see the relationship of their work to other operations?
- Provide access to all the information they need to do their work?

- Have a satisfactory work cycle – neither too long nor too short?
- Give people feedback on how well they are doing?
- Enable them to see how they contribute to the usefulness of the product for the customer?

Controlling. Can the individual or group –
- State customer quality requirements and reasons for these standards?
- Keep their own records of quality and quantity?
- Check quality and quantity of work and revise procedures?
- Evaluate and modify work layout on their own initiative?
- Identify and correct unsafe working conditions?
- Obtain information from people outside the group as a means of evaluating performance?

Sample Items from Job Incumbent Checklist for Describing Meaningfulness of Work

	No	Sometimes	Yes
Planning			
• Does my job allow me to set my own performance goals?	( )	( )	( )
• Is setting my own goals essential to good job performance?	( )	( )	( )
• Do I want more opportunity to set my own performance goals?	( )	( )	( )
Doing			
• Does my job provide variety?	( )	( )	( )
• Is variety in my job essential to good job performance?	( )	( )	( )
• Do I want more variety in my work?	( )	( )	( )
Controlling			
• Does my job allow me to measure my work performance?	( )	( )	( )
• Is opportunity to evaluate my own work essential?	( )	( )	( )
• Do I want more opportunity to measure my own job performance?	( )	( )	( )

Fig. 12.2 Questions to determine the meaningfulness of a job

(From Scott Myers, M., 'Every Employee a Manager' © [1968] by the Regents of the University of California. Reprinted from the *California Management Review*, vol. 10, no. 3, By permission of the Regents.)

Work and psychological well-being

As part of a study of the psychological importance of work undertaken by the Social and Applied Psychology Unit at the University of Sheffield, *Warr* has examined variations among jobs, and aspects and types of work which enhance or impair psychological well-being.[15] Controlled experiments are carried out to change the content of jobs in a direction predicted to increase employee well-being.

One example of the study set out to examine consequences of increasing the control which lower-level production workers have over their work tasks and interrelationships. Jobs were redesigned to shift responsibilities from supervisors to teams of shop-floor workers. The workers were given greater control over the pacing of their work, distribution of tasks among themselves, and general organisation of their time and effort.

These changes increased the scope of workers' decision making, and introduced wider opportunities for skill use, work variety and constructive interpersonal contacts. Information on employee attitudes, well-being and performance was gathered before the changes, and then 6 and 18 months later. Results indicated that employee well-being increased substantially. Overall job satisfaction was significantly greater and psychological distress declined significantly.

The Social and Applied Psychology Unit contains a psychological clinic which receives workers referred by their medical practitioners as suffering from neurotic problems linked to their jobs. From studies of people in the clinic, and in jobs, Warr has derived a perspective on features of paid work which are psychologically 'good' or 'bad'. (*See* Table 12.1.) Many of these features are desirable only up to a point. For example: most people want a reasonable, but not excessive, degree of interpersonal contact; and some psychological threat is inherent in the development of skills and pursuit of challenging goals. Warr points out that one of the tasks of occupational research is to determine the optimum level of these variables.

Table 12.1 Characteristics of psychologically 'good' and 'bad' jobs.

	'Good' jobs have	'Bad' jobs have
1 Money	more	less
2 Variety	more	less
3 Goals, traction	more	less
4 Decision latitude	more	less
5 Skill use/development	more	less
6 Psychological threat	less	more
7 Security	more	less
8 Interpersonal contact	more	less
9 Valued social position	more	less

(From Peter Warr, 'Work, Jobs and Unemployment', *Bulletin of the British Psychological Society*, vol. 36, 1983, p. 309.)

JOB DESIGN

The application of motivational theories, and greater understanding of dimensions of job satisfaction and work performance, have led to increasing interest in job design. The nature of the work organisation and the design of jobs can have a significant effect on the job satisfaction of staff and on the level of organisational performance.

Job design is concerned with the relationship between workers and the nature and content of jobs, and their task functions. It attempts to meet people's personal and social needs at work through the reorganisation or restructuring of work. There are two major reasons for attention to job design;

- to enhance the personal satisfaction that people derive from their work;
- to make the best use of people as a valuable resource of the organisation and to help overcome obstacles to their effective performance.

Individual job redesign

Earlier approaches to job design concentrated on the restructuring of individual jobs and the application of three main methods: (i) job rotation; (ii) job enlargement; and (iii) job enrichment. (*See* Fig. 12.3.)

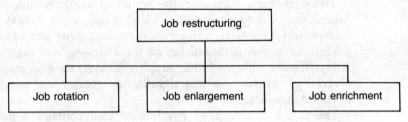

Fig. 12.3 Main methods of individual job redesign

Job rotation

This is the most basic form of individual job design. Job rotation involves moving a person from one job or task to another. It attempts to add some variety and to help remove boredom, at least in the short term. However, if the tasks involved are all very similar and routine, then once the person is familiar with the new task the work may quickly prove boring again.

Job rotation may lead to the acquisition of additional skills but does not necessarily develop the level of skills. Strictly, job rotation is not really job design because neither the nature of the task nor the method of working is restructured. However, job rotation may help the person identify more with the completed product or service. It can also be used as a form of training.

Job enlargement

This involves increasing the scope of the job and the range of tasks that the person carries out. It is usually achieved by combining a number of related operations at the same level. *Job enlargement is horizontal job design*, it makes a job structurally bigger. It lengthens the time-cycle of operations and may give the person greater variety.

Job enlargement, however, is not always very popular and may often be resisted by workers. Although it may give the person more to do, it does little to improve intrinsic satisfaction or a sense of achievement. Workers may see job enlargement as simply increasing the number of routine, boring tasks they have to perform. Some workers seem to prefer simple, routine tasks which they can undertake almost automatically, and with little thought or concentration. This enables them to day-dream and to socialise with colleagues without affecting their performance.

Job enrichment

This is an extension of the more basic job rotation and job enlargement methods of job design. Job enrichment arose out of *Herzberg*'s two-factor theory. It attempts to enrich the job by incorporating motivating or growth factors such as increased responsibility and involvement, opportunities for advancement and the sense of achievement.

Job enrichment involves vertical job enlargement. It aims to give the person greater autonomy and authority over the planning, execution and control of their own work. It focuses attention on intrinsic satisfaction. Job enrichment increases the complexity of the work and should provide the person with a more meaningful and challenging job.

Methods of achieving job enrichment include the following:

* permitting workers to build a complete product, or a complete component of a larger product, undertake a full task cycle, or provide a complete service;
* giving workers the opportunity to have direct contact with the users of the product or service provided;
* allowing workers greater freedom over the scheduling and pacing of their own work; and
* providing workers with direct feedback on their performance, and increased responsibility for checking and control of their own work.[16]

An example of giving people freedom over the scheduling of their work is flexible working hours, or flexitime. Within certain stated limits ('core' times) people are free to vary arrival and departure times at work to suit their own individual needs and wishes.

BROADER APPROACHES TO IMPROVED JOB DESIGN

Approaches to improved job design now take on a broader perspective. For example, in the context of technological change the focus of attention has spread from manipulating the tasks of individual jobs to the wider organisational context. Attention needs to be given to improving the effectiveness of the organisation in achieving its goals and objectives; and helping the development of skills and resources to manage successfully changes in the way the organisation functions.

Desirable task and job characteristics

The Work Research Unit has summarised evidence about desirable task characteristics and job characteristics as follows.

Tasks should:

* combine to form a coherent whole job, either independently or with related jobs, whose performance makes a significant contribution which is visible to the job-holder;
* provide some variety of pace, method, location and skill;
* provide feedback on performance both directly and through other people;
* provide some degree of discretion and control in the timing, sequence and pace of work effort;
* include some degree of responsibility for outcomes.

Some needs are, in the short run, easily satisfied. In fact, it is feasible to have *too much* variety, which is experienced as unpredictability or incompatibility.

Jobs should:

- provide opportunity for learning and problem solving within the individual's competence;
- be seen as leading towards some sort of desirable future;
- provide opportunity for development in ways that are relevant to the individual;
- enable people to contribute to decisions affecting their jobs and their objectives;
- ensure that the goals and other people's expectations are clear and provide a degree of challenge;
- provide adequate resources (training, information, equipment, materials);
- provide adequate support from the contact with others.

Again, it is possible, temporarily at any rate, to be faced with too much challenge, too many new problems to solve, which are experienced as stress resulting from overload or conflicting objectives.

As an essential background and context to the design of tasks and jobs:

- industrial relations policies and procedures should be agreed and understood and issues handled in accordance with these arrangements;
- payment systems should be seen as fair and reflect the full contribution of individuals and groups;
- other personnel policies and practices should be fair and adequate; and
- physical surroundings, health and safety provisions should be satisfactory.[17]

These are general statements which need to be translated in practice, taking account of how people perceive their present tasks and what they regard as improvements, and involving them in changes which affect them and their jobs.

Autonomous work groups (socio-technical approach)

An important development in job design is a form of work organisation based on autonomous work groups and team working. This involves a socio-technical approach with technological processes, production methods and the way work is carried out integrated with the social system of the organisation, including the informal group structure.

The group assume greater responsibility for effective performance of the work. Specific goals are set for the group, but members decide the means by which these goals are to be achieved. Group members have greater freedom and choice, and wider discretion over the planning, execution and control of their own work. The level of external supervision is reduced and the role of the supervisor becomes more that of giving advice and support to the group.

The Volvo project

A famous example of a socio-technical, team-working approach is the Kalmar car plant opened in Sweden in 1974. Workers are arranged in self-contained teams of 15–20 members with their own workshop area, changing room and rest area. Instead of the traditional assembly-line system, the work remains stationary and materials are brought to the work stations. A special carrier transports a car and positions it for assembly work. Should problems arise, a car can be withdrawn from the production flow for extra attention.

The aim is to increase the work content of individual workers through greater use of team working. The teams of workers are responsible for the assembly and checking of a complete sub-system – for example electrical system, steering and control, heating system, instrumentation, interior – at one station. Work cycles can last up to 40 minutes. The group conduct their own inspection which is monitored by a television screen at their work station. The members of each group are free to manage themselves, elect their own leader, and organise and distribute work among themselves. Provided sufficient units are in the central stockpile the team also have some control over the pacing of their work.[18]

In addition to the improved working environment of the plant and the lower noise levels, the quality of working life was reportedly improved. Turnover, absenteeism and sickness were reduced. Also, ten years after the start of the project, the vice-president of organisation development at Volvo stated that the Kalmar plant had achieved 20 per cent higher productivity than the goal set for the project.[19] Volvo have now extended the concepts of Kalmar to most other plants.

Goal setting

Goal setting, which was discussed in the previous chapter, is sometimes viewed as another approach to job design. Goal setting involves building goals, feedback and incentives into the structure of the job.[20]

Associated factors in job design

The different methods of job design are not necessarily separate approaches. They are interrelated and there is some overlapping among them. In addition, there are many other associated (contextual) factors which affect job design; for example, organisation structure; the system of management and style of leadership; trade unions; personnel policies and procedures; the nature of technology; group norms; and the working environment. (*See* Fig. 12.4.)

Job design: a continuous movement

Whatever form job design takes, it should be augmented by:

- developmental design; and
- organisational supports.[21]

Job design should be a continuous and progressive movement in order to satisfy people's needs for growth and learning. It should be seen as a cumulative process which does not end until individuals have reached, but not exceeded, their growth capacity.

Organisational supports are also necessary to maintain and aid the development of job design. This involves management commitment and support for the idea of job design. It also involves structural support such as the availability of accurate information for decision making. Attention must be given to 'hygiene' factors, such as pay and working conditions, and to the removal of the causes of dissatisfaction in order to provide the right environment for job design.

A COMPREHENSIVE MODEL OF JOB ENRICHMENT

Attempts to improve intrinsic motivation must not only include considerations of job characteristics but also take account of individual differences

345

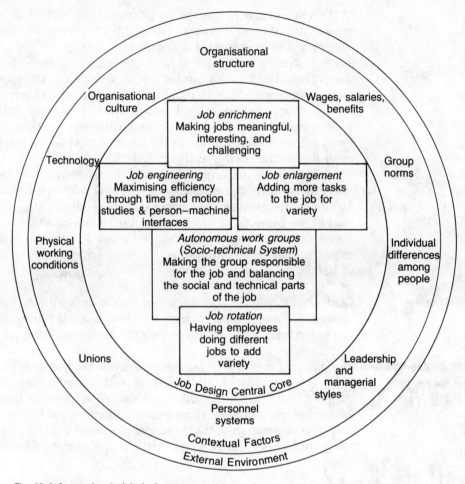

Fig. 12.4 Approaches to job design
(Reprinted by permission from *Organizational Behavior Fourth edition*, by Hellriegel, D., Slocum, J. W. and Woddman, R. W., p. 363. Copyright © 1986 by West Publishing Company. All rights reserved.)

and attributes, and people's orientation to work. A popular and comprehensive model of job enrichment has been developed by *Hackman* and *Oldham* (Fig. 12.5).[22] The model views job enrichment in terms of increasing five core job dimensions; skill variety, task identity, task significance, autonomy and feedback. These core job characteristics create three psychological states:

- experienced meaningfulness of the work;
- experienced responsibility for the outcomes of the work; and
- knowledge of the actual results of the work activities.

Five core dimensions

The five core job dimensions can be summarised as follows:

- *Skill variety* – the extent to which a job entails different activities and involves a range of different skills and talents.
- *Task identity* – the extent to which a job involves completion of a whole piece of work with a visible outcome.
- *Task significance* – the extent to which a job has a meaningful impact on

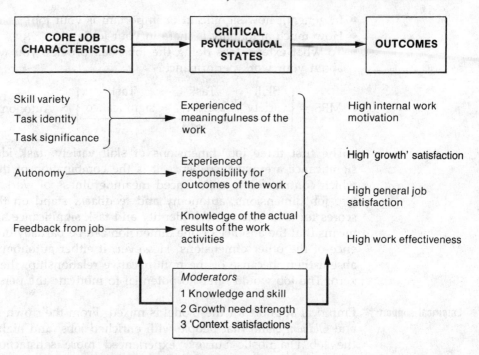

Fig. 12.5 A job characteristics model of work motivation
(Reprinted with permission from Hackman, J. R. and Oldham, G. R., *Work Redesign*, © (1980) Addison-Wesley, Reading, Massachusetts, p. 90, fig. 4.6.)

other people, either inside or outside the organisation.

- *Autonomy* – the extent to which a job provides freedom, independence and discretion in planning the work and determining how to undertake it.
- *Feedback* – the extent to which work activities result in direct and clear information on the effectiveness of job performance.

An example of a job with little enrichment could be that of a mass production assembly-line worker, or a copy typist, where all five core characteristics are likely to score low. An example of an enriched job could be that of a parish priest who draws upon a wide range of social skills and talents, who can usually identify with the whole task, and whose job has clear and important meaning and significance. There is a very high level of autonomy, and likely to be direct and clear feedback.

Motivating potential score

From these five core job dimensions *Hackman* and *Oldham* have developed an equation which gives a single index of a person's job profile. By answering a questionnaire – the Job Diagnostic Survey (JDS) – and by giving a score (between 1 and 7) to each job dimension, the person can calculate an overall measure of job enrichment, called the motivating potential score (MPS).

Examples of questions from the JDS are:

- How much variety is there in your job?
- To what extent does your job involve doing a whole and identifiable piece of work?

- In general, how significant or important is your job?
- How much autonomy is there in your job?
- To what extent does doing the job itself provide you with information about your work performance?

$$MPS = \left\{ \frac{\text{Skill variety} + \text{Task identity} + \text{Task significance}}{3} \right\} \times \text{Autonomy} \times \text{Feedback}$$

The first three job dimensions of skill variety, task identity and task significance are averaged, since it is the combination of these dimensions which contributes to experienced meaningfulness of work. The remaining two job dimensions, autonomy and feedback, stand on their own. Since scores for skill variety, task identity and task significance are additive, this means that the absence of one dimension can be partially offset by the presence of the other dimensions. However, if either autonomy or feedback is absent then, because of the multiplicative relationship, the MPS would be zero. The job would offer no potential to motivate the person.

Empirical support

Empirical support for the model is mixed. From their own studies *Hackman* and *Oldham* claim that people with enriched jobs, and high score levels on the Job Diagnostic Survey, experienced more satisfaction and internal motivation. The core job dimensions of skill variety, task identity and task significance combined to predict the level of experienced meaningfulness of the work.

The core dimensions of autonomy and feedback did not relate so clearly to experienced responsibility and knowledge of results. Some of the other dimensions were as good, or better, in predicting these psychological conditions. In general, however, the results of their studies showed that jobs which scored high on the core dimensions were associated with high levels of personal and work outcomes.

Although the core job dimensions do appear to influence personal and work outcomes, there is some doubt as to the validity of the causal relationships – that is the extent to which the job characteristics influence critical psychological states, and the psychological states then influence outcomes.[23] There is also some doubt as to the extent to which high correlations might be expected on the basis of people's desire for consistency in their approach, rather than as a result of any other links among the measures involved.[24]

JOB ENRICHMENT AND JOB SATISFACTION

In general, there appears little doubt that restructuring the nature of work itself, and providing job enrichment by making it more interesting and challenging, does increase job satisfaction.[25]

From a review of developments in the field, and case study evidence, *Taylor* concludes that theories of job enrichment and employee motivation do work.[26] The factors which affect motivation to work are shown in Fig. 12.6.

The inner circle relates to job content and the motivators. The outer circle relates to the job context, the environment in which the job is carried out.

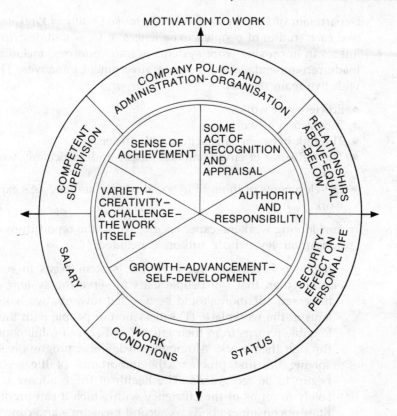

Fig. 12.6 What motivates individuals to work
(Reproduced with permission from Taylor, L. K., *Not for Bread Alone: An Appreciation of Job Enrichment*, 3rd edition, Business Books (1980) p. 31.)

From the case studies, Taylor found that the situations people find most satisfying and rewarding are invariably those which provide the opportunities to satisfy job content (shown in the inner circle). If any of the job context factors (shown in the outer circle) are allowed to deteriorate in any way, a climate of dissatisfaction and tension, frustration and friction will prevail and people will not perform at their best.

Job satisfaction and personnel management

Theories of work motivation and job satisfaction have influenced management systems and styles of leadership, and developments in personnel policies and procedures. The personnel management function is centred on people's needs while working in an organisation, and ways in which their work promotes or frustrates the fulfilment of these needs.[27] The practice of modern personnel management is directed towards providing conditions under which people work willingly and effectively, and contribute to the success of the organisation. This involves concern for employee motivation and job satisfaction.

THE QUALITY OF WORKING LIFE[28]

Increased interest in job design has been associated with the development of a broader social concern for the quality of working life (QWL). In 1973 a

Department of Employment report, *On the Quality of Working Life*, summarised case studies of people's experiences of work and descriptions of experiments in improving work systems in four countries, including the UK.[29] It made recommendations for future government initiatives. The report dealt with five main themes:

- Efficiency at work;
- Satisfaction at work;
- The link between satisfaction and efficiency;
- The influence of environmental factors and particularly work technology; and
- Developments of thought in social science and people's expectations from work.

In considering workers' experience of work, the report drew attention to an American survey, whose authors concluded:

> If one believes that our economic system exists to serve the people rather than that the people exist to serve the system, it follows that increased attention should be directed towards two basic human problems in the workplace: (1) satisfaction of people with the economic and tangible returns from their efforts: and (2) self-fulfillment of individuals through their work. Although considerable progress has been made in solving the first problem, the importance of the second has barely begun to be recognized. The health of the economy is still measured solely in terms of the efficiency with which it can produce large quantities of consumer goods. A second measure – and concern – is needed: one which considers the contribution work is making to the quality of life and to the growth and happiness of the worker.[30]

Two of the main recommendations of the report were accepted and implemented, together with a 'vitally important measure'.

- A co-ordinated programme of projects in a range of industrial and commercial settings, in which experience of job redesign could be monitored and used as a demonstration of what might be achieved.
- A small unit within the Department of Employment to manage the programme of research, to collate and make widely available information about successful experiences, and also (although this was not an explicit recommendation) to provide information and advice for organisations. The unit was called the Work Research Unit (WRU).
- The 'vitally important measure' was the setting up of a mechanism for involving representatives of trade unions, employers and government in planning and monitoring these activities. This was the Tripartite Steering Group on Job Satisfaction. Its role was to advise the secretary of state for employment on ways of stimulating interest in the quality of working life, and on ways of encouraging management and trade unions to take action to increase the job satisfaction of employees. It was chaired by a minister of state and its ten members were representatives of the Confederation of British Industry (CBI), the Trade Union Congress (TUC) and government, with a secretariat provided by the WRU.

THE WORK RESEARCH UNIT

The WRU was transferred in 1985 to the independent Advisory, Conciliation and Arbitration Service (ACAS), where it forms part of the Advisory Services. The role of the Tripartite Steering Group has been taken on by the ACAS Council whose members also represent the CBI and the TUC; in addition there are three independent members.

The unit's principal objective is to encourage industry and commerce to adopt measures that will improve the quality of working life and thereby increase organisational effectiveness. Four interrelated activities contribute to this task:

- creating awareness about QWL through mounting and participating in conferences and courses;
- providing information in response to inquiries and publishing papers, including a bimonthly bulletin, *News and Abstracts*, which contains special bibliographies and occasional papers;
- monitoring QWL activities and research; and
- providing advice and assistance for management and unions in organisations. The aim here is to help people move to ways of working that are more satisfying for them and more effective for their organisations, and to help more individuals to become skilled and experienced in the joint management of change. (*See* Fig. 12.7.)

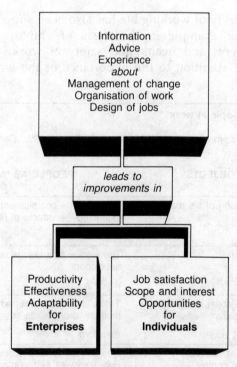

Fig. 12.7 The approach of the work research unit

(Taken from the Department of Employment/Work Research Unit leaflet. Crown copyright. Reproduced with permission of the Department of Employment and the Controller of Her Majesty's Stationery Office.)

Design of jobs and management style

The potential benefits of improved job design are unlikely to be realised if attention is focused on the content of jobs alone. Equal, if not more important, is the *process* by which re-design is carried out. This has led to recognition of the importance of management style and, increasingly, of organisation culture. Central to improving the quality of working life is a participative, open style of management involving employees in decisions that affect them, including the design or choice of the technology itself. Personnel policies, including, for example, those relating to pay and benefits, should facilitate and help new concepts of improved job design.

The management of change

The focus of the WRU is on the management of change. At the same time, the increasing pace of technological and structural change has made it imperative to address the issues of managing change in ways that would ensure the best outcomes for organisations and for the people in them. An important issue is still the jobs which people are asked to do. When change is being planned, particularly if new technology is to be introduced, a 'window of opportunity' exists to think about the work that people will do and the design of their jobs. The aim is to ensure that the quality of working life is enhanced rather than undermined.[31]

Views about people at work

Improving job design needs to take account of how people perceive their present tasks, and involving them in changes which affect them and their jobs. It involves the ways of thinking about people at work set out in Fig. 12.8.

Concern of the quality of working life has also been supported by government legislation, for example in the areas of employment protection, employee involvement, and health and safety at work. Such legislation directs management attention to the importance of the work environment

---

Alternative views of people at work

Derived and developed from presentations made at 'QWL in the 80s' Conference, Toronto, 30 August 1981

PEOPLE AS 'OBJECTS'	PEOPLE AS 'AGENTS'
Workers	
The worker is an extension of his machine	The machine complements the worker by extending the effects of his or her skills
and	and
A dispensable spare part	The worker is a unique resource to be developed
which implies	which suggests
Work should be broken down into single tasks requiring narrow skills	Tasks should be grouped and require multiple, broad skills
therefore	therefore
Design jobs to the lowest common denominator to enhance control	Design jobs to take account of people's needs as well as technical requirements
Because	with

Workers require and like laid down rules and external controls, for example supervisors, specialist staffs and procedures *and so*	A degree of self-determination individually or in groups which will be more creative, flexible and effective *taking into account that whilst*
Rewards suitable for workers are wages, benefits and security *as*	Economic rewards remain the major concern, there are other factors; the individuals' and the community's needs require to be met *because*
Workers cannot and do not want to think about their work, they like repetitive tasks and they do not want responsibility *because*	People have a wide range of talents which if work structures are right they can and will use *and*
Workers work, managers think	The ideas of everyone there can be applied to improve the enterprise

Managers

Management's sources of power are its prerogative and status *which requires*	A manager's authority is earned through competence *entailing*
Autocratic management with many layers of authority *because*	Flat organisation charts and a participative style *so that*
The organisation's objectives are paramount *and*	Members' and the community's goals count *and*
Financial management is more important than human resource management, because without profits there is no enterprise	Both financial performance *and* human asset management can be measured and both contribute to the survival of the enterprise

Unions

A union's job is to improve the terms and conditions of employment of its members *thus*	The union's job is not only to improve the terms and conditions of workers in real terms, but to enhance the quality of working life in every respect *and*
The 'adversarial' stance is the only suitable one for a union	It is appropriate for unions to encourage and take part in participation at many levels on many subjects as well as to bargain
attitudes and behaviour which lead to:	
Organization competitiveness and gamesmanship *with*	Co-operative collaboration *towards*
Alienation and combat	Commitment and effectiveness

An important task for the Work Research Unit is and will continue to be to make the ideas associated here with 'people as agents' operational.

Fig. 12.8 Extract from the *1981 Report of the Tripartite Steering Group on Job Satisfaction to the Secretary of State for Employment (1982)*
(Reproduced with the permission of The Department of Employment and the Controller of Her Majesty's Stationery Office.)

and the context in which work is carried out, which in turn can have a direct effect on job satisfaction.

An example of a WRU assignment in new technology, QWL and organisation culture is given in the appendix.

QUALITY CIRCLES

One particular feature increasingly associated as a part of the quality of working life movement is the concept of quality circles. A quality circle is a group of people within an organisation who meet together on a regular basis to identify, analyse and solve problems relating to quality, productivity or other aspects of day-to-day working arrangements using problem-solving techniques. Quality circles are broadly compatible with the quality of working life in that they provide an opportunity for people at work to become more involved in matters which have a bearing on the jobs that they do.[32]

Although quality circles actually originated in America they were exported to Japan and are more usually associated with their wide applications (since 1962) in Japanese manufacturing industries, as well as in some white-collar operations. Since the refinement of the quality circle process in Japan there has been increasing interest in their use in America and Britain as well as in many other countries. In America, quality circles appear to have been first implemented in 1974.[33]

Essential features of a quality circle group

The essential features of a quality circle group include the following.

- Membership is voluntary;
- The group usually number between five and ten members;
- Membership is normally drawn from people undertaking similar work or from the same work station;
- The group select the problems to be tackled;
- Leadership can be decided from within the group but is usually the immediate supervisor;
- The group members receive training in communication and problem-solving skills, quality control techniques and group processes;
- The group recommend solutions to management and where possible have authority to implement agreed solutions.

The introduction of quality circles

The development of effective quality circle groups requires consideration of a number of important criteria.

- Commitment and support of top management;
- Full consultation with staff;
- A participative approach by management, and appropriate systems and style of managerial behaviour;
- Delegation of decision making;
- Trust and goodwill on all sides;
- An effective support structure of consultation and negotiation;
- Support of trade unions;
- An effective training programme including development of quantitative skills;

● Continuous monitoring and review of results.

In assessing the potential for introducing quality circles into an organisation, *Collard* suggests four broad areas for consideration: (i) the existing management style of the organisation; (ii) the industrial relations climate; (iii) the current state of the organisation; and (iv) the scope for reducing non-productive time. These should be considered first at the organisational level, and second at the individual department level. It is then necessary to have an action plan, and a pilot study which allows the evaluation of quality circles.[34]

There are a number of potential limitations on the effectiveness of quality circles.

● Any attempt at solving organisational problems cannot be considered as a single dimension. The promotion of quality circles needs to be approached in terms of possible effects on related sub-systems of the organisation, for example personnel management and industrial relations procedures.
● Quality circles can rely too heavily on intrinsic motivation and the assumption that involvement and recognition are sufficient rewards in themselves. This reflects a major difference between the operation of quality circles in the West and in Japan. Workers in Japan appear to accept that financial gains will go to the organisation.[35]
● The greater involvement of members in problem solving and decision making may be resented by some groups, for example quality control departments, or by managers or trade union officials who may be suspicious of possible challenges to their traditional authority.

Applications of quality circles

The application of quality circles does appear simple and straightforward, but early experience must be viewed in the context of Japanese culture and management systems. However, quality circles offer a number of potential benefits. They provide problem solving at a more local level and the participation of employees in work-related decisions which concern them. They help supervisors keep control of the shop/office floor and encourage the use of supervisors as communicators.[36] Quality circles do work and are used successfully by a number of British organisations including Rolls-Royce (the UK pioneer in 1978), IBM, Duracell, British Telecom and Wedgwood.

The Work Research Unit, whilst cautious in its response to quality circles, is supportive of the principle and a broader participative approach. In appropriate applications, quality circles can be part of a broad, long-term strategy for organisational change aimed both at improved economic performance and the quality of working life.[37]

Quality circles at Wedgwood

One of the leading exponents of quality circles in Britain is the Wedgwood pottery group. They have more than 100 circles of up to ten workers each.[38] The following extract outlines the company's approach.

About two years ago we were in the state that I think many companies are today, we had heard something about Quality Circles, we were wondering whether it would help us if we introduced them at Wedgwood, but we had not decided one way or the other. So what I want to do is to describe why and how we did so, and the enjoyment and the benefits all the participants have since derived from them.

Why did we eventually decide to go ahead? And the reason, the real reason, was for the survival of our company. About three years ago the company had about 8,000 employees; now that has now gone down to under 5,000. They are divided among 12 factories, all within a five mile radius. Now those may not sound very large numbers compared with some firms, but we felt that with what for us seemed a quite large factory, management, the senior management, was losing touch with shop floor operatives and also with middle management and supervision. And the person who started us on the road to Quality Circles was the man at the very top – the Chairman of the company.

Total commitment

I believe the fact that Quality Circles have been successful at Wedgwood – and they have been remarkably successful – is basically for one reason and one reason only: that there has been absolute and total commitment from the very beginning, from the top and right down to the bottom. And that, I believe, is absolutely essential for any company that is considering Quality Circles – total commitment. If you start off at half-cock, your Circles will go off at half-cock, and one failing Circle can do more damage than 20 good ones can achieve.

Involving the people who do the jobs

Why did the Board decide to go ahead? As I have already mentioned, there was the feeling that senior management was losing touch with the shop floor. In much of British industry we are stuck with a 'we and they' attitude that somehow has to be stopped – and Quality Circles is one way of getting round it, because for the first time ever, Quality Circles enable the people who are doing a regular job in the factory – in our case, such as making plates or decorating cups – to play a very important part in the running of the factory, and to know that they are doing so. It is, after all, the people who have spent much of their lives sticking handles on cups, who know more about that job, and its problems and possibilities for improvement, than anyone else, often even than their managers. Managers, certainly in our industry, are basically administrators, and we tend to change them around from one job to another, so that often they have no real down to earth knowledge of the jobs their people are actually doing – and they are often very tricky jobs requiring a great deal of skill and practice. So through Quality Circles, we believed that we might find out from the people who are actually doing the job, what are the problems associated with it, and how they can be solved – and this has proved to be the case: we are now getting answers to many of the problems that we had never been able to solve before.

Voluntary participation

We wanted eight to ten members of each Circle and they were to be entirely voluntary. So the Circle leaders went around the members of their work-group saying something like: 'Look, Mary, I think you are the sort of person who might enjoy this'. And the response might be: 'Well, I'll come if Bill and his wife will come too', and so on. But it was made absolutely clear to everyone that it was entirely voluntary; if they came and didn't like it, they could leave at any time; or they could even leave half way through a project and come back three months later.

So we got the nucleus of the first six Circles, and we started to train them as to what it was all about, with me sitting in the whole time. And then the second six Circles on the same basis. All the time we emphasised not only that it was voluntary, but that it was a thing to enjoy. It shouldn't be looked upon as hard work. It in enjoyment. And it is of interest that, of all Circles we started with, the original members are all still with us – so they are still enjoying it.

Extending the programme

Then we did a repeat of the whole thing, choosing another 12 leaders, training them and getting two more successive groups of six Circles started. Now we are up to 104 Circles altogether, which is a large number for this country, but not large compared with America where the Circle movement originally started, and miniscule compared with some companies in Japan.

Circle presentations to senior management

Once the Circles have chosen their own problems that they want to tackle, and have analysed the causes, they come up with a solution and make their presentation to senior management – and this is a very important part of the programme. The presentation may be made to the Company Chairman if the Circle thinks it is important enough; a lot of them are made to other Board members or General Managers. So far there have been 297 such individual presentations. The average time between presentations – ie the time it takes a Circle to identify, analyse and solve a problem – is five weeks. Some have been as short as three weeks – but in one case as long as nine months. That was a problem that involved a lot of hard work and a great deal of data gathering.

Problems solved by Circles at Wedgwood

Now to convert that picture of a Quality Circle into our factories at Wedgwood, to show the kinds of problems that have been solved, but without going into technical details that probably only other pottery people could follow.

One problem that has been common to the whole pottery industry throughout its history, is that when you make top quality bone china plates, you can only make 40 plates from each mould, and you have always had to throw the first three away because they were no good. And nobody had ever come up with a solution. But the mould makers' Quality Circle in one of our factories decided to tackle this problem, and they came up with something that was absolutely novel, that no-one had ever even thought of before – and now we don't throw those first three plates away any more.

Nor do any of the other factories in our Wedgwood group – and of course it didn't take long before it got to our competitors as well, but I am quite pleased about that, because it all helps the industry as a whole – and we are a very close-knit community. But this is just one of the things that would never have happened except for the people who have actually been making the moulds all their lives, getting together and putting their minds to the problem.

Eliminating spoilt plates

Another problem which was tackled by one of our earliest Circles was the identification marks on the back of plates. It is perhaps a rather strange thing that every hand-painted plate has an identification mark on its back to show who painted it. Now these marks, which were chosen by each individual for herself, vary greatly in complexity and therefore in the time it took to make them, but they also had a nasty habit of sometimes partly flaking off or falling off during firing, and therefore ruining the plate below. The Circle came up with these solutions – a simple dot rather than a complicated mark, with the positioning of the dot in relation to the backstamp as the individual identifying device.

The same Circle then tackled another problem – the elimination of colour specks and 'crawl' that ruined so many plates, the cause of which had been absolutely unknown previously. And with some of the larger plates that sell at £100 or so each, the saving here was quite extraordinary.

Another Circle designed a new trolley for moving the unfired pottery to the kiln, that greatly reduced the risk of pieces of pottery knocking together and being broken.

Working with manufacturers to improve quality of material

Another designed a quite different and much more effectively shaped brush for painting plates. This they did in co-operation with the brush manufacturer, by going to visit his factory in London and explaining their problems with the traditional type of brush. This was a wonderful experience both for the manufacturer and for our Circle members – the people who actually used the product discussing with the people who made it, what their real problems and needs were. And as a result of this experience, most of our suppliers now have to work with the Circles that use their materials – and there is no better judge of the quality of materials coming into a factory than the people who are actually got to use them!

One Circle has even tackled the question of the factory bus service, and the loading and unloading points – and in conjunction with the bus company, significantly improved the service and facilities for the very many of our employees who depend on it to get to and from work.

What are the pitfalls?

With over 100 Circles now operating I could give innumerable examples of Quality Circle achievements. But perhaps I should mention also what the pitfalls are, because it is also important to know what these may be, in order to steer clear of them. In fact, we have not had any really serious problems. We have had some people who drop out of a Circle because someone else is in it, or perhaps because they have not agreed with the solution the Circle put forward. Often it only needs the facilitator to keep his ear to the ground and know what is going on, to smooth out that sort of difficulty before it gets serious.

Management inadequacies revealed

I think the only genuine trouble we have had is with some of our junior managers who have tended to feel pilloried when they have taken on the role of Circle leader. This we have found particularly with some of the older people who are perhaps not quite as good as they like to think they are; and in many cases they have been superseded by up and coming operatives who have shown remarkable signs of being just the right people to run the Circle. This has undoubtedly caused a certain amount of aggro.

But the really good people among our junior managers and supervisors have derived great benefit from the Circles, and the improvement in personal relations, and the fact that people now feel very much a part of the factory, is what is so very encouraging.

Improvements from Circles at Wedgwood

Wedgwood is not just a factory full of people painting flowers on the sides of cups. It is a very tightly controlled factory – that is why it is so successful. Even in the days when we were having so many cutbacks, our turnover and profit figures have been maintained.

The introduction of Quality Circles has been accepted as one of the main reasons why our quality and our productivity have improved. In addition our industrial relations have improved out of all measure – because people now once again, even though we have grown so big, feel they are back in a smaller unit where they can speak directly to people they couldn't speak to before. Quality Circles have certainly done something for all our Circle members at Wedgwood, that otherwise I believe could never have happened.

Extracted with permission of the Industrial Participation Association from: Dick Fletcher 'Quality Circles at Wedgwood', *Industrial Participation*, no. 578, Summer 1982, pp. 2–9

Failure of quality circles

Quality circles do not always succeed, however, and there is frequent opposition from top management and first line management, but most particularly from middle management. Because the basic concept of quality circles is so deceptively simple, not enough thought is always given to their formation. Many quality circles have malfunctioned because of insufficient preparation and management support, or because of union opposition of a range of other difficulties.[39] (*See* Fig. 12.9.)

JOB SATISFACTION AND PRODUCTIVITY

Despite many theories and studies of the relationship between satisfaction and performance there are still doubts as to how to manage an organisation so that staff have both high job satisfaction and productivity. *Staw* suggests

Top Management	Middle Management	First-line Management
Difficulties in distinguishing circles from techniques such as task-forces, committee structure, management–employee 'rap' sessions, departmental meetings	Fear that circles will show up their own shortcomings as work organisers	Workers taken off the job to solve problems are not really working – time-wasting potential
Superficial and a gimmick	Fear of some loss of control	Existing workload
Threat to the established pattern of organisation hierarchy and to management prerogative	Scepticism about the concept being a 'vogue' management technique	Part of some management ploy
Introduction of circles would be an admission of bad management	Encroach on areas of traditional authority and responsibility	They do not know how circles operate
The company is sufficiently well organised to cope promptly with situations at management and shop-floor levels	Threat to their respective patterns of power	Quality circles would be used by employees for knocking other people and getting their own back
It is not the right time	They were expected to solve problems the circles had 'dumped' on them	Fear of being exposed as a poor leader
Changes required in management style	Circles cause us extra problems because they do not know the ripple effect their actions cause in other parts of the organisation	Merely an extension of the company's existing suggestion scheme
Introduction of circles might disturb the present good relations with the unions	Threat to legitimacy and authority	Conflict with suggestion scheme
Alien culture argument	Fear the increased knowledge of circle members through circle training – unfamiliar with the circle analysis techniques	Fear the increased knowledge of circle members through circle training
Anticipated resistance from middle management	We don't need circles attitude	Fear of redundancies
Because it is a personnel department initiative	Unnecessary powers being given to the circles	
Fear of interference from the union	Increased data available to members and potentially through them to the rest of the workforce	
	Circles do not follow prescribed organisational channels	
	The facilitator goes around me	

Fig. 12.9 Reasons for management resistance to quality circles
(Reproduced with permission of MCB University Press from Dale, Barrie and Barlow, Eric, 'Quality Circles: The View From Within', *Management Decision*, vol. 25, no. 4, (1987) p. 7.)

that it is difficult to bring about changes in both satisfaction and performance and that it is necessary to lower expectations in the pursuit of the 'happy/productive worker'.[40]

Instead of the alternating practice of fanfare and despair, Staw puts forward three approaches that may make for sustained slow progress in overcoming forces for stability in both job attitudes and performance.

- *The individually oriented system.* This is based on traditional good management and would emphasise, for example: extrinsic rewards linked to performance; realistic and challenging goals; accurate employee performance; equitable promotions policy; training and skills development; job enlargement and job enrichment.

The major principle underlying such features is to structure work and/or reward systems so that high performance is either intrinsically or extrinsically rewarding to the individual, and to create a situation in which high performance contributes to job satisfaction. However, to be effective the individually oriented system needs to be implemented correctly, and into a well-run organisation with an efficient structure and motivational system.

• *The group-oriented system*. This is where satisfaction and performance are derived from group participation. This would include methods such as: work organised around intact groups; resources distributed on a group basis; greater group autonomy for selection, training and reward systems; the use of the group to enforce norms of behaviour; and encouraging inter-group rivalry to build within-group solidarity.

Group-oriented systems may be difficult to control but they can be very powerful. Because individuals will work to achieve group praise and loyalty, an effectively managed group-oriented system can make a potential contribution to high job satisfaction and performance.

• *The organisationally oriented system*. This is where working conditions are organised so that individuals gain satisfaction from contribution to the welfare of the organisation as a whole, for example, through applying the principles of Theory Z organisation. If individuals can identify closely with the organisation as a whole, then organisational performance will be intrinsically rewarding to the individual.

This system would include common features such as: effective socialisation into the organisation; job rotation in different units; long training periods with the development of skills specific to the organisation; long-term or protected employment; decentralised operations; few status distinctions; education and sharing of information about the organisation; linking individual rewards to organisational performance through profit sharing, bonuses and share options.

| Synopsis | Motivation to work well is usually related to job satisfaction, but the nature of this relationship is not clear. Although the level of job satisfaction may well affect the strength of motivation this is not always the case. Job satisfaction is more of an internal state and could, for example, be associated with a feeling of personal achievement. The relationship between job satisfaction and work performance is an issue of continuing debate and controversy.

Job satisfaction is a complex concept and difficult to measure objectively. The level of job satisfaction is affected by a wide range of individual, social, organisational and cultural variables. Dimensions of job satisfaction include consideration of: alienation at work; the nature of technology; mass production work and stress; meaningful work and psychological well-being. The application of motivational theories and a greater understanding of dimensions of job satisfaction has led to increasing interest in improving job design.

Earlier approaches to job design concentrated on the restructuring of individual jobs and application of job rotation, job enlargement and job enrichment. Approaches to improving job design now take a broader perspective, and in the context of technological change, for example, focus attention on the wider organisational issues. Whatever form job design takes it should be a continuous and progressive movement and augmented by (i) developmental design and (ii) organisational supports. One popular and comprehensive model of job enrichment has been developed by Hackman and Oldham. The model views job enrichment in terms of five core job dimensions: skill variety, task identity, task significance, autonomy and feedback.

Increased interest in job design has been associated with the development of a broader social concern for the quality of working life, including consideration of workers' experience of work. The Work Research Unit encourages industry and commerce to adopt measures that will improve the quality of working life and thereby increase organisational effectiveness. The WRU provides advice and assistance for management and unions in organisations. The aim is to help people move to ways of working that are more satisfying for them and more effective for their organisations, and to help more individuals to become skilled and experienced in the joint management of change.

One particular feature increasingly associated as a part of the quality of working life movement is the concept of quality circles. These are groups within an organisation who meet together to identify, analyse and solve problems relating to quality, productivity or other aspects of day-to-day working arrangements using problem-solving techniques. There are a number of important considerations relating to the effective introduction of quality circles, but they do appear to work. In appropriate applications, quality circles can be part of a broad strategy for organisational change aimed at improving both economic performance and the quality of working life.

Despite many theories and studies there are still doubts as to how to manage an organisation so that staff have both high job satisfaction and productivity. It may be necessary to lower expectations in the pursuit of the 'happy/productive worker' and to make for sustained, slow progress in overcoming forces for stability in both job attitudes and performance. Three possible approaches are: the individually oriented system, the group oriented system and the organisationally oriented system.

| **Appendix** | A WRU assignment in new technology, QWL and organisation culture |

Pirelli Plc, Building Wires Business Unit, Aberdare, South Wales

In the early 80's the company found it increasingly difficult to operate profitably in a keenly priced competitive market. Withdrawal being strategically undesirable, various options were considered:

- To upgrade an existing UK production unit introducing individual computer controlled machines
- To upgrade this existing UK production unit installing a computer integrated manufacturing system (CIM)
- To construct a computer integrated manufacturing unit on a greenfield site in the UK
- To transfer production overseas.

The choice of option was influenced by two conflicting considerations:

- The desirability of transferring the special cables facility at the Aberdare site, South Wales, nearer to the research centre of the company in Hampshire
- The social responsibility felt by the company for the local community at Aberdare.

Towards the end of 1984 the company decided to construct a computer integrated manufacturing unit at an existing location at Aberdare, but in essence as a 'greenfield' site. This decision was linked with a determination to pursue an improved industrial relations climate incorporating flexibility of operation and removal of demarcation as a means of ensuring maximum competitive advantage from the new technology.

Early in 1985 the company approached the Work Research Unit requesting assistance with the development of an organisation designed to maximise operational effectiveness. Advice was sought for example on whether to 'de-skill' or 'up-skill', whether to harmonise terms and conditions of employment, and a range of other issues. Following preliminary discussions the Unit produced a paper discussing alternative options available within different organisation design parameters. It particularly stressed features which would progress an involved, participative cultured based on Quality of Working Life goals and processes. It addressed the greenfield site option, considering in particular the implications for job design, work organisation, organisational structure, the opportunity for greater employee involvement, and the consequences for management style and payment systems. The Unit arranged visits to companies operating team working and provided advice on integrated payment systems and the development of skill modules and skill related pay.

Following preliminary discussion with the Unit about the nature of employee representation within an involved organisation culture, the assistance of ACAS Wales was sought. A meeting was arranged between company representatives, the Wales TUC, a local ACAS adviser and a member of the Unit. Employee representation, trade union recognition, single union agreements and other industrial relations issues were discussed in the context of the proposed organisation culture. The company subsequently decided upon the single union option and consulted with a number of individual trade unions before negotiating an agreement with one of these unions. The agreement expressly states that the advanced technology incorporated in the manufacturing and administrative systems combined with characteristics of the product market will require unique approaches to operational matters, on the part of the company, employees and the Union.

The installation of the computer integrated production equipment is currently at an advanced stage and recruitment, selection and training of staff is proceeding. The careful deliberations of the company have resulted in the specification of an organisation culture which is designed to ensure the operational and commercial success of the company through its employees, to the mutual benefit of both. The opportunity presented by the greenfield site enabled the company to introduce new technology and organisation structure and complementary human resource strategies.

Key features of the management of change were:

- The commitment of top management to an organisation culture which emphasises high employee involvement
- The early involvement of a trade union to provide an employee representative structure and an industrial relations base for joint co-operation
- The care taken to design an organisation structure which takes account of both technical and people needs
- The emphasis on and commitment to the training and development of all employees in the new technology and new ways of working
- The option of single status removing possible sources of division in the integrated culture
- A selection procedure which focusses on the congruence of individuals' attitudes with the organisation culture
- An integrated company wide payment structure incorporating skill related pay supporting flexibility and individual development within a teamworking approach
- A profit related payment of equal amounts to all employees giving visible support to teamworking an emphasis on two way communication harnessing interactive use of the computer system where appropriate the recognition and encouragement of the contribution which employees can make by the use of a task force approach to problem solving.

In the interim period before the new organisation is fully operational, the WRU is continuing to maintain advisory contact. Emphasis is currently directed to selection, teambuilding, training and the development of the participative management style which is crucial to the new culture.

Reprinted from ACAS 1987 Annual Report pp. 51–53 with permission of John Cove, Administration Manager, Building Wires Business Unit, Pirelli General and the Controller of Her Majesty's Stationery Office.

Review and discussion questions

1. What exactly do you understand by job satisfaction? What are the main dimensions of job satisfaction?
2. Explain what you see as the relationship between job satisfaction and improved work performance. Give supporting reasons for your views.
3. What factors are likely to influence job design and what factors might affect its potential success? Contrast different approaches to job design and give examples of situations in which these approaches might be appropriate, and acceptable, to the staff concerned.
4. Why do you think that increasing attention is being given to the quality of working life? As a manager, detail the main areas in which you could take action in order to improve the quality of working life of staff.
5. Explain the work of the Work Research Unit. Detail what you believe are the main desirable task characteristics and job characteristics, and give examples from your own experience.
6. Outline the core dimensions of a job. Estimate the approximate Motivating Potential Score (MPS) for any job that you have held and/or attempt to establish the likely MPS for a job that you hope to have in the future.

7. Explain the essential features of a quality circle group. What are some of the main reasons for management resistance to quality circles?
8. Discuss the extent to which you believe theories of job enrichment lead to improved job satisfaction. Where possible, give practical examples in support of your answer.

| Case study 1 | THE WIDE OPEN SPACES

Rio Cosmetics Ltd.

Rio Cosmetics have chosen to concentrate their effort on what they regard as the most lucrative section of the market. As their Marketing Manager says, 'We've gone for short-term profit maximisation – rather than for diversification.' Their production is therefore concentrated on a single tube of deodorant marketed under the brand name 'Freche'. The product is heavily advertised on TV and Rio have made considerable profits over the past 5 years. However, a substantial competitor has now entered the market, and Rio's share of the market has dropped to 18%, its lowest level in 3 years.

The Board are now looking for explanations. They have asked for reports from the Sales and Production Departments. They have also asked Personnel Department to report on some disturbing statistics regarding the workforce. In particular:

1. There has been a dramatic increase in absenteeism over the last year.
2. Although the number of line workers has remained fairly stable (at around 2115 during the last four or five years), weekly average output has fallen from 312,000 to 287,000 units.
3. During the last year 21% of the line workers have been late at least once a week, in spite of the fact that they lose a quarter of an hour's pay when this happens. (Before this year the figure was fairly constant at around 10%.)

In addition:

Within the past four months, the number of consumers complaining direct to the company have doubled according to the information supplied by the Quality Control Department, who keep a record of the number of letters received each week. They advise that the majority of these complaints have been traced back to what they describe as 'human errors' on the production line. Furthermore, three serious cases of pilfering have been notified by the Security Section within the past week.

Other Information Available

The rate of pay is approximately 10% higher than could be obtained by the line workers elsewhere.

Older women are not discouraged, but the average age of the workforce is only 19 years. It is increasingly difficult to find acceptable line supervisors.

Production starts at 8 a.m. and finishes at 5 p.m. – 5 days a week – with an hour lunch break and two 20-minute tea breaks.

The graphs shown in Fig. 12.10 have been prepared covering Labour Turnover and Absenteeism over the past five years.

What explanations and recommendations would you offer the Board of Directors?

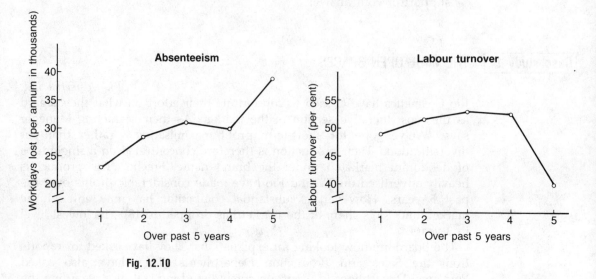

Fig. 12.10

Case study 2

You are a management consultant called in to advise an organisation which has undergone significant change, involving both voluntary and compulsory redundancies, in the last two years. Employee members have reduced by 60% whilst the work load has remained unchanged for the organisation as a whole. Employees, including managers and supervisors now work under significantly increased work pressure. Senior management are concerned about the low morale and commitment to the organisation which they now perceive amongst the remaining workforce. Six months ago the senior management team decided to introduce a major exercise to improve communication within the organisation. They wished employees at all levels to understand better the problems of the organisation, the management strategy adopted to deal with these problems, and the senior management team's growing confidence that the situation was now improving significantly. Productivity and cost effectiveness had improved substantially. Moreover major programmes of technical improvement and investment were now underway.

One important element of this programme was a training course in interactive skills for first-line supervisors. The personnel manager has told you that this programme has failed.

Personnel Manager: 'We wanted to build up the supervisors' role with their own people. Therefore we wished the supervisor to talk with his people about our plans and to get their ideas and views. We put them through a one week course in interactive skills and human relations skills. But it failed. They enjoyed the course. They all said they gained a lot from it. But when we asked them to communicate to their people about plans for this year, they said they did not feel confident enough.'

Consultant: 'Do they understand the plans? Do you feel that the plans have been presented to them in a clear enough way? Are their own managers communicating effectively with the supervisors? Do their managers provide support and encouragement to the supervisors?'

Personnel Manager: 'I'm not sure, possibly not. We give them copies of our detailed plans. They see everything. In any case I think they are afraid of being criticised by their staff. They don't want arguments with them and they don't feel sure enough about the plans. They wonder about job losses in the future.'

The role of first-line supervisors had been changed with the introduction of a professional Personnel Function in the 1960s. Supervisors no longer fully understood the terms and conditions of employment, bonus schemes, job evaluation systems and employment legislation relevant to the organisation. Moreover the manpower reductions had meant that supervisors were increasingly taking on tasks once carried out by their subordinates. Thus the role of the supervisor had come to be solely a technical, and no longer a managerial role.

(1) Assess the effectiveness of the training programme identifying the problems experienced.
(2) Identify the main issues you feel will need attention if communications within this organisation are to be improved.
(3) State what advice you will offer to the organisation about how to proceed from the current situation.

Notes and references

1. Herzberg, F. 'One More Time: How do you Motivate Employees?' *Harvard Business Review*, vol. 46, 1968, pp. 53–62. Abridged in Davis, L. E. and Taylor, J. C. (eds) *Design of Jobs*, Penguin (1972).
2. Herzberg, F. 'Orthodox Job Enrichment'. *Defense Management Journal*, vol. 13, April 1977, pp. 21–7. Abridged in Davis, L. E. and Taylor, J. C. (eds) *Design of Jobs*, Second edition, Goodyear (1979).
3. Myers, M. S. 'Who are Your Motivated Workers?' *Harvard Business Review*, vol. 42, January–February 1964, pp. 73–88.
4. Vroom, V. H. *Work and Motivation*, Wiley (1964). (Also published by Krieger (1982).)
5. Argyle, M. *The Social Psychology of Work*, Penguin (1974).
6. Luthans, F. *Organizational Behavior*, Third edition, McGraw-Hill (1981).
7. Grunberg, M. M. *Understanding Job Satisfaction*, Macmillan (1979).
8. Marx, K. 'The Notion of Alienation', in Coser, L. A. and Rosenburg, B. *Sociological Theory*, Collier Macmillan (1969) pp. 505–10.
9. Blauner, R. *Alienation and Freedom*, University of Chicago Press (1964).
10. See: Gerth, H. H. and Wright, M. C. 'Marx and Weber', in *From Max Weber Essays in Sociology*, Routledge and Kegan Paul (1970), pp. 46–50.
11. Walker, C. R. and Guest, R. H. *The Man on the Assembly Line*, Harvard University Press (1952).

12. Karasek, R. A. 'Job Demands, Job Decision Latitude and Mental Strain: Implications for Job Redesign', *Administrative Science Quarterly*, vol. 24, no. 2, 1979, pp. 285–308.
13. Myers, M. S. 'Every Employee a Manager', *California Management Review*, vol. 10, no. 3, Spring 1968, pp. 9–20.
14. Ibid. p. 17.
15. Warr, P. 'Work, Jobs and Unemployment', *Bulletin of the British Psychology Society*, 36, 1983, pp. 305–11.
16. Hackman, J. R. and Oldham, G. R. *Working Redesign*, Addison-Wesley (1980).
17. White, G. *Effective and Satisfactory Work Systems*, Work Research Unit, Occasional Paper, no. 27. HMSO (December 1983).
18. Gyllenhammar, P. G. *People at Work*, Addison-Wesley (1977).
19. Jönsson, B. *New Management*, School of Business Administration, University of Southern California, vol. 1, no. 2, 1983, pp. 30–3. See also: Ferguson, A. 'Volvo Plant's Smooth Path to 1,000', *Management Today*, June 1988, p. 27.
20. Luthans, F. *Organizational Behavior*, Fourth edition, McGraw-Hill (1985).
21. Cooper, R. *Job Motivation and Job Design*, Institute of Personnel Management (1974).
22. Hackman, J. R. and Oldham, G. R. *Work Redesign*, Addison-Wesley (1980).
23. Wall, T. D., Clegg, C. W. and Jackson, P. R. 'An Evaluation of the Job Characteristics Model', *Journal of Occupational Psychology*, vol. 51, no. 2, 1978 pp. 183–96.
24. Algera, J. A. 'Objective and Perceived Task Characteristics as a Determinant of Reactions by Task Performers', *Journal of Occupational Psychology*, vol. 56, no. 2, 1983, pp. 95–107.
25. Grunberg, M. M. *Understanding Job Satisfaction*, Macmillan (1979).
26. Taylor, L. K. *Not for Bread Alone: An Appreciation of Job Enrichment*, Third edition, Business Books (1980).
27. See, for example: Cuming, M. W. *The Theory and Practice of Personnel Management*, Sixth edition, Heinemann (1989).
28. I am grateful for the help of Auriol Blandy, Principal Research Officer, Work Research Unit, with the sections on the quality of working life and the Work Research Unit.
29. Wilson, N. A. B. *On the Quality of Working Life*: report prepared for the Department of Employment, Manpower Paper no. 7, HMSO (1973).
30. Herrick, N. Q. and Quinn, R. P. 'The Working Conditions Survey as a Source of Social Indicators', *Monthly Labor Review*, US Department of Labor, April 1971.
31. See, for example: Work Research Unit publications *Meeting the Challenge of Change: Guidelines for the Successful Implementation of Changes in Organisations*, HMSO (1982), and *Meeting the Challenge of Change, Case Studies*, HMSO (1982)
32. Russell, S. *Quality Circles in Perspective*, Work Research Unit, Occasional Paper, no. 24, HMSO (February 1983).
33. Meyer, G. W. and Stott, R. G. 'Quality Circles: Panacea or Pandora's Box', *Organizational Dynamics*, Spring 1985, pp. 34–50.
34. Collard, R. 'The Practical Applications of Quality Circles', *Management Review and Digest*, vol. 8, no. 4, January 1982, pp. 3–5.
35. Jones, W. G, 'Quality's Vicious Circles', *Management Today*, March 1983, pp. 97–8, 100, 102.
36. Middleton, R. 'Team Briefing and Quality Circles Prove Their Value', *British Journal of Administrative Management*, vol. 34, no. 7, November 1984, pp. 255–7.
37. Russell, S. *Quality Circles in Perspective*, Work Research Unit, Occasional Paper, no. 24, HMSO (February 1983).
38. Fletcher, D. 'Quality Circles at Wedgwood', *Industrial Participation*, no. 578, Summer 1982, pp. 2–9.
39. Dale, B. and Barlow, E. 'Quality Circles: The View From Within', *Management Decision*, vol. 25, no. 4, 1987, pp. 5–9.
40. Staw, B. M. 'Organizational Psychology and the Pursuit of the Happy/Productive Worker', *California Management Review*, vol. 28, no. 4, Summer 1986, pp. 40–53.

13. THE NATURE OF GROUPS

Groups are a major feature of organisational life. The organisation and its sub-units are made up of groups of people. Most activities of the organisation require at least some degree of co-ordination through the operation of group working. An understanding of the nature of groups is vital if the manager is to influence the behaviour of people in the work situation. The manager must be aware of the impact of groups and their effects on organisational performance.

Objectives

To:
(i) Explain the meaning and nature of groups;
(ii) Distinguish between formal and informal groups;
(iii) Explain the main reasons for the formation of groups;
(iv) Examine factors which influence group cohesiveness;
(v) Assess the impact of technology on the attitudes and behaviour of work groups;
(vi) Analyse the nature of role relationships and role conflict;
(vii) Appreciate the important of groups for effective organisational performance.

THE MEANING AND IMPORTANCE OF GROUPS

Individuals seldom work in isolation from others. Groups are a characteristic of all social situations and almost everyone in an organisation will be a member of one or more groups. The working of groups and the influence they exert over their membership is an essential feature of human behaviour and of organisational performance. The manager must use groups in order to achieve a high standard of work and improve organisational effectiveness.

There are many possible ways of defining what is meant by a group. The essential feature of a group is that its members regard themselves as belonging to the group. A group consists of a number of people who have:

a common objective or task,
an awareness of group identity and 'boundary',
a minimum set of agreed values and norms, which regulates their relatively exclusive mutual interaction.[1]

Another useful definition defines the group in psychological terms as: 'any number of people who

(1) interact with one another;
(2) are psychologically aware of one another; and
(3) perceive themselves to be a group'.[2]

Essential feature of work organisations Groups are an essential feature of the work pattern of any organisation. Members of a group must co-operate in order for work to be carried out, and managers themselves will work within these groups. People in groups influence each other in many ways and groups may develop their own hierarchies and leaders. Group pressures can have a major influence over the behaviour of individual members and their work performance. The activities of the group are associated with the process of leadership (which is discussed in Chapter 15). The style of leadership adopted by the manager has an important influence on the behaviour of members of the group.

The classical approach to organisation and management tended to ignore the importance of groups and the social factors at work. The ideas of people such as *F. W. Taylor* popularised the concept of the 'rabble hypothesis' and the assumption that people carried out their work, and could be motivated, as solitary individuals unaffected by others.

The human relations approach, however, gave recognition to the work organisation as a social organisation and to the importance of the group, and group value and norms, in influencing behaviour at work. The power of group membership over individual behaviour and work performance was illustrated clearly in the famous Hawthorne experiments at the Western Electric Company in America,[3] already referred to in Chapter 2.

Group values and norms

One experiment involved the observation of a group of 14 men working in the bank wiring room. It may be remembered that the men formed their own sub-groups or cliques, with natural leaders emerging with the consent of the members. Despite a financial incentive scheme where workers could receive more money for the more work they did, the group decided on 6000 units a day as a fair level of output. This was well below the level they were capable of producing. Group pressures on individual workers were stronger than financial incentives offered by management.

The group developed its own pattern of informal social relations and codes and practices ('norms') of what constituted proper group behaviour.

- *Not to be a 'rate buster'* – not to produce at too high a rate of output compared with other members or to exceed the production restriction of the group.
- *Not to be a 'chiseller'* – not to shirk production or to produce at too low a rate of output compared with other members of the group.
- *Not to be a 'squealer'* – not to say anything to the supervisor or management which might be harmful to other members of the group.
- *Not to be 'officious'* – people with authority over members of the group, for example inspectors, should not take advantage of their seniority or maintain a social distance from the group.

The group had their own system of sanctions including sarcasm, damaging completed work, hiding tools, playing tricks on the inspectors, and ostracising those members who did not conform with the group norms. Threats of physical violence were also made, and the group developed a system of punishing offenders by 'binging' which involved striking someone a fairly hard blow on the upper part of the arm. This process of binging also became a recognised method of controlling conflict within the group.

Another finding of the bank wiring room experiment was that the group did not follow company policy on the reporting of production figures. It was company policy that each man's output should be reported daily by the supervisor. However, the workers preferred to do their own reporting, and in order to remain in favour with the group the supervisor acquiesced to this procedure. On some days the men would actually produce more than they reported to 'build up' extra units for those days when they produced less than reported. Although actual production varied the group reported a relatively standard amount of output for each day. The men would also exchange jobs with each other even though this was contrary to management instructions.

Socio-technical system

The systems approach to organisation and management also gave recognition to the importance of groups in influencing behaviour at work. The concept of the organisation as a socio-technical system is concerned with the interactions between the psychological and social factors, as well as structural and technical requirements. Again, it may be remembered that technological change in the coal-mining industry had brought about changes in the social groupings of the miners.[4]

New methods of working disrupted the integration of small self-selecting groups of miners who worked together as independent teams. The change had undesirable social effects and as a result the new method did not prove as economically beneficial as it should have done with the new technology. The result was a 'composite' method of working with more responsibility taken by the team as a whole. The composite method proved to be not only more rewarding socially to the miners but also more efficient economically than the previous new method of working. (Recall the importance of autonomous work groups as a feature of job design, discussed in Chapter 12.)

WORK PATTERN OF ORGANISATIONS

Groups therefore, help shape the work pattern of organisations, and the attitudes and behaviour of members of their jobs. The formation and operation of work groups, and the behaviour of their members, has an important significance for the manager. *Likert*, for example, has developed a theory of organisation based on work groups. In his discussion of group processes and organisational performance he concludes that: 'Group forces are important not only in influencing the behavior of individual work groups with regard to productivity, waste, absence and the like, they also affect the behavior of entire organizations.'[5]

Overlapping group membership

Likert suggests that organisations function best when members act not as individuals but as members of highly effective work groups. He proposes a structure based on overlapping group membership with a *'linking-pin' process* by which the superior of one group is a subordinate member of the next group. The superior is, therefore, the linking-pin between a group of subordinates and the next authority level group (Fig. 13.1).

A structure of vertical overlapping groups helps to develop a committed team approach and would improve the flow of communication, co-

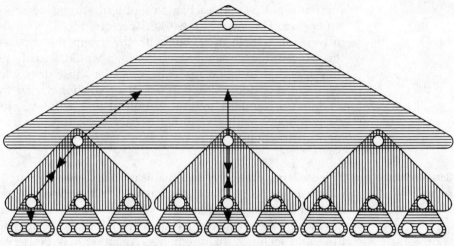

(The arrows indicate the linking pin function)

Fig. 13.1 Overlapping group structure and the linking-pin
(Reproduced with permission from Likert, L., *New Patterns of Management*, McGraw-Hill (1961) p. 113.)

ordination and decision-making. The use of the overlapping group structure together with a participative style of management form part of the criteria for System 4 management, discussed in Chapter 9.

Horizontal linking-pin

Likert also recognises the position of subordinates serving as horizontal linking-pins (Fig. 13.2) between different groups, such as functional or line work groups, and product-based work groups.[6]

Likert recognises that sooner or later the subordinate is likely to be caught in a conflict between membership of both groups and the provision of information for decision making. He suggests that both groups would need to be involved in group decision making to resolve differences and that this is more likely to occur with System 4 management.

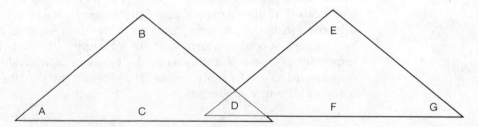

Fig. 13.2 D is a member of both groups and acts as a linking-pin for horizontal communication

Organisation structure

Groups are formed as a consequence of the pattern of organisation structure and arrangements for the division of work, for example the grouping together of common activities into sections. Groups may result from the nature of technology employed and the way in which work is carried out, for example the bringing together of a number of people to carry out a sequence of operations on an assembly line. Groups may also develop when a number of people of the same level or status within the organisation see themselves as a group, for example departmental heads of an industrial organisation, or chief officers of a local authority.

Groups are deliberately planned and created by management as part of the formal organisation structure. But groups will also arise from social processes and the informal organisation. The informal organisation arises from the interaction of people working within the organisation and the development of groups with their own relationships and norms of behaviour, irrespective of those defined within the formal structure. This leads to a major distinction between groups – formal and informal.

FORMAL GROUPS

Formal groups are created to achieve specific organisational objectives and are concerned with the *co-ordination of work activities*.

People are brought together on the basis of defined roles within the structure of the organisation. The nature of the tasks to be undertaken is a predominant feature of the formal group. Goals are identified by management, and certain rules, relationships and norms of behaviour established.

Formal groups tend to be relatively permanent, although there may be changes in actual membership. However, temporary formal groups may also be created by management, for example the use of project teams in a matrix organisation.

Formal work groups can be differentiated into team groups, task groups and technological groups.[7]

- *Team groups* – these are fairly autonomous groups with broad terms of reference and limited supervision. The team designate the positions to be filled and the allocation of members, and instigate changes as necessary. Examples are problem-solving groups, research teams, maintenance crews.
- *Task groups* – jobs are defined clearly and individuals assigned to specific positions. The group has some flexibility over methods of work and the pace of work, but otherwise limited discretion. Examples could include many administrative or clerical workers.
- *Technological groups* – members have very limited autonomy to determine or change the operational activities. The pace of work is also likely to be controlled. Content and method of work are specified and individuals assigned to specific jobs. There is little scope for individual discretion, and often limited opportunities for interaction among members. A typical example is people working on assembly-line operations.

Another possible categorisation is *decision-making and problem-solving groups*, such as committees and working parties.[8]

INFORMAL GROUPS

Within the formal structure of the organisation there will always be an informal structure. The informal organisation was discussed in Chapter 3.

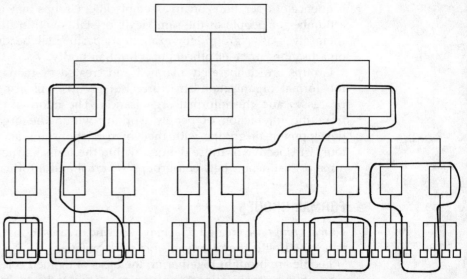

Fig. 13.3 Examples of informal groups within the formal structure of an organisation

The formal structure of the organisation, and system of role relationships, rules and procedures, will be augmented by interpretation and development at the informal level. *Informal groups* are based more on personal relationships and agreement of group members than on defined role relationships. They serve to satisfy psychological and social needs not related necessarily to the tasks to be undertaken. Groups may devise ways of attempting to satisfy members' affiliation and other social motivations which are lacking in the work situation, especially in industrial organisations.[9]

The membership of informal groups can cut across the formal structure. They may comprise individuals from different parts of the organisation and/or from different levels of the organisation, both vertically and diagonally, as well as from the same horizontal level. An informal group could also be the same as the formal group, or it might comprise a part only of the formal group. (*See* Fig. 13.3.)

The members of informal group may appoint their own leader who exercises authority by the consent of the members themselves. The informal leader may be chosen as the person who reflects the attitudes and values of the members, helps to resolve conflict, leads the group in satisfying its goals, or liaises with management or other people outside the group. The informal leader may often change according to the particular situation facing the group. Although not usually the case, it is possible for the informal leader to be the same person as the formal leader appointed officially by management.

REASONS FOR FORMATION OF GROUPS

Individuals will form into groups, both formal and informal, for a number of different reasons relating to both work performance and social processes.

- *Certain tasks can be performed only through the combined efforts of a number of individuals working together*. The variety of experience and expertise among members of the group provides a synergetic effect which can be applied to the increasingly complex problems of modern organisations.

- *Groups may encourage collusion between members* in order to modify formal working arrangements more to their liking, for example by sharing or rotating unpopular tasks. Group membership therefore provides the individual with opportunities for initiative and creativity.

- *Groups provide companionship and a source of mutual understanding and support from colleagues.* This can help in solving work problems, and also to mitigate against stressful or demanding working conditions.

- *Membership of the group provides the individual with a sense of belonging.* The group provides a feeling of identity, and the chance to acquire role recognition and status within the group.

- *The group provides guidelines on generally acceptable behaviour.* It helps to clarify ambiguous situations such as, for example, the extent to which official rules and regulations are expected to be adhered to in practice, the rules of the game, and what is seen as the correct actual behaviour. The informal organisation may put pressure on group members to resist demands from management on such matters as, for example, higher output or changes in working methods. Group allegiance can serve as a means of control over individual behaviour. The group may discipline individuals who contravene the norms of the group; for example, the process of 'binging' in the bank wiring room, mentioned above.

- *The group may provide protection for its membership.* Group members collaborate to protect their interests from outside pressures or threats.

Expectations of group membership   Individuals have varying expectations of the benefits from group membership. Groups are a potential source of motivation and of job satisfaction, and also a major determinant of effective organisational performance. It is important, therefore, that the manager understands the reasons for the formation of groups and is able to recognise likely advantageous or adverse consequences for the organisation.

GROUP COHESIVENESS

The manager's main concern is that members of a work group co-operate in order to achieve the results expected of them. Co-operation among members is likely to be greater in a united, cohesive group. Membership of a cohesive group can be a rewarding experience for the individual and can contribute to the promotion of morale. Members of a high-morale group are more likely to think of themselves as a group and work together effectively. *Strong and cohesive work groups can, therefore, have beneficial effects for the organisation.*

Cohesive groups do not necessarily produce a higher level of output. Performance varies with the extent to which the group accept or reject the goals of the organisation. The level of production is likely to conform to a standard acceptable as a norm by the group.[10] However, cohesive groups may result in greater interaction between members, mutual help and social satisfaction, lower turnover and absenteeism, and often higher production.[11]

Factors affecting cohesiveness

In order to develop the effectiveness of work groups the manager will be concerned with those factors that contribute to group cohesiveness, or that may cause frustration or disruption to the operation of the group.

The manager needs to consider, therefore, both the needs of individual members of staff, and the promotion of a high level of group identity and cohesion.

There are many factors which affect group cohesiveness and performance, which can be summarised under four broad headings:

(i) *Membership*

- size
- compatibility
- permanence

(ii) *Work environment*

- nature of task
- physical setting
- communications
- technology

(iii) *Organisational*

- management and leadership
- success
- external threat

(iv) *Group development and maturity*, for example:

- forming
- storming
- norming
- performing

Membership

- *Size of the group* As a group increases in size, problems arise with communications and co-ordination. Large groups are more difficult to handle and require a higher level of supervision. Absenteeism also tends to be higher in larger groups. When a group becomes too large it may split into smaller units and friction may develop between the sub-groups.

  It is difficult to put a precise figure on the ideal size of a work group. Much will depend upon other variables, but it seems to be generally accepted that cohesiveness becomes more difficult to achieve when a group exceeds 10–12 members.[12] Beyond this size the group tends to split into sub-groups.

- *Compatibility of the members* The more homogeneous the group in terms of such things as shared backgrounds, interests, attitudes and values of its members, the easier it is to promote cohesiveness. Variations in other individual differences, such as the personality or skills of members, may serve to complement each other and help make for a cohesive group. On the other hand, such differences may be the cause of disruption and conflict. Conflict can also arise in a homogeneous group where members are in competition with each other. Individual incentive payment schemes, for example, may be a source of conflict.

- *Permanence of group members* Group spirit and relationships take time to develop. Cohesiveness is more likely when members of a group are together for a reasonable length of time, and changes occur only slowly. A frequent turnover of members is likely to have an adverse effect on morale, and on the cohesiveness of the group.

Work environment

- *The nature of the task* and the way in which work is carried out. Where workers are involved in similar work, share a common task, or face the same problems, this may assist cohesiveness. The nature of the task may serve to bring people together when it is necessary for them to communicate and interact regularly with each other in the performance of their duties, for example members of a research and development team.

  Even if members of a group normally work at different locations they may still experience a feeling of cohesiveness if the nature of the task requires frequent communication and interaction; for example, security guards patrolling separate areas who need to check with each other on a regular basis. However, where the task demands a series of relatively separate operations or discrete activities, for example on a machine-paced assembly line, it is more difficult to develop cohesiveness. Individuals may have interactions with colleagues on either side of them but little opportunity to develop a common group feeling.

- *Physical setting* Where members of a group work in the same location or in close physical proximity to each other this will generally help cohesiveness. However, this is not always the case. For example, in large open-plan offices staff often tend to segregate themselves from colleagues and create barriers by the strategic siting of such items as filing cabinets, book cases or indoor plants. The size of the office and the number of staff in it are, of course, important considerations in this case. Isolation from other groups of workers will also tend to build cohesiveness. This often applies, for example, to a smaller number of workers on a night shift.

- *Communications* The more easily members can communicate freely with each other the more likelihood of group cohesiveness. Communications are affected by the work environment, by the nature of the task, and by technology. For example, difficulties in communication can arise with production systems where workers are stationed continuously at a particular point with limited freedom of movement. Even when opportunities exist for interaction with colleagues, physical conditions may limit effective communication.

  In their study of the effects of the assembly line on workers' behaviour in a new car factory, *Walker* and *Guest* found that in some jobs the technological layout and high level of noise severely limited the amount of contact between workers.[13] This restricted the possibilities for social interaction and hampered internal group unity. It also influenced the form of contact workers had with supervisors. Where opportunities existed for interpersonal relationships workers took advantage of them, and when such opportunities were absent the workers felt deprived.

- *Technology* The nature of technology has an important effect on cohesiveness. The importance of technology has already been discussed in Chapters 3 and 12. Technology also has wider implications for the operation and behaviour of groups and therefore is considered in a separate section below.

Organisational

- *Management and leadership* The activities of groups cannot be separated from management and the process of leadership. The form of management and style of leadership adopted will influence the relationship between the group and the organisation, and is a major determinant of group cohesiveness. In general terms, cohesiveness will be affected by such things as the manner in which the manager: gives guidance and encouragement to the group; offers help and support; provides opportunities for participation; attempts to resolve conflicts; and gives attention to both employee relations and task problems.

- *Success* The more successful the group, the more cohesive it is likely to be; and cohesive groups are more likely to be successful. Success is usually a strong motivational influence on the level of work performance. Success, or reward, can be perceived by group members in a number of ways; for example, the satisfactory completion of a task through co-operative action; praise from management; a feeling of high status; achievement in competition with other groups; benefits gained, such as high wage payments from a group bonus incentive scheme.

- *External threat* Cohesiveness may be enhanced by members co-operating with one another when faced with a common external threat, such as changes in their method of work, or the appointment of a new manager. Even if the threat is subsequently removed, the group may still continue to have a greater degree of cohesiveness than before the threat arose. Conflict between groups will also tend to increase the cohesiveness of each group and the boundaries of the group become drawn more clearly.

GROUP DEVELOPMENT AND MATURITY

The degree of cohesiveness is affected also by the manner in which groups progress through the various stages of development and maturity. *Bass* and *Ryterband* identify four distinct stages in group development: mutual acceptance and membership; communication and decision making; motivation and productivity; and control and organisation.[14]

- *First stage – developing mutual acceptance and membership* Members have an initial mistrust of each other and a fear of inadequacies. They remain defensive and limit their behaviour through conformity and ritual. The priority is with questions of likes and dislikes, and power or dependency of group members.

- *Second stage – communication and decision making* Once members have learnt to accept each other they begin to express their feelings and conflicts. Norms of procedure are established and there is acceptance of legitimate influence over the group. Members develop a liking, or at least a sense of caring for each other. There are more open communications and reactions. More constructive problem-solving and decision-making behaviour strategies develop.

- *Third stage – motivation and productivity* Problems of members' motivation have been resolved. Members are involved with the work of the group.

They co-operate with each other instead of competing. Members are motivated by intrinsic rewards to achieve a high level of productivity.

- *Fourth stage – control and organisation* The final stage of group development. Work is allocated by agreement and according to the members' abilities. Members work independently and the organisation of the group is flexible and adaptable to new challenges.

Group development and relationships

An alternative, and more popular, model by *Tuckman* also identifies four main successive stages of group development and relationships: forming, storming, norming and performing.[15]

- *Stage 1 – Forming* The initial formation of the group and the bringing together of a number of individuals who identify, tentatively, the purpose of the group, its composition and terms of reference.

  At this stage consideration is given to hierarchical structure of the group, pattern of leadership, individual roles and responsibilities, and codes of conduct.

  There is likely to be considerable anxiety as members attempt to create an impression, to test each other, and to establish their personal identity within the group.

- *Stage 2 – Storming* As members of the group get to know each other better they will put forward their views more openly and forcefully.

  Disagreements will be expressed and challenges offered on the nature of the task and arrangements made in the earlier stage of development. This may lead to conflict and hostility.

  The storming stage is important because, if successful, there will be discussions on reforming arrangements for the working and operation of the group, and agreement on more meaningful structures and procedures.

- *Stage 3 – Norming* As conflict and hostility start to be controlled members of the group will establish guidelines and standards, and develop their own norms of acceptable behaviour.

  The norming stage is important in establishing the need for members to co- operate in order to plan, agree standards of performance and fulfil the purpose of the group.

  This co-operation and adherence to group norms can work against effective organisational performance. It may be remembered, for example, that, in the bank wiring room experiment of the Hawthorne studies, group norms imposed a restriction on the level of output of the workers.

- *Stage 4 – Performing* When the group has progressed successfully through the three earlier stages of development it will have created structure and cohesiveness to work effectively as a team.

  At this stage the group can concentrate on the attainment of its purpose and performance of their common task is likely to be at its most effective.

The analysis of behaviour in groups, and group dynamics are discussed in Chapter 14.

General formulation of group cohesiveness

Based on an analysis of research studies, *Cartwright* suggests a general formulation of the nature of group cohesiveness, its determinants and its consequences.[16] (*See* Fig. 13.4).

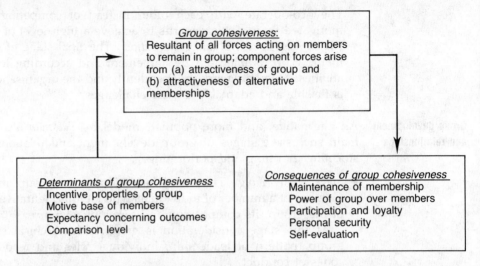

Fig. 13.4 A scheme for analysing group cohesiveness
(From Cartwright, D., 'The Nature of Group Cohesiveness', in Cartwright, D. and Zander, D. A. (eds) *Group Dynamics: Research and Theory*, Harper & Row (1968) p. 92.)

Potential disadvantages of strong, cohesive groups

If the manager is to develop effective work groups then attention should be given to those factors which influence the creation of group identity and cohesiveness. But, strong and cohesive groups also present potential disadvantages for management. The goals of the group may be at variance with the goals of the organisation. Again, for example, in the bank wiring room experiment, group norms and pressures on individual members led to restrictions on production and a low level of output.

Once a group has become fully developed and created cohesiveness, it is more difficult for the manager to change successfully the attitudes and behaviour of the group. It is important that the manager should attempt to influence the group during the norming stage when members are establishing guidelines and standards, and their own norms of acceptable behaviour.

Strong, cohesive groups may develop a critical or even hostile attitude towards people outside the group or members of other groups. This can be the case, for example, when group cohesiveness is based on common status, qualifications, technical expertise or professional standing. Group cohesiveness may result in lack of co-operation with, or opposition to, non-members. As a result, resentment and inter-group conflict may arise to the detriment of the organisation as a whole.

In order to help prevent, or overcome, unconstructive inter-group conflict, the manager should attempt to stimulate a high level of communication and interaction between the groups, and to maintain harmony. Rotation of members among different groups should be encouraged.

On the other hand, inter-group rivalry may be deliberately encouraged as a means of building stronger within-group cohesiveness.[17] A competitive element may help to promote unity within a group. However, inter-group rivalry and competition need to be carefully handled by the manager. Groups should not normally be put in a situation where they have to compete for resources, status or approval.[18]

The manager should attempt to avoid the development of 'win–lose' situations. Emphasis should be placed on overall objectives of the organisation and on superordinate goals. These are goals over and above the issues at conflict and which, if they are to be achieved, require the co-operation of the competing groups.

THE EFFECTS OF TECHNOLOGY ON WORK GROUPS

The nature of technology and the work flow system of the organisation is a major determinant of the operation of groups, and the attitude and behaviour of their members. Low morale and a negative attitude towards management and the job are often associated with a large number of workers undertaking similar work.

A number of different studies have drawn attention to the relationship between technology and work groups. For example, *Walker* and *Guest* referred to effects of technology on work groups. The character or type of group is determined largely by the technological requirements of the organisation. They found that the technological layout and pacing of work by the assembly-line operation was a source of dissatisfaction to the workers.[19]

Scott undertook a study of a large steel plant which appeared to have an unusual history of assimilating large-scale technical change with the minimum of resistance or overt conflict despite problems with demarcations, wage differentials and redundancies.[20] One of the main reasons for this was the nature of the work groups. Operators worked in close co-operation with group members. The groups were 'self-regulating', they allocated functions to their members and established a hierarchy of skill and authority based on seniority. New members of the group started at the lower level of the hierarchy and worked their way up. They felt it to be in their long-term interests to stay with the organisation and to remain in the same group.

Production systems and group behaviour The type of production system determines the nature of work groups and the manner in which they conduct themselves. On the basis of a study of 300 work groups in a number of different industrial organisations, *Sayles* identified four main types of group, each with distinctive technological features and characteristic patterns of behaviour: apathetic, erratic, strategic and conservative.[21]

- *Apathetic groups* Tended to be relatively low skilled, and poorly paid. Members performed a range of different functions with little task interdependence. There was a lack of enthusiasm, little sense of internal unity, lack of a clearly defined leader, individual rather than group problems, low morale. Tended to accept management decisions with few pressure devices. Members felt suppressed and discontented.
- *Erratic groups* Also tended to be low skilled and with low status. Members performed identical or very similar tasks requiring frequent interaction with each other. Work was often physically demanding. Tended to be unpredictable. Developed occasional cohesion. Mixed relationship with management, but easily inflamed in handling grievances. Tended to have authoritarian leadership.
- *Strategic groups* Relatively skilled, well paid and self-assured. Usually a

good production record. Generally individual jobs but with a high degree of interaction and internal group unity. Jobs were often important to management. Tended to be active and influential with continual union participation and pressure on management. Shrewd in use of grievance procedures and in improving their own position.

- *Conservative groups* Skilled workers with high status. Mainly individual operation. Wide dispersion throughout the organisation and low level of interaction, but strong sense of identity and a reasonable degree of internal unity. Tended to be conservative in negotiations but exert strong pressure for specific objectives, for example maintenance of traditional differentials and wage levels. Often associated with professional bodies and tended to be ambivalent regarding trade unions.

There was a marked similarity of behaviour among the different types of groups with similar technological features across a wide range of industrial settings. The work organisation and production technology determines the type of work group that emerges, and restricts the form of action taken by the group. Sayles suggests that the relationship between work groups, management and the form of grievance behaviour, and the collective activity of the group, is influenced by five major variables:

- relative position of the group on the internal promotion ladder;
- relative size and importance of the group;
- similarity of jobs within the group;
- extent to which the work is indispensable to the functioning of the department or organisation; and
- precision with which management can measure the workload and work pace for the group.

These variables are determined largely by the nature of technology. Technology also influences the differentiation of the task and division of work, and the internal social structure of the group. The greater the task differentiation and the more complex the internal structure of the group, the less likely the effects of grievance behaviour.

| Differences in behaviour of social groupings | *Lupton* undertook a study of the organisation of two contrasting workshops at different companies termed Wye and Jay.[22] Wye Garment Company made waterproof garments and also embraced other manufacturing activities. The workers were mainly female. Jay's Electrical Components was founded originally for the manufacture of equipment for the generation and transmission of electricity. The workers were mainly male. |

Differences in behaviour of social groupings

Lupton undertook a study of the organisation of two contrasting workshops at different companies termed Wye and Jay.[22] Wye Garment Company made waterproof garments and also embraced other manufacturing activities. The workers were mainly female. Jay's Electrical Components was founded originally for the manufacture of equipment for the generation and transmission of electricity. The workers were mainly male.

In both companies there were clear social groupings, but marked differences in their behaviour. At Wye the social groupings had no influence on the work situation, they appeared to accept management norms and there was no solidarity or control aimed at determining the level of output or earnings.

At Jay's the social groupings coincided with the work groups and actually shaped their pattern. They established norms of output, sanctions to control individual behaviour, and an informal division of labour which affected output and earnings. In attempting to explain the differences in the pattern of behaviour between the two workshops, Lupton examined a number of factors such as the sex of the workers, the wage payment system, external conditions, and technology and the work organisation.

At Wye there was a detailed breakdown of operations, the work flow was based on the individual, and jobs had a short time-span. At Jay's there was no detailed breakdown of operations, the production unit was based on the section, and each job had a reasonably long time-span with opportunities for manipulation. There was more scope for the workers and more opportunities for worker control. Lupton suggests that the layout of the job, the work flow pattern, the method of job allocation and the time-span of the operational cycle, are important to a comparative analysis of the degree of control which can be exercised by the workers.

Technology and alienation

The nature of technology and the work organisation can result in a feeling of alienation, especially among manual workers. Factors which have been shown to affect alienation include the extent to which the work of the individual or the group amounts to a meaningful part of the total production process, and the satisfaction which workers gain from relationships with fellow workers and group membership.

In a study of assembly-line and other factory work, *Goldthorpe* found that the technology was unfavourable for the creation of work groups.[23] However, he also found a group of workers who, although alienated, were still satisfied. Membership of a meaningful work group was not necessarily an important source of job satisfaction. The workers, all married men, aged between 21 and 46, were not interested in maintaining close relationships with fellow workers or supervisors. Their earnings were well in excess of the average manual wage at the time – the 'affluent' workers.

Orientations to work

Goldthorpe's study is an example of the social action approach to organisational behaviour. His findings were based on a study of more than 200 manual workers from three different firms in Luton. Information was collected about the work situation, organisational participation and involvement with work colleagues, and life outside of the work organisation. Goldthorpe suggested that responses to work resulted largely from the individual's orientation to work. He suggested the existence of three main types of orientation to work: instrumental, bureaucratic and solidaristic.

- Individuals with an *instrumental orientation* defined work not as a central life issue but in terms of a means to an end. There is a calculative or economic involvement with work and a clear distinction between work related and non-work related activities.
- Individuals with a *bureaucratic orientation* defined work as a central life issue. There is a sense of obligation to the work of the organisation and a positive involvement in terms of a career structure. There is a close link between work-related and non-work-related activities.
- Individuals with a *solidaristic orientation* defined the work situation in terms of group activities. There is an ego involvement with work groups rather than with the organisation itself. Work is more than just a means to an end. Non-work activities are linked to work relationships.

Goldthorpe claimed that the workers had an instrumental orientation to work. Their primary concern was with economic interests – pay and security

– rather than the nature of the work, or the satisfaction of social needs at work. Goldthorpe suggests that the different orientation to work in certain industries may help to explain the importance of work groups. He recognises that in other situations where there is the opportunity for team-work, the workers will have greater social expectations and the membership of work groups will be very important to them.

Technology and group behaviour

Technology is clearly a major influence on the pattern of group operation and behaviour. The work organisation may limit the opportunities for social interaction and the extent to which individuals are able to identify themselves as members of a cohesive work group. This in turn can have possible adverse effects on attitudes to work and the level of job satisfaction. In many assembly-line production systems, for example, relationships between individual workers are determined by the nature of the task, the extent to which individual jobs are specified, and the time cycle of operations.

In recent years there have been attempts to remove some of the alienating aspects of mass production and assembly-line work by increasing the range of tasks and responsibility allocated to small groups. These attempts include greater use of team working and of group technology.

An example of team working is the famous 'Volvo experiments' in Sweden, discussed in Chapter 12.

Group technology involves changes to the work flow system of production. With the traditional 'functional layout' of production, lines of similar machines or operations are arranged together so that components are passed back and forth until all activities are completed. However, with 'group technology' production, the work flow system is based on a grouping of workers and a range of machines. This enables work groups to perform series of successive operations using a group of machines on a family of similar components.

Impact of information technology

The impact of information technology is likely to lead to new patterns of work organisation, and affect the formation and structure of groups. Movement away from large-scale centralised organisation to smaller working units can help create an environment in which workers may relate more easily to each other. Improvements in telecommunications mean, for example, that support staff need no longer be located within the main production unit. On the other hand, modern methods of communication mean that individuals may work more on their own, or even from their own homes, or work more with machines than with other people.

ROLE RELATIONSHIPS

In order that the organisation can achieve its goals and objectives the work of individual members must be linked into coherent patterns of activities and relationships. This is achieved through the 'role structure' of the organisation.

A 'role' is the expected pattern of behaviours associated with members occupying a particular position within the structure of the organisation. It also describes how a person perceives their own situation. The formal organisational relationship discussed in Chapter 5 (line, functional, staff or lateral) can be seen as forms of role relationships. These individual authority relationships determine the pattern of interaction with other roles.

The concept of 'role' is important to the functioning of groups and for an understanding of group processes and behaviour. It is through role differentiation that the structure of the work group and relationships among its members are established. The development of the group entails the identification of distinct roles for each of its members. Some form of structure is necessary for team-work and co-operation. The concept of roles helps to clarify the structure and to define the pattern of complex relationships within the group.

The role, or roles, that the individual plays within the group is influenced by a combination of:

- *situational factors*, such as the requirements of the task, the style of leadership, position in the communication network; and
- *personal factors* such as values, attitudes, motivation, ability and personality.

The role that a person plays in one work group may be quite different from the role that person plays in other work groups. However, everyone within a group is expected to behave in a particular manner and to fulfil certain role expectations.

In addition to the role relationships with members of their own group – peers, superiors, subordinates – the individual will have a number of role-related relationships with outsiders, for example members of other work groups, trade union officials, suppliers, consumers. *This is a person's 'role-set'*. The role-set comprises the range of associations or contacts with whom the individual has meaningful interactions in connection with the performance of their role. (*See* Fig. 13.5.)

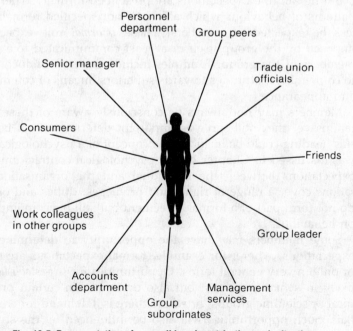

Personnel department
Group peers
Senior manager
Trade union officials
Consumers
Friends
Work colleagues in other groups
Group leader
Accounts department
Management services
Group subordinates

Fig. 13.5 Representation of a possible role-set in the work situation

Role congruence   An important feature of role relationship is the concept of 'role congruence'. This means that a member of staff should not be perceived as having a high and responsible position in one respect but a low standing in another respect. Difficulties with role congruence can arise from the nature of group-ings and formal relationships within the structure of the organisation, discussed in Chapter 5.

An example of this is with staff relationships. For instance, a young and comparatively junior personal assistant passes on the superior's instructions to one of the superior's more senior subordinates. Although the subordinate will understand that the personal assistant is speaking on behalf of the superior, the senior subordinate may still feel that instructions are coming from a more junior member of staff.

Another example could be with the line-staff relationship. For instance, a relatively junior member of the personnel department informing a senior departmental manager that a certain proposed action is contrary to the policies of the organisation.

Problems over role congruence can also lead to the possibility of role stress; see below.

Role expectations   Many role expectations are *prescribed formally* and indicate what the person is expected to do and their duties and obligations. Formal role prescriptions provide guidelines for expected behaviours. Examples are a written contract of employment, rules and regulations, standards, policy decisions, job description, or directives from superiors. Formal role expectations may also be derived clearly from the nature of the task. They may, in part at least, be defined legally, for example the obligations of a company secretary under the Companies Acts, or the responsibilities of a district auditor under the Local Government Acts.

But not all role expectations are prescribed formally. There will be certain patterns of behaviour which although not specified formally will none the less be expected of members. These *informal* role expectations may be imposed by the group itself or at least communicated to a person by other members of the group. Examples include general conduct, mutual support to co-members, attitudes towards superiors, means of communicating, dress and appearance.

Members may not always be consciously aware of these informal expec-tations yet they still serve as important determinants of behaviour. Under this heading could be included the concept of a psychological contract which was discussed in Chapter 1. The psychological contract implies a variety of expectations between the individual and the organisation. These expec-tations cover a range of rights and privileges, duties and obligations which do not form part of a formal agreement but still have an important influence on behaviour.[24]

Some members may have the opportunity to determine their own role expectations, where, for example, formal expectations are specified loosely or only in very general terms. Opportunities for *self-established roles* are more likely in senior positions, but also occur within certain professional, tech-nical or scientific groups, or where there is a demand for creativity or artistic flair. Such opportunities will also be influenced by the style of leadership adopted, for example where a *laissez-faire* approach is adopted.

ROLE CONFLICT

The concept of role focuses attention on aspects of behaviour existing independently of an individual's personality. Patterns of behaviour result from both the role and the personality. Role conflict arises from inadequate or inappropriate role definition and needs to be distinguished from personality clashes. These arise from incompatibility between two or more people, *as individuals*, even though their roles may be defined clearly and understood fully.

In practice, the manner in which a person actually behaves may not be consistent with their expected pattern of behaviours. This inconsistency may be a result of role conflict. Role conflict as a generic term can include role incompatibility, role ambiguity, role overload and role underload. These are all problem areas associated with the creation of role expectations. (*See* Fig. 13.6.)

- *Role incompatibility* arises when a person faces a situation in which simultaneous different or contradictory expectations create inconsistency. Compliance with one set of expectations makes it difficult or impossible to comply with other expectations. The two role expectations are in conflict. A typical example concerns the person 'in the middle', such as the supervisor or section head, who faces opposing expectations from workers and from management.[25]

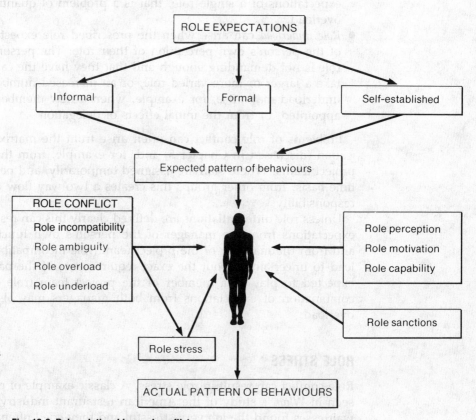

Fig. 13.6 Role relationships and conflicts
(Adapted and reproduced with permission from Miner, J. B., *Management Theory*, Macmillan (1971) p. 47.)

387

Another example might be the situation of a manager who believes in a relaxed, participative style of behaviour more in keeping with a Theory Y approach, but whose superior believes in a Theory X approach and expects the manager to adopt a more formal and directive style of behaviour.

- *Role ambiguity* occurs when there is lack of clarity as to the precise requirements of the role and the person is unsure what to do. The person's own perception of their role may differ from the expectations of others. This implies that insufficient information is available for the adequate performance of the role.

  Role ambiguity may result from a lack of formally prescribed expectations. It is likely to arise in large, diverse groups or at times of constant change. Uncertainty often relates to such matters as the method of performing tasks, the extent of the person's authority and responsibility, standards of work, and the evaluation and appraisal of performance.

- *Role overload* is when a person faces too many separate roles or too great a variety of expectations. The person is unable to meet satisfactorily all expectations and some must be neglected in order to satisfy others. This leads to a conflict of priority.

  Some writers distinguish between role overload and work overload. Role overload is seen in terms of the total role-set, and implies that the person has too many separate roles to handle. Where there are too many expectations of a single role, that is a problem of quantity, this is work overload.[26]

- *Role underload* can arise when the prescribed role expectations fall short of the person's own perception of their role. The person may feel their role is not demanding enough and that they have the capacity to undertake a larger or more varied role, or an increased number of roles. Role underload may arise, for example, when a new member of staff is first appointed, or from the initial effects of delegation.

Problems of role conflict can often arise from the matrix form of organisation (discussed in Chapter 5) and, for example, from the use of flexible project teams. Where staff are assigned temporarily, and perhaps on a part-time basis, from other groups this creates a two-way flow of authority and responsibility.

Unless role differentiations are defined clearly this can result in conflicting expectations from the manager of the person's own functional grouping, and from the manager of the project team (role incompatibility). It can also lead to uncertainty about the exact requirements of the part the person is expected to play as a member of the project team (role ambiguity). The combination of expectations from both managers may also result in role overload.

ROLE STRESS

Role conflict can result in role stress. A classic example of role stress can be seen in *Whyte*'s study of the American restaurant industry.[27] A number of waitresses found the job very stressful and they cried often. One reason for this was the constant conflict between the demands of the customer to be served quickly and pressure from the chefs who were unable to produce the food in time. The waitresses were caught between two incompatible expectations and were pulled both ways.

Also, the chefs, who regarded themselves to be of high status and generally recognised as such by the staff, resented being 'told' what to do by the waitresses who were generally regarded to be of lower status. (An example of role congruence, discussed above.) As a result arguments resulted, disrupting performance. The conflict of status was resolved by the introduction of an ordering process by which the chefs received customers' orders without the appearance of taking instructions from the lower status waitresses.

Although a certain amount of stress can be a good thing and helps to bring out a high level of performance, it is also potentially very harmful. Stress is a source of tension, frustration and dissatisfaction. It can lead to difficulties in communication and interpersonal relationships. For example, a review of research by *Filley* and *House* into the consequences of role conflict concluded that job satisfaction is lower and there is an adverse effect on the level of individual performance.[28]

In a survey of a representative sample of 725 male industrial workers in America, *Kahn* found widespread feelings of role conflict and role ambiguity.[29] Forty-eight per cent of the sample reported experience of role conflict, for example between the demands of management and the unions, or between the requirements of superiors and subordinates. Fifteen per cent reported this as a frequent and serious concern. Thirty-five per cent reported having been disturbed by lack of clarity about the scope and responsibilities of the job. Twenty-nine per cent were concerned about what co-workers expected of them. Thirty-two per cent expressed feelings of tension arising from uncertainty about their superior's evaluation of them.

Reducing role conflict and role stress

There is increasing evidence concerning stress-related illnesses, such as cardiovascular diseases, and social problems which can have stress as a factor, for example marriage breakdowns. And decreasing efficiency resulting from work stress is extremely costly to organisations.[30] It is important, therefore, that managers make every effort to minimise the causes of stress.

There are a number of ways in which management might attempt to avoid or reduce role conflict, and the possibilities of role stress.

- Increased specification and clarity of prescribed role expectations, for example through written statements on objectives and policy, use of manuals and set procedures, introduction of appropriate rules, detailed job descriptions. However, such measures may be resented by staff. They may restrict the opportunity for independent action and personal development, giving rise to even more role conflict.
- Improved recruitment and selection and the careful matching of abilities, motivation, interests and personalities to the demands of a particular role.
- Medical examinations and health screening may give early indications of potential stress-related problems.

- The creation of new roles or assimilation of existing roles. The reallocation or restructuring of tasks and responsibilities. The clarification of priorities, and the elimination or down-grading of minor roles.
- Attention to induction programme, job training and retraining, staff development and career progression plans.
- Giving advance notice and explanation of what is likely to happen, for example of an expected, additional heavy workload which must be completed urgently. Where possible and appropriate provide an opportunity for practice or experience.
- Attention to factors which may help improve group structure and group cohesiveness, and help overcome inter-group conflict.
- Change in management system and leadership style, for example the move towards System 4 management, or the possible use of Management by Objectives. (*See* Chapter 9.)
- Review of organisation structure, information flow and communication networks; for example, members of staff being answerable to more than one superior, bureaucratic interference and poor delegation are all common causes of work stress; whereas, greater autonomy and the introduction of autonomous work groups can result in a marked reduction in stress.[31]

Other influences on behaviour

Even if there is an absence of role conflict and role stress, a person's actual behaviour may still be inconsistent with their expected pattern of behaviours. *Miner* gives three reasons that may account for this disparity.[32]

- The person does not perceive their job in the way the role prescriptions specify. This is a form of role ambiguity but may arise not because the role prescriptions themselves are unclear, but because the person misunderstands or distorts them
- Motivation is lacking, and the person does not want to behave in the way prescribed.
- The person does not have the capabilities – knowledge, mental ability or physical skills – required to behave in the way the role prescriptions specify.

Application of sanctions

Organisations apply a number of both positive and negative sanctions as inducements for members to contribute and behave in accordance with their prescribed roles. Typical examples are: an increase in salary or wages; promotion; a sideways or downwards move in the organisation structure; the threat of dismissal.

There are also a number of less direct sanctions which may be adopted. These include; the size of office or work area; the allocation of unpopular tasks; giving opportunities for paid overtime work; level of supervision; the amount of information given or the extent of consultation; granting or withholding privileges.

Role sanctions may also be applied through the operation of the informal organisation. Members of the group may impose their own sanctions and discipline individuals who contravene the norms of the group or expected standards of behaviour.

| Synopsis |

Groups are a major feature of human behaviour and of organisational performance. Members of a group must co-operate with one another for work to be carried out. Groups help shape the work pattern of organisations, and the attitudes and behaviour of members regarding their jobs. Groups develop their own values and norms of behaviour. Organisations function best when members act not as individuals, but as members of highly effective work groups.

Groups are formed as a consequence of the pattern of organisation structure and arrangements for the division of work. There are two main types of groups at work, formal and informal. Formal groups are deliberately planned and created by management as part of the organisation structure, and to achieve specific organisational objectives. They are concerned with the co-ordination of work activities. Informal groups are based on personal relationships and develop irrespective of the formal structure. Informal groups serve to satisfy members' psychological and social needs. Groups are formed, therefore, for a number of reasons relating to both work performance and social processes.

The manager's main concern is that members of a work group co-operate with one another. Factors which affect group cohesiveness can be considered under the broad headings of: membership; work environment; organisational; and group development and maturity. Membership of strong and cohesive groups can be a rewarding experience for the individual and have beneficial effects for the organisation. There are, however, potential disadvantages and the manager should attempt to prevent unconstructive inter-group conflict. On the other hand, inter-group rivalry may be deliberately encouraged as a means of building stronger within-group cohesiveness.

The nature of technology and the work flow system of the organisation is a major influence on the operation of groups, and the manner in which they conduct themselves. Four main types of groups, each with distinctive technological features and patterns of behaviour, are: apathetic, erratic, strategic and conservative. There may also be differences in behaviour between social groupings. The nature of technology can be unfavourable for the creation of work groups and a source of alienation, especially for manual workers. The impact of information technology is likely to lead to new patterns of work organisation, and affect the formation and structure of groups.

The concept of 'role' is important to the functioning of groups, and for an understanding of group processes and behaviour. It is through role differentiation that the structure of work groups and relationships among members is established. Role expectations may be established formally, they may be informal or they may be self-established. Inadequate or inappropriate role definition can result in role conflict including: role incompatibility, role ambiguity, role overload and role underload. Role conflict can result in role stress. It is important that the manager makes every effort to minimise role conflict and the causes of role stress.

Review and discussion questions

1. What is a group? Explain the importance of group values and norms, and give practical examples from within your own organisation.
2. Explain what is meant by a 'linking-pin' process of group membership. Illustrate your answer with a simple diagram.
3. Distinguish between formal and informal groups. What functions do groups serve in an organisation?
4. Identify different stages in group development and maturity. What other factors influence the cohesiveness of work groups? Give examples by reference to a work group to which you belong.
5. Assess the impact of technology as a determinant of group behaviour and performance. What action might be taken by management to help remove some of the alienating aspects of technology?
6. What is meant by the role structure of an organisation? Construct a diagram which shows your own role-set within a work situation. Give examples of informal role expectations to which you are, or have been, a party.
7. Explain different forms of role conflict which can result in role stress. Give an account of a work situation in which you have experienced role conflict/role stress. As manager, what action would you have taken in an attempt to rectify the situation?
8. What are the characteristics of an effective work group? As a manager, how would you attempt to develop effective group relationships and performance?

Assignment

Attempt, *preferably*, to observe a small group or project team at work; *alternatively*, recall the working of any small group of which you have recently been a member.

  (a) Explain the extent to which the group progressed through the stages of: forming; storming; norming; performing.

  (b) Complete the following grid by giving a tick in the appropriate box to denote each contribution by individual members.

Names of group members (or reference numbers)

Forming					
Storming					
Norming					
Performing					

  (ii) (a) Give examples of the group values or norms which constituted 'proper' behaviour of group members.

      (b) Explain sanctions applied to those members who did not conform to the group norms and the apparent effectiveness of these sanctions.

  (iii) Explain the factors which influenced the cohesiveness of the group.

  (iv) Give your views, with supporting reasons, on:

(a) the apparent satisfaction derived by individuals from membership of the group; and

(b) the effectiveness of the group as a whole.

Case study

BACKGROUND INFORMATION

Hovertec PLC is a large public company which has been manufacturing civilian and military helicopters for nearly 50 years. The company is very successful in its field and during 198–/198–achieved total sales of over £280 million. Profits before taxation exceeded £16½ million. Hovertec PLC employs over 6000 people, most of whom work in three manufacturing plants which are situated in South-West England, Scotland and Northern Ireland.

The company has developed two main types of helicopters since World War 2. These are the 'Falcon' range of small helicopters, which are sold to civilian operators, and the 'SX/Hawk' range of small and large military helicopters which are produced for government defence projects. Some export orders of 'SX/Hawk' helicopters are manufactured for NATO countries and other friendly countries. The precise number and size of Ministry of Defence contracts is not published and is regarded as classified information by Hovertec PLC.

Nevertheless, it is possible to gain some insight into the close relationship between the Ministry of Defence and the company from the details of the research and development (R&D) expenditure which is published in the Hovertec PLC Annual Report and Accounts. During 198–/ 8–, the R&D expenditure exceeded £43 million, of which £13 million was 'raised from private venture expenditure', £2½ million was 'funded in civilian helicopter sales prices' and £28 million was 'covered by classified research contracts'. All the research and development projects as well as all the military and some civilian contracts, are undertaken at the largest plant in South-West England. The remaining civilian helicopter contracts are shared between the two smaller factories in Scotland and Northern Ireland.

The Manufacture of a Helicopter

Without going into technical details, the manufacture of a helicopter can be divided into five inter-connected processes:

- (i) *The power unit*, which 'drives' the helicopter like an engine drives a motor car.
- (ii) *The helicopter loom*, which is an inter-woven collection of between 1200 and 2000 insulated copper wires and electrical cables, connecting the power unit with the various 'control' switches, dials, buttons and levers in the cockpit and passenger/crew compartment, and can be compared, in human terms, with the function of the spinal cord in linking the brain with the arms and legs, etc.
- (iii) *The external rotor blades*, which are mounted over the cockpit and passenger/crew compartment, and also above the tail of the helicopter.
- (iv) *The cockpit and passenger/crew compartment*, which has a different lay-out, services and accessories (viz. electronic weapon systems), depending on whether the helicopter is intended for civilian or military purposes.

(v) *The superstructure or 'shell'*, which encases the helicopter in a similar manner as the 'bodywork' on a motor car.

Although the latest technology is used in these production and assembly processes, the manufacture of a complete helicopter is a relatively slow process, taking 3 weeks for a civilian unit and 4 weeks for the larger, more sophisticated military helicopter. The main 'bottle-neck' in the process is the long time taken to assemble the helicopter loom and complete the 1200–2000 connections between the power unit and the numerous helicopter systems and services.

Assembling a Helicopter Loom

Because of the complexity of the task and the high risk of error, the assembly of each helicopter loom is normally carried out by one loom technician who takes up to two weeks (10 working days) to assemble a complete loom unit. Production output is maintained by a team of 24 loom technicians who work in two shifts of 12 technicians per shift. The loom technicians are all qualified maintenance fitters who have received extensive training from the company in loom-assembly procedures. They are the highest-paid section of the workforce after the supervisors and management, and they receive other benefits, such as membership of the company pension scheme, free BUPA medical insurance and additional holiday entitlement which is related to length of service with the company. All of these technicians are men, aged between 36 and 50 years with between 8 and 15 years service with the company. Many were recruited from either the Royal Navy or the Army Engineering Corps, where they received their basic training as maintenance fitters. This form of recruitment is adopted, firstly, because the loom technicians help to assemble both civilian and military helicopters and possible security risks have to be minimised on Ministry of Defence contracts. Secondly, the majority of Hovertec PLC managers possess Army or Naval backgrounds and strong links are maintained with the Armed Services. Perhaps the one striking difference between the working conditions at the Hovertec PLC factory in South-West England and those at their previous employment in the Armed Services is that all the loom technicians belong to a trade union which is recognised by the company. Although in practice the Hovertec PLC management frequently circumvent the union representatives by informing the workforce directly of changes in procedures, policy, etc., using 'briefing' procedures.

An improved Helicopter Loom assembly method

The 198– company Corporate Plan concluded that: 'Because of the constricting squeeze on defence projects and on the finances of civilian helicopter operators, which appears likely to continue until the world recession ends and general demand picks up, future activity in the three factories will be at a lower level during the next two to three years than seemed likely a few years ago.'

A detailed cost-cutting exercise was introduced on the strength of this plan, with particular emphasis on the helicopter loom workshop. For example all overtime working was withdrawn in September 198–   Meanwhile, the Research and Development Laboratories had divised a radically new method of assembling helicopter looms which, under pilot-scheme conditions, reduced the assembly time from 2 weeks (10 working days) to 3 working days. The new method had the added advantage of allowing unskilled labour to be employed on loom assembly.

Instead of one technician assembling a single loom, by following a blue-print in a painstaking way, the new method relies upon a team of five operatives working together and following a sequence of 'instructions' provided by a computer. The 1200–2000 insulated copper wires and elec-trical cables are previously 'colour coded' in terms of the ten main helicopter operating systems. Each operative is given responsibility for two sets of colour-coded wires and cables and is required to thread the leads of one colour through the loom, one at a time, by following a 'map' which is set out on a personal visual display unit. The total computerised lay-out, which appears on a separate large screen, resembles a coloured map of the London Underground 'Tube' system. For example, as one operative threads each blue electrical cable through the loom, a blue light flicks on as each correct 'station' is reached. If an error is made, the appropriate light fails to appear and a buzzing alarm sounds continuously until the mistake is corrected and the correct 'route' is re-established. At the same time, the computer-directed system can also be used for the other 'colour-coded' electrical connections and the team is therefore able to assemble the loom simultaneously, without slowing down or interfering with each other's work.

Further trials conducted by the Research and Development Laboratories indicated that small groups of five female workers achieved, on average, 40 per cent higher productivity than similar teams of male operatives. The highest productivity was consistently achieved under laboratory conditions by a team of 16–17 year old female school-leavers, who were permitted to choose their working partners and were also allowed to change from one 'colour code' to another whenever they became bored with one colour or started to make errors. This team was given ten-minute 'rest pauses' every hour to change 'colour codes' and was supervised by a member of the Research and Development Laboratory team, who also collected data on the group's productivity, etc.

Proposed changes in the helicopter loom workshop

Within six months, a decision was taken by the Hovertec PLC senior management to transfer the new computerised system pilot-scheme to the loom workshop on a 3 months trial basis. Management informed the work-force about the proposed trials beforehand and the loom technicians accepted the proposed change after receiving a personal assurance that no redundancies would occur as a result of the trials. The company wrote to their trade union about 10 days later, during the week when the trials began, to inform them of the new situation; and also pointed out that the trials would allow full-time employment to be offered to five female school-leavers, who would otherwise be out of work.

Outcome of the trials

Within two weeks of the new computerised system being installed, three of the five girls in the work group handed in their notice because of continual abuse from and arguments with the loom technicians. Productivity fell far below the expected targets on every day after the first loom was completed (in 4 days). The cause of low productivity was invariably due to breakdowns of equipment (loss of VDU pictures was the most frequent fault) which, according to the Research and Development Department, was the direct result of vandalism. A serious argument broke out on one occasion between a loom technician and the Research and Development Supervisor, who had earlier asked the technician to leave the VDU area and return to his own work-area, and the outcome was that disciplinary action had to be taken against the loom technician.

Three days later, the trade union representing the loom technicians advised the company that the men were unwilling to work alongside the girls on classified defence contracts in future. The reason given was that the girls were considered to be irresponsible and were more of a 'security risk' than the service-trained loom technicians. Management were swift to point out that none of the girls possessed any expertise in engineering or electronic systems and, in fact, three of the girls were close relatives of different loom technicians.

Output in the loom workshop fell during April and May and the company began to fall behind on outstanding defence contracts. A senior Ministry of defence official visited the plant in South-West England to advise senior management of the 'Whitehall View' that the new computerised loom assembly trials should be suspended on all defence contract helicopters until further notice.

(i) Using your knowledge of different approaches to organisation and management, comment on the Research and Development Laboratory trials carried out by Hovertec with the team of young, female workers.
(ii) Discuss the conditions which contributed to the cohesiveness of the loom technicians as a work group.
(iii) What factors might explain the difficulties between the group of loom technicians and the team of female workers?
(iv) What action would you propose should be taken by the management of Hovertec?

Notes and references

1. Drake, R. I. and Smith, P. J. *Behavioural Science in Industry*, McGraw-Hill (1973) p. 46.
2. Schein, E. H. *Organizational Psychology*, Third edition, Prentice-Hall (1980) p. 145.
3. Roethlisberger, F. J. and Dickson, W. J. *Management and the Worker*, Harvard University Press (1939).
4. Trist, E. L. *et al. Organizational Choice*, Tavistock Publications (1963).
5. Likert, R. *New Patterns of Management*, McGraw-Hill (1961) p. 38.
6. Likert, R. *The Human Organization*, McGraw-Hill (1967).
7. Dubin, R. *The World of Work*, Prentice-Hall (1958).
8. Argyle, M. *The Social Psychology of Work*, Penguin (1974).
9. See, for example: Argyris, C. *Integrating the Individual and the Organization*, Wiley (1964).
10. Seashore, S. E. *Group Cohesiveness in the Industrial Work Group*, Institute for Social Research, University of Michigan (1954).
11. Argyle, M. *The Social Psychology of Work*, Penguin (1974).
12. See, for example: Jay, A. *Corporation Man*, Penguin (1975) In an amusing historical account of the development of different forms of groups, Jay suggests that ten is the basic size of human grouping.

13. Walker, C. R. and Guest, R. H. *The Man on the Assembly Line*, Harvard University Press (1952). See also: Walker, C. R., Guest, R. H. and Turner, A. N. *The Foreman on the Assembly Line*, Harvard University Press (1956).
14. Bass, B. M. and Ryterband, E. C. *Organizational Psychology*, Second edition, Allyn and Bacon (1979).
15. Tuckman, B. W. 'Development Sequence in Small Groups', *Psychological Bulletin*, vol. 63, 1965, pp. 384–99.
16. Cartwright, D. 'The Nature of Group Cohesiveness', in Cartwright, D. and Zander, D. A. (eds) *Group Dynamics: Research and Theory*, Harper and Row (1968) pp. 91–109.
17. See, for example: Staw, B. M. 'Organizational Psychology and the Pursuit of the Happy/Productive Worker', *California Management Review*, vol. 28, no. 4, Summer 1986, pp. 40–53.
18. For example, see: Schein, E. H. *Organizational Psychology*, Third edition, Prentice-Hall (1980).
19. Walker, C. R. and Guest, R. H. *The Man on the Assembly Line*, Harvard University Press (1952).
20. Scott, W. H. *et al. Technical Change and Industrial Relations*, Liverpool University Press (1956).
21. Sayles, L. R. *Behavior of Industrial Work Groups*, Wiley (1958).
22. Lupton, T. *On the Shop Floor*, Pergamon Press (1963).
23. Goldthorpe, J. H. *et al. The Affluent Worker*, Cambridge University Press (1968).
24. See, for example: Schein, E. H. *Organizational Psychology*, Third edition, Prentice-Hall (1980).
25. For example, see: Dunkerley, D. *The Foreman: Aspects of Task and Structure*, Routledge and Kegan Paul (1975).
26. See, for example: Handy, C. B. *Understanding Organizations*, Third edition, Penguin (1985).
27. Whyte, W. F. *Human Relations in the Restaurant Industry*, McGraw-Hill (1948).
28. Filley, A. C. and House, R. J. *Managerial Process and Organizational Behavior*, Scott Foresman (1969).
29. Kahn, R. L. *et al. Organizational Stress*, Wiley (1964).
30. Hall, K. and Savery, L. K. 'Stress Management', *Management Decision*, vol. 25, no. 6, 1987, pp. 29–35.
31. Ibid.
32. Miner, J. B. *Management Theory*, Macmillan (1971).

14. GROUP PROCESSES AND BEHAVIOUR

If the manager is to make the most effective use of groups, then it is important to have an understanding of group processes and behaviour. It is necessary to understand the nature of group functions and roles, and factors which influence group performance and effectiveness. Attention must be given to the analysis of behaviour of individuals in group situations. The manager must be aware of the functioning and operation of work groups.

Objectives

To: (i)   Explain patterns of communication networks in groups;
    (ii) Examine methods of analysing behaviour of individuals in group situations;
    (iii) Distinguish different functions and member roles in the study of group behaviour;
    (iv) Explain the use of frameworks of behavioural analysis in groups;
    (v) Assess the nature of group performance and effectiveness;
    (vi) Explain the nature and value of group dynamics;
    (vii) Recognise the importance of understanding the functioning and operation of work groups.

PATTERNS OF COMMUNICATION

Group performance and the satisfaction derived by individuals are influenced by the interactions among members of the group. The level of interaction is determined by the structuring of channels of communication. Laboratory research by *Bavelas*[1] and subsequent studies by other researchers such as *Leavitt*[2] have resulted in the design of a series of communication networks.

These networks were based on groups of five members engaged in a number of problem-solving tasks. Members were permitted to communicate with each other by written notes only, and not everyone was always free to communicate with everyone else.

Main communication networks

There are five main types of communication networks – Wheel, Circle, All-channel, Y and Chains (*see* Fig. 14.1).

The wheel, also sometimes known as the star, is the most centralised network. This network is most efficient for simple tasks. Problems are solved more quickly with fewer mistakes and with fewer information flows. But as the problems of the group become more complex and demands on the link person increase, effectiveness suffers. The link person is at the centre of the network and acts as the focus of activities and information flows, and the co-ordinator of group tasks. The central person is perceived

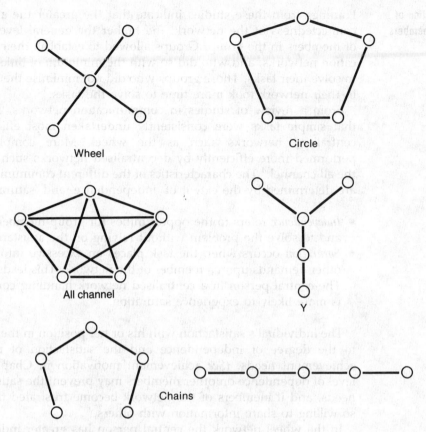

Fig. 14.1 Communication networks

as leader of the group and experiences a high level of satisfaction. However, for members on the periphery, the wheel is the least satisfying network.

The circle is a more decentralised network. Overall it is less efficient. The group is unorganised, with low leadership predictability. Performance tends to be slow and erratic. However, the circle is quicker than the wheel in solving complex problems, and also copes with change or new tasks more efficiently. The circle network is most satisfying for all the members. Decision making is likely to involve some degree of participation.

The all-channel network involves full discussion and participation. This network appears to work best where a high level of interaction is required among all members of the group in order to solve complex problems. Leadership predictability is very low. There is a fairly high level of satisfaction for members. The all-channel network may not stand up well under pressure, in which case it will either disintegrate or reform into a wheel network.

A '*Y*' *or chain network* might be appropriate for more simple problem-solving tasks, requiring little interaction among members of the group. These networks are more centralised, with information flows along a predetermined channel. Leadership predictability is high to moderate. There is a low to moderate level of satisfaction for members.

Satisfaction of group members

Findings from these studies indicate that the greater the amount of inter-connectedness of the network, the higher the general level of satisfaction of members in the group. Groups allowed to establish their own communication networks, and who did so with the minimum of links, took less time to solve their tasks. Those groups who did not minimise the number of links in their network took more time to solve the tasks.[3]

From a review of studies in communication networks, *Shaw* confirmed that simple tasks were consistently undertaken most efficiently in more centralised networks such as the wheel. More complex tasks were performed more efficiently by decentralised networks such as the circle or the all-channel.[4] The characteristics of the different communication networks are determined by the extent of 'independence' and 'saturation'.

- *Independence* refers to the opportunities for group members to take action and to solve the problem without relying on the assistance of others.
- *Saturation* occurs when the task places an excessive information load or other demands upon a member of the network. This leads to inefficiency. The central person in a centralised network handling complex problems is more likely to experience saturation.

The individual's satisfaction with his or her position in the network relates to the degree of independence and the satisfaction of recognition and achievement needs. (*See* achievement motivation in Chapter 11.) A high level of dependence on other members may prevent the satisfaction of these needs, and if members of the network become frustrated they may not be so willing to share information with others.

In the wheel network the central person has greater independence than the other members, but in the circle network all members have a moderate degree of dependence upon each other. Leadership is also important because this can influence the opportunity for independent action by the group members, and can also control the possibility of saturation.

Implications for the manager

Despite the artificiality of these communication network studies, they do have certain implications for the manager. A knowledge of the findings may be applied to influence the patterns of communication in meetings and committees. They also provide a reasonable representation of the situations that might apply in large organisations. Members of the group may be located in different parts of the organisation or have only limited opportunities for face-to-face contact with each other. The majority of communications may only be indirect or by means of written notes or telephone.

It will be interesting for the manager to observe the patterns of communication adopted by different groups in different situations. The manager can also note how communication networks change over time and how they relate to the performance of the group.

No one network is likely to be effective for a range of given problems. It is the manager's job to ensure the most appropriate communication network for the performance of a given task. Problems which require a high level of interaction among members of the group may not be handled efficiently if there are inadequate channels of communication or sharing of information.

The choice of a particular communication network may involve trade-offs between the performance of the work group and the satisfaction of its members.

ANALYSIS OF BEHAVIOUR IN GROUPS

In order to understand and to influence the functioning and operation of a group it is necessary to study patterns of interaction, and the parts played by individual members. Two of the main methods of analysing the behaviour of individuals in group situations are sociometry and interaction process analysis.

SOCIOMETRY

Originally developed by *Moreno*,[5] sociometry is a method of indicating the feelings of acceptance or rejection among members of a group. A sociogram (*see* Fig. 14.2) is a diagrammatical illustration of the pattern of interpersonal relationships derived from sociometry. The sociogram depicts the choices, preferences, likes or dislikes, and interactions between individual members of a group. It can also be used to display the structure of the group and to record the observed frequency and/or duration of contacts among members.

The basis of sociometry, however, is usually 'buddy rating' or 'peer rating'. Each member in the group is asked to nominate or to rate, privately, other members in terms of some given context or characteristic, for example with whom they communicate, how influential or how likeable. Questions may relate to either work or social activities, for example: who would you most prefer or least prefer as a work-mate? or who would make a good leader of the group? or with whom would you choose and not choose to go on holiday?

Positive and negative choices may be recorded for each person, although sometimes positive choices only are required. The choices may be limited to a given number or they may be unlimited. Sometimes individuals may be asked to rank their choices.

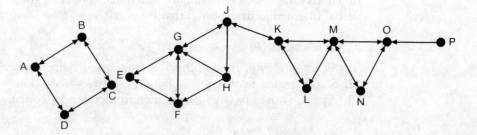

Fig. 14.2 A simple sociogram illustrating interaction among 15 members of a group. Positive choices only

(i)   G and M are popular (the stars) and most often chosen by members.
(ii) M is the link between two overlapping cliques, KML and MNO.
(iii) H and P are unpopular (isolated) and chosen least by members.
(iv) JKMO is a chain.
(v)   ABCD is a sub-group and separated from the rest of the members.

Constructing a sociogram

In constructing the sociogram the distance between the points may be arranged to indicate the degree of positive attraction. If two people choose each other the points representing these individuals will be closer together than if neither person chooses the other. If both positive and negative choices are recorded some distinguishing feature, such as different colours or the use of solid and broken lines, can be used to differentiate clearly between selection and rejection.

Members' choices could be tabulated, but the advantage of the sociogram is that it provides a visual description of the sociometric structure of a group. It indicates cliques and sub-groups, compatibility, and members who are popular, isolated or who act as links. However, sociograms can become complicated and unwieldy especially for larger groups or where there is an unlimited number of nominations, if rankings are given, or where both positive and negative choices are recorded. Individuals express desired choices and may indicate what they feel should happen. This does not always correspond with actual patterns of behaviour.

Buddy rating is used sometimes as part of a staff selection procedure, usually as a basis for judgement of candidates' 'sociability' rating, discussed in Chapter 7. This method can only be used, of course, if a group of candidates have been together long enough to become well acquainted with each other.

INTERACTION ANALYSIS

The basic assumption behind interaction analysis is that behaviour in groups may be analysed from the viewpoint of its function. This approach has developed largely from the work of *Bales* on methods for the study of small groups. This aim is to provide ways of describing group process and indications of factors influencing the process.[6]

In Bales's, 'Interaction Process Analysis' every act of behaviour is categorised, as it occurs, under twelve headings. These differentiate between 'task' functions and 'socio-emotional' functions. The categories apply to both verbal interaction and non-verbal interaction.

A. Socio-Emotional: Positive Reactions

1. *Shows solidarity*, raises others' status, gives help, reward.
2. *Shows tension release*, jokes, laughs, shows satisfaction.
3. *Agrees*, shows passive acceptance, understands, concurs, complies.

B. Task: Attempted Answers

4. *Gives suggestion*, direction, implying autonomy for others.
5. *Gives opinion*, evaluation, analysis, expresses feeling, wish.
6. *Gives orientation*, information, repeats, clarifies, confirms.

C. Task: Questions

7. *Asks for orientation*, information, repetition, confirmation.
8. *Asks for opinion*, evaluation, analysis, expression of feeling.
9. *Asks for suggestion*, direction, possible ways of action.

D. Socio-Emotional: Negative Reactions

10. *Disagrees*, shows passive rejection, formality, withholds help.
11. *Shows tension*, asks for help, withdraws out of field.
12. *Shows antagonism*, deflates others' status, defends or asserts self.

In an extension of interaction process analysis, Bales gives 27 typical group roles which are based on various combinations of these original main behavioural categories.[7]

Task and maintenance functions

If the group is to be effective, then, whatever its structure or the pattern of interrelationships among members, there are two main sets of functions or processes that must be undertaken – task functions and maintenance functions.

- *Task functions* are directed towards problem solving, the accomplishment of the tasks of the group and the achievement of its goals. Most of the task-oriented behaviour will be concerned with 'production' activities, or the exchange and evaluation of ideas and information.
- *Maintenance functions* are concerned with the emotional life of the group and directed towards building and maintaining the group as an effective working unit. Most of the maintenance-oriented behaviour will be concerned with relationships among group members, giving encouragement and support, maintaining cohesiveness and the resolution of conflict.

Task and maintenance functions may be performed either by the group leader or by members. Ultimately it is the leader's responsibility to ensure that both sets of functions are carried out and the right balance is achieved between them. The appropriate combination of task-oriented behaviour and maintenance-oriented behaviour is essential to the success and continuity of the group.

In addition to these two types of behaviour members of a group may say or do something in attempting to satisfy some personal need or goal. The display of behaviour in this way is termed *self-oriented behaviour*. This gives a classification of three main types of functional behaviour which can be exhibited by individual members of a group: task-oriented, maintenance-oriented and self-oriented.

Classification of member roles

A popular system for the classification of member roles in the study of group behaviour is that devised originally by *Benne* and *Sheats*.[8] The description of member roles performed in well-functioning groups is classified into three broad headings: group task roles, group maintenance roles and individual roles.

Group task roles These assume that the task of the group is to select, define and solve common problems. Any of the roles may be performed by the various members or the group leader.

(i)	The *initiator-contributor*	(vii)	The *co-ordinator*
(ii)	The *information seeker*	(viii)	The *orienter*
(iii)	The *opinion seeker*	(ix)	The *evaluator-critic*
(iv)	The *information giver*	(x)	The *energiser*
(v)	The *opinion giver*	(xi)	The *procedural technician*
(vi)	The *elaborator*	(xii)	The *recorder*

Group building and maintenance roles The analysis of member-functions is oriented towards activities which build group-centred attitudes, or maintain group-centred behaviour. Contributions may involve a number of roles, and members or the leader may perform each of these roles.

(i)	The *encourager*	(v)	The *standard setter or ego ideal*
(ii)	The *harmoniser*	(vi)	The *group-observer and commentor*
(iii)	The *compromiser*	(vii)	The *follower*
(iv)	The *gate-keeper and expediter*		

Individual roles These are directed towards the satisfaction of personal needs. Their purpose is not related to either group task or to the group functioning.

(i)	The *aggressor*	(v)	The *playboy*
(ii)	The *blocker*	(vi)	The *dominator*
(iii)	The *recognition-seeker*	(vii)	The *help-seeker*
(iv)	The *self-confessor*	(viii)	The *special interest pleader*

FRAMEWORKS OF BEHAVIOURAL ANALYSIS

Several frameworks have been designed for observers to categorise patterns of verbal and non-verbal behaviour of group members. Observers chart members' behaviour on specially designed forms. These forms may be used to focus on single individuals, or used to record the total group interaction with no indication of individual behaviour.

The system of categorisation may distinguish between different behaviours in terms of the functions they are performing. The completed observation forms can be used as a basis for discussion of individual or group performance in terms of the strengths/weaknesses of different functional behaviour.

In the following framework there are two observation sheets, one covering six types of leader–member *task-function behaviour* and the other covering six types of leader–member *group building and maintenance function behaviour*.

Task functions

1. *Initiating*: Proposing tasks or goals; defining a group problem, suggesting a procedure or ideas for solving a problem.
2. *Information or opinion seeking*: Requesting facts, seeking relevant information about a group concern, asking for suggestions and ideas.
3. *Information or opinion giving*: Offering facts, providing relevant information about group concern; stating a belief; giving suggestions or ideas.

4. *Clarifying or elaborating*: Interpreting or reflecting ideas and suggestions; clearing up confusions; indicating alternatives and issues
before the group, giving examples.

5. *Summarising*: Pulling together related ideas, restating suggestions
after group has discussed them; offering a decision or conclusion for
the group to accept or reject.

6. *Consensus testing*: Sending up 'trial balloons' to see if group is nearing
a conclusion; checking with group to see how much agreement has
been reached.

Group building and maintenance functions

1. *Encouraging*: Being friendly, warm and responsive to others,
accepting others and their contributions, regarding others by giving
them an opportunity for recognition.

2. *Expressing group feelings*: Sensing feeling, mood, relationships within
the group, sharing one's own feelings with other members.

3. *Harmonising*: Attempting to reconcile disagreements, reducing
tension through 'pouring oil on troubled waters', getting people to
explore their differences.

4. *Compromising*: When own idea or status is involved in a conflict
offering to compromise own position, admitting error, disciplining
oneself to maintain group cohesion.

5. *Gate-keeping*: Attempting to keep communication channels open,
facilitating the participation of others; suggesting procedure for
sharing opportunity to discuss group problems.

6. *Setting standards*: Expressing standards for group to achieve, applying
standards in evaluating group functioning and production.

Source: National Training Laboratory, Washington DC (1952).

Frameworks of behaviour analysis concerned with 'collecting behavioural
data' as a basis for interactive skills training are given by *Rackham, Honey* and
Colbert.[9] They emphasise the importance of identifying behaviours that are
susceptible to development and change. For example, Fig. 14.3 relates to an
activity which members agree serves a useful purpose, and categorises
behaviours of importance to the group situation.

In a second framework, Fig. 14.4, the categories are paired to provide a
framework of behavioural feedback and a link to supervisory style.

**Use of different
frameworks**

Different frameworks use a different number of categories for studying
behaviour in groups. The interaction analysis method can become complex,
especially if non-verbal behaviour is included. Many of the categories in
different frameworks may at first sight appear to be very similar.

It is important, therefore, to keep the framework simple, and easy to
understand and complete. The observer's own personality, values and attitudes can influence the categorisation of behaviour. For these reasons it is
preferable to use trained observers, and wherever possible and appropriate
to use more than one observer for each group. The observers can then
compare the level of consistency between their categorisations.

Observation sheets can be designed to suit the particular requirements of
the group situation and the nature of the activity involved. An example of

Start time: 14.50   Finish time: 15.35   Any time absent: None

SEEKING SUGGESTIONS (ideas and proposals)	卌 卌 I / II		II	IIII	II		I
CAUGHT PROPOSALS	III	卌 II	卌 卌 III	IIII		卌 卌 卌 / 卌 II	卌 卌 / 卌 IIII
ESCAPED PROPOSALS	I	I	I	IIII	卌 III / II	I	
BUILDING	I	I		III			
DISAGREEING and CRITICISING	III	卌 III	卌 卌 IIII / II	II	卌 I	III	
SEEKING CONFIRMATION (agreement and support)	卌 卌 / 卌 I	III	卌 卌 III / I	II	III	卌 卌 / II	
SUPPORTING	II	II	卌 卌 卌 IIII III / I				卌 卌
SEEKING CLARIFICATION EXPLANATION AND INFORMATION	卌 卌 / 卌 II	卌 卌 / 卌	卌 卌 / I	卌 II	卌 卌 / III	III	III
OTHER BEHAVIOUR (including providing info. and explanations in response to requests)	卌 IIII	卌 卌 / II	卌 卌 / II	卌 卌 / 卌 III	卌 卌 / II	卌 I	卌 卌 / 卌 卌
OFFERING (uninvited) EXPLANATIONS, REASONS and DIFFICULTIES	II	卌 卌 / I	卌 卌 / 卌 卌 / I	卌	III	III	卌 II
UNSTRUCTURED CONTRIBUTIONS (thinking aloud, rambling on and contradicting oneself, etc.)	II	卌	I	I	卌	III	IIII
MULTI-SPEAK (Talking over and interrupting)	卌 卌 / 卌 II / I	卌 II	卌 卌 / 卌 / 卌	卌 III III / II	II	II	卌 卌 / 卌 卌 / II

Fig. 14.3 Behaviour analysis in a group situation

(Extracted from Rackham, N., Honey, P. and Colbert, M. J., *Developing Interactive Skills*, Wellen's Publishing (1971), p. 99. Reproduced with permission of the publishers.)

a reasonably simple, ten-point observation sheet used by the author is given in Fig. 14.5.

Where appropriate it may be helpful to note the initial seating, or standing, arrangements of the group. This will help in the identification of group members. Depending on the nature of the activity involved, it might also be possible to indicate main channels of interaction among individuals

SUPPORTING
DISAGREEING
BUILDING
CRITICISING
BRINGING IN
SHUTTING OUT
INNOVATING
SOLIDIFYING
ADMITTING DIFFICULTY
DEFENDING/ATTACKING
GIVING INFORMATION
SEEKING INFORMATION
OTHER

Fig. 14.4 A framework of behavioural feedback

(Extracted from Rackham, N., Honey, P. and Colbert, M. J., *Developing Interactive Skills*, Wellen's Publishing (1971). Reproduced with permission of the publishers.)

– for example to whom eye contact, hand movements, or ideas and questions are most frequently directed. A note could also be made of changes in arrangements during, and at the end of, the activity.

Headings of the observation sheet are not necessarily exclusive. For example, leadership could be included under Taking Initiative, or under Performing Group Roles. Similarly, the role of humorist could be included under Performing Group Roles, but might also appropriately be included under the heading of Harmonising.

Observers will tend to use their own methods for completing the sheet. For example, a simple stroke or tick for each contribution and perhaps a thick stroke for a particularly significant contribution. Some observers might use some other distinguishing mark to indicate non-verbal behaviour such as body movements, smiles or eye contact. The most important point, however, is that the charting should not become too complex. The observer should feel happy with the framework and be capable of explaining the entries in a meaningful way. Where more than one observer is present there should be some degree of consistency between them.

Nature of group
Nature of activity
Date   Name of observer(s)

Initial arrangement of group

Names of group members (or reference letters)

	A	B	C	D	E	F
Taking initiative – e.g. attempted leadership, seeking suggestions, offering directions						
Brainstorming – e.g. offering ideas or suggestions however valid						
Offering positive ideas – e.g. making helpful suggestions, attempting to problem-solve						
Drawing in others – e.g. encouraging contributions, seeking ideas and opinions						
Being responsive to others – e.g. giving encouragement and support, building on ideas						
Harmonising – e.g. acting as peacemaker, calming things down, compromising						
Challenging – e.g. seeking justification, showing disagreement in *constructive* way						
Being obstructive – e.g. criticising, putting others down, blocking contributions						
Clarifying/summarising – e.g. linking ideas, checking progress, clarifying objectives/proposals						
Performing group roles – e.g. spokesperson, recorder, time keeper, humorist						
Other comments						

Fig. 14.5 Observation sheet for behaviour in groups

GROUP PERFORMANCE AND EFFECTIVENESS

Groups are an essential feature in the life of the organisation. It is, however, difficult to draw any firm conclusions from a comparison between individual and group performance. An example of this can be seen from a consideration of decision making. Certain groups, such as committees, may be concerned more specifically with decision making, but all groups must make some decisions. Group decision making can be costly and time consuming, but would appear to offer a number of advantages.

- Groups can bring together a range of complementary knowledge and expertise.
- Interaction among members can have a 'snowball' effect and provoke further thoughts in the minds of others.
- Group discussion leads to the evaluation and correction of possible decisions.
- Provided full participation has been facilitated, decisions will have the acceptance of most members and they are more likely to be committed to decisions made and their implementation.

Risky-shift phenomenon

One might expect, therefore, a higher standard of decision making to result from group discussion. However, on one hand there is the danger of compromise and decisions being made in line with the 'highest common view'; and on the other hand is the phenomenon of the so-called *risky-shift*. This suggests that instead of the group taking fewer risks and making safer or more conservative decisions, the reverse is often the case. There is a tendency for groups to make more risky decisions than would individual members of the group on their own. Studies suggest that people working in groups generally advocate more risky alternatives than if they were making an individual decision on the same problem.[10]

Presumably, this is because members do not feel the same sense of responsibility for group decisions or their outcomes. 'A decision which is everyone's is the responsibility of no one.' Other explanations offered for the risky-shift phenomenon include:

(i) people inclined to take risks are more influential in group discussions than more conservative people; and
(ii) risk taking is regarded as a desirable cultural characteristic which is more likely to be expressed in a social situation such as group working.[11]

However, groups do appear to work well in the evaluation of ideas and to be more effective than individuals for problem-solving tasks requiring a range of knowledge and expertise. From a review of the research *Shaw* suggests that the evidence supports the view that groups produce more solutions and better solutions to problems than do individuals.[12]

BRAINSTORMING

A brainstorming approach involves the group adopting a 'freewheeling' attitude and generating as many ideas as possible, the more wild or apparently far-fetched the better.[13] There are a number of basic procedures for brainstorming.

- The initial emphasis is on the quantity of ideas generated, not the quality of ideas.

- No individual ideas are criticised or rejected at this stage, however wild or fanciful they may appear.
- Members are encouraged to elaborate or build on ideas expressed by others, and to bounce suggestions off one another.
- There is no comment or evaluation of any particular idea until all ideas have been generated.

Brainstorming is based on the assumptions that creative thinking is achieved best by encouraging the natural inclinations of group members and the free association of ideas; and that quantity of ideas will lead to quality of ideas.

Effectiveness of brainstorming groups

One might reasonably expect that members of a brainstorming group would produce more creative problem-solving ideas than if the same members worked alone as individuals. Availability of time is an important factor. Over a longer period of time the group may produce more ideas through brainstorming than individuals.[14] Perhaps surprisingly, however, there appears to be doubt about the effectiveness of brainstorming groups over an individual working under the same conditions. Research findings suggest that brainstorming groups can inhibit creative thinking.

Taylor compared 12 groups of four people who were participating together, with 12 'groups' of four people working separately. Performance was measured in terms of the number of alternative solutions to a series of given problems, generated through 'brainstorming' over a given period of time. In each case the group with people working on their own produced more solutions and generally of a higher quality.[15]

In another study, by *Maginn* and *Harris*, 152 students were divided into groups of four and asked to brainstorm two problems. Some of the groups were informed that their ideas would be evaluated for originality and quality, and that they would be observed by judges, either from behind a one-way mirror or by tape recording. Other groups were told that although they would be listened to, their ideas would not be subject to evaluation.[16]

Although it was predicted that the groups facing evaluation would perform less well, the findings indicated that the performances of both sets of groups were similar. Maginn and Harris concluded that individual members put less effort into a task when responsibility for the outcome is shared with other members of the group. Unless this feeling of diminished responsibility can be overcome, individual brainstorming, although lonelier, is better.

VARIETY OF INTERRELATED FACTORS

Whatever the results of a comparison between individual and group performance, groups will always form part of the pattern of work organisation. It is a matter of judgement for the manager as to when, and how best, to use groups in the execution of work.

Any framework for viewing the performance and effectiveness of groups must take into account a variety of interrelated factors. These include:

- the composition, cohesiveness and maturity of the group;

- its structure, the clarification of role differentiation and channels of communication;
- patterns of interaction and group process, and attention to both task and maintenance functions;
- the task to be undertaken and nature of technology;
- management system and style of leadership;
- organisational processes and procedures;
- the social system of the group and the informal organisation; and
- the environment in which the group is operating.

These are the factors that the manager must attempt to influence in order to improve the effectiveness of the group. Ultimately, however, the performance of the group will be determined very largely by the characteristics and behaviour of its members.

GROUP DYNAMICS

Interest in the study of group process and behaviour has led to the development of group dynamics and a range of group training methods aimed at increasing group effectiveness through improving social interaction skills.

Group dynamics is the study of interactions and forces within small face-to-face groups.

One such method is *sensitivity training*, in which members of a group direct attention to the understanding of their own behaviour and to perceiving themselves as others see them. The objectives are usually stated as:

- to increase sensitivity (the ability to perceive accurately how others react to oneself);
- diagnostic ability (the skill of assessing behavioural relationships between others and reasons for such behaviour); and
- behavioural flexibility, or action skill (the ability to relate one's behaviour to the requirements of the situation).

T-GROUPS

A usual method of sensitivity training is the *T-group* (training group), sometimes called laboratory training.

A T-group has been defined as: 'an approach to human relations training which, broadly speaking, provides participants with an opportunity to learn more about themselves and their impact on others, and in particular to learn how to function more effectively in face-to-face situations.'[17]

The original form of a T-group is a small, leaderless, unstructured, face-to-face grouping. The group normally numbers between 8 to 12 members who are strangers to each other. A deliberate attempt is made to minimise any status differentials among members. There is no agenda or planned activities. Trainers are present to help guide the group, but not to take an active role or to act as formal leader. The agenda becomes the group's own behaviour in attempting to cope with the lack of structure or planned activities. Training is intended to concentrate on process rather than content,

411

that is on the feeling level of communication rather than the informational value of communication.

Faced with confusion and lack of direction, individuals will act in characteristic ways. With the guidance of the trainers these patterns of behaviour become the focus of attention for the group. Feedback received by individuals from other members of the group is the main mechanism for learning.

This feedback creates a feeling of anxiety and tension, and the individual's own self-examination leads to consideration of new values, attitudes and behaviour. Typically, the group meets for a $1\frac{1}{2}$ hour–2 hour session each day for up to a fortnight. The sessions are supported by related lectures, study groups, case studies and other exercises.

Self-insight in T-group process

A simple framework for looking at self-insight, which is used frequently to help individuals in the T-group process, is the 'Johari window' (Fig. 14.6). This classifies behaviour in matrix form between: what is known–unknown to self; and what is known–unknown to others.[18]

A central feature of the T-group is reduction of the individual's 'hidden' behaviour through self-disclosure and reduction of the 'blind' behaviour through feedback from others.

Hidden behaviour is that which the individual wishes to conceal from, or not to communicate to, other group members. An important role of the group is to establish whether members conceal too much, or too little, about themselves from other members.

The blind area includes mannerisms, gestures, tone of voice and represents behaviour of which the individual is unaware of the impact on others. The group must establish an atmosphere of openness and trust in order that hidden and blind behaviours are reduced and the public behaviour enhanced.

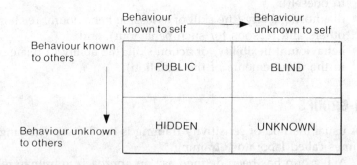

Fig. 14.6 The Johari window

Value and effectiveness of T-groups

Reactions to the value and effectiveness of T-group training are very mixed. Specific benefits and changes in behaviour from T-group training are listed by *Mangham* and *Cooper* as:

> *Receiving Communications*: more effort to understand, attentive listening
> *Relational Facility*: co-operative, easier to deal with
> *Awareness of Human Behaviour*: more analytic of others' actions, clear perceptions of people
> *Sensitivity to Group Behaviour*: more conscious of group process

Sensitivity to Others' Feelings: sensitivity to the needs and feelings of others

Acceptance of Other People: more tolerant, considerate, patient

Tolerant of New Information: willing to accept suggestions, less dogmatic[19]

However, the experience can be very disturbing and unpleasant, at least for some members. For example, participants have described it as: 'a blood-bath and a psychological nudist colony in which people are stripped bare to their attitudes'.[20]

T-group training is difficult to evaluate objectively and there is still a main problem of the extent to which training is transferred 'back home' to practical work situations. However, a number of studies do suggest that participation as a member of a T-group does increase interpersonal skills, induces change, and leads to open communications and more flexible behaviour.[21]

T-groups now take a number of different forms. Some place emphasis on the understanding of group processes, others place more emphasis on the development of the individual's self-awareness and feelings towards the behaviour of other people. They are now used frequently as a means of attempting to improve managerial development and organisational performance.

The *Blake* and *Mouton* managerial grid seminars, discussed in Chapter 9, can be seen as an applied, and refined, form of T-group. A number of different training packages have been designed, often under the broad heading of interpersonal skills, which are less disturbing for participants. The training often involves an analysis of group members' relationships with one another and the resolution of conflict.[22]

Synopsis

Group performance and the satisfaction derived by individuals are influenced by the interactions among members of the group. The level of interaction is determined by the channels of communication (communication networks). There are five main types of communication networks – wheel, circle, all-channel, Y and chains. Despite the artificiality of communication network studies, they do provide a reasonable representation of situations that might apply in large organisations. No one network is likely to be effective for a range of given problems, and the choice of a particular communication network may involve a trade-off between group performance and member satisfaction.

In order to understand and to influence the functioning and operation of a group, it is necessary to study the behaviour of individual members. Two main methods are (i) sociometry, and (ii) interaction analysis. Sociometry is usually based on 'buddy rating' or 'peer rating'. It is a method of indicating feelings of acceptance and/or rejection among members of a group. A sociogram gives a diagrammatical illustration of the pattern of interpersonal relationships derived from sociometry.

Interaction analysis is based on the assumption that behaviour in groups may be analysed from the viewpoint of its function or process. Two essential functions necessary for the success and continuity of a group are: (i) task-oriented behaviour; and (ii) maintenance-oriented behaviour. In addition, members of a group may display self-oriented behaviour. Several frameworks have been designed for observers to categorise patterns of verbal and non-verbal behaviour of group members. Observers chart members' behaviour on specially designed forms. Different frameworks use a different number of categories for studying behaviour in groups. It is important, however, that the frameworks do not become too complex.

Groups are an essential feature in the life of the organisation. It is, however, difficult to draw firm conclusions from a comparison between individual and group performance. Group decision making would appear to offer a number of advantages, but the 'risky-shift' phenomenon suggests that there is a tendency for groups to make more risky decisions than would individual members of the group on their own. There also appears to be some doubt about the effectiveness of brainstorming groups over an individual working under the same conditions. Viewing the performance and effectiveness of groups must take into account a variety of interrelated factors, especially the characteristics and behaviour of their members.

Interest in the study of group process and behaviour has led to the development of group dynamics and a range of group training methods aimed at improving social interaction skills. A usual method is the T-group. This approach provides participants with an opportunity to learn more about themselves and their impact on others. Reactions to the value and effectiveness of T-group training is mixed. There are a number of potential benefits but some participants can find the experience disturbing and unpleasant.

Review and discussion questions

1. Contrast different types of communication networks in small groups. Give examples of a situation in which each type of network is likely to be most appropriate.
2. What methods are available for analysing the behaviour of individuals in group situations? Assess the practical value to the manager of the analysis of group behaviour.
3. Explain what you understand by sociometry. How would you go about constructing a sociogram?
4. Distinguish between: (i) group task roles; (ii) group building and maintenance roles; and (iii) individual roles. Give examples of each type of these group member roles.
5. Suggest a framework for the categorisation of patterns of behaviour in group situations. What considerations need to be kept in mind when using such frameworks?
6. Explain what is meant by: (i) the risky-shift phenomenon; and (ii) brainstorming. Assess the likely standard of individual, compared with group, problem solving and decision making.
7. Explain the meaning and purpose of sensitivity training. Give your views on the practical value of group dynamics as a means of increasing the effectiveness of work groups.
8. In what ways might a manager expect to benefit from an understanding of the behaviour of people in work groups? Give practical examples relating to your own experience.

Assignment 1 Attempt, *preferably*, to observe a small group or project team at work; *alternatively*, next time you are involved in a small group discussion observe the members of your group.

(i) (a) Explain the nature of the *content* of the group's discussion and contrast this with the *process* of the discussion.

(b) Complete the following grid by giving a tick in the appropriate box to denote the behaviour of individual members in terms of:
- Group task roles;
- Group building and maintenance roles;
- Individual roles.

NAMES OF GROUP MEMBERS (OR REFERENCE NUMBERS)

							Totals
Group task roles							
Group building/ maintenance roles							
Individual roles							
Totals							

(ii) Explain the conclusions you draw concerning the conduct and apparent effectiveness of the group.

(iii) Depict the *communication network(s)* adopted by the group and comment on its apparent effectiveness.

Assignment 2 ## WILDERNESS SURVIVAL WORK SHEET

Here are twelve questions concerning personal survival in a wilderness situation. Your first task is *individually* to select the best of the three alternatives given under each item. Try to imagine yourself in the situation depicted. Assume that you are alone and have a minimum of equipment except where specified. The season is fall. The days are warm and dry, but the nights are cold.

After you have completed this task individually, you will again consider each question as a member of a small group. Your group will have the task of deciding, *by consensus*, the best alternative for each question. Do not change your individual answers, even if you change your mind in the group discussion. Both the individual and group solutions will later be compared with the 'correct' answers provided by a group of naturalists who conduct classes in woodland survival.

415

1. You have strayed from your party in trackless timber. You have no special signalling equipment. The best way to attempt to contact your friends is to:
   a. call 'help' loudly but in a low register.
   b. yell or scream as loud as you can.
   c. whistle loudly and shrilly.

2. You are in 'snake country'. Your best action to avoid snakes is to:
   a. make a lot of noise with your feet.
   b. walk softly and quietly.
   c. travel at night.

3. You are hungry and lost in wild country. The best rule for determining which plants are safe to eat (those you do not recognize) is to:
   a. try anything you see the birds eat.
   b. eat anything except plants with bright red berries.
   c. put a bit of the plant on your lower lip for five minutes; if it seems all right, try a little.

4. The day becomes hot and dry. You have a full canteen of water (about one litre) with you. You should:
   a. ration it – about a cupful a day.
   b. not drink until you stop for the night, then drink what you think you need.
   c. drink as much as you think you need when you need it.

5. Your water is gone; you become very thirsty. You finally come to a dried-up watercourse. Your best chance of finding water is to:
   a. dig anywhere in the stream bed.
   b. dig up plant and tree roots near the bank.
   c. dig in the stream bed at the outside of a bend.

6. You decide to walk out of the wild country by following a series of ravines where a water supply is available. Night is coming on. The best place to make camp is:
   a. next to the water supply in the ravine.
   b. high on a ridge.
   c. midway up the slope.

7. Your flashlight glows dimly as you are about to make your way back to your campsite after a brief foraging trip. Darkness comes quickly in the woods and the surroundings seem unfamiliar. You should:
   a. head back at once, keeping the light on,

    hoping the light will glow enough for you to
make out landmarks.

  b. put the batteries under your arm-pits to warm
them, and then replace them in the flashlight.

  c. shine your torch for a few seconds, try to get
the scene in mind, move out in the darkness,
and repeat the process.   _____   _____

8. An early snow confines you to your small tent.
You doze with your small stove going. There is
danger if the flame is:

  a. yellow

  b. blue

  c. red.   _____   _____

9. You must ford a river that has a strong current,
large rocks, and some white water. After carefully
selecting your crossing spot, you should:

  a. leave your boots and pack on.

  b. take your boots and pack off.

  c. take off your pack, but leave your boots on.   _____   _____

10. In waist-deep water with a strong current, when
crossing the stream, you should face:

  a. upstream.

  b. across the stream.

  c. downstream.   _____   _____

11. You find yourself rimrocked; your only route is
up. The way is mossy, slippery rock. You should
try it:

  a. barefoot.

  b. with boots on.

  c. in stocking feet.   _____   _____

12. Unarmed and unsuspecting, you surprise a large
bear prowling around your campsite. As the bear
rears up about ten metres from you, you should:

  a. run.

  b. climb the nearest tree.

  c. freeze, but be ready to back away slowly.   _____   _____

WILDERNESS SURVIVAL GROUP BRIEFING SHEET

Decision by consensus is a method of problem solving and decision making
in groups in which all the parties involved actively discuss the issues
surrounding the decision. The group thus pools the knowledge and experience of all its members. Any final decision must be supported by each
member of the group. The ideas and feelings of all the members are integrated into a group decision, thus allowing several people to work together
on a common problem, rather than producing a 'we–they' stand-off.

As you might imagine, decision by consensus is usually difficult to attain and will consume more time than other methods of deciding an issue. As the energies of the group become focused on the problem at hand (rather than on defending individual points of view), the quality of the decision tends to be enhanced. Research indicates, in fact, that this approach to problem solving and decision making results in a significantly higher-quality decision than other methods such as the use of majority power (voting), minority power (persuasion), and compromise.

In the decision-by-consensus process, each group member is asked to:

1. Prepare his/her own position as well as possible prior to meeting with the group (but to realize that the task is incomplete and that the missing pieces are to be supplied by the other members of the group).
2. Recognize an obligation to express his/her own opinion and explain it fully, so that the rest of the group has the benefit of all members' thinking.
3. Recognize an obligation to listen to the opinions and feelings of all other group members and be ready to modify his/her own position on the basis of logic and understanding.
4. Avoid conflict-reducing techniques such as voting, compromising, or giving in to keep the peace and to realize that differences of opinion are helpful; in exploring differences, the best course of action will make itself apparent.

You have just completed an individual solution to Wilderness Survival: A Consensus-Seeking Task. Now your small task group will decide on a group solution to the same dilemmas. Remember, decision by consensus is difficult to attain, and not every decision may meet with everyone's unqualified approval. There should be, however, a general feeling of support from all members before a group decision is made. Take the time you need to listen for understanding, consider *all* members' views, make your own view known, and be reasonable in arriving at a group decision.

Notes and references

1. Bavelas, A. 'A Mathematical Model for Group Structures', *Applied Anthropology*, vol. 7, 1948, pp. 19–30, and Bavelas, A. 'Communication Patterns in Task-oriented Groups', in Lasswell, H. N. and Lerner, D. (eds) *The Policy Sciences*, Stanford University Press (1951).
2. Leavitt, H. J. 'Some Effects of Certain Communication Patterns on Group Performance', *Journal of Abnormal and Social Psychology*, vol. 46, 1951, pp. 38–50. See also: Leavitt, H. J. *Managerial Psychology*, Fourth edition, University of Chicago Press (1978).
3. Guetzkow, H. and Dill, W. R. 'Factors in the Organizational Development of Task-oriented Groups', *Sociometry*, vol. 20, 1957, pp. 175–204.
4. Shaw, M. E. 'Communication Networks', in Berkowitz, L. (ed.) *Advances in Experimental Social Psychology*, vol. 1, Academic Press (1964).
5. Moreno, J. L. *Who Shall Survive?* Beacon House (1953). See also: Moreno, J. L. and Jennings, H. H. *The Sociometry Reader*, Free Press of Glencoe (1960).
6. Bales, R. F. 'A Set of Categories for the Analysis of Small Group Interaction', *American Sociological Review*, vol. 15, April 1950, pp. 257–63.
7. Bales, R. F. *Personality and Interpersonal Behaviour*, Holt, Rinehart and Winston (1970).
8. Benne, K. D. and Sheats, P. 'Functional Roles of Group Members'. *Journal of Social Issues*, vol. 4, 1948, pp. 41–9.
9. Rackham, N., Honey, P. and Colbert, M. J. *Developing Interactive Skills*, Wellen's Publishing [Guilsborough, Northampton NN6 8PY. Tel.: (0604) 740379] (1971).

10. Kogan, N. and Wallach, M. A. 'Risk-taking as a Function of the Situation, the Person and the Group', in Newcomb, T. M. (ed.) *New Directions in Psychology III*, Holt, Rinehart and Winston (1967).

11. For a comprehensive review of the 'risky-shift' phenomenon, see, for example: Clarke, R. D. 'Group Induced Shift Towards Risk: A Critical Appraisal', *Psychological Bulletin*, vol. 76, 1971, pp. 251–70.

12. Shaw, M. E. *Group Dynamics*, McGraw-Hill (1976).

13. The idea of brainstorming was developed by Osborn. See: Osborn, A. F. *Applied Imagination*, Scribner's (1957).

14. Shaw, M. E. *Group Dynamics*, McGraw-Hill (1976).

15. Taylor, D. W., Berry, P. C. and Block, C. H. 'Does Group Participation when Using Brainstorming Facilitate or Inhibit Creative Thinking?' *Administrative Science Quarterly*, vol. 3, no. 1, June 1958, pp. 23–47. See also: Dunnette, M. D., Campbell, J. and Jaastad, K. 'The Effect of Group Participation on Brainstorming Effectiveness for Two Industrial Samples', *Journal of Applied Psychology*, vol. 47, 1963, pp. 30–7.

16. Maginn, B. K. and Harris, R. J. 'Effects of Anticipated Evaluation on Individual Brainstorming Performance', *Journal of Applied Psychology*, vol. 65, no. 2, 1980, pp. 219–25.

17. Cooper, C. L. and Mangham, I. L. (eds) *T-Groups: A Survey of Research*, Wiley (1971) p. v.

18. Luft, J. *Group Processes: An Introduction to Group Dynamics*, Second edition, National Press (1970). (The term 'Johari Window' was derived from a combination of the first names of the original authors, Joseph Luft and Harry Ingham.)

19. Mangham, I. and Cooper, C. L. 'The Impact of T-Groups on Managerial Behaviour', *Journal of Management Studies*, February 1969, vol. 6, no. 1, p. 57.

20. Davis, K. *Human Behavior at Work*, Fifth edition, McGraw-Hill (1977) p. 183.

21. See, for example: Campbell, J. P. and Dunnette, M. D. 'Effectiveness of T-group Experiences in Managerial Training and Development', *Psychological Bulletin*, vol. 70, no. 2, 1968, pp. 73–103.

22. For an overview of experimental small group methods and training needs, see, for example: Smith, P. B. *Group Processes and Personal Change*, Harper and Row (1980). See also: Brown, R. *Group Processes: Dynamics Within and Between Groups*. Basil Blackwell (1988).

15. THE NATURE OF LEADERSHIP

The organisation is made up of groups of people. An essential part of management is co-ordinating the activities of groups and directing the efforts of their members towards the goals and objectives of the organisation. This involves the process of leadership and the choice of an appropriate form of behaviour. The manager must understand the nature of leadership and factors which determine the effectiveness of the leadership process.[1]

Objectives

To: (i)   Explain the meaning of leadership and the nature of the leadership relationship;

(ii) Outline different approaches to leadership;

(iii) Identify the functions and responsibilities of leadership;

(iv) Distinguish different styles of leadership and examine leadership as an aspect of behaviour;

(v) Detail patterns of managerial leadership and the main studies of leadership;

(vi) Examine contingency theories of leadership and situational factors which determine the characteristics of leadership;

(vii) Appreciate the importance of leadership in work organisations and variables which determine effective leadership.

THE MEANING OF LEADERSHIP

There are many ways of looking at leadership and many interpretations of its meaning. Leadership might be interpreted in simple terms, such as 'getting others to follow' or 'getting people to do things willingly', or interpreted more specifically, for example as 'the use of authority in decision making'. It may be exercised as an attribute of position, or because of personal knowledge or wisdom.

Leadership might be based on a function of personality, or it can be seen as a behavioural category. It may also be viewed in terms of the role of the leaders and their ability to achieve effective performance from others. Leadership is related to motivation and to the process of communication.

It is difficult, therefore, to generalise about leadership, but essentially it is: *a relationship through which one person influences the behaviour of other people.* This means that the process of leadership cannot be separated from the activities of groups.

But the leadership relationship is not limited to leader behaviour resulting in subordinate behaviour. Leadership is a dynamic process. The leader–follower relationship is reciprocal and effective leadership is a two-way process.

A more specific definition, which draws attention to the relationship between leadership and communications, sees leadership as interpersonal influence which is exercised in a situation and directed through the communication process towards the attainment of a specified goal.[2]

Leadership and management

What is the relationship between leadership and management? Sometimes management and leadership are seen as synonymous. There is, however, a difference between the two and it does not follow that every leader is a manager.

Management is more usually viewed as getting things done through other people in order to achieve stated organisational objectives. The manager may react to specific situations and be more concerned with solving short-term problems. Management is regarded as relating to people working within a structured organisation and with prescribed roles. To people outside of the organisation the manager might not be seen in a leadership role.

The emphasis of leadership is on interpersonal behaviour in a broader context. It is often associated with the willing and enthusiastic behaviour of followers. Leadership does not necessarily take place within the hierarchical structure of the organisation. Many people operate as leaders without their role ever being clearly established or defined. A leader often has sufficient influence to bring about longer-term changes in people's attitudes and to make change more acceptable. Leadership can be seen primarily as an inspirational process.[3]

Other differences

There are other differences between leadership and management. For example, *Zaleznik* explores difference in attitudes towards goals, conceptions of work, relations with others, self-perception and development.[4]

- Managers tend to adopt impersonal or passive attitudes towards goals. Leaders adopt a more personal and active attitude towards goals.
- In order to get people to accept solutions, the manager needs continually to co-ordinate and balance in order to compromise conflicting values. The leader creates excitement in work and develops choices that give substance to images that excite people.
- In their relationships with other people, managers maintain a low level of emotional involvement. Leaders have empathy with other people and give attention to what events and actions mean.
- Managers see themselves more as conservators and regulators of the existing order of affairs with which they identify, and from which they gain rewards. Leaders work in, but do not belong to, the organisation. Their sense of identity does not depend upon membership or work roles and they search out opportunities for change.

The differences between leadership and management have been applied by *Watson* to the 7-S organisational framework of: strategy, structure, systems, style, staff, skills and superordinate (or shared) goals. Watson suggests that whereas managers tend towards reliance on

- strategy,

- structure and
- systems;

leaders have an inherent inclination for utilisation of the 'soft' Ss of

- style,
- staff,
- skills and
- shared goals.

Watson also suggests, although cautiously, that 7-S management could be seen as the province of leaders. Managers will not ordinarily be capable of achieving sufficient mastery of all seven factors to attain a consistently high level of organisational performance.[5]

Despite the differences, there is a close relationship between leadership and management in work organisations.[6] For example, the method of management training known as the Managerial Grid (discussed in Chapter 9) can also be used as a means of measuring leadership style. To be an *effective* manager it is necessary to exercise the role of leadership. A common view is that the job of the manager requires the ability of leadership and that leadership is in effect a sub-set of management; although leadership is a special attribute which can be distinguished from other elements of management.

THE LEADERSHIP RELATIONSHIP

A leader may be imposed, formally appointed or elected, chosen informally, or emerge naturally through the demands of the situation or the wishes of the group. Leadership may be attempted, successful or effective.[7]

- *Attempted leadership* is when any individual in the group attempts to exert influence over other members of the group.
- *Successful leadership* is when the influence brings about the behaviour and results that were intended by the leader.
- *Effective leadership* is when successful leadership results in functional behaviour and the achievement of group goals.

The leader may exercise authority as an attribute of position. In this case the manager is seen as a leader because of a stated position in the hierarchy. Leadership, however, is more than just adherence to a formal role prescription. It is more than eliciting mechanical behaviour which results from a superior–subordinate relationship in a hierarchical structure.

Leadership may also be exercised through greater knowledge or expertise, or by reputation (sapiential authority). It may also be based on the personal qualities, or charisma, of the leader and the manner in which authority is exercised. This view of leadership gives rise to the question of 'born' or 'natural' leaders. Leadership may also focus on the role of the leader in terms of the relationship with followers and the adoption of a particular style of leadership.

Leadership influence and power Within an organisation, leadership influence will be dependent upon the type of power that the leader can exercise over other people. The exercise of power is a social process which helps to explain how different people can influence the behaviour/actions of others. Five main sources of power upon which the influence of the leader is based have been identified by *French* and *Raven*.[8] We shall consider these in terms of the manager (as a leader) and subordinate relationship.

- *Reward power* is based on the subordinate's *perception* that the leader has the ability and resources to obtain rewards for those who comply with directives; for example, pay, promotion, praise, recognition, increased responsibilities, allocation and arrangement of work, granting of privileges.

- *Coercive power* is based on fear and the subordinate's *perception* that the leader has the ability to punish or to bring about undesirable outcomes for those who do not comply with directives; for example, withholding pay rises, promotion or privileges; allocation of undesirable duties or responsibilities; withdrawal of friendship or support; formal reprimands or possibly dismissal.

- *Legitimate power* is based on the subordinate's *perception* that the leader has a right to exercise influence because of the leader's role or position in the organisation. Legitimate power is based on authority, for example that of managers and supervisors within the hierarchical structure of an organisation. Legitimate power is therefore 'position' power because it is based on the role of the leader in the organisation, and not on the nature of the personal relationship with others.

- *Referent power* is based on the subordinate's *identification* with the leader. The leader exercises influence because of perceived attractiveness, personal characteristics, reputation or what is called 'charisma'. For example, a particular manager may not be in a position to reward or punish certain subordinates, but may still exercise power over the subordinates because the manager commands their respect or esteem.

- *Expert power* is based on the subordinate's *perception* of the leader as someone who is competent and who has some special knowledge or expertise in a given area. Expert power is based on credibility and clear evidence of knowledge or expertise; for example, the expert knowledge of 'functional' specialists such as the personnel manager, management accountant or systems analyst. The expert power is usually limited to narrow, well-defined areas or specialisms.

These sources of power are based on the subordinate's *perception* of the influence of the leader, whether it is real or not. For example, if a leader has the ability to control rewards and punishments but subordinates *do not believe this*, then in effect the leader has no reward or coercive power.

French and Raven point out that the five sources of power are interrelated and the use of one type of power (for example, coercive) may affect the ability to use another type of power (for example, referent). Also the same person may exercise different types of power, in particular circumstances and at different times.

A dynamic form of behaviour

Leadership is, therefore, a dynamic form of behaviour and there are a number of variables which affect the leadership relationship. Four major variables are identified by *McGregor* as:

- the characteristics of the leader;
- the attitude, needs and other personal characteristics of the followers;
- the nature of the organisation, such as its purpose, its structure, the tasks to be performed; and
- the social, economic and political environment.

McGregor concludes that 'leadership is not a property of the individual, but a complex relationship among these variables'.[9]

APPROACHES TO LEADERSHIP

There are many ways of analysing leadership. It is helpful, therefore, to have some framework in which to consider different approaches to study of the subject.[10]

One way is to examine leadership in terms of:

- the qualities or traits approach;
- the situational approach; and
- the functional or group approach.

Other main headings under which to study leadership are:

- style theories and leadership as a behavioural category; and
- contingency theories.

These are discussed later in this chapter.

THE QUALITIES OR TRAITS APPROACH

The first approach assumes that leaders are born and not made. Leadership consists of certain inherited characteristics, or personality traits, which distinguish leaders from their followers: the so-called 'Great Person' theory of leadership. The qualities approach focuses attention on the man or woman in the job and not on the job itself. It suggests that attention is given to the selection of leaders rather than to the training for leadership.

Search for common traits of leadership

There have been many research studies into the common traits of leadership. However, attempts at identifying common personality, or physical and mental, characteristics of different 'good' or 'successful' leaders have met with little success. For example, *Byrd*, in a study of trait theory research up to 1940, identified a long list of traits which studies had shown differentiated leaders and the led, but found that only 5 per cent of the traits were common to four or more of the studies.[11] Another study, by *Jennings*, concluded: 'Fifty years of study have failed to produce one personality trait or set of qualities that can be used to discriminate between leaders and non-leaders.'[12]

Later studies have identified some correlation between leadership and certain personality traits, for example a significant correlation between leadership effectiveness and the traits of intelligence, supervisory ability, initiative, self-assurance and individuality in the manner in which work was done.[13] *Stogdill* discovered that the average person occupying a position of leadership exceeded the average member of the group in characteristics such as intelligence, scholarship, dependability in exercising responsibility, originality, social participation and socio-economic status.[14]

It is noticeable that 'individuality' or 'originality' usually features in the list of traits. This itself suggests that there is little in common between specific personality traits of different leaders. It is perhaps possible therefore to identify general characteristics of leadership ability, such as self-confidence, initiative, intelligence and belief in one's actions, but research into this area has revealed little more than this. Investigations have identified lists of traits which tend to be overlapping or contradictory and with little significant correlation for most factors.

Limitations of the traits approach

There are two further limitations with this approach.

- First, there is bound to be some subjective judgement in determining who is regarded as a 'good' or 'successful' leader.
- Second, the lists of possible traits tend to be very long and there is not always agreement on the most important.

Even if it were possible to identify an agreed list of more specific qualities, this would provide little explanation of the nature of leadership. It would do little to help in the development and training of future leaders. Although there is still some interest in the qualities, or traits, approach, attention has been directed more to other approaches to leadership.

THE SITUATIONAL APPROACH

The second approach concentrates on the importance of the situation in the study of leadership. A variety of people with differing personalities and from different backgrounds have emerged as effective leaders in different situations. The person who becomes the leader of their work group is thought to be the person who knows best what to do and is seen by the group as the most suitable leader in the particular situation.

The situational approach places emphasis on the importance of professional knowledge or technical expertise, and relates to the idea of sapiential authority. With this approach the focus is on what the leader actually does rather than on the personality characteristics, or qualities, of the leader.

The situational approach, therefore, provides a sounder base for training in leadership. This is despite the uncertainty about whether leaders are born or made, or whether leadership is an art or a science. The important point is that these are not mutually exclusive alternatives. Even if there are certain inborn qualities which make for good leadership, these natural talents need encouragement and further development. Even if leadership is an art, it still requires knowledge and the application of special skills or techniques.

Limitations of the situational approach A limitation of the situational approach is that there are people who possess the appropriate knowledge and skills, and appear to be the most suitable leaders in a given situation, but who do not emerge as leaders.

Another limitation is that it does not explain fully the process of inter-personal behaviour or the different styles of leadership and their effect on the people being led.

Finally, in the work organisation it is not usually practicable to allow the situation continually to determine who should act as a leader.

THE FUNCTIONAL OR GROUP APPROACH

The third approach to leadership focuses attention not on the personality of the leader, nor on the particular situation in which the leader emerges, but on the functions of leadership. Leadership is always present in any group engaged in a task. The functional approach views leadership in terms of how the leader's behaviour affects, and is affected by, the group of followers. This approach concentrates on the nature of the group, the followers or subordinates. It focuses on the content of leadership.

Greater attention can be given to the training of leaders and to the means of improving the leaders' performance by concentrating on the functions which will lead to effective performance by the work group. The advantages of the functional approach to leadership have been well expressed by *Miles*.

> The functional approach does not get bogged down (as other theories tend to) on the issue of the appointed leader versus the emergent leader. Both the official leader and the group member who happens to come up with the right function at the right time are doing the same thing: supplying functions needed by the group. The appointed leader who does not do so will become leader in name only, even though he may retain his authority until he retires twenty years hence. Most groups do have appointed leaders as a kind of 'safety net' or guarantee that someone will fill needed functions, but the approach taken here assumes that the appointed leader and members alike may exert leadership.[15]

Action-centred leadership A general theory on the functional approach is associated with the work of *John Adair* and his ideas on action-centred leadership.[16] The effectiveness of the leader is dependent upon meeting three areas of need within the work group. The need to achieve the common *task*, the need for *team maintenance*, and the *individual needs* of group members. Adair symbolises these needs by three overlapping circles (*see* Fig. 15.1).

Task functions involves

- achieving the objectives of the work group;
- defining group tasks;
- planning the work;
- allocation of resources;
- organisation of duties and responsibilities;
- controlling quality and checking performance;
- reviewing progress.

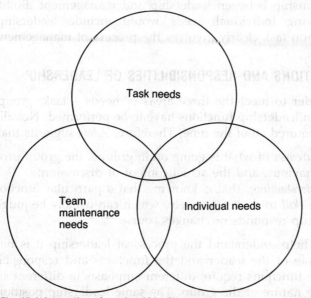

Fig. 15.1 Interaction of needs within the group
(Reproduced with permission from Adair, J., *Action-Centred Leadership*, Gower Press (1979) p. 10.)

Team functions involve;

- maintaining morale and building team spirit;
- the cohesiveness of the group as a working unit;
- setting standards and maintaining discipline;
- systems of communication within the group;
- training the group;
- appointment of sub-leaders.

Individual functions involve:

- meeting the needs of the individual members of the group;
- attending to personal problems;
- giving praise and status;
- reconciling conflicts between group needs and needs of the individual;
- training the individual.

The action by the leader in any one area of need will affect one or both of the other areas of need. The ideal position is where complete integration of the three areas of need is achieved. In any work group the most effective leader is the person who sees that the task needs, the needs of the group and those of the individual are all adequately met. The effective leader elicits the contribution of members of the group and draws out other leadership from the group to satisfy the three interrelated areas of need.

Leadership training   Based on the work of *Adair*, the Industrial Society has developed a system of leadership training for helping managers to develop and improve their ability as leaders.[17] The action-centred leadership approach to leadership training is currently used by a number of organisations in this country.

The three-circle approach used by Adair also serves to illustrate the close relationship between leadership and management. Building the team and satisfying individual needs would include leadership. Achieving the common task clearly involves the process of management.

FUNCTIONS AND RESPONSIBILITIES OF LEADERSHIP

In order to meet the three areas of needs – task, group and individual – certain leadership functions have to be performed. Not all of these functions are required all of the time. Therefore, *Adair* suggests that the leader needs:

- *awareness* of what is going on in groups, the group process or underlying behaviour, and the actual content of discussion;
- *understanding*, that is knowing that a particular function is required; and
- the *skill* to do it effectively, which can usually be judged by whether the group responds or changes course.[18]

To help understand the process of leadership it is necessary to analyse the role of the leader and the functions and responsibility of leadership. These functions require different emphasis in different situations according to the nature of the group. The same leadership position may also change over a period of time. It is possible, however, to list a range of general functions which are served by the leadership position. A useful summary is provided by *Krech* who identifies fourteen functions.[19]

- *The leader as executive* – top co-ordinator of the group activities and overseer of the execution of policies.
- *The leader as planner* – deciding the ways and means by which the group achieves its ends. This may involve both short-term and long-term planning.
- *The leader as policy maker* – the establishment of group goals and policies.
- *The leader as expert* – a source of readily available information and skills, although there will be some reliance on technical expertise and advice from other members of the group.
- *The leader as external group representative* – the official spokesperson for the group, the representative of the group and the channel for both outgoing and incoming communications.
- *The leader as controller of internal relations* – determines specific aspects of the group structure.
- *The leader as purveyor of rewards and punishment* – control over group members by the power to provide rewards and apply punishments.
- *The leader as arbitrator and mediator* – controls interpersonal conflict within the group.
- *The leader as exemplar* – a model of behaviour for members of the group, setting an example of what is expected.
- *The leader as symbol of the group* – enhancing group unit by providing some kind of cognitive focus and establishing the group as a distinct entity.
- *The leader as substitute for individual responsibility* – relieves the individual member of the group from the necessity of, and responsibility for, personal decision.
- *The leader as ideologist* – serving as the source of beliefs, values and standards of behaviour for individual members of the group.

- *The leader as father figure* – serving as focus for the positive emotional feelings of individual members and the object for identification and transference.
- *The leader as scapegoat* – serving as a target for aggression and hostility of the group, accepting blame in the case of failure.

These fourteen functions could readily be consolidated into a shorter number of more general functions. But they help to illustrate the range of roles and responsibilities that the leader may be expected to fulfil, and the complexity of the nature of leadership.

It is important to note that leadership *resides in the functions and not a particular person*. The various functions of leadership can be shared among members of the group. If a member provides a particular function which is relevant to the activities of the group, and accepted by group members, then in those circumstances this could become a leadership function.

STYLES OF LEADERSHIP

In the work situation it has become increasingly clear that managers can no longer rely solely on the use of their position in the hierarchical structure as a means of exercising the functions of leadership. In order to get the best results from subordinates the manager must also have regard for the need to encourage high morale, a spirit of involvement and co-operation, and a willingness to work. This gives rise to consideration of the style of leadership and provides another heading under which to analyse leadership behaviour.

Leadership style is the way in which the functions of leadership are carried out, the way in which the manager typically behaves towards members of the group.

The development of behavioural science has drawn attention to the processes of interpersonal behaviour in the work situation and to the effects of leadership on those being led. The attention given to leadership style is based on the assumption that subordinates are more likely to work effectively for managers who adopt a certain style of leadership than they will for managers who adopt alternative styles.

Broad classification of leadership style Styles of leadership are usually classified under the two extreme headings of authoritarian (or autocratic) and democratic. Sometimes a third heading of *laissez-faire* is included. There are of course many dimensions within these broad headings and a number of other styles may be identified, such as, for example, dictatorial, bureaucratic, benevolent, charismatic, consultative, participative and abdicatorial.

- *The authoritarian style* is where the focus of power is with the manager, and all interactions within the group move towards the manager. The leader alone exercises decision making and authority for determining policy, procedures for achieving goals, work tasks and relationships, control of rewards or punishments.
- *The democratic style* is where the focus is more with the group as a whole and there is greater interaction within the group. The leadership functions are shared with members of the group. The group members have

a greater say in decision making, determination of policy, implementation of systems and procedures.

- *A genuine* laissez-faire *style* is where the manager observes that members of the group are working well on their own. The manager consciously makes a decision to allow them freedom of action and not to interfere, but is readily available if help is needed. This is to be contrasted with the manager who could not care, who deliberately keeps away from the trouble spots and does not want to get involved. The manager just lets members of the group get on with the work in hand. This is more a non-style of leadership or it could perhaps be labelled as abdication.

Importance of participative approach

The importance of a more participative approach to leadership style and its effect on group performance was seen after publication of the research findings of the relay assembly test room experiment at the Hawthorne plant of the Western Electric Company of America.[20] Later work by *Maslow*, who theorised that individuals possess a hierarchy of needs, resulted in greater research into the motivation and behaviour of individuals in the work situation.[21]

The subsequent attention given to theories of individual motivation gave rise to a more psychological approach to the study of work organisations. The main focus of concern was on the personal adjustment of the individual and the effects of group relationships and leadership styles. The style of leadership adopted is a function of the manager's attitude and assumptions about human nature and behaviour.

Work by such writers as *McGregor, Likert*, and *Blake* and *Mouton* (discussed in Chapter 9) appear to support the value of participative managerial leadership in improving organisational effectiveness.

The law of the situation

A somewhat different approach was put forward many years ago by *Follett* who considered the problem of avoiding the two extremes of (i) too great bossism in giving orders; and (ii) practically no orders given. Follett's solution was what she called the 'depersonalising of orders and obeying the law of the situation'.

> My solution is to depersonalize the giving of orders, to unite all concerned in a study of the situation, to discover the law of the situation and obey that. Until we do this I do not think we shall have the most successful business administration. . . . This is, ideally, what should take place between foreman and rank and file, between any head and his subordinates. One *person* should not give orders to another *person*, but both should agree to take their orders from the situation. If orders are simply part of the situation, the question of someone giving and someone receiving does not come up. Both accept the orders given by the situation.[22]

Attention to style of leadership

Attention to the manager's style of leadership has come about because of a greater understanding of the needs and expectations of people at work. It has also been influenced by such factors as:

- changes in the value system of society;
- broader standards of education and training;

- the influence of trade unions;
- pressure for a greater social responsibility towards employees, for example through schemes of participation in decision making; and
- government legislation, for example in the areas of employment protection.

All of these factors have combined to create resistance against purely autocratic styles of leadership.

LEADERSHIP AS A BEHAVIOURAL CATEGORY

One of the most extensive research studies on behavioural categories of leadership was the *Ohio State Leadership Studies* undertaken by the Bureau of Business Research at Ohio State University. The focus was on the kinds of behaviour of people in leadership positions and the effects of leadership styles on group performance.

Questionnaires were designed which comprised a list of descriptive items each dealing with a specific aspect of leadership behaviour. The questionnaires were used repeatedly in different kinds of organisations and in a variety of leader–group member situations.

Consideration and structure

Results of the Ohio State studies indicated two major dimensions of leadership behaviour, labelled 'consideration' and 'initiating structure'.[23]

- *Consideration* reflects the extent to which the leader establishes trust, mutual respect and rapport with the group and shows concern, warmth, support and consideration for subordinates. This dimension is associated with two-way communication, participation and a human relations approach to leadership.
- *Structure* reflects the extent to which the leader defines and structures group interactions towards attainment of formal goals and organises group activities. This dimension is associated with efforts to achieve organisational goals.

Consideration and initiating structure can be seen as the same as maintenance function (building and maintaining the group as a working unit and relationships among group members) and task function (accomplishment of specific tasks of the groups and achievement of goals) discussed in the previous chapter.

Four types of leadership behaviour

Consideration and initiating structure were found to be uncorrelated and independent dimensions. They are separate behavioural categories and give rise to four types of leadership behaviour. Leaders may be:

- low on consideration and low on structure;
- low on consideration and high on structure;
- high on consideration and high on structure, or
- high on consideration and low on structure.

Leadership behaviour could, therefore, be shown on two separate axes instead of along a single continuum. As a result four quadrants were developed which illustrated the different combinations of 'consideration' and 'structure' (*see* Fig. 15.2).

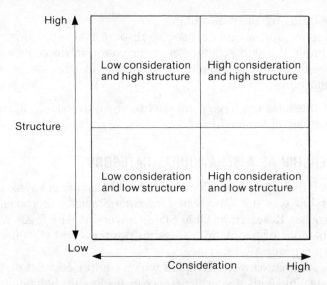

Fig. 15.2 The Ohio State quadrants of leadership behaviour

Research into the effects of these four types of leadership behaviour suggests that some balance is needed between consideration and structure in order to satisfy both individual needs and organisational goals. A high consideration, high structure style appears to be generally more effective in terms of subordinate satisfaction and group performance, but the evidence is not conclusive and much seems to depend upon situational factors.

Employee-centred and production-centred supervisors

Another major research study was carried out at the *University of Michigan Institute for Social Research* at the same time as the Ohio State studies. Effective supervisors (measured along dimensions of group morale, productivity and cost reduction) appeared to display four common characteristics:

- delegation of authority and avoidance of close supervision;
- an interest and concern in their subordinates as individuals;
- participative problem solving; and
- high standards of performance.

Likert, who has summarised the findings of the University of Michigan studies, used the terms *employee-centred* and *production-centred* supervisors.[24] These terms are similar to the dimensions of consideration and structure. The first three of these supervisory characteristics are examples of consideration. The fourth characteristic exemplifies structure.

Like consideration and structure, employee-centred and production-centred supervision need to be balanced. Likert concluded that employee-centred supervisors who get best results tend to recognise that one of their main responsibilities is production. Both the Ohio State studies and the University of Michigan studies appear to support the idea that there is no single behavioural category of leadership which is superior. There are many types of leadership behaviour and their effectiveness depends upon the variables in any given situation.

Major dimensions of leadership behaviour Despite the many types of actual leadership behaviour, we have seen that there appears to be general agreement on two major dimensions of leadership (*see* Fig. 15.3).

Group interaction analysis	Task functions	Maintenance functions
Blake and Mouton managerial grid	Concern for production	Concern for people
Ohio State leadership studies	Structure	Consideration
University of Michigan studies (Likert)	Production-centred supervision	Employee-centred supervision

Fig. 15.3 Summary of major dimensions of leadership

CONTINUUM OF LEADERSHIP BEHAVIOUR

One of the best known works on leadership style is that by *Tannenbaum* and *Schmidt* (Fig. 15.4).[25] They suggest a continuum of possible leadership behaviour available to a manager and along which various styles of leadership may be placed. At one extreme of the continuum is boss-centred leadership (authoritarian) and at the other extreme is subordinate-centred leadership (democratic).

The continuum presents a range of action related to the degree of authority used by the manager and to the area of freedom available to subordinates in arriving at decisions. The Tannenbaum and Schmidt continuum can be related to *McGregor's* supposition of Theory X and Theory Y. Boss-centred leadership is towards Theory X and subordinate-centred leadership is towards Theory Y.

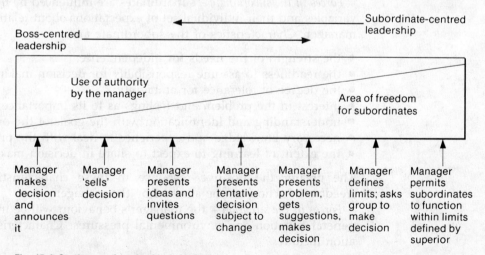

Fig. 15.4 Continuum of leadership behaviour

(Reprinted by permission of the *Harvard Business Review*, from 'How to Choose a Leadership Pattern' by Robert Tannenbaum and Warren H. Schmidt (May/June 1973). Copyright © 1973 by the President and Fellows of Harvard College. All rights reserved.)

433

Four main styles of leadership

Moving along the continuum, the manager may be characterised according to the degree of control that is maintained over subordinates. Neither extreme of the continuum is absolute as there is always some limitation on authority and on freedom. This approach can be seen as identifying four main styles of leadership by the manager: tells, sells, consults, joins.

- *Tells* – the manager identifies a problem, chooses a decision and announces this to subordinates, expecting them to implement it without an opportunity for participation.
- *Sells* – the manager still chooses a decision but recognises the possibility of some resistance from those faced with the decision and attempts to persuade subordinates to accept it.
- *Consults* – the manager identifies the problem but does not choose a decision until the problem is presented to the group, and the manager has listened to the advice and solutions suggested by subordinates.
- *Joins* – the manager defines the problem and the limits within which the decision must be chosen and then passes to the group, with the manager as a member, the right to make decisions.

Three main forces

Tannenbaum and *Schmidt* suggest that there are three factors, or forces, of particular importance in deciding what types of leadership are practicable and desirable. These are: forces in the manager; forces in the subordinates; forces in the situation.

Forces in the manager – the managers' behaviour will be influenced by their own personalities, backgrounds, knowledge and experiences. These internal forces will include:

- value systems;
- confidence in subordinates;
- leadership inclinations; and
- feelings of security in an uncertain situation.

Forces in the subordinate – subordinates are influenced by many personality variables and their individual set of expectations about relationship with the manager. Characteristics of the subordinate are:

- the strength of the needs for independence;
- the readiness to assume responsibility for decision making;
- the degree of tolerance for ambiguity;
- interest in the problem and feelings as to its importance;
- understanding and identification with the goals of the organisation;
- necessary knowledge and experience to deal with the problem; and
- the extent of learning to expect to share in decision making.

The greater the positive response to these characteristics, the greater freedom of action can be allowed by the manager.

Forces in the situation – the manager's behaviour will be influenced by the general situation and environmental pressures. Characteristics in the situation include:

- type of organisation;
- group effectiveness;

- nature of the problem; and
- pressure of time.

Tannenbaum and Schmidt conclude that successful leaders are keenly aware of those forces which are most relevant to their behaviour at a particular time. They are able to behave appropriately in terms of their understanding of themselves, the individuals and the group, the organisation, and environmental influences. Successful managers are both perceptive and flexible.

Interdependency of forces

In the second publication of their work, originally written in 1958, *Tannenbaum* and *Schmidt* add a retrospective commentary in which they suggest how they would update their original ideas to reflect social developments and new concepts of management.[26] More attention would be given to the interdependency of the forces in the manager, in the subordinates and in the situation. (*See* Fig. 15.5.)

Forces lying outside the organisation would now also be included. Recognition is given to the possibility of the manager and/or subordinates taking initiative to change the boundaries of the rectangle through interaction with external forces. Recognition is also given to the power available to all parties in the organisation (for example individual workers and trade unions) and to the factors which underlie decisions on the use of power by the manager.

The term 'non-manager' is now preferred to 'subordinate' as the terminological difference between 'manager' and 'non-manager' is functional rather than hierarchical. Tannenbaum and Schmidt suggest a new continuum of patterns of leadership behaviour in which the total area of freedom shared between managers and non-managers is redefined constantly by interactions between them and the forces in the environment.

CONTINGENCY THEORIES OF LEADERSHIP

Situational factors are important in considering the characteristics of leadership. The interactions between the variables involved in a leadership situation and patterns of leadership behaviour provide another general approach to the study of leadership–contingency theory. Major contingency models of leadership include:

Favourability of leadership situation	– *Fiedler*
Quality and acceptance of leader's decision	– *Vroom* and *Yetton*
Path–goal theory	– *House*, and *House* and *Dessler*
Maturity of followers	– *Hersey* and *Blanchard*, and *Nicholls*

FIEDLER'S CONTINGENCY MODEL

One of the first leader-situation models was developed by *Fiedler* in his contingency theory of leadership effectiveness.[27]

Fiedler's contingency model was based on studies of a wide range of

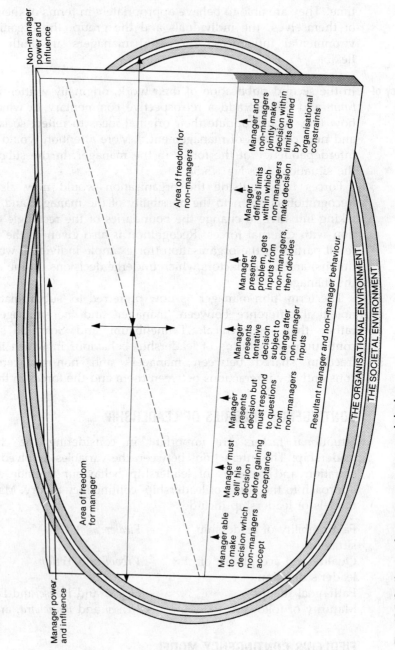

Fig. 15.5 Continuum of manager–non-manager behaviour

(Reprinted by permission of the *Harvard Business Review*, from 'How to Choose a Leadership Pattern' by Robert Tannenbaum and Warren H. Schmidt (May/June 1971). Copyright © 1973 by the President and Fellows of Harvard College. All rights reserved.)

group situations, and concentrated on the relationship between leadership and organisational performance. In order to measure the attitudes of the leader, Fiedler developed a 'least preferred co-worker' (LPC) scale. This measures the rating given by leaders about the person with whom they could work least well. The questionnaire contains up to twenty items. Examples of items in the LPC scale are pleasant/unpleasant, friendly/ unfriendly, helpful/frustrating, distant/close, co-operative/unco-operative, boring/interesting, self-assured/hesitant, open/guarded.

Each item is given a single ranking of between one to eight points, with eight points indicating the most favourable rating. For example:

Pleasant : _____:_____:_____:_____|_____:_____:_____:_____ Unpleasant
                8   7   6   5 | 4   3   2   1

The LPC score is the sum of the numerical ratings on all the items for the 'least preferred co-worker'. The less critical the rating of the least preferred co-worker and the more favourably evaluated, the higher the leader's LPC score.

The original interpretation of the LPC scale was that the leader with a high LPC score derived most satisfaction from interpersonal relationships, and the leader with a low LPC score derived most satisfaction from performance of the task. It was thought that high LPC scores would be associated with effective performance by the group. However, the interpretation of LPC has changed a number of times and there is still uncertainty about its actual meaning.

Favourability of leadership situation

Fiedler suggests that leadership behaviour is dependent upon the favourability of the leadership situation. There are three major variables which determine the favourability of the situation and which affect the leader's role and influence.

- *Leader–member relations* – the degree to which the leader is trusted and liked by group members, and their willingness to follow the leader's guidance.
- *The task structure* – the degree to which the task is clearly defined for the group and the extent to which it can be carried out by detailed instructions or standard procedures.
- *Position power* – the power of the leader by virtue of position in the organisation, and the degree to which the leader can exercise authority to influence (for example) rewards and punishments, or promotions and demotions.

From these three variables, Fiedler constructed eight combinations of group–task situations through which to relate leadership style (Fig. 15.6).

When the situation is *very favourable* (good leader–member relations, structured task, strong position power) *or very unfavourable* (poor leader–member relations, unstructured task, weak position power), then a *task-oriented leader* (low LPC score) with a directive, controlling style will be more effective.

When the situation is *moderately favourable* and the variables are mixed, then the leader with an interpersonal relationship orientation (high LPC score) and a *participative approach* will be more effective.

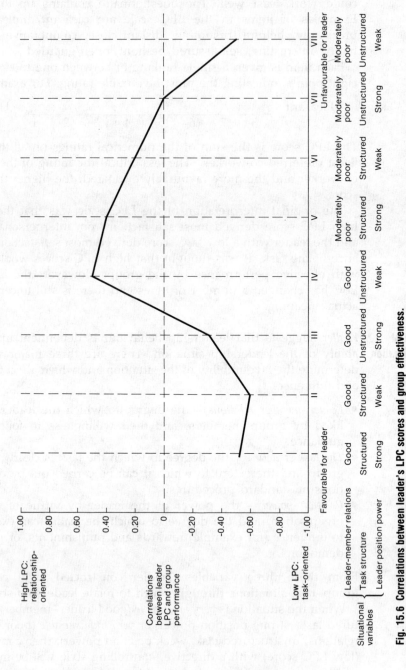

Fig. 15.6 Correlations between leader's LPC scores and group effectiveness.

── = leadership style. The appropriateness of leadership style for maximising group performance is dependent upon the three variables in the leadership situation

(Adapted and reproduced with permission from Fiedler, F. E., *A Theory of leadership Effectiveness*, McGraw-Hill (1967) p. 146.)

Fiedler is suggesting, therefore, that leadership style will vary as the favourability of the leadership situation varies.

Organisational variables

Fiedler's work has been subject to much criticism[28] but it does provide a further dimension to the study of leadership. It brings into consideration the organisational variables which affect leadership effectiveness and suggests that in given situations a task-orientated, or structured, style of leadership is most appropriate. The 'best' styles of leadership will be dependent upon the variable factors in the leadership situation.

Fiedler argues that leadership effectiveness may be improved by changing the leadership situation. Position power, task structure and leader–member relations can be changed to make the situation more compatible with the characteristics of the leader. Leaders with a low LPC score could be placed in a leadership situation which is very favourable or very unfavourable. Leaders with a high LPC score could be placed in a leadership situation which is of moderate favourability.

VROOM AND YETTON CONTINGENCY MODEL

Another contingency model of leadership is provided by *Vroom* and *Yetton*.[29] They base their analysis on two aspects of a leader's decision: its quality and its acceptance.

- *Decision quality*, or rationality, is the effect that the decision has on group performance.

- *Decision acceptance* refers to the motivation and commitment of group members in implementing the decision.

A third consideration is:

- The amount of *time required* to make the decision.

The Vroom and Yetton model suggests five main management decision styles:

Autocratic

A.I. Leader solves the problem or makes the decision alone using information available at the time.

A.II. Leader obtains information from subordinates but then decides on solution alone.

Consultative

C.I. The problem is shared with relevant subordinates, individually. The leader then makes the decision which may or may not reflect the influence of subordinates.

C.II. The problem is shared with subordinates as a group. The leader then makes the decision which may or may not reflect the influence of subordinates.

Group

G.II. The problem is shared with subordinates as a group. The leader acts as chairperson, rather than an advocate. Together the leader and subordinates generate and evaluate alternatives and attempt to reach group consensus on a solution.

Decision rules

Vroom and *Yetton* suggest seven decision rules to help the manager discover the most appropriate leadership style in a given situation. The first three rules protect the quality of decisions and the last four the acceptance of decisions. These rules indicate decision styles that the manager should *avoid* in a given situation and indicate the use of others. Decision tree charts have been produced to help in the application of the rules and to relate the situation to the appropriate leadership style. (*See* Fig. 15.7.)

PATH–GOAL THEORY

A third contingency model of leadership is the path–goal theory, the main work on which has been undertaken by *House*,[30] and by *House* and *Dessler*.[31] The model is based on the belief that the individual's motivation is dependent upon expectations that increased effort to achieve an improved level of performance will be successful, and expectations that improved performance will be instrumental in obtaining positive rewards and avoiding negative outcomes. This is the 'expectancy' theory of motivation, which was discussed in Chapter 11.

Satisfaction of expectations

The path–goal theory of leadership suggests that the performance of subordinates is affected by the extent to which the manager satisfies their expectations. Path–goal theory holds that subordinates will see leadership behaviour as a motivating influence to the extent that it means:

- satisfaction of their needs is dependent upon effective performance; and
- the necessary direction, guidance, training and support, which would otherwise be lacking, is provided.

House identifies four main types of leadership behaviour.

- *Directive leadership* involves letting subordinates know exactly what is expected of them and giving specific directions. Subordinates are expected to follow rules and regulations. This type of behaviour is similar to 'initiating structure' in the Ohio State Leadership Studies.
- *Supportive leadership* involves a friendly and approachable manner and displaying concern for the needs and welfare of subordinates. This type of behaviour is similar to 'consideration' in the Ohio State Leadership Studies.
- *Participative leadership* involves consulting with subordinates and the evaluation of their opinions and suggestions before the manager makes the decision.
- *Achievement-oriented leadership* involves setting challenging goals for subordinates, seeking improvement in their performance and showing confidence in subordinates' ability to perform well.

Path–goal theory suggests that the different types of behaviour can be practised by the same person at different times in varying situations. (*See* Fig. 15.8.)

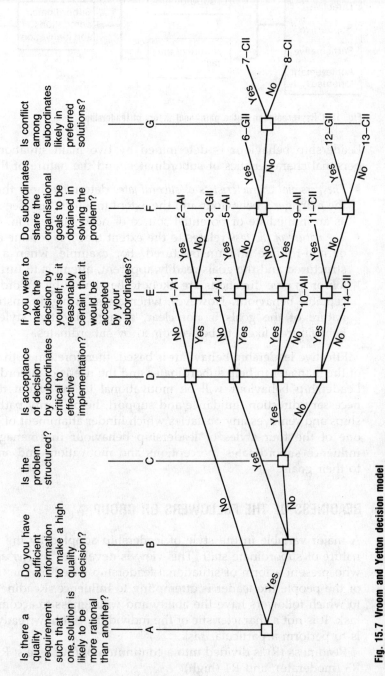

Fig. 15.7 Vroom and Yetton decision model

(Reprinted, by permission of the publisher, from 'A New Look at Managerial Decision Making', Victor H. Vroom, *Organizational Dynamics*, Spring 1973, © 1973, American Management Association, New York. All rights reserved.)

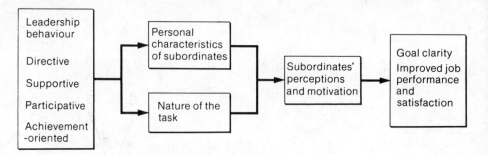

Fig. 15.8 Representation of the path–goal theory of leadership

Two main situational factors

Leadership behaviour is determined by two main situational factors: the personal characteristics of subordinates; and the nature of the task.

- *The personal characteristics of subordinates* determine how they will react to the manager's behaviour and the extent to which they see such behaviour as an immediate or potential source of need satisfaction.
- *The nature of the task* relates to the extent that it is routine and structured, or non-routine and unstructured. For example, when a task is highly structured and the goals readily apparent, attempts to further explain the job or to give directions are likely to be viewed by subordinates as unacceptable behaviour. However, when a task is highly unstructured or the nature of the goals is not clear, a more directive style of leadership behaviour is likely to be welcomed by subordinates.

Effective leadership behaviour is based, therefore, on both the willingness of the manager to help subordinates and the needs of subordinates for help. Leadership behaviour will be motivational to the extent that it provides necessary direction, guidance and support, helps clarify path–goal relationships and removes any obstacles which hinder attainment of goals. By using one of the four styles of leadership behaviour the manager attempts to influence subordinates' perceptions and motivation, and smooth the path to their goals.

READINESS OF THE FOLLOWERS OR GROUP

A major variable in the style of leadership adopted by the manager is the nature of subordinate staff. This view is developed by *Hersey* and *Blanchard* who present a form of situational leadership based on the 'readiness' level of the people the leader is attempting to influence. Readiness is the extent to which followers have the ability and willingness to accomplish a specific task. It is not a characteristic of the individual, but how ready the individual is to perform a particular task.[32]

Readiness (R) is divided into a continuum of four levels: R1 (low), R2 and R3 (moderate), and R4 (high).

- *R1 – low follower readiness* – refers to followers who are both *unable and unwilling*, and who lack commitment and motivation; or who are *unable and insecure*.
- *R2 – low to moderate follower readiness* – refers to followers who are *unable*

but willing, and who lack ability but are motivated to make an effort; or who are *unable but confident*.

- *R3 – moderate to high follower readiness* – refers to followers who are *able but unwilling*, and who have the ability to perform but are unwilling to apply their ability, or who are *able but insecure*.
- *R4 – high follower readiness* – refers to followers who are both *able and willing*, and who have the ability and commitment to perform, or who are *able and confident*.

Task behaviour and relationship behaviour

For each of the four levels of maturity, the appropriate style of leadership is a combination of task behaviour and relationship behaviour.

- *Task behaviour* is the extent to which the leader provides directions for the actions of followers, sets goals for them, and defines their roles and how to undertake them.
- *Relationship behaviour* is the extent to which the leader engages in two-way communication with followers, listens to them, and provides support and encouragement.

From the combination of task behaviour and relationship behaviour, *Hersey* and *Blanchard* present four leadership styles (S): telling (S1), selling (S2), participating (S3) and delegating (S4). The appropriate leadership style corresponds with the readiness of the followers. (*See* Fig. 15.9.)

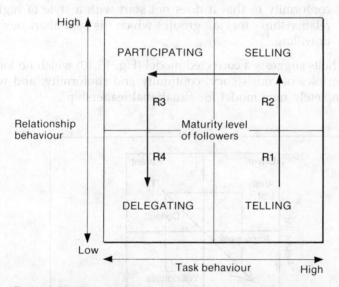

Fig. 15.9 Situational leadership model
(Adapted from Hersey, P. and Blanchard, K., *Management of Organizational Behavior*, 5th edition, Prentice-Hall (1988) p. 171.)

- *S1 – telling* – emphasises high amounts of guidance (task behaviour) but limited supportive (relationship) behaviour. This style is most appropriate for *low follower readiness* (R1).
- *S2 – selling* – emphasises high amounts of both directive (task) and relationship behaviours. This style is most appropriate for *low to moderate follower readiness* (R2).
- *S3 – participating* – emphasises a high amount of two-way communication

and supportive (relationship) behaviour but low amounts of guidance (task behaviour). This style is most appropriate for *moderate to high follower readiness* (R3).

- *S4 – delegating* – emphasises little direction or support with low levels of both task and relationship behaviours. This style is most appropriate for *high follower readiness* (R4).

Application and validity

Hersey and *Blanchard* suggest that the key to using situational leadership is that any leader behaviour may be more or less effective according to the readiness of the person the leader is attempting to influence. The manager should help subordinates to develop in readiness to the extent that they are able and willing to go. This development should take place by adjusting leadership behaviour through the four styles of telling, selling, participating and delegating.

Revised model of situational leadership

The validity of Hersey and Blanchard's basic model has been challenged by *Nicholls* who claims that the model violates three logical principles – consistency, continuity and conformity.

> It is inconsistent in the way it connects concern for task/relationships with ability/willingness. The development level continuum lacks continuity since it requires willingness to appear, disappear and re-appear as the development level increases. Finally, it runs counter to conformity in that it does not start with a style of high task and high relationship for a group which is simultaneously unable and unwilling.[33]

Nicholls suggests a corrected model (Fig. 15.10) which no longer violates the principles of consistency, continuity and conformity, and which presents a completely new model for situational leadership.

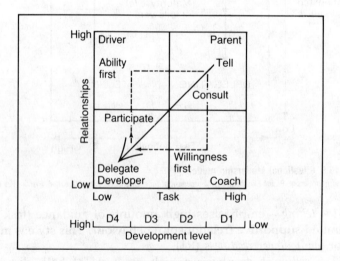

Fig. 15.10 New situational leadership model

(From Nicholls, J. R., 'A New Approach to Situational Leadership', *Leadership and Organization Development Journal*, vol. 6, no. 4, (1985) p. 60.)

Explanation   *Nicholls*'s situational leadership model can be explained as follows.

(i)   For groups at low development level, that is both unable and unwilling, the leader acts in the same role as a *parent* who wishes to develop simultaneously the ability and the social skills of a child. As both ability and willingness increase, activity connected with both task and relationships can be reduced in a symmetrical way. This allows progression from 'tell', through 'consult' to the role of a *developer* (bottom left quadrant).

(ii) The developer role of leadership continues with a light touch to use 'participation' and 'delegation' in order to develop further the ability and willingness of the group.

(iii) However, if willingness develops more quickly than ability, the leader will have the opportunity to act more in the role of a *coach* who is anxious to improve ability.

(iv) If, however, ability develops more quickly than willingness, the leader may wish to revert to the role of *driver* in order to push the group to achieve results up to its potential and to prevent unwillingness causing a shortfall in performance.

(v)   *Summary* The model requires a smooth progression of the leader from parent, using a high task and high relationship leadership style; following the usual progression 'tell–sell (or consult)–participate–delegate; to the leader as developer and using a low task and low relationship leadership style.

But if ability and willingness do not develop in harmony, the leader may find it appropriate to act more like a coach to develop ability, or more like a driver to overcome unwillingness.

Response   In the latest edition of their work, *Hersey* and *Blanchard* appear to make reference to the points raised by *Nicholls*.

Some people have difficulty understanding the development of followers from R1 to R2 to R3. How can one go from being insecure to confident and then become insecure again? The important thing to remember is that at the lower levels of readiness, the leader is providing the direction – the what, where, when and how. Therefore, the decisions are *leader directed*. At the higher levels of readiness, *followers* become responsible for task direction, and the decisions are *follower-directed*. *This transition from leader-directed to self-directed may result in apprehension or insecurity*. As followers move from low levels of readiness to higher levels, the combinations of task and relationship behavior appropriate to the situation begin to change.[34]

NO ONE BEST STYLE OF LEADERSHIP

Research studies tend to indicate that democratic styles of leadership are more likely to produce effective performance from work groups. A human relations, people-oriented approach is more likely to lead to job satisfaction and to group cohesiveness. For example, *Likert* found that authoritative, task-centred systems of management can result in high productivity in the short term because of compliance based on fear. However, long-term improvements in high productivity and in labour turnover are more likely to result from a participative, group-oriented approach.[35]

Many forms of leadership

However, it is not always the case that democratic styles of leadership are best. There are occasions when an autocratic style of leadership is more effective. For example, we have seen from the studies by *Fiedler* that when the situation is very favourable or very unfavourable in terms of leader–member relations, task structure and position power, then a task-oriented style of leadership is most effective. Some subordinates appear to prefer a more directive, task-oriented approach and respond better to more autocratic styles of leadership. Recall also the discussion on managerial behaviour in Chapter 9.

Contingency models demonstrate that there are many forms of leadership. Within an organisation different individuals may fulfil the functions of leadership and there are many different styles of leadership.

A potential danger with the contingency approach is that the manager may appear to lack consistency in leadership style. However, although subordinates may reasonably expect some degree of consistency from the manager in approaching the same type of problem with the same style, this is not to say that different types of problems should be approached in the same manner. Subordinates would ordinarily expect a different style of managerial leadership according to the contingencies of the situation.

Different styles at different stages of a business

Different types of leadership may also be most appropriate at different stages in the development of a business organisation. For example, *Clarke* and *Pratt* identify four different styles of managerial leadership required at different stages of business: champion, tank commander, housekeeper and lemon-squeezer.[36]

- *Champion* – as a new corporate venture develops into a business it needs a champion to fight for and defend the seedling business. The champion must be able to drive a small team to win orders, provide a wide range of management skills, and have the dash and energy to deal with a range of different matters.
- *Tank commander* – as the business enters its growth stage the manager must develop a strong, supportive team and have leadership qualities to be able to drive into readily exploitable parts of the market.
- *Housekeeper* – as the business runs up against boundaries erected by other growing businesses it enters the mature stage. The housekeeper has to ensure the efficient and economic management of the business. This involves skills in planning, cost control and the development of soundly based personnel policies.
- *Lemon-squeezer* – although the mature stage might last for many years, sometimes a business goes into premature decline. At this stage the need is for the kind of leader who can extract the maximum benefit from the situation. The lemon-squeezer needs to be both tough and innovative in order, for example, to cut costs, and improve productivity and staffing levels.

Finding and fitting the manager best suited to each stage of a business is a delicate task. Clarke and Pratt suggest that most managers are one type of leader or another. Although there are exceptions, few managers are flexible enough to switch between such different leadership roles.

Variables affecting leadership effectiveness

Clearly, there is no one 'best' style of leadership which will result in the maintenance of morale among group members and high work performance. Three main aspects to be considered in determining the most appropriate style of leadership are: the manager, the group and the work environment.

However, there are many variables which underlie the effectiveness of leadership in work organisations. More specifically, these include:

- the characteristics of the manager, personality, attitudes, abilities, value system, and the personal credibility of the manager;
- the type of power of the manager and the basis of the leadership relation;
- the characteristics of the subordinates, their needs and expectations, attitudes, knowledge and experience, and their motivation and commitment;
- the relationship between the manager and the group, and among members of the group;
- the nature of the tasks to be achieved, technology and methods of work organisation;
- organisation structure and systems of management;
- the type of problem and the nature of the manager's decisions;
- the nature and influence of the external environment.

Education and training in management needs to emphasise not only interpersonal skills, but a flexibility of approach, diagnostic ability and the realisation that the most effective form of leadership behaviour is a product of the total leadership situation.

Synopsis

There are many ways of looking at leadership, but essentially it is a relationship through which one person influences the behaviour of other people. The leader–follower relationship is reciprocal and effective leadership is a two-way process. Leadership is related to motivation, the process of communication and the activities of groups. There is a close relationship between leadership and management, especially in work organisations. However, there are differences between the two, and it does not follow that every leader is a manager. Leadership may be viewed in more general terms with emphasis on interpersonal behaviour in a broader context.

Leadership is a dynamic form of behaviour and there are many variables which affect the nature of the leadership relationship. Within an organisation, leadership influence will be dependent upon the type of power which the leader can exercise over other people. Leadership may be examined in terms of the qualities or traits approach, the situational approach, and the functional or group approach. There is a wide range of general functions and responsibilities served by the leadership position. Leadership resides in the functions and not a particular person. The various functions of leadership can be shared among members of the group.

Increasing attention has been given to style theories and leadership as a behavioural category, and to contingency theories. Leadership style is the way in which the functions of leadership are carried out. Greater emphasis has been placed on more democratic styles of leadership. There is, however, a wide range of possible leadership behaviour available to the manager. Two major dimensions of leadership are consideration, concerned with relationships with the group; and structure, concerned with efforts to achieve organisational goals. Leadership style can be measured along a continuum between boss-centred (authoritarian) at one extreme and subordinate-centred (democratic) at the other extreme.

Contingency theories draw attention to the interactions between the variables involved in a leadership situation and patterns of leadership behaviour. The most appropriate form of leadership is dependent upon the variables in a particular leadership situation. Different contingency theories have concentrated on different situational variables. These include: favourability of the leadership situation; decision acceptance and decision quality; path–goal theory; and the 'readiness' of followers.

Research studies tend to indicate that democratic styles of leadership are more likely to produce effective group performance. However, this is not always the case and there is no one 'best' style of leadership. Contingency models demonstrate that there are many forms of leadership. Within an organisation different individuals may fulfil the functions of leadership. Different types of leadership may also be needed at different stages of a business. There are many variables which underlie the effectiveness of leadership in work organisations. The most effective form of leadership behaviour is a product of the total leadership situation.

Review and discussion questions

1. What do you understand by the meaning of leadership? Distinguish leadership from management.

2. Explain the main sources of leadership influence and power. Give a practical example of each of these main sources of influence and power within your own organisation.

3. Distinguish among different approaches to the study of leadership and discuss what you see as the relevance of each of these approaches.

4. Explain what is meant by leadership style. What are the major dimensions of leadership behaviour? Suggest why greater attention has been given to more participative styles of leadership.

5. Assume you are a departmental manager in an organisation. Using the Tannenbaum and Schmidt continuum identify, with reasons, your preferred style of leadership. Give an example of a situation in which you might need to adopt an alternative style of leadership.

6. What do you understand by leader–situation models of leadership? Assess the practical value to the manager of: (i) Fiedler's contingency model of leadership effectiveness; and (ii) Vroom and Yetton's contingency model of leadership.

7. Explain Hersey and Blanchard's model of situational leadership. Give your own views, with supporting reasons, on the validity of this model.

8. List the main situational variables which are likely to influence the most appropriate form of leadership behaviour. Detail three different work situations in which a different style of leadership is likely to be most effective.

9. If you were a consultant on leadership, what areas of needs would you include in designing a leadership training programme for a large work organisation?

Assignment 1   LEAST PREFERRED CO-WORKER (LPC) SCALE (Fig. A)

1. Think of the person with whom you can work least well. This person may be someone you work with now or someone you knew in the past. The person does not have to be someone you like least.

2. Describe this person as he or she appears to you by completing the following scale. Place an 'X' in one of the eight spaces according to how well the adjective fits the person. Look at the words at both ends of the line before placing your 'X'.

3. There are no right or wrong answers. Work rapidly; your first answer is likely to be the best. Do not omit any items and mark each item only once.

Pleasant	:__:__:__:__ __:__:__:__:	Unpleasant
	8 7 6 5 4 3 2 1	
Friendly	:__:__:__:__ __:__:__:__:	Unfriendly
	8 7 6 5 4 3 2 1	
Rejecting	:__:__:__:__ __:__:__:__:	Accepting
	1 2 3 4 5 6 7 8	
Helpful	:__:__:__:__ __:__:__:__:	Frustrating
	8 7 6 5 4 3 2 1	
Unenthusiastic	:__:__:__:__ __:__:__:__:	Enthusiastic
	1 2 3 4 5 6 7 8	
Tense	:__:__:__:__ __:__:__:__:	Relaxed
	1 2 3 4 5 6 7 8	
Distant	:__:__:__:__ __:__:__:__:	Close
	1 2 3 4 5 6 7 8	
Cold	:__:__:__:__ __:__:__:__:	Warm
	1 2 3 4 5 6 7 8	
Cooperative	:__:__:__:__ __:__:__:__:	Uncooperative
	8 7 6 5 4 3 2 1	
Supportive	:__:__:__:__ __:__:__:__:	Hostile
	8 7 6 5 4 3 2 1	
Boring	:__:__:__:__ __:__:__:__:	Interesting
	1 2 3 4 5 6 7 8	
Quarrelsome	:__:__:__:__ __:__:__:__:	Harmonious
	1 2 3 4 5 6 7 8	
Self-assured	:__:__:__:__ __:__:__:__:	Hesitant
	8 7 6 5 4 3 2 1	
Efficient	:__:__:__:__ __:__:__:__:	Inefficient
	8 7 6 5 4 3 2 1	
Gloomy	:__:__:__:__ __:__:__:__:	Cheerful
	1 2 3 4 5 6 7 8	
Open	:__:__:__:__ __:__:__:__:	Guarded
	8 7 6 5 4 3 2 1	

Fig. A

After you have completed the scale compare your responses with those of your colleagues.

Case study

Tony Jackson was first employed in a busy branch office of a building society on a Youth Training Scheme but left after two years because there was no permanent position available at that time. However, nine months later and following a period of continual rapid growth in business a new position was established in the branch. Jackson applied and got the job. After speaking on the telephone to the personnel department at head office, Mary Rogers the branch manager told her staff that she had always got on well with Tony Jackson. He seemed very bright, did everything asked of him and never caused her any trouble.

Jane Taylor had been employed with the branch for the past four years, since leaving sixth form college. Her main duties were those of a cashier and assisting with mortgage advance accounts. Two weeks before Jackson was due to start work Mary Rogers asked to see her.

'From now on, Jane, I would like you to act as senior branch assistant. I need someone to take some of the weight off my shoulders. Your main task will be to be responsible for the quality and accuracy of the work of the staff and to look after things when I'm not here.'

'Well . . . er . . . thank you, Miss Rogers. This is unexpected. It sounds exciting, but I wonder if. . . .'

'Oh, I know you can manage, Jane,' continued Mary Rogers. 'You know I tend to rely on you already. Anyway I've arranged for you to attend a refresher course at head office the week after next. It's all about our systems and procedures, and new ideas on automated technology, I think they called it. I am sure you will cope. And I know the extra money for the job will be helpful, won't it?'

'Yes, that's true enough – the money will certainly be helpful.'

'Good, that's fine then. I'm glad we got that settled. Now you must excuse me,' said Mary Rogers standing up. 'I have to attend to these returns due at head office by the end of next week. Then I have some new ideas for introducing even more business and providing a detailed analysis schedule of advances that I am working on. And I am due to see Pat Gray at the solicitors some time. Always plenty to do, Jane. We must have another chat sometime.'

As Jane left the manager's office she reflected upon the extra money. With the new house and a large mortgage it would be very welcome.

Approximately two months later

Jane Taylor is speaking with Mary Rogers in her office.

'I am sorry to trouble you, Miss Rogers, but it seems that Tony Jackson and I may have a clash of personalities.'

'What do you mean, Jane?' asked Mary Rogers.

'Putting my own feelings to one side, I made a conscious effort not to let it affect my work or responsibilities. But he does not accept jobs I give him without a fuss and tries to pass his work onto the YTS. He also tries to embarrass other members of staff when they are serving customers,' explained Jane.

'How do you mean he embarrasses you?'

'Among other things, he shouts to other assistants at the far end of the office and refers to customers by nicknames to try and make us laugh.'

'Oh dear, well we can't have that, can we now, Jane? What have you done about it?'

'I did try to tell him about it and told him not to be so stupid and childish, but it didn't seem to do any good.'

'All right, Jane, you had better leave it to me,' sighed Mary Rogers. 'I suppose I had better see what I can do. In the meanwhile I think you should try to learn to exercise your authority more.'

Lunchtime, three weeks later

Jane Taylor is with a friend in a local public house.

'What's the matter, Jane? You seem a bit down lately. You're not still annoyed about that assistant, are you?' asked the friend.

'It's not just that, but, oh I don't know . . . but, yes it does upset me,' replied Jane. 'You remember I told you about me seeing the branch manager; well, afterwards I had another go at Jackson. I told him to concentrate on his own work, but this is often below standard and when I showed him his mistakes he just said, "What do you expect, I'm only human."'

'But you didn't just leave it like that?' inquired the friend.

'No, A couple of days later to try and overcome the problem I took him to the staff kitchen. I told him we all had to work together and as assistant manager I had a responsibility to keep the office running smoothly, and that an effort should be made for all of us to get on with each other. If not, I would take the matter further and report it to Miss Rogers. He just shrugged his shoulders and said, "Yeah, all right, let's go and see Mary."'

'So then what happened?' asked the friend expectantly.

'His reaction was unsuspecting. It threw me a bit. I think I said something like "when I'm ready" and walked away. Mind you, his work did seem to improve for a time. But then last week I told him I needed his help with this urgent job and he got all huffy with me. When I told him it was about time he grew up and stopped behaving like that he just said, "If you treat me like a piece of dirt, I'll behave like a piece of dirt" or words to that effect.'

'So did you go to see Miss Rogers, then?' the friend asked.

'I was going to. But, no, not yet. I know I really should go and see her again sometime before too long,' replied Jane.' Anyhow, sorry, must dash now. We are still so busy at work – business seems to be growing all the time. See you again sometime.'

Later that same week

Mary Rogers is on the telephone to head office.

'. . . By the way, I have a member of staff we appointed who I think would benefit from a reminder about the importance of good supervision. I see you are running a course on Human Relations next month. Can you do your usual perfect organisation and fit her in? At least we can suggest she might like to attend. She can be a bit prickly at times but I am sure with all your experience you will know how to use the best words when you write to her.'

Ten days later

Jane Taylor meets her friend in the public house again.

'I'm glad to see you, Veronica. I was hoping I might find you here,' Jane said to her friend.

'What's up, work still troubling you?' asked Veronica. 'I seem to remember you were going to sort things out with the manager. What did she do about that assistant of yours?'

'Yes, I was thinking of going to see her, but then Miss Rogers called me in to see her. She said that she had spoken with Tony Jackson and explained that as senior assistant I had more experience and authority than Tony, and that he should do as he was asked from now on.'

'Good! Quite right too. That's the way it should be,' said Veronica. 'So what's the matter now?'

'Well his concentration and work had appeared to improve again but his attitude got even worse. Then this last week Miss Rogers has been off sick and I am temporarily in charge of the office once again. I usually distribute the work equally in the morning and then carry out the branch manager's duties. Sometimes work comes in during the day and I distribute that straight away. When I leave work in Jackson's tray he usually 'tuts' or makes some sort of sarcastic comment as I am returning to the manager's office. It is so unsettling and you can sense an unpleasant atmosphere in the whole office. And it looks like another assistant, Graham Wilkins, is thinking of leaving. That would be a pity. He is so good at his job. I don't know what to do next. Oh, and I have also been told about a course on management in a couple of weeks at head office. I suppose I shall have to go.'

(i) Discuss the various issues of leadership and related matters raised by this case study.
(ii) Explain what actions you think should be taken in order to help improve the situation. Give supporting reasons.

| Assignment 2 | LEADERSHIP QUESTIONNAIRE |

The following items describe aspects of leadership behaviour. Respond to each item according to the way you would most likely act if you were leader of a work group. Circle whether you would most likely behave in the described way:
always (A); frequently (F); occasionally (O); seldom (S); or never (N).

Scoring

1. Circle the item number for items 8, 12, 17, 18, 19, 30, 34 and 35.
2. Write the number 1 in front of a *circled item number* if you responded S (seldom) or N (never) to that item.
3. Also write a number 1 in front of *item numbers not circled* if you responded A (always) or F (frequently).

4. Circle the number 1s which you have written in front of the following items: 3, 5, 8, 10, 15, 18, 19, 22, 24, 26, 28, 30, 32, 34 and 35.

5. *Count the circled number 1s.* This is your score for concern for people. Record the score in the blank following the letter P at the end of the questionnaire.

6. *Count the uncircled number 1s.* This is your score for concern for task. Record this number in the blank following the letter R.

A F O S N   1. I would most likely act as the spokesperson of the group.

A F O S N   2. I would encourage overtime work.

A F O S N   3. I would allow members complete freedom in their work.

A F O S N   4. I would encourage the use of uniform procedures.

A F O S N   5. I would permit the members to use their own judgment in solving problems.

A F O S N   6. I would stress being ahead of competing groups.

A F O S N   7. I would speak as a representative of the group.

A F O S N   8. I would needle members for greater effort.

A F O S N   9. I would try out my ideas in the group.

A F O S N   10. I would let the members do their work the way they think best.

A F O S N   11. I would be working hard for a promotion.

A F O S N   12. I would tolerate postponement and uncertainty.

A F O S N   13. I would speak for the group if there were visitors present.

A F O S N   14. I would keep the work moving at a rapid pace.

A F O S N   15. I would turn the members loose on a job and let them go to it.

A F O S N   16. I would settle conflicts when they occur in the group.

A F O S N   17. I would get swamped by details.

A F O S N   18. I would represent the group at outside meetings.

A F O S N   19. I would be reluctant to allow the members any freedom of action.

A F O S N   20. I would decide what should be done and how it should be done.

A F O S N   21. I would push for increased production.

A F O S N   22. I would let some members have authority which I could keep.

A F O S N   23. Things would usually turn out as I had predicted.

A F O S N   24. I would allow the group a high degree of initiative.

A F O S N   25. I would assign group members to particular tasks.

A F O S N   26. I would be willing to make changes.

A F O S N   27. I would ask the members to work harder.

A F O S N   28. I would trust the group members to exercise good judgment.

A F O S N   29. I would schedule the work to be done.

A F O S N   30. I would refuse to explain my actions.

A F O S N   31. I would persuade others that my ideas are to their advantage.

A F O S N   32. I would permit the group to set its own pace.

A F O S N   33. I would urge the group to beat its previous record.

A F O S N   34. I would act without consulting the group.

A F O S N   35. I would ask that group members follow standard rules and regulations.

T _____   P _____

After you have recorded your total scores compare your responses with those of your colleagues

Assignment 2 | Interpretation: T-P LEADERSHIP STYLE PROFILE SHEET

To determine your style of leadership, mark your score on the *concern for task dimension* (T) on the left-hand arrow below.

Next, move to the right-hand arrow and mark your score on the *concern for people dimension* (P).

Draw a straight line that intersects the P and T scores. The point at which that line crosses the *shared leadership* arrow indicates your score on that dimension.

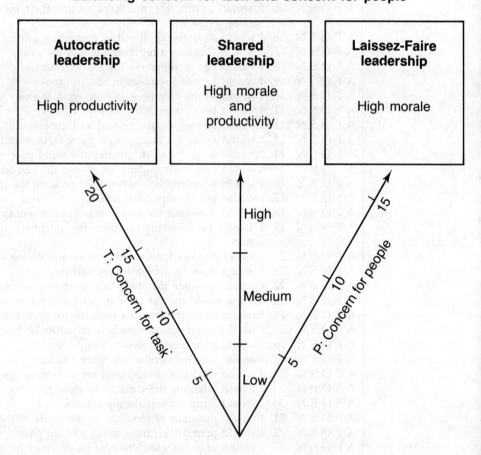

Shared leadership results from balancing concern for task and concern for people

Autocratic leadership	Shared leadership	Laissez-Faire leadership
High productivity	High morale and productivity	High morale

Source: Pfeiffer J. W. and Jones J. E. (eds) *A Handbook of Structured Experiences for Human Relations Training*, Vol. 1, revised, University Associates Inc., San Diego, CA (1974) p. 12.

Compare your style on the T-P Profile Sheet with your score from Assignment 1.

Assignment 3

1. Think of:

   (a) one of the 'best' leaders, *and*
   (b) one of the 'worst' leaders

   that you have experienced, *preferably in a work situation.*

2. Identify and list those specific qualities, or lack of them, which were character-istic of *each* leader. Where possible, draw up your list under three broad head-ings of:

   (a) personal attributes – for example, intelligence, appearance;
   (b) social relationships – for example, approachability, interests;
   (c) task performance – for example, delegation, discipline.

3. Give a brief description of an actual situation which illustrates the behaviour/actions of *each* leader, and the results of such behaviour/action.
   Keep your answer balanced. Bear in mind that even the 'best' leader is likely to have some weak points; and even the 'worst' leader some good points. Try to be as objective as possible and avoid personal bias.

4. Draw up your *own* list, with brief supporting descriptions, of the main character-istics you would expect to be exhibited by a 'good' leader.
   Be prepared to justify your lists and descriptions in class discussion.
   See how your answers relate to your responses to Assignment 1 and Assign-ment 2 of this chapter.

Notes and references

1. This chapter is based in parts on a development of the author's article: Mullins, L. J. 'Approaches to Leadership', *The British Journal of Administrative Management*, vol. 32, no. 8, November 1982, pp. 263–9.
2. Tannenbaum, R., Weschler, I. R. and Masserik, F. *Leadership and Organization*, McGraw-Hill (1961).
3. See, for example: Hunt, J. W. *Managing People at Work*, Second edition, McGraw-Hill (1986).
4. Zaleznik, A. 'Managers and Leaders: Are They Different?' *Harvard Business Review*, May–June 1977, pp. 67–78.
5. Watson, C. M. 'Leadership, Management and the Seven Keys', *Business Horizons*, March–April 1983, pp. 8–13.
6. See, for example: Newman, N. 'Management Navy-Fashion', *Management Today*, January 1981, pp. 34–41, 114–17.
7. For example, see: Bass, B. M. *Leadership, Psychology and Organizational Behavior*, Harper and Row (1960).
8. French, J. R. P. and Raven, B. 'The Bases of Social Power', in Cartwright, D. and Zander, A. F. (eds) *Group Dynamics: Research and Theory*, Third edition, Harper and Row (1968).
9. McGregor, D. *The Human Side of Enterprise*, Penguin (1987) p. 182.
10. For a review of theoretical and empirical research study or leadership, see: Vroom, V. H. 'Leadership', in Dunnette, M. D. (ed). *Handbook of Industrial and Organizational Psychology*, Rand McNally (1976).
11. Byrd, C. *Social Psychology*, Appleton-Century-Crofts (1940).
12. Jennings, E. E. 'The Anatomy of Leadership', *Management of Personnel Quarterly*, vol. 1, no. 1, Autumn 1961, p. 2.
13. Ghiselli, E. E. 'Management Talent', *American Psychologist*, vol. 18, October 1963, pp. 631–42.
14. Stogdill, R. M. *Handbook of Leadership*, Free Press (1974).
15. Miles, M. B. *Learning to Work in Groups*, Columbia University (1959) p. 19.
16. Adair, J. *Action-centred Leadership*, Gower (1979). See also: Adair, J. *The Skills of Leadership*, Gower (1984).
17. For a summary, see: Smith, E. P. *The Manager as a Leader* (Notes for Managers). The Industrial Society (June 1983).
18. Adair, J. *Effective Leadership*, Pan Books (1983).
19. Krech, D., Crutchfield, R. S. and Ballachey, E. L. *Individual in Society*, McGraw-Hill (1962).
20. Roethlisberger, F. J. and Dickson, W. J. *Management and the Worker*, Harvard University Press (1939).
21. Maslow, A. H. 'A Theory of Human Motivation', *Psychological Review*, 50, July 1943, pp. 370–96, and Maslow, A. H. *Motivation and Personality*, Third edition, Harper and Row (1987).
22. Follett, M. P. 'The Giving of Orders', in Metcalf, H. C. and Urwick, L. (eds) *Dynamic Administration*, Harper (1941). Reprinted in Pugh, D. S. (ed.) *Organization Theory*, Penguin (1971) pp. 154–5.
23. Fleishman, E. A. 'Leadership Climate, Human Relations Training and Supervisory Behavior', in Fleishman, E. A. and Bass, A. R. *Studies in Personnel and Industrial Psychology*, Third edition, Dorsey (1974).
24. Likert, R. *New Patterns of Management*, McGraw-Hill (1961).
25. Tannenbaum, R. and Schmidt, W. H. 'How to Choose a Leadership Pattern', *Harvard Business Review*, May–June 1973, pp. 162–75, 178–80.
26. Ibid. Retrospective commentary, pp. 166–8.
27. Fiedler, F. E. *A Theory of Leadership Effectiveness*, McGraw-Hill (1967).
28. For example, see: Filley, A. C., House, R. J. and Kerr, S. *Managerial Process and Organizational Behavior*, Second edition, Scott, Foresman (1976). They refer to the uncertainty of the interpretation of LPC and to what aspects of leadership behaviour it actually represents.
29. Vroom, V. H. and Yetton, P. W. *Leadership and Decision-Making*, University of Pittsburgh Press (1973).
30. House, R. J. 'A Path-Goal Theory of Leadership Effectiveness', *Administrative Science Quarterly*, vol. 16, September 1971, pp. 321–38.

31. House, R. J. and Dessler, G. 'The Path–Goal Theory of Leadership', in Hunt, J. G. and Larson, L. L. (eds) *Contingency Approaches to Leadership*, Southern Illinois University Press (1974).
32. Hersey, P. and Blanchard, K. *Management of Organizational Behavior*, Fifth edition, Prentice-Hall (1988).
33. Nicholls, J. R. 'A New Approach to Situational Leadership', *Leadership and Organization Development Journal*, vol. 6, no. 4, 1985, pp. 2–7.
34. Hersey, P. and Blanchard, K. *Management of Organizational Behavior*, Fifth edition, Prentice-Hall (1988) p. 177.
35. Likert, R. and Likert, J. G. *New Ways of Managing Conflict*, McGraw-Hill (1976).
36. Clarke, C. and Pratt, S. 'Leadership's Four-part Progress', *Management Today*, March 1985, pp. 84–6.

16. THE NATURE OF MANAGEMENT CONTROL

> An important feature of the people–organisation relationship is the need for control. Control systems exist in all spheres of the operations of the organisation and are a necessary part of the process of management. Control completes the cycle of managerial activities. It is concerned with gauging the measure of success in achieving the goals and objectives of the organisation. The manager needs to understand the nature of control and how best to implement control systems in order to improve organisational performance.[1]
>
> ## Objectives
>
> To: (i) Explain the meaning of control and different approaches to management control;
> (ii) Identify the essential elements in a management control system;
> (iii) Examine different forms of control and strategies of management control;
> (iv) Detail characteristics of an effective control system;
> (v) Examine the importance of behavioural factors in management control systems;
> (vi) Assess the nature of financial and accounting systems of management control;
> (vii) Appreciate the effects of management control systems on individual behaviour and organisational performance.

THE MEANING OF CONTROL

The word control may be interpreted in a number of different ways with varying connotations. *Tannenbaum*, for example, sees control as an inherent characteristic of the nature of organisations. The process of control is at the centre of the exchange between the benefits that the individual derives from membership of an organisation and the costs of such benefits.

> Organization implies control. A social organization is an ordered arrangement of individual human interactions. Control processes help circumscribe idiosyncratic behaviors and keep them comformant to the rational plan of the organization. Organizations require a certain amount of conformity as well as the integration of diverse activities. It is the function of control to bring about conformance to organizational requirements and achievement of the ultimate purposes of the organization.[2]

Interpretations of 'control'

Control often has an emotive connotation and is interpreted in a negative manner to suggest direction or command by the giving of orders. People

458

may be suspicious of control systems and see them as emphasising punishment, an indication of authoritarian management, and a means of exerting pressure and maintaining discipline. Some writers seem to take this view, and even to suggest organisational control as exploitation of employees.[3]

This is too narrow an interpretation, however. There is far more to control than simply a means of restricting behaviour or the exercise of authority over others. Control is not only a function of the formal organisation and a hierarchical structure of authority. It is also a function of interpersonal influence. Control is a general concept which is applied to both individual behaviour and organisational performance. Control systems can have positive as well as negative effects. They can be designed and implemented in a constructive and rewarding way.

Control can stand for reliability, order and stability. Whenever a person inquires 'I would like to know how well I am doing', this in effect can be seen as asking for control. Members of staff want to know what is expected of them and how well they are performing. This places emphasis on the exchange of information, and feedback and comparison of actual results against planned targets. At the same time, management need to exercise 'control' over the behaviour and actions of staff in order to ensure a satisfactory level of organisational performance.[4]

Most people show an ambivalence towards control. While they may not wish to have them applied to their own performance they recognise the need for, and usefulness of, control systems. Under certain conditions, however, people may actually desire control. *Lawler* gives three reasons why employees might want to be subject to a control system:

- to give feedback about task performance;
- to provide some degree of structure of tasks, definition of how the tasks are to be carried out, and how performance will be measured; and
- where reward systems, for example pay, are based on performance.[5]

Control, then, can be interpreted in different ways. Our concern is with managerial control systems as a means of checking progress to determine whether the objectives of the organisation are being achieved. Control completes the cycle of managerial activities. The whole purpose of management control is the improvement in performance. (*See* Fig. 16.1.)

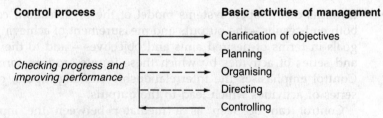

Control process

Checking progress and improving performance

Basic activities of management

Clarification of objectives
Planning
Organising
Directing
Controlling

Fig. 16.1 The purpose of management control

APPROACHES TO MANAGEMENT CONTROL

Different approaches to organisation and management have illustrated different approaches to the nature of control.

Classical writers

The classical writers placed emphasis on structure and formal organisation, sets of principles to guide managerial actions, standardised procedures, and the assumption of rational and logical behaviour. Writers who place emphasis on the technical requirements of the organisation tend to support a high level of control as necessary for efficiency. For example, *Fayol* describes control as:

> In an undertaking, control consists in verifying whether everything occurs in conformity with the plan adopted, the instructions issued and principles established. It has for object to point out weaknesses and errors in order to rectify them and prevent recurrence. It operates on everything, things, people, actions.[6]

It may also be recalled that the ideas of 'Taylorism' and scientific management (discussed in Chapter 2) can be seen as representing a form of management control over the workers and the actual process of work. A distinctive feature of *Taylor*'s thought was that workers should be controlled not only by the giving of orders and maintenance of discipline, but also by removing from them any decisions about the manner in which their work was to be carried out.[7]

Human relations approach

The definition given by *Fayol* illustrates the far-reaching nature of control and the technical requirements of a management control system. But it tends to ignore the behavioural implications. *While the need for some suitable form of control is constant, the extent and manner of control is variable.* This raises the question of how much control over people and actions, that is over behaviour, is necessary and in what form in order to help improve organisational effectiveness.

The human relations approach placed emphasis on the social organisation, and on the importance of groups and informal relationships. Those writers who place emphasis on the social needs of individuals within the work organisation see a high level of control as self-defeating. It produces a negative response, increases internal conflict or results only in short-term improvement in performance. Control should not be seen, therefore, only in the sense that it suggests close and constant supervision or as an organisational constraint on freedom of action by the individual.

Open-systems model

In terms of the open systems model of the organisation, control relates to both end-results – the outputs and measurement of achieving organisational goals in terms of desired aims and objectives – and to the means – inputs and series of activities by which these inputs are transformed to outputs. Control emphasises the interrelationships among inputs, outputs and the series of activities which lead to the outputs.

Control can be seen as a mediator between the input and output processes. It helps to maintain the working of the organisational system. For example, budgetary control is a mediator relating to financial resources. Inventory control and production control relate to material resources. Staff appraisal is a control mediator in the area of human resources.[8] The organisation as an open system is subject to changes in its environment. The operation of management control systems will need, therefore, to be responsive to external influences.

Contingency approach

The contingency approach takes the view that there is no one, best structure. The most appropriate organisation structure and system of management, including methods of control, depend upon contingencies of the situation. Recall the discussion on the organisational setting (Chapter 3) and consider likely variations in the extent and form of management control among such diverse organisations as, for example, a prison, local government department, mass production factory, polytechnic.

The nature of management control is an organisational variable. It may even be that control systems provide a better means of predicting certain facets of organisational behaviour than the classification of technology. See discussion on classification of control systems later in this chapter.

ELEMENTS OF A MANAGEMENT CONTROL SYSTEM

Whatever the nature of control there are five essential elements in a management control system (*see* Fig. 16.2):

- planning what is desired;
- establishing standards of performance;
- monitoring actual performance;
- comparing actual achievement against the planned target; and
- taking corrective action.

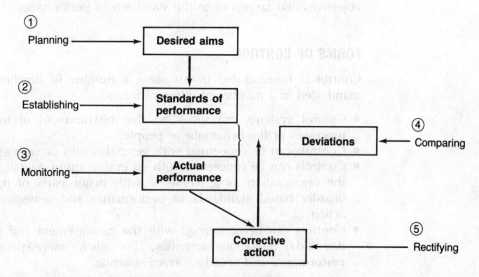

Fig. 16.2 The five essential elements of management control

Planning what is desired involves clarification of the aims to be achieved. It is important that people understand exactly what is required of them. This requires that objectives and targets are specified clearly, and given some measurable attribute. Planning provides the framework against which the process of control takes place.

Related to planning is *the establishment of defined standards of performance* against which the level of success can be determined. This requires realistic measurements by which the degree and quality of goal achievement can be determined. Planning and measurement are prerequisites of control. Without them there can be no control. Objectives and targets, and standards of performance need to be communicated to those concerned and to those who are subject to the operation of the control system.

The third aspect of control is the need for a means of *monitoring actual performance*. This requires feedback and a system of reporting information which is accurate, relevant and timely, and in a form that enables management to highlight deviations from the planned standard of performance. Feedback also provides the basis for decisions to adjust the control system, for example the need to revise the original plan. Feedback should relate to both the desired end results and the means designed to achieve them.

Next, it is necessary *to compare actual performance against planned targets*. This requires a means of interpreting and evaluating information in order to give details of progress, reveal deviations, and identify probable causes. This information should be fed back to those concerned to let them know how well they are getting on.

The final element of a management control system is the *taking of corrective action* to rectify the situation which has led to the failure to achieve objectives or targets, or other forms of deviations identified. This requires consideration of what can be done to improve performance. It requires the authority to take appropriate action to correct the situation, to review the operation of the control system and to make any necessary adjustments to objectives and targets or to the standards of performance.

FORMS OF CONTROL

Control is far-reaching, it can serve a number of functions and can be manifested in a number of different forms.

- Control systems can focus on the measurement of inputs, outputs, processes or the behaviour of people.
- Controls can be concerned with general results or with specific actions.
- Controls can be concerned with an evaluation of overall performance of the organisation as a whole or with major parts of it. This requires broadly based standards of performance and remedies for corrective action.
- Controls can be concerned with the measurement and performance of day-to-day operational activities. This calls for more specific standards of performance and speedy corrective action.

Traditional assumptions of organisation and management

One view of control is based on the traditional assumptions of organisation and management. Control is a feature of the formal organisation and a hierarchical structure of authority. This traditional view assumes that the amount of control is fixed and shared, in varying proportions, between the manager and subordinates.

Another view of control is based on behavioural assumptions. Control is a feature of interpersonal influence and takes place within a network structure of communication. The amount of control is variable and is a function of the common commitment to the objectives of the organisation.

It may be recalled that in Chapter 3 we saw that one form of classification of organisations (coercive, remunerative and normative) was based on the nature of control and the power used by superiors to obtain the compliance of subordinates.

Control can be achieved by the use of routine procedures and the exercise of rules and regulations in an attempt to create consistency and predictability in behaviour. This form of control is related to *Weber*'s model of bureaucracy. Control can be achieved by planning, and through innovation and revision of objectives, in order to maintain the continued existence of the organisation. Control is therefore a general concept. It can be viewed in a number of ways and it can take a variety of forms.

Behavioural control and output control

Ouchi and *Maguire* suggest that the study of control in organisations includes selection and training, socialisation processes, bureaucracy, formalisation and the measurement of outputs.[9] They refer to two independent forms of control that serve different functions.

- *Behavioural control*, which is based on direct personal surveillance; and
- *output control*, which is based on the measurement of outputs.

From a study of data collected from retail department stores, Ouchi and Maguire conclude that the control mechanism in an organisation is not a limited, single-purpose process.

Output measures serve the control needs of the organisation as a whole and are used largely as a result of the demand for a quantifiable, simple measure of results achieved.

Behavioural control serves the needs of the individual manager in charge of one department or section.

The use of behavioural control is responsive to the particular needs of the task, the abilities of the manager and the norms of the organisation. Ouchi and Maguire suggest that if organisations could develop suitable output measures sensitive to the particular needs of each manager, these could serve both departmental and organisational needs. In practice, and in the absence of an all-powerful chief executive or a fully comprehensive set of output measures, it is necessary for organisations to have two complementary means of control: one to serve organisational needs; the other to serve departmental needs.

Action planning and performance control

An alternative approach is suggested by *Mintzberg* who distinguishes between two fundamentally different types of planning and control systems: action planning and performance control.[10] These are two ways in which the organisation can regulate output, although there are a number of inter-relationships between the two systems.

The planning system establishes output standards for each department or section. The control system assesses whether or not these have been met.

Action planning is concerned with the specification of activities that *will* take place, and seeks to regulate specific actions.

Performance control is concerned with *after-the-fact* monitoring of results, and focuses on the regulation of overall performance for a given department or section for a given period of time. (*See* Fig. 16.3.)

Action planning can be used to determine in advance what specific decisions or actions are required; for example, to introduce an additional

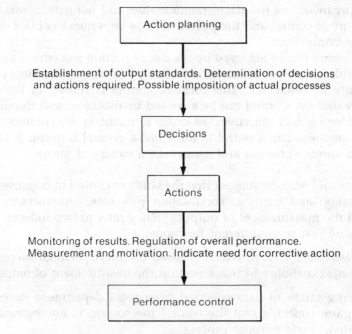

Fig. 16.3 Action planning and performance control
(Adapted from Mintzberg, H., *The Structuring of Organizations*, Prentice-Hall (1979) p. 149.)

product range, or to create a new market, or holes should be drilled with a diameter of z centimetres. Action plans specify decisions that call for specific actions, and these actions may cut across departmental boundaries. At its extreme, action planning may impose the actual processes or means by which decisions and actions are to be carried out. In this case, action planning resembles formalisation of behaviour.

Performance control can serve two functions: measurement and motivation. Performance control systems can be used to measure results of a whole series of actions and is a means of standardising outputs. For example, profitability should increase by X per cent or the number of holes drilled should increase by Y per cent per day. They can be used to indicate to management the need for corrective action to improve performance. Performance control systems can also be used as a motivator to elicit higher performance.

CLASSIFICATION OF CONTROL SYSTEMS

Reeves and *Woodward* propose a classification of control systems based on seven case studies of differing industrial organisations.[11] They concluded that there was little likelihood of classifying control systems along a simple scale in one dimension, but from a large number of possible parameters they described two main aspects of control of particular relevance to the study of organisational behaviour:

- *personal–mechanical*; and
- *unitary–fragmented*.

Personal–mechanical control

Organisations might be positioned on a scale ranging from the extremes of: completely personal hierarchical control; to completely mechanical control; with administrative but impersonal control processes between the two extremes. This scale relates to how control is exercised within an organisation and the degree to which it is personal or impersonal.

An example of personal managerial control is the owner-employer who decides what should be done and monitors the work of employees to see that it is done. Personal hierarchical control becomes more difficult to exercise with increases in the size and technical complexity of organisations. In order to control various specialised and complex processes of the manufacturing task, management introduces impersonal systems of control to influence and regulate the behaviour of those employed in the organisation.

These impersonal control systems may be administrative or mechanical. Examples of administrative controls, which are based on formal standardised procedures, are production planning and cost control. An example of mechanical control is the automatic control system of machine tools or continuous flow production plant which is built into the production process and operates through mechanical or electronic devices.

Unitary–fragmented control

A second characteristic of management control systems of importance in its behavioural effects, identified by *Reeves* and *Woodward*, is the extent to which the various control systems are linked with each other and integrated into a single system of managerial control.

Firms may be positioned on a scale ranging between the two extremes of: a single integrated system of control; and multi-system, fragmented control. Some firms attempt to relate the different control systems set for various departments into a unitary (integrated) system of managerial control. At the other end of the scale some firms do not establish a relationship between standards for such factors as cost or quality and time, and control is fragmented.

With multi-system control, standards of control are set independently by different functional specialists. People in the organisation are trying to satisfy a number of control criteria at the same time. For example, a particular task has to meet the demands of the production controller, the work study person, the personnel manager, the inspector and the cost accountant.

Four categories of control

Using the two scales together, *Reeves* and *Woodward* identify four categories of control. (*See* Fig. 16.4.)

A1 Firms with unitary and mainly personal controls.

A2 Firms with unitary and mainly impersonal administrative or mechanical controls.

B1 Firms with fragmented and mainly personal controls.

B2 Firms with fragmented and mainly impersonal administrative or mechanical controls.

Reeves and Woodward suggest that the normal processes of industrial and technical development would move a firm in the direction of:

$$A1 \rightarrow B1 \rightarrow B2 \rightarrow A2$$

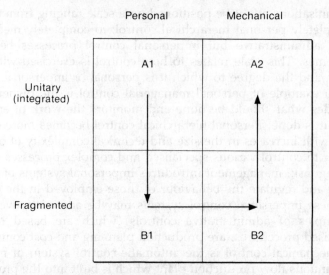

Fig. 16.4 Categorisation of control systems
(Adapted and reproduced with permission from Woodward, J., *Industrial Organization: Theory and Practice*, 2nd edition, Oxford University Press (1980) p. xxi.)

From a further analysis of the data collected from Woodward's south Essex study of 100 manufacturing firms, clear links emerged between the original classification of technology (unit and small batch production; large batch and mass production; and process production) and the above categorisation of managerial control systems (*see* Table 16.1).

Unit and small batch production firms tended to have unitary and mainly personal controls.

Process production firms tended to have unitary and mainly impersonal controls.

The similarities in some organisational characteristics between unit production firms and process firms identified in Woodward's south Essex study could be explained by the fact that in both groups unitary control systems predominated.

In the case of large batch and mass production firms, those with predominantly personal controls had similar organisational characteristics to unit

Table 16.1 Relationship between control system and classification of technology

	Control system A1 (%)	Control system B1 (%)	Control system B2 (%)	Control system A2 (%)
Unit and small batch production	75	25	–	–
Large batch and mass production	15	35	40	10
Process production	–	–	5	95
Total firms	28	21	18	33

(Reproduced with permission from J. Woodward, *Industrial Organization: Theory and Practice*, 2nd edition, Oxford University Press (1980) p. xxi.)

firms; and those with predominantly mechanical controls had an organisation structure similar to process firms.

From the analysis, Reeves and Woodward suggest that control systems may be the underlying variable which links organisational behaviour and technology, and that the classification of control systems they propose might provide a better means of predicting certain facets of organisational behaviour than the classification of technology.

STRATEGIES OF MANAGEMENT CONTROL

Four particularly significant strategies of control in organisations are explained by *Child* (*see* Fig. 16.5):

* personal centralised;
* bureaucratic;
* output; and
* cultural.[12]

---

1 *Personal centralised control*
   1.1 centralised decision-taking
   1.2 direct supervision
   1.3 personal leadership: founded upon ownership or charisma, or technical expertise
   1.4 reward and punishment reinforce conformity to personal authority

2 *Bureaucratic control*
   2.1 breaking down of tasks into easily definable elements
   2.2 formally specified methods, procedures and rules applied to the conduct of tasks
   2.3 budgetary and standard cost-variance accounting controls
   2.4 technology designed to limit variation in conduct of tasks, with respect to pace, sequence and possibly physical methods
   2.5 routine decision-taking delegated within prescribed limits
   2.6 reward and punishment systems reinforce conformity to procedures and rules

3 *Output control*
   3.1 jobs and units designed to be responsible for complete outputs
   3.2 specification of output standards and targets
   3.3 use of 'responsibility accounting' systems
   3.4 delegation of decisions on operational matters: semi-autonomy
   3.5 reward and punishment linked to attainment of output targets

4 *Cultural control*
   4.1 development of strong identification with management goals
   4.2 semi-autonomous working: few formal controls
   4.3 strong emphasis on selection, training and development of personnel
   4.4 rewards oriented towards security of tenure and career progression

---

Fig. 16.5 Four strategies of management control
(From Child, John, *Organization: A Guide to Problems and Practice*, 2nd edition, Paul Chapman (1984) p. 159.)

Personal centralised control This is an approach often found in small owner-managed organisations. The approach is characterised by the centralisation of decision making and initiative around a leadership figure. Control consists very largely of personal inspection to see that decisions are carried out, and the leader may spend a high proportion of time supervising the work personally. Once the organisation grows large enough to employ someone to undertake detailed supervision of everyday tasks, the locus of decision making and close supervision will tend to become separated. A major criterion for the allocation of rewards and punishment is likely to be obedience to the leader's authority. The authority of the leader will usually rest upon the rights of ownership, special personal qualities (charisma) or technical expertise.

As organisations grow in size and technological complexity, a heavy centralised approach to control becomes increasingly difficult to maintain. In a large, complex organisation top managers will find increasing external demands on their time. In the development of an organisation, a combination of factors will move management away from personal centralised control towards bureaucratic control or output control.

Bureaucratic control This approach to control is familiar in public sector organisations and in many other types of large organisations. The approach is based on the specification of how members should behave and carry out their work. There is an attempt to ensure predictability through formal job descriptions and procedures, the breaking down of tasks into constituent elements, and the specification of standard methods for the performance of tasks. Reward and punishment systems can be designed to reinforce this control strategy. Compliance can be rewarded by upgrading, improved status, favourable employment benefits and job security.

Bureaucratic control will make use of accounting control systems such as budgetary control (discussed later in this chapter) and standard cost variances. The bureaucratic strategy also permits delegation without loss of control. Managers can delegate routine decision making within formally prescribed limits of discretion.

Output control This approach relies upon the ability to identify specific tasks having a measurable output or criterion of overall achievement; for example, an end-product, a part manufactured to agreed standards, batch production or a sub-assembly. Once outputs or criteria for achievement have been identified, management can specify output standards and targets. Rewards and sanctions can be related to performance levels expressed in output terms. The efficiency of incentives will largely depend on the degree of trust in management's intentions to honour the relationship between performance and rewards.

Output control can make use of 'responsibility accounting' systems. Responsibility accounting assigns financial responsibility to specified sub-units of the organisation, measures the performance of the units and provides feedback on performance for those persons assigned the responsibility and to their supervisors. The assignment of responsibility may be in terms of investment centres, profit centres or cost centres. Output control strategy is aimed at facilitating the delegation of operational decision making without the need for bureaucratic controls or relying on close personal supervision. Once output standards have been agreed, subordinates can work with a 'semi-autonomous' relationship to management, free from detailed control over how tasks are carried out.

The strategy of output control can stand in the way of introducing technological advances which require a more integrated system of operation.

However, in such a situation it may be possible to move the level of output control from group output to plant output. Output control may be difficult to apply to certain activities, such as the legal department of a business organisation. Although it may be difficult to establish suitable and agreed measures of output, and it may be difficult for management to codify the activities involved, output control may be more appropriate than the application of a bureaucratic control strategy.

Cultural control

This approach tends to be exemplified by organisations offering professional services and staffed by professional people. The basis of cultural control strategy is the acceptance and willing compliance with the requirements of management, for example through strong professional identification and acceptance of the values and beliefs of the organisation. Provided members have the necessary skills and ability they can be given wide freedom of action in deciding how to undertake their responsibilities. There may not be any readily appropriate way of assessing the quality of output, especially in the short term, for example management development work of a personnel department.

There is likely to be careful selection, training and socialisation of staff in order to permit the use of semi-autonomous methods of working, with only limited formal controls. The combination of elements of cultural and output control could lead to self-managing units or teams with responsibility for completing projects and meeting agreed targets. This approach to control can only work with agreement on operating objectives and depends upon some shared culture among members of the organisation. Although a cultural control strategy may help identification with the objectives of corporate management, it is usually supported by substantial material inducements such as high salaries, fringe benefits and job security.

CHARACTERISTICS OF AN EFFECTIVE CONTROL SYSTEM

Whatever the nature or form of control there are a number of characteristic features of an effective control system. *Hicks* and *Gullett* state: 'Control systems should be understandable and economical, be related to decision centres, register variations quickly, be selective, remain flexible and point to corrective action.'[13] Developing the suggestion of Hicks and Gullett, we can identify a number of important characteristics of an effective control system.

Understandable

For a control system to be meaningful *it must be understood by those involved in its operation*. The purpose of the control system and the information it provides must be fully comprehensible to those who have to act on the results. The level of sophistication of a control system should be related to the nature of the activities involved and to the technical competence of the staff. For example, a detailed and sophisticated analysis of financial ratios may have little significance for an industrial shop-floor supervisor. Information must be presented in a suitable format. If information is presented in a way which people do not understand they are likely to disregard it, and the full potential of the control system will not be realised. Equally, a too simplistic system of reporting which does little to help pinpoint the cause of deviations will not be of much value to the manager.

The control system should, wherever possible, yield objective information based on appropriate quantitative or qualitative units of measurement which cannot easily be questioned or subject to different interpretations and possible misunderstanding.

Related to decision centres

Controls should *conform with the structure of the organisation and be related to decision centres responsible for performance*. Information should be supplied to those managers who have the responsibility for specified areas of activity and who are capable of using this information to evaluate the degree of success in achievement of objectives; for example, the cause of excess expenditure in a manufacturing operation. Is this a result of increases in prices of raw materials? Is it because of the need to use substitute materials or suppliers? Is it because of problems with the manufacturing process? Or is it because of lower productivity by certain workers?

The information should enable managers to control their area of responsibility, and should be presented in a form which shows clearly when corrective action is necessary.

Reporting deviations quickly

An effective control system should *report deviations from the desired standard of performance as quickly as possible*. Ideally, indications of likely deviations should be discovered before they actually occur. It is important for deviations from the plan to be reported in good time so that corrective action to remedy the situation can be undertaken promptly. For example, information that the budget is likely to be overspent or underspent should arrive in sufficient time to enable the manager to do something about it and avoid drastic last-minute action.

Critical activities of the organisation

The control system should *draw attention to the critical activities which are important to the success of the organisation*. An unnecessary number of controls over comparatively unimportant activities are uneconomic and time consuming, they can have a demoralising effect on staff and may possibly result in lack of attention to the key control points. Certain control points are more important than others. Careful control must be maintained in key result areas and in those activities which are crucial to the success of the organisation.

For example, a restaurant manager would need to have information on the number of orders taken at different times, and the number and type of meals provided, in order to deploy staff in the most effective manner. Information will also be needed to ensure adequate cash flow.

Flexibility

To be effective, *a control system must be flexible*. It must yield information which is not influenced by changes in other factors unconnected to the purpose of the control system. For example, a control system established five years ago which specifies that reports to top management should be made whenever expenditure exceeds the budget by more than £x, is unlikely to be effective if no account has been taken of the effects of inflation. As prices rise over a period of time the excess expenditure will be an increasingly less serious matter.

Also, if the same amount is applied in all cases, large spending departments may be subject to excessive control and small spending departments not monitored closely enough. Control systems should not become an end in themselves. They should be designed to improve the operations of the organisation and be adaptable to changing environmental circumstances.

Nature of activity to which it relates

The control system should be *consistent with the objective of the activity to which it relates*. In addition to locating deviations from the planned standard of performance, the control system should be sophisticated enough to indicate ways in which performance can be improved.

For example, in the field of social services it may not be sufficient just to know that expenditure has been kept within the budget, without any under- or over-spending. It would be more helpful to know in what areas expenditure has been incurred. It might be that the highest share of expenditure has gone to the financially better-off, who may be more knowledgeable of their rights and the procedures involved, than those who may be in greater financial need.

The control system should therefore address itself to causes of deviations rather than to symptoms. Controls may point to a number of possible problem areas for corrective action. Management will need to investigate these possibilities, and to determine the most appropriate form of corrective action which will deal with the causes of the deviation and solve the problems identified.

Continual review

Control systems should themselves *be subject to a continual review* to ensure that they are effective and appropriate in terms of the results they produce. They should not be too costly or elaborate, but should satisfy the characteristic features suggested above.

Behavioural implications

An important additional feature underlying all aspects of an effective management control system is *the need to consider the behavioural implications*. 'The broad objective of the control function is to effectively employ all the resources committed to an organization's operations. However, the fact that non-human resources depend on human effort for their utilization makes control, in the final analysis, the regulation of human performance.'[14]

Control often provokes an emotional response from those affected by it. It should be recognised, therefore, that the activities of a management control system raise important considerations of the human factor and of the management of people.

BEHAVIOURAL FACTORS IN MANAGEMENT CONTROL SYSTEMS

The effectiveness of management control systems will depend upon both their design and operation, and the attitudes of staff and the way they respond to them. Control systems provide an interface between human behaviour and the process of management.

According to *Tannenbaum*: 'Research suggests that the manner in which control is exercised, or the amount that is exercised, has significant effects on the adjustment of organisation members and on the performance of the organisation.'[15] Tannenbaum puts forward five general propositions which help explain some of these effects.

- Control has both practical and symbolic implications. Control implies what an individual must or must not do, restrictions and areas of freedom of choice. It also has a special meaning or significance to individuals by implying something about their importance and standing within the organisation.
- The exercise of control has a positive value for most members of the organisation. Most people prefer to exercise some control and authority in their work situations, and they experience greater satisfaction than when they are powerless and do not exercise control.
- The exercise of control helps the member to identify with the organisational system. The exercise of control implies compatibility with the intentions of the controller. Psychologically, the system is an extension of the person exercising control. The person who exercises control is less alienated and is more likely to identify with, and support the aims of, the organisation.
- The exercise of control can result in frustrating as well as satisfying consequences. Individuals who are unable to exercise control tend to be less satisfied with their work situations and are often alienated and apathetic. People who exercise control have a greater sense of personal involvement and interest in the success or failure of decisions taken.
- People who exercise control in organisations may be more willing to accept control over themselves. Because of the greater loyalty to, and identification with, the organisation people may more readily accept increased control, and the need to conform to the regulations and norms of the organisation.

Resistance to control systems

Control gives rise to a number of important behavioural considerations. Control systems can help fulfil people's needs at work and their presence may be welcomed by some members of staff. Often, however, control systems are perceived as a threat to the need satisfaction of the individual. Control over behaviour is resented and there is a dislike of those responsible for the operation of the control system. Even when control systems are well designed and operated there is often strong resistance, and attempts at non-compliance, from those affected by them.

The amount of resistance is determined by both the nature of the control system and the characteristics of the individuals involved. For example, *Lawler* suggests that resistance to control systems is most likely to be present when:

1. The control system measures performance in a new area.
2. The control system replaces a system that people have a high investment in maintaining.
3. The standards are set without participation.
4. The results from the control system are not fed back to the people whose performance is measured.
5. The results from the control system are fed to higher levels in the organization and are used by the reward system.
6. The people who are affected by the system are relatively satisfied

with things as they are and they see themselves as committed to the organization.

7. The people who are affected by the system are low in self-esteem and authoritarianism.[16]

OVERCOMING RESISTANCE TO MANAGEMENT CONTROL SYSTEMS

Control systems are bound to be viewed with a certain amount of suspicion, and possible resentment, by members of staff. Therefore, if control systems are to be successful in leading to improved performance and organisational effectiveness, they require attention to factors which influence human behaviour.

There are a number of factors which can affect the successful implementation of management control systems, including:

- consultation and participation;
- motivation;
- groups and the informal organisation;
- organisation structure;
- leadership style and systems of management.

Consultation and participation

The manager should attempt to enlist the co-operation of staff and help them to feel that decisions which are taken are in their own interests. This calls for a high level of consultation and encouragement for staff to participate in the decision-making process. If staff are committed personally to particular objectives they are more likely to direct themselves and to exercise self-control over their level of performance. Staff should understand, and accept, the purpose and nature of control systems. This should help to make for better employee relations.

Motivation

Motivation is an important aspect in the operation of a control system. Lack of positive motivation can lead to frustrated behaviour resulting in lack of commitment to the aims of the organisation and poor job performance. This may lead to increased control.

People are influenced by the expected results of their actions. Motivation is a function of the relationship between effort expended and likely outcomes, and the expectation that reward will be related to performance.[17] People want to know how well they are performing. This places emphasis on the need for reporting of information and feedback, and the comparison of actual performance against planned targets.

Recognition given for a satisfactory level of attainment coupled with a suitable reward system, as integral parts of control, can do much to motivate staff and encourage improved performance. Motivation is an important aspect in the operation of a control system. As *Brech*, for example, points out: 'No method of control will prove effective unless the (organisation's) employees are motivated in some way to achieve good results.'[18]

Groups and the informal organisation

The operations of groups and the informal organisation can influence the functioning of control systems. It may be recalled that one of the findings of the bank wiring room experiment in the famous Hawthorne studies was that the group did not follow company policy on the reporting of production

473

figures. Although actual production varied the workers officially reported a relatively standard amount of output each day, and in order to remain as a member of the informal group the supervisor acquiesced to this.

Recall, also, the discussion on the value of group working as an approach to job design and improving job satisfaction (Chapter 12). With the development of autonomous work groups, members have greater freedom and wider discretion over the planning, execution and control of their own work.

In order to maintain co-operation and commitment of staff the manager must continually review at both the individual and group level the operation of the control system and the progress made in achieving objectives. This includes full participation of staff in discussions on the operation of control systems which affect them, on the difficulties and problems experienced, and on decisions concerning remedial action and future plans.

Organisation structure

The structure of an organisation and its pattern of management can affect the implementation of control systems. Organisation structure can be distinguished in terms of two divergent systems of management practice at extreme ends of a continuum – the *mechanistic* and the *organic* systems.[19] These two systems imply differences in the total amount of control.

The mechanistic system is a more rigid structure and is appropriate to relatively stable conditions. It is characterised by specialisation, a clear hierarchical structure of authority, closely defined duties and responsibilities, and the downward flow of information. Organisations with a mechanistic structure are more readily suited, therefore, to the operation and implementation of traditional systems of control.

The organic system, however, is a more fluid structure and appears to be required for conditions of change and for uncertain environmental influences. This system is characterised by a network structure of control, authority and communication, the continual adjustment and redefinition of jobs and communication based on information and advice rather than instructions. New problems constantly arise and require actions which cannot be allocated among defined roles in the hierarchical structure. The effectiveness of control is more dependent upon individual involvement and commitment to the aims of the organisation. Traditional systems of control are therefore less suited to organisations with an organic structure.

The nature and form of management control systems are also influenced by specific features of organisational design. For example, the extent of divisionalisation and delegation, and the shape of the hierarchical pyramid structure, will affect the means of control over the behaviour of staff.[20]

An example of this can be seen in Richard Branson's Virgin Group.

> The group's organizational structure reflects the decentralized arrangements at the top. Virgin's 2,500 employees worldwide work in small units of up to 80 people, each with its own director. In London alone there are 25 offices spread across the three divisions. 'People can dress as they feel comfortable, they work out of pleasant surroundings, and in small groups. There isn't a clock-in, clock-out mentality as there is in some companies, and because we have that attitude people are quite willing to work long hours.'[21]

Leadership style and systems of management

The exercise of control is an expression of leadership style and systems of management. The style of managerial leadership is a function of the manager's attitudes towards people, and assumptions about human nature and behaviour – for example *McGregor*'s Theory X and Theory Y.[22]

The central principle of Theory X is direction and control through a centralised system of organisation and the exercise of authority. By contrast, Theory Y is based on the principle of the integration of individual and organisational goals. People can learn to accept and to seek responsibility, and will exercise self-direction and self-control in the service of objectives to which they are committed.

The character of control processes is one of the organisational variables identified in *Likert*'s four-fold model of management systems: System 1 (exploitive–authoritative), System 2 (benevolent–authoritative), System 3 (consultative) and System 4 (participative–group).[23]

In System 1 the major concern with regard to the performance of the control function is at the top hierarchical level in the organisation, the review and control functions are concentrated in top management, and there is an informal organisation opposing the goals of the formal organisation. In System 4 the concern for performance of control functions is spread throughout the organisation, review and control functions are carried out at all levels, and the formal and informal organisation share the same goals.

Likert found that in Systems 1 and 2 organisations, high performance goals by superiors, coupled with high-pressure supervision using tight budgets and controls, yield high productivity initially because of compliance based on fear. However, because of unfavourable attitudes, poor communications, lack of co-operative motivation and restriction of output, the long-term result is high absence and turnover, and low productivity and earnings.

On the other hand, the nearer the behavioural characteristics of an organisation approach to System 4, efficiency improves. Organisational decisions are improved since they are based on more accurate information and there is greater motivation to implement the decisions.

Management by Objectives

A system of Management by Objectives may allow staff to accept greater responsibility and to make a higher level of personal contribution. Participation is inherent if Management by Objectives is to work well, and there is an assumption that most people will direct and control themselves willingly if they share in the setting of their objectives.[24]

The main features of Management by Objectives are: the setting of objectives; the specification of jobs and key tasks by discussion between the manager and staff; identification of key result areas; agreement on standards of performance; control, review and adjustment of objectives. The concept of Management by Objectives is therefore closely related to the general principles of a management control system.

Management by Objectives can be applied as a modern and effective method of control (Table 16.2). It could, for example, be used in a positive and constructive way to provide a control system related to performance appraisal and career progression.

Table 16.2 Management by Objectives as a control system.

Activities in Management by Objectives	Management control system
Agree what you expect from me	Planning what is desired.
	Specification of objectives and targets.
Give me an opportunity to perform	Establishing defined standards of performance.
Let me know how I'm getting on	Monitoring and reviewing actual performance.
	Control information and feedback.
Give me guidance where I need it	Comparing actual performance against planned targets.
	What can be done to improve performance?
Reward me according to my contribution	Recognition of achievement.
	Motivation for further improvement in performance.
Control, review and adjustment	Taking corrective action.

(Adapted and reproduced with permission from J. W. Humble, *Management by Objectives*, Management Publications Limited for the British Institute of Management (1972) p. 46.)

FINANCIAL AND ACCOUNTING SYSTEMS OF MANAGEMENT CONTROL

Management control systems are frequently thought of in terms of financial or accounting systems. The reasons for this are easy to understand.

- The stewardship of financial resources is of vital concern to the majority of organisations. In both private enterprise and public sector organisations there is an increasing need to demonstrate value for money expended.
- Organisational aims, objectives and targets are often expressed in financial terms and measured in terms of profitability. Results are measured and reported in financial terms.
- Money is quantifiable and is a precise unit of measurement. It is easily understood, and is often used as a common denominator and as a basis for comparison.
- Financial limits are easy to apply as a measure of control and easy to relate to. For example, the need for control is an integral part of the process of delegation. This control may easily be applied where, for example, a manager gives a subordinate the authority, without prior reference, to incur expenditure on certain items up to a given financial cost limit.

It is understandable, therefore, that so much attention is given to financial and accounting systems of control. But management control embraces far more than just financial or accounting considerations. It is concerned with the whole process of management: with the extent to which organisational aims are achieved and with improvement in performance. Control includes considerations of such factors as quality, judgement, consumer satisfaction, market share, social responsibilities, and the human factor and management of people.

Objective of profit maximisation

Although the objective of profit maximisation is undoubtedly of great importance, it is not by itself a sufficient criterion for the effective management of a business organisation. In practice, there are many other considerations and motivations which affect the desire for the greatest profit or maximum economic efficiency and the accompanying assumptions which underlie the economic theory of the firm.

The objective of profit maximisation must be considered over a period of time. It is also important to give full attention to the non-financial factors which affect organisational performance.

> A company can increase its short-term profit very easily. Cut down vital capital expenditures, reduce essential services, slash depreciation, and the return on investment will look splendid – for a time. The question is, for how long? . . . There is a point also to be made about non-financial factors, some of which indicate a great deal about the future performance of a company. Such factors as the industrial relations record, absenteeism, productivity performance, the ability or otherwise to meet deadlines, product quality and design and the extent to which customers are satisfied, are obviously eloquent pointers to the company's prospects, both for the present and the future.[25]

Behavioural factors   To what extent do financial and accounting systems of control take account of behavioural factors and motivate people to improve their performance?[26]

Accounting control systems such as internal audit, management by exception and budgetary control tend to operate in a negative way and to report only on the unfavourable, or on favourable variances which may have adverse consequences, for example less spent than budgeted. 'Success' for the accounting staff may be equated with the 'failure' of other staff. As a result there is no specific recognition from management. There is only a limited sense of achievement or self-esteem for favourable performance or where no corrective action is required. There is little, if any, positive motivation.

Budgets, for example, are accounting techniques designed to control costs through people.[27] Budgets are used as a medium for personality expression and may also be used as a pressure device. Budgetary control can also be seen as imposing restriction on freedom of action by the individual.

> Budgetary control was originally intended to quantify liberty: The idea was that you said to a man, 'We are not going to tether you to this post any more. We are going to fix a financial fence, which you have agreed, and within this fence you can do whatever you like – trot, canter, gallop just as you please.' But the accountants got hold of budgetary control, and now it's universally regarded as just another form of head office restriction.[28]

Design and implementation of accounting systems of control   There is, of course, nothing wrong with the use of accounting systems of control such as internal auditing, management by exception and budgetary control, or with associated techniques such as time and motion studies. What needs to be considered is the manner in which these controls and techniques are applied, and the differences in use as a result of the attitudes adopted and the motives felt to be important in influencing behaviour.

For example, research by *Cammann* explored the moderating effects of subordinate participation in decision making and subordinate job difficulty on their responses to different uses of control systems by superiors. The use of control systems for problem solving was positively related to job satisfaction under conditions of low job difficulty and low participation. The use of control systems for goal setting was positively related to satisfaction under conditions of high subordinate participation and high job difficulty. Results of the study indicate that responses to different uses of control systems will vary as a function of the contexts in which they are used.[29]

Hopwood distinguishes alternative approaches to information processing in terms of official or unofficial, and routine or non-routine. Unofficial strategies reflect attempts by non-senior members of the organisation to satisfy their own information needs. Official, routine approaches include most accounting systems. But 'even routine information systems can be designed to consciously encourage the exercise of self-control by organisational participants rather than merely facilitate the exercise of control by others'.[30]

Control systems can have positive as well as negative effects. Financial and accounting control systems, as with other forms of control, should be designed and implemented in a constructive and rewarding way. To do this, they must take account of individual, social and organisational factors which determine people's patterns of behaviour.

MANAGEMENT SERVICES AND TECHNIQUES

In the search for improved organisational effectiveness there is an increasing range of specialist skills to help managers, whether in business, public sector or other organisations. When striving to achieve the goals and objectives of the organisation there are a number of 'tools' which can assist the manager in the execution of work and the process of control. Many of these tools come under the heading of management services and techniques. These services and techniques aid management by providing relevant information to enable improved decision making and more effective control. (*See* Fig. 16.6.)

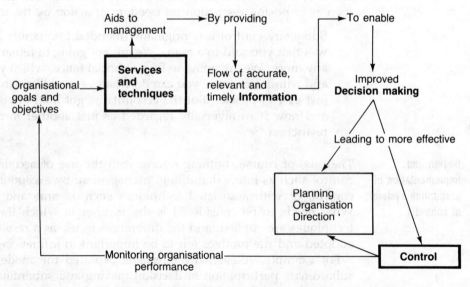

Fig. 16.6 The role of management services and techniques as part of the control process

The meaning of management services and techniques

'Management services' and 'management techniques' tend to be overworked terms and there are considerable differences in the interpretations placed upon them. Although it is not the purpose here to explain the particular tools of management, it is important to understand what is implied by the terms management services and management techniques.

One simple approach is to a regard management services as the generic term covering the grouping of a number of specialist, advisory activities or services to management. It is the emergence of various new specialisations and techniques which has given rise to the term management services. In ideas of 'hierarchical' levels, management services might be regarded as the more comprehensive and embracing term covering aids to management in the broader sense; while management techniques are particular specialisations and skills for dealing with individual problems.

On this basis computerisation, organisation and methods, management information systems, programme budgeting and management accounting could be quoted as examples of management services. Simulation, critical path analysis, discounted cash flow, and cost–benefit analysis could be quoted as examples of management techniques. However, terminology is confused. There is no clear distinction between the use of the word services or of the word techniques. The two words are often used synonymously or interchangeably. There are different connotations in different publications and different organisations, and varying interpretations on the range of activities properly placed under each heading.[31]

The use of management techniques

Whatever the debate on terminology, the important thing is the use of techniques as aids to management and the process of control. Many techniques are based on a high level of mathematics or statistics, and they have been surrounded with an aura of mystique and glamour. Because of their apparent complexity many techniques may seem to the manager to lack practical application. Some techniques are by their nature complex and not easy to describe in simple terms. This may further confuse the manager. There is, therefore, the danger of using sophisticated techniques for their own sake when simpler methods might be just as satisfactory. Used in appropriate circumstances, however, management services and techniques can assist in the execution of work and the process of control.

The manager will not usually be expected to have a detailed technical knowledge of all the individual techniques. This is a job for the specialist. The manager should, however, be aware of their main features, advantages and limitations; and have sufficient understanding of how different techniques might be applied to help the process of management and the development and operation of control systems. The responsibility for the implementation of these techniques should rest with the manager. An understanding of management services and techniques will aid the activity of management, including the control process, and help to improve organisational effectiveness.

Synopsis

There are varying connotations of the meaning of control. It is often interpreted in a negative manner to suggest direction or command, the restriction of behaviour or even exploitation of employees. However, control is not only a function of the formal organisation. It is also a function of inter-personal influence and can have positive effects. Most people recognise the need for control and in certain circumstances may actually desire control. The whole purpose of management control is improvement in performance. Different approaches to organisation and management have illustrated different approaches to the nature of control.

The essential elements in a management control system are: planning what is desired; establishment of standards of performance; monitoring actual performance; comparison with planned targets; and taking corrective action. Control is a general concept. It can serve a number of functions and take a variety of forms. Control systems can be classified in terms of two main aspects: personal–mechanical and unitary–fragmented. Four signifi-cant strategies of management control are personal centralised, bureaucratic, output and cultural.

There are a number of important characteristics of an effective control system. The system should be understood, conform with the structure of the organisation, report deviations quickly, draw attention to critical acti-vities of the organisation, be flexible, consistent with the activity to which it relates and subject to continual review. If control systems are to be successful in leading to improved performance then attention must also be given to the factors which influence human behaviour.

Control gives rise to a number of important behavioural considerations. Control systems can help fulfil people's needs at work and their presence may be welcomed. Often, however, control over behaviour is resented and perceived as a threat. The manager should, therefore, enlist the co-operation and commitment of staff, and provide for participation in the operation of control systems. The effective functioning of control systems is also influ-enced by: the motivation of staff; the operation of groups and the informal organisation; organisation structure; leadership style and systems of management. The system of Management by Objectives can be applied as an effective method of control related to performance appraisal and career progression.

Management control systems are frequently thought of in terms of finan-cial and accounting systems. There are a number of reasons for this. However, management control embraces more than just financial or accounting considerations. Accounting control systems tend to operate in a negative way, and to give little specific recognition from management and only a limited sense of achievement. What needs to be considered is the manner in which financial and accounting control systems, as with other forms of control, motivate people to improve their performance. To do this, they must take account of individual, social and organisational factors which determine people's patterns of behaviour.

Review and discussion questions

1. Explain what you understand by the meaning of control. What do you see as the purposes of control in work organisations?
2. Outline how different approaches to organisation and management have

viewed the nature of control. What are the essential elements of a management control system?

3. Explain the various forms of control. How might management control systems be classified?

4. Identify, with your own supporting examples, the characteristic features of a good control system.

5. Explain the importance of the behavioural implications of management control. What factors are likely to influence the amount of resistance to control systems?

6. Suggest how: (i) Management by Objectives (MBO), and (ii) management services and techniques, might be applied to help improve the process of control in work organisations.

7. Discuss what you see as the likely consequences of a manager exercising close personal supervision as a means of maintaining control over the work of subordinate staff.

8. Discuss the main factors which are likely to affect the successful implementation of management control systems.

9. Why is it that many systems of control in work organisations tend to be financial or accounting in nature? To what extent do you think it is justified that they should be, and what other factors should be considered?

Practical assignment

(i) For your own or some other organisation, identify:

(a) the various areas of control of the activities of the organisation; and
(b) the type of control systems adopted.

Explain how you would classify the different forms of control.

(ii) Examine a particular management control system of your choice and assess the extent to which it satisfies:

(a) the essential elements of a control system; and
(b) the characteristic features of a good control system.

Give your views, with supporting reasons, on the apparent effectiveness of the control system.

(iii) Attempt to discover, and explain, a particular situation in which a management control system was welcomed by staff and/or where lack of a control system was the source of frustration to staff.

Case study

You are the recently appointed Chief Executive of the Omega organisation. Your organisation is located in a large town and comprises five operating units and a head office with personnel, client service, management services and finance divisions. It employs a total of 5,000 people.

The organisation has been successful in recent years. Clients report receiving good service and the financial performance of the organisation is good. The organisation has been run on centralised lines with tight financial controls applied by the Finance Division.

You have concluded that a more decentralised approach to management is needed, mainly to give unit managers greater discretion. The clients served by the five operating units have different and changing needs. You feel that greater discretion will allow a more flexible response to these various needs at unit level.

One of the ways you have decided to achieve decentralisation is to decentralise the management accounting function. Each operating unit will have a management accountant responsible to the unit General Manager for operational matters. The Finance Director will retain overall professional responsibility for the finance discipline, for financial accounting, planning and reporting. Unit management accountants will therefore report to the Finance Director for professional purposes but to the relevant General Manager for operational purposes.

In line with these changes, the Finance Director has proposed a number of changes to the role of the head office Finance Division. In particular, he wishes to encourage a more constructive and co-operative approach by finance staff to staff in other divisions. In the past, finance staff have identified inefficiencies in the utilisation of resources and generally called the various unit management teams to account. He wishes to move toward a more problem-solving style through which finance staff help others both to identify problems and develop solutions. As part of this, he wishes to see a change in the extent to which the Finance Division relies solely on traditional financial control techniques, often as a means of preventing change and limiting expenditure. Finally, he wishes to reduce the use of financial and accounting jargon.

These are significant organisational and professional changes. You accept the need for them and are fully committed to decentralisation. However, you are concerned about a number of issues.

Write a paper for circulation to your top management colleagues covering the following issues.

(1) What are likely to be the main problems and advantages of decentralised management accounting?
(2) What measures should be adopted to support the changed professional role for the Finance Division?
(3) What actions should be taken with the top management team (the General Managers of the five operating units, and the directors of the personnel, client service, management services and finance divisions) in preparation for the changes?

Notes and references

1. This chapter is based in parts on a development of the author's article: Mullins, L. J. 'Improving Management Control Systems', *Management Accounting*, vol. 61, no. 5, May 1983, pp. 30–32.
2. Tannenbaum, A. S. *Control in Organizations*, McGraw-Hill (1968) p. 3.
3. See, for example: Salaman, G. *Class and the Corporation*, Fontana (1981).
4. For example, see: Mullins, L. J. and Banks, G. 'How Well am I Doing?', *Euhofa Journal*, Association Internationale des Directeurs d'Ecoles Hoteliers, Lausanne, Switzerland, no. 18, June 1986.
5. Lawler, E. E. 'Control Systems in Organizations', in Dunnette M. D. (ed.) *Handbook of Industrial and Organizational Psychology*, Rand McNally (1976).
6. Fayol, H. *General and Industrial Management*, Pitman (1949) p. 107. See also: Gray, I. *Henri Fayol's General and Industrial Management*, Pitman (1988).

7. Gospel, H. F. and Littler, C. R. (eds) *Managerial Strategies and Industrial Relations*, Heinemann (1983).

8. Miner, J. B. *Management Theory*, Macmillan (1971).

9. Ouchi, W. G. and Maguire, M. A. 'Organizational Control: Two Functions', in Litterer, J. A. *Organizations: Structure and Behavior*, Third edition, Wiley (1980).

10. Mintzberg, H. *The Structuring of Organizations*, Prentice-Hall (1979).

11. Reeves, T. K. and Woodward, J. 'The Study of Managerial Control', in Woodward, J. (ed.) *Industrial Organization: Behaviour and Control*, Oxford University Press (1970). See also: Introduction to Woodward, J. *Industrial Organization: Theory and Practice*, Second edition, Oxford University Press (1980).

12. Child, J. *Organization: A Guide to Problems and Practice*, Second edition, Harper and Row (1984).

13. Hicks, H. G. and Gullett, C. R. *The Management of Organizations*, Third edition, McGraw-Hill (1976) p. 502.

14. Reeser, C. and Loper, M. *Management: The Key to Organizational Effectiveness*, Scott, Foresman (1978) p. 437.

15. Tannenbaum, A. S. *Control in Organizations*, McGraw-Hill (1968) p. 307.

16. Lawler, E. E. 'Control Systems in Organizations', in Dunnette. M. D. (ed.) *Handbook of Industrial and Organizational Psychology*, Rand McNally (1976) p. 1274.

17. Based on expectancy theory and the work of, for example: Vroom, V. H. *Work and Motivation*, Wiley (1964). (Also published by Krieger (1982).)

18. Brech, E. F. L. *The Principles and Practice of Management*, Third edition, Longman (1975) p. 669.

19. Burns, T. and Stalker, G. M. *The Management of Innovation*, Tavistock Publications (1966).

20. For a more detailed discussion on organisation and control, see, for example: Child, J. *Organization: A Guide to Problems and Practice*, Second edition, Harper and Row (1984).

21. Foster, A. 'Virgin's New-Found Modesty', *Management Today*, March 1988, p. 57.

22. McGregor, D. *The Human Side of Enterprise*, Penguin (1987).

23. Likert, R. and Likert, J. G. *New Ways of Managing Conflict*, McGraw-Hill, (1976).

24. Humble, J. W. *Management by Objectives*, Management Publications Limited for the British Institute of Management (1972).

25. Bhallacharya, K. 'Accountancy's Faulty Sums', *Management Today*, February 1985, p. 37.

26. See, for example: Mullins, L. J. 'Behavioural Implications of Management Accounting', *Management Accounting*, vol. 59, no. 1, January 1981, pp. 36–9.

27. Argyris, C. 'Human Problems with Budgets', in Solomans, D. (ed.) *Studies in Cost Analysis*, Second edition, Sweet and Maxwell (1968).

28. Prior, P. (in conversation with Strong, F.) 'Communicating: An Enthusiast's View', *Accountancy*, vol. 95, no. 1089, May 1984, p. 69.

29. Cammann, C. 'Effects of the Use of Control Systems', *Accounting, Organizations and Society*, vol. 1, no. 4, 1976, pp. 301–13.

30. Hopwood, A. G. 'Accounting and Organisational Behaviour', in Carsberg, B. and Hope, T. (eds) *Current Issues in Accounting*, Second edition, Philip Allan (1984) p. 269.

31. For a discussion on the difficulties of defining management services and techniques, and their organisation, see: Mullins, L. J. 'Understanding Management Services and Techniques', *Industrial Management & Data Systems*, January/February 1983, pp. 3–7.

PART SIX

ORGANISATIONAL DEVELOPMENT AND EFFECTIVENESS

17. ORGANISATION DEVELOPMENT

> Organisation development (OD) is concerned with the diagnosis of organisational health and performance, and the ability of the organisation to adapt to change. It involves a range of intervention strategies into the social processes of an organisation. The organisation must be responsive to change. The manager needs to understand the nature of OD, the importance of organisational climate and employee commitment, and organisational conflict.
>
> ### Objectives
>
> To: (i) Explain the main features and implementation of OD;
> (ii) Identify the characteristics of organisational climate and explain the concept of employee commitment;
> (iii) Explain the meaning and nature of organisational conflict;
> (iv) Examine sources of conflict and strategies for managing organisational conflict;
> (v) Explain the nature of organisational change and the forces of change;
> (vi) Detail reasons for resistance to change and examine the management of organisational change;
> (vii) Recognise the importance of organisational health and performance, and the ability of the organisation to adapt to change.

THE MEANING AND NATURE OF OD

Organisation development (OD) is a generic term embracing a wide range of intervention strategies into the social processes of an organisation. These intervention strategies are aimed at the development of individuals, groups and the organisation as a total system.

Because OD is a generic term there are many possbile ways in which it can be defined. A popular definition of OD in the behavioural science sense of the term is given by *French* and *Bell*:

> a top-management supported, long-range effort to improve an organization's problem-solving and renewal processes, particularly through a more effective and collaborative diagnosis and management of organization culture – with special emphasis on formal work team, temporary team, and intergroup culture – with the assistance of a consultant-facilitator and the use of the theory and technology of applied behavioural science, including action research.[1]

Top management support involves the general direction, support and active involvement of the chief executive and members of top management.

Problem-solving and renewal processes refers to the way in which an organisation adapts to opportunities and challenges of its environment; for example, the extent to which the organisation sees its environment in terms of the past or continuously redefines its purpose and methods in terms of the present and the future. Renewal processes are concerned with the viability of the organisation, generating technical and human resources for organisational survival, and the avoidance of organisational decay and senility.

Collaborative diagnosis and management of culture refers to a shared examination and management of organisation culture, and not to a traditional management structure with orders imposed through a hierarchy of levels. The culture of an organisation includes prevailing patterns of behaviour, values, attitudes, beliefs, norms, sentiments and technology. These characteristics enable the differentiation among organisations. OD recognises that problems and solutions should be viewed in terms of the long-range goals of the organisation and its members, rather than in meeting the needs of a particular group. OD is a process of people managing the culture of an organisation rather than the organisation being managed by that culture.

Formal work team is the key unit in OD activities. Rather than attention being centred on the individual manager or supervisor, the focus is on the work group. Emphasis is given to team development and the dynamics of small work group situations.

Consultant-facilitator (or change agent or catalyst) refers to the services of a third party as an internal or external consultant. The third party can be a member of the organisation but should be external to the particular subsystem initiating an OD programme. The facilitating role of the change agent will involve a range of consultation skills depending on the nature of the OD programme.

Action research involves the diagnosis of the organisation's problems, gathering data from the client group, feedback and analysis of data, and action by members of the client group to resolve the problems. Action research is the basic intervention model which is common to most OD programmes.

The broad nature of OD

The broad nature of OD means that many interrelated topic areas could be included under this heading or 'label'.[2] For example many of the topics discussed in previous chapters such as socio-technical systems, the Managerial Grid, Management by Objectives, job design, T-groups and quality circles could be seen as part of OD. In a very general sense, OD is concerned with attempts to improve the overall performance and effectiveness of an organisation. Essentially it is an applied behavioural science approach to planned change and development of an organisation.[3]

THE IMPLEMENTATION OF OD

In order to bring about effective change OD makes use of a number of approaches – often referred to as intervention strategies – including: survey research and feedback, T-groups, team building and grid training.

Survey research and feedback

This involves the use of questionnaire surveys to help determine the attitudes of members to the functioning of the organisation. Results of the surveys are fed back to top management and then to work groups for interpretation and analysis. Group members participate in discussions on the implications of the information, the diagnosis of problems and the development of action plans to help overcome the problems identified.

T-groups (or sensitivity training)

This involves small, unstructured, face-to-face groupings who meet without a planned agenda or set activities. Training is intended to concentrate on process rather than content: that is on the feeling level of communication rather than the informational value of communication. With the guidance of the trainers, participants' patterns of behaviour become the focus of attention for the group. The objectives are usually to increase participants' sensitivity to the emotional reactions in themselves and others, their diagnostic ability, and their behavioural flexibility and effectiveness. (T-groups were discussed in Chapter 14.)

Team building

This is the process of diagnosing task procedures and patterns of human interaction within a work group. The basic objective is to improve the overall performance of the organisation through improvements in the effectiveness of teams. Attention is focused on work procedures and interpersonal relationships, and especially the role of the leader in relation to other members of the group.

Grid training

This is a development from the *Blake* and *Mouton* Managerial Grid approach (discussed in Chapter 9). An implied goal of grid training is that changes are aimed at attaining a 9,9 orientation (maximum concern for both production and people) on the Grid. As part of OD, grid training involves six overlapping phases.

(i) *Grid seminar* – a five-day seminar where participants learn more about the Grid and about their own personal style of managing. The goals of the grid seminar are: to increase self-understanding; to experience problem-solving effectiveness in teams; to learn about managing interface conflict; and to comprehend organisation implications.

(ii) *Team building* – follows the grid seminar and is concerned with the diagnosis of barriers to sound team-work and the identification of opportunities for improvements within actual work teams. A major goal is to establish objectives for team and individual development.

(iii) *Interface development* – marks the start of overall OD. This phase is concerned with inter-group relations, analysing barriers to interface co-operation and co-ordination, and applying problem-solving and decision-making skills. Conflicts and frictions among groups are identified and analysed.

(iv) *Ideal strategic organisational model* – in this phase participants of the top team study and diagnose the current goals, needs and business activity of the organisation. The top team then design an ideal corporate model and specify a blueprint for the redesign of the organisation.

(v) *Implementing development* – this phase is concerned with implementation of the ideal corporate model. This involves the examination of existing activities, identification of those that are sound, and the design of specific action as necessary to change activities to meet the ideal model.

(vi) *Consolidation* – is the overall evaluation phase. It is concerned with stabilising and consolidating progress achieved in the earlier phases, (i)–(v). The organisation continues to adapt and it is necessary to monitor environmental changes which may call for a shift in the model.[4]

OD action-oriented No two organisations are the same. Each organisation has its own types of problems and most appropriate remedies. OD is action-oriented and tailored to suit specific individual needs. It concerns itself with the examination of organisational health and the implementation of planned change. This may include training in interpersonal skills, sensitivity training, and methods and techniques relating to motivational processes, patterns of communication, styles of leadership and managerial behaviour.

Although an OD programme is legitimised by the formal system it focuses

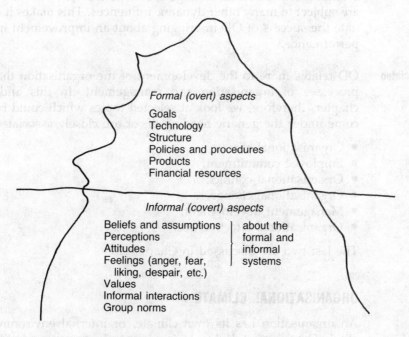

Fig. 17.1 The organisational iceberg
(From French, W. L. and Bell, C. H., *Organization Development*, 3rd edition, Prentice-Hall (1984) p. 19.)

on both the formal and the informal system. The initial intervention strategy is usually through the informal system, which includes feelings, informal actions and interactions, group norms and values, and which forms part of the culture of an organisation. The informal aspects of organisational life are in some respects the hidden or suppressed domain – the covert part of the 'organisational iceberg'.[5] (*See* Fig. 17.1.)

The value of OD

As with any management situation, the value of OD programmes is open to debate. In particular, the use of certain forms of sensitivity training is subject to strong criticism, and the claim that they can result in unwanted side-effects and have an unacceptably high cost in mental stress for some individuals.[6] However, although part of an OD programme may involve personal relationships, less threatening techniques can be employed to help bring about a mutual understanding of the disruptive influences of personality clashes.

Another potential problem with OD is the application of borrowed techniques such as small leaderless groups, attitude surveys and indicators of management style. OD consultants should be subject to the same scrutiny which they apply to their client organisations.[7]

Whilst OD consultants have their failures, this is also true of most practitioners in organisation and management. Clearly OD does have a constructive role to play. It can help to increase personal competence and responsibility, team building and a sense of commitment to the results of the organisation.

The success and effectiveness of OD may not always be readily apparent. But it should be remembered that OD is usually a long-term process and changing the climate of an organisation is a major task. Also, organisations are subject to many other dynamic influences. This makes it difficult to evaluate the success of OD in bringing about an improvement in organisational performance.

Topics associated with OD

OD relates more to the development of the organisation than to the actual processes of organisation and management. In this and the following chapter, therefore, we look at selected topics which could be considered to come under the generic heading of, or are closely associated with, OD.

- Organisational climate;
- Employee commitment;
- Organisational conflict;
- Organisational change;
- Management development;
- Organisational effectiveness.

The last two are discussed in Chapter 18.

ORGANISATIONAL CLIMATE

An organisation has its own climate, or internal environment or 'personality'. Organisational climate is a general concept and difficult to define precisely. It can be likened to our description of the weather and the way in which the climate of a geographical region results from the combination of environmental forces. Some of these forces are better understood than others. Applied to organisations, climate can be said to relate to the prevailing atmosphere surrounding the organisation, to the level of morale, and to the strength of feelings of belonging, care and goodwill among members.

Organisational climate is based on the *perception* of members towards the organisation.

> Organizational climate is a relatively enduring quality of the internal environment of an organization that (a) is experienced by its members, (b) influences their behavior, and (c) can be described in terms of the values of a particular set of characteristics (or attributes) of the organization.[8]

Climate also relates to the recognition of the organisation as a social system and the extent to which membership is a psychologically rewarding experience. It can be seen as the state of mutual trust and understanding among members of the organisation. Organisational climate is characterised, therefore, by the nature of the people–organisation relationship and the superior–subordinate relationship. These relationships are determined by interactions among goals and objectives, formal structure, styles of leadership, the process of management, and the behaviour of people.

Characteristics of organisational climate

Although similar types of organisations will share certain common features and norms, each organisation will have its own different and distinctive features. The normative climate of a particular organisation reflects the history of its internal and external struggles, its work processes and physical layout, patterns of communication, the type of people employed and the exercise of authority. Distinctive features of collective feelings and beliefs will be passed on to new group members.[9]

A healthy organisational climate might be expected to exhibit such characteristic features as:

- the integration of organisational goals and personal goals;
- a flexible structure with a network of authority, control and communications, and with autonomy for individual members;
- styles of leadership appropriate to particular work situations;
- mutual trust, consideration and support among different levels of the organisation;
- recognition of individual differences and attributes, and of people's needs and expectations at work;
- attention to job design and the quality of working life;
- challenging and responsible jobs with high performance standards;
- equitable systems of rewards based on positive reinforcement;
- opportunities for personal development, career progression and advancement;
- justice in treatment, and fair personnel and industrial relations policies and practices;
- the open discussion of conflict with emphasis on the settlement of differences without delay or confrontation;
- democratic functioning of the organisation with full opportunities for genuine consultation and participation;

● a sense of identity with, and loyalty to, the organisation and a feeling of being a needed and important member of the organisation.

In addition to arrangements for carrying out organisational processes and the execution of work, management has a responsibility for creating an organisational climate in which people are motivated to work willingly and effectively. If organisational climate is to be improved, then attention should be given to the above features.

Importance of a healthy climate

Organisational climate will influence the level of morale and attitudes which members of the organisation bring to bear on their work performance and personal relationships. Morale, however, is another general concept which is difficult to measure objectively. A carefully designed and conducted description questionnaire, or attitude survey, will help to establish the true feelings of members on factors contributing to organisational climate. When morale is low, and feelings of frustration or alienation are found to exist, it is important that positive action is taken to remedy the causes.

A healthy climate will not by itself guarantee improved organisational effectiveness. However, an organisation is unlikely to attain optimum operational performance unless the climate evokes a spirit of co-operation throughout the organisation, and is conducive to motivating members to work willingly and effectively.

Among the factors which contribute to a healthy organisational climate, high morale and motivation, is the extent to which employees have a sense of commitment to the organisation. The extent of their commitment will have a major influence on the level of work performance.

EMPLOYEE COMMITMENT

The concept of commitment itself, and the manner in which it is actually created, is difficult to describe. *Martin* and *Nicholls* view commitment as encapsulating 'giving all of yourself while at work'. This entails such things as, for example, using time constructively, attention to detail, making that extra effort, accepting change, co-operation with others, self-development, respecting trust, pride in abilities, seeking improvements and giving loyal support.[10]

A three-pillar model of commitment

Based on case studies of 14 British companies, including Jaguar, Royal Bank of Scotland, British Steel, Pilkingtons, Rothmans, Raleigh, Schweppes and Burton, *Martin* and *Nicholls* present a 'model of commitment' based on three major pillars, each with three factors. (*See* Fig. 17.2.)

(i) *A sense of belonging to the organisation*
This builds upon the loyalty essential to successful industrial relations. The sense of belonging is created by managers through ensuring that the workforce is:

● informed
● involved
● sharing in success

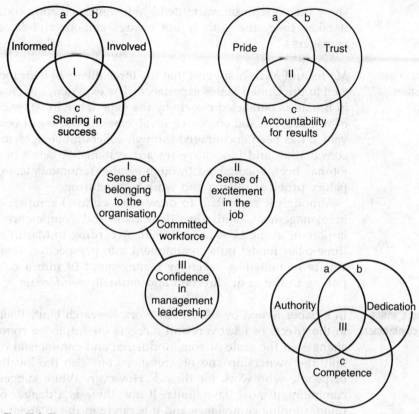

Fig. 17.2 The three-pillar model of commitment
(From Martin, P. and Nicholls, J., *Creating a Committed Workforce*, Institute of Personnel Management (1987) p. 27.)

(ii) *A sense of excitement in the job*

Improved results will not be achieved unless workers can also feel a sense of excitement about their work which results in the motivation to perform well. This sense of excitement can be achieved by appealing to the higher level needs of:

- pride
- trust
- accountability for results

(iii) *Confidence in management*

The senses of belonging and excitement can be frustrated if workers do not have respect for, and confidence in, management leadership. This respect is enhanced through attention to:

- authority
- dedication
- competence

A large measure of the success of the companies studied derives from their management of people and from creating a climate for commitment. For example: 'If people feel trusted, they will make extraordinary efforts to show the trust to be warranted.'[11] However, creating commitment is hard. It takes time, the path is not always smooth and it requires dedicated managers.

Comparison with United States experience

Martin and *Nicholls* suggest that the three pillars of their model apply equally well to the United States experience. The experience in creating commitment in Britain is paralleled closely by the experience in America with the quality of working life and employee involvement. A sense of belonging and being valued has been encouraged through collaborative agreements with unions, consultation and innovative reward systems. A sense of excitement in the job has been encouraged through semi-autonomous team working, participatory problem solving and work restructuring.

Although it is difficult to draw cross-cultural comparisons of confidence in management, authority, dedication and competence appear to be as important in the USA as in Britain. According to Martin and Nicholls: 'The three-pillar model puts commitment into perspective. It shows how a wide variety of initiatives taken by management fit into a coherent picture, all pulling in the same direction and mutually reinforcing.'[12]

Behaviours which denote commitment

In a paper issued by the ACAS Work Research Unit, *White* draws attention to the effects of takeovers and mergers on employee commitment. Massive changes in the scale of some industrial and commercial concerns affect not only the ownership and organisation, but also the loyalty and attachment of people who work for them.[13] However, White suggests that employee commitment must have limits. If not, there is a danger of fanatical zeal or unquestioning compliance and it is rarely in the interests of an organisation to confine recruitment to people who appear willing to become committed to such an extent.

In contrast to 'involvement', White suggests three kinds of feelings or behaviours which denote 'commitment' to the organisation in which a person works:

- belief in, and acceptance of, the organisation itself and/or its goals and values;
- willingness to exert effort on behalf of the organisation above the contract of employment;
- desire to remain with the organisation.

Commitment is also always both *voluntary and personal*. It cannot be imposed, it cannot be initiated by others, and it can be withdrawn.

Commitment is reciprocated by the organisation

From a review of ways in which organisational policies can influence commitment, *White* concludes that a high level of employee commitment implies willingness to work for the organisation's benefit: but that its continuation depends on a reciprocal commitment by the organisation to its members.

In the current industrial climate, there needs to be concern not only for producing goods or services, but also for the encouragement of innovative, exploratory and creative ideas that go beyond what can be prescribed for the job, and for the application to work of intuitive as well as explicit knowledge. These multiple objectives can only be achieved if managers consider with care exactly what kinds of commitment they are aiming for, and design policies and practices accordingly.[14]

ORGANISATIONAL CONFLICT

It might be expected that a healthy organisational climate would be reflected by complete harmony in working relationships, and loyalty and common commitment to the goals and objectives of the organisation. This view of work organisations as 'happy families' is perhaps a worthwhile and creditable ideal and as such appears to be implied by a number of management writers.

For example, *Drucker* makes the following point:

> Any business enterprise must build a true team and weld individual efforts into a common effort. Each member of the enterprise contributes something different, but they must all contribute towards a common goal. Their efforts must all pull in the same direction, and their contributions must fit together to produce a whole – without gaps, without friction, without unnecessary duplication of effort. . . . The manager must know and understand what the business goals demand of him in terms of performance, and his superior must know what contribution to demand and expect of him – and must judge him accordingly. If these requirements are not met, managers are misdirected. Their efforts are wasted. Instead of teamwork, there is friction, frustration and conflict.[15]

Such views appear to imply *a unitary perspective* of the organisation. With the unitary approach, the organisation is viewed as a team with a common source of loyalty, one focus of effort and one accepted leader. Conflict can be explained, for example, by poor communications, personality clashes or the work of agitators. But, if one accepts the views of, for example, the social action writers and the idea of a pluralistic approach to work organisations, then conflict among competing sub-groups will be seen as inevitable.[16] From *the pluralistic approach*, conflict is seen as an inherent feature of organisations and induced, in part, by the very structure of the organisation. Restrictive practices may be seen as a rational response from a group which regards itself as being threatened.[17]

THE MEANING OF CONFLICT

Conflict is a reality of management and organisational behaviour. Most of us will understand what is commonly meant by organisational conflict and be aware of its existence and effects. Yet conflict is another term which can be defined and interpreted in a number of ways. For our purpose we can see conflict as: *behaviour intended to obstruct the achievement of some other person's goals*. Conflict is based on the incompatibility of goals and arises from opposing behaviours. It can be viewed at the individual, group or organisation level.

Conflict and competition

The terms conflict and competition are often used synonymously. Conflict and competition do have common aspects. Both involve at least some degree of opposing behaviour and the belief that one party is attempting to deprive others of something which they value. But conflict can be seen to differ from competition.

Conflict situations denote both incompatible goals *and* opposing behaviour.

Competition may still arise when there is a greater commonality of goals and may involve only limited opposing behaviour, or even some co-operative behaviour. In competition, individuals or groups do not obstruct or interfere with each other in attempting to satisfy their goals.

An example of a conflict situation could be where two managers are in contest with each other to avoid compulsory redundancy. An example of competition could be members of staff vying for promotion. The unsuccessful members will not lose their present level of pay, status or responsibilities and still have other options open including the opportunity for promotion into some other position.

In conflict situations one or both of the parties may be drawn or forced into the confrontation. The situation may arise spontaneously with no ground rules and little knowledge of how far the situation could escalate. The outcomes are potentially dysfunctional for at least one of the parties. *In competition* the parties are usually willing participants. Competition implies that certain ground rules apply and that there has been some prior planning by a higher authority.[18]

Competition might, initially at least, be comparatively friendly. But if the situation develops into one of greater antagonism, and behaviour intended to obstruct the other person, then a conflict situation could develop.

Argument, competition and conflict

Handy refers to three kinds of differences within organisations: argument, competition and conflict.[19] Argument and competition are potentially fruitful and beneficial aspects of differences. Conflict is the harmful side of difference.

Argument is the resolution of differences through discussion. The expression of differing opinions and viewpoints usually helps in reaching a better solution. Effective argument depends upon the characteristics of the group involved in the discussion and the logic of the argument.

Competition can be productive in three principal ways: (i) in setting standards; (ii) in stimulating and channelling energies, and giving a common sense of purpose; and (iii) in distinguishing better from worse.

The productive outcomes of competition will depend to a large extent upon whether it operates in a closed or open manner. If it is closed (the zero-sum competition) one person wins at the expense of the other. When competition is open there is no finite amount. All parties can increase their gains without being at the expense of the others. There is competiton but not out of a fixed amount.

However, Handy points out that in most organisations it is likely to be difficult to satisfy the conditions for fruitful competition and there are not unlimited resources or opportunities. As a result, competition, if left to itself, is very likely to produce organisational conflict. If not properly managed, both argument and competition can become disruptive or degenerate into conflict.

CONTRASTING VIEWS OF CONFLICT

Common definitions of conflict tend to be associated with negative features and situations which give rise to inefficiency, ineffectiveness or dysfunctional consequences. The traditional view of conflict is that it is bad for organisations and represents a form of deviant behaviour which should be controlled and changed. Clearly, extreme cases of conflict in organisations can have very upsetting, or even tragic, consequences for some people and have adverse effects on organisational performance. Conflict situations can give rise to excessive emotional or physical stress.

Positive and negative outcomes

Properly managed, however, conflict can have potentially positive outcomes. It can be an energising and vitalising force in groups and in the organisation. Conflict can be seen as a 'constructive' force and in certain circumstances it can be welcomed or even encouraged. For example, conflict can be seen as an aid to incremental improvement in organisation design and functioning, and to the decision-making process. Properly identified and handled, conflict can help to minimise the destructive influences of the win–lose situation.[20]

From a survey of practising managers, who reported that they spend approximately 20 per cent of their time dealing with conflict situations, *Schmidt* records a number of both positive and negative outcomes of conflict.[21]

Positive outcomes include:

- better ideas produced;
- people forced to search for new approaches;
- long-standing problems brought to the surface and resolved;
- clarification of individual views;
- stimulation of interest and creativity;
- a chance for people to test their capacities.

Negative outcomes include:

- some people felt defeated and demeaned;
- the distance between people increased;
- a climate of mistrust and suspicion developed;
- individuals and groups concentrated on their own narrow interests;
- resistance developed rather than team-work;
- an increase in turnover.

The current view appears to recognise that conflict can be interpreted more broadly than in the traditional view. Conflict, *per se*, is not necessarily good or bad but an inevitable feature of organisational life. Even if organisations have taken great care to try and avoid conflict it will still occur. Conflict will continue to emerge despite attempts by management to suppress it.

THE SOURCES OF CONFLICT

Much has been written about the implications of conflict as a social process. Whilst recognising the importance of this debate, it is not the intention here to enter into a detailed discussion of the ideologies of conflict. The important point is not so much whether competing sub-groups and conflict are seen as inevitable consequences of organisation structure, but how conflict, when found to exist, is handled and managed.

There are many potential sources of organisational conflict including the main ones summarised below.

- *Differences in perception*. We all see things in different ways. We all have our own, unique picture of image of how we see the 'real' world. Differences in perception result in different people attaching different meanings to the same stimuli. As perceptions become a person's reality, value judgements can be a potential major source of conflict. (The importance of perception was discussed in Chapter 1.)
- *Limited resources*. Most organisational resources are limited, and individuals and groups have to fight for their share; for example, at the time of the allocation of next year's budget or when cutbacks have to be made. The greater the limitation of resources, then usually the greater the potential for conflict. In an organisation with reducing profits or revenues the potential for conflict is likely to be intensified.
- *Departmentalisation and Specialisation*. Most work organisations are divided into separate departments with specialised functions. Because of familiarity with the manner in which they undertake their activities, departments tend to turn inwards and to concentrate on the achievement of their own particular goals. When departments need to co-operate with each other this is a frequent source of conflict.

  Differing goals and internal environments of departments are also a potential source of conflict. For example, a research and development department is more likely to be concerned with the long-run view and, confronted with pressures for new ideas and production innovation, the department is likely to operate in a dynamic environment and with an organic structure. A production department, however, is concerned more with short-term problems such as quality control and meeting delivery dates. The department tends to operate in a more stable environment and with a bureaucratic structure.
- *The nature of work activities*. Where the task of one person is dependent upon the work of others there is potential for conflict; for example, if a worker is expected to complete the assembly of a given number of components in a week but the person forwarding the part-assembled components does not supply a sufficient number on time. If reward and punishment systems are perceived to be based on keeping up with performance levels, then the potential for conflict is even greater.

  If the work of a department is dependent upon the output of another department a similar situation could arise, especially if this situation is coupled with limited resources; for example, where the activities of a department, whose budget has been reduced below what is believed necessary to run the department efficiently, are interdependent with those of another department, who appear to have received a more generous budget allocation.
- *Role conflict*. A role is the expected pattern of behaviours associated with members occupying a particular position within the structure of the

organisation. In practice, the manner in which people actually behave may not be consistent with their expected pattern of behaviour. Problems of role incompatibility and role ambiguity arise from inadequate or inappropriate role definition and can be a significant source of conflict. (Role conflict was discussed in Chapter 13.)

- *Inequitable treatment.* A person's perception of unjust treatment, such as in the operation of personnel policies and practices, or in reward and punishment systems, can lead to tension and conflict. For example, according to the equity theory of motivation (discussed in Chapter 11) the perception of inequity will motivate a person to take action to restore equity, including changes to inputs or outputs, or through acting on others.

- *Violation of territory.* People tend to become attached to their own 'territory' within work organisations; for example, to their own area of work, or kinds of clients to be dealt with; or to their own room, chair or parking space. Jealousy may arise over other people's territory; for example, size of room, company car, allocation of a secretary or other perks; through access to information; or through membership of groups. A stranger walking into a place of work can create an immediate feeling of suspicion or even resentment because people do not usually like 'their' territory entered by someone they do not know, and whose motives are probably unclear to them.[22]

  Ownership of territory may be *conferred formally*, for example by organisation charts, job descriptions or management decisions. It may be *established through procedures*, for example circulation lists or membership of committees. Or it may *arise informally*, for example through group norms, tradition or perceived status symbols. The place where people choose to meet can have a possible, significant symbolic value. For example, if a subordinate is summoned to a meeting in a manager's office this might be taken that the manager is signalling higher status. If the manager chooses to meet at the subordinate's place of work, or on neutral territory, this may be a signal that the manager wishes to meet the subordinate as an equal.

  If a person's territory is violated this can lead to the possibility of retaliation and conflict. For example, in *Woodward*'s study of management organisation of firms in this country (discussed in Chapter 5) she comments on the bad relationships between accountants and other managers. One reason for this hostility was the bringing together of two quite separate financial functions.

  > People concerned with works accounting tended to assume responsibility for end results that was not properly theirs; they saw their role as a controlling and sanctioning one rather than as a servicing and supportive one. Line managers resented this attitude and retaliated by becoming aggressive and obstructive.[23]

- *Environmental.* Changes in an organisation's external environment, such as shifts in demand, increased competition, government intervention, new technology or changing social values, can cause major areas of conflict. For example a fall in demand for, or government financial restrictions on, enrolments for a certain discipline in higher education can result in conflict for the allocation of resources. If the department concerned is a large and important one, and led by a powerful head, then there could be even greater potential for conflict.

- *Other sources.* There are many other potential sources of organisational conflict, including:

  - *individual* – such as attitudes, personality characteristics or particular personal needs, illness or stress;
  - *group* – such as group skills, the informal organisation and group norms;
  - *organisation* – such as communications, authority structure, leadership style, managerial behaviour.

The possible sources of conflict have been summarised by *Bryans* and *Cronin* as:

1. Differences between corporate and individual goals.
2. Conflicts between different departments or groups within the organization.
3. Conflict between the formal and informal organization.
4. Conflict between manager and managed.
5. Conflict between individual and job.
6. Conflict between individuals.[24]

STRATEGIES FOR MANAGING CONFLICT

Although a certain amount of organisational conflict may be seen as inevitable, there are a number of ways in which management can attempt to avoid the harmful effects of conflict. Many of these ways have been discussed in previous chapters. The strategies adopted will vary according to the nature and sources of conflict outlined above.

- *Clarification of goals and objectives.* The clarification and continual refinement of goals and objectives, role definitions and performance standards will help to avoid misunderstandings and conflict. Focusing attention on superordinate goals, that are shared by the parties in conflict, may help to defuse hostility and lead to more co-operative behaviour.
- *Resource distribution.* Although it may not always be possible for managers to increase their allocated share of resources, they may be able to use imagination and initiative to help overcome conflict situations; for example, making a special case to higher management; flexibility in virement headings of the budget; delaying staff appointments in one area to provide more money for another area.
- *Personnel policies and procedures.* Careful and detailed attention to just and equitable personnel policies and procedures may help to reduce areas of conflict. Examples are: job analysis, recruitment and selection, job evaluation; systems of reward and punishment; appeals, grievance and disciplinary procedures; arbitration and mediation; recognition of trade unions and their officials.
- *Non-monetary rewards.* Where financial resources are limited, it may be possible to pay greater attention to non-monetary rewards. Examples are job design; more interesting, challenging or responsible work; increased

delegation; flexible working hours; attendance at courses or conferences; unofficial perks or more relaxed working conditions.

- *Development of interpersonal/group process skills.* This may help to encourage a better understanding of one's own behaviour, the other person's point of view, communication processes and problem solving. It may also encourage people to work through conflict situations in a constructive manner.

- *Group activities.* Attention to the composition of groups and to factors which affect group cohesiveness may reduce dysfunctional conflict. Over-lapping group membership with a 'linking-pin' process, and the careful selection of project teams or task forces for problems affecting more than one group, may also be beneficial.

- *Leadership and management.* A more participative and supportive style of leadership and managerial behaviour is likely to assist in conflict management; for example, showing an attitude of respect and trust; encouraging personal self-development; creating a work environment in which staff can work co-operatively together. A participative approach to leadership and management may also help to create greater employee commitment.

- *Organisational processes.* Conflict situations may be reduced by attention to such features as: the nature of the authority structure; work organisation; patterns of communication and sharing of information; democratic functioning of the organisation; unnecessary adherence to bureaucratic procedures, and official rules and regulations.

- *Socio-technical approach.* Viewing the organisation as a socio-technical system, in which psychological and social factors are developed in keeping with structural and technical requirements, will help in reducing dysfunctional conflict.

ORGANISATIONAL CHANGE

An organisation can only perform effectively through interactions with the broader external environment of which it is part. The structure and functioning of the organisation must reflect, therefore, the nature of the environment in which it is operating. Factors such as uncertain economic conditions, fierce world competition, the level of government intervention, scarcity of natural resources and rapid developments in new technology create an increasingly volatile environment. In order to help ensure its survival and future success the organisation must be readily adaptable to the external demands placed upon it. The organisation must be responsive to change. OD itself is a response to organisational change.

Change also originates within the organisation itself. Much of this change is part of a natural process of ageing; for example, as material resources such as buildings, equipment or machinery deteriorate or lose efficiency; or as human resources get older, or as skills and abilities become outdated. Some of this change can be managed through careful planning; for example, regular repairs and maintenance; choice of introducing new technology or methods of work; effective manpower planning to prevent a large number of staff retiring at the same time; management succession planning; training and staff development.

But the main pressure of change is from external forces. The organisation must be properly prepared to face the demands of a changing environment. It must give attention to its future development and success.

The nature of change

Change is a pervasive influence. We are all subject to continual change of one form or another. It is an inescapable part of both social and organisational life. The effects of change can be studied over different time scales, from weeks to hundreds of years, and they can be studied at different levels. Change can be studied in terms of its effects at the individual, group, organisation, society, national or international level. However, because of its pervasive nature, change at any one level is interrelated with changes at other levels, and it is difficult to study one area of change in isolation. But our main focus of attention is on the management of organisational change.

Organisational change can be initiated deliberately by managers, it can evolve slowly within a department, it can be imposed by specific changes in policy or procedures, or it can arise through external pressures. Change can affect all aspects of the operation and functioning of the organisation.

Planned organisational change

Most planned organisational change is triggered by the need to respond to new challenges or opportunities presented by the external environment, or in anticipation of the need to cope with potential future problems; for example, intended government legislation, a new product development by a major competitor or further technological advances. Planned change represents an intentional attempt to improve, in some important way, the operational effectiveness of the organisation. The basic underlying objectives can be seen in general terms as: (i) modifying the behavioural patterns of members of the organisation; and (ii) improving the ability of the organisation to cope with changes in its environment.

Behaviour modification

A programme of planned change and improved performance involves the management of a three-phase process of behaviour modification:

- *Unfreezing* – reducing those forces which maintain behaviour in its present form, recognition of the need for change and improvement to occur;
- *Movement* – development of new attitudes or behaviour and the implementation of the change;
- *Refreezing* – stabilising change at the new level and reinforcement through supporting mechanisms, for example policies, structure or norms.[25]

French, Kast and *Rosenzweig* list eight specific components of a planned-change effort related to the above process.[26] (*See* Fig. 17.3.)

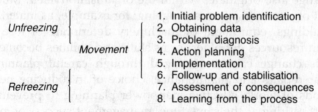

Unfreezing		1. Initial problem identification
		2. Obtaining data
		3. Problem diagnosis
Movement		4. Action planning
		5. Implementation
Refreezing		6. Follow-up and stabilisation
		7. Assessment of consequences
		8. Learning from the process

Fig. 17.3 Stages in a planned-change effort
(Adapted from French, W. L., Kast, F. E. and Rosenzweig, J. E., *Understanding Human Behavior in Organizations*, Harper & Row (1985) p. 569.)

A systems approach to organisational change

One strategy of change is through the adoption of a systems approach. The organisation can be viewed as a system and analysed in terms of its major interrelated variables (sub-systems). The variables can be identified in a number of ways including: task, technology, structure, people and management. (The organisation as a system and the identification of sub-systems were discussed in Chapter 3.)

These variables serve as 'entry points' and organisational change can be initiated by alteration of any one, or a combination, of these variables.[27] In practice, change in any one variable is likely to involve changes in the other variables. The implementation of change can be approached, therefore, in terms of a choice of strategies relating to modifications of the task, the technology, the structure, the people or the management. Applying a systems approach involves managers understanding the interrelationships among all major variables (sub-systems) of the organisation.

Overlooking the systems nature of organisations can result in the failure of even well-conceived change programmes.

> No unit is an island, and changes planned for one part of an organisation invariably have knock-on effects on the other parts. It is crucial in planning any changes to be aware of the likely impact of those changes on other parts of the organisation. If a change has an unanticipated effect on a unit, a considerable amount of resistance to the change will develop. It is better to consider the effects of any changes with all the units concerned and to plan the changes in consultation with them to minimise the adverse effects.[28]

THE FORCES OF CHANGE

There are a wide range of forces acting upon organisations and which make the need for change inevitable. These forces of change can be summarised under five broad headings: changing technology; knowledge explosion; rapid product obsolescence; changing nature of the workforce; and quality of working life.[29]

- *Changing technology.* The rate of technological change is greater now than at any time in the past; for example, advances in information technology, automation and robotics.
- *Knowledge explosion.* The amount of knowledge is increasing continually; for example, the number of people in some form of education, the number of scientific journals and new books. With this rapid explosion of knowledge, knowledge in a particular field quickly becomes outdated or obsolete.
- *Rapid product obsolescence.* Changes in consumer preferences, together with rapidly changing technology, have shortened the life-cycle of many products and services. Many products and services available today did not exist a few years ago and many do not remain available for long.
- *Changing nature of the workforce.* These include changes in the composition of the working population, broader educational opportunities, part-time working, changes in family life-styles, equal opportunities.
- *Quality of working life.* Increased importance attached to the quality of working life has drawn attention to the satisfaction of people's needs and

expectations at work; and to such factors as frustration and alienation, job design and work organisation, styles of managerial behaviour. It has also drawn attention to relationships between the quality of working life and employee commitment, levels of work performance and productivity.

RESISTANCE TO CHANGE

Despite the potential positive outcomes, change is often resisted at both the individual and at the organisational level. Resistance to change – or the thought of the implications of the change – appears to be a common phenomenon. People are naturally wary of change. 'Among many there is an uneasy mood – a suspicion that change is out of control.'[30]

Individual resistance Resistance to change can take many forms and it is often difficult to pinpoint the exact reason for the resistance. The forces against change in work organisations include: ignoring the needs and expectations of members; when members have insufficient information about the nature of the change; or if they do not perceive the need for change. Some common reasons for individual resistance to change within organisations include the following.

- *Selective perception.* People's own interpretation of stimuli presents a unique picture or image of the 'real' world and can result in selective perception. This can lead to a biased view of a particular situation, which fits most comfortably into a person's own perception of reality, and can cause resistance to change. For example, trade unionists may have a stereotyped view of management as untrustworthy and therefore oppose any management change however well founded might have been the intention. Managers exposed to different theories or ideas may tend to categorise these as either: those they already practice and have no need to worry about; or those of no practical value and can be discarded as of no concern to them.

- *Habit.* People tend to respond to situations in an established and accustomed manner. Habits may serve as a means of comfort and security, and as a guide for easy decision making. Proposed changes to habits, especially if the habits are well established and require little effort, may well be resisted. However, if there is a clearly perceived advantage, for example a reduction in working hours without loss of pay, there is likely to be less, if any, resistance to the change. Although some people may, because of habit, still find it difficult to adjust to the new times.

- *Inconvenience or loss of freedom.* If the change is seen as likely to prove inconvenient, make life more difficult, reduce freedom of action or result in increased control, there will be resistance.

- *Economic implications.* People are likely to resist change which is perceived as reducing either directly or indirectly their pay or other rewards, requiring an increase in work for the same level of pay or acting as a threat to their job security. People tend to have established patterns of working and a vested interest in maintaining the status quo.

- *Security in the past.* There is a tendency for some people to find a sense of security in the past. In times of frustration or difficulty, or when faced with new or unfamiliar ideas or methods, people may reflect on the past. There is a wish to retain old and comfortable ways. For example, in bureaucratic organisations, officials often tend to place faith in well-established ('tried and trusted') procedures and cling to these as giving a feeling of security.

- *Fear of the unknown*. Changes which confront people with the unknown tend to cause anxiety or fear. Many major changes in a work organisation present a degree of uncertainty; for example, the introduction of new technology or methods of working. A person may resist promotion because of uncertainty over changes in responsibilities or the increased social demands of the higher position.

Organisational resistance

Although organisations have to adapt to their environment, they tend to feel comfortable operating within the structure, policies and procedures which have been formulated to deal with a range of present situations. To ensure operational effectiveness, organisations often set up defences against change and prefer to concentrate on the routine things they perform well. Some of the main reasons for organisational resistance against change are:

- *Maintaining stability*. Organisations, especially large-scale ones, pay much attention to maintaining stability and predictability. The need for formal organisation structure and the division of work, narrow definitions of assigned duties and responsibilities, established rules, procedures and methods of work, can result in resistance to change.
- *Investment in resources*. Change often requires large resources which may already be committed to investments in other areas or strategies. Assets such as buildings, technology, equipment and people cannot easily be altered. For example, a car manufacturer may not find it easy to change to a socio-technical approach and the use of autonomous work groups (such as with the Volvo project), because it cannot afford the cost of a new purpose-built plant and specialised equipment.
- *Past contracts or agreements*. Organisations enter into contracts or agreements with other parties, such as the government, other organisations, trade unions, suppliers and customers. These contracts and agreements can limit changes in behaviour; for example, organisations operating under a special licence or permit, or a fixed-price contract to supply goods/services to a government agency. Another example might be an agreement with trade unions which limits the opportunity to introduce compulsory redundancies, or the introduction of certain new technology or working practices.
- *Threats to power or influence*. Change may be seen as a threat to the power or influence of certain groups within the organisation, such as their control over decisions, resources or information. For example, managers may resist the introduction of quality circles or worker-directors because they see this as increasing the role and influence of non-managerial staff, and a threat to the power in their own positions. Where a group of people have, over a period of time, established what they perceive as their 'territorial rights' they are likely to resist change.

THE MANAGEMENT OF ORGANISATIONAL CHANGE

As we have seen, people tend to be resistant to change. It is important, therefore, for management to adopt a clearly defined strategy for the initiation of change. The successful management of change is an increasingly important managerial responsibility. New ideas and innovations should not be perceived as threats by members of the organisation. The efforts made by management to maintain the balance of the socio-technical system will influence people's attitudes, the behaviour of individuals and groups, and thereby the level of organisational performance and effectiveness.

Style of managerial behaviour

Most people feel threatened by the challenge of change. One of the most important factors in the successful implementation of organisational change is the style of managerial behaviour. In certain situations, and with certain members of staff, it may be necessary for management to make use of hierarchical authority and to attempt to impose change through a coercive, autocratic style of behaviour. Some members may actually prefer, and respond better, to a directed and controlled style of management. (Recall, for example, the discussion on Theory X and Theory Y styles of managerial behaviour in Chapter 9.)

In most cases, however, the introduction of change is more likely to be effective with a participative style of managerial behaviour. If staff are kept fully informed of proposals, are encouraged to adopt a positive attitude and have personal involvement in the implementation of the change, there is a greater likelihood of their acceptance of the change.

> With the participative change cycle, a significant advantage is that once the change is accepted it tends to be long lasting. Since everyone has been involved in the development of the change, each person tends to be more highly committed to its implementation. The disadvantage of participative change is that it tends to be slow and evolutionary – it may take years to implement a significant change. An advantage of directive change, on the other hand, is speed. Using position power, leaders can often impose change immediately. A disadvantage of this change strategy is that it tends to be volatile. It can be maintained only as long as the leader has position power to make it stick. It often results in animosity, hostility, and, in some cases, overt and covert behavior to undermine and overthrow.[31]

Organisational effectiveness

The successful management of change is a key factor of organisational effectiveness, which is discussed in the following chapter.

HUMAN AND SOCIAL FACTORS OF CHANGE

Activities managed on the basis of technical efficiency alone are unlikely to lead to optimum improvement in organisational performance. A major source of resistance to change arises from the need of organisations to adapt to new technological developments. The following discussion on how to minimise the problem of change centres on the example of the impact of information technology.[32] The general principles, however, apply equally to the management of change arising from other factors.

- *An important priority is to create an environment of trust and shared commitment, and to involve staff in decisions and actions which affect them.* There is a considerable body of research and experience which demonstrates clearly the positive advantages to be gained from participation. Government encouragement has come through the Employment Act 1982 which requires all companies with more than 250 employees to report annually on steps taken to introduce, maintain or develop arrangements of employee consultation and involvement, information sharing, employee share schemes and related matters. It is important to remember, however, that the implications of information technology will need to be faced even by small organisations.

- *There should be full and genuine participation of all staff concerned as early as possible, preferably well before the actual introduction of new equipment or systems.* Information about proposed change, its implications and potential benefits should be communicated clearly to all interested parties. Staff should be actively encouraged to contribute their own ideas, suggestions and experiences, and to voice openly their worries or concerns. Managers should discuss problems directly with staff and handle any foreseen difficulties in working practices or relationships by attempting to find solutions agreed with them. The use of working parties, liaison committees, steering groups and joint consultation may assist discussion and participation, and help to maintain the momentum of the change process.

- *Team management, a co-operative spirit among staff and unions and a genuine feeling of shared involvement will help create a greater willingness to accept change.* A participative style of managerial behaviour which encourages supportive relationships between superiors and subordinates, and group methods of organisation, decision making and supervision, are more likely to lead to a sustained improvement in work performance. A system of Management by Objectives (MBO) may allow staff to accept greater responsibility and to make a higher level of personal contribution. Participation is inherent if MBO is to work well, and there is an assumption that most people will direct and control themselves willingly if they share in the setting of their objectives.

- *As part of the pre-planning for new technology there should be a carefully designed 'personnel management action programme'.* The development of information technology together with the growth of service organisations may, in the longer term, lead to the creation of new jobs. However, it must be recognised that the extra efficiency of new technology and automation can result in the more immediate consequence of job losses. The action programme should be directed to a review of: recruitment and selection; natural wastage of staff; potential for training, retraining and the development of new skills; and other strategies to reduce the possible level of redundancies or other harmful effects on staff. Where appropriate, arrangements for a shorter working week, and redeployment of staff with full financial support, should be developed in full consultation with those concerned. If job losses are totally unavoidable, there should be a fair and equitable redundancy scheme and provision for early retirement with protected pension rights. Every possible financial and other support should be given in assisting staff to find suitable alternative employment.

- *The introduction of incentive payment schemes may help in motivating staff by an equitable allocation of savings which result from new technology and more efficient methods of work.* Incentive schemes may be on an individual basis, with bonuses payable to each member of staff according to effort and performance; or on a group basis, where bonus is paid to staff in relation to the performance of the group as a whole. An alternative system is 'measured day work'. Staff receive a regular, guaranteed rate of pay in return for an agreed quantity and quality of work based on the capabilities of new equipment and systems. Management may also be able to negotiate a productivity bargain with unions. By accepting changes in work methods and practices, staff share in the economic benefits gained from the improved efficiency of information technology and automated systems.

- *Changes to the work organisation must maintain the balance of the socio-technical system.* Increased technology and automation may result in jobs becoming more repetitive and boring, and providing only a limited challenge and satisfaction to staff. It is important, therefore, to attempt to improve the quality of work, to remove frustration and stress from jobs, and to make them more responsible and interesting. New working practices should take account of how best to satisfy people's needs and expectations at work through the practical application of behavioural science.

- *Careful attention should be given to job design, methods of work organisation, the development of cohesive groups, and relationships between the nature and content of jobs and their task functions.* The introduction of new technology has also highlighted the need to give attention to the wider organisational context including the design of technology itself, the development of skills and problem-solving capacity, and the effective management of change. The ACAS Work Research Unit provides management and trade unions, in a range of different organisations, with direct assistance in taking practical steps to improve the design of jobs and the way work is organised. The unit publishes papers on a variety of issues concerned with improving the quality of working life, including the introduction of new technology, details of actual projects, developments in the field of job satisfaction, special bibliographies and case studies.

The successful implementation of new work methods and practices is dependent upon the willing and effective co-operation of staff, managerial colleagues and unions. Continued technological change is inevitable and likely to develop at an even faster rate. Managers must be responsive to such change. The full, potential benefits of information technology and automation will only be realised if the management of change takes proper account of human and social factors, as well as technical and economic factors.

Synopsis

Every work organisation is concerned with being effective. Organisation development (OD) is concerned with the diagnosis of organisational health and performance, and adaptability to change. OD is a generic term embracing a wide range of intervention strategies into the social processes of an organisation. The broad nature of OD means that many interrelated topic areas could be included under this heading.

In order to bring about effective change OD makes use of a number of approaches, or intervention strategies, including survey research and feedback, T-groups, team building and grid training. OD is action-oriented and tailored to suit specific organisational needs. It is usually a long-term process and changing the climate of an organisation is a major task. This makes it difficult to evaluate the success of OD in bringing about an improvement in organisational performance.

Organisational climate is a general concept and difficult to define precisely. It is based on the perception of members towards the organisation, and can be seen as the state of mutual trust and understanding among members of the organisation. A healthy organisational climate might be expected to exhibit a number of characteristic features. Among the factors which contribute to a healthy climate is the extent to which employees have a sense of commitment to the organisation. The concept of commitment is difficult to describe but can be put into perspective in terms of a three-pillar model based on: a sense of belonging to the organisation; a sense of excitement in the job; and confidence in management. Employee commitment, however, must have limits and be reciprocated by the organisation.

It might be expected that a healthy organisational climate would be reflected by complete harmony in working relationships, but conflict is a reality of management and organisational behaviour. Conflict can be distinguished from argument and competition. There are contrasting views of conflict and it can be seen to have both positive and negative outcomes. There are many potential sources of organisational conflict related to individual, group, organisational and environmental factors. Although a certain amount of conflict may be seen as inevitable, the important point is how conflict, when found to exist, is handled and managed. Management need to adopt appropriate strategies for dealing with the harmful effects of conflict.

Organisations operate within an increasingly volatile environment. In order to perform effectively they must be responsive to change. OD itself is a response to organisational change. Change is a pervasive influence and an inescapable part of social and organisational life. There are a wide range of forces acting upon organisations which make the need for change inevitable. One strategy of change is through the adoption of a systems approach. Despite the potential positive outcomes, change is often resisted at both the individual and the organisational level. It is important, therefore, for management to adopt a clearly defined strategy for the initiation of change, including attention to the human and social factors of change.

Review and discussion questions

1. Explain what you understand by organisation development (OD). What are the main features of OD and how would you attempt to assess its value?
2. Outline the Blake and Mouton grid training strategy as a means of implementing OD. What other intervention strategies might be used in an OD programme?
3. What do you understand by organisational climate and what do you

think are its main characteristic features? From your own organisation, give examples of features that have contributed to and/or detracted from a healthy climate.

4. Explain the concept of employee commitment and suggest how it might actually be created. Give examples of factors which have contributed to your own strength of commitment in a work situation.

5. To what extent do you accept the view that conflict is an inevitable feature of management and organisational behaviour? Distinguish between contrasting views of organisational conflict, and outline potential positive and negative outcomes of conflict.

6. Outline main potential sources of organisational conflict and give examples from your own organisation. Suggest how management can attempt to avoid the harmful effects of conflict.

7. Discuss, with supporting practical examples, some of the major changes confronting work organisations today. What is the need for planned organisational change?

8. Why do people in organisations tend to resist change? Explain instances of resistance to change in your own organisation and the effectiveness of management strategies to overcome the resistance.

| Case study |

The Wakewood organisation comprises seven units, each of which has been managed autonomously over the last five years. Each unit is managed by a General Manager and comprises one or more product/service departments and other staff departments. Each unit is, in effect, an autonomous division of Wakewood.

The Chief Executive has managed the organisation from a small headquarters building using a participative style. He has become increasingly concerned about the performance of one of the seven units. The unit employs 700 people and accounts for 20% of Wakewood's activities. He perceives the following internal and external pressures on this unit and believes that the General Manager responsible for it cannot deal with the problem. The Chief Executive has been unable to devote much time to this unit during the last years because of other pressures on his time. During the last four years, he has achieved significant changes and improvements in other units within the organisation. This has absorbed much of his time but has created a very positive reputation for him throughout Wakewood. He is seen as up-to-date and concerned for his employees.

External Pressures
Increasing client/customer
  dissatisfaction
New technology
Increasing competition in the
  provision of the products/services
  provided
Rapidly increasing costs

Internal Pressures
Fear of change
Limited management skills in the
  introduction of change
Lack of experience with new
  technology
Low productivity and quality
Poor staff morale

The unit is managed by a General Manager with functional managers responsible to the General Manager for three product/service departments, an administration department, finance and a small personnel department.

The General Manager has worked with Wakewood for eighteen years now. His approach to managing the unit has been always to control costs and activities fairly tightly and to concentrate on developing an efficient and professional team working for him. He has paid little or no attention to the needs of clients. There has been a growing number of complaints from clients about the service provided by the unit. Long waits are often involved and staff are said not to handle clients too well.

New computer technology is being deployed by Wakewood. However, progress in this unit has been slow. The General Manager seems largely disinterested and the staff reluctant to adapt. However, the pressure to introduce the technology is strong. Staff costs are high and many routine tasks seem likely to be capable of computerisation.

The Chief Executive wishes to introduce marketing and quality audit ideas into the unit as a means of responding to some of the pressures identified above. Moreover, be believes that new technology must be introduced over the next few years, particularly in the product/service departments. To do so he has concluded that three major problems must be faced, as follows:

(i)   attitudes to change and the organisation must be changed;
(ii) attitudes to, and knowledge of new technology, must be improved dramatically.
(iii) the organisation structure must be reviewed in order to introduce marketing and quality audit ideas into the unit.

You have been asked to advise on how to proceed. Outline a strategy for change designed to achieve the following objectives:

(a) to prepare people for change, convincing them that significant organisational changes are needed;
(b) to plan and monitor a programme of organisational change;
(c) to help people at all levels in the unit cope with the problems of change;
(d) to achieve improvement in the unit's performance.

(You may deal with this case study from *either* a private sector or a public sector perspective. If you adopt a public sector standpoint you can interpret 'marketing and quality audit ideas' to mean to develop an approach in which concern for the client and the quality of services provided becomes more important than previously.)

Notes and references

1. French, W. L. and Bell, C. H. *Organization Development*, Third edition, Prentice-Hall (1984) p. 17.
2. For example, see: Pritchard, W. 'What's New in Organisation Development', *Personnel Management*, vol. 16, no. 7, July 1984, pp. 30–3.
3. See, for example: Mumford, E. 'Helping Organizations Through Action Research: The Sociotechnical Approach', *Quality of Work Life*, vol. 3, nos 5–6, September–December 1986, pp. 329–44.
4. Blake, R. B. and Mouton, J. S. *The Managerial Grid III*, Gulf Publishing Company (1985).
5. French, W. L. and Bell, C. H. *Organization Development*, Third edition, Prentice-Hall (1984).
6. See, for example: Rowlandson, P. 'The Oddity of OD', *Management Today*, November 1984, pp. 90–2.
7. Fitzgerald, T. H. 'The OD Practitioner in the Business World: Theory Versus Reality', *Organizational Dynamics*, Summer 1987, pp. 20–33.

8. Tagiuri, R. and Litwin, G. H. (eds) *Organizational Climate*, Graduate School of Business Administration, Harvard University (1968) p. 27.
9. Katz, D. and Kahn, R. L. *The Social Psychology of Organizations*, Second edition, Wiley (1978).
10. Martin, P. and Nicholls, J. *Creating a Committed Workforce*, Institute of Personnel Management (1987).
11. Ibid. p. 97.
12. Ibid. p. 184.
13. White, G. *Employee Commitment*, ACAS Work Research Unit, Occasional Paper no. 38, HMSO (October 1987).
14. Ibid. pp. 17–18.
15. Drucker, P. F. *The Practice of Management*, Pan Books (1968) p. 150.
16. For example, see: Salaman, G. *Class and Corporation*, Fontana (1981).
17. Fox, A. *Industrial Sociology and Industrial Relations*, HMSO (1966).
18. French, W. L., Kast, F. E. and Rosenzweig, J. E. *Understanding Human Behavior in Organizations*, Harper and Row (1985).
19. Handy, C. B. *Understanding Organizations*, Third edition, Penguin (1985).
20. Argyris, C. *Intervention Theory and Method: A Behavioral Science View*, Addison-Wesley (1970).
21. Schmidt, W. H. 'Conflict: A Powerful Process for (Good or Bad) Change', *Management Review*, 63, December 1974, pp. 4–10.
22. See, for example: Ardrey, R. *The Territorial Imperative*, Collins (1967) (Ardrey suggests that principles of territory which motivate animal behaviour can also be applied to society).
23. Woodward, J. *Industrial Organization: Theory and Practice*, Second edition, Oxford University Press (1980) p. 113.
24. Bryans, P. and Cronin, T. P. *Organization Theory*, Mitchell Beazley (1983) p. 103.
25. Lewin, K. *Field Theory in Social Science*, Harper and Row (1951).
26. French, W. L., Kast, F. E. and Rosenzweig, J. E. *Understanding Human Behavior in Organizations*, Harper and Row (1985).
27. Leavitt, H. J. 'Applied Organizational Change in Industry: Structural, Technological and Humanistic Approaches', in March, J. G. (ed.) *Handbook of Organizations*, Rand McNally (1965).
28. Wilson, B. 'The Challenge of Change', *Industrial Management & Data Systems*, November/December 1987, p. 21.
29. Hellreigal, D., Slocum, J. W. and Woodman, R. W. *Organizational Behavior*, Fourth edition, West Publishing (1986).
30. Toffler, A. *Future Shock*, Pan Books (1970) p. 27.
31. Hersey, P. and Blanchard, K. *Management of Organizational Behavior*, Fifth edition, Prentice-Hall (1988) pp. 342–3.
32. Based on extracts from the author's article: Mullins, L. J. 'Information Technology – The Human Factor', *Administrator*, vol. 5, no. 8, September 1985, pp. 6–9.

18. MANAGEMENT DEVELOPMENT AND ORGANISATIONAL EFFECTIVENESS

Every work organisation is concerned with being effective. Upon the attainment of its aims and objectives rests the success and ultimate survival of the organisation. The quality of management is one of the most important factors in the success of any organisation. There are, however, a multiplicity of variables which impinge upon organisational effectiveness. The manager needs to understand the importance of improving the overall performance and effectiveness of the organisation.

Objectives

To: (i)   Explain the importance of effective management to organisation development;

(ii)   Detail an integrated model of managerial behaviour and development;

(iii)   Explain the main features and requirements of the management development process;

(iv)   Examine the importance of management education, training and development;

(v)   Assess the nature of organisational effectiveness and basic attributes for organisational success;

(vi)   Outline criteria for an evaluation of organisational effectiveness;

(vii)   Recognise the importance of management development, and attempts to improve organisational performance and effectiveness.

THE IMPORTANCE OF EFFECTIVE MANAGEMENT

Effective management is at the heart of organisation development and improved performance, and the contribution to economic and social needs of society. This applies as much to service organisations as to any other industry. The quality of management is one of the most important factors in the success of any organisation. Managers need a balance of technical, social and conceptual knowledge and skills, acquired through a blend of education and experience. There is, therefore, a continual need for managerial development. The organisation must ensure the development of both present and future managers.

AN INTEGRATED MODEL OF MANAGEMENT DEVELOPMENT

The wide variety of organisational settings found within the work situation makes special demands upon its managers. There is a dichotomy between the application of general management theory in influencing the behaviour and performance of managers, while at the same time accepting the need for individuals to manage according to situational demands. Particular models of managerial behaviour applied to specific types of organisations have little relevance, and if anything provide a constraint on the need for an open and fluid interpretation of management development.

Using accumulated knowledge of management theory, *Mullins* and *Aldrich* have constructed an integrated model of managerial behaviour and development. The model relies on basic management and behavioural theories for its structure, and situational demands for its adaptation.[1] (*See* Fig. 18.1.)

Past knowledge and experience

Development involves a combination of knowledge and varied experience. These are seen as taking place through a combination of both theoretical and practical involvement. The advancement of human relations skills is ideally seen as stemming from deliberate and constructive self-development.

The manager as an individual

Behavioural and social variables provide a framework for conceptualising behaviour in organisations, and include:

- Links with other individuals and groups within and outside the organisation. These links may be formal or informal.
- Personality and people perception.
- Values.
- Attitudes.
- Opinions.
- Motivation: needs and expectations.
- Intelligence and abilities: learning and skill acquisition and the assimilation and retention of past knowledge and experiences.[2]

Any organisation

The organisation can be analysed in terms of five main interrelated sub-systems. Two of these, people and management, can be considered within the context of the 'behavioural and social variables' above.

(i) *Task* – includes the goals and objectives of the organisation, the nature of its inputs and outputs, and work to be carried out during the work process.

(ii) *Technology* – describes the manner in which the tasks of the organisation are carried out and the nature of the work performance. The materials, techniques and equipment used in the transformation or conversion process.

(iii) *Structure* – defines the patterns of organisation and formal relationships among members. The division of work and co-ordination of tasks by which any series of activities can be carried out.

(iv) *People* – the nature of the members undertaking the series of activities as defined by the behavioural and social variables.

(v) *Management* – is therefore the integrating activity working to achieve the 'tasks', using the 'technology' through the combined efforts of 'people'

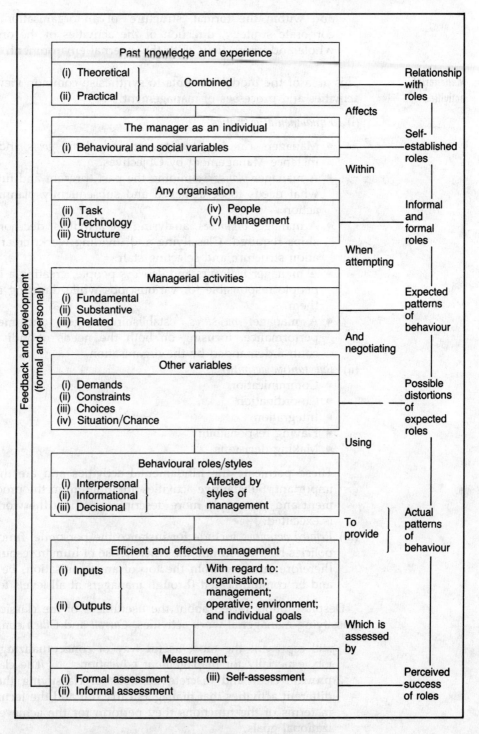

Fig. 18.1 An integrated model of managerial behaviour and development

(From Mullins, Laurie and Aldrich, Paul, 'An Integrated Model of Management and Managerial Development', *Journal of Management Development*, vol. 7, no. 3, (1988) p. 30.)

and within the formal 'structure' of an organisation. This involves corporate strategy, direction of the activities of the organisation as a whole and interactions with the external environment.

Managerial activities

This area of the model attempts to synthesise common views on the basic activities and processes of management.

(i) *Fundamental activities*

- Managers can be seen to set and *clarify goals* and *objectives*. For instance Management by Objectives.
- A manager *plans*, examining the past, present and future; describing what needs to be achieved and subsequently planning a course of action.
- A manager *organises*, analysing the activities, decisions and relationships required. Classifying and dividing work, creating an organisation structure and selecting staff.
- A manager *motivates* and *develops* people, creating a team out of the people responsible for various jobs while directing and developing them.
- A manager *measures*, establishing targets and measurements of performance, focusing on both the needs of individuals and the control demanded by the organisation.

(ii) *Substantive activities*

- Comminication
- Co-ordination
- Integration
- Having responsibility
- Making decisions

These permeate the fundamental activities and are therefore no less important. Substantive activities are inherent in the process of management and are simply more descriptive of how the work of a manager is executed.

(iii) *Related activities* include for instance the personnel function. Personnel policies help determine the efficient use of human resources and should therefore emanate from the top of an organisation, be defined clearly and be communicated through managers at all levels to their staff.

Despite doubts raised about the usefulness of the classical functions for classifying managerial work activities, *Carroll* and *Gillen* conclude that they:

> still represent the most useful way of conceptualizing the manager's job, especially for management education. . . . The classical functions provide clear and discrete methods of classifying the thousands of different activities that managers carry out and the techniques they use in terms of the functions they perform for the achievement of organizational goals.[3]

Other variables

Stewart has developed a model based on studies of managerial jobs which it is suggested provides a framework for thinking about the nature of managerial jobs and about the manner in which managers undertake them.[4]

(i) *Demands* are what anyone in the job has to do. They are not what the manager ought to do but only what must be done.
(ii) *Constraints* are internal and external factors limiting what the manager can do.
(iii) *Choices* are the activities that the manager is free to do but does not have to do.

'Chance' is one of the factors which determine dominant Managerial Grid style: where, for instance, a manager has no experience of, or sets of assumptions about, how to manage a particular situation.[5]

Behavioural roles and styles

According to the contingency approach, the task of the manager is to identify which style, role or technique will in a particular situation, in particular circumstances, within a particular organisation and at a particular time contribute best to the attainment of corporate, managerial, social and individual goals.

The activities of managers can be classified into ten interrelated roles.[6]

(i) *Interpersonal* – relations with other people arising from the manager's status and authority. These include *figurehead*, *leader* and *liaison* roles.
(ii) *Informational* – relate to the sources and communication of information arising from the manager's interpersonal roles. These include *monitor*, *disseminator* and *spokesperson* roles.
(iii) *Decisional* – involve making strategic, organisational decisions based on authority and access to information. These include *entrepreneurial*, *disturbance handler*, *resource allocator* and *negotiator* roles.

It is emphasised that this set of roles is a rather arbitrary synthesis of a manager's activities. These roles are not easy to isolate in practice but they do form an integrated whole. As such, the removal of any one role affects the effectiveness of the manager's overall performance.

This area has strong links with *Miner*'s 'role expectations and expected pattern of behaviours' theory which is adopted in the model.[7]

The variables already described within the model will determine which form of management is appropriate in any given situation. For example, *McGregor*'s Theory X and Theory Y attempt to develop a predictive model for the behaviour of individual managers.[8] Most managers have a natural inclination towards one basic style of behaviour, with an emergency or 'back-up' style. The dominant style is influenced by one or several of the following: organisation, values, personal history and chance.[9]

Another influential model of management style is centred on 'exploitive authoritative', 'benevolent authoritative', 'consultative' and 'participative group' systems. These systems can then be related to a profile or more specific organisational characteristics.[10]

Efficient and effective management

Managerial efficiency can be distinguished from managerial effectiveness.[11]

(i) *Efficiency* is concerned with doing things right and relates to *inputs* and what a manager does.
(ii) *Effectiveness* is concerned with doing the right things and relates to *outputs* of the job and what the manager actually achieves.

Performance is related to the goals of the organisation and the informal and formal goals of all its individual participants, including managers. The need to take into account external, environmental variables must not be forgotten.

Measurement

Managerial effectiveness is a difficult concept either to define or to measure. Managerial effectiveness cannot be measured simply in terms of achievement, productivity or relationships with other people. The manager must be adaptable in adopting the appropriate style of behaviour which will determine effectiveness in achieving the output requirements of the job. What is also important is the manner in which the manager achieves results, and the effects on other people.

Managerial effectiveness may be assessed in three ways.

(i) *Formal assessment* – the pursuit of the systematic development of managers is not possible without the support of an appraisal scheme providing for periodic assessment on the basis of the best obtainable objectivity.[12] An assessment form is often used as a valuable aid to objectivity and covers among other areas: personal skills, behaviour and attitudes; performance in the allocated role; management knowledge and competence; and performance related to potential. Assessment should point out strengths and weaknesses and suggest ways of resolving the latter.

(ii) *Informal assessment* – may be given as advice by other managers, or by the behaviour and attitudes of staff. The willingness to accept a manager's authority will manifest itself through the strength of motivation and therefore measured levels such as staff turnover, incidence of sickness, absenteeism and poor time keeping.

(iii) *Self-assessment* – the more managers understand about their job and themselves the more sensitive they will be to the needs of the organisation. Sensitivity should also extend to the needs of members. This understanding cannot come simply from studying the results of formal appraisals. Managers must be receptive to the reactions of others and focus consciously on their own actions to try and develop an understanding of what specifically they do and why.[13]

Feedback and development

There are two basic kinds of feedback: intrinsic and augmented.[14]

(i) *Intrinsic* – includes the usual visual and kinaesthetic cues occurring in connection with a response; for example, the perception of other people's visual reactions towards a management style in a given situation.

(ii) *Augmented* – may be concurrent or terminal, and may occur with performance or after it. The frequency, details and timing of each illustrate the differences between the two; for example, continuous, interim reviews as part of a system of Management by Objectives, compared with the annual performance appraisal interview.

Feedback is largely associated with the measurement area of the model but should be seen as part of the manager's development package. The specific elements in the programmes for individual managers are determined by a variety of.circumstances including the outcome of periodic appraisals.

Stewart has commented on the move towards a more individual approach to management development. There should be a greater emphasis on the individual's own setting and needs, and the growing interest in promoting self-development encourages the individual to adopt general management theories to his or her particular needs.[15] This has more recently been extended by the idea of 'mentoring' – a process of nurturing the growth of other people within their jobs – and by the allocation of senior management to support the development of individual juniors within the organisation. Mentoring is part of a self-managed learning process.[16]

MANAGEMENT DEVELOPMENT PROCESS

The process of management development should be related to the nature, objectives and requirements of the *organisation as a whole*. A prerequisite of management development is *effective manpower planning* coupled with procedures for *recruitment and selection*.

Performance review An essential feature of management development is performance review. The systematic review of work performance provides an opportunity to highlight positive contributions from the application of acquired knowledge, skills, qualifications and experience. An effective system of performance review will help identify individual strengths and weaknesses, potential for promotion, and training and development needs. A key activity is *Management by Objectives* (MBO) which attempts to relate organisational objectives to individual performance and development through the involvement of all levels of management.

For example, the performance review system of the Abbey National Building Society provides a framework for:

- measuring results;
- identifying and meeting training and development needs;
- personal career planning;
- agreeing objectives and standards of performance; and
- organisational succession planning.

Details of the Abbey National performance review system are given in the appendix to this chapter.

Training and learning Management development also requires a combination of *on-the-job training*, through, for example, delegation, project work, coaching and guided self-analysis, trial periods and simulation; and *off-the-job learning*, through, for example, external short courses, or study for a Diploma in Management Studies or MBA qualification. This training and learning should be aimed at providing a blend of technical competence, social and human skills, and conceptual ability.

The British Institute of Management, in conjunction with the Open University, has launched a new Diploma in Management Practice which aims to improve the working effectiveness of individual managers. This new BIM diploma programme is the first to be based on the development of practical skills in the workplace in conjunction with a business school's academic training and teaching.

Succession planning and career progression

Management succession planning aims to ensure that a sufficient supply of appropriately qualified and capable men and women are available to meet the future needs of the organisation.

Allied to management development and succession planning should be a programme of *planned career progression*. This should provide potential managers with:

● training and experience to equip them to assume a level of responsibility compatible with their ability; and
● practical guidance, encouragement and support so that they may realise their potential, satisfy their career ambition and wish to remain with the organisation.

Requirements of a management development programme

The requirements of a management development programme have been identified as providing:

● an effective method of defining expected results from managers;
● the continuous improvement in the performance of managers;
● the recruitment and retention of suitable calibre staff;
● first class training, for tomorrow's jobs as well as today's at lower cost;
● a reliable means of judging the performance of managers;
● a flexible succession plan for the future staffing of the organisation;
● the motivation of managers and fair rewards in relation to results achieved;
● improved flow of communications up, down and across the organisation.[17]

MANAGEMENT EDUCATION, TRAINING AND DEVELOPMENT

The importance of management education, training and development in this country has been highlighted by two recent reports sponsored by the British Institute of Management.

THE CONSTABLE AND McCORMICK REPORT

The first report, *The Making of British Managers*, examines the development of managers in Britian and warns that many managers need broad professional training and education if they are to compete successfully.[18]

There is widespread recognition of effective management as a key factor in economic growth. But Britain's 2.75 million managers lack the development, education and training opportunities of their competitors in other countries. The great majority of people entering management roles each year have no prior formal management education and training.

Recommendations for action

The report lists 23 recommendations for action, centred on four main areas.

(i) Ensuring an adequate flow of educated and trained entrants into management.

(ii) Providing a new Diploma in Business Administration to be taken by young people during their first three to four years of work after higher education. The diploma should be the primary qualification for membership of BIM, but it should not be created by a simple repackaging of the existing Diploma in Management Studies.

(iii) Growth in MBA programmes should be concentrated on flexible and modular programmes, integrated with career development and work experience. Provision for open and distance learning should be expanded for both the diploma and the MBA.

(iv) Management development should be a career-long process with both internal and external training. There should be co-operation among employers, academic and professional institutions, government and individual managers. A credit transfer system should be established covering both academic courses and company programmes.

The report recommends that the government should be responsible for the costs of expanding the infrastructure of university, polytechnic and college management schools. Two new management teacher training programmes should be established and employer organisations should encourage managers to teach part-time.

THE HANDY REPORT

A second report, *The Making of Managers: A Report on Management Education, Training and Development in the United States, West Germany, France, Japan and the UK*, questions why enterprises in these other countries are economically more successful than those in Britain, and whether there is something special about the particular contribution by management.[19] Although there are differences in the approach taken to management development by the other countries, overall there is a much more positive approach than in this country. The main similarity is that, in the four competitor countries, most managers have been educated to a higher level than British managers. In contrast to other professions, for example medicine, law and accountancy, there is no clear, relevant and prestigious route into management in Britain.

The report warns that in future technical and functional skills alone will not be enough. Managers will require business knowledge, and human and conceptual skills. Main proposals in the report include the following.

(i) A move to a two-part qualification, on the professional model, with periods of early study leading to a preliminary qualification, followed by work experience interleaved with more specialised study leading to a full qualification, which could be a (revised) MBA.

(ii) For management development there could be a 'Development Charter' setting out a code of good practice including, for example, a personal development plan for every manager and a system for experience-based learning. Major organisations should commit themselves to the charter and form a charter group to set examples, take initiatives and help disseminate good practice.

A ten-point agenda The report outlines a ten-point agenda for Britain based on the best aspects of management education, training and development in the other countries.

The agenda includes: educating more people more broadly, if possible up to first degree level; encouraging some form of work experience to be undertaken as part of this education; establishing a tradition of apprenticeship or 'articles of management'; encouraging good practice in management development by promoting larger organisations as trendsetters; improving co-operation in training between companies, and between companies and business schools; establishing an information base on the provision of management education.

A key conclusion of the report is that, by comparison with the other countries, Britain has yet to find an appropriate form of management education to suit its culture. Many more of the managers in the four competitor countries have benefited from formal, systematic policies for continuous education and development.

THE NATURE OF ORGANISATIONAL EFFECTIVENESS

The underlying theme of this book has been the need for organisational effectiveness and the role of management as an integrating activity. Organisational effectiveness is affected by a multiplicity of variables. For example, *Handy* identifies over 60 factors that impinge on any one organisational situation and which illustrate the complicated nature of the study of organisational effectiveness.[20] (*See* Fig. 18.2.)

Basic attributes for organisational success

In their study of 62 American companies with outstandingly successful performance, *Peters* and *Waterman* identify eight basic attributes of excellence and which appear to account for success.[21]

- *A bias for action*; that is action oriented and a bias for getting things done.
- *Close to the customer*; that is listening and learning from the people they serve, and providing quality, service and reliability.
- *Autonomy and entrepreneurship*; that is innovation and risk taking as an expected way of doing things.
- *Productivity through people*; that is treating members of staff as the source of quality and productivity.
- *Hands-on, value driven*; that is having well-defined basic philosophies and top management keeping in touch with the 'front lines'.
- *Stick to the knitting*; that is, in most cases, staying close to what you know and can do well.
- *Simple form, lean staff*; that is simple structural forms and systems, and few top-level staff.
- *Simultaneous loose–tight properties*; that is operational decentralisation but strong centralised control over the few, important core values.

The companies were marked, above all, by the 'intensity itself' which stemmed from their strongly held beliefs.

The McKinsey 7-S framework

From their research *Peters* and *Waterman* report that:

> any intelligent approach to organizing had to encompass, and treat as interdependent, at least seven variables: structure, strategy, people, management style, systems and procedures, guiding concepts and

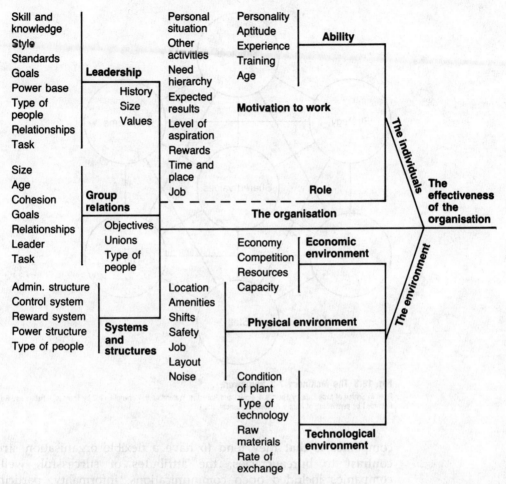

Fig. 18.2 Some factors affecting organisational effectiveness
(From Handy, C. B., *Understanding Organizations*, 3rd edition, Penguin Books Ltd. (1985) p. 15). Reproduced by permission of Penguin Books Ltd.

shared values (i.e. culture), and the present and hoped-for corporate strengths or skills. We defined this idea more precisely and elaborated what came to be known as the McKinsey 7-S Framework. With a bit of stretching, cutting and fitting, we made all seven variables start with the letter S and invented a logo to go with it.[22]

(*See* Fig. 18.3.)

ORGANISATIONAL EFFECTIVENESS AND THE MANAGEMENT OF CHANGE

A key factor in organisational effectiveness is the successful management of change. Diagnosing and solving organisational problems involves the interaction of a multiplicity of factors influencing an organisation's ability to change and its proper mode of change.[23]

The importance of innovation

In the *Peters* and *Waterman* study a common thread among the successful companies is *innovation*. A common characteristic of excellently managed

521

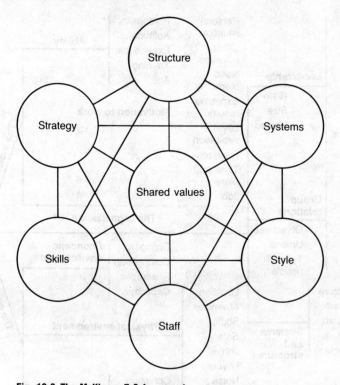

Fig. 18.3 The McKinsey 7-S framework
From *In Search of Excellence* by Thomas J. Peters and Robert H. Waterman Jr. Copyright 1982 by Thomas J. Peters and Robert H. Waterman. Reprinted by permission of Harper & Row, Publishers, Inc.)

companies is that they tend to have a flexible organisation structure. In contrast to bureaucracies, the attributes of successful, well-managed companies included open communications, informality, participative decision making and freedom of expression. The flexible nature of organisation led to a bias for quick action rather than inertia, and emphasis was placed on risk taking and innovation.

When looking at management excellence itself, Peters and Waterman chose a double meaning for 'innovation'. 'In addition to what might normally be thought of – creative people developing marketable new product and services – . . . *innovative companies are especially adroit at continually responding to change of any sort in their environments*'[24]

When their environments change, innovative companies change too. As a whole culture, they innovate to meet changes in the needs of their customers, the skills of competitors, the mood of the public, forces of international trade or government regulations. The concept of innovation defined the task of the truly excellent manager or management team. Companies that appeared to have attained that kind of innovative performance were the ones Peters and Waterman labelled as 'excellent companies'.

CRITERIA OF ORGANISATIONAL EFFECTIVENESS

There is a wide range of interrelated individual, group, organisational and environmental influences on behaviour in work organisations, and therefore many different criteria which might be applied in an attempt to assess organisational performance and effectiveness. In addition to those discussed in the last two chapters, we can mention some examples that have been discussed in previous chapters of this book.

Open systems framework

An organisation may be analysed in terms of an open systems framework: inputs; the series of activities involved in the transformation or conversion process: outputs; interactions with the environment; and performance of the system (organisation) in achieving its aims and objectives. The organisation may also be examined in terms of interrelated sub-systems, for example tasks to be undertaken, technology employed, formal structure, behaviour of people and the process of management. The state of the sub-systems will reflect upon the effectiveness of the organisation as a whole.

Key areas of performance and results

The effectiveness of an organisation might be assessed against *Drucker*'s eight key areas in which objectives need to be set in terms of business performance and results: market standing; innovation; productivity; physical and financial resources; profitability; manager performance and development; worker performance and attitude; and public responsibility.

Profile of organisational characteristics

The overall effectiveness of an organisation could also be gauged against *Likert*'s profile of organisational characteristics, and the extent to which these meet the fundamental concepts of System 4 (participative group) management practices, that is: the principle of support relationships; group decision making, and methods of organisation and supervision; and high performance aspiration for all members of the organisation. The human organisation and operation of the firm can be examined in terms of the relationships among causal, intervening and end-result variables.

The role of management

There are also a number of criteria which could be applied, more specifically, to an evaluation of the role of management. The activities of management could be judged, for example, against *Bourn*'s set of ten interrelated activities, or against *Mintzberg*'s set of ten integrated roles which comprise the essential functions of a manager's job. Style of management could be assessed, for example, by the *Blake* and *Mouton* Managerial Grid in terms of an appropriate mixture of concern for production and concern for people.

Managerial effectiveness

This can be evaluated by *Reddin*'s three-dimensional model of managerial behaviour: task orientation, relationship orientation and the demands of the situation. Or by *Langford*'s criteria of: the manager's work; the manager himself/herself; the manager's relationship with other people; the manager as part of the organisation; and a single overall criterion of general effectiveness.

Organisation audit

A programme of organisation audit (or management audit) involves a review of the operations of the organisation as a whole and an examination of the full range of management activities. Organisation audit is concerned with the identification of problems which are encountered in achieving organisational goals and disparities between strategy formulation and policy decisions, and actions necessary for their successful implementation.

Such a review may be undertaken by members of the organisation, external consultants on organisation and management, or a combination of both internal members and external consultants. Organisation audit tends to be concerned more with the current state of the organisation, and with what must be done now in order to meet set objectives and targets. But an organisation must also be properly prepared to face the demands of a changing environment. It must give attention to its future development and success.

Synopsis

Effective management is at the heart of organisation development and improved performance. There is a continual need for managerial development. Using accumulated knowledge of management theory it is possible to construct an integrated model of managerial behaviour and development. Attention needs to be given to the process of management development, including performance review and management by objectives, training and learning, management succession planning and career progression. Attention also needs to be given to the requirements of a management development programme.

Recent reports sponsored by the British Institute of Management have highlighted the importance of, and shortcomings in, management education, training and development in this country. The Constable and McCormick report warns that many more managers need broad professional training and education if they are to compete successfully, and lists 23 recommendations for action. The Handy report suggests that there is a much more positive approach in the four main competitor countries than in Britain. The report outlines a ten-point agenda for Britain based on best aspects of management education, training and development in the other countries.

There are a multiplicity of variables which impinge on any one organisational situation and which illustrate the complicated nature of the study of organisational effectiveness. In their study of 62 American companies with outstandingly successful performance, Peters and Waterman identify eight basic attributes of excellence. One approach to organising is the McKinsey 7-S framework of interdependent organisational variables – structure, strategy, skills, staff, style, systems and shared values.

A key factor in organisational effectiveness is innovation and the successful management of change. Diagnosing and solving organisational problems involves the interaction of a multiplicity of factors influencing an organisation's ability to change and its proper mode of change. There are, however, many different criteria which might be applied in an attempt to assess organisational performance and effectiveness.

For example, an organisation may be analysed in terms of an open systems framework. The effectiveness of an organisation might be assessed in terms of key areas of performance and results, or against a profile of organisational characteristics. There are also a number of criteria which could be applied more specifically to an evaluation of the role of management and managerial effectiveness. A programme of organisation audit involves a review of the operations of the organisation as a whole. However, in addition to concern for the current state of the organisation, attention must be given to its future development and success.

| Appendix | ABBEY NATIONAL BUILDING SOCIETY – PERFORMANCE REVIEW

Introduction

The Performance Review system provides a framework for

- Measuring results
- Identifying and meeting training and development needs
- Personal career planning
- Agreeing objectives and standards of performance
- Organisational succession planning

The system is not an isolated appraisal process, but is a key component of the Society's manpower planning and personnel policy: it is therefore especially important that all Abbey National staff understand what they can expect from the process, and what they need to do to keep it working effectively.

Objectives and standards of performance

What is an objective?

An objective is a statement of what an individual is aiming to achieve, in a key area of responsibility during the coming review period.

Objectives will normally fall into three main areas:

- *Business results*
- *Special business tasks or projects*
- *Personal development or performance improvements.*

These should be set within a broad objective which expects the person to manage his/her activity in a cost effective, controlled (by audit reports, procedures, instructions etc.) manner, within the defined budgets and standards of service. Objectives do not just repeat the job description, but should define priorities for the period in question, recognising that no two jobs (or job holders) are exactly alike. Objectives may occasionally repeat the normal job requirements, where performance has fallen below an acceptable level and the objectives form part of a recovery plan.

When should objectives be set?

Ideally, objectives should be set just before the start of the next review period, and should cover the next 12 months. However, for some jobs it may be more appropriate to set objectives for shorter periods. For example, with project-based jobs, you might find it more helpful to agree new objectives at the start of a new project. This is particularly true if the change of project also involves a change of management.

What is a standard of performance?

A standard of performance is what enables you to decide whether a job has been done well. It allows you to measure the achievements of an objective against predetermined standards.

Every objective should have several measurable standards of performance attached to it. You might consider measuring in terms of:

- *quality* e.g. accuracy, audit results, feedback from users
- *quantity* e.g. number of accounts, letters typed
- *timeliness* e.g meeting agreed deadlines
- *cost* e.g. within agreed budgets.

Some standards of performance already exist for jobs, but they are not always stated openly, or discussed. For example, you might be expected to equal the performance of other staff doing similar jobs, or there might be external standards applicable to your job (professional bodies or similar organisations often lay these down). The Performance Review System asks everyone to define the acceptable standards of performance for each objective, and to agree these with their manager, so that expectations are known, and performance can be monitored against these.

It is sometimes useful particularly for objectives of high priority to define what is an 'Effective', 'Highly Effective', and 'Exceptional' level of performance. The levels at which these ratings are agreed are likely to vary with changing circumstances and it is the manager's task to evaluate an individual's performance taking all factors into consideration.

Where possible, standards of performance should be based on observable *Results*: amount of mortgage lending, numbers of transactions processed.

As well as these obvious measures, you will often want to set standards for less quantifiable aspects of success – a good example of this is where you want to measure the quality of work, as well as the amount. You might then look at *Symptoms*: complaints rates, staff turnover etc.

When objectives and standards of performance have been set it is advisable for the manager and the reviewee to agree an Action Plan. This incorporates the actions to be taken to achieve the final result. It is the achievement of the agreed objective and standard that is rewarded through the Performance Review System, not the level of activity, nor the completion of individual action steps.

Example

Objective	Standards of Performance	Effective	Highly Effective	Exceptional
To reduce the percentage of arrears cases	By 31st Dec arrears to be reduced to	0.9%	0.5%	0.2%

Action Plan

- Arrears statistics to be analysed monthly and emerging trends commented on at quarterly meetings.

- Feeder branches to be involved in personal calls where appropriate.
- After 2 or more letters, all arrears cases to be contacted by telephone.
- Personal telephone contact to be made with all cases of 3+ months and file to be noted accordingly.
- By the time arrears reach 4+ months, all cases to be written off, arrangements made, or solicitors instructed.

How to set objectives and performance standards

Defining objectives is an essential part of the planning process, and of the Performance Review System. Individuals should propose their own objectives, once they understand Corporate, Divisional and Departmental/Regional plans.

- Identify your key areas of responsibility, thinking about what your particular priorities will be for the coming period. Ideally, aim for 5 or 6; more than this might mean that you are going into too much detail, fewer suggests that you are keeping things too general, or not doing yourself justice.
- For each area of responsibility, consider what result or end-point you could achieve during the review period (or another relevant timeframe, e.g. before moving to another project). Draft a standard to express the result which you think is realistic, but challenging.
- Think about how you could measure success in the objective. Set standards based on quantity, quality, cost and deadlines. Try first of all to measure actual *results* then consider whether you might include some *symptoms* of success.

Once you have drafted your objectives and standards of performance, these should be discussed with your reviewer, amended if necessary, and agreed upon. Objectives should then be prioritised to ensure the individual focuses on the key requirements of the business and his/her job. Make sure that you both understand and agree about what you are expected to achieve, and how this will be measured.

Summary

- Objectives state *what* should be achieved.
- Standards of performance define *how* achievement will be measured.
- They both relate to priority areas, not just to ordinary job requirements.
- They are agreed by both the reviewer and the person being reviewed.
- Standards should be measurable, specific and unambiguous.
- Objectives and standards should be realistic and achievable, but challenging.
- Action Plans relate to the action steps to be taken to achieve the objectives and the standards of performance.
- The Performance Review System rewards the achievement of objectives and agreed standards, not the level of activity nor, individual action steps.

Performance rating definitions

Rating	Definition
Exceptional	Standards for priority objectives were substantially exceeded and performance was exceptional in every respect. All other objectives were achieved to the agreed standard. All job requirements were maintained. Working beyond their normal job the individual has made a significant contribution to the business.
Highly Effective	Standards for priority objectives were exceeded. All other objectives were achieved to the agreed standard. All job requirements were maintained. A significant contribution was made to the department or area.
Effective	All objectives were achieved to the agreed standards taking into account all the circumstances. All job requirements were maintained.
Less than Effective	Some objectives were met or, All objectives were met but were below the agreed standard. Basic job requirements were maintained.
Unacceptable	Few objectives were met or, Objectives were well below the agreed standard. Basic job requirements were not maintained.

- There is an element of managerial judgement attached to deciding on the accurate rating to choose. Whilst the rating definitions are quite specific, circumstances must be taken into account as well. For example, someone who achieves all major objectives, but does not exceed them might still in some circumstances merit a 'highly effective' rating if the reviewer knows that
  a) the objectives were particularly challenging
  b) the person had to overcome major obstacles which were not foreseen at the time of setting the original objectives.
  c) the person initiated an activity which had a significant impact on the business, while still maintaining effective performance in their objectives.

- It is expected that the full range of 5 ratings will each be appropriate to some individuals. Any significant variation in performance should be pointed out to the individual concerned as soon as it is noticed, and steps taken to correct any decline in standards. Unacceptable performance should not be tackled for the first time at the annual review meeting.

'Effective' means that the individual has met agreed standards in relation to the objectives set and agreed. It is seen as good performance, making a **Valuable** *and* **Positive** *contribution.*

Management performance factors

This appendix defines performance factors which are relevant to jobs at management levels. Their relative importance will vary with the location and nature of the job. The list is not intended to be exhaustive: there may be other factors which you consider appropriate to particular individuals.

The factors suggested represent those identified for Career Assessment Programmes, and full definitions together with examples of behaviour are attached.

1 Communication – oral and written skills
2 Planning, Organising and Controlling
3 Self-motivation
4 People Management
5 Specialist Knowledge
6 Customer Service

1 Communication

The clear, concise and effective expression of ideas and other information in a persuasive manner.

Oral
- *Explains technical matters in an understandable way*
- *Succeeds in getting the message across*
- *Demonstrates enthusiasm, interest and conviction, e.g. smiles, good eye contact, open body posture, tone of voice*
- *Uses examples and analogies appropriate to the listener's experience and understanding*
- *Summarises and uses questions to check understanding*
- *Listens and correctly interprets the spoken word AND non-verbal behaviour*

Written
- *Uses simple, concise, grammatically correct English to produce understandable written work*
- *Uses a clear structure which includes key information at the appropriate level of detail*
- *Use of headings, paragraphs, introduction and conclusions to highlight the main themes, analysis and recommendations.*

2 Planning, organisation and controlling

Establishing a course of action and effective procedures to monitor and control one's own activities and responsibilities, and that of subordinates.

Structuring & co-ordinating work
- *Actively schedules own time and activities*
- *Prioritises work according to overall objectives*
- *Updates plans as necessary*
- *Plans resources to implement activities e.g. who works on what, budgets, time-scales and performance standards*
- *Ensures plans are clearly documented*
- *Ensures projects are planned to appropriate levels of accuracy and precision*
- *Allocates all tasks to specific individuals*

- *Establishes procedures to monitor job activities of self and/or others*
- *Delegates responsibility and ownership of key decisions to others*
- *Delegates with end result and standards of performance clearly explained*

Controlling
- *Makes sure projects stay on target, and renegotiates those targets when necessary*
- *Ensures accurate records are kept*
- *Monitors results and takes appropriate action*
- *Measures results against objectives*
- *Ensures vital figures are correct*
- *Involved in subordinates' activities at a level appropriate to the individual's need for guidance*

3 Self-motivation

Sets high work standards, and maintains a high level of energy and motivation at all times.

- *Maintains effectiveness in varying environments, tasks, and responsibilities*
- *Responds positively to constructive criticism*
- *Sets self high personal standards or performance and strives to attain them*
- *Maintains a consistently high level of activity across all tasks*
- *Maintains a high level of performance and activity over extended periods.*

4 People Management

Uses appropriate styles and methods of interpersonal behaviour. Influences through skill and enthusiasm rather than from his/her formal position.

Individual
- *Provides regular feedback*
- *Takes time out to praise effective performance*
- *Constructively confronts poor performance*
- *Objectively identifies skills and weaknesses in staff*
- *Creates opportunities for others to develop skills, pursue interests, and use initiative*
- *Actively encourages others to fulfil their potential*

Group
- *Explains and sells groups goals, to build loyalty and commitment to these goals*
- *Keeps others informed and up-to-date on branch/area/regional/departmental and organisational issues*
- *Regularly talks and listens to others, actively seeking their views*
- *Co-ordinates work areas, ensuring close liaison between teams working towards common objectives*
- *Provides group with regular feedback on progress towards achieving goals*
- *Involves all members in decisions which affect the group's objectives*
- *Clarifies and helps to resolve problems or conflicts*

5 Specialist Knowledge

The appropriate application and use of specialist and professional expertise.
- *Keeps up-to-date with new approaches and methods within his/her specialist area*

- *Always provides accurate and reliable specialist advice; will not offer advice if she/he lacks knowledge*
- *Continually increases the depth of his/her specialist knowledge; knows his/her subject to the finest level of detail*
- *Draws on a fund of background specialist knowledge to highlight technical problems and opportunities which others do not readily see*
- *Actively seeks to maintain the highest standards of technical quality*

6 Customer Service

There are now defined standards of service concerning a number of activities, which can be applied across the Society. Beyond this, Customer Service is concerned with a willingness to respond to the needs of others in terms of business and relationships, within a broad definition of the Society's purpose and the individual's job function.

- *Shows concern for the person as well as the rules*
- *Meets commitments and produces results*
- *Demonstrates personal involvement*
- *Contributes to team support*

Senior Management performance factors

The management performance factors are also relevant for senior managers, however the following were defined as being particularly concerned with success at the senior management level.

1 Use of Authority
2 Influencing Skills
3 Judgement
4 Adaptability and Flexibility
5 Organisational Awareness
6 External Perspective
7 Strategic Thinking
8 Personal Impact

1 Use of Authority

Readily taking responsibility for all aspects of a situation, rather than passively accepting it.

- *Takes accountability for ensuring results are achieved*
- *Uses authority to give direction to a team, but maintains appropriate distance when authority not needed*
- *Willingly and confidently accepts new responsibilities*
- *Takes decisions quickly and on own initiative when appropriate*
- *Accepts corporate decisions positively, and actions the policies*
- *Actively challenges others' views, regardless of their position or status*
- *On issues of key importance, sticks to own view even against tough opposition*
- *Makes his/her point of view known*

2 Influencing Skills

Gaining acceptance of his/her proposals

- *Puts forward proposals and gives explanations which are clearly defined*
- *States what she/he wants and expects to achieve*
- *Questions others to identify their needs and reflects these back*
- *Overcomes objections and persuades others to accept his/her viewpoint*
- *Compromises his/her position to reach acceptable solutions*
- *Gains acceptance by explicitly asking for agreement*
- *Adjusts his/her style to respond to the feelings and needs of others*

3 Judgement

Identifying issue and problems, developing alternative courses of action and taking sound decisions based on sound analysis and interpretation of the implications. NB Judgement is concerned with the quality rather than the speed of decisions.

Analysis
- *Identifies all important parameters, and the information needed to tackle a problem.*
- *Evaluates complex problems in a logical and in-depth manner.*
- *Focuses analysis on key areas which need to be tackled in order to solve problems.*
- *Questions basic assumptions to identify the nature of a problem.*
- *Critically evaluates and draws correct inferences from numerical information.*
- *Assimilates new information and understands arguments quickly.*

Producing Solutions
- *Original, versatile approach to problem solving.*
- *Provides a number of practical, workable solutions where possible.*

Decision Making
- *Takes decisions on the basis of his/her analysis when there is uncertainty and risk.*
- *Takes decisions with sufficient, rather than complete, information.*
- *Willing to initiate action involving deliberate risk, in order to achieve a recognised benefit or advantage.*

4 Adaptability/Flexibility

Maintaining effective performance in changing situations, environments, priorities, tasks and responsibilities.

- *Responds positively to new ideas, willing to give new approaches a try*
- *Makes progress on tasks when final objectives are still unclear*
- *Looks for alternative ways to achieve objectives when faced with obstacles*
- *Looks for ways of improving quality of work*
- *Originates action on own initiative*
- *Maintains stability of performance when faced with unforeseen changes*

5 Organisational Awareness

Knowledge of how the organisation operates and how his/her area of work relates to each part of the organisation.

- *Bases decisions for own Department/Region on the requirements of the Divisional strategy*
- *Takes into account the priorities and needs of other areas within the Society when making decisions*
- *Uses informal channels of communication when appropriate to achieve objectives*

6 External Perspective

Having and using knowledge of changing situations and pressures both inside and outside the organisation (social, environmental, financial and business).

- *Bases decisions for own area on the major influences affecting the Society's position in the market place*
- *Proposes ideas in the light of major external influences*
- *Actively bases decisions on enhancing the image and impact of the Society in the market place*
- *Develops strategies to achieve the key commercial objectives of the Society*
- *Keeps up-to-date on latest developments in technological, economic and social fields*

7 Strategic Thinking

Taking a broad, long-term view and having the ability to stand back from daily activity to see the whole picture and focus on major goals.

- *Identifies long-term objectives and sets strategic goals. Integrates the detail into an overall corporate perspective*
- *Actively shapes work on the basis of a personal vision of what she/he would like to achieve*
- *Puts forward new ideas which influence the overall direction of the Society, and finds new ways of improving on established approaches*
- *Concentrates proposals on what is important to the business and its changing priorities*
- *Stands back and spots possibilities which others have not noticed; provides fresh insight into problems*

8 Personal Impact

Having personal credibility. Commanding respect from others.

- *Respected for his/her contribution to the business by people at all levels*
- *Inspires others to have confidence in his/her own judgement and ability*
- *Holds the attention of others, has presence*
- *Conducts himself/herself with assurance when dealing with senior colleagues*
- *Delivers presentations to groups in a confident and concise manner and at the appropriate level of detail*
- *Takes immediate, positive steps to resolve a crisis*

Staff performance factors

This appendix defines performance factors which are relevant to staff jobs. Their relative importance will vary with the location and nature of the job. The list is not intended to be exhaustive: there may be other factors which you consider appropriate to particular individuals.

The factors suggested are:
1 Job knowledge
2 Planning and organising
3 Consistency of work standards
4 Relationships/working with others
5 Customer Service

1 Job Knowledge

Obviously how much work-related knowledge someone has will reflect their ability to do their job. A review of this performance factor provides an opportunity to highlight where thorough knowledge and practical application of it have contributed positively; for example, in helping to train new staff. Equally there may have been occasions where gaps in knowledge have led to work being delayed, or completed incorrectly. This should indicate a training need.

2 Planning and Organising

This factor relates to the way in which an individual approaches tasks. It is concerned with the practice of planning ahead; scheduling activities for oneself and where applicable for others and allowing sufficient time for completing them; identifying priorities and working systematically; keeping colleagues and supervisors/managers informed of progress. Maintaining proper and secure systems for storing and retrieving information.

3 Consistency of Work Standards

This factor is concerned with the extent to which the individual consistently applies him/herself to the job. The quantity and quality of work produced defined by standards of performance are key aspects of reliability which contribute to effective and accurate levels of output in the job. The maintenance of security procedures and retaining confidentiality come under this heading, as does compliance with operating procedures e.g. keeping proper records.

4 Relationships/Working with Others

This factor is concerned with 'getting on' with other people. This includes relationships with subordinates, supervisors and other staff members. An individual may contribute to effective performance by consideration for the needs of others and an awareness of the effect that one's own behaviour is likely to have on other people.

5 Customer Service

There are now defined standards of service concerning a number of activities which can be applied across the Society. Beyond this, customer service is concerned with a willingness to respond to the needs of others in terms of business and relationships, within a broad definition of the Society's purpose and the individual's job function.

- *Shows concern for the person as well as the rules*
- *Meets commitments and produces results*
- *Demonstrates personal involvement*
- *Contributes to team support*

Extracted from Abbey National Building Society, Performance Review Guidenotes, October 1987.

I am grateful to Mr Tony Fraser, Manager Manpower Development, and Mr John King, Personnel Manager, Abbey National Building Society, for providing the above information.

Review and discussion questions

1. Explain the importance of effective management to organisation development.
2. Outline the main elements of an integrated model of managerial behaviour and development. Use this model to examine the process of management development in your own organisation.
3. Detail the main features in the process of management development. What are the main factors to consider in the implementation of a successful management development programme?
4. Explain the importance and main features of a performance review system as an essential part of management development.
5. What are your views on the nature of management education, training and development in this country? Comment on the apparent effectiveness of management education, training and development in your own organisation.
6. Summarise what you believe are the main variables which affect organisational effectiveness and successful performance.
7. Explain what you see as the main attributes for organisational success and give examples from your own or some other organisation. Discuss the importance of innovation as a key factor in organisational effectiveness.
8. Detail the specific criteria you would consider in attempting to evaluate the performance and effectiveness of your own organisation.

| **Practical assignment** | Imagine you are the managing director or chief executive of your organisation, and complete the following checklist. |

(a) *Structure*
   Does your organisation have:

	Yes	No	Maybe
(1) an outdated structure, for example: geared to forgotten objectives, old markets, retired top managers;			
(2) an over-extended structure, for example: no adaptation to business growth, technical change or to the competition;			
(3) changed organisational objectives, but structure and staffing basically unchanged;			
(4) formal structure which is an impediment to business performance, and out of touch with reality;			
(5) flexibility, adaptability and delegation impeded by bureaucracy or detailed built-in procedures?			

	Yes	No	Maybe
(b) *Managerial staffing* Does your organisation have:			
(6) unclear top management succession; or does it offer only a 'Hobson's Choice' for several senior positions;			
(7) a general and unduly heavy loss of managers, especially the younger or better ones;			
(8) quite numerous examples of badly under-employed managers in 'non jobs';			
(9) development clearly held back by a lack of good people;			
(10) fairly widespread managerial job dissatisfaction and frustration;			
(11) managerial vacancies frequently difficult to fill, from either within or outside the organisation?			
(c) *Performance* Does your organisation have:			
(12) poor organisational performance, due to ineffective management controls;			
(13) poor performance because of a generally low level of managerial competence for present-day tasks;			
(14) poor performance which arises from blurred or badly drawn managerial responsibilities;			
(15) widespread over-burdening of managers, which undermines performance;			
(16) extensive waste of managerial time, for example in board meetings, committees, working groups;			
(17) widespread delays in obtaining either decisions, or the information needed to make decisions;			
(18) frequent failure to seize opportunities, or to react speedily to new challenges?			

Although the object of this exercise is to help you to master this section of your study, it is hoped that this approach and checklist will be of some interest and value to you in the practical management situations which you face in your job – either now or in the future.

Notes and references

1. Mullins, L. J. and Aldrich, P. 'An Integrated Model of Management and Managerial Development', *Journal of Management Development*, vol. 7, no. 3, 1988, pp. 29–39.
2. Payne, R. and Pugh, D. S. 'Organizations as Psychological Environments', in P. B. Warr (ed.) *Psychology at Work*, Penguin (1971).
3. Carroll, S. J. and Gillen, D. J. 'Are the Classical Management Functions Useful in Describing Managerial Work?' *Academy of Management Review*, vol. 12, no. 1, 1987, pp. 38–51.
4. Stewart, R. *Choices for the Manager*, McGraw-Hill (1982).
5. Blake, R. B. and Mouton, J. S. *The Managerial Grid III*, Gulf Publishing Company (1985).
6. Mintzberg, H. *The Nature of Managerial Work*, Harper and Row (1973).
7. Miner, J. B. *Management Theory*, Macmillan (1971).
8. McGregor, D. *The Human Side of Enterprise*, Penguin (1987).
9. Blake, R. B. and Mouton, J. S. *The Managerial Grid III*, Gulf Publishing Company (1985).
10. Likert, R. and Likert, J. G. *New Ways of Managing Conflict*, McGraw-Hill (1976).
11. Drucker, P. F. *The Effective Executive*, Pan Books (1970), and Reddin, W. J. *Managerial Effectiveness*, McGraw-Hill (1970).
12. Brech, E. F. L. (ed.) *The Principles and Practice of Management*, Third edition, Longman (1975).
13. Mintzberg, H. *The Nature of Managerial Work*, Harper and Row (1973).
14. Ribeaux, P. and Poppleton, S. E. *Psychology and Work: An Introduction*, Revised edition, Macmillan (1983).
15. Stewart, R. *The Reality of Management*, Second edition, Pan Books (1986).
16. Mumford, A. 'What's New in Management Development', *Personnel Management*, vol. 17, no. 5, May 1985, pp. 31–2, and Zey, M. G. 'Mentor Programs: Making the Right Moves', *Personnel Journal*, vol. 64, no. 2, 1985, pp. 53–7.
17. Humble, J. W. *Management by Objectives*, Management Publications Limited for the British Institute of Management (1971).
18. *The Making of British Managers* (the Constable and McCormick report), British Institute of Management (1987).
19. *The Making of Managers: A Report on Management Education, Training and Development in the United States, West Germany, France, Japan and the UK* (The Handy Report), National Economic Development Office (1987).
20. Handy, C. B. *Understanding Organizations*, Third edition, Penguin (1985).
21. Peters, T. J. and Waterman, R. H. *In Search of Excellence*, Harper and Row (1982).
22. Ibid. p. 9.
23. Waterman, R. H., Peters, T. J. and Phillips, J. R. 'Structure is not organization', *Business Horizons*, June 1980, pp. 14–26.
24. Peters, T. J. and Waterman, R. H. *In Search of Excellence*, Harper and Row (1982) p. 12.

CONCLUSION

This book has presented a managerial approach to organisational behaviour. It has been concerned with interactions among the structure and operation of organisations, the process of management and the behaviour of people at work. The underlying theme has been the need for organisational effectiveness and the importance of the role of management as an integrating activity.

No single book could hope to have covered adequately all aspects of such a wide and multi-disciplinary field of inquiry. In order to attain a reasonable level of depth, therefore, this book has concentrated on selected topics of particular relevance to problems of organisation and management in work situations.

It is hoped that this book has provided you with an improved understanding of management and organisational behaviour, and the nature of the people–organisation relationship. It is also hoped that the book has encouraged you to be more aware of, and sensitive to, the organisational factors and management processes influencing the behaviour and performance of people at work.

LJM

INDEX

Page numbers in **bold type** refer to the Notes and references at the end of each chapter. Only names that appear in both the text and the reference lists have been indexed.